# THE LIFE OF OUR LORD
# JESUS CHRIST IN MEDITATIONS

## VOLUME I

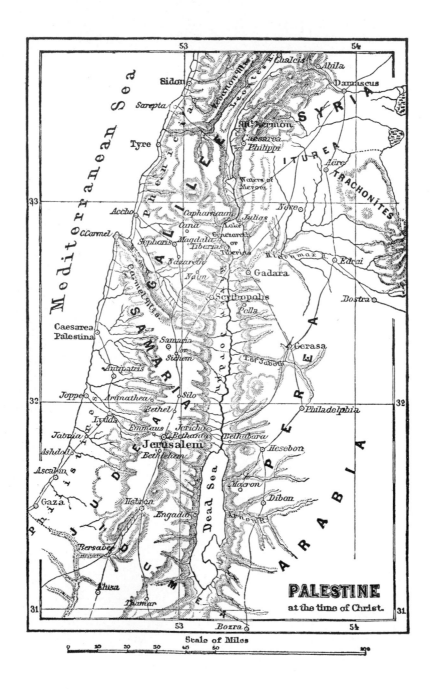

PALESTINE
at the time of Christ.

Scale of Miles

# THE LIFE OF OUR LORD
# JESUS CHRIST

IN MEDITATIONS

BY

MAURICE MESCHLER, S.J.

TRANSLATED BY SISTER MARY MARGARET, O.S.B.

VOLUME I

B. HERDER BOOK CO.

15 & 17 SOUTH BROADWAY, ST. LOUIS 2, MO.

AND

33 QUEEN SQUARE, LONDON, W. C.

1953

NIHIL OBSTAT

Rt. Rev. Wm. Fischer, S.T.D.

Censor Librorum

IMPRIMATUR

✠ Joseph E. Ritter

Archiepiscopus

Sti. Ludovici, die 23 Nov. 1949

Tenth Printing

Library of Congress Catalog Card Number: 50-1304

Vail-Ballou Press, Inc., Binghamton and New York

# CONTENTS

Maps

# CONTENTS

―――

# I

## THE FIRST LIFE OF JESUS

### I. IN THE BOSOM OF THE FATHER

### II. THE LIFE OF JESUS IN THE PROPHECIES

# II

## THE TEMPORAL LIFE OF JESUS

### I. THE YOUTHFUL LIFE OF JESUS

#### A. THE INCARNATION

the time of his death, at the advanced age of 82, he was superintending the publication of a "Life of Our Lady," a companion volume to his "Life of St. Joseph." To the last he continued to contribute to the well-known "Stimmen aus Maria-Laach," the last effort of his pen being a posthumous article in that magazine. He died a holy and peaceful death at Exaeten on the 2nd of December 1912.

R. I. P.

# TRANSLATOR'S PREFACE

---

In the work of preparing this translation I was fortunate in securing the cooperation of the Benedictines of St. Mary's Priory, Princethorpe, whose disinterested and sisterly kindness I am glad to take this opportunity gratefully to acknowledge. The arduous labor of finally revising our work was most kindly undertaken by the Rev. F. E. Ross, of St. Mary's College, Oscott, without whose friendly encouragement and practical help the undertaking would certainly have had to be abandoned. The other kind friends who have interested themselves in the work and rendered assistance in various ways are so numerous that I am obliged to be content with thanking them all in general; but I cannot refrain from adding a word of gratitude to Father MESCHLER, whose ever ready advice and help has been a great encouragement to me throughout. If, as it is hoped, this work should prove of some assistance to persons seeking a deeper insight into the life and teaching of our Divine Saviour, I feel sure that all who have contributed to the production of the work will consider themselves amply rewarded.

## BIOGRAPHICAL SKETCH

Father MAURICE MESCHLER was born in the little town of Brig, Canton of Valais in Switzerland, at the foot of the Simplon Pass, on the 16th of September 1830. Brought up amidst the magnificence of Alpine scenery, he always possessed and manifested in his writings a richness and power of description which gave a peculiar charm to his works and won for them a wide and devoted circle of readers. He was educated at the Jesuit College in his native town until the Fathers were sent into exile in 1847; he then went with his brother to the Benedictine Monastery of Engelberg to continue his studies. But although he here acquired the great love and devotion for St. Benedict to which he so often gives expression in his writings, he retained all his affection for his former instructors; and in October 1850 he entered the noviciate of the Society at Münster. His bright and joyous disposition soon made him a great favorite with his companions in religion, and won him the hearts of all. The first years of his scholastic life were passed at Paderborn, Bonn, Gorheim and Feldkirch; he then returned to Paderborn for his theological course, and was ordained priest in 1862. He completed his studies by a further course of dogmatic theology at Maria Laach, now a Benedictine Monastery, but then belonging to the Society of Jesus. From 1867 till 1892, with an interval of a few years during which he filled the post of Provincial, Father MESCHLER was charged with the spiritual training of the novices and young priests of the German province. A second persecution, which followed close upon the unjust "May Laws" passed under Bismarck, drove him into Holland; and it was during this second exile at Blyenbeck that he composed the "Life of Our Lord Jesus Christ," which is perhaps the most familiar of his writings, having been translated into several other languages. In 1892 Father MESCHLER was appointed Assistant for the German Province to the Father General of the Society, until whose death in 1906 he remained in Italy, first at Fiesole and then in Rome. The last years of his life were spent at Luxemburg and then at Exaeten in Holland. Father MESCHLER's years as novice-master and later as Assistant in Rome afforded him ample opportunity for collecting his material and giving ripeness to his reflections upon spiritual subjects, while his editorial connection with the "Stimmen aus Maria-Laach" promoted his literary activity. He was a master in the spiritual life, and his works continue after him, not only in the books which he wrote, but likewise in the countless souls whom he led to perfection. Among his other works we may mention the "Gift of Pentecost" and his charming booklet on the devotion of the Rosary, entitled "Our Lady's Garden of Roses." He is also the author of a "Life of St. Aloysius," of volumes of meditations upon the saints and upon the ecclesiastical year, of many brief devotional treatises and of essays upon ascetical subjects, which have recently been gathered and published in book form. His explanation of the Spiritual Exercises of St. Ignatius is a treasure highly valued by the Society, for which it was written. One of his latest works was a clear and succinct account of the Society of Jesus, of which he had been so long a faithful and distinguished member; and at the life of Jesus, and to meditate well is such a high art that no pains should be considered too great in order to acquire it. The grace of God and earnest, continual practice will accomplish it. Our gracious Lord will have regard to our desire and meet it half-way. "Wisdom is glorious and never fadeth away, and is easily seen by them that love her, and is found by them that seek her. She preventeth them that covet her. . . . He that awaketh early to seek her, shall not labor; for he shall find her sitting at his door. . . . For she goeth about seeking such as are worthy of her, and she showeth herself to them cheerfully in the ways, and meeteth them with all providence. For the beginning of her is the most true desire of discipline. And the care of discipline is love; and love is the keeping of the laws; and the keeping of the laws is the firm foundation of incorruption; and incorruption bringeth near to God. Therefore the desire of wisdom bringeth to the everlasting kingdom" (Wisd. 6:13–21). We may well apply these words to our gracious Lord, the Incarnate Wisdom, on that occasion when He so tenderly and sweetly turned to those two disciples who were timidly following Him, and, in reply to their question as to where He lived, invited them, saying: "Come and see." "And they stayed with Him" (John 1:39).

meditation should be overcharged with a number of practical applications and resolutions. If, at its close, we succeed in taking one good, special resolution, in arriving at something beautiful and uplifting, and in forming the energetic resolve to pass the day with renewed fervor, to serve such a good Master at all costs, and to do our duty, then the meditation has been a good one. It has gained its end.

An excellent and indispensable fruit of meditation is, lastly, the actual prayer or colloquy with God, by adoration, thanksgiving, praise, petition and reparation, speaking with Him according to the subject of meditation and the frame of mind we are in, either asking grace, accusing ourselves, communicating our heart's desires, thoughts, doubts, difficulties, hopes, plans and resolutions, interceding for others, or placing our train of thought and the whole course of the meditation before God in the form of a colloquy. In doing this it is not necessary to be borne along by a special feeling of devotion and consolation. Neither the essence of prayer nor its real good consists in this sensible devotion, nor can we command it ourselves, because it does not depend upon us, but upon God. Prayer is simply speaking with God, telling Him our thoughts and sentiments, just as they come from our hearts, and as simply as we speak to our fellow-men. Such outpourings and colloquies can be brought in anywhere, whenever and wherever the heart prompts thereto, as often as we are more forcibly struck by some thought and form some resolution. In fact, we must apply ourselves with diligence to this colloquy, because it is not so much in the reflections as in the actual prayer that negligence creeps in. At all events a prayer of this kind, and a good, heartfelt prayer too, must close the meditation, or else the main object has been lost. The prayer is the last and most important act of the meditation. The whole idea of meditation—or of the use of the intellect—is to enable us to make a really fervent and devout prayer. In the prayer we already practise the virtues we have resolved upon, and moreover gain for ourselves the grace to practise them in the future and to live up to what we have learned.

What has been said here about the fruit of meditation has found beautiful and eloquent expression in the scenes from the Life and Passion of our Saviour with which the immortal Fra Angelico has decorated the cells and cloisters of what was once the Dominican convent of St. Mark in Florence. Our Lord is everywhere surrounded by a group of Saints, who are meditating upon the mystery and applying it to themselves, each in his own way. St. Dominic, in peaceful, quiet meditation, with thoughtful devotion, transfigured by grief of soul, is lost in contemplation of the scenes of the Life and Passion of Jesus; St. Francis, with his poor, thread-bare habit and the wounds in his hands, brings into actual, every-day life the poverty and sufferings of our Lord. Sometimes the application becomes most realistic. At the Scourging of our Lord, St. Dominic bares his shoulders and lacerates them with bloody stripes. In the mystery of the Nativity there stands apart from the other Saints the crowned figure of a woman, who does nothing but gaze upon the scene; but this she does with folded hands, and with an expression of such heartfelt, childlike sympathy, with such attention, love and joy, that one cannot look at her without emotion. So at any rate ought the mysteries of our Lord to be meditated upon. It should be enough that our Saviour has said, done or suffered something, for us to dwell upon and find pleasure in it. For love everything is of importance!

After the meditation it is well to cast a brief glance over the whole course of it, and to examine how it has passed, whether well or ill, and why well or ill. In this way the art of meditating is acquired and the recurrence of mistakes or negligence is effectually prevented. It will not be without use to return to the meditation now and then in the course of the day, especially in moments of recollection and prayer, and to take the matter of the meditation as the subject of our intercourse with God. It is often only then that beautiful and consoling thoughts and upliftings of heart occur, for God is the Lord of grace, and the riches of grace contained in these mysteries are inexhaustible. Thus the meditation exerts its influence over the whole day, whereas otherwise it would pass away and disappear without leaving a trace, like a cloud in the morning sky; and thus, lastly, we live in constant union with our Saviour and approach the succeeding meditation with much more recollection. Yes, indeed, we ought always to be occupied with some mystery from the Life and Passion of our Lord. This would be the true way to live with Christ and in Christ. The angels of God are always ascending and descending upon the Son of Man (John 1:51), and it is their sweetest delight to gaze into the mysteries of the God-Man. So also must it be our joy to be constantly thinking over and meditating upon what our Lord has done and suffered for us.

We find such gain, such refreshment of soul in meditation upon work of art; mental prayer, on the other hand, like an earnest study of it.

This exercise of the interior faculties of the soul is the essential thing in meditation. In practice a few supplemental acts are added to it. The preceding night or immediately before the meditation, the points are quietly read through. Before proceeding to the meditation itself we recollect ourselves for a moment, reflecting that we are now about to pray, and remembering the presence of God. We then kneel down, briefly offer the meditation for the glory of God, cast a cursory glance over the historical course and scene of the mystery, ask fervently and in few words for the grace to know, love and serve our Saviour ever better; and then begins the actual work of meditation.

Within this general frame of the technique of meditation may be distinguished three ways of considering the mysteries of our Saviour. The first is more concerned with the intellect, when for example the aim of the mystery is chiefly kept in view, then the means, and finally the result or effects, and the matter of the mystery, the place, persons, words and actions are made use of with regard to this aim. The second way is to picture to oneself the principal features of the mystery in their successive order, and to attach the work of the understanding and the will to the persons, their words and actions. That is to go through the mystery with the intellect and the senses. The third way is chiefly the work of the senses and the imagination, or a so-called application of the senses to the mystery, by which a sort of picture is made of the place, the persons, their probable thoughts, feelings, words, actions and virtues, as particularly and vividly as if one were actually a witness of and sharer in the mystery. The mode of procedure in this kind of meditation consists in letting the senses take the chief share of the work, and then following them up with the intellect and the will. This method of meditation may be facilitated by thinking of similar occurrences in life, and representing to oneself what one usually thinks, feels, says and does on such occasions, and on the other hand what our Saviour thought, said and did. The utility of this way of meditating lies in the fact that we often penetrate much further into the actual meaning of the mystery, gain much more abundant matter for practical application, and more quickly obtain consolation. The fundamental principle of this kind of meditation is certainly a right one, and the

masters of prayer confirm it, viz. that the more we accustom
ourselves to picture our Saviour and His actions in a vivid and
detailed manner, to rest and feel ourselves at home in them,
the easier, better and more perfect our prayer becomes.

As regards the means of obtaining a good result from meditation, the first means is God's grace; and we must always humbly
acknowledge this, by unceasingly asking God to help us more and
more to pray with ease and from the heart. The second means is
the cooperation and exercise especially of our will in prayer and
meditation. If the meditation is to turn out well, then this desire
of finding something beautiful, some incentive, must always be
present, urging and spurring on the various faculties of the soul
and keeping them in lively activity. In each mystery we must say
to ourselves: "There is certainly much that is beautiful and inspiring hidden here; now let us seek, and take pains to find it."
In truth, every mystery is like Moses' rock; in it an abundant
source of enlightenment and inspiration is enclosed. It is only
necessary to strike the rock, and that forcibly and repeatedly. Each
mystery should therefore be approached with great sympathy and
love, and regarded and treated as an artist treats a favorite study.
This hint is of infinite importance when meditating upon the life
of Jesus, in order to avoid a sort of routine or mechanical process,
or even weariness. He who has attained to this liking and attraction has found the key to meditative prayer.

Now just a word more about the fruit of meditation. Every
advance in the knowledge and love of God and in zeal for His
service is a fruit. As the theologians say, the real fruit and result of
prayer is devotion: this is of two kinds, accidental devotion, which
consists in feelings and in the enjoyment of sweet consolation,
and essential devotion, which is nothing else than the readiness
of the will for everything relating to the service of God. Consequently every special resolution either to practice a particular
virtue or to overcome a fault, according to whatever the mystery
in question happens to be, is a fruit of meditation, and generally
the best fruit, for we have quite definite and pressing needs that
must be satisfied. A more general fruit of meditation consists in
joy in our Saviour and love of Him, and in realizing how good and
blessed it is to be with Him and to serve Him. This general fruit
must not be underestimated, for it draws us away from the world
and brings us to our Saviour, and makes our hearts familiar and at
home with Him. It is therefore by no means necessary that our

# AUTHOR'S PREFACE

---

In writing this book the author had three chief objects in view. First, in the presentation of each mystery, it has been his aim to bring out into bold relief whatever it contains that may aid to a deeper appreciation of our holy religion, its doctrine on faith and morals, the marvelous development of the Church, and the beauty of the Christian life. The Gospel is God's last and loftiest revelation, the ground-plan, as it were, of His Church; it is therefore replete with ideas of great moment, destined in the course of time to develop the organism of the Church and thereby transform the life of the world. How often has a word, a hint which our Lord lets fall in an apparently unintentional manner, a transient act which He performs at an opportune moment, become, in the shadow of a distant time and in a strange land, the type, the prophecy and the seed of institutions, vocations and states of life in the Church! To follow up these hidden treasures of life and blessing in the Gospel, to discover therein the world-renewing thoughts of God and expose them to view, was the first intention in the meditation of each mystery.

The second object in view was to make the Person and character of Jesus stand out in full and strong relief. As the sun's wealth of light and color is revealed in the rainbow, so also is the splendor of the portrait of Jesus scattered throughout the mysteries of His life in a thousand charming and majestic revelations. In every fragment of these mysteries this central Sun breaks through in single flashes of light, each with its own splendor of color. Now it is His great wisdom, now His noble, kingly Heart, strong to endure and yet quick to feel; here His divine power, there His lovable humanity, and ever again His holiness and virtue, which gleam forth in the most varied rays and tints, and serve for our admiration, instruction and edification. It is in this that the infinite advantage and gain of this final revelation lies, that God comes in person and speaks by His Son (Hebr. 1:2). It is no longer a lifeless law in brass and stone that points out to us the way of salvation, it is not lifeless virtue preached and held up to us by a sage; a true, living Child of the human race stands before us as virtue embodied, and lays hold upon us and carries us away by the charm and sublimity of His gracious and majestic appearance. "That which was from the beginning . . . the life, was manifested, and we have seen, and do bear witness, and declare unto you the life eternal, which was with the Father, and hath appeared to us" (I John 1:2). There is a way to Jesus through virtue, and a way to virtue through Jesus, and the latter is indisputably sublimer, sweeter, shorter and surer. To point out this way by unveiling the portrait of Jesus was the second aim of these meditations.

The third object was to present each mystery in a fixed arrangement and number of points, in logical or historical order. There are many interpretations of the Gospel which are confined to the sense and explanation of the words and phrases, and also many which represent, grouped together or in broad outlines, the contents and connection of a Gospel; but there are not so many which give each single mystery in clear, sharply defined and individual detail. And yet this, so to speak, architectural division and representation of the mysteries is of great importance. It facilitates meditation, gives clearness and comprehensiveness, assists the memory, and affords special help in giving out points of meditation before a large number of hearers.

These, then, were the objects kept in view during the preparation of the present interpretation of the Gospels. Its end is not exegetical instruction, but edification; not study, but aid to prayer. It was to be before all things a book of meditation. For this reason all discussions which are a matter of indifference for the spiritual life were omitted. On the other hand everything, as far as possible, that could be of practical service in works old and new on Holy Scripture has been utilized. Nothing that leads to a more detailed knowledge and deeper comprehension of divine truth must be neglected. To know is to love, say the old masters. It is certainly the glorious result and undisputed merit of modern Scriptural research and interpretation, that it throws into relief and pieces together the life of our Saviour,—both in itself, by the historical grouping and successive arrangement of the mys-

teries, and also in its relation to the history of the period, country
and people. What this little book offers, then, are only treasures
of old and new researches in Holy Writ, put together and pieced
into a mosaic.[1] That which others have skilfully and laboriously
done for the promotion of knowledge is here to be turned to account for assistance in prayer, as our Saviour said to the Apostles
with reference to their labors: "It is one man that soweth, and
it is another that reapeth. . . . Others have labored, and you
have entered into their labors" (John 4:37, 38).

The meditations are preceded by a survey of the scene and time
of the ministry of Jesus. Then follows, first, the Divine life of
Jesus before the beginning of time, and during the Old Covenant;
secondly, the Divine and human life of our Saviour throughout
His earthly course; and thirdly, His mystical life in the Church.

So far as to the aim, the leading thoughts and the arrangement
of the following meditations.

It only remains to wish the little book every blessing on its way!
Where there is a heart longing to learn to know Jesus; where there
is a soul casting itself down at our Lord's feet in recollection, to
hear from His lips the word of life; wherever there may be a human heart cultivating the sweet habit of prayer, and wishing to
push its way upwards to the heights, to the strong and living
God: there may it pause, offer and communicate what it has
gathered together. May Almighty God and the unction of the
Holy Spirit bless these poor little germs of thought, work upon
them and cause them to spring up and bear in souls the beautiful
fruit of the knowledge and love of Jesus! A pious German artist,
a master in colors, once sat long before his easel, as though lost
and rapt in mental contemplation of his conception. At last he
laid down his brush discouraged, and cried out: "Oh, I see colors
and lights that I cannot reproduce; there are none such in this
world." So it is with all who gaze upon the face of the glory of the
Lord, and undertake to describe it. It is simply impossible, here
below. In heaven we shall see Him as He is, in His light we shall
see light (Ps. 35:10), and be infinitely happy and blessed. But
only to try just to picture Him to ourselves, to speak of Him, to
catch but one ray of His truth and beauty and goodness,—this is

---

[1] Among the more modern writers those chiefly made use of were: Loch and
Reischl, Grimm, Keppler, Faber, Schanz, Holzammer, Cornely, Lohmann,
Knabenbauer, Corluy. The Gospel text which has been adopted in this transla-
tion is that of the Douay Bible.

already the rosy dawn of blessedness and the brightness of eternal life.

## II. HOW TO MEDITATE UPON THE MYSTERIES OF OUR LORD

It may perhaps be of use to place here a few preliminary thoughts upon meditative prayer, and especially upon meditation on the mysteries of our Lord.

Meditative prayer in general is a serious reflection upon points of faith, in order to direct our lives in accordance with them; in other words, in order to exert an improving influence upon our will. Without this direction of intention and influence upon the will and life, reflection upon points of faith is merely a theological study, and not meditative prayer.

It follows from this definition that meditative prayer consists in a particular exercise of the interior powers of the soul. The memory must place the ideal and historical matter of the point of faith before the understanding. The understanding endeavors to convince itself of the truth of the mystery, and to make itself master of whatever beauty, depth, sublimity, and practical utility for daily life is contained therein. But the will, touched by the truth, immediately makes acts either of aversion, repugnance and abhorrence, or of pleasure, joy and desire. It seeks to gain possession of the good placed before it by the means which practical common-sense suggests: viz. by resolutions, determinations, and prayer for the necessary grace to put these resolutions into practice. This exercise of the interior faculties of the soul is to be observed in meditation on abstract as well as on historical truths, with this difference, that the memory and the imaginative faculty come more into play with historical events than with abstract truths. The comparison of mental prayer with vocal shows how far more penetrating and more earnest the exercise of the interior faculties of the soul is in the former. We exercise the memory, the intellect and the will in vocal prayer also, but not so thoroughly and earnestly. We call to mind this or that point of faith briefly and cursorily, just as it happens to be contained in the words of the formula of prayer, and let the will make a few appropriate acts; whilst in mental prayer we hold fast to one single truth and consider it in detail, in order that it may work upon our will powerfully and deeply. Vocal prayer is like a mere fleeting glance at a

# INTRODUCTION

---

## THE SCENES AND TIMES OF CHRIST'S MINISTRY

A short sketch of the country, time and nation which formed the background and surroundings of the life of Jesus may serve as an introduction to this life, and assist us to obtain a deeper and more complete comprehension of it.

### DESCRIPTION OF THE COUNTRY

1. Palestine, called also the Promised or Holy Land, comprises that stretch of country which is bounded on the north by the ranges of Libanus and Anti-Libanus and on the south by the Arabian Desert, and which is shut in to east and west by the Desert of Syria and the Mediterranean Sea. The whole country is divided into two distinct regions—the East and West Jordan districts respectively—by the River Jordan, which, rising in Mount Hermon (a spur of the Anti-Libanus range), flows in a straight course from north to south and thus unites the Lake of Genesareth with the Dead Sea.

2. The East Jordan district extended from the eastern shore of the Dead Sea northwards to Great Hermon, and comprised Peraea on the south, reaching from the Dead Sea almost up to the Lake of Tiberias or Genesareth; Decapolis on the eastern shore of the Lake; and lastly Ituraea and Trachonitis between the north-eastern shore of the Lake and the range of Hermon (Luke 3:1).

Trachonitis reached on the north to the lofty and magnificent range of Hermon, whose snow-capped summits gleam over the Lake of Genesareth far away towards Galilee and Samaria. It is a region imposing in its grandeur, yet at the same time fertile and delightful. Within its limits lay Caesarea Philippi (Paneas), the summer resort of the Herodian princes, with the celebrated temple of Pan and Augustus and other magnificent buildings; here too

1

is found one of the sources of the Jordan. In this district our Saviour received from St. Peter the confession of His Divinity (Matt. 16:13; Mark 8:27; Luke 9:18). Another place, celebrated through the miracles of Christ, was Bethsaida (Julias), said to have been situated near the eastern opening of the Jordan into the Lake of Genesareth, where our Lord restored a blind man to sight (Mark 8:22). Not far from this town lies the little plain so famous for the first (and perhaps also the second) miracle of the multiplication of loaves (Matt. 14:14; 15:32; Mark 6:32; 8:1; Luke 9:12; John 6:2). Trachonitis was the principality of Herod Philip.

Decapolis, which adjoined the southern boundary of Trachonitis, was a confederation of towns immediately under the Roman supremacy; to it belonged the territory of the Gerasenes, which lay on the east coast of the Lake of Genesareth. There our Lord healed the two men possessed with devils (Matt. 8:28; Mark 5:1; Luke 8:26). At another place in Decapolis He cured a deaf-mute (Mark 7:31).

The upper part of Peraea, which adjoined the south of Decapolis, is a fertile plateau rich in grain and pasture land; the southern part, along the eastern shore of the Dead Sea, presents the most beautiful scenery. It is the mountainous Galaad, with Mount Nebo and magnificent woods of oak, fir and pistachio trees. Here, on the east coast of the Dead Sea, was situated the Castle of Machaerus, in which probably St. John the Baptist was imprisoned and beheaded. On the other side of the Jordan, in Peraea, he baptized and preached (John 1:28). Our Saviour Himself repeatedly exercised His ministry in Peraea, especially during a considerable time after the Feast of the Dedication of the Temple (Luke 13:23 to 16:31; John 10:40), and then again on His last journey from Ephrem, by way of Jericho, to Jerusalem (Luke 18:35; 19:1). Peraea belonged to the territory ruled by Herod Antipas. The population of all the districts east of the Jordan, and especially that of Decapolis and Trachonitis, contained a large admixture of Gentiles.

3. The land west of the Jordan rose in three terraces or ascents from south to north: viz. Judaea, Samaria, and Galilee. Galilee was the most beautiful and fertile part of Palestine. Here all is green, shady and smiling. The mountains are moderately high, with gently-rounded summits. In the spring-time the land is like a flower-bed of exceptional beauty. Side by side the pomegranate,

the date-palm, the nut, the fig-tree and the vine grow and flourish in the gardens. The woods and fields swarm with turtle-doves and crested larks. The inhabitants are vigorous, frank, vivacious and industrious, and great lovers of freedom.

But the most beautiful part of Galilee was the district around the Lake of Genesareth. This lake, four or five leagues in length and three in breadth, stretches from north to south in an oval shape, like a hanging cluster of grapes. The rocky banks of the eastern shore, only slightly curved, fall precipitously down to the Lake; the west coast, on the other hand, widens out from the new and magnificently-built town of Tiberias to the vicinity of the entrance of the Jordan, forming a little bay of about three leagues. The moderate heights now slightly project into the Lake, forming rocky capes or little promontories crowned by oleanders, and now again recede, thus leaving space for three little plains, which (especially the middle one, called Genesar—Matt. 14:34) were dotted with springs, gardens, baths, country-houses, castles and towns. Among these latter, along the shore of the Lake, may be named Tiberias, Magdala (Matt. 15:39), Bethsaida, the native town of the Apostles Peter, Andrew and Philip (John 1:44; 12:21), Capharnaum and Corozain, which latter was situated not far from Capharnaum, but probably rather more inland (Luke 10:13). Owing to the low level of the Lake (600 feet below the sea), its basin enjoys a uniformly warm climate, and possesses quite a tropical vegetation; whilst the excessive heat is mitigated by the shade of the trees. The waters of the Lake are transparent and clear as crystal, its depths are peopled by innumerable fish, and its surface is alive with waterfowl. The caravan road from Damascus to Acre (Ptolemais), which passed close by, brought what the Lake and its surroundings failed to produce. On the north may be seen Great Hermon, sparkling with its drifts of snow; on the east the Lake is shut in by the long row of the terraced heights of Peraea, extending almost in a straight line southwards; on the west are the gently-rising heights of the central chain of the Galilean mountains with their luxuriant vegetation; and over all this stretches the blue vault of a clear, unclouded sky with a never exhausted flood of light and warmth. It was here along the shores of the Lake that our Saviour passed the greater part of His public life; here, that He preached in the synagogues, on the mountains and on the shore itself, and worked countless miracles of all kinds. To the west of the Lake, traversing the West Jordan country in all directions, runs the central chain of the Galilean mountains, a spur of the Libanus range. In its charming valleys are situated the villages of Nazareth and Cana, the latter of which was the home of Nathanael (John 21:2), and is celebrated for the first great miracle wrought by Jesus at the marriage feast (John 2:1) and for the cure of the ruler's son (John 4:46). A kind of gap in this mountain-land is made by the beautiful and fertile plain of Esdrelon, which stretches from the sea-coast towards the interior and is watered by the little river Kison. It is enclosed on the northeast by the majestic Thabor, on the south and south-east by Lesser Hermon, the town of Naim (Luke 7:2) and the heights of Gelboe, and on the south-west by the Carmel range. It opens out towards Acre and the Mediterranean Sea, and then, skirting the coast, extends northwards towards Tyre and Sidon. Our Saviour once visited the neighborhood of these towns, and worked there the miraculous cure of the daughter of the Syrophenician woman (Matt. 15:21). The beautiful province of Galilee was part of the territory ruled by Herod Antipas.

The center of the West Jordan country was occupied by Samaria. It formed, with its long fertile dales and innumerable transverse valleys, a central chain of very varied aspect, which was called the Ephraim range. The Samaritans, who peopled this country at the time of Christ, were a mixed race which had originated after the Assyrian captivity from those Israelites who had remained behind, and from immigrant Gentiles. Repulsed as inferiors from the common place of worship in Jerusalem by the Jews who returned from the Babylonian captivity (I Esdr. 4:1), the Samaritans built themselves a pseudo-temple on Mount Garizim, near Sichem. They accepted of the Holy Scriptures only the five books of Moses. Their religion at first was a compound of heathenism and Judaism, but later on they worshiped the true God. Their temple on Mount Garizim had been destroyed by the Jews 120 years before the time of Christ, and so they lived on without priests or altar, without right religious knowledge, and yet ever in the persuasion that they belonged to Israel, and in expectation of a Messias; in constant feud with the Jews, they were more bitterly hated and persecuted by these than the heathens were, and in their turn they hated and persecuted the Jews. The pilgrims to Jerusalem especially had to suffer from them (Luke 9:53). We find our Saviour three times in Samaria: once after the first Feast of the Pasch, in Sichar (Sichem), at Jacob's well (John 4:5);

again after His departure from Galilee, on His way to Jerusalem, to the Feast of Tabernacles (Luke 9:52); and finally on the last journey before His Passion (Luke 17:11).

There were three main roads from Galilee to Jerusalem. The first led along the coast of the Mediterranean Sea, by Ptolemais, Caesarea and Joppe, then inland over the plains of Saron and Lydda into the mountain region of Judaea. The second went straight through the interior, passing the towns of Samaria, Sichem, Silo and Bethel. The third swerved twice to the left— once in Galilee, and again farther on in Samaria, to the two passages of the Jordan—and led along the deeply-jagged east bank of this river as far as the neighborhood of Jericho, and from Jericho through the desert of Juda over Bethania and the Mount of Olives to Jerusalem. This desert of Juda is a belt of steppes and bare gray hills which, torn, cut and cleft by a thousand precipices, fall steeply down to the Jordan valley and the Dead Sea. Among the sites identified in the north-east of this desert are the town of Ephrem (John 11:54) and Mount Quarantine, upon which our Lord began His fast (Matt. 4:1). This third road was generally chosen by the pilgrims from Galilee, in order to avoid the territory of the hated Samaritans. All these roads might be easily traversed in four or five days.

4. In contrast to green, shady Galilee and its frank, warm-hearted and susceptible inhabitants was the sterner land of Judaea. Its very natural characteristics, the bare heights of the Juda range, the valleys and the ravines, the dry, stony soil and frequent desert regions, gave it an aspect wild and imposing rather than friendly or attractive, which was quite in accordance with the grave, stern character of its inhabitants. Jerusalem itself, in the interior highlands of Judaea and on the watershed, surrounded by peaks of a considerable height, lay opposite the Mount of Olives on a plateau which, gently sloping from north to south, fell on the south and south-east very abruptly down to the vale of Hinnom, and eastwards to the valley of Josaphat, or Cedron valley. A slighter depression of the plateau (Tyropoeon), running also from north to south, divided the city into two parts: Lesser Moriah or the Temple Hill on the east and the more elevated upper town on the west. In the bottom of this depression, not far from where the vale of Hinnom opens into that of Cedron, but still within the city wall and encompassed by it, lay the pool of Siloe, the waters of which flowed from the Temple Hill. What first caught the eye,

looking from the Mount of Olives, was the magnificent Temple edifice, which rose on the south and east from massive stone foundations and, with its gilded central buildings, its large forecourts, extensive and beautiful wings and intervening erections, its splendid colonnades, mighty outer walls and fortress towers, presented the aspect at once of a wonderful temple and of an invincible stronghold. From the comparatively small building by which Zorobabel had replaced the Temple of Solomon, which had been destroyed by fire, Herod had (18 years before Christ) raised, enlarged and embellished it till it became one of the most important, rich and beautiful buildings of the ancient world.

The Temple area consisted of the Holy of Holies, which was empty; the Sanctuary, with the altar of incense, the seven-branched candlestick and the table of the loaves of proposition. Adjoining the Sanctuary, lengthwise towards the east, was the court of the priests with the great altar of holocausts, and farther on in the same direction the court of Israel and of the women, with the treasury. Finally the Temple itself and the three courts were surrounded on all sides by the great court of the Gentiles, with magnificent colonnades towards the interor. The city, with its numerous large buildings and palaces of marvelous, imposing and magnificent architecture, was divided into four separate parts and surrounded the Temple on three sides. Adjoining it on the south lay the lower town, the most ancient part, said to have been the real historical Sion or former Jebusite city; on the west was the suburban and the upper city, also traditionally called Sion, which rose from the Temple upwards to the western heights and included the palace of David and the Coenaculum; and on the north the Temple was bounded by the stronghold of Antonia and the newest part of the city, called Bezetha, with Herod's palace. Finally the entire city was surrounded on all sides by a gigantic rampart, a very armor of massive walls of hewn stone, with numerous towers and battlemented bulwarks. Thus Jerusalem with its strong position and its 100,000 inhabitants was a great and mighty city, truly the capital of the country, still more by its intellectual and religious significance than by its natural strength and warlike importance. Here the entire intellectual and religious life of the people was focused, and from there it went forth again to the more outlying parts of the country itself and of the whole Jewish world. Indeed, as the only true place of worship of the ancient world, the dwelling-place of God and the seat of revelation for many ages, Jerusalem with its Temple was not only the pride and delight of the Jewish people, but a true subject of religious veneration for the whole world and the entire human race. And now it was to witness the last and most glorious revelation of God, the revelation through the Messias.

5. About two leagues south of Jerusalem, on the road to Hebron, Abraham's city, lies the small but royal town of Bethlehem. It is a charmingly situated little place, rising amidst vineyards, fig and olive plantations, high above smiling valleys, fields and grass-grown dales, and extending over a mountain ridge with two elevations, joined by a narrow strip or saddle of land. The saddle itself and the western hill are covered with rows of white houses. On the eastern elevation, over against Jerusalem, stands the Church of the Nativity. Here, then, was the grotto in which our Saviour came into the world. From Bethlehem onwards the landscape is again diversified (as in the north) by considerable heights, which form the range of Juda; then it slopes down towards the deserts of Egypt and Arabia, forming the southern boundary of the country.

6. Such was the land in which our Lord lived and worked; in truth a beautiful and, though small, yet in very deed a Promised Land, blessed with the beauties, the variety and riches of nature. The rainy season began towards the end of October with the so-called early rains, after which the winter seed was sown; it lasted, with interruptions, till the end of April, when the late rains fell, maturing thus early the winter harvest. The actual winter fell within the months of January and February, during which snow lay upon the mountains, whilst the rose-bushes blossomed in the lowlands. With May began the dry season, the scorching heat of which was tempered by copious night-dews. The harvest of the winter crops took place in the course of May; that of the summer productions, with the fruit crop and vintage, in September. The landscape presented a most wonderful variety of pastures and grass-grown wastes, barren deserts and fertile arable land, luxuriant vineyards and beautiful garden-plots. Lakes and sea, heights and lowlands, charming valleys and mighty mountains with the most ravishing views alternated in never-ending variety. The produce of the land in its wonderful abundance corresponded to these happy conditions of soil and altitude. In this small area the product of every climate was represented: the vine of fruit-trees, the olive, fig, pomegranate, orange, lemon, and palm; of lofty trees, the cedar, plane, terebinth, cypress, maple and acacia;

of lower shrubs, the oleander, mustard and cotton tree; and of sweet-smelling spices, myrrh, saffron, balsam and frankincense. The lakes and rivers abounded in fish, the air and the fields were peopled with all kinds of wild fowl; and, lastly, on the magnificent pastures were fed large herds of every species. It was indeed the land flowing with milk and honey, an earthly garden, such as God could give only to His beloved people (Deut. 8:7, 10; 11:10–12), and as though expressly made to be the seat and starting-point of revelation for the entire human race. It lay in the midst of the civilized nations of the ancient world (Ez. 5:5), on the one hand so shut off from land and sea by high mountains, extensive wastes, and undeveloped, uncultivated seashore, that it was protected against the incursions of the heathen; and on the other hand, on all sides so close and easy of access to all the heathen lands that it could send its messengers without difficulty to all parts of the world, after Christ had once broken through the narrow bounds of the old religion by the world-embracing destiny of His revelation and His Church.

## Political Position of the Nation

1. In the period preceding the birth of our Saviour the nation had undergone certain political changes. After the return from the Babylonian captivity the original division of the people into twelve tribes had disappeared, whilst the house of David had gradually sunk into obscurity. The bloody wars with the Syrian kings, which the nation had fought in defense of religion and political freedom after the death of Alexander the Great, had finally resulted in the establishment of Jewish independence and in the union of civil and religious authority in the family of the Machabees or Hasmonaeans (140 B.C.).

2. The bloody strife for the throne in this unhappy family led to a twofold catastrophe: first, the interference of the Romans, who, under Pompey, conquered Jerusalem (62 B.C.) and reduced the country to a vassal state; secondly, the rise and influence of the Herodian family, first of Herod Antipater as counselor to the crown, and then of his son, Herod the Great, as actual rival and pretender to the throne. This latter Herod, a man of considerable importance, experienced, full of energy and skilled in the affairs of state, began by procuring at Rome his installation as king (38 B.C.). He then stormed Jerusalem, extirpated the ancient royal family of the Hasmonaeans, and united under his sovereignty all

the lands on both sides of the Jordan, together with Idumaea. It was under the reign of Herod the Great that the Messias was born. After the death of Herod, a few months or perhaps a year after the birth of our Lord, the kingdom was divided among his sons Archelaus, Herod Antipas and Herod Philip. Archelaus received Samaria, Judaea and Idumaea, but was soon deposed and banished by the Romans on account of his cruelty (A.D. 7). His lands were incorporated with the Roman province of Syria, but had a special governor, who resided at Caesarea (on the sea-coast), but usually came to Jerusalem at the time of the Pasch. Pontius Pilate, an imperious, hard, unscrupulous and untrustworthy man, was the fifth Roman governor of Judaea. To Herod Antipas, the brother of Archelaus, were assigned as his dominions Galilee and Peraea; and to Herod Philip, Ituraea and the remaining upper East Jordan territory. Both maintained possession of their principalities during the time of Christ's ministry.

3. Augustus Caesar had confirmed Herod the Great as king (28 B.C.). After the death of Augustus (A.D. 14; Luke 3:1) Tiberius Caesar succeeded him on the throne of the Roman Empire, and reigned until A.D. 36. Such was the political situation of the nation at the time of Christ. Independence was completely gone. A few years before our Saviour's death the Jews had lost even the right of capital punishment, and were no longer allowed to carry out executions (John 18:31).

## MORAL AND RELIGIOUS CONDITION OF THE PEOPLE

In the spheres of morals and religion the people had in many respects greatly changed for the better since their return from captivity; in others they had deteriorated, and the future threatened still more serious dangers.

1. The chief element of good was the final disappearance of the former tendency to idolatry, prime sin against the fundamental truth of the Israelite religion. Its destruction was wrought partly by the sufferings of exile and the efforts of the prophets Daniel and Ezechiel, partly and still more effectively through the hardships of the wars under the Machabees against their heathen oppressors, the kings of Syria (Jer. 30:18; Osee 2:17; Mich. 5:10; 5:12; Zach. 13:2; Ez. 14:17).

Further, the religious views of the people had in many respects been purified and refined. The Temple was venerated as God's dwelling-place, though it no longer possessed the Ark of the

Covenant, the Shechina, the Urim and Thummim, or prophecy
(Jer. 3:16). The people had learned to appreciate the spiritual
side of sacrifice and religion.

The divine service, moreover, was everywhere celebrated, and
well ordered for the maintenance of the true worship of God,
by remembrance of His past wonderful deeds and revelations and
by prefiguration of those to be expected. The synagogues were
numerous and often really beautiful, with vestibules of Greek
architecture. In them the Sabbath was zealously celebrated by
common prayer, reading and interpretation of the Holy Scriptures. The priesthood was once more duly ordered (Luke 1:58),
and the morning and evening sacrifices were offered with scrupu-
lous care. The great national feasts (the Pasch, Pentecost, the Day
of Atonement, the Feast of Tabernacles, the Dedication of the
Temple) were solemnized with great pomp and attended by an
immense concourse of people. Even the daily private devotions
had taken a more definite form since the exile.

Finally, the Great Synagogue (a supreme council of learned
and distinguished men, under the presidency of the High Priest)
had already been instituted by Esdras (453 B.C.) for the maintenance of the law and of civic order. Since the rule of the Hasmonaeans the Great Synagogue had been replaced by the Great
Council or Sanhedrim, which consisted of seventy-one members
under the presidency of the High Priest or some other prominent
man. The members were chosen from among the former High
Priests, the heads of the priestly families, the lawyers and scribes,
and the oldest among the heads of the tribes and families.

2. All this, then, was favorable to religion and morals. But the
unfavorable circumstance was, above all, the cessation of prophecy, which, together with the law and public worship, had formed
one of the three main constituents of the Old Covenant. The last
prophet (Malachias, 450 B.C.) foretold the advent of the Forerunner of the Messias, and then the prophetic voices were silent.
With the cessation of prophecy the fate of religion was placed
more upon a natural basis, and the possibility of a decline was
brought near.

With this a second circumstance was connected, namely the
rise of the "scribe" class in place of the prophets and (one may
well say) of the priesthood, whose province it properly was to
impart instruction in the law (II Par. 19:10; Lev. 10:11; Deut.
21:5; Mal. 2:7). The scribes were really the lawyers, preachers

and teachers of knowledge, and ruled as such in the schools, courts of justice and synagogues. Their method of teaching was by conversation and discussion, and all questions were decided according to the maxims of the old masters. Thus were formed the so-called "traditions" or human precepts, which superseded the great truths and the spirit of the law; and these fanciful additions and inventions crowded out, disfigured and in many respects falsified even the law itself (Mark 7:8; Matt. 23:4). Instead of preserving and communicating to others the substance of the law and the prophecies, these scribes to a great extent withheld the Scriptures from the people (Luke 11:52). The very essence of their character was hair-splitting, miserable casuistry, sophistry, boundless perversity, wrangling and hatred without end. One may say with truth that, after the captivity, Judaism with both its good and bad sides proceeded from the synagogue. But the public worship in the synagogues was often of great service to our Saviour and the Apostles for the spread of their doctrine (Matt. 4:23; 9:35; Mark 1:39; Luke 4:15; John 6:60; 18:20; Acts 13:5).

A third fatal circumstance was the degradation of the high priestly office. Since Onias (175 B.C.) the legitimate succession to this office had been interrupted. The kings of Syria gave it away to the highest bidders. The dignity of this important post had suffered no less from the fact that, since Simon the Hasmonaean, the high-priestly office and the political sovereignty were united in one person, and were hereditary (I Mach. 14:41). Finally, Herod and the Romans degraded the office completely by their arbitrary deposition and installation of High Priests.

The fourth and worst circumstance was the rise and increase of sects that combined political with religious aims. The chief of these were the Pharisees and the Sadducees, who represented the two opposing phases of popular opinion at the time of Christ.

The Sadducees were the representatives of the Hellenizing, free-thinking, materialistic tendency which had been developed amongst the Jews through the influence of heathenism. They held fast, it is true, to the more essential points of the law—to circumcision, the Sabbath, the Temple service and sacrifices—but rejected all traditions, especially those of the Pharisees, and denied the spiritual nature and immortality of the soul, the resurrection of the dead and the existence of the spirit-world (Acts 23:8). As their adherents belonged for the most part to the richer, more aristocratic and official classes, they possessed influence, but were nevertheless regarded by the people with distrust and dislike.

The Pharisees, on the other hand, formed the Jewish national religious party. They presented in a degenerate form the praiseworthy zeal of the first years after the captivity, for the preservation of the law in all its purity and integrity; they watched jealously, therefore, over its strict observance. In order to keep the law intact, they surrounded it with an intolerable "hedge" of customs, regulations and human precepts, laid down by the scribes, forming an accumulated mass of observances which made life a burden. In their idea, the law was made for its own sake, the letter of it was everything. Thus was developed by degrees a system of heartless rigor, hypocrisy, self-sufficient pride, cant and dissimulation beyond compare; none the less galling that the supporters of it (for the most part) made a display of outward observances only in order to win esteem, whilst in other respects they indulged their caprice. Thus they were given to avarice and sensuality, and by their teaching and decisions relaxed the law in many ways (for example with regard to vows, oaths, the strictness of the marriage bond), in this way undermining the whole religious life of the nation. Since the time of Herod their influence in political life had ceased, but they sought to assert themselves upon religious ground by putting forward men of their party for the office of High Priest and for membership in the Sanhedrim. At the time of Christ they held sway in the schools, in the Great Council and in the Synagogue, and were greatly esteemed by the people. The scribes in particular, who formed the learned class among the Pharisees, were looked up to as the guardians by profession of the spiritual blessings of Judaism, the custodians of pure doctrine and of the institutions and mode of life prescribed by the law, as the defenders of national freedom and dignity, and as scions of pure Jewish blood. They were beyond question the representatives and speakers of the nation. One may therefore say in a certain sense that the whole nation was tainted with Pharisaism, since the Pharisees were the predominant party. The most powerful means for the preservation and renewal of religious life were in such wise misused for party ends. These parties under the cloak of religion strove against each other for political power and position. Such a state of affairs could not be otherwise than ruinous for the people.

Lastly, in addition to these internal abuses, there was external oppression, which was to a great extent inimical to religion; of this oppression much was due to Herod, the alien and Edomite, a man whose selfishness, craft and cruelty inspired all with horror. He ruled with an iron hand. Half Jew, half heathen, on the one hand from political motives he rebuilt the Temple on a large and magnificent scale; on the other, he erected heathen temples, assisted at idolatrous sacrifices, and covered the country with theaters, monuments and other degrading marks of heathenism. He was merely a creature of Rome, and flattered in every way the Roman potentates, who, after their first interference, did not let the unfortunate nation out of their power again, but ensnared it more and more. It was indeed the "iron age" of Daniel which had commenced (Dan. 2:40).

3. All these circumstances developed amongst the people a spirit of discontent and inward rancor, together with an immoderate desire for revenge. There was no longer trusting faith, but a wide-spread murmuring against (not to say defiance of) God Himself. It is no marvel that amidst these evil dispositions ideas took firm root as to the coming Messias which were a mere distortion of the truth, and the fruit of their stubbornness and estrangement from God. They did not want a Redeemer from sins, but a deliverer from the oppressive yoke of foreign government—a secular ruler who would place them at the head of the nations, an avenging, avaricious, pleasure-loving and ambitious saviour. That the Messias, according to the prophecies, would have a Forerunner and work miracles, was the universal expectation; but that He would be God was clear probably to very few,— and to fewer still, that He would suffer and die. The sufferings and sacrifices which the prophets had foretold of Him may very likely have been understood to be the sufferings and sacrifices of the whole nation. Nevertheless there was still, amidst the corrupt and degenerate majority of the people, a good and healthy nucleus of law-abiding Judaism to be found in all classes; a chosen few who longed for the true consolation of Israel. But that the Messias would come soon was universally expected.

Such was the internal and external, political and religious condition of the people at the time of Christ; such the brighter and darker sides of the epoch of the Messias.

# ADVENT MEDITATION

We cannot begin our meditations upon the life of our Saviour, and especially upon the first beginnings of that life, better than by some thoughts on the season of Advent.

With Advent a new cycle of the ecclesiastical year begins, under the beautiful sign of the star of Jacob, the founder of the age of peace and joy. There was deep meaning and piety in that old name of the "Christ-month" which our forefathers gave to this season. Just as the sun gilds the darkening days, the hoary treetops and frosted windows of winter, so in the mystery of the Incarnation does the Sun of Justice arise, sending his bright and cheery rays into our hearts, awakening our souls to joyous summer activity. A few instructions for the Advent season cannot, therefore, be otherwise than in keeping with meditations upon the life of Jesus.

## 1. WHAT THE HOLY SEASON OF ADVENT IS

Advent is a preparation for the coming of the Lord. But there is a threefold coming, or advent of our Lord: the first, in human weakness; the second, in the souls and hearts of Christians; and the last, in power and glory, to judge the world. These three kinds of advent are very intimately connected with each other. Each is either a preparation for or a result of the others. Christmas reminds us of the true birth of our Lord which once took place, effects His spiritual birth in the hearts of the faithful, and thus prepares us for His future coming to judgment.

Advent is above all the preparation for Christmas, in the same way as the Old Covenant was a preparation for the true coming of the Saviour. This preparation reminds us of two things: first of a great misfortune, and secondly of a still greater happiness.

The misfortune was the fall of our first parents. In these the entire human race fell, estranged itself, without grace or faith,

14

more and more from God, and became a prey to a state of most terrible deterioration, sin and misery. From that one trespass sin steadily progressed till it acquired a veritable empire in heathendom, where Satan ruled the whole world through unbelief, fornication and cruelty, and hurled it from abyss to abyss of temporal misfortune down to despair and eternal damnation. Even with God's chosen people, to whom the inheritance of faith and grace remained, the pressure of the law was heavy, light scanty, assistance weak, apostasy frequent, degeneracy and discontent universal, and the desire for the Redeemer ardent. All classes lay under the tyranny of sin, the passions and death, all were shut out from heaven; it was one great migration of the human race to hell. The misery was great, universal and incurable, had God not taken compassion and come down to earth.

But He took compassion on us, and came. And that is the happiness of which Advent reminds us. The more the human race estranged itself from God, the nearer did the promised Saviour approach, and prepared a special place for Himself in the human race, in a particular nation, tribe and family, until at last He appeared in visible form, in the fulness of time, and repaired all. He overcame the darkness of unbelief by the light of His doctrine, the passions by His grace and example; He blotted out sin by His atonement, and saved us all from eternal death by His own Death and Resurrection. He set up His kingdom in souls through faith, grace and love, and founded, in opposition to the great empire of Satan, the visible kingdom of His Church—a kingdom which embraces all quarters of the globe and all nations; which includes time and eternity; in which all, freed from the ban of sin and the passions, protected by His law and by His power, enriched by the proper administration of His means of grace, and led by His visible government, are to serve God in justice and holiness, peace and joy, and to journey towards the heavenly kingdom. This kingdom of Christ is among us; its works, prayers and struggles take place in our midst. The holy Advent bells, which are now constantly ringing, bear witness of it. They proclaim it to the whole world, and invite all men to open their hearts and receive it. They proclaim our unhappiness, but also our happiness, our incomparably greater happiness in and through Christ. The holy season of Advent coming before Christmas is like the majestic vestibule leading into an old German cathedral, which is called Paradise. There we are bidden to gaze upon our first parents with the fatal tree of temptation, upon the patriarchs and prophets, telling us of their unsatisfied longings, and pointing trustfully to the coming of our Saviour to be ever with us in the Tabernacle, not in figure, but really and bodily, as the Lamb that once worked and still works their and our redemption.

## 2. HOW ADVENT SHOULD BE KEPT

From this character of the Advent season we may deduce the way in which it should be kept, and this way is exactly the same as that in which the Old Covenant prepared for the actual coming of Christ. It consists of three things. The first is penance. This is appropriate to the remembrance of sin. Sin is always atoned for by penance, and penance must in fact prepare the way for all that is good in us, and make God propitious to us. This is the unanimous preaching of the prophets, St. John the Baptist and our Saviour Himself: "Do penance." Penance itself is interior and exterior. Interior penance consists in contrition for the sins we have committed and a resolution not to commit them again, and especially in the use of the holy Sacrament of Penance. Exterior penance is practised by bodily austerities, by fasting, vigils and abstinence from sensual pleasures. The Church comes to our aid in this respect by the prescribed Advent fasts, and by her prohibition of marriage solemnities during this period. She vests herself in the color of sorrow, and thereby indicates to us that we should renounce vain pleasures, as we do during an obligatory time of mourning. Everyone must, then, see if he cannot put a restraint on his indulgence in earthly delights and sensual pleasures.

The second characteristic of the Advent observance is recollection, retirement and prayer. Everything at this season invites us to retire within ourselves. Nature recollects herself, as it were, and gazes into her mysterious depths; only in the heavens above, where the world of stars unfolds its splendor, is life to be found, which draws our thoughts away from this earth and upwards to heaven and eternity. Advent is like a solemn vigil before a great feast. The Church too prays more at this time, and all earnest souls are lost in loving, devout contemplation of the mysteries of the Advent and Incarnation of Jesus. There they build their tabernacles. The mysteries of His youthful life are like a rose of Jericho. Throughout the year it shrivels up and looks very insignificant. Now, in Advent, moistened with fresh water, it begins to show signs of life, blossoms, and becomes a familiar adornment of the room at Christmas. So it is with the youthful life of Jesus. Now, in Advent, fostered by loving meditation, it blossoms anew, much sweeter and more beautiful than the rose of Jericho, and exhales a perfume by which every sick heart is healed of sorrow and distress. St. Paul says in the Epistle of the first Sunday in Advent that we must "put on the Lord Jesus Christ" (Rom. 13:14). This, then, must be our occupation during Advent: meditation upon the Incarnation, and many prayers and intercessions for the salvation of the world, the conversion of sinners, the necessities of the Church, and the realization of God's intentions in the institution of the holy season of Advent.

The third thing that we must do in Advent is to long and to trust. The patriarchs of the Old Covenant are in this especially our models. The coming Redeemer was the object of their faith, hope, love and desire. From heart to heart, from mouth to mouth passes this longing, and the loud cry rings down the whole line of patriarchs and prophets: "O come!" (Ps. 79:3.) "O that Thou wouldst rend the heavens!" (Isa. 64:1.) "Drop down dew, ye heavens, from above, and let the clouds rain the just" (Isa. 45:8). With what confidence and happy trustfulness they await Him! Yes, for they had the divine promise. "God Himself will come and save you" (Isa. 35:4). And the more intense their longing grew, the more emphatically did God, on His side, answer by His sure promise and encourage them to confidence and joy. It is especially from the prophet Isaias, the prophet of trust in the Redeemer, that the Church in her daily Hours takes the words of longing and confidence. At this season the Alleluia is never absent from the songs of the Church, for it is a season of longing and jubilant hope. The subject of this confidence of the Church is the constant fulfilment of the effects of our Saviour's first advent, as seen in ourselves. "To Thee, O Lord, have I lifted up my soul. . . . I shall not be confounded!" (Ps. 24:1, 2.) Thus the Mass of the first Sunday in Advent begins; and with these words the key-note for the entire Advent season is struck.

So, then, penance, prayer, and trustful longing! Let everyone now reflect as to what he can and will do in this respect.

### 3. WHAT MOTIVES WE HAVE FOR SPENDING ADVENT IN THIS MANNER

There are both interior and exterior motives.

The interior motives spring from the three different advents of our Lord, which stand in most intimate relation to one another. The first motive is the greatness of the benefit which accrues to us in the first, actual coming of our Saviour, of which Christmas reminds us. It is "a faithful saying, and worthy of all acceptation, that Christ Jesus came into this world" (I Tim. 1:15). How fitting it is to think of it, and to reflect that He, He Himself, came to save us, that He did it at the cost of so many sacrifices, and that His coming brought us so many and such great blessings! What should we be without Him? Would life be worth living, if He had not redeemed us? Is it not a joy to be a human being, now that the goodness and loving kindness of God has appeared and we look for the blessed hope and coming of the glory of our great God and Saviour? (Titus 2:11, 13.) And yet how few think of this goodness and these benefits! Is it not meet and right that we should pay for others also the debt of thanks to our loving Redeemer? The second motive is the spiritual coming of our Lord, which is now to take place in our hearts by our appropriation of the graces of the redemption. How abundantly this redemption is offered to us! All that the first coming brought to the world stands at our disposal. We can appropriate it just as well and as truly as the shepherds, the Magi, Simeon and Anna, and all those who have believed in Christ and sanctified themselves by this faith. The blood of Christ washes away our sins now, just as it once did those of St. Mary Magdalen; faith and the peace of Christ, and the happiness of finding Him, fall to our lot just as to that of the good, simple shepherds and the Magi; we can fold Christ in our arms, as Simeon and Anna did; He can be born in our hearts spiritually, just as in the flesh He was once born in the womb of the Blessed Virgin. These are not pious opinions and imaginations, but truths and facts. The mystery of the Incarnation and Redemption is a reality, it takes place, only in another form and under other circumstances. And is not the need of redemption just as great and urgent as at the time of Christ's coming? Is there not sin of every kind, private and public? Is not the devastation wrought by the passions as great still, and is there not a whole army of temporal evils? Do not unbelief and heathenism exist? Does not the heathenism of the past still hold sway over the greater part of the earth's surface? And, in the midst of Christendom, has not a modern heathenism developed, which would like to deprive the world of the grace and comfort of faith in Christ, and throw her 1900 years backwards into heathen times and customs? How sorely our world needs redemption and peace in Christ, and how easily it might have it! The third motive is the future coming of our Lord to judgment, for which we must prepare ourselves by the spiritual reception of Him into our hearts, and by the use of the graces of redemption which are offered to us in the Christmas mystery. Does not the world, do not we need to be prepared for this last advent of our Lord? Would that the Advent bells might carry this truth out into the whole world, and arouse all men to bear a hand in the building up of Christ's kingdom by prayer and penance!

The exterior motives are to be found in the example of all good Catholics and of the Church, which has observed from time immemorial the custom of preparing by prayer and penance for our Lord's coming, in order thus to apply the grace of redemption to all ages and generations. The Church's office in the world is to pray, to do penance and to strive for the advancement of Christ's kingdom, just as the Church of the Old Covenant did before her. For this reason she takes from the lips of the prophets and saints of old the accents of longing and desire of the Redeemer, and offers them to God in the name of the whole human race. They are the same prayers and sighs that went up to the Saviour of the world before His actual coming in the flesh. Yes, the Church regards the mystery of the Incarnation and Nativity of Christ as though it were to take place again, and as if this event were now impending. "Let us adore the approaching King. . . . The Lord is near, let us adore Him," she says in her Office. Now she hopes, now she rejoices, then she fears lest our sins should delay His coming; in short, she gives herself up to the contemplation of the mystery of her Divine Spouse with all her loving heart, with all her thoughts and endeavors.

We too will keep Advent in the same manner, and follow in the step of our Mother when she teaches us to meditate upon the mysteries of the Incarnation and at the same time asks of our hearts a little sacrifice for our own good and for the comfort of the poor world. Who knows if we shall live to see another Advent, if this be not the last, and if we may not soon meet as our Judge the Saviour whom we are now about to meet with joy as our Redeemer?

# I

# THE FIRST LIFE OF JESUS

The first life of Jesus may be divided into two parts: the eternal life of the Word in the bosom of the Father, and the earthly life in the prophecies.

## I. IN THE BOSOM OF THE FATHER

### BEFORE TIME AND THE CREATION OF THE WORLD

JOHN 1:1. "In the beginning was the Word, and the Word was with God, and the Word was God.—2. The same was in the beginning with God."

The preparation for the Incarnation embraces the eternal, heavenly life of the Word, and also the earthly life of the God-Man from the creation of the world until His visible advent; that is, the time in which He began to live in the faith and expectation of mankind, and (according to the flesh) in the existence of His ancestors and forefathers. The Saviour is at once God and man, and as such He fills up time and eternity. In order to learn to know Him, we must first raise our minds to His life before the creation, and try to comprehend it as far as possible.

### 1. MOTIVES FOR MEDITATING UPON CHRIST'S LIFE BEFORE THE CREATION

The first motive for turning our attention with loving sympathy towards this life is, that it is the life of the Divine Person and Nature of our Lord and Saviour, and this life of His before the creation is far more sublime and significant than His temporal life, because it is a thoroughly essential, absolutely necessary, glorious, eternal, purely divine life. As far as God is above the creature, so far is this divine life of the God-Man above His

20

created life. Great and sublime as this latter is, it is supported, bounded and surrounded on all sides by the divine life, and derives thence all its glory.

Secondly, our Saviour Himself repeatedly draws our attention to this life of His before the creation. "Before Abraham was, I am" (John 8:58). "Father, glorify Me with the glory which I had, before the world was, with Thee" (John 17:5, 24). Some are of opinion that the words of our Saviour: "I saw Satan like lightning falling from heaven" (Luke 10:18), "I am the beginning, who also speak unto you" (John 8:25), also refer to this former life. They are only a few words; but, full of majesty and endless depth, they light up like vivid flashes of lightning the mysterious darkness of the life before the creation, and open out long vistas of incalculable distances. The Apostles also often refer to this life; St. John, for example, in the beginning of his Gospel, and St. Paul in his Epistles (Col. 1:15, 16, 17; Hebr. 1:2, 8, 10).

Thirdly, this life is not without its relation to us. It is our beginning and our great end, and it will be our reward and eternal joy at the close of our life.

### 2. NATURE OF THIS LIFE BEFORE THE CREATION

This life before the creation presents two points of view: first its own peculiar characteristics, and secondly its relation to creatures. Its own peculiar characteristics are revealed to us in a few words by St. John (1:2). It is of eternal duration. This newborn Child that rests upon the Virgin's knee has lived from all eternity. Long before the giving of the law on Sinai, long before the epochs of the creation and development of our terrestrial globe, long before the creation and fall of the angels, long before all the twilight of history, before all history and before all time, at the beginning of all things, consequently before all created things, Himself uncreated and without beginning, He is the Ancient of Days (Dan. 7:9), the Alpha and Omega, the beginning and the end of all things (Apoc. 22:13).

The abode of this life is no earthly home; it has no walls, no form; it is not in space, but far beyond the ends of the world and the rising and setting of the planets (Job 28:12, 20). "The Word was with God." In the bosom of the Father is His home, the beautiful land whence all good comes and whither all things beautiful go. The light of the Godhead, the abyss of inexhaustible beauty, the sanctuary of undisturbed peace, the glowing sea of infinite love and joy is His birthplace and His dwelling. There He is with God, as a distinct Person, equal to His Father in dignity, having the one Divine Nature and possessing equally with Him all power, honors and joys. "With Thee is the principality in the brightness of the saints" (Ps. 109:3).

And He is there in His quality of "the Word." "God was the Word." He is the Person of the Word, the Second Person of the Trinity. The First is the Father, Who proceeds from none, and Who has the Divine Nature and the divine life from Himself. But He knows Himself from all eternity, thinks Himself, begets a living and perfect image of His Being, and utters it as an essential and eternal Word, which perfectly and exhaustively represents Him. This is the Second Person, the Son, the Word, Wisdom, the expression and comprehension of His wisdom. Therefore the Scriptures call Wisdom the image of His Being, the brightness of eternal light, the unspotted mirror and the image of His goodness (Wisd. 7:26). In union with the Father, the Son produces the Holy Spirit, as the Person of love, the unending exhalation of divine exultation and joy, and the seal of eternal peace. There, then, the Son lives and reigns in union with the two other Persons, in eternal bliss, in social unity and all-transcendent joy.

Whilst the Father is grandeur, majesty and power, the Holy Spirit love, goodness, joy and delight in the Godhead, the Son is life, wisdom and beauty. And what is brighter, more peaceful, joyous and genial than wisdom? What sweeter than life? What more charming than light? What, lastly, more ravishing to the heart than beauty? The Son is all this. These are the special attributes of His Person, which result from the manner of His proceeding from the Father, which is a true generation.

A second feature of this life before the creation is its relation to creatures. God was not alone in His retirement and eternity. He recognized not only His uncreated goodness, beauty, power and wisdom, but also His creative goodness, capable of communication to creatures. He knew all the ways and means by which He can impart Himself, and all the aims of His creative power. Thus He was surrounded by innumerable and wonderful circles and orders of possible creations, the one higher and more glorious than the other—another side, as it were, or another world of the Divine Being. Where, then, were all these images and glories of God's communications? In the Son. He is the image of God's goodness, of the uncreated as well as of the created.

He is the wisdom of the Father, and in Him were to be found the ideas of all possible beings; in Him they lived. Indeed, He Himself proceeds also from the knowledge of all possible created things. He, then, was the treasure-house in which were stored the creative riches of God in their manifold and wondrous types; the gigantic mirror in which the glory of God was reflected in innumerable orders of creatures; the great Book of Life which lay ever open before the Father and in which He read with indescribable complacency.

We see, then, that this inner life of God was not without a most intimate relation to us. There we were, and there we lived, from all eternity. There we were thought of, there we were loved as possible images, reflections and radiations of the glory and goodness of God. How sweet it is to think that the Word proceeds from the knowledge of us also, and that we were a part, however small and insignificant, of His eternal occupation and joy! We, like many other creatures, were drops in the heavenly rainbow which surrounded Him with a million rays, and in which His divine light was reflected; little waves in the sea of possibilities in which the countenance of His beauty was mirrored; pearls in the crown of His wisdom. How wonderful and how glorious is this life, and the occupation of the Word in the midst of His possible creations! Although not yet created, still there rolled before His eye an unending series of worlds, with wonderful vegetation, strange forms of animal life, and immense mountain-throes; limitless seas roared the mighty song of their waves; hosts of stars and suns displayed themselves before His view, greeting Him with the flashing lances of their rays and the youthful vigor of their impetuous course; souls, human souls, innumerable and manifold, blossomed out before His eye like flowers before the sun in spring-time, and hovered about Him, as if attracted by a mysterious familiarity, like beautiful angelic figures without number, waiting around His throne to serve Him. A wonderful world, much greater, more manifold and splendid than the real creation, in perpetual change and renewed variety, surrounded Him like a royal court and reflected His glory and beauty.

Such was the life before the creation, a wondrous life, full of light, of majestic repose, of unity, retirement and communion, of silence and astonishing converse, of simplicity and vastness, of necessary spontaneity and unbounded freedom and independence; a life in the splendor of uncreated holiness and the exultation of all divine perfections; an adorable, divine life, the type and source of all life.

## 3. CONCLUSIONS

There are two conclusions to be drawn from meditation on this life before the creation.

First, we owe to this life our admiration, adoration, and the cordial sympathy of joy and congratulation. It is really the life of our God, His most peculiar and essential life, infinitely great, wonderful and adorable in itself. Indeed, the only adequate tribute which can be offered to this life is the exultation of the Holy Trinity Itself, and the joy which the Eternal Word Himself takes in it. "Yea, blessed art Thou, O Lord, . . . and worthy to be praised, and glorified, and exalted above all for ever; and blessed is the holy name of Thy glory, and worthy to be praised, and exalted above all in all ages. Blessed art Thou in the holy temple of Thy glory, and exceedingly to be praised, and exceeding glorious for ever. Blessed art Thou on the throne of Thy kingdom, and exceedingly to be praised, and exalted above all for ever. Blessed art Thou, that beholdest the depths, and sittest upon the Cherubim, and worthy to be praised and exalted above all for ever." "Blessed art Thou, that walkest upon the wings of the wind, and upon the waves of the sea, and exceedingly to be praised and exalted above all for ever. All angels and all Thy saints shall praise Thee, and bless and extol Thee for ever. Heaven and earth, and the sea, and all that therein is, shall bless Thee, and praise and extol Thee for ever." (Dan. 3:52–55; liturgy for Saturday in the Ember week of Advent.) We must have a tender, heart-felt love for this life, because it is also the first home, the oldest and most beautiful scene of our own life.

Secondly, we must always keep in view this life before the creation in our intercourse with our Divine Saviour, and regard His created life in the light and glory of His uncreated life. Thus we must contemplate Him in the manger, at Nazareth, in the desert, in His intercourse with men, and dying on the Cross; and bend our knees and receive Him into our hearts every time that we draw near to Him in prayer. A moment old, just after his birth, and dying for us on the Cross, He is ever the same Eternal; the Beginning without beginning, our Creator and our God, blessed for ever!

### The Eternal Decree of the Incarnation

To recognize the innumerable and glorious possibilities, how and to whom the divine goodness can impart itself, was only one part of the occupation of the life of God and of His Word before the creation. Another part consisted in the various decrees and selections which were to carry out these communications to creatures. All such communications that have taken place during time in the order of nature, grace and glory, were determined upon and settled in eternity, even the highest and last of all communications, which is above grace and glory; namely, the communication of a Divine Person to a creature. This eternal decree is the subject of our present meditation.

### 1. THE SUBJECT OF THE DECREE

The decree consisted in this, that the Second Person of the Most Holy Trinity should, in the course of time, form an essential union with a definite human nature; or rather, should raise the latter to an essential union with Himself.

It was, then, the Second Person of the Most Holy Trinity who was to assume this human nature; not the First, and not the Third. The reasons of this choice might perhaps be as follows: The Second Person is the Word, the internal, substantial Word of God. The outward creation is also a word of God, but a finite and accidental word. This second word was spoken by the First, and according to His own likeness (Gen. 1:26). It was therefore fitting that prototype and copy should be essentially united and thus present a perfect image of God, such as the God-Man is. Again, the Second Person is the Son. Because God has created the creature, His relation to it is a sort of fatherhood, and the highest aim of the creature is that of a kind of sonship. Now, by the fact that the Son of God united Himself essentially to the creature, it has become the true son of God, and the First Person of the Deity its true Father. In the God-Man the creature attains to its true sonship, and it was fitting that this sonship should be imparted to it through the Divine Son. Thus the Father finds through the Son access to the creature as a father, and the creature access to the Father as a son. Lastly, the Second Person is Wisdom. Wisdom had created the world; by Wisdom the world must be restored and perfected. The first man, in his criminal desire of wisdom, had formed an alliance with the impious wisdom of Satan,

in order to unravel God's mysteries. It was therefore very fitting
that he should now be led to this glorious goal by union with the
Wisdom of God, the source of all wisdom.

With regard to the nature which the Son of God was to assume,
the choice could lie only within the limits of the beings gifted
with reason; that is to say, between the angelic and the human
nature. How important and momentous for us the result of this
choice was! Its superiority, sublimity and purity, as well as its
nearness to God, pleaded for the angelic nature. Then, too, the
assumption of their nature by God would comfort and reward
those angels who had remained faithful to Him and be a glorious
compensation for the humiliation they had sustained in the fall of
so many of their number. On the other hand, the very lowliness
of the human nature had its claims for assumption. God would
thus descend deeper into His creation, and raise it to Himself.
Besides, the nature of man, being both material and spiritual,
included in itself the two great kingdoms of the spiritual and the
material creation; and thus, in it, the whole creation would be as it
were drawn up into God. Another reason for choosing our human
nature was pity and compassion for its fall, which had been
brought about by the wiles of the fallen angel. Thus it was to
our nature that the Son of God graciously stooped, and the choice
was determined for all eternity, as the Apostle says: "Nowhere
doth He take hold of the angels; but of the seed of Abraham He
taketh hold" (Hebr. 2:16).

And now this decision was followed by other decrees. The
Eternal Word chose for Himself a definite human soul, a definite
body; He chose His Mother, the nation, tribe and family to which
He should belong; He chose our little, insignificant earth as His
country and His earthly home; He chose His faithful, His apostles
and companions in glory. Sin also He permitted, in all its power
and terror, and on its account chose the circuitous path of poverty,
humiliation and death. He chose Bethlehem and Calvary. Such
were the decrees made by the Eternal Word, together with the
Father and the Holy Ghost; made in all perfection, freedom,
precision, with infinite joy in their number, beauty and efficacy,
and with infinite love for us. They were eternal and unalterable,
yet made with full knowledge of the caprice and fickleness of
the human will; they were marvelously adapted to promote God's
honor and our welfare; they were common to all the Divine Persons, though they concerned more especially the Second Person.

Thus this great decree, with its many decisions, penetrates, takes root in, supports and embraces the whole of creation, like a mighty tree of life, under whose immense shade the whole host of the elect may rest secure. These decrees laid the foundation of our salvation, and they will be the object of our joy in heaven for ever.

## 2. THE MOTIVES FOR THIS DECREE

There were two principal motives.

The first motive consists in the task of the God-Man, or the external object of the Incarnation. This is in fact, and is acknowledged to be, the redemption of mankind. Nothing is more clearly and frequently enunciated by the holy Fathers, in Holy Scripture, and in the words of our Divine Saviour. He Himself said that He came to seek that which was lost (Luke 19:10), to give His life for many (Matt. 20:28), in short, to save His people (Matt. 1:21); and as our holy Church so powerfully expresses it in the Creed: "For us men and for our salvation He came down from Heaven." The whole plan and arrangement of the nature and life of the God-Man, His Passion and Death and all the circumstances of His life agree with this. Indeed, many of the Fathers and great theologians say that, but for the Fall, the Incarnation would never have taken place. According to them, then, the actual and sufficient reason for it was the redemption, or the exceeding mercy of God: His will to remedy our chief evil, sin. In truth, this motive shows His mercy in a marvelously bright light, repaying an injury by so great a benefit, causing so much that is good and glorious to arise from such a terrible evil, and deciding even in the prevision of sin upon this, the greatest of all benefits. Thus this divine mercy reveals itself in the most perfect manner.

A second motive lay in the greatness and magnificence of the work itself, for the very reason that the outcome of it was the God-Man, and in consequence the love of God for the God-Man. As a matter of fact Holy Scripture does not exclude this motive, and great theologians say that there is no contradiction in presuming that God may have had several different motives, each of which would alone have sufficed for the execution of the work. Indeed, some of them go still farther, and say that the consideration of the greatness and magnificence of its result, namely the God-Man, was the first and principal motive; so that even if Adam had not fallen, God would nevertheless, out of regard for this motive, have accomplished the work of the Incarnation, because Christ is of greater value than all creatures together, and God on this account loved Him more than all others. If the God-Man had come only on account of sin and to remedy sin, He would lose the great significance which He has in Himself and sink down, as it were, to the level of contingent beings. But this is by no means the case with our Saviour, and this gives occasion to the theologians who hold this opinion to develop their magnificent view of the greatness and splendor of the Word Incarnate.

They say the God-Man was the first being of which God thought and which He willed, Himself excepted. Therefore He planned the God-Man so that He embraced in His being all classes and kinds of creatures, and all the splendors of God's communications to creatures, and included in Himself all the treasures of nature, grace and glory, and even the participation in the Divine Nature, by means of the union with the Second Person of the Godhead. All other beings, say they, whether purely material, purely spiritual, or material and spiritual combined, were created not only on His account but after His likeness, and are merely partial copies of His being and sharers in a part of His glory. The ground for this assumption is that God does not, like us, rise from the individual to the universal, in thinking and creating, but comprehends and appoints at once each individual in the generality of things. Besides, the dignity of the God-Man, on account of the personal union with God, is so great that we may and must of right concede to Him all that is not contrary to faith and reason, especially when there is sufficient foundation for it in revelation. And this foundation we find in the Scriptures, where the God-Man is called "the first-born of every creature," for whom all things were made, "that He might hold the primacy in all things, because in Him it hath well pleased the Father that all fulness should dwell" (Col. 1:15, 18, 19); "the heir of all things" (Hebr. 1:2); the "bud of the Lord" (Isa. 4:2; Jer. 23:5), that is, as it were, the flower of all creation. There is certainly nothing more glorious and magnificent than this view of the God-Man. He is, so to speak, God's first step outwards, the beginning of His ways, the design and sketch of the whole plan of creation; He is the origin and center of all creatures, their model and their aim. The different spheres of creation, material, human, and angelic, group themselves around the God-Man like the planets round the sun, and receive from Him their glory, beauty and significance; He is the rule and guide of all God's works.

### 3. THE FIRST CONCLUSIONS TO BE DRAWN FROM THIS MEDITATION

We ought, above all, to be filled with admiration at the greatness and splendor of the divine decree. It is certainly the most beautiful of all God's ideas, the most glorious of His counsels, a summary and abridgment of all His creative thoughts. There is no other of these thoughts in which the riches of the divine wisdom, power and goodness are so gloriously reflected, whether it was conceived before or after the prevision and permission of sin (Ps. 39:6; Rom. 11:34).

Secondly, we must thank the Most Holy Trinity for the glory which accrues to It from this decree; also on our Saviour's account, because upon it all His greatness rests; and lastly, for ourselves, since it is so intimately connected with us. Our happiness, our salvation, our greatness and predestination wholly depend upon the predestination of Jesus. We must also thank the Second Person of the Godhead in particular, because He consented to the union with our nature, and offered Himself for it. Herein lies a peculiar and intimate relation of our nature to the Second Person of the Deity. The Church thanks the Son of God so touchingly in the Te Deum, that He "did not abhor the Virgin's womb." And since the Divine Wisdom said of Himself that it was His delight to dwell with the children of men (Prov. 8:31), we may call Him in a special manner the great Friend of mankind.

Lastly, it is but fitting that we should think often of this eternal decree and speak of it to the Blessed Trinity. Great consolation and an inexhaustible source of courage in all sadness may be derived from this truth, and our petitions will have a special power to obtain the wished-for graces if we remind the Persons of the Holy Trinity of this great counsel of their goodness and mercy, which has made us rich in all things. Advent is a season especially appropriate to devout thought on this mystery. At this time we may with St. John the Evangelist raise our eyes and contemplate the Word "in the beginning" and in the bosom of the Father, destined from all eternity to be the Child of Bethlehem.

## THE CREATION

JOHN 1:3. All things were made by him, and without him was made nothing that was made.—4. In Him was life, and the life was the light of men.—10. He was in the world, and the world was made by Him.

At length came the time for the realization of the eternal decrees. These decrees embraced not merely the God-Man, but also innumerable other creatures, which stood in the closest relations to Him. The present meditation is occupied only with the relations of the God-Man to creation in general. It will open out to us many of the marvelous counsels of God.

### 1. WHAT IS UNDERSTOOD BY CREATION

By creation is understood everything that exists besides God, and that is created, preserved and brought to its end by Him. This creation is in truth simply the outward kingdom of God, the visible expression of His creative, communicative goodness, a created image of His divine beauty and glory. And since this uncreated glory is infinite and inexhaustible, the expression of it will also be extremely varied in every respect, whether as regards the physical nature of creatures or as regards the manner of their existence.

Creation may be divided, according to nature and essence, into irrational and rational beings; the former, again, into animate and inanimate creatures, the rational into purely spiritual beings and such as are in part material and in part spiritual. The whole universe—including alike matter, vegetation, the animal, human and angelic worlds—is grouped in vast, manifold circles around God, the eternal and unending origin and source of all life and light; so many rays and reflections, as it were, of Himself. As regards their manner of existence, rational beings belong either to the order of nature or to that of grace, according as they remain within the limits of their innate wants, sufficiencies and spheres of action, or are raised by the pure grace of God to a manner of existence, a life and an activity which stand entirely or partially above the sphere, capability, consciousness and wants of nature, and which are instead a created communication of the nature, life and activity of God Himself. This is the supernatural state, or state of grace. This state of grace consists here below in the communication of the divine adoption by the gift of sanctifying grace, with the right of inheritance to the heavenly kingdom; and in the world to come in the entrance upon and possession of this heavenly inheritance, by the glory in which we shall behold, possess and love God, as He beholds, possesses and loves Himself and is infinitely happy in this love. According to God's eternal decree, men and angels are called to this sublime life; and to this end He created, in His goodness, an abundance of supernatural means for the communication, preservation and development of this sanctifying grace, in the magnificent arrangements and institutions which are to be found, in their entirety, in the Church, and whose existence and development embrace earth and heaven, and extend over the whole period of the world's existence. All created things center round this glorious economy of grace, and the entire kingdom of nature serves as its support and its aid. Even purely material things become, in the Sacraments of the Church, channels of grace and supernatural blessings. This is but a superficial glance at the work of creation, and yet what glorious counsels it reveals!

### 2. THE RELATIONS OF THE GOD-MAN TO CREATION

In our meditations on the God-Man it will be necessary to distinguish carefully between His Divine Person and Nature, which were from all eternity, and His human nature, which was created and began to exist in time.

As the Eternal Word of God, or Second Person of the Godhead, He is simply the author, type and last end of all creation, and this in common with the Father and the Holy Ghost, because every divine action *ad extra* is an operation of the Divine Nature, which is the same in all the Three Persons, and as such it is to be ascribed to them all in the same manner. Nevertheless the creation is ascribed to the Son in an especial manner, inasmuch as it is the work of life, wisdom and beauty. The Second Person is always represented to us in Scripture as the author of light, life, truth and wisdom, in the natural as well as in the supernatural order. Here we have above all the magnificent testimony of St. John (1:3, 4, 9, 10). He first bears witness to the authorship of the Word with regard to all creatures, and he begins with the physical order of nature. "All things were made by Him, and without Him was made nothing that was made" (John 1:3). He does not say "of Him," but "by Him," and this denotes quite a peculiar relation to the Son, inasmuch as He is Wisdom, and embraces the prototypes of all things in Himself, and executes them by the divine power which He has received from the Father by His generation.

Thus the denotation "by Him" is quite peculiar to the Son, while of the Father it is said that all things are "of Him," and of the Holy Ghost, "in Him." Further, St. John attests the authorship of the Word with regard to the supernatural order of things (John 1:4, 9, 10): "In Him was life, and the life (the Word) was the light of men." The life which He had in Himself was the life of the Divine Nature and Divine Sonship, and of beatitude in the vision and possession of God; and this supernatural life the Word imparts to mankind by revelation, by the grace of faith, by sanctifying grace and the brightness of glory (John 1:12, 13; Apoc. 3:14). The same truth is confirmed by St. Paul (Hebr. 1:2, 3; Col. 1:16). This action or operation of Eternal Wisdom is gloriously and magnificently described in the books of the Old Testament. Wisdom is the author of the physical and moral order (Prov. 8:22 seq.; Job 28; Wisd. 7:21 seq.); she leads to the perfection of righteousness (Wisd. 6:19, 20), instructs kings and guides nations (Wisd. 6; 7; 10), and saves them (Wisd. 16:12; Ps. 106:20). It is often difficult to distinguish the action of the divine wisdom from the Person of Wisdom, in these magnificent passages. But this very emphasis and stress which is laid upon Wisdom as the creative Word and supreme wisdom of the Father is precisely the reason why the creation and government of the world are ascribed in an especial manner to the Son.

Regarded as God-Man, the Saviour could not of course be the author of creation, because He did not yet exist. He could however, according to the opinion of those who say that He was the first being which God recognized and willed, be so to speak the type of creation, by virtue of His divine and human nature, which includes in a certain sense all orders of creation in germ. This is beyond all doubt with regard to the supernatural state of grace, with the entire splendor of which He is endowed, so that upon His model all the elect are formed (Eph. 1:3, 9 seq.; Rom. 8:29). And just as assuredly was He in the prevision of His Death, for mankind at least, the meriting cause of all graces of supernatural life and glory. For this reason St. John calls Him the Lamb which was slain from the beginning (Apoc. 13:8). Finally, the God-Man is the last end of the whole creation, that in all things He might rank supreme (Col. 1:16; Hebr. 1:2; Eph. 1:5). Even the material creation finds in Him its end and fulfilment. Our world was to become His earthly home. For Him the continents of this earth rose and sank; for Him marble, gold and precious stones were secreted in the bosom of the mountains; for Him the springs and rivers flowed, the seas were formed; and for Him the earth was peopled with its animals and plants. In Him and through Him oil, corn and wine were to convey the most priceless blessings of earth, and even a glorious immortality. And for Him in a special manner were formed the beautiful Promised Land, Egypt with its marvels, and the mighty city of Rome. Throughout creation Wisdom worked, continually interweaving, in thought and intention, her every work with the destiny of the coming God-Man and His kingdom.

### 3. CONCLUSIONS TO BE DRAWN FROM THIS MEDITATION

Our origin, then, is from the Son, and for Him we are created; we bear within us His image, His life and His destiny. What can follow from this but, in the first place, homage, adoration and gratitude, as is due to the Author of our being? We owe all to Him, in the natural as well as in the supernatural order. And it is especially in the supernatural order that we bear the image of His divine goodness and adoption, and have received "of His fulness grace for grace" (John 1:16).

Moreover there follows from what has been said a lofty idea of the splendor and divinity of the Word. What a world of truth, beauty and goodness this creation is! By this Word it has been called into existence, and it is but a feeble image of His power, wisdom, goodness and beauty. In Him all these treasures are essential and original (Col. 2:3).

The third conclusion may be a great esteem and regard for the image of the God-Man within us. "If we examine sincerely and prudently into the origin of our creation," says St. Leo, "we find that man was created after the image of God, in order that he might imitate his Creator. This is the natural nobility of our race, when the image of the divine goodness is reflected in us as in a mirror."

Lastly, we may also find in this meditation the motive of affection and love towards the Second Person of the Deity. In the description of the action of Wisdom in this world, as the Holy Scriptures of the Old Testament trace it out for us, we are struck by the benevolence, the loving kindness, one might almost say the motherly tenderness with which this royal Wisdom devotes herself to the guiding and training of man. Man appears there as her favorite, her pupil, her child, whom she protects with touching condescension and care (Eccli. 24; Wisd. 6:13, 14, 15 seq.; 7:22 seq.; Prov. 1:20 seq.; 8:1 seq.; 9:1 seq.) against the seduction and persecution of the world (Wisd. 2 seq.) and the corruption of sin and heathenism (Wisd. 13:14, 15). It is a faithful picture of the spirit, the action and the fulness of blessings in which the Incarnate Wisdom appeared and revealed Itself (Matt. 12:18).

## The Angel World

The first part of this divine plan to be realized was the creation of the world of angels.

### 1. THE CREATION OF THE ANGELS

The angels are incorporeal beings, pure spirits, with deep, penetrating intellect and enormous will-power, by which they influence even the material world. They were created in great number and glorious variety, endowed with sanctifying grace, and destined to enjoy the vision of God as their supernatural end. No mere creature, save the Mother of God, is equal to this first work of divine power. The angels burst from the bosom of the Almighty like streams of light, numerous as the stars of heaven and the sands of the sea; a vast world, with innumerable hierarchies of knowledge and power, of spiritual and supernatural beauty.

They also were created by the Word, as St. Paul (Col. 1:16) expressly points out in his enumeration of several classes of angels created by the Eternal Word. By virtue of their profound knowledge and grace, these "morning stars of the creation and first sons of God" (Job 38:7) are in a special way images of uncreated Wisdom and of the Son of God.

### 2. THE TRIAL OF THE ANGELS AND ITS RESULT

Although created in the grace of God, the angels were not, at the time of their creation, as yet in their final state. They, like ourselves, were to merit the vision of God by undergoing a test, in which they should prove themselves worthy of heaven. For them, as for us, heaven was to be a reward.

It has not been revealed to us in what this test consisted. In general it may be said that they were to make use of their freedom to acknowledge God as their Lord and last end, to submit to Him, and to reach their destiny by that path and by those means which He had appointed for them. The opinion of St. Bernard (Sermo 17 in Cant.) and several other theologians may be considered very probable; namely, that the test consisted in this, that God revealed to the angels the future Incarnation of His Son and required them, as a just consequence, to recognize Him (the Son) as their Lord and Advocate, and to submit to Him. This opinion, although not to be found in Holy Scripture or in the more ancient writings of the holy Fathers, has nothing incongruous in it, and presents the advantage of one great uniform idea, comprising all the elements of creation and ranging them about the God-Man; whilst on the other hand it explains very easily, naturally, and with peculiar facility all that Holy Scripture says concerning the fall of the angels. The result of the trial was that a part of the angelic host submitted to God and stood the test, but the other part, led astray by Lucifer, resisted the will and command of God, and thus fell into mortal sin. This sin is designated in the Holy Scriptures and in the writings of the holy Fathers as pride (Eccli. 10:15; Tob. 4:14; Isa. 14:13; Ez. 28:2, 17), hatred of mankind (John 8:44), and envy (Wisd. 2:24). It may be that this pride consisted in striving to attain a resemblance to God, and that the rebellious angel wished to win for himself by his own natural strength the goal of heaven, or to arrogate to himself some other power that belongs to God alone. But the most natural explanation is the supposition that he envied the God-Man His personal union with the Second Person of the Godhead, claiming it for himself, and refusing to pay homage to Him. Thence also the fierce hatred and envy of the fallen angels towards the God-Man and the whole human race, whose nature attained in Him to the honor of personal union with God. As it appears, the mighty angel, who may probably have been one of the highest order (Ez. 28:12–15), seduced a great number of the angels into disobedience (Apoc. 12:4).

The other angels, apparently under the leadership of St. Michael (Apoc. 12:7), by God's grace stood firm, resisted the tempter and submitted humbly to God. If the subject of the test really was the mystery of the Incarnation, then their submission was also a homage to the future God-Man, and it may be easily understood how, as theologians say, all gifts of grace and glory came to them from Him. They believed in Him, hoped in Him, and thus grace could flow to them from His merits, though not from His Death. He is not their Redeemer, because they did not need any reconciliation or satisfaction, but He is their Head (Col. 1:18; Eph. 1:22). In Him all were to be united (Eph. 1:10). Angels and men form one order, one body in Christ; and thus it is natural that all graces should flow to them from the common source, the common head. The grace of Christ extends to all times and all orders of the creation.

### 3. CONSEQUENCES OF THE RESULT OF THE TEST

Judgment was at once passed upon the fallen angels. Their condemnation was sudden, terrible and eternal. The heinousness of their sin was in proportion to the perfection of their intellect and the decision and stubbornness of their will; and, not being allowed time and grace, it was irreparable. Thus, then, the fallen angels, deprived of grace, stripped of all consoling, supernatural truth, hardened and obdurate in sin, have lost heaven for ever and incurred the twofold punishment of the damned; some of them being banished for a time to our earthly sphere for the trial of mankind (Eph. 2:2; 6:11, 12), the remainder to the abyss of hell for the punishment of the lost. To abide in hell is assuredly the portion which awaits them after the Last Judgment (II Peter 2:4). They are the most abject and unhappy of creatures. From being the brightest ornaments of God's Court, they have become the seducers of mankind and the jailers and executioners of divine justice; detestable on account of their wickedness and hatred of God and His image. Temptation is their business (II Cor. 11:3; I Thess. 3:5; I Peter 5:8; Apoc. 12:9). And how terribly they have succeeded in their work of destruction, and in their hatred of God, the God-Man and mankind! They prompted original sin, and with it death; they brought heathenism and a flood of temporal evils into the world. Even the Death of the God-Man was their work (John 13:2). Fearful is the devastation they have wrought and still work in Christ's kingdom. Nevertheless all their efforts do but accomplish, in a certain sense, the decrees of God. By temptations God's wisdom and the power of His grace are glorified; virtue is practiced, sin atoned for, and victories and merits gained, and all turns at length to the confusion and torment of the tempters (Apoc. 12:10, 11). In this manner the evil spirits, even after their fall, cooperate indirectly at least in the universal good and the order of Divine Providence. They are in truth a power desirous ever of evil, but producing good.

The good angels, on the contrary, were beatified immediately after the test; they enjoy for all eternity the vision of God, and exercise a great activity for His honor and the salvation of mankind, by opposing the efforts of the evil spirits, restraining men from evil and leading them to good, and defending, enlightening and purifying the kingdom of Christ. Thus we see them everywhere, in the Old Covenant as well as in the New, busied with the Church, the Person of the God-Man, and the accomplishment of His mysteries. They truly ascend and descend continually upon Christ and upon the Body of Christ, the Church (John 1:51; Hebr. 1:14).

Thus this mystery of the angel world is of great significance with regard to the whole life of our Saviour. Here is the beginning of sin, the first resistance and strife against the God-Man and His kingdom. Later on the sin of the angels caused sin in the world also. It is the same devil who ever sins (I John 3:8). But this sin brought us the Saviour. He came to destroy the works of the devil (I John 3:8); namely sin, death, and the empire of concupiscence (Hebr. 2:14). Here, then, all is explained, and in particular the reason of the devil's hatred and enmity against the human race, for which cause our Lord says that he "was a murderer from the beginning" (John 8:44). But we have also a motive for loving the holy angels, in their affection for the God-Man and our human nature, which is so strikingly manifested in their exertions for us and for the Church. These exertions are also an encouragement to us to resist with all our might the animosity of the devil against mankind and the Church, and to work for souls and the kingdom of Christ.

## II. THE LIFE OF JESUS IN THE PROPHECIES

### THE CREATION OF MAN, AND HIS FALL

#### (GEN. 3)

The visible world, with man as its head and adornment, was God's second creation.

#### 1. THE CREATION OF MAN

The very manner in which the creation of man is related shows that an important work is in process. God first takes counsel with Himself (Gen. 1:26); He Himself makes man, with a body and a soul (Gen. 1:27; 2:7, 22), and the words that He speaks at the consultation denote a special similarity and likeness of man to God (Gen. 1:26, 27). In fact man, as a spiritual and material being, unites in himself the excellence of the material and the spiritual creation, and is by virtue of his rational soul a true, natural image of God. To this was added the supernatural likeness, by grace, which makes man a child of God and opens out and ensures to him all the glory of the supernatural life. Other wondrous gifts were added to this supernatural grace; especially freedom from concupiscence (Gen. 2:25), immortality (Gen. 2:17), complete control over the visible world (Gen. 1:26, 28, 29), and the pleasant sojourn in Paradise (Gen. 2:15). Thus was man created. He went forth from the hand of God as a wonderful being, and moreover presented a magnificent image of the Second Person of the Godhead, in virtue of his intellect and his supernatural quality of child of God and representative on earth of His royal wisdom. Not only were our first parents to enjoy these splendid gifts, but all their descendants also, provided that they obeyed God's command. It was a glorious plan of God's wisdom and goodness towards mankind. Beyond all, this earthly kingdom was to be the pledge of the eternal, heavenly kingdom, into which they were to be received without suffering or death (cf. Ps. 8).

## 2. THE FALL OF MAN

In the fall of man there are two things to be considered: first, the cause of sin, and secondly, sin itself.

The remote cause, or rather occasion, was the permission of God. He left to subordinate causes the freedom with which He had endowed them, notwithstanding which He still gained His end, viz. the revelation of His power, wisdom and goodness, and in particular the realization of the eternal decree of the Incarnation, as St. Augustine says: "God preferred to permit evil, rather than not to take occasion from evil to do good." Another occasion on the part of God was the command not to eat of the fruit of the forbidden tree (Gen. 2:16, 17). He made the compact with mankind conditional upon the observance of this single and simple command. The second cause, a very powerful one, although only external, was the devil, in his hatred of God and His image; his envy of the human race, whose happiness he intended to destroy; his pride, in which he wished to rule over mankind; his malice and likewise the cunning with which he devised the gradual steps of his temptation. He concealed himself under the form of a serpent; he tempted Eve as being weaker, and first laid siege to the spiritual part of her being, because the senses presented no point for an attack, on account of their freedom from irregular concupiscence. He sought to seduce her soul to distrust of God (Gen. 3:4), curiosity, pride (Gen. 3:5), and lastly sensuality. He intended that Eve should then play the part of temptress to the man. The third and actual cause is the weakness and inconstancy of man, the limitation of his intellect, and especially the feebleness of his will. It would appear that Eve, at any rate, believed the lying words of Satan (Gen. 3:13), and allowed herself to be duped and led into interior and exterior sin. Adam may have fallen rather through compliance with the wish of Eve (Gen. 3:12, 17).

The sin itself consisted, in the first place, in disobedience to the strict command of God, and then in distrust of His truthfulness; then again in pride, since our first parents strove after an unlawful similarity to God, whether it was that they wished to know the mysteries of God and their own future, or to determine for themselves the way to beatitude, all of which may be understood in the words: "You shall be as gods, knowing good and evil" (Gen. 3:5); finally, the sin consisted also in sensuality, by the enjoyment of the fruit, and in Adam's case in guilty compliance with the wish of Eve. The sin was not in itself of the greatest, even as regards pride; for our first parents aspired to a similarity to God in knowledge, not in power like the fallen angels, and specifically there are other sins of pride greater than this, such as atheism and blasphemy. But taking circumstances into consideration, the sin of our first parents was very great, on account of the elevation and perfection of their state, of the grace with which they were endowed, and of their position as parents of the human race; further, on account of the ease of observing the precept, and of their ingratitude and frivolity; and lastly, on account of the terrible consequences, if these were foreseen by them. This, then, was the first sin committed upon earth; a reproduction of the sin of the angels, because it was a sin of pride and brought about by them, and the type and origin of all human sin.

### 3. THE PUNISHMENT

The punishment fell upon all the guilty, on Satan as well as on our first parents.

The severest punishment fell upon Satan, because he was the real instigator of the sin. His hatred and malice had succeeded in ruining our first parents, and in them the whole human race, thus frustrating God's original plan; and he was already about to set his foot in triumph upon the neck of poor humanity, when he was for the second time overtaken by judgment and punishment, and that the worst that his pride could meet with. No sooner has he accomplished the downfall of humanity by means of a woman, than his own defeat by a woman and her seed is announced to him (Gen. 3:14, 15). This woman, according to the interpretation of the Church, is Mary, the second Eve, and Christ is the second Adam; the second parents of our race. Satan encountered this defeat first in the Immaculate Conception of the Mother of God, and then in the Death of Christ. This Death was brought about by Satan. He was to be the mortal sting in the heel of the Redeemer, and this heel crushed his head. The contemptible crawling of the animal that he had used as an instrument of temptation was to be to Satan a token of this defeat, disgrace and shame. As the serpent crawls upon the earth and is an abomination to all, so shall he also be degraded and abhorred.

The punishment of our first parents had features peculiar to each of them, as well as those which are shared by the whole human race. The deprivation of sanctifying grace and of the dignity of being children of God fell upon both in common, and upon all of us, so that all their descendants are born in original sin, in a state of exclusion—and guilty exclusion—from grace. This punishment made itself felt in the deprivation of sensible gifts, which all depended upon the possession of sanctifying grace. These gifts were freedom from irregular concupiscence, immortality, and the enjoyment of Paradise. Irregular concupiscence showed itself in our first parents at once, in their shame at being naked (Gen. 3:7, 10, 11); death was formally announced to them (Gen. 3:19, 22); and the banishment from Paradise to the curse-laden earth followed immediately (Gen. 3:23, 24). The particular punishments took into account the difference of sex and office. Pain in childbirth and subjection, reluctant subjection to the man in domestic life were imposed as the woman's portion (Gen. 3:16). The man, who had to provide for the maintenance of the family, and who was destined to rule over nature, was punished by heavy, humiliating and often fruitless labor, and by the contumacy of nature (Gen. 3:17, 18, 19). He was now obliged to wrest from the earth by painful labor all that he was henceforth to subsist upon. Although by virtue of his position the sin of Adam was the greater, yet relatively Eve's transgression weighed heavier, because she had not only sinned herself but also led another into sin, and because she had done wrong not as a concession to a friend, but by yielding to the enemy.

Such, then, is the sad history of the fall of our first parents, and of us all. It is certainly fitting that we should conclude by making acts of hatred and horror of mortal sin and its instigator. Sin it is by which the Evil One destroys the works and plans of God, and plunges His creatures into unspeakable misery. Already the second of God's creations is disfigured and devastated by sin; and how terrible has Adam's sin proved itself, in its range over all mankind, in the wild and devastating torrent of the passions, in the flood of crimes and temporal evils, in the punishment of death for all without exception, and eternal death for countless numbers! God and the human race have no greater enemy than mortal sin. Indeed, it is their only enemy. Without sin, even hell can do no harm.

But even here God's goodness and mercy are revealed in a touching manner. First of all, He does not let the human race, like the fallen angels, remain in its ruin, but wills to save it. It had been overreached and overcome by one more powerful than itself. The guilt passes down to all the descendants of Adam and Eve without their personal fault, whilst with the angels each one sinned in person. Secondly, it is another feature of His mercy that the very punishment, in its various forms (e.g. work, temporal evils), is a bridle upon strong passions and sin. Thirdly, His mercy is shown especially in the promise of a Saviour. This Saviour is Satan's condemnation. Satan's plot against the human race is overthrown, and turns against himself. He would have made us unhappy, and has occasioned our greatest happiness; he would have robbed us of all supernatural blessings, and has enriched us with still greater ones; he would have humiliated us, and has raised us above himself and all created things. This Saviour is no other than the Messias, at once God and man. He will repair and restore everything: sin by His Death, the ravages of the passions by His grace, and death by His Resurrection. Thus Satan's condemnation is our salvation. God became our shield and defender against our malicious and insolent oppressor (Isa. 49:25, 26). We may well exclaim with the Church: "O happy fault, which deserved to have such and so great a Redeemer!" The Redeemer promised to us is to be of our own race. Poor humanity can now depart from Paradise consoled, and set out on its pilgrimage through the unfriendly world; it has a staff upon which to lean, a star to guide, rejoice and comfort it, the sign of the woman trampling on the serpent, with the promise of Emmanuel. The words spoken by God as He expelled Adam from Paradise, "So Adam is become as one of us" (Gen. 3:22), are no longer a mockery, but a consoling truth, realized in Christ, in whom the human nature and the divine are hypostatically united.

## ISRAEL AND THE MESSIAS

JOHN 1:11. He came unto His own.

MATT. 1:1. The book of the generation of Jesus Christ, the son of David, the son of Abraham.—2. Abraham begot Isaac. And Isaac begot Jacob. And Jacob begot Judas and his brethren.—3. And Judas begot Phares and Zara of Thamar. And Phares begot Esron. And Esron begot Aram.—4. And Aram begot Aminadab. And Aminadab begot Naasson. And Naasson begot Salmon.—5. And Salmon begot Booz of Rahab. And Booz begot Obed of Ruth. And Obed begot Jesse. And Jesse begot David the king.—6. And David the king begot Solomon, of her that had been (the wife) of Urias.—7. And Solomon begot Roboam. And Roboam begot Abias. And Abias begot Asa.—8. And Asa begot Josaphat. And Josaphat begot Joram. And Joram begot Ozias.—9. And Ozias begot Joatham. And Joatham begot Achaz. And Achaz begot Ezechias.—10. And Ezechias begot Manasses. And Manasses begot Amon. And Amon begot Josias.—11. And Josias begot Jechonias and his brethren in the transmigration of Babylon.—12. And after the transmigration of Babylon: Jechonias begot Salathiel. And Salathiel begot Zorobabel.—13. And Zorobabel begot Abiud. And Abiud begot Eliakim. And Eliakim begot Azor.—14. And Azor begot Sadoc. And Sadoc begot Achim. And Achim begot Eliud.—15. And Eliud begot Eleazar. And Eleazar begot Mathan. And Mathan begot Jacob.—16. And Jacob begot Joseph the husband of Mary, of whom was born Jesus, who is called Christ.

LUKE 3:23. And Jesus himself was beginning about the age of thirty years, being, as it was supposed, the son of Joseph, who was of Heli, who was of Mathat,—24. Who was of Levi, who was of Melchi, who was of Janne, who was of Joseph,—25. Who was of Mathathias, who was of Amos, who was of Nahum, who was of Hesli, who was of Nagge,—26. Who was of Mahath, who was of Mathathias, who was of Semei, who was of Joseph, who was of Juda,—27. Who was of Joanna, who was of Resa, who was of Zorobabel, who was of Salathiel, who was of Neri,—28. Who was of Melchi, who was of Addi, who was of Cosan, who was of Elmadan, who was of Her,—29. Who was of Jesus, who was of Eliezer, who was of Jorim, who was of Mathat, who was of Levi,—30. Who was of Simeon, who was of Judas, who was of Joseph, who was of Jona, who was of Eliakim,—31. Who was of Melea, who was of Menna, who was of Mathatha, who was of Nathan, who was of David,—32. Who was of Jesse, who was of Obed, who was of Booz, who was of Salmon, who was of Naasson,—33. Who was of Aminadab, who was of Aram, who was of Esron, who was of Phares, who was of Juda,—34. Who was of Jacob, who was of Isaac, who was of Abraham, who was of Thare, who was of Nachor,—35. Who was of Sarug, who was of Ragau, who was of Phaleg, who was of Heber, who was of Sale,—36. Who was of Cainan, who was of Arphaxad, who was of Sem, who was of Noe, who was of Lamech,—37. Who was of Mathusale, who was of Henoch, who was of Jared, who was of Malaleel, who was of Cainan,—38. Who was of Henos, who was of Seth, who was of Adam, who was of God.

To Adam had been promised a Redeemer, who should be one of his own race. This Redeemer was to be a definite Person, and was therefore to belong to a definite family and, since the descendants of Adam had separated into tribes and nations after the building of the tower of Babel, also to a definite nation. This nation was that of the Israelites, which was sprung from Abraham, had increased to a numerous people in Egypt, and had been delivered from its oppressors by Moses. Strengthened by the direct government of God, it had conquered the Promised Land. Established there, it later on took a monarchic form of constitution under Saul, and reached the highest summit of its power under David and Solomon. It was then split into two kingdoms, and led away to captivity in Ninive and Babylon, returned to its own land under the Persian monarchy, won for itself independence from the neighboring Greek kingdoms, and was again ruled by its own princes. Finally, at the time of Christ, it had become incorporated into the Roman Empire. The chief task of this nation was to prepare the world for the Messias, to give Him to the world, and to make all nations participators in its own hereditary blessings, as St. Paul says: "The words of God were committed to them" (Rom. 3:2), to them "belongeth the adoption as of children, and the glory, and the testament, and the giving of the law, and the service of God, and the promises; whose are the fathers, and of whom Christ is according to the flesh, who is over all things God blessed for ever" (Rom. 9:4, 5). The Israelite nation prepared the way for the Messias in a threefold manner.

### 1. ISRAEL PRESERVES IN THE WORLD THE BELIEF IN THE FUTURE MESSIAS AND PREACHES HIM

The belief in the Messias pervaded the whole existence of this nation and was, as it were, its very soul. The expression of this belief was manifested in four distinct ways. First, in the prophecies and promises. After God had given to Abraham in general and obscure terms the promise of the Messias, saying that in his seed all nations of the earth should be blessed (Gen. 12:3), which was only possible through Christ, and had repeated this promise to Isaac (Gen. 26:4) and Jacob (Gen. 28:14), He declared to the latter in more express terms that the Messias should belong to the tribe of Juda (Gen. 49:10), later on specifying the family of David as the branch from which He should proceed (II Kings 7:16; 23:5; Ps. 88:29; Osee 3:5; Amos 9:11, 12). The Messias is of the very essence of the prophecies, and in them His whole portrait is sketched in broad outlines. He is the Son of God (Ps. 2:7) and Son of Man, David's Son and Lord (Ps. 109:1, 3; Jer. 23:5); He is the Saviour from sin, by His Passion (Ps. 39; 68); He is born of a virgin (Isa. 7:14), and in Bethlehem (Mich. 5:2); His advent occurs at the time of the second Temple (Agg. 2:8), about seventy weeks of years after Daniel's prediction (Dan. 9); He is announced by a Forerunner who preaches salvation (Isa. 40:3; Mal. 3:1); He works first in Galilee (Isa. 9:1) and without ostentation (Isa. 42:1–4; 61:1–3); He founds an eternal kingdom over all nations (Dan. 2:44; Isa. 49); He enters Jerusalem in triumph (Zach. 9:9); He is misunderstood, despised, persecuted and slain by His own people (Ps. 21; 117:22; Zach. 12:10; Isa. 53); He rises again from the dead (Ps. 15:10) and comes to judge the world (Mal. 3:3; Joel 2:2). Thus the idea of the Messias was essentially interwoven with God's revelation. The two points upon which the faith of the Old Testament hinged were the coming of the Messias and the unity of God.

Secondly, many theologians see in the theocratic constitution of the Israelites a revelation of the Son of God, inasmuch as the guidance and government of the people was principally carried on by means of the "Angel of the Testament" (Mal. 3:1). This angel gives the promise to Abraham (Gen. 22:16–18), wrestles with Jacob (Gen. 32:24 f.), calls Moses (Ex. 3), leads the people in the pillar of cloud (Gen. 14:19; 33:2, 14, 15; Isa. 63:9). The guidance of Adam, Noe, Abraham, Jacob, Joseph and of the whole nation is described in the Book of Wisdom as the work of the wisdom of the Word of God (Wisd. 10; 11; 16; 17; 18; 19). This Angel of the Covenant is explained by the holy Fathers to be an angel according to his office, but God according to his nature (St. Hilary, De Trinit. 50:4; 100:22–34). However this may be, the national constitution, with its priestly, prophetic and kingly character, was a type of the Messias.

Thirdly, the belief in the Messias was expressed in the divine service of the Old Covenant, in its sacrifices, feasts and means of grace. The sacrifices and means of grace, such as circumcision and the purifications prescribed by the law, were only effective through faith in the coming Messias, and were types of His Sacrifice and Sacraments (Hebr. 10:1–14; Col. 2:17–19). The feasts, especially the principal ones, such as the Feast of the Pasch (I Cor. 5:7) and the Feast of Tabernacles, were Messianic feasts, and in the solemn Hallel took the form of an explicit confession of faith and hope with regard to the Messias. This faith was constantly confirmed and reanimated by the divine service.

Fourthly, the history of the people was most intimately connected with the Messias, and heralded Him by innumerable types, which appeared partly in historical events, partly in the character and lives of the great men and saints of the Old Testament, and which plainly pointed to the future Messias. Such were the deliverance from Egypt, the passage through the Red Sea, the pillar of cloud, the water issuing from the rock, the manna, the brazen serpent (John 3:14), the sacrifice of Melchisedech, the sacrifice of Isaac; then also Moses, Samson, David, Solomon, Jeremias, Elias (I Cor. 10:1–6). Thus many things in the Old Testament foretold the coming of Christ.

## 2. ISRAEL MERITS THE MESSIAS FOR THE WORLD

We have to consider here both in what respects and in what manner the patriarchs of the Old Testament may be said to have merited with regard to the Incarnation.

They could not in any way merit the Incarnation itself, because it is a pure grace, indeed the greatest grace, and the source of all graces for mankind. But they could in some measure merit, though not in the strict sense of the term, certain minor points with regard to the accomplishment of the Incarnation, e.g. its acceleration, the circumstances of time, place and family. They could also merit the effects of our Saviour's life and Passion for their nation and for us.

And how did they merit this? First, by their ardent desire, their fervent prayer and continual supplication. This longing pervaded the whole of the Old Covenant, and showed itself in the ardent prayers which were offered up. Thus Abraham rejoiced to see the day of the Messias (John 8:56), and Jacob sighed for His coming (Gen. 49:18); thus, too, David (Ps. 84:8; Isa. 45:8; 64:1), Daniel (Dan. 9), the faithful at the time of the Machabees (I Mach. 14:41; II Mach. 2:18); and again, in the days of the Messias, Simeon (Luke 2:25). Secondly, the patriarchs merited the advent of the Messias in an especial way by their virtues, so magnificently described by St. Paul (Hebr. 11). Thirdly and lastly, by the sufferings which they had to endure on account of Christ (Hebr. 11:26). It was precisely on account of this faith and hope that the nation was always hated and persecuted by the powers of hell. The Church of the Old Covenant was, as it were, the woman who bore Christ, the God-Man, in her womb; for whom the dragon lay in wait, and whom he threatened to devour (Apoc. 12:1–4). This was the way in which the patriarchs, in a certain broad, moral sense, made way for and merited the Incarnation, and rightly, for all the conditions of merit were present: first, the state of grace, which establishes some slight parity of rank with the mystery of the Incarnation, and which was to be the adornment even of the Word Incarnate; further, great sanctity, ardent prayer and desire, which were inspired by the Holy Ghost; and finally the will of God, who vouchsafed to apply these merits to this end.

### 3. ISRAEL PREPARES FOR THE MESSIAS ACCORDING TO THE FLESH

It is, according to St. Paul (Rom. 1:3; 9:4, 5), the greatest privilege of the Israelites, that the Saviour, Who was the Son of God and of man, belonged (according to the flesh) to this people. Christ is the descendant of Abraham and David. St. Matthew and St. Luke give us the genealogy of Christ up to Adam (Matt. 1:1–17; Luke 3:23–38).[1]

The importance of the genealogy consists in this: first, that it gives us the certainty that Christ was truly man, and that He assumed our human nature from Adam through the family of David, in accordance with the promises and prophecies. Secondly, the history of the descent from Adam is a splendid manifestation of God's attributes. We realize His omnipotence, which continually preserved this nation and this tribe, from which the Redeemer was to proceed, and always delivered and guided them, throughout so many thousand years, through the most various destinies and events, through persecutions, wars, and repeated captivity and exile. Again, we see His wisdom, which gives us in this genealogy an indisputable proof of the true humanity of our Divine Saviour, and in the choice of the recipients of the hereditary blessing often interferes with the course of nature, that special grace, favor and preference may predominate (Gen.

---

[1] The differences in the names contained in these genealogies are due to two circumstances. In the first place, St. Matthew traces the descent from David through Solomon, and St. Luke, through Nathan. Secondly, we must take into consideration the custom of levirate marriage (the brother of a man who died childless being obliged to marry his deceased brother's widow). Thus the actual father of St. Joseph was Jacob; the legal father, Heli.

25:25; 27:27 seq.; 38:29). Further, God's fidelity is also revealed in the genealogy of Jesus, inasmuch as He kept the promise so often repeated to this people and especially to the family of David (Ps. 131:11; III Kings 11:12, 32; Ez. 7:22, 23; Agg. 2:24), in spite of the unworthiness, unbelief and corruption of so many of His ancestors, and indeed of the whole nation. Lastly, the genealogy is a touching proof of God's goodness, condescension and mercy, since He unites Himself so closely to our race and becomes one with it. "Behold," says Moses (Deut. 10:14, 15), "heaven and earth are the Lord's . . . and yet the Lord has been closely joined to thy fathers and loved them." "As the girdle sticketh close to the loins of a man, so have I brought close to Me all the house of Israel and all the house of Juda . . . that they might be My people, and for a name, and for a praise" (Jer. 13:11). On this account God called the Israelite nation His son, His firstborn (Ex. 4:22). Sinners, even heathens are to be found in the pedigree of our Lord; but that did not prevent His goodness from making Him by their means one of our race. Thirdly, the genealogy has its importance for our Saviour Himself, inasmuch as it displays to us the whole glory of His work and its significance, the splendor of His dignities and offices, revealing to us the kingly, prophetic, and priestly office, the office of Redeemer and Head of the chosen people, indeed (as St. Luke shows) of the whole human race.

This was the great significance of the Israelite nation for the whole world. Israel was to be the moral and physical medium by which the Redeemer was given to it. She was by her laws the pedagogue of the world in Christ (Gal. 3:24). Christ was the end of her law and existence (Rom. 10:4); Christ was her hope (Acts 28:20), her faith, her history, her greatness and her glory. Unhappily she was afterwards broken off from the glorious olive-tree on account of her unbelief, and the Gentiles were grafted into it in her stead (Rom. 11:17, 24).

## THE HEATHEN WORLD AND THE REDEEMER

JOHN 1:5. The light shineth in darkness, and the darkness did not comprehend it.—9. That was the true light, which enlighteneth every man that cometh into this world.—10. He was in the world, and the world was made by him, and the world knew him not.

Whilst Israel enjoyed all the benefits of the revelation, by far the greater part of the human race were in the way of unbelief.

Nevertheless they were not excluded from the salvation effected by Jesus Christ.

### 1. RISE OF HEATHENISM AND UNHAPPY STATE OF THE HEATHEN WORLD

That idolatry had already broken out among the grandchildren of Adam, is scarcely probable; but it certainly existed at the time of Abraham (Gen. 31:19, 30, 34; Judith 5:7; Jos. 24:2; Gen. 35:2), and spread farther and farther. The rise of idolatry was due mainly to original sin, which had already wrought such fearful havoc (Gen. 4:8). Other causes at work were the fleshly lusts and earthly cravings of the children of Cain (Gen. 4:19, 21, 22; 6:1, 2, 11) and, after the flood, of Cham (Gen. 10:8 seq.); to these may be added pride, which already showed itself so undisguisedly at the building of the tower of Babel (Gen. 11:4). All this could not fail to dim by degrees the clear perception of God and render the heart susceptible to all evil. To this was added the influence of the Evil One, who alienated men from God by temptation and probably also by demonstrations of great power, and seduced them to adore his mysterious might (Apoc. 12:9). Thus polytheism arose from ungodliness; and from polytheism, by the deification of the passions, of the powers of nature, and of the world's heroes, proceeded actual idolatry and worship of images, with services and sacrifices. It received an abiding and legalized form in idolatrous state constitutions. Thus the satanic empire, heathendom, came into existence; and the "prince of the world" exercised his tyranny far and wide over the races and nations (Wisd. 14:12–31; 15:1–19).

How sad and wretched was the state of the poor heathen world, how great its bewilderment, its weakness, its immorality and unhappiness, is sufficiently told by St. Paul (Rom. 1:18–32; 3:10–19). That world, in the enjoyment of all temporal goods, was yet poor in truth, unhappy through slavery and immorality; and the end was the shipwreck of its religious and moral life. Nowhere was hope to be found. The priesthood was everywhere dumb, and the searcher after truth was stranded on the sand-bank of doubt. Unchastity was part of religion, and cruelty, part of public worship and service. Thus life had grown cheap and was regarded as a burden; the last word of paganism was weariness of life, agony of death, and despair. Either a divine intervention must take place, or all was lost.

And why did God permit this? Just because evil had to develop and live itself out; hindrances had to be heaped up; the cup of worldly lust had to be drained; every remedy had to be proved insufficient, every hope to be deceived, every moral restraint broken down; the wisdom and power of men had to be demonstrated unsuccessful and impotent in the struggle against corruption; then was God's time to step in and prove that He alone is able to help. He allowed all to be "concluded in unbelief," that He might have mercy on all (Rom. 11:32), and that no man could boast of sharing in the achievement.

## 2. RELATIONS OF THE REDEEMER TO THE HEATHEN WORLD

These relations were three in number.

First, the heathen world was comprised by the Messias in the decree of salvation. All nations were included in the hereditary blessing of our Saviour. This was promised by God to Abraham (Gen. 12:3; 18:18; 22:18), Isaac (Gen. 26:4), and Jacob (Gen. 28:14). "The whole earth shall be filled with the glory of the Lord" (Num. 14:21). "The mountain of the house of the Lord shall be prepared . . . and all nations shall flow unto it" (Isa. 2:2). The Saviour is "the Light which enlighteneth every man that cometh into this world" (John 1:9); He is the Light of the Gentiles (Luke 2:32), their Shepherd (John 10:16), and so He sends His Apostles to all nations (Matt. 28:19). God wishes to save all men, Jews and Gentiles; that is the ever recurring thought of St. Paul in his Epistles (Rom. 3:29; I Tim. 2:4).

Secondly, God gave to the nations the means to obtain salvation. In the first place, He disposed them for this end by the natural law (Rom. 2:14, 15, 16); then again by notorious chastisements, such as were inflicted upon Sodom, upon the Egyptians, the Chanaanites (Jos. 12), Sennacherib (Isa. 37:29), Balthasar (Dan. 5) and Antiochus (I Mach. 6:11). Further, explicit revelations were made to the Gentiles concerning the true God and the Messias; e.g. by Job and Balaam (Num. 24:4). Two heathen women, Rahab (Jos. 6:25) and Ruth (1:16), were received into the Covenant and have a conspicuous place in the pedigree of our Lord (Matt. 1:5). Moreover God so ordered things that through the very situation of the land which He had allotted to Israel as a dwelling-place, every nation one after another—the Egyptians, Assyrians, Chaldees, Persians, Greeks and Romans—came into closest contact with the chosen people. In the frequent exiles of their people, Jewish princes, prophets and saints, prominent men like Jonas, Tobias, Ezechiel, Daniel (3:98 seq.; 4:31; 6:26) were introduced to the courts of the ancient rulers, and there disseminated the knowledge of the true God and of the Holy Scriptures. Still more was this the case later on, by the great emigration of the Jews into Egypt, to the Greek colonies of Asia Minor, and to the Occident, where they established communities and gathered around themselves a group of Gentiles in every settlement they made. In Alexandria, as is well known, the translation of the Holy Scriptures was made by the Seventy (the Septuagint). The Sibylline Books also contributed to the knowledge and expectation of the Messias among the Gentiles. Thus the Promised Land proved itself to be indeed the bridge and way of the nations, the center and focus of the earth (Ez. 38:12); and the Israelite nation, in its priestly vocation (Ex. 19:6), was the missionary and apostle of the ancient world.

Thirdly, God made use of the political development and religious decline of the nations themselves to prepare them for Christ (Isa. 45; Hab. 2:14). One dynasty after another, each mightier than the other, arose to absorb the rest, so that at the time of the Roman Empire the whole of the known earth formed one great political union. Differences of nationality, speech and worship were becoming less separatist. The world had one head in Rome, and all roads led to this point of union. What a union, indeed! But this also was a means for the extension of Christ's kingdom and a preparation of the world for Him. The religion of paganism had fallen into disrepute, and the result was a general indifference. By degrees people came to see in idolatry, and even in the oracles, only human invention and human fraud; the philosophers and poets, especially, made the entire mythology ridiculous and childish. Only State interests upheld the exterior worship of the gods, and a corrupt state of morals the interior. Thus there reigned everywhere a deep-felt dissatisfaction, a seeking and longing for surer truth, for a clear and definite moral law, and above all for an elevating model. All the apotheoses forced upon people, all the introduction of new mysteries and foreign cults served only to increase the confusion, discontent and wistful longing. It is touching to hear from the depths of paganism the echoes of this longing: "We must wait until someone comes to teach us how to offer sacrifice" (Plato, in Phaedon).

"Why was I born now? Why not a little later?" (Hesiod, Virgil.) The Stoic declares that the ideal of virtue has not yet appeared, even after so many thousand years. How ravished Tullius would have been, if it had been granted to him to see it! It was also the universal expectation that a great ruler should go out from the East (Tacitus, Suetonius).

Thus did God prepare heathendom for the Messias. The harvest was ripe. As a matter of fact, the Gentiles accepted Christianity more readily than the Jews. The need of redemption was more deeply felt and better recognized by the Gentiles, and their gratitude much more humble.

### 3. CONCLUSIONS

There are three conclusions to be drawn from what has been said.

First, we see very clearly in the unhappy condition of heathendom what the forsaking of God by sin makes of a man and of the whole human race. "Sin maketh nations miserable" (Prov. 14:34). Heathenism marks the paths of the creature without God; they are a descent from step to step of misery, degradation and ungodliness. What had the culture of several thousand years availed against the corruption of sin and the passions? The finest product of its work and efforts was perhaps the Stoic, that personification of callousness, pride and self-worship. Could he be the deliverer? Without Christ nothing availed. He alone is our wisdom, our justification, our sanctification and our redemption (I Cor. 1:30; cf. Bar. 3:9, 14).

Secondly, we see how worthy of love is God, our Redeemer. He is not the God and Redeemer of the Jews alone, but also of the Gentiles and of all men. A notable error of the Jews was that they wished to have sole part in the Redeemer, to monopolize Him, so to speak, and to keep all others away from salvation. Not so our God. He is the God of all, because all are His creatures, as it is so beautifully written: "For the whole world before Thee is as the least grain of the balance, and as a drop of the morning dew, that falleth down upon the earth. But Thou hast mercy upon all, because Thou canst do all things, and winkest at the sins of men for the sake of repentance. For Thou lovest all things that are, and hatest none of the things which Thou hast made; for Thou didst not appoint or make anything hating it. And how could anything endure, if Thou wouldst not? Or be preserved, if not called by Thee? But Thou sparest all; because they are Thine, O Lord, who lovest souls!" (Wisd. 11:23–27.)

Thirdly, we must remember that heathenism has not yet died out in the world. It is still there, ruling over the greater part of humanity, and holding it fast bound in the chains of the same misery. There is still, then, much to do and much to pray for. The holy season of Advent is a time especially suited to intercession for the poor heathen, of which our holy Mother the Church sets us such a beautiful example in her song of praise the "Benedictus," in the O-antiphons and in the 88th Psalm.

### THE MOTHER OF THE REDEEMER

The proximate and direct preparation for the advent of the Redeemer was the election, creation and preparation of His Mother. This blessed Mother was Mary. The preparation for her, as for Christ, was threefold; and a threefold life of Mary answers to this preparation.

#### 1. THE LIFE OF THE MOTHER OF JESUS IN ETERNITY

Mary's life in eternity consists in her eternal predestination in the thoughts and counsels of God. Predestination in general is shared with Mary by all creatures, but not in the same manner. She was, after Christ, the first chosen by God; not according to time, but according to dignity and elevation. For God chose her from eternity, not only for grace and glory, but also for the dignity of Mother of God; if one may so speak, rather for the dignity of Mother of God than for grace and glory, because the measure of her grace and glory was proportioned to the sublimity of this dignity. Thus those theologians who are of the opinion that Christ was foreseen and predestinated before all creatures and before sin, use similar terms of His Mother. However this may be, she is at all events the first in rank after Christ. She and her Divine Son are the principal and most sublime beings of the whole creation in the divine thoughts and counsels; indeed, they are always together in God's thoughts. They form, as it were, a distinct order, united in the closest intimacy, and thence also bear the greatest similarity to each other in nature, grace, glory, duties in life and destiny. And this relation extends to their predestination. That is the reason why the Church applies to Mary those passages of Holy Scripture which depict the life and activity of the

God-Man before the creation, as the Son of God and Eternal Wisdom. "The Lord possessed me in the beginning of His ways, before He made anything, from the beginning. I was set up from eternity, and of old before the earth was made. . . . When He prepared the heavens, I was there . . . forming all things, and was delighted every day, playing before Him at all times" (Prov. 8:22 seq.). "I came out of the mouth of the Most High, the first-born before all creatures. . . . I dwelt in the highest places, and my throne is in a pillar of a cloud" (Eccli. 24:5 seq.).

It is charming to contemplate the Mother of God in the divine ideas, enveloped in the splendor of the predestination of Jesus. Just as the Child of Bethlehem is one of God's first ideas, and was ever present to Him at the origin of the whole creation, so also was His Virgin Mother; and as the God-Man was the first and most glorious of all ideas, so after Him comes Mary; and as she was the sweetest, the purest and holiest creature that ever gladdened this earthly life, so also was the thought and imagination of the future Mother of God the joy of the divine creative goodness. Her beautiful life on earth and the glory of her life in heaven are but the actual reflection of her glory in the creative thoughts of God.

### 2. THE MOTHER OF GOD IN THE OLD COVENANT

As the Saviour had been prepared for and typified in the Old Covenant, so too was His Mother.

Mary belonged, in the first place, to the faith of the Old Testament, in consequence of the prophecies. She was already promised to our first parents, as the woman whose son should overcome the serpent (Gen. 3:15). Especially and expressly, however, was the virginal birth of the Emmanuel promised to Achaz and the whole people, as a sign of deliverance from the danger which was impending upon the House of David and upon Jerusalem, through the alliance of the king of Israel with the king of Assyria. "Behold, a virgin shall conceive and bear a son, and his name shall be called Emmanuel" (Isa. 7:14). Almost the same promise is given by Jeremias, though in more obscure terms: "The Lord hath created a new thing upon the earth; a woman shall compass a man" (Jer. 31:22). The prophet Micheas also points to the delivery of the "woman that travaileth" as the end of oppression and the fulness of salvation (Mich. 5:3). Thus she was received into the revelation of the Old Covenant, as the Virgin Mother of the Messias.

She was also interwoven with its history, by the numerous types which, partly in inanimate things, partly in persons, foretold her virtues, privileges, graces, her position and office towards the new people of God. Thus the burning bush (Ex. 3:2), Gedeon's fleece (Judg. 6:37), Aaron's blossoming rod (Num. 17:8) were types of her Immaculate Conception; the seven-branched candlestick and the Tabernacle, of the rich treasures of her graces; and the Ark of the Covenant, of her priestly vocation as the medium of God's real presence among His people. Not less brilliantly are her types unfolded in the array of the great women of Israel—in Eve, Sara, Rachel, Judith, Esther—who reveal the virtues of the Mother of God and her position towards Christ's kingdom.

Finally, she also belonged to the family of David, and was thus united by a new bond with the most glorious period of the Israelite nation. That she was a descendant of the family of David is the testimony of several of the holy Fathers, e.g. St. Ignatius of Antioch (Ad Eph., 18), the holy martyr St. Justin (Contra Tryph., 100). St. Paul says that the Son of God "was made to him of the seed of David according to the flesh" (Rom. 1:3), and "made of a woman" (Gal. 4:4); and St. Peter, that "God had sworn to him (David) with an oath that of the fruit of his loins one should sit upon his throne" (Acts 2:30; Ps. 130:11). Besides this, the holy Fathers say that Mary was the heiress-daughter of a line of David, and was expected, according to the law (Num. 36:6), to marry one of her own kindred. And this is very probable, considering that on account of her vow of virginity Mary would otherwise never have consented to a betrothal. Thus the pedigree of St. Joseph was in great part identical with that of Mary; and she was a true daughter of David, and heiress not only of the glory of his family, but also of his race, and of the whole nation and the whole Covenant. As an aloe sprouts forth its leaves and sheds them again, season after season, for a hundred years, until at last the flower appears, so also the Old Covenant sprouted and flourished, and bore leaves of royal, priestly and prophetic honors. They were all on Mary's account, in whom the varied splendors of the preparation reached their culminating point and perfection. For this reason the Church applies to Mary the words: "Then the Creator of all things commanded, and said to me . . . Let thy dwelling be in Jacob, and thy inheritance in Israel, and take root in My elect. . . . And so was I established in Sion, and in the holy city likewise I rested, and my power was in Jerusalem.

And I took root in an honorable people and in the portion of my God His inheritance, and my abode is in the full assembly of saints" (Eccli. 24:12–16). So "has God," says St. Bernard (*Hom. 2 Miss.*), "not taken to Himself a mother of today or at random, but a mother chosen from the beginning, foreseen by the Most High, guarded by the angels, foretold by the prophets and typified by the patriarchs; in a word, a mother of whom God Himself appears to have foretold: 'I will put enmity between thee and the woman.' "

### 3. THE EARTHLY LIFE OF MARY

At last Mary, the blessed child of St. Joachim and St. Anne, appeared on earth. Her earthly life was the proximate preparation for Christ, and similar to His. The way was prepared for Christ in her, first, with regard to her natural qualities. Mary had a body noble in form, perfect in its strength and the grace of its proportions, so pure that Christ might share her blood, so beautiful that He might bear in His own features the stamp of her grace and comeliness. If God made the bodies of Adam and Eve so perfect, because He thought of Christ, who was to be their image (Tertull., *De carn. Chr.* 6), how much more perfect and beautiful must Mary's body have been, from which He was actually to be born! Her intellect and her heart alike were incomparable. After Christ's there has probably never been a more splendid intellect or a better and more harmonious disposition than Mary's; for it was necessary that she should resemble our Saviour and be a fitting companion for Him. Mary was a daughter of kings, and even in the natural order the masterpiece of God's creation.

But what of the order of grace? As Christ was always sinless, because He was never touched by a breath of evil concupiscence; as He always possessed grace, and that in an all-surpassing measure: so also Mary, with this difference only, that all of this belonged to Christ by right, whilst it was only granted to Mary on account of Him and His merits, and always in a subordinate degree. The beginning and foundation of this holiness was laid in her Immaculate Conception, by which she not only remained free from original sin, but also received the plenitude of sanctifying grace and all the gifts of grace, to such a degree as has never fallen to the lot of any other created being, together with the gift of perseverance and freedom from all concupiscence. This Immaculate Conception is the most glorious fruit of the redemption by Christ and its most splendid victory, the first complete victory over Satan. In this Conception, Satan's head was already crushed. Mary was thus the first and most magnificent creation of the new order, worthily endowed for the office of Mother of God, to fit her for which she received these wonderful prerogatives.

Her subsequent life also, until the Conception of our Lord, was a worthy preparation for Christ. According to tradition she spent her youth in the Temple among other virgins, in work for the divine service, in prayer, and in the practice of all virtues. This life was a true school of the Holy Ghost. He was her Master and Teacher; her heart, His pure temple, and He accomplished His way therein in a marvelous manner, and prepared her for the Divine Motherhood with masterly skill. Thus these words of the Book of Wisdom may be applied to her: "I was exalted like a cedar in Libanus, and as a cypress-tree on Mount Sion; I was exalted like a palm-tree in Cades, and as a rose-plant in Jericho; as a fair olive-tree in the plains, and as a plane-tree by the water in the streets was I exalted. I gave a sweet smell like cinnamon and aromatical balm; I yielded a sweet odor like the best myrrh; and I perfumed my dwelling . . . as the frankincense. . . . As the vine I have brought forth a pleasant odor; and my flowers are the fruit of honor and riches" (Eccli. 24:17–23).

The final preparation of Mary for Christ was her betrothal to St. Joseph, before the Annunciation of the angel and the Incarnation (Luke 1:27). It may well be assumed that Mary, who would not know man (Luke 1:34), was not induced to enter upon a betrothal by her own mere natural inclination, but only by the Will of God. And this Will of God was probably revealed to her by the priests and by the law, according to which she, as the heiress-daughter (in all probability) of a line of David, must enter upon an alliance with a man of the same family. She submitted to this Will of God, and in so doing acted under Divine Providence, which made of this betrothal the final preparation for the advent of the Son of God.

Nazareth in Galilee was the place where Mary, this noble scion of the root of David, bloomed and grew up in preparation for her high and important vocation for Israel and for the whole world (Luke 1:26). The little town lies, quiet and peaceful, as though hidden in the hollow of a shell, in the midst of a circle of hills, between the heights which form the northern boundary of the plain of Esdrelon. From the depths of the oblong valley rise, row upon row, the white houses of the little town, reaching half-way up the mountain, whence the eye roams over the beautiful view across Galilee to the sea, and over the Lake of Genesareth. Olive, pomegranate and fig-trees, tall green cactus-plants and a few scattered date-palms give to Nazareth and the whole landscape a certain grace and charm of appearance. Nazareth is called for this reason the "white town" and the "flower of Galilee."

Such was Mary's life up to the time of the Incarnation. How beautiful, how sublime and sweet it is! In very truth the life of a future Mother of God, full of purity and virtue. Theologians say also that, though she could not merit the dignity of Mother of God, she was nevertheless worthily prepared for it, and that she merited this preparation by her cooperation with grace and by her virtues. So Christ and His kingdom are already founded and prepared in her. What the dawn is to the sun, that is Mary to Christ. Christ shares everything with her: His life before the creation, in the bosom of the Father, by her eternal predestination; His existence in the Old Covenant, and His privileges of nature and grace. What a fitting subject is Mary for our thoughts and aspirations during the holy season of Advent! We too, in our degree, must prepare ourselves and the world for Christ.

## ST. JOSEPH

MATT. 1:16. And Jacob begot Joseph, the husband of Mary, of whom was born Jesus, who is called Christ.

LUKE 1:26. The angel Gabriel was sent from God . . . —27. to a virgin espoused to a man whose name was Joseph, of the house of David.

LUKE 3:23. And Jesus himself was beginning about the age of thirty years, being, as it was supposed, the son of Joseph.

Through his betrothal with Mary, St. Joseph also comes into the closest intimacy with the coming Messias, since he too, in the plan of the divine wisdom, forms a necessary part of the preparation for the Incarnation.

### 1. THE VOCATION OF ST. JOSEPH

It was the vocation and office of St. Joseph to be the legal father of the Divine Saviour. This is his peculiar duty and his most honorable title.

It was necessary that St. Joseph should be the legal father of our Saviour, but this dignity sufficed. It was necessary, in order that our Saviour might have at least a legal father here on earth, and through him an honorable, legal existence; but it was also sufficient, because this kind of fatherhood was recognized by the law, and gave to St. Joseph all the rights and privileges of a father both within and without the family, and this in a higher degree than a mere adoptive fatherhood would have done. The fatherhood of St. Joseph, however, might not be more than a legal one; for it had been prophesied that the Conception of our Saviour should be virginal (Isa. 7:14), and no other was fitting for the Son of God, Who had His natural Father in heaven, and could not have a second here upon earth. The temporal generation of the Son of God was to be a pure representation of His eternal generation in Heaven.

This legal fatherhood of St. Joseph was nevertheless a high and glorious office. In the first place, St. Joseph was the representative of the Heavenly Father of the Divine Child, as well in dignity, authority and power, as in purity, holiness and love; an image of the Heavenly Father, at once sublime and winning. In the second place, this dignity placed St. Joseph over our Divine Saviour and His Blessed Mother as their head, guardian and support, and ensured him their obedience, respect and love. This office raised him above all other grades of vocation and rank, and assigned to him, after the Mother of God, the first place in the economy of the hypostatic union. His position was solely concerned with the person of our Divine Saviour. The Heavenly Father too always regarded him as His representative and the head of the Holy Family, and always sent His commands and directions to him (Matt. 1:20; 2:13, 22). Great graces accrued to St. Joseph himself in consequence of this legal fatherhood. It ensured him the privilege of purity and virginity; it caused him much labor and inconvenience; it offered him the most splendid advantages for the active and for the contemplative life, in the care of his family and in his intimate, familiar intercourse with Jesus and Mary. Lastly, it was a part of St. Joseph's duty to conceal by his legal fatherhood, at least for a time, the Divinity of Christ and the glory of the Divine Fatherhood, and this brought him the advantage of serving the Saviour and His kingdom in humility, obscurity and unselfishness. Thus St. Joseph's vocation was on all sides glorious and wonderful.

## 2. QUALIFICATIONS FOR THIS VOCATION

There were three principal qualifications.

First, St. Joseph, as legal father, had to be of David's family. The Saviour had been announced in the prophecies as the Son of David, and could only prove Himself legally such if His father belonged to this family. That this was the case, is proved by the two genealogies of St. Matthew and St. Luke (Matt. 1:6–16; Luke 1:27; 3:23–31). It was because St. Joseph was from Bethlehem, and of the family of David, that he had to go to Bethlehem for the census (Luke 2:4, 5). The angel also calls him the son of David (Matt. 1:20). Yes, he was the son of David, and the happy heir to all the blessings and splendors of the House of David and of the whole Covenant. The prophetic spirit of the Old Covenant passed in him into actual vision; his office was in the highest degree a noble one, because it was entirely concerned with the Person of Jesus; and though the kingdom of his ancestors had passed into other hands, still his word was law for the King of kings and the Queen of heaven and earth.

Secondly, St. Joseph was the truly affianced bridegroom and spouse of Mary. Only thus could he become the legal father of our Saviour; but, granting this, he really is the legitimate father of Jesus. If Mary was his betrothed bride, then they were, according to the expression of Holy Scripture, "one flesh," and what was born of Mary, belonged by right to him as the father. For this reason God so disposed matters that the betrothal took place before the Conception of our Saviour (Matt. 1:18; Luke 1:27). This betrothal was, according to the custom of the time, no less binding than marriage, and therefore our Saviour was the son of Joseph more truly than the issue born of a levirate marriage (Deut. 25:5, 6) was the son of his deceased legal father. The betrothal of Mary to St. Joseph was, then, a true marriage, and St. Joseph the father of our Saviour. Not only is he so called by the Jews (Luke 3:23; John 6:42; Matt. 13:55; Mark 6:3), but also by Mary herself (Luke 2:48). How much then our Saviour owed to St. Joseph, on this account alone! It was also His will to be thus conceived and to grow up under the shadow of the marriage state; for He wished by this very means to honor and sanctify this state, which He had instituted and made the source of all human life.

The third qualification of St. Joseph for his vocation as legal father of Jesus was holiness. How great his holiness must have been, we may already conclude from his office, which surpassed all others in sublimity. It was a necessary part of the dispensations of Providence to place at the head of the Holy Family a man who was to some extent on a level with it in holiness. Before St. Joseph had taken Mary to himself, he is already called in the Scriptures a "just," i.e. holy man (Matt. 1:19), and his self-restraint on the occasion of the serious doubt with regard to Mary's purity shows that he was so in fact. What fruits of holiness may he not have gained later on by his intercourse with Jesus and Mary, by his care and labor for them, and by the grateful love which they on their part showed to him! If a cup of cold water given in the name of Christ does not pass unrewarded (Matt. 10:42), how much greater is the reward due to the tokens of love which St. Joseph showed to Jesus and Mary themselves, and for so long a time! How gloriously he outshines, by his spirit of faith, obedience, purity and patience, his forefathers, who from the time of Solomon down to the exile had fallen, in numerous instances, into unbelief and corruption!

### 3. FULFILMENT OF HIS VOCATION

How, in truth, did St. Joseph fulfil his vocation?

First, with great skill. Like his prototype, the Egyptian Joseph, he was a man who succeeded in what God called him to do, "a prosperous man in all things" (Gen. 39:2). The cause of this success was assuredly nothing else than St. Joseph's humility, piety, and conformity to the Will of God.

Further, he applied himself to his vocation with great fidelity and unselfishness. He is and will ever be the Saint of the Holy Childhood, and this office caused him much labor, and gained him little honor from men. He was to conceal the great secret of Almighty God, and no ray of the glory of Jesus in His public career brightened St. Joseph's life, which was led in quiet and humble obscurity.

Lastly, he fulfilled his vocation with exceeding love. We have no idea how great was the love of St. Joseph's heart for Jesus and Mary. Assuredly the Heavenly Father, Whose representative he was, gave him a share of His love for them, and the intensity of his love for Jesus and Mary grew stronger day by day until the very hour of his death.

Thus St. Joseph appears in the life of our Saviour. We must thank him above all for this beautiful example of fidelity to life's duties, for all that he did for our Saviour, for the Mother of God and the whole of Christ's kingdom. Secondly, we must honor him on account of the high dignity with which he was invested, the magnificent treasures of grace and virtue which fell to his lot, and the power which he now exercises. God has rewarded him for his unselfishness, humility and lowliness during his earthly life, by making him to be the patron of the whole Church. He not merely equals but surpasses his prototype, the Egyptian Joseph. Lastly, we must have confidence in St. Joseph. Everything about him invites our confidence. He is the very expression of the most lovable fatherliness. To be a father was his task in life; for our Blessed Saviour and His holy Mother were to find in him a father. His virtues are those of a father: tranquillity, reflection, fidelity, unselfishness and love. And to be a father to the Church and to everyone is now his reward. We can therefore in all confidence commend to him all our affairs, both temporal and eternal. What he takes in hand is blessed by God, and is safe. Let us say then, uniting ourselves with the prayer of the Church: "Sanctissimae Genitricis tuae Sponsi, quaesumus, Domine, meritis adjuvemur; ut, quod possibilitas nostra non obtinet, ejus nobis intercessione donetur."

## THE ANNUNCIATION AND CONCEPTION OF ST. JOHN THE BAPTIST

LUKE 1:5. There was in the days of Herod, the king of Judaea, a certain priest named Zachary, of the course of Abia, and his wife was of the daughters of Aaron, and her name Elizabeth.—6. And they were both just before God, walking in all the commandments and justifications of the Lord without blame.—7. And they had no son, for that Elizabeth was barren, and they both were well advanced in years.—8. And it came to pass, when he executed the priestly function in the order of his course before God,—9. According to the custom of the priestly office, it was his lot to offer incense, going into the Temple of the Lord;—10. And all the multitude of the people was praying without at the hour of incense.—11. And there appeared to him an angel of the Lord, standing on the right side of the altar of incense.—12. And Zachary seeing him was troubled, and fear fell upon him.—13. But the angel said to him: "Fear not, Zachary, for thy prayer is heard, and thy wife Elizabeth shall bear thee a son, and thou shalt call his name John;—14. And thou shalt have joy and gladness, and many shall rejoice in his nativity;—15. For he shall be great before the Lord, and shall drink no wine nor strong drink, and he shall be filled with the Holy Ghost even from his mother's womb.—16. And he shall convert many of the children of Israel to the Lord their God;—17. And he shall go before him in the spirit and power of Elias, that he may turn the hearts of the fathers unto the children, and the incredulous to the wisdom of the just, to prepare unto the Lord a perfect people."—18. And Zachary said to the angel: "Whereby shall I know this? for I am an old man, and my wife is advanced in years."—19. And the angel answering, said to him: "I am Gabriel, who stand before God; and am sent to speak to thee, and to bring thee these good tidings.—20. And behold, thou shalt be dumb, and shalt not be able to speak until the day wherein these things shall come to pass, because thou hast not believed my words, which shall be fulfilled in their time."—21. And the people were waiting for Zachary; and they wondered that he tarried so long in the Temple.—22. And when he came out, he could not speak to them, and they understood that he had seen a vision in the Temple. And he made signs to them, and remained dumb.—23. And it came to pass, after the days of his office were accomplished, he departed to his own house.—24. And after those days Elizabeth his wife conceived, and hid herself five months, saying:—25. "Thus hath the Lord dealt with me in the days wherein he hath had regard to take away my reproach among men."

John the Baptist, by his annunciation and conception, shared in the preparation for the advent of the Saviour in a most intimate and proximate way.

## 1. CIRCUMSTANCES OF THIS ANNUNCIATION

The time of his annunciation is strikingly expressed in the words: "In the days of Herod, the king of Judaea" (Luke 1:5); for the reign of Herod was a time of decadence, unbelief and faction (cf. Introduction 9–16).

The picture of the family to which St. John was to owe his origin stands out in bright contrast against the dark background of these days. This gives us the second circumstance of his annunciation. He was born of the noble, priestly family of Zachary and Elizabeth. These two were models of the faithful practice of Judaism down to its smallest details (Luke 1:6), even to the very circumstance that Elizabeth also was of a priestly family (Luke 1:5; Ex. 6:23). They sought comfort in the Holy Scriptures, in prayer and visits to the Temple. However, they had only one sorrow and one humiliation (Luke 1:7; Deut. 7:14; Ex. 23:26), that they were childless. For a marriage to be fruitful in several children was considered one of the greatest blessings of God. And to be without children was looked upon as a grievous affliction. Elizabeth had now reached an advanced age, at which she could no longer hope for offspring.

The third circumstance of the annunciation is the place and time chosen for it. It took place in the inner, holy part of the Temple, in the Sanctuary, which faced the Holy of Holies itself. Here stood the table with the loaves of proposition and the seven-branched candlestick, and between these was the altar of incense, upon which incense had to be offered morning and evening. Thus it was in the very place where God dwelt and revealed Himself (cf. Introduction, p. 6). The time was that of the public, official worship, and it would seem to have been a Sabbath, since all the people were present outside (Luke 1:10). On this day the duty of offering incense had fallen to Zachary. Each day lots were drawn for the various duties among the priests who had the weekly service in the Temple; that is to say, who offered the bloody sacrifice and the incense, and attended to the maintenance of the altar, the holy fire and the candlestick. The offering of incense was an especially honorable service.

Under these circumstances, then, the annunciation took place. They are not without significance. Priestly descent was a most fitting element in the priestly vocation of St. John, whilst the piety of his parents and the circumstance that the annunciation took place at the time of public worship suggest that he was not only the gift of God's mercy, but also the fruit of his parents' sanctity and of public prayer. "Thy prayer is heard," said the angel (Luke 1:13). These words refer certainly to the constant prayer of Zachary for the blessing of progeny, but also and still more to the prayer of the priest for the great necessities of the people and for the greatest of all needs, the advent of the Messias, with which the advent of the Forerunner was so intimately connected. Thus holiness and prayer, especially prayer for the common wants, bring about all great things.

### 2. THE ANNUNCIATION ITSELF

The messenger of the annunciation is the angel Gabriel (Luke 1:19), who appears to be one of the angels of high rank who stand before God ready to fulfil particularly important missions (Luke 1:19; Tob. 12:15; Apoc. 1:4). It is the same who revealed to Daniel the time of the advent of the Messias (Dan. 9:21). He appeared to Zachary at the right side of the altar of incense, that is to say between the altar and the golden candlestick.

The subject of the annunciation itself was St. John, and it foretold first his birth, race and name (Luke 1:13). Secondly, the angel announces John's task and office: he is to go before the Messias in the power of Elias, and to "prepare unto the Lord a perfect people" (Luke 1:17). He will therefore be the Forerunner who is prophesied by Malachias and Isaias (Isa. 40:3; Mal. 3:1; Matt. 11:10; 17:11, 12; Mark 1:2; 9:12). The angel foretells, thirdly, John's holiness and virtues: he will be "great before the Lord," "filled with the Holy Ghost even from his mother's womb"; he will live as a Nazarite, in great outward austerity, drinking neither wine nor other fermented drink (Luke 1:15); his life will be, in short, entirely a priestly one (Lev. 10:9). Fourthly, the angel also prophesies the great success of St. John's life and mission. His birth will be a great joy to many (Luke 1:14), to his parents, to Mary, to Christ, to a great part of Israel, and to the whole Church (cf. the "Benedictus"). He will effect a great religious movement, convert many to God (Luke 1:16), bring many to the knowledge of salvation, reconcile the hearts of fathers to their children, and unite both in the same faith and love (Luke 1:17). The angel here uses words which Malachias had actually spoken of Elias (Mal. 4:6; Eccli. 48:10); but they apply to St. John also, because his vocation is in one respect the same (Mark 9:12; Matt. 17:12). St. John is the Forerunner of Christ's first advent, and Elias of His second.

This, then, is the vocation of St. John, depicted in a few masterly strokes. What a glorious vocation, with regard to the Saviour, to mankind, whom he makes so happy, and to himself! Here we have true greatness: intimate union with our Saviour, the possession of the Holy Ghost and His grace, and abundance of virtues.

### 3. CONFIRMATION OF THE ANNUNCIATION

Zachary was troubled at the sight of the angel (Luke 1:12), and although encouraged by the latter (Luke 1:13), he still doubts the possibility of the fulfilment of the promise, because it would necessitate a very miracle, on account of his wife's barrenness and of their advanced age. He points out these circumstances and desires a pledge in confirmation of the promise (Luke 1:18).

The angel gives him a threefold confirmation of it. First, he reveals to Zachary his name and dignity, declaring his message to be a mission from God (Luke 1:19). Secondly, he gives Zachary another confirmation, in the punishment of his incredulity. He is to be dumb until the birth of the promised son (Luke 1:20). And from that moment he could not speak; for on coming out of the sanctuary he could only by signs give the people to understand that he had seen a vision (Luke 1:22). Thirdly, the angel insists again on the promise (Luke 1:22). And it was fulfilled to the letter (Luke 1:23, 24). Elizabeth "hid herself," or withdrew from ordinary social intercourse, until the fifth month, to prepare herself in prayer and greater quiet for the birth of the child of grace (Luke 1:24, 25). So St. John began his life of solitude and recollection even in his mother's womb, until Mary rejoiced both him and his mother by the visit which brought them such blessings. The mother now recognized clearly her child's relation to the Redeemer, and did not hesitate to divulge the secret. God had indeed not only taken away her reproach, but given her singular honor before men (Gen. 30:23; Luke 1:25).

The annunciation and conception of St. John have an important bearing on our Saviour in three ways. First, on account of St. John's personal relations to the Redeemer. John's coming was a sign of the advent of the Messias. Two prophets had foretold this (Isa. 40:3; Mal. 3:1). Our Saviour Himself often appealed to this sign in His arguments with the Jews (Matt. 11:10; 21:24; John 5:33 seq.). The morning star had risen; the sun itself must soon appear. Secondly, the wonderful events by which St. John's annunciation was accompanied prepared the minds of the people, and drew their attention to the coming of the Messias. God permitted Zachary's incredulity in order to make the event public through his punishment. His sudden dumbness after the offering of incense (Luke 1:22), and the circumstance that he could not again serve in the Temple, on account of being speechless, were of a nature to strike everyone, and the wonder of it was increased by the news that a child had been born to him at such an advanced age. Thus, by his birth, John was already preparing the hearts of the people for the Saviour. Thirdly, John's annunciation, like the cheerful gleam of dawn, brightens the dark horizon of the time at which our Saviour was to appear. The days of Herod were dark and sad. After a silence of 400 years Heaven once more speaks to earth, and again sends down its messengers. John appears, and his person, his task, and the results which he attained are so many rays piercing the darkness. The family of John is in every respect a pleasing feature in the midst of such desolation. Even amid the corruption of this period there were still believing and law-abiding Jews; and Zachary's family is a good representation and expression of this faithful remnant. It is with this remnant that God begins the realization of His plan. From the sound kernel of this true representative of Judaism He draws the man who is to prepare the world for the coming new order of things. His annunciation takes place in Jerusalem, in the Temple, during public worship; that is to say, in the very center of the ancient theocratic life.

# II

# THE TEMPORAL LIFE OF JESUS

---

The Life of Jesus may be divided into four periods: His youth, the public life, the life of suffering and death, and His glorious life.

## I. THE YOUTHFUL LIFE OF JESUS

The mysteries of the youthful life of Jesus include the Incarnation itself, the revelation of the same, and the hidden life of our Saviour.

### A. THE INCARNATION

#### THE ANNUNCIATION AND CONCEPTION OF CHRIST

LUKE 1:26. And in the sixth month the angel Gabriel was sent from God into a city of Galilee, called Nazareth,—27. To a virgin espoused to a man whose name was Joseph, of the house of David, and the virgin's name was Mary.—28. And the angel being come in, said unto her: "Hail, full of grace; the Lord is with thee; blessed art thou among women."—29. Who, having heard, was troubled at his saying, and thought with herself what manner of salutation this should be.—30. And the angel said to her: "Fear not, Mary, for thou hast found grace with God: —31. Behold, thou shalt conceive in thy womb, and shalt bring forth a son, and thou shalt call his name Jesus;—32. He shall be great, and shall be called the Son of the Most High, and the Lord God shall give unto him the throne of David his father; and he shall reign in the house of Jacob for ever,—33. And of his kingdom there shall be no end."—34. And Mary said to the angel: "How shall this be done, because I know not man?"—35. And the angel answering said to her: "The Holy Ghost shall come upon thee, and the power of the Most High shall overshadow thee. And therefore also the Holy which shall be born of thee shall be called the Son of God.—36. And behold, thy cousin Elizabeth, she also hath conceived a son in her old age, and this is the sixth month with her that is called barren,—37. Because no word shall be impossible with God."—38. And Mary said: "Behold the handmaid of the Lord; be it done to me according to thy word." And the angel departed from her.

JOHN 1:14. And the Word was made flesh, and dwelt among us.

Daniel's "weeks of years" drew to a close. The preparation was made; the earthly home of the Eternal Word stood ready, inviting the Son of God by its beauty and charm. Then at last the moment came—that moment most important and significant for time and eternity,—the end and conclusion of all history, the fulness of time, the moment in which the Eternal Word was made Man. The mystery is so great that we must choose the most simple words to represent to ourselves its purport.

## 1. THE MESSAGE

God would not act in this great mystery without the consent of His creature. He did not therefore make use of His infinite power, but of His wisdom, goodness and condescension, and offered to Mary the choice of cooperating in the work of the Incarnation. And why so? It was fitting that Mary should first receive the Saviour in spirit, and then in body; for she was not a mere instrument without free-will, but a free and rational being, and as such was to cooperate with God. Her freedom was to be a reflection of the freedom and spontaneity of God in this work. Lastly, the Incarnation was to be the espousal of the Son of God with human nature, and Mary was to give her assent to it in the name of humanity. God sent therefore the angel Gabriel to gain Mary's consent. He sent an angel as intermediary, because it is the office of the angels to announce supernatural events to men, and to be the medium between God and mankind. Moreover, since an angel was the accessory cause of our fall, an angel was to be the accessory cause of our elevation. Lastly, Christ is also the Head of the angels, and therefore it was fitting that an angel should announce His advent. But why God chose the angel Gabriel and no other, it is not easy to ascertain. He appears to have been specially appointed to bear the messages concerning the Messias, as this had already been the case with Daniel and Zachary.

And how did Gabriel appear to Mary? Certainly in visible form. The reason of this visible appearance might be, on the one hand, that he announced Christ, Who was to appear in a visible shape; and on the other, that Mary possessed a human nature, and would thus receive, by the visible appearance and the sound of audible words, a double certainty, of the senses as well as of the intellect, with regard to the truth of the message. This may be seen from all that is recorded concerning the mystery of the Annunciation, the appearance and disappearance of the angel, and the colloquy between him and Mary.

How then does the angel fulfil his errand? Assuredly with great joy, on Christ's account as well as on Mary's and ours. It was a great honor for him to be the intermediary between such persons, and in such a matter. Then, too, he carried out the commission with great reverence and humility in word and gesture towards the future Mother of God, whom God honored so highly and who stood so far above himself. Lastly, with as great skill as any ambassador or intermediary could possess or display. We may distinguish three parts in this address of the angel. The first part contains the glorious salutation by which the angel attracts Mary's attention and favorable regard. In this greeting, in the "Ave," he wishes her happiness, welfare and joy, and depicts in a few mysterious words the whole magnificent share which she takes in the work of the Incarnation, namely her worthy preparation for it by fulness of grace: "(Thou art) full of grace." He then praises her participation in it by the intimate union with Christ, which does not consist merely in a united activity, but in the kind of unity that exists between mother and child: "The Lord is with thee." Finally, he extols the results of this motherhood; she is "blessed among women," not only above all women of her own nation, however renowned by their holiness, their exploits, or their position, but above all the women of the entire human race, since Mary alone unites motherhood with virginity, and thereby co-operates in the greatest and most important of works, for which reason she will receive the praise of all generations: "Blessed art thou among women" (Luke 1:28).

Then the angel explains to Mary the object of his errand, namely the Conception and Birth of a Son, who is no other than the Messias; and Mary is now to consent to become His Mother (Luke 1:31). The third part contains motives calculated to persuade Mary to accept the proposal. These motives are partly negative, partly positive. The angel first sets aside the doubt of the Virgin with regard to the manner of the Conception (Luke 1:34). He answers that it will take place by the direct action of God (Luke 1:35). This action is ascribed to the Holy Ghost, because the Incarnation is the highest work of natural and supernatural perfection, the masterpiece of nature and grace; for which reason also the Saviour is called the "Holy One." The manner in which the Incarnation is effected is a simple descent and overshadowing, a dwelling, resting upon and protecting, as of yore the cloud descended upon the Tabernacle of the Covenant (Ex. 40:35, 36). The positive motives lie in the subject of the message itself, viz. in the sublimity and glory of the Son whose Mother Mary is to become. The angel tells her the name of this Son (Luke 1:31) and His divine and human nature: He is the Son of God (Luke 1:32, 35). Further, he declares His holiness, together with His office and dignity as king and ruler of the family of David and Jacob, according to the promises made to them (Luke 1:32, 33, 35). This divine motherhood, which contains everything that can touch a believing heart (Isa. 7:14), is urged by the angel as a motive. Lastly, Gabriel adds as a sign of the truth of his message the tidings of John's conception, and reminds Mary of the omnipotence of God (Luke 1:34–37). We now hear for the first time the holy names of Jesus and Mary. "Jesus" denotes "God is help, Saviour, salvation" (Gen. 49:18); "Mary" denotes "Mistress, lady, the shining one, the bitter one, fragrant with myrrh."

Thus Gabriel fulfils his mission in a manner at once perfect, imposing and magnificent, worthy of an angel. He sketches in a few words the most glorious portrait of the Messias, His character, His duty as Priest and King, His central importance in the gradual development of the work of salvation, tracing it backwards to the foundation of the kingdom by David and Jacob, the first founder of the chosen people, and forwards to the splendor and eternity of the Church Triumphant. We certainly owe the heavenly messenger deep gratitude for having taken such a glorious part in the foundation of our salvation.

### 2. THE CONSENT

This salutation of the angel, his message to Mary, and her liberty to consent to it were an unheard-of honor. But she shows herself quite equal to such an honor and distinction, by the glorious virtues which she practices and reveals on this very occasion. Not to speak of the fervent prayer in which she was probably engaged at this moment, there are three special virtues which she here practices, and by which she performs her part in the accomplishment of the Incarnation.

First, the great humility with which she receives this extraordinary praise and unheard-of honor. Let us consider in detail the message that Mary received. Every word is a tribute of honor truer and higher than any on earth. From whose lips did these praises flow? And in whose name were they bestowed? When was ever a human being the subject of such praise? And what does Mary do? No word, no smile from her; no self-complacency. She is silent and rapt in thought; she is afraid (Luke 1:29), as it were, at her own greatness and beauty, which are revealed to her for the first time. What a depth of wisdom and humility such conduct presupposes! Eve did not act thus, nor Lucifer. Their privileges and greatness were a stumbling-block to them. Not so in Mary's case. The more she is praised, the more she retires into herself and her lowliness, doing nothing rashly. What a sterling, humble heart, what an earnest mind, to be found in a young maiden who was probably not more than fifteen or sixteen years old!

Secondly, no less admirable are the faith, prudence and purity which Mary reveals in the few words uttered by her. As the angel has announced to her that she is to become a mother, she asks how that is to take place (Luke 1:34). The question does not proceed from incredulity or slowness of belief, as with Zachary, who asked in quite a different manner (Luke 1:18). She believed, and believed firmly (Luke 1:45). But she had evidently, notwithstanding her betrothal, offered to God the vow of virginity, and so she asked if this offering was to hold good or not. What beauty and excellence of mind and heart Mary reveals in these words! Faith, good sense, prudence and chastity, all these lie in this question; in short, a liberty of spirit and high-mindedness such as became a being whom God had raised to such an elevation.

Thirdly, Mary crowns all by the most magnificent act of submission to God (Luke 1:38). After she has received from the angel the explanation that her vow of virginity is not to be broken, but only sealed and glorified by a virginal motherhood, she does not hesitate an instant. She yields herself entirely, with blind and childlike trust, to God's Will as regards the important consequences which her consent might have for herself. And this consent was to have great consequences, not only with relation to St. Joseph but to the whole nation. It meant for her the first step in the hard and painful path of the Messias, of which she probably had a good general idea from the prophecies. She was to become both an Agar and a Sara, but in a way more sublime. Blind to all else, she regarded only the Will of God and the salvation of men. With unbounded love for us, and with complete, unconditional compliance with God's thoughts and plans, she gave her consent. Humility, submission, obedience, trust, devotion, adoration, all lay in this act. It gave existence to a God-Man, made her the Mother of God and made us God's children. Never had God been glorified by such an act, which in beauty, power, depth and effectiveness, is closely associated with the act with which the Word Incarnate was just about to begin His life here on earth as the God-Man.

Such was the ever memorable dialogue between Mary and the angel, by far more important and momentous than any negotiation between the great personages of this earth. All in Mary is virtue, whether she speaks or is silent; all is virtue, and that a great, heroic virtue, which renders her a worthy Mother of God. It is the last preparation for the Incarnation; in it all the faith, desire, and longing of the preceding ages of humanity, and all the abundance of graces that had fallen to Mary's lot since her Conception, reached their culminating point and perfection.

### 3. THE FULFILMENT

Mary has given her consent, and the Incarnation is accomplished at the same instant. The effecting of the Incarnation is, as a work *ad extra*, common to all three of the Divine Persons; but it is nevertheless ascribed to each Person according to His distinctive peculiarity. The result only of the accomplishment of the Incarnation, inasmuch as it is the union of the human nature with a Divine Person, belongs in particular to the Son. Thus the old theologians say that the Incarnation was like an investiture with our human nature; the Father and the Holy Ghost assisted at the Incarnation, but it was the Son alone who assumed our human nature.

This then was the moment in which the Most Holy Trinity accomplished this great exterior work, a work in which It created, in the Sacred Humanity of Jesus, a kind of presence that was quite new here in this world, such as had never been before; the moment in which the Father sent His Son into the world, in order that He might give Him to us; in which the Holy Ghost, as the principle of perfection, holiness and love, accomplished the most magnificent work of nature, grace and love; the moment in which the Second Person of the Godhead assumed our human nature, and raised it to a union of life and being with Himself. At this moment, then, began this precious and glorious life, so perfect, true, and real; this life without any defect; this life that always attained its ends, fully and surely; this life of incomparable moral excellence, unsurpassed wisdom, and ineffable holiness; this life, overflowing with mysteries, merits and satisfactions; this life which embraces, forms, bears, strengthens, supplements, ennobles and perfects all other lives; this life so deep and wide and tremendous that all other lives appear petty and insignificant in comparison with it; this life of simply infinite value (Faber). "Et verbum caro factum est, et habitavit in nobis" (John 1:14). Who can fathom the depth of the mysteries of this moment, and embrace them with the affections of his heart? If we were to remain on our knees our whole lives long, rapt in grateful adoration of its glory and its miracles, we should still fail to comprehend it, and no effort of ours could ever be sufficient acknowledgment. Only in adoration and gratitude should heaven and earth think of this moment.

Such is the mystery of the Incarnation. What can we, what shall we do but thank, and thank again without ceasing? First of all the holy angel, who conducted the preliminaries of our redemption with so much love and zeal. What another angel had robbed us of, this one has abundantly restored. Then we will thank the blessed Mother of God. O wonderful, sublime creature, in whose hand and heart God laid our redemption, on whose consent He made everything depend! We were not to have Jesus, we were not to be redeemed, without her. She gave her consent, and gave it freely, with boundless love for us. She thereby broke the seal and opened the way to God's plans for our salvation. Like the floods of the sea the waters of salvation descended, grace upon grace, the grace of graces, Christ Himself. How can we ever thank her enough for it? Lastly thanks, the greatest and most heartfelt thanks be to the Most Holy Trinity, the Father of mercies and God of all consolation, Who in His love has given us His Only-begotten Son, and in Him has blessed us with all the riches of His pardon! Thanks be to the Holy Ghost, Who presided at the espousals of the Word with our nature, and blessed the alliance with the treasures of His grace. Finally thanks to the Divine Son, Who desired our poor mortal nature with inexplicable love and longing, and established a new home for Himself among us; Who overwhelms us, so to speak, with His love, clothes us with the treasures of His being and His glory, and draws us to the bosom of His Father as children and co-heirs with Himself. O beautiful, blessed power of His love! How shall we thank Him for it? May He Himself be our thanks, for we have all become rich in Him. We will close this meditation with a heartfelt Te Deum.

## THE MYSTERY OF THE INCARNATION

In order to become well acquainted with our Saviour and His life, it is necessary that we should have a clear idea of the mystery of the Incarnation. We must therefore penetrate a little further into it, and consider it in its essential character, in the way in which it was effected, and the results which it brought about.

### 1. ESSENTIAL CHARACTER OF THE INCARNATION

By the Incarnation we understand in general the mystery of the union of the divine and human natures, or the union of Divinity and humanity in one Person, in Christ; the mystery which is simply and strikingly expressed by the term "the God-Man." It is of the first importance to know in what this union consists. And in order to make the matter plain, we must first see in what it does not consist, and then what it really is, and how it took place.

This union of the divine and the human nature did not take place by direct combination of the two natures, that is, by amalgamation, or fusion, or by dissolution, the change of the one into the other, or by a transformation into a third nature. This is not what happened. Faith tells us that Christ possessed and retained fully and truly both natures, divine and human, and therefore there can be no question of a change or decrease of either the one or the other. The Divine Nature cannot possibly gain or lose anything; it cannot descend, lower itself or combine directly with anything outside itself. Hence theologians say that the Incarnation is not a descent and lowering of the Divinity, but rather the assumption and reception of the human nature into the Divinity. But while our human nature was assumed, it still remained what it was.

How then did the union of the two natures take place? Simply in and through the Second of the Divine Persons. The Second Divine Person was the Person in whom both natures met; in this way, that the Second Person in the Godhead became at the same time a Person with a human nature. Hence we must recognize two true and perfect natures in Christ, the divine and the human, the human nature complete, just as we have it, having body and soul, intellect and will, and under quite the same conditions and relations as with us. Never did the Divinity take the place of the human soul. Nothing was wanting to this human nature but its natural and appurtenant personality. When we come into the world, we have a complete, separate, independent existence; we are the bearers, owners, possessors of our powers and capabilities, and the masters of our actions; in a word, we have a personality, we are persons. With Christ the Second Divine Person took the place of the human personality, and this Person was from the first moment the owner, bearer and possessor of this nature; everything in it concerned Him, He did everything. But this Divine Person did not change the human nature in any way, just as any personality has no other effect upon the nature which it possesses than to render it independent, to complete and perfect it. So also here, the Divine Person had no effect upon the human nature, except that the latter existed in and belonged to the Second Person. That the human nature in Christ was holier and more powerful than ours, in consequence or on account of this union, is only a difference in degree of perfection, and not in essential character. There are, then, two entirely different natures in Christ, the divine and the human, but only one Person, namely that of the Son of God. This one Divine Person unites both natures in Himself, possesses them both as His own, and commands the powers and resources of both as their master and independent owner.

It follows from this that this union is the most intimate possible, in fact an essential one, because it makes, in Christ, one Being who is composed of different natures; further, that it is the greatest, last and highest of unions, not merely an assimilation to God by the communication of His nature, grace and glory, but by the communication of a Divine Person Himself. It follows, further, that this union is most glorious and magnificent, because its result is the God-Man; and lastly, that it is a purely supernatural one, the source and type of all supernatural union with and similarity to God.

### 2. MANNER IN WHICH THE INCARNATION WAS EFFECTED

It follows from the essential character of this union of the human nature with the Second Person of the Godhead that the said union was effected, first, with perfect freedom, out of pure goodness and benevolence on God's part, because it is entirely supernatural, and stands above all exigencies, capabilities and aspirations of our nature. "Who," indeed, "shall ascend into heaven, to bring Christ down?" (Rom. 10:6.)

Secondly, this union was effected in a manner most gracious towards us men; for this reason, that the human nature which is received into union with the Divine Person of the Son was taken from the blood of Adam, as it flowed in his actual descendants. Christ did not come into the world like Adam, directly from the hand of God. He had human ancestors, and they may be traced up to the first man (Luke 3:38). He is not, then, a stranger to us; He is really one of our race, our blood flows in His veins, and thus He is indeed our Brother. Moreover this assumption of our nature was an act of peculiar grace, because our Saviour assumed it with all the physical weaknesses that usually appertain to it. His Body was passible, subject to hunger, thirst, weariness and pain; and this because He willed it so, for He could have been freed from these conditions in consequence of the hypostatic union. So also His soul, like ours, was susceptible to love, joy and mercy, as well as to the sensations of sorrow, fear, repugnance and all the natural emotions of the sensual appetite, only with the difference that these sensations were entirely dependent upon His will as regards their origin and strength, and were therefore always good and meritorious. In these manifestations of His feelings on the part of our Saviour we have a new proof of the reality of His human nature, and also a beautiful example of control of the passions and patience in suffering; and on the other hand these very traits and their exercise became a new instrument in the hand of our Saviour in effecting our redemption by the Passion.

Thirdly, He assumed our nature indissolubly and for ever. No power will break this alliance. Even Death, the great divider, did not sever the Godhead from our Saviour's Body and Soul.

### 3. EFFECTS OF THE INCARNATION

The Incarnation embraces heaven, earth, all the orders of creation in nature and in grace, and the Creator Himself. It is incontestably the greatest of God's exterior works, and thus its consequences and effects must also be immeasurable. We will touch at least upon the nearest and most immediate of these. They relate to our Saviour and to Mary, to mankind, the universe, and God.

There were three immediate effects produced upon our Saviour by the Incarnation.

The first effect is the communication of the divine dignity, title and privileges to our human nature, by means of the Divine Person. The God-Man is, then, before all, the true, natural Son of God, generated in the bosom of the Father from all eternity. Like the Father and the Holy Ghost, He is the object of religious veneration, adoration, faith, hope and love, and must be honored and adored in the same manner as they are. All that this human nature does, suffers and says is divine; it is God Who acts and suffers, and all is of infinite intrinsic value and merit. This natural, Divine Sonship of the God-Man is based upon the eternal generation in the bosom of the Father. This Son is the Person of the God-Man. We meet with frequent assertions of this belief in the life of our Saviour (John 1:34, 49; 5:23; 6:70; 9:37 seq.; 11:27; Matt. 16:16; 27:54).

The second effect upon our Saviour was a special and most glorious endowment of His human nature, such as beseemed the Son of God. The intellect of Christ's soul possessed a threefold order of knowledge and science. First, our Saviour enjoyed from the first moment the beatific vision of God, as He Himself testifies: "We speak what we know, and we testify what we have seen" (John 3:11; 8:38). He is "full of grace and truth" (John 1:14). This was only becoming to His dignity as Son of God, Head of the angels, and Teacher of men. Further, He possessed from the moment of His Conception the fulness of supernatural (infused) knowledge (Hebr. 10:5 seq.); but natural (acquired) knowledge probably only in proportion to His age and the development of His faculties. The saints and we ourselves have also infused and acquired knowledge. By virtue of this threefold knowledge the God-Man comprehended (without this consciousness being omniscience), from the very first and at every moment, all spheres of truth, natural and supernatural, God's being, all mysteries of grace, glory and nature, all free actions of men in the past, present and future. All this was due to Him by right, as Head of the angels and of men, King of the universe, Lord, Judge and Mediator of mankind, and Last End of the whole creation.

A second endowment was holiness. Essential holiness consisted, in Christ's case, in the union of the human nature with the Second Divine Person, by virtue of which He was impeccable, sanctified and well-pleasing to God. In this sense Christ is anointed, sanctified, the Holy One, the Holy of Holies (Ps. 44:8; Luke 1:35; John 10:36). His soul derived additional holiness from the possession of sanctifying grace, infused virtues, and the gifts of the Holy Ghost (Isa. 11:1–5; John 1:14). His endowment with holiness served to perfect Him and to make Him in every supernatural respect our Model and Author. All this abundant grace of our Saviour is called, with relation to other creatures, "the grace of the Head" (or Chief), and consists partly in the superabundance and excellence of this wealth of grace, partly in the power and authorization to impart and communicate all graces to all those whose Head He is; that is, to the Church and to all men in this world (John 1:16), and to the angels, at least as far as concerns their service.

The third endowment was an extraordinary fulness of power. This power was not omnipotence, but still astonishingly great, and was bestowed upon Christ's Humanity as inherent to it, as a gift of grace for the accomplishment of supernatural and even miraculous effects, at least as cooperative instrument (Luke 6:19). This power was in accordance with the dignity of the Son of God, and with His task as teacher and prophet; for He was thus enabled to emphasize His doctrine by miracles. Our Saviour Himself repeatedly appeals to this divine proof of His mission to teach (John 5:36; 10:37, 38).

Moreover, even the Body of the God-Man was not excluded from the effects of the immediate union of the human nature with the Person of the Word. On account of this union and of the tasks which this Body had to fulfil, it excelled in its purity, its beauty, the delicacy of its constitution, and its powers of endurance. It was subject to sufferings only inasmuch as these are the common lot of human nature and of all creatures; but otherwise it had no trace of physical defect. A marvelous creation in itself alone, it was, as it were, a light but majestic wrapping of the Divinity, the instrument (or rather the hand) of the soul and of the Godhead for wonderful supernatural effects; as it still is, in the holy Sacraments. His Body was a sort of docile agent of His divine Person.

The third effect of the hypostatic union upon the God-Man was that He possessed the fulness and comprehensiveness of honors, dignities and offices. He inherited and united them all in Himself. As God-Man He is the born Head of the human race and of the entire creation, because He comprehends all their splendor in Himself, and because all power to rule and to sanctify proceeds from Him. By virtue of His twofold nature and of God's appointment, He is the natural Mediator between God and the world; through Him all creation reaches to God, and through Him all things—love, truth and grace—come from God to us. From the moment of His Conception He is Teacher, Prophet (John 1:17; 3:2; 6:14; Matt. 22:16; 23:8 seq.; Luke 7:16), Lawgiver and Redeemer, High Priest (Ps. 109:4) and King (Ps. 2:6; Matt. 2:2; John 18:37; Apoc. 1:5; 19:16), all in one Person. The hypostatic union itself was the unction which made our Saviour a Prophet, High Priest and King, and endowed Him with all that we see in Him of the great and the glorious.

### EFFECTS OF THE INCARNATION UPON MARY

The immediate effect of the Incarnation upon Mary was that she became really the Mother of God. Mary is really the Mother of God, precisely because she is the Mother of Jesus. She is often called the Mother of Jesus in the Holy Scriptures (Matt. 1:18, 21; Luke 2:33, 51; John 2:1); Elizabeth, Simeon and others, even our Saviour Himself, recognize her as such (Luke 1:43; John 6:42; 19:25 seq.). Besides, what the Holy Scripture adds about this relationship expresses nothing short of actual motherhood (Luke 1:31) and actual conception, and the fruit of this conception is the Son of God (Luke 1:32). Just as we are the sons of our mothers, so is the Saviour the Son of Mary; and the more so, that He was conceived in a virginal manner.

This is a most sublime and wonderful dignity. As regards its character, it is entirely supernatural, as well in the manner in which the motherhood was realized as with regard to the Son, who is the Son of God; with regard to the Son indeed it is simply infinite, because the dignity of this Son is infinite. It is a blood-relationship with the Son of God. He is in her, not, as in other creatures, in figure and by presence, but in a certain sense in identity, because His Flesh and Blood are the flesh and blood of Mary.

It is the highest and most intimate alliance with God, with the Son in the first place, and through Him, in a special manner, with the Father and the Holy Ghost also. There can be no comparison of this dignity with other dignities (with sanctifying grace, for example), inasmuch as the dignity of Mother of God belongs to quite another and a higher order, and at the same time contains in itself the glory of grace. It is not merely a carnal, but also a spiritual relationship with God. With regard to its effects, this dignity includes the highest power, viz. that of giving commands to the Son of God; and also the greatest advantage, viz. a special right to His love, gratitude and respect, a right to all blessings of grace and glory for herself, and the power to impart them to others. Thus this divine motherhood is the source of all the graces and privileges that Mary had received from the moment of her Conception, and the source of all her power to help us. She is by virtue of this motherhood our Advocate, the Queen of heaven and earth, and our spiritual Mother. Consequently this motherhood is also, on our side, the foundation of a special veneration for and childlike trust in her. This position of Mary as Mother of Jesus is simply her prerogative and distinguishing feature, the stand-point from which alone one can understand and judge of her wondrous life. Everything comes thence and returns thither. We honor in her, before all things, the Mother of God; or more properly speaking, we honor our God and Saviour in her.

That is what the Incarnation means for Mary. How sublime she is in this motherhood, standing at Christ's side! Quite otherwise than Eve beside the first Adam. Here the second Adam proceeds from the second Eve; she gives Him His Name, and He is subject to her. By this motherhood Mary is an essential and inseparable element of the Church of Christ; she enters into its faith, as the Mother of God; into its morals, as the unrivaled model of virtue and holiness; and into its economy of grace as, after Christ, the chief Mediatrix of assisting grace.

### EFFECTS OF THE INCARNATION UPON THE HUMAN RACE

There were three special, immediate effects of the Incarnation upon the human race.

The first effect is the elevation of our nature and our race. By the alliance of the Son of God with our nature we are all elevated, ennobled, and, so to speak, deified, made blood-relations of God. The Son of God becomes one of us by a natural birth, an honor which makes even the angels reverence us. He is indeed their Lord and Head, but not their Brother according to nature. In Christ our nature is raised above all the orders of the heavenly hierarchy to the right hand of God, and shares with the Father and the Holy Ghost the throne of glory itself; and thereby we also are, as it were, transported into the vicinity of the divine throne.

The second effect is the bestowal of gifts. The Son of God possesses supernatural life, grace and glory, naturally and by right. By the Incarnation all these blessings are conveyed to our race; it owns them now in Christ as its possession and right, and God owes them to us in consequence of His gracious decree of the Incarnation and Redemption, if we on our side fulfil the conditions laid down by Christ. More than this; His merits are our merits, and we can lay claim to them at our pleasure. For Christ is not merely our Brother, but also our Head; we are His mystical Body, and as head and members help each other and share their gifts, and as the human nature in Christ (as far as this is possible) shares in the honors and properties of the Divine Person and Nature, so also a mutual exchange of goods takes place between Christ and ourselves, so that we have our part in the sonship of God and in the prophetic, priestly and kingly office of Christ. Yes, even with relation to God we have grown rich and powerful in Christ; for He enables us to honor and adore God worthily. In and through Christ we can offer to God adoration and worship of infinite value, and satisfy all His claims. And this worship is our very own and proceeds from us; for Christ exercises this office of glorifying God through us and in our nature.

The third advantage which the Incarnation brings us is a sweet consolation and heartfelt trust, which arises from the truth that Christ is true Man and has a nature like our own. He is indeed God also; but that does not hinder His being Man, and entire Man, with all that appertains to humanity, sin excepted. It is true and infinitely sweet to think that He is really Man like ourselves, and that we may draw nigh to Him without fear and tell Him all our natural infirmities. He knows all, He has experienced all; He was tried in all, and was "compassed with infirmity," that He might be a merciful High Priest (Hebr. 5:2). Nothing therefore must come between us and Him, no shyness, no feeling of absolute distance and dissimilarity. He is not a strange, vast Being whom we can only adore, but is one like ourselves, related to us, so that we can love and embrace Him familiarly and without constraint.

With no claim save that of being men and His brethren, we may be assured of the special and unbounded love of His Heart, however wretched and sinful we are. Loving confidence in all our necessities—that is the incomparable advantage and blessing of this mystery, and the echo of the glorious songs in which the prophets proclaimed the advent of the God-Man (Isa. 12).

### CONSEQUENCES OF THE INCARNATION FOR THE ENTIRE CREATION

It is a beautiful thought of profound theologians, that God may also have carried out the Incarnation with a view to the completion, embellishment and perfection of the universe. The Incarnation does, as a matter of fact, effect this design in two ways. First, in the increase of variety which results throughout all orders of creation. We have now not only the marvelous variety of beings of the material and the spiritual orders, and beings partaking of both natures; not only a natural and a supernatural order, not only the kingdom of grace and that of glory; not only beings consisting of one person and one nature, and a Being Who consists of several Persons and one Nature; we have not only human beings originating from man and woman, and also one woman (Eve) originating only from a man; we have not only created beings and an Uncreated Being: but, by the Incarnation, the creation acquires also a Being in Whom two natures exist in one Person, a Being Whose human nature proceeds from a woman only, a Being Whose Person and divine Nature are uncreated. God as regards His Person and Divine Nature. Thus the creation is completed on all sides by this mystery, and perfected in variety and richness.

Thence results secondly the advantage, that the multiformity and variety of creatures attains to a most wonderful unity and essential connection with God. Before the Incarnation, there was nowhere in the various orders of creation a living link with God; everywhere was immeasurable distance and absolute difference of nature, dignity and excellence. Everywhere was lacking a living link, which, so to speak, growing out of the Godhead and taking root in God and in nature, should unite everything in itself, and bring all into a real, living connection with God. This took place in the Incarnation. One Who sits as God on the throne of glory stretched forth His Hand towards a created, individual nature, and took it to Himself. This individual nature was a human one, in which all the elements and orders of the creation are represented, and which therefore, being the central point of all things created, became also the point of contact and union between God and them. Thus nothing more is wanting. The organization and connection is completed by a sublime, Divine Being, Who is the adornment, honor and glory of all the others.

### CONSEQUENCES OF THE INCARNATION FOR GOD

This mystery so truly glorifies and honors God, because it reveals His attributes as no other of all the mysteries of our faith can do. It reveals in the first place Wisdom, in the variety and unity of her creations. Wisdom here completes her work by the glorious key-stone and crown of all creation. Then omnipotence. Omnipotence creates here not stars and worlds, earth, sea, men and angels, but a human nature which it unites with a divine nature, a human nature which a Divine Person assumes to Himself. Further, bounty and mercy, which are nowhere more gloriously displayed than in giving and forgiving. Where does God give more generously than in the Incarnation? He gives not only His blessings, nature, grace and glory, but Himself; and not merely to be used, enjoyed, contemplated and possessed, but to be substantially united with us, in a union that surpasses all other unions and brings with itself the whole abundance of God's natural and supernatural gifts. It is not a created gift, but the Uncreated and Infinite Person of the Son of God. And this bounty glorifies God's justice also. The end and aim of the Incarnation is the propitiation and satisfaction of justice. In the Incarnation man's debt is paid fully and completely, by a representative head, as the debt was originally incurred also by a representative head. Through God's bounty this very debt was a motive for drawing nearer to humanity by the Incarnation, so that man attained to higher graces and honors than he had possessed before his fall. And we are the heirs to these benefactions.

But God is glorified not only by the revelation of His divine attributes, but also by the praise and honor which mankind offers Him in consequence of these attributes. This praise and the adoration that is due to God from His creatures are gained in the Incarnation in an entirely new manner, most worthy of God. By the Incarnation He receives an infinite adoration and satisfaction, such as could not have been offered to Him by the whole of creation unaided. In the Incarnation it is God Who adores and satisfies, God Who offers everything in an infinite manner. And had this infinite glorification of God been capable of increase, it would have been augmented by the circumstance that this same God renders the satisfaction out of pure love, in the lowest depths of privation and humiliation, by delivering Himself to a most ignominious and painful death; that He continues this sacrifice mystically in innumerable souls whom His example encourages to imitation, and in the Eucharistic sacrifice that never ceases on the altars of the Catholic Church. These three sacrifices—the sacrifice of the Cross, the Eucharistic sacrifice, and the mystical sacrifice in the hearts of men—are radiations from the priestly spirit of sacrifice of Jesus, and make the terrestrial globe a living temple of God's honor and glory. With the Incarnation, then, a new and glorious era began for God's glory, and therefore the angels sang at the birth of the God-Man: "Glory to God in the highest" (Luke 2:14).

Such is the mystery of the Incarnation. Its very essence is the wonderful union of the human nature with the Second Divine Person, and the assumption of humanity into the Godhead. Its result is the God-Man, that great and wondrous Being, the model, author and end of the whole creation; that mysterious Being Who stands first in all ages and marches at the head of all the nations; Who unites in Himself all phases of existence as well as all dignities; at Whose name every knee in heaven and on earth should bow; that Being Who is the despair of His opponents, the love and admiration of heaven, and the life and consolation of earth. The effects of the Incarnation extend everywhere; the universe is aglow with the light of this divine work. It surrounds the whole creation, time, eternity, even the throne of the Godhead, with a beautiful halo of glory that rejoices the Holy Trinity and procures for earth Its blessing and eternal complacency.

We are always reminded of this great and consoling mystery by the holy season of Advent, with its hymns of expectation and longing, the sweet prayers of its matins, and the clear-tongued voices of its bells. What comfort they have rung out over this old world! Into how many hearts have they brought better desires, increasing hope and new confidence! The world is so rich in pain and sorrow, and so bitterly poor in consolation. There are ills and wounds for which no remedy is to be found except in the God-Man. He is not merely a physician, but also medicine; medicine for our intellect, for our hearts, for our sins, and even for death. The God-Man heals everything. If our religion is a religion of consolation, it is so through this mystery. What should we be without it? We could only regret having lived. But now we have Him, and therefore let us rejoice and thank God for having given Him to us; let us love Him and make use of the blessings He has brought us for His honor and our salvation, and impart them to others also as well as we can.

## The First Pulsations of the God-Man's Life

The life of the Incarnate God began, then, with His Conception; and it expressed itself in glorious manifestations of intellect and will from the first moment of its existence. It is both sweet and instructive to meditate upon the first manifestations of this life of the God-Man. There were three principal objects to which these acts were directed.

### 1. GOD

God Himself was the first object which occupied the life of the God-Man; and in the first place He adored Him. Adoration is the first duty to God. By adoration we acknowledge Him to be the Supreme Being, the source of all our possessions, and the Author and Creator of our being, and resign ourselves to Him with all that we have and are. That was in the natural order of things the first act which the great and glorious soul of the God-Man poured out before God. It was a glorious and majestic act, such as the entire creation had never yet accomplished.

The second act was thanksgiving and joy. Our Saviour often gave thanks during His life, and especially whenever He received from God the opportunity to do some good work. How much greater and more glorious must His thanksgiving have been at this moment, the very beginning of His life, in which He received everything from God, and in which the whole force of His faculties, like the gushing waters of a spring when first freed from restraint, exulted in the Living God!

The third act was love; love toward God, the Supreme Good, His Father. The Divine Son had in His assumed humanity a new instrument, a new source of His old, eternal love for His Father, and the Holy Ghost had endowed this instrument with all the might of His love. What can equal this first outburst of love? Now at last, so many thousand years after the creation, was attained creation's aim: to love God with the whole heart, the whole soul and the whole strength.

Each of these acts had three properties. In the first place, they were infinite in dignity and value and absolutely perfect. It was the mighty soul of the God-Man which produced them, and the object of them was God Himself. By virtue of the direct contemplation of God, the Word Incarnate knew and saw all the grounds for adoration and love of God; He saw all God's claims on the creature; He knew them better and in quite another light than we, and fulfilled them most perfectly; He glorified all God's attributes magnificently by the wealth of His praise and adoration. Further, these acts never ceased henceforth in His Heart. God, and the adoration and love of God, became the absorbing idea and the purport of His life. The precious censer of His heart and soul unceasingly sent up this sweet odor of affections to God's throne, and filled the earth with its fragrance. It burned perpetually and never went out. Lastly, these acts were not of a merely private nature; they were accomplished and offered to God in the name of the whole creation. The love and adoration of the God-Man embraced not only their Infinite Object, but also the whole extent of the creation. It was the new and mighty voice with which the whole creation now praised and blessed God.

### 2. MARY AND MANKIND

Mary and mankind were the second object of the occupation of the God-Man's life. The Son of God willed in His exceeding graciousness to become our brother and the child of a human mother, and entered immediately into the inheritance of love for her and for us. He must of necessity love her, as His mother, and He did so easily and willingly. It was a joy to Him to be Mary's child, and He embraced her with the arms of His love. He owed to her His human existence, and she owed all to Him. Everything came to her from Him; her wisdom, her virtue and her holiness were a reflection of Him. Thus in her He only loved, as it were, His own beauty and loveliness. In her He had truly "come into His own."

But He also loved us men. At the moment of His Conception He felt and recognized Himself to be the Head of all mankind and of the whole creation, and embraced us all with the love at once of a brother and a Creator. Even at this time He already longed for our salvation, and our names were mentioned in His prayers. What a joy for us! We were all present in the first thoughts and loving impulses of the Sacred Heart.

### 3. THE GOD-MAN HIMSELF

But the God-Man also knew Himself, and comprehended His relations to God and to us; and the result of this perception was the deepest humility and self-abasement. "Being in the form of God," says the Apostle, "He emptied Himself, taking the form of a servant . . . and humbled Himself" (Phil. 2:7, 8). Never was an act of such deep humility made as by the God-Man at the moment in which He became conscious that He, in His human nature, constituted one united life with the Second Person of the Godhead. How clear to Him were the infinite height and sublimity of the Godhead, to the participation in which His human nature was now raised, and on the other hand the poverty, baseness and unworthiness of our nature! None knew so well as He that it was only unmerited grace and goodness which raised His human nature to such a height. With regard to us, also, He saw how it was only this same free gift that raised Him above all the misery of our sin. Of Himself, according to His human nature, He could not have been more than we are. For this reason He did not consider it beneath His dignity to make Himself the servant of God and of us. And this lively feeling of humility was never extinguished in His heart, not even when He saw and communed with us men and perceived us to be so wretched and full of degrading weaknesses. It was this very humility which made Him so gentle, so engaging, so mild and so full of divine compassion in His intercourse with us men, even with the greatest sinners; and it began in His Heart at the first instant of His existence.

Lastly, there followed from this humility and love towards God and us another precious act. Theologians say that God set before our Saviour at the first moment of His Conception all the ways of redeeming us, and left Him free to choose which He pleased; whatever He then chose was to become the will and command of the Father. According to this view, then, our Saviour made at that moment with absolute freedom the choice of His path in life, and appointed the details and circumstances of His earthly career. His manner of life as we now see it in the Gospels was the result of this choice.

The reality and probability of this choice has solid support in Holy Scripture. St. Paul says of this very moment: "When He cometh into the world, He saith: Sacrifice and oblation Thou wouldst not, but a body Thou hast fitted to Me; holocausts for sin did not please Thee. Then said I: Behold, I come; in the head of the book it is written of Me, that I should do Thy will, O God" (Hebr. 10:5, 6, 7; Ps. 39:7–10). Another passage of St. Paul is also pertinent here: "Let us run by patience to the fight proposed to us, looking on Jesus, the author and finisher of faith, Who, having joy set before Him, endured the cross, despising the shame" (Hebr. 12:1, 2). The meaning of these last words is, that the path of honor and joy was placed before our Saviour, but that He despised it and chose instead the path of suffering and humiliation. This interpretation lies within the literal meaning of the words, and is confirmed by the context as also by the aim of the passage, which is nothing else than to encourage Christians, by the example of our Saviour, to courageous endurance of the sufferings of life. Now, there is no more powerful motive than this, that our Saviour Himself embraced the way of suffering, of His own free choice and out of love for us. This is quite in keeping with the love which the Father bears to His Divine Son. He treats Him with respect, and allows Him to make His choice with freedom. Even to us He allows this freedom in the choice of a path in life. In this manner too Christ's freedom and the obedience in which He accomplished the work of the Redemption are best reconciled.

The magnificence of the act consists, first, in the greatness of the joys and honors which would have been His portion from the very first instant, and which He renounces for the period of His life on earth. He could have appeared in an impassible state, or even in a passible one He could have entered public life as a King and High Priest, with power and honor, like a David, a Solomon or a Moses, and thus have redeemed us. Secondly, the magnificence of this act consists in the greatness of the sufferings and abasement which our Saviour chose for Himself. We see, indeed, how the path that He chooses leads through poverty, sufferings and humiliations, grows ever more narrow, more difficult and forbidding, till it ends on Mount Calvary. Who can ever comprehend the greatness of the sacrifice which lay in this resolution? By this act He stamps His whole life with the character of sacrifice. Indeed, He says so Himself: "Holocausts for sin did not please Thee . . . behold, I come" (Hebr. 10:6, 7), i.e. as a sacrifice, instead of these typical sacrifices. His whole life was decided by this act. All that followed was only the fulfilment of this great vow of sacrifice. The program of His life was traced out: a life of suffering and self-annihilation throughout. Thirdly, the magnificence of the act lay in the motive which induced our Saviour to take this resolution. It could not, after all, be simply God's glory that decided Him to this excess of sacrifice. Each one of His works was of infinite merit before God, and the infinite admits of no augmentation. He could choose what He pleased; God's honor would receive an infinite reparation in any case. Neither was it regard for Himself, to gain merits and increase His essential glory; this was allotted to Him from the first moment, as God-Man, and was not essentially increased by all that He suffered and sacrificed. And as regards the accidental glory which proceeds to Him from the love and gratitude we bear to Him (which is greater in proportion to the bitterness He suffered for us), He could have obtained it by actual graces which, by making us understand His grandeur and majesty, would have sufficed to make us capable of the greatest sacrifices. What was it, then, that inspired Him with this resolve? Love for us, nothing but love, and a love noble above all other love. We were in sin, and under the ban of evil passions and the love of transitory things. In order to be saved we must take the path of penance, renunciation, suffering and poverty. To find this road passable and less difficult we need a model, and also courage and comfort. On this account our Saviour went through the whole of human life, and took into His career all the suffering and distress that can come upon a human heart. Thus we have the advantage of having Him with us everywhere as our model and companion; by uniting ourselves to Him we can always sanctify our actions and sufferings, make them meritorious, and always derive the most abundant consolation from His example and His love. What a true and generous love our Saviour showed for us at the very first moment of His life! How can we ever thank Him enough for it? Even now that He has of His own free choice taken and followed up the path of poverty, humiliation and suffering, in order to set us an example and encourage us to imitate Him, we still find it so hard to follow. What would it have been if He had gone another way, the way of honors and joys, as He might have done unhindered? We should never have believed that we must take an opposite road, and that would have been our ruin. Let us render Him everlasting thanks for His love and generosity.

We may now examine the important consequences of these acts of adoration, devotion and intense love for God and for us, with which our Saviour began His life. By these acts was founded the kingdom of Christ, God's kingdom here below. They are our honor and our joy, and by them God was adored and loved as He deserves to be. In truth He "put a new canticle into the mouth" of creation (Ps. 39:4) by the song of praise in the Heart of the God-Man, and never throughout all eternity will it die away. These acts of the God-Man at His entrance into this world are also our comfort when we see how we always fall short of our endeavor, or when our inadequacy and sinfulness oppress us. The wealth and magnificence of these acts belong to us. In this one oblation He has perfected us all (Hebr. 10:14); we can supply for our poverty before God by His superabundant riches. Lastly, these acts are the glorious model of our life. This act of choice by which the God-Man decided His whole life was to be the pattern of all our decisions. We should always imitate His choice, that is, prefer whatever tends towards the abasement and privations of the God-Man and away from self-love. The spirit of love and humility from which this choice proceeded was to be the spirit in which we were to serve God and man.

## In the Womb of His Mother

So, then, the Lord had become Man, and passed according to the ordinary course of nature nine months in the womb of His Mother. This is a new proof of His true human nature. And His life in His Mother's womb was just as wonderful and glorious as His Conception.

### 1. THE LIFE OF JESUS

In this life that our Saviour led in His Mother's womb there are two things to be considered.

First, we must consider the characteristics of this life. It is, in the first place, a life of concealment, darkness and captivity, whilst He Himself is infinite, the light of the angels and of the whole world, the light that streamed in rays of beauty over the entire creation. It is further a life of silence. He, the Word of the Father, the expression of His glory, the teacher of the prophets, veils Himself in His Mother's womb in silence, and preludes that reserve and moderation in speech which was to mark Him throughout His whole life, and which was also a marked feature in Mary and Joseph. Lastly, it is a life of weakness and helplessness, notwithstanding His divine strength. Is there a greater helplessness and dependency than that of the child in its mother's womb? So it was here. It is as if this extreme weakness and dependency had a charm for His omnipotence. These were the general characteristics of this life.

Secondly, we must also consider the manifestation of this life. What, then, did our Saviour do during this long period of concealment? In the first place, He perfected His bodily faculties for our benefit. He formed His Body, in order to give it for us in death and in the Blessed Sacrament. He formed His eyes, to look upon us with mild and pitying glance and to weep over us. He formed His lips, to teach us. He formed His feet, to go after us and seek us as a Good Shepherd; His hands to heal us and be pierced for us on the Cross, His shoulders to carry it; He formed His Heart, to love us; and His Precious Blood, to shed it for us and give it to be our drink. He formed His whole body, to die for us as a sacrificial Lamb. The second form of His activity is adoration and praise of God; joy in God, His Heavenly Father, and in the Holy Ghost; joy in all the attributes and counsels of God. The third object with which He was occupied was Himself; joy in His Divine Sonship and glorious human nature; joy in His intellect, with its immeasurable spheres of knowledge and the contemplation of God; joy in His will, with its freedom, sinlessness, holiness and unbounded power; joy also in His relationship to us and His destiny as our Redeemer; joy, lastly, in the future kingdom of His Church, which was to arise from His life and death. But with these joys were also mingled bitter sorrows. He saw that monster, sin, with its terrible devastations in God's kingdom and in individual souls; He saw our sufferings and the sufferings of His Church; He saw His own sufferings, and the Cross. It was already present to His mind and heart; fear and anguish already force their way into the depths of His sensitive soul, like a rushing stream through rocky defiles. Fourthly, He constantly sanctified His Mother, Mary, transforming her ever more and more into Himself by wondrous graces of knowledge of the mystery of the Incarnation, and by graces of love which united her to Him. She became more and more filled with His spirit, grew into Him, as it were, and became in her soul ever more the Mother of God and Mother of Jesus. The same thing holds good proportionately with regard to St. Joseph, who had already become His father through betrothal to Mary. Lastly, He was occupied with the sanctification and government of the world. From the first moment of His Conception He began to reign, and was the center and heart of the government of heaven and earth. From Him there flowed heavenwards an unceasing stream of glory; the waves of His grace ever poured over the earth, the poor heathen world, over faithful Israel, the tempted and the dying; and the rays of His consolation penetrated even into the dim region of Limbo. He occupied Himself with the salvation of all souls; and as the invisible, hidden Ruler of the world He judged all who departed this life. It was indeed a divine life that He led in His Mother's womb, a life most active, and yet one of unbroken calm.

## 2. THE LIFE OF THE MOTHER OF GOD

The Mother's life during this period presents both an inward and an outward aspect.

The interior life of Mary was before all things a life of closest union with Jesus. It was a union of body as well as of soul. There is no more intimate bodily union than that of mother and child. They are one life. One pulsation sustains the life of both. Mary's life was almost the same as the life of those who already possess God in heaven. The Supreme God rested and worked in her. Secondly, her life was a life of deepest recollection, which gathered all the powers of her soul around the God-Man. She saw ever more with His eyes, loved with His Heart, and His taste became her taste. It was a life of marvelous enlightenment, which led her deeper and deeper into the mystery of the Redemption, its essential character, its effects in the past and in the future, its connection with the history of the chosen people and the entire human race; and which initiated her more and more, as Mother of God, into its compass and sublimity. It was a life of the purest, most fervent, most perfect emotions of love for God, Whom she encompassed within herself; of emotions of joy, because all divine things are joy and bring joy, and she possessed God Himself; emotions, lastly, of desire, longing and most eager expectation of the Birth of the Divine Child. The Church celebrates this expectation by a special feast in the Advent season. And how great must have been that longing! This trait of longing for the countenance of God, yearning to see it and be happy in the vision, goes through the whole creation. Mary was soon really to see the Face of God, the created image of divine perfection, the sight of which rejoices heaven and earth, from which all beings derive life and joy; the Face whose features God beheld from all eternity; the Face for which all ages had expectantly looked; she was to see it unveiled, face to face, in all the beauty and grace of childhood, as the face of her own child (Faber). Indeed, all were awaiting Christ: the world, to gain rest and peace; the angels, to see God's counsels accomplished; the Heavenly Father Himself, if we may so speak, to behold His created Image; and all this longing was united in Mary's heart and had to find expression in her, all the more now, the nearer the moment came. It was a life of the noblest activity, of deepest emotion, and most glorious; a life of the highest spiritual perfection and heavenly grandeur, thrilling with vibrations that began in the deepest sources of heavenly existence.

And yet the outward aspect of this interior life of Mary was full of deep repose and charming naturalness. Everything in her was so sublime, so unusual and extraordinary, and yet it did not overpower her nature. Her life with her Divine Son seemed to be as natural as the life of the Son in the bosom of the Father. Whilst she bore the Author of all things in her womb, and her heart was beating quickly with love, adoration and longing, still her face told nothing of this, and the world had no suspicion that such marvelous things were taking place in her. This very fact shows how great and glorious and queenly was the nature of our Blessed Lady, that she bore so many heavenly favors thus lightly and easily.

### 3. OUR LIFE

Great and wonderful as this life of Jesus in Mary is, it yet approaches and resembles our life as Christians, our supernatural life. It is the beautiful model of the interior Christian life; it must also be our life. Christ is in us. Through sanctifying grace we bear within us the supernatural image of the Divine Sonship; and, after Holy Communion, not merely in figure but in all reality. Christ works in us also by His grace; He forms Himself in us by supernatural principles, which He implants in our minds, by supernatural intentions, supernatural actions, and good, meritorious works. He follows up in our hearts also the aim that brought Him into Mary's womb. He wishes to be born in us, to grow, rule, and reveal Himself. Thus the soul of a Christian in sanctifying grace is always, in a spiritual manner, like the womb of Mary.

And as Mary led an interior life and concentrated all her thoughts and life upon the Word Incarnate in her womb, so we too must lead an interior, supernatural life, always guided and directed by supernatural principles, having always supernatural intentions and performing supernatural actions. These actions of the interior, supernatural life consist above all in watchfulness over self, custody of the exterior and interior senses, avoidance of all outward haste and inward passion, the endeavor to make a virtuous action of everything we do, and lastly frequent converse with God by prayer. Thus our life will be a copy of the life of Jesus and Mary during this period. The motives are not far to seek. They are contained in our mystery. There is nothing more sublime than this life, because it has God for its aim and object and is the life of God Himself. There is nothing of more solid value, because everything in it has merit for eternal life. There is nothing more powerful, because it bears in itself the strength of God and can extend its influence over the whole human race. The weapon of this life, prayer, is the greatest power in the world. Lastly, there is nothing sweeter and more joyous than this interior life, because it arises from sacrifice and brings purity and divine consolation with it. Purity, merit, joy, and power, these are the beautiful results of the interior life which makes the soul pleasing in the sight of God.

## B. Revelation of the Incarnation

### The Visitation

Luke 1:39. And Mary rising up in those days went into the hill country with haste, into a city of Juda;—40. And she entered into the house of Zachary, and saluted Elizabeth.—41. And it came to pass that, when Elizabeth heard the salutation of Mary, the infant leaped in her womb. And Elizabeth was filled with the Holy Ghost;—42. And she cried out with a loud voice, and said: "Blessed art thou among women, and blessed is the fruit of thy womb.—43. And whence is this to me, that the mother of my Lord should come to me?—44. For behold, as soon as the voice of thy salutation sounded in my ears, the infant in my womb leaped for joy.—45. And blessed art thou that hast believed; because those things shall be accomplished that were spoken to thee by the Lord."—46. And Mary said: "My soul doth magnify the Lord;—47. And my spirit hath rejoiced in God my Saviour. —48. Because he hath regarded the humility of his handmaid; for behold from henceforth all generations shall call me blessed.—49. Because he that is mighty hath done great things to me; and holy is his name.—50. And his mercy is from generation unto generations, to them that fear him.—51. He hath shown might in his arm; he hath scattered the proud in the conceit of their heart.—52. He hath put down the mighty from their seat, and hath exalted the humble.—53. He hath filled the hungry with good things; and the rich he hath sent empty away.—54. He hath received Israel his servant, being mindful of his mercy,—55. As he spoke to our fathers, to Abraham and to his seed for ever."—56. And Mary abode with her about three months; and she returned to her own house.

Our Blessed Lady's visit to Elizabeth falls within the nine months preceding the Birth of our Lord.

### 1. THE VISITATION, ITS OCCASION AND OBJECT

It is evident that this visit was occasioned by the words of the angel Gabriel, announcing to Mary that her kinswoman Elizabeth was blessed with a child, in spite of her barrenness and advanced age. The angel's statement was not merely a token of the truth of his message to Mary, but also an invitation to visit Elizabeth, especially since Mary may have recognized, either through divine inspiration or through information from the angel, the relation in which Elizabeth's child stood to her Divine Son, as also that her visit was to be the means of conveying to John the blessing of grace, and that Zachary's family was to be made happy by the revelation of the advent of the Messias. Apart from this divine inspiration Mary would scarcely have consented to this visit, especially as she withheld the secret even from St. Joseph.

In God's design, then, this mystery had the significance of revealing the fact of the Incarnation and conveying to St. John its first gift of grace, because his task was so intimately connected with the Person of our Saviour. This mystery is therefore the first revelation of the Incarnation and the first application of its graces, and also a real proof of the bounty and wisdom of Jesus. He reveals His bounty, because He cannot rest inactive. He has brought grace upon earth, and He must bestow it at once. As yet incapable of going Himself, He causes Himself to be taken to John by His Mother. And He shows His wisdom by the valid reasons which lead Him to choose this object for the bestowal of grace.

### 2. HOW THE OBJECT OF THE MYSTERY WAS ATTAINED

It was in reality the Holy Ghost Who directed and acted. But He made use of an instrument to carry out His ends.

This instrument was the Mother of God; the means, her beautiful virtues. It was above all her faith, and also her reverence and gratitude for the token given to her. She would have considered it as a mark of gross indifference not to follow the divine sign. Further was her habitual readiness to obey divine inspirations. Hence she started off with all speed on her way to the highlands of Judaea, and hastened to the place where Zachary and Elizabeth dwelt, perhaps the "St. John's Mount" or "Ain Karim" of today (Luke 1:39). The little village lies two leagues west of Jerusalem, on a stony hill in the midst of a valley, surrounded by rocky slopes. The white houses stand out in bold relief against the dark background of slender cypress-trees, with olive and vine plantations sloping gradually down to the bed of a little brook. Surrounded as they are by gray masses of rock, crowned only by a few watch-towers and castles, with here and there scanty groups of terebinth-trees, they form a scene of beauty and grace, quite in keeping with the character of the mystery. Finally, the modesty and friendliness with which the Blessed Virgin first greeted her cousin, on her entrance into the house (Luke 1:40). It was just this humble and loving word of greeting that the Holy Ghost made use of for the work of revelation and of saving grace.

Scarcely had Elizabeth heard the greeting when the babe under her heart leaped, a sign that it was filled with abundant divine grace, and perhaps also that it already recognized the Redeemer Who had come to sanctify it, and was hailing Him with joy. It was probably at this moment that John, as the angel had foretold (Luke 1:15), was freed from original sin and raised to a wonderful height of sanctity. This was the first act of revelation and bestowal of saving grace by the mediation of our Blessed Lady.

This grace passed on from John to Elizabeth. As the babe leaped, she was filled with the Holy Ghost (Luke 1:41). With Elizabeth, probably, this grace included not only an increase of holiness and sanctifying grace, but also revelation and the spirit of prophecy, in which, by the special enlightenment of the Holy Ghost, she beheld the accomplishment and the essential character of the Incarnation. The essential character of the Incarnation she enunciates in terms most unmistakable and to the point, by calling Mary "the Mother of the Lord" and the fruit of her womb "blessed" (Luke 1:42, 43). And Mary received in these words a confirmation of the angel's message; Elizabeth even takes up the angelic salutation and continues it, as if she had been listening in spirit to the quiet dialogue in the little chamber at Nazareth (Luke 1:42). Thus all the objects of the visit were gained, and the house of Zachary was filled with grace and blessing, not only by Mary's first greeting to Elizabeth, but still more by her three months' sojourn there. Where Mary is, there is grace; there the springs of heavenly blessings flow more quickly and more abundantly. She bears the Source of all grace in herself, and imparts it to others.

### 3. THE RESULTS OF THE VISIT

A very natural result of this revelation and operation of divine grace was, first, the glorification of the Mother of God; and secondly, the glorification of God through Mary.

Elizabeth was the mouth-piece of the homage paid to Mary. She is not merely the first who honored Mary, but also a true pattern and model of all veneration of Our Lady, since she reveals to us the true motives and the manner of this cult, and lastly the blessings accruing from it. St. Elizabeth tells us three reasons for her veneration of Mary. The first is her dignity as Mother of God. She greets Mary as the Mother of her Lord (Luke 1:43), and calls the fruit of her womb blessed (Luke 1:42). The second motive is Mary's holiness, and Elizabeth lays especial stress upon this holiness as displayed in the spirit of faith (Luke 1:45), contrasting her perhaps with Zachary. The privileges and graces of the Mother of God are the third motive, and Elizabeth sums them up in a word, when she says with the angel that Mary is "blessed among women" (Luke 1:42), because in her position as Mother of the Redeemer and channel of grace she surpasses in greatness all other holy women. Elizabeth is also our model for the manner in which Mary should be honored. Her veneration of Mary is interior and exterior, a veneration expressed in thought, word and deed. The interior veneration is a great respect for Mary. It is worthy of note how Elizabeth humbles herself before her cousin. She finds it inexplicable that the latter comes to her and greets her, and yet Mary was much younger, and as yet unknown and without position; Elizabeth was venerable by her age, her holiness, and the position of her husband, favored by God with a child of miracles, the greatest among those born of women, and yet she regards Mary's visit as a favor. And she gives loud expression to this respect and veneration, in terms full of enthusiasm (Luke 1:43). Thus Elizabeth is a perfect model of the true cult of Mary, as well as of the blessings derived from it, since she and her household received such graces through Mary. She is the first to do honor to her after the Incarnation, and her sentiments of veneration for Our Lady, as well as her enthusiastic greeting, still perpetuate their work in the human race.

God and our Saviour in turn receive their homage from Mary, who, in sweet and touching humility and piety, transfers the

praises conferred upon her to God, and breaks forth into the
glorious "Magnificat" (Luke 1:46–55). The Magnificat is in its
character and substance the most appropriate song of praise of
the Redemption, as she herself says: "My spirit hath rejoiced in
God, my Saviour" (Luke 1:47). This canticle extols the greatness and glory of the work of Redemption, on all sides. First,
with regard to God. The Redemption is a work of God's power
(Luke 1:49, 51), of God's mercy (Luke 1:50, 54), and lastly of
God's fidelity (Luke 1:55). Further, Mary extols the glory of
the Redemption with regard to herself. From the lowliness of her
nature, rank and sex, she is raised by her share in the work of the
Redemption to an inconceivable height of dignity, inward holiness and external glory, which has no limits either in time or space
(Luke 1:48, 49). She then reveals the glory of the Redemption
with regard to the heathen world and the kingdom of Satan, to
which, unhappily, a part of the Israelite nation also belonged.
This kingdom of arrogance, diabolical self-sufficiency, earthly
might and independence is confounded, cast down and ignomini-
ously stripped of its power (Luke 1:51, 52, 53). Finally, she
extols the work of Redemption in that wondrous kingdom of God,
the Church (of which the corner-stone is laid in the Incarnation),
in its existence from times of yore (Luke 1:54, 55), its foundation
and realization (Luke 1:54), and lastly in its marvelous laws and
means of power. It is a wondrous song, this canticle of God's
Mother, full of simplicity and unfathomable depth, the bird-
song heralding the dawn of Christ on earth. Marvelous notes
they are and, though mingled with chords from ancient times,
yet new and strange and mysterious, on account of their relation to Christ's kingdom. It is a song infinitely dear to all children of Mary, for the very reason that she sang it, under the
guidance of the Holy Ghost. Would that we might always sing
and recite it with the same devotion, piety, and loving enthusiasm
with which the great soul of the Mother of God poured it forth
before Him!

The visitation of Mary is a charming mystery, charming as an
idyl; it consists of a friendly, cousinly visit to the beautiful village
of St. John's Mount, and is accompanied and animated by the
sweet virtues of family affection, humility, modesty and heavenly
piety. And it is withal a mystery rendered so great, so deep and
significant, by the revelation not only of the fact of the Incarna-

tion, but also of its object, which is no other than the pardon and sanctification of the world and of sinners. The sanctification of John is the fruit and the first known effect of the Incarnation in this direction. How appropriate that the first act of the advent of our Saviour, Who came to seek that which was lost and to call sinners, is the pardon of a sinner! And this pardoned sinner is of all others John, the purport of whose preaching was: "Behold the Lamb of God. . . . Who taketh away the sin of the world" (John 1:29). John is now a child of God, baptized, so to speak, with the Holy Ghost by Jesus Himself, and already the Forerunner of the Lord; for from him the revelation of Jesus passes over to his mother. He has, as it were, announced the Redeemer to her.

But of all this Mary is the instrument and medium; she appears here for the first time in her important position as mediatrix of grace. At her word John is justified. At the very moment that Mary's greeting was heard, his sanctification came to pass. Her word was the decree, as it were, of his deliverance from original sin. The pardon and grace came from our Lord; but the communication of it was Mary's work, and that a public one. The sanctification could have taken place in silence, without any outward sign, as was the case with Jeremias; but it was not to be so here. Doubtless our Saviour wished to reveal Mary as the mediatrix of grace, and to establish a law which was henceforth to remain in force. Even the great St. John is, like countless others, the child of the Mother of God in grace. We also see in this mystery the Source and Author of the veneration of Mary. That Source is no other than the Holy Ghost. Moreover we see the foundation, the practice and the blessings of this devotion to the Mother of God, wonderfully and beautifully revealed.

## The Birth and Youth of St. John

LUKE 1:57. Now Elizabeth's full time of being delivered was come, and she brought forth a son.—58. And her neighbors and kinsfolk heard that the Lord had shown his great mercy towards her, and they congratulated with her.—59. And it came to pass that on the eighth day they came to circumcise the child, and they called him by his father's name Zachary.—60. And his mother answering, said: "Not so, but he shall be called John."—61. And they said to her: "There is none of thy kindred that is called by this name."—62. And they made signs to his father, how he would have him called.—63. And demanding a writing-table, he wrote, saying: "John is his name." And they all wondered.—64. And immediately his mouth was opened, and his tongue loosed, and he spoke, blessing God.—65.

And fear came upon all their neighbors, and all these things were noised abroad over all the hill-country of Judaea;—66. And all they that had heard them laid them up in their heart, saying: "What an one, think ye, shall this child be?" For the hand of the Lord was with him.—67. And Zachary his father was filled with the Holy Ghost; and he prophesied, saying:—68. "Blessed be the Lord God of Israel, because he hath visited and wrought the redemption of his people;—69. And hath raised up an horn of salvation to us, in the house of David his servant.— 70. As he spoke by the mouth of his holy prophets, who are from the beginning; —71. Salvation from our enemies, and from the hand of all that hate us;—72. To perform mercy to our fathers; and to remember his holy testament.—73. The oath which he swore to Abraham our father, that he would grant to us:—74. That being delivered from the hand of our enemies, we may serve him without fear,— 75. In holiness and justice before him, all our days.—76. And thou, child, shalt be called the prophet of the Highest; for thou shalt go before the face of the Lord to prepare his ways;—77. To give knowledge of salvation to his people; unto the re- mission of their sins.—78. Through the bowels of the mercy of our God, in which the Orient from on high hath visited us;—79. To enlighten them that sit in dark- ness and in the shadow of death; to direct our feet into the way of peace."— 80. And the child grew, and was strengthened in spirit; and was in the deserts until the day of his manifestation to Israel.

## 1. THE BIRTH OF ST. JOHN

There are two things to be considered about the birth of St. John.

The first thing is the marvelous nature of this birth in itself. It was above all rich in grace; a privilege, as we know, such as was never accorded to any other saint. For this reason the Church celebrates in his case the day of birth into this world, and applies to him in the liturgy the words of Isaias: "The Lord hath called me from the womb, from the bowels of my mother he hath been mindful of my name" (Isa. 49:1).

Secondly, the birth of St. John was marvelous on account of several extraordinary outward events. Some of the holy Fathers reckon among these the circumstance that the Holy Ghost re- vealed to Elizabeth the name of the child (Luke 1:60), as it had been communicated to Zachary by the angel; though we may rather presume, as is more probable, that Zachary had imparted the name to Elizabeth in writing. The relatives who had assembled to perform the circumcision or to assist as witnesses at the cere- mony, wished to name the child Zachary; but Elizabeth insisted that it should be called John, and Zachary confirmed this in writ- ing, declaring that the child already had a name (Luke 1:59–63).

Further, it was a marvelous thing that Zachary suddenly re- covered his speech and, filled with the Holy Ghost, broke forth into a song of praise. This song also is a hymn of praise of the Redemption. It contains two parts. In the first part (Luke 1:68–

75) God is praised on account of the accomplishment of the Redemption, which had begun to take place. The nature of this Redemption is especially emphasized, and designated as a gracious visitation of God (Luke 1:68), as the advent of the great salvation and of the strong deliverer in the house of David (Luke 1:69; Ps. 131:17). Then are mentioned the causes which brought about the Redemption, which causes are none other than God's mercy (Luke 1:72, 78) and fidelity to His promises (Luke 1:70, 72, 73). Lastly, the results of the Redemption are extolled, which consist first in deliverance from enemies (Luke 1:71, 74),—not, however, from exterior enemies, but from the enemies of salvation;—and secondly in the bringing about of justice and true holiness before God (Luke 1:75). The second part is occupied with St. John's relations to the work of Redemption and to the Redeemer Himself. John is to precede the Redeemer as the herald and prophet of the Most High and the preparer of the way of the Lord (Luke 1:76), by proclaiming His advent and imparting light and knowledge of salvation to sinners, thus preparing them for the remission of their sins and directing them into the way of peace (Luke 1:76, 77). In these words is expressed John's whole glorious vocation as Forerunner of the Lord and preacher of penance. The conclusion of the hymn is a thrilling cry to the approaching Messias for help, that He may lead poor humanity, by His consoling presence, from its condition of exhaustion and despair into the way of peace and salvation (Luke 1:78, 79).

The "Benedictus" is a sublime canticle, full of the priestly spirit. It celebrates the introduction and dawn of the Messianic period; not however according to Jewish expectations, but in the spirit of truth and humility. The kingdom of the Messias is a kingdom of peace, through reconciliation to God and remission of sins; a kingdom therefore of true holiness and justice, a kingdom of light and knowledge of salvation for all who sit in the shadow of death, and for the whole world. The Messias is the dawn of light, the Sun of Justice (Isa. 9:2; Mal. 4:2), or the Orient (Zach. 3:8; 6:12), heralding a time of peace and of the light of faith, such as Christianity did actually bring in its train. For this reason the Church repeats these two songs of praise of the Redemption, the "Benedictus" and the "Magnificat," every day in her Hours. The "Benedictus" is moreover her song at the burial of her dead, and the prayer which she bids her children say when traveling. Christ is her light and the horn of salvation whose graces and consolations accompany her whole life, up to the gates of eternity. Such were the occurrences which made the birth of John a marvelous event.

## 2. THE YOUTH OF ST. JOHN

Holy Scripture records two circumstances touching the youth of St. John (Luke 1:80).

The first circumstance is his growth, and his being strengthened in spirit. It was only to be expected that the great graces which were bestowed upon St. John even before his birth would show themselves afterwards no less powerful to promote and accomplish their work. Mary perhaps remained until the birth of St. John (Luke 1:56). In that event the tokens of affection which she showed the wonderful child will certainly have brought him as many graces as the first word of greeting, and so St. John would be our Lord's Forerunner even in the arms of His Mother.

The second circumstance is that St. John remained in the desert from his youth upwards, until his public appearance; either because the Holy Ghost urged him into the desert at an early age, or that the danger at the time of Herod's murder of the Innocents made it necessary for him, as a child, to flee thither and conceal himself. A barren, rocky district is pointed out as this desert, about a league west of St. John's Mount, where the cave and spring of St. John are still shown on the steep slope of a mountain. In this hermitage he is supposed to have passed his boyhood and youth, in retirement, prayer, and that austere penance which is described to us on his appearance in public. The garment of camel's hair had certainly been his clothing ere this, and locusts and wild honey his food (Matt. 3:4). A slab of stone in the cave is said to have served during the hours of the night as the couch of this innocent penitent, this angel in the flesh.

## 3. SIGNIFICANCE OF THE BIRTH AND YOUTH OF ST. JOHN

The significance of this double mystery lies in the fact of its being a preparation for the coming of Christ, and this in a twofold manner.

The wonderful occurrences at St. John's birth attracted the attention of the people, and aroused an intense expectation of the coming of the Messias. His wonderful conception, then the giving of his name and the miraculous cure of Zachary's dumbness, all gave evidence of "the hand of the Lord" (Luke 1:66); that is, of a special intervention of God, such as had not taken place for a long period. And these signs pointed to other events in the future, namely to the advent of the Messias, as the words of the "Benedictus," that priestly song of praise, clearly show. The relatives who were present spread this rumor abroad, and everywhere in the highlands of Judaea the arrival of this wonderful child was spoken of (Luke 1:65, 66). Thus this circumstance was also a revelation, if only an obscure one, of the coming of Christ.

The sojourn in the desert, in prayer, penance and retirement, was for John himself the proximate preparation for his great vocation. That is God's way of preparing His great instruments for His ends. By retirement the divine instrument gains in purity, by penance it is strengthened and tempered, and by prayer it is united to God. Everything must be bought by prayer and penance, our own salvation and that of our neighbor. The world-reformers always come out of solitude. For this reason the Church applies to John the words of the prophet Isaias: "He hath made my mouth like a sharp sword; in the shadow of His hand He hath protected me, and hath made me as a chosen arrow; in His quiver He hath hidden me" (Isa. 49:2).

## ESPOUSALS OF ST. JOSEPH WITH MARY

MATT. 1:18. Now the generation of Christ was in this wise: When his mother Mary was espoused to Joseph, before they came together, she was found with child of the Holy Ghost.—19. Whereupon Joseph her husband, being a just man and not willing publicly to expose her, was minded to put her away privately.—20. But while he thought on these things, behold the angel of the Lord appeared to him in his sleep, saying: "Joseph, son of David, fear not to take unto thee Mary thy wife; for that which is conceived in her is of the Holy Ghost.—21. And she shall bring forth a Son, and thou shalt call his name Jesus; for he shall save his people from their sins."—22. Now all this was done that it might be fulfilled which the Lord spoke by the prophet, saying:—23. "Behold a virgin shall be with child and bring forth a son; and they shall call his name Emmanuel, which being interpreted is: God with us."—24. And Joseph, rising up from sleep, did as the angel of the Lord had commanded him, and took unto him his wife.—25. And he knew her not till she brought forth her first-born Son; and he called his name Jesus.

Mary had returned to Nazareth after her visit to Elizabeth, and now Joseph, her affianced husband, was to lead her home. But the espousals were to be the occasion of a severe trial.

### 1. HOW HARD AND PAINFUL THE TRIAL WAS

Mary had told St. Joseph nothing of the supernatural Conception of our Saviour, whilst all the time the natural results were becoming more evident (Matt. 1:18). This was a bitter trial for Mary as well as for St. Joseph. First of all, it was a cross which two persons on the most loving and intimate terms, through no fault of theirs, caused each other. An exterior cross can usually be laid partly on the shoulders of others; but this was not the case here. The cross of the one was the cross of the other. What is more painful to a virginal heart than the loss of honor and the good repute of virginity? In all probability Mary and Joseph had consented to a betrothal only on condition of perpetual virginity. And now Mary saw herself exposed to such a terrible doubt of her virginity, and St. Joseph felt himself wounded in his honor, shaken in his confidence, and deceived in his previous esteem for Mary. It was certainly a heavy cross for them both.

### 2. HOW MARY AND JOSEPH CONDUCT THEMSELVES UNDER THE TRIAL

Naturally Mary must have perceived or suspected the anxiety and grief of St. Joseph; but how does she behave in this sad hour? How admirable is her silence under these circumstances, where it was a question not only of her own peace and honor, but also of her bridegroom's, and even of the honor of God and her Son! It would have cost her only a little word of explanation. But she does not speak it. And why not? Probably on account of the indescribable delicacy of her humility and confidence in God. The mystery is God's affair, and she will not expose it. He had already revealed it to Elizabeth. So she trusts in Him, waits, prays and suffers. Any step towards solving the mystery seems to her like a want of trust in God. The Saints are always very reluctant to anticipate His action and proceed in their own cause.

And St. Joseph? First, he does not let himself be carried away by passion, anger or jealousy. He too prays and reflects what is best to be done, and chooses the expedient that does him in every respect the greatest honor. He might have delivered her up to justice (Deut. 22:23), or at least have brought her into ill-repute; but his kind heart could not endure this. Yet he was just as unwilling to be a party to apparent evil (Prov. 18:22). He therefore decided upon a private separation, which should be declared only before a few witnesses and without specification of the reason of separation; or he intended simply to leave her and go away. He is indeed "a just man," as Holy Scripture says (Matt. 1:19), not only because he will have nothing to do with sin, but also because he is full of forbearance and charity. That St. Joseph did not venture to inquire into the matter, bears quite as much witness to his dignity, delicacy, and respect for Mary. There are even some among the holy Fathers who think that St. Joseph may have had a suspicion of the mystery of the Incarnation, and have wished to part from the Blessed Virgin because he did not consider himself worthy to be her spouse. The most natural acceptation, and the one most in keeping with the words of the angel (Matt. 1:20), seems to be that St. Joseph, in his esteem for Mary, could never convince himself that there could be a fault on her side; and yet, on the other hand, he could not close his eyes to the evidence of his senses. In this divided state of mind, he decided upon the expedient most honorable and considerate for Mary.

### 3. HOW GOD PUTS AN END TO THE TRIAL, AND REWARDS MARY AND JOSEPH

God tries, but does not forsake His own, who suffer on His account and put their trust in Him. He hears their prayers, delivers them and glorifies them (Ps. 90:15), even though He should have to send angels for the purpose. In fact, God does send an angel, and the latter comforts and rewards St. Joseph in a prophetic dream. The angel addresses him, first, with great respect, and with the title of his dignity and rank of "Son of David," which is here of special significance, now that the great promises of David are to be fulfilled by the Saviour (Matt. 1:20; Luke 1:32, 69). Secondly, he reveals to him the mystery of the Incarnation and the supernatural Conception of our Saviour (Matt. 1:20), together with His name and task, viz. to redeem the people from their sins (Matt. 1:21); and thirdly, he removes every doubt from his mind, and encourages him to take to himself Mary, his wife (Matt. 1:20). St. Joseph, then, is to be the legal father of our Saviour, and to give Him His name; and Jesus and Mary are to be subject to him. How suddenly he is freed from all anxiety and overwhelmed with honors and dignities!

Mary too is rewarded with honors and distinctions by the message of the angel. How does she stand now in St. Joseph's eyes? As a perfect Saint, and as the Mother of the Messias. And how she rejoiced over St. Joseph, and how indebted she felt to him for his noble-heartedness! Thus the hard trial only served to strengthen their mutual esteem and the bond of love and trust between them.

This love was now sealed by the public and solemn act of leading Mary to her home (Matt. 1:24). St. Joseph thus took up his position as Mary's husband, the legal father of our Saviour, and the head of the Holy Family; he gained the advantage of daily and familiar intercourse with Jesus and Mary, and a special love and reverence from them both. Mary, on her side, received in him a support, a shield and protector, a witness to her virginity, and a consoler in her difficult vocation. The honor of both is preserved, our Saviour proven to be the Son of David. Both Mary and Joseph are henceforth the models and protectors of the virginal as well as of the married state. So, since God willed it thus, they celebrated their marriage with all the decorum, joy, and modesty usual on such occasions. Here, as nowhere else, it was verified that holy marriages are made in heaven.

We must therefore thank God for His wise and loving providence. The fruits of this marriage-bond are enjoyed by all Christendom. We must also congratulate our Lady and St. Joseph with all our hearts, that God gave them the great grace to stand the hard test so gloriously, and that He caused such magnificent fruits to proceed from it for them and for us. The resolution to follow the beautiful example of virtue which we see in Mary and Joseph, and especially to submit in a childlike manner to the dispensations of Providence, which orders all things so wisely and sweetly, is certainly appropriate here. This mystery is also a new revelation of the Incarnation (viz. to St. Joseph), and the last preparation for the visible entrance of the Saviour into this world. The tabernacle of David is now erected (Amos 9:11), and the Ruler of the House of David can appear.

## The Journey to Bethlehem

Luke 2:1. And it came to pass that in those days there went out a decree from Caesar Augustus, that the whole world should be enrolled.—2. This enrolling was first made by Cyrinus, the governor of Syria.—3. And all went to be enrolled, every one into his own city.—4. And Joseph also went up from Galilee out of the city of Nazareth into Judaea, to the city of David, which is called Bethlehem, because he was of the house and family of David,—5. To be enrolled with Mary his espoused wife, who was with child.

The day of Mary's delivery drew ever nearer. It was not, how-ever, to take place in Nazareth, but in Bethlehem.

### 1. OCCASION OF THE JOURNEY TO BETHLEHEM

The occasion of the journey was twofold.

The first, most immediate and exterior occasion came from the order of the Roman Emperor Augustus, enjoining a census and enrolment of the whole Empire, including therefore the conquered kingdoms, to which Judaea, the kingdom of Herod, also belonged (Luke 2:1). Cyrinus, the governor of Syria, made the enrolment in Herod's dominions (Luke 2:2), and, as was the immemorial custom of the nation and country (Num. 1:2; 26:2; II Kings 24:2), according to tribes, houses and families, so that the head of every family had to go to the place where his ancestors had originally been settled (Luke 2:3). For the family of David this place was Bethlehem. Joseph and Mary therefore betook them-selves thither. The reason why Mary accompanied St. Joseph may possibly have been the circumstance that she was the last scion of a branch of the family of David, or that St. Joseph had some thought of settling permanently in Bethlehem; but in any case there were also other and higher reasons.

The design of God in permitting this census to be taken just at the time of Christ's Birth provides another motive for the journey. It is plainly to be seen from the fact of this census being taken by Roman officials in Herod's own kingdom, that the scepter was taken from Juda, indeed that the government of Herod himself was as good as absorbed in the great Roman Em-pire, according to the prophecy of Daniel (Dan. 2:40; 7:23). The Saviour was thus to be officially recorded as the Son of David, and entered as a member of the last great world-kingdom, which He was to win for Himself and incorporate in His eternal dominion. Tertullian (Contr. Marc., 4, 19) and St. Justin (Apol., 1, 4) bear witness to the enrolment of Jesus in the registers of the kingdom. Further, the prophecy of Micheas, which designates Bethlehem as the birthplace of the Messias (Mich. 5:2), was thus to be ful-filled. Lastly, Christ was to come into the world in poverty and obscurity. In order to bring about these circumstances, there was no better or more natural opportunity than the concourse of people in Bethlehem in consequence of the census. Humble and full of the spirit of Jesus as Mary was, still she would scarcely have brought herself to await her delivery in a stable. All this was now provided for, and without any angel's message. The government order for the enrolment of the people, then, was only an instrument to satisfy the preference of Jesus for poverty, humility and obedience. It was probably for these higher reasons that God put it into Mary's heart to undertake the journey to Bethlehem with Joseph; and these certainly were the considerations which finally persuaded her to do so under such circumstances. Whilst perhaps not a few of the Jews gnashed their teeth over the new order of the foreign ruler, Mary and Joseph probably saw therein only the Divine Providence which was preparing the way for the Saviour. These two holy persons accepted the circumstances of time and place and thus cooperated in the designs of God, who in such hidden ways prepares for the momentous events of His Providence.

### 2. THE JOURNEY

So Mary and Joseph started on their journey (Luke 2:4, 5), in connection with which we find three subjects of meditation.

The first is the patience of the Holy Family. The journey was fairly long, four days and a half at the least, and brought many discomforts with it. Their way led either by Sichem, Bethel and Jerusalem, or along the banks of the Jordan by Jericho and Jerusalem to Bethlehem. It was in the month of December, during which it can be bitterly cold in the mountainous districts of the Promised Land, with west wind, rain and snow. At all events the journey was not a mere pleasant outing. But they bore everything with patience.

Secondly, their modesty and humility must be considered. Since every family had to register in the census rolls, their number included persons of wealth and prominence, who probably traveled with ostentation and a display of their importance. But Mary and Joseph traveled humbly, as became people of the working class. And yet who are they? The noblest and holiest of beings. What ancestress of our Saviour ever journeyed so unassumingly through the country? Think of the pomp with which the Ark of the Covenant was once carried through these districts! Here is the living Ark of the Lord.

The third thing to be noted is the spirit of recollection and prayer in which the Holy Family made this journey. Men become more recollected and more silent, the nearer God approaches

them. What could be compared to the recollection in which our
Saviour attracted all the thought and attention of His Mother and
St. Joseph to Himself! Of all the multitude making this journey
along the road to Jerusalem they were the only souls who knew of
the mystery; the only ones who, by their prayer and longing, could
represent the human race. So they probably spoke little and prayed
much; indeed, they were constantly lost in quiet prayer, in the
midst of the disturbance and tumult of the journey.

### 3. THE ARRIVAL IN BETHLEHEM

So Joseph and Mary came to Bethlehem (see Introd. p. 7).
Perhaps the setting sun was just lighting up the white rows of
houses on the hills, as Mary and Joseph with their ass approached
the little town, coming through the terraces of vineyards; and in
all probability they first directed their steps to the inn for travelers.
But the inn was already occupied, and the town full of strangers.
By many a house may the little family have passed, seeking shelter,
and at many a door may St. Joseph have given a humble knock;
they were overlooked in the crowd, or coldly repulsed. In the
meantime the evening was drawing in; the doors closed, and no
lodging was found. So at last they turned their steps away from
the little town, outside of which St. Joseph found a kind of
cave, a shelter for animals. They arrived at it, tired out, and
settled themselves to rest for the night, and to wait for the ever
memorable hour of our Lord's Birth. In the East, it is nothing
unusual to pass the night in caves and grottoes, and some people
live continually in them. The inner part of the dwelling is often
hewn out of the rocks; but in this case this sojourn has something
especially touching about it. They are the holiest, the best and the
highest of God's creatures, and they are so inhospitably lodged,
everything is so unprepared, so poor and desolate, whilst the little
town there offers hospitable reception and the comforts of home to
hundreds of less worthy persons. They are the heirs of the House
of David, and Bethlehem is the town of David; the Bethlehemites,
descendants of Hur and Mary (Ex. 17:10; 24:14; Par. 4:4), of
Booz and Jesse, do not take them in, but let them seek shelter
where the animals find theirs, outside the town. What a touching
contrast! They were God's nearest and dearest, and yet God
Himself seems to forsake them and not to think of them. He
provides for all others on this evening, but for them nothing is
prepared, not even the barest necessaries, and that after a long

journey and on a winter evening. There seems scarcely to be a Providence for them. Thus are the chosen friends of God tried, that by their faithfulness under trial they may grow in holiness and merit an increase of reward. We, too, can advance in the love of God by the same road.

And how did Mary and Joseph bear the trial? Certainly quite in the spirit of our Saviour. It was the first slight and humiliation that He met with in this world. The world does not want Him, does not know Him, because He does not come as it had expected Him to come. The Heart of our Saviour rejoices at this, and He imparts His thoughts and sentiments to His parents. Assuredly it was only with reluctance that they had asked hospitality, because they feared to be troublesome. They knew how to excuse every refusal; full of gentleness, patience and charity, they left the little town, and only God knew of their quiet sadness. This is the second shadow that the Cross and Mount Calvary cast over Jesus and Mary. It was the first meeting of the Messias with His people, with His own, His fellow-citizens of Bethlehem, and they received Him not (John 1:11). In the East, hospitality is otherwise as common as the flower of the field; only for God it does not seem to exist. He receives no hospitality, either at His Birth or at His Death.

So the holy night drew on, apparently insignificant as any other night, and wrapped Bethlehem and the world in its shades. The nations under the scepter of the Roman rule, and the pagan world, wearied with its earthly and sinful work, lay down to rest as usual, and had no suspicion how near their God was. Except for the dreary consciousness of sin, the weariness of earthly strivings, and the universal peace which had at last succeeded to the cruel wars, there was scarcely any preparation made by the human race for the visible coming of God. Only there in the poor cave Joseph and Mary watched by the dim light of a little fire. They are the praying heart of the world. So it was, and so it is. The world does not know God or think of Him. There must always be holy, chosen souls, who form the point of contact between heaven and earth. Their prayers, their supplications, their longings are the clock of the divine counsels (Faber). This was the case here with Joseph and Mary. We will unite ourselves to them. It is Christmas Eve. Let us sanctify ourselves (so the Church exhorts us in the holy Office), and let us prepare ourselves. In a few hours the Lord will be with us, and we shall see the glory of God. The misdeeds

of the earth will be blotted out, and the Redeemer of the world
will rule over us. Fiat! Fiat!

## THE BIRTH OF OUR LORD

LUKE 2:6. And it came to pass that when they were there, her days were accomplished, that she should be delivered.—7. And she brought forth her first-
born Son, and wrapped him up in swaddling-clothes, and laid him in a manger;
because there was no room for them in the inn.

"In the 5199th year after the Creation of the world, when in the
beginning God created heaven and earth, 2957 years after the
Flood, 2015 after the birth of Abraham, 1510 after Moses and the
Exodus of the Israelite nation from Egypt, 1032 after the anointing of David as king, in the 65th week of years according to the
prophecy of Daniel, in the 194th Olympiad, 752 years after the
building of the city of Rome, in the 42nd year of the reign of
Octavianus Augustus, while the whole world was at peace, Jesus
Christ, Eternal God and Son of the Eternal Father, wishing to
sanctify the world by His gracious advent, having been conceived
of the Holy Ghost, was born of the Virgin Mary in Bethlehem,
nine months after His Conception, being made Man." In these
words the Roman Martyrology announces the Birth of our
Saviour, in a manner as solemn as it is touching. Later ages recognized this date as the most important in all human history.

### 1. SIGNIFICANCE AND IMPORTANCE OF THE BIRTH
### OF OUR LORD

Birth is the visible entrance of a man into the world and human
society. In the case of a man who exercises great influence, his first
appearance is significant and important. How much more must
this be the case with our Saviour, with Whom nothing is without
conscious volition, but every detail is well thought out, carefully
prepared, and of infinite significance! It is therefore of the greatest
importance to consider what were the circumstances of His first
appearance and entrance into the world. And this all the more,
when we reflect how believing Israel pictured to itself the coming
of the Messias, and what hopes and expectations it entertained
with regard to this appearance. With what awful might, with
what terrifying majesty had God appeared in Egypt and on
Mount Sinai! Now it was a question of deliverance from a much
worse fate, of the salvation of all races, of the extension of the

kingdom of God to all nations, of legislation for the whole world.
Compare what the prophets had foretold of the coming and ap-
pearance of the Messias (Hab. 3; Mal. 3; 4; Joel 2:28 seq.; Agg. 2:7;
Dan. 7:13 seq.; Isa. 63). And how does He now appear in reality?

## 2. CIRCUMSTANCES OF CHRIST'S BIRTH

There are two features to be considered about the circumstances of Christ's appearance; one is exterior, the other interior.

With regard to the exterior circumstances: Christ appears
at the place and the time that had been prophesied, at the
expiration of Daniel's weeks of years (Dan. 9:24 seq.), and in
Bethlehem, the city of David (Mich. 5:2). Secondly, He appears in a most lovable form, no longer as a flame of fire, as the
Angel of the Covenant, as the splendor of brightness, but as man,
as a child (Luke 2:12). What is more lovable than a child? Here
there is nothing of the sternness of the lawgiver, nothing tells us He
is either the Victim or the Judge of our sins. The sweet Child Himself does not seem to think of our sins, nor of the fate they have
prepared for Him; and so nothing troubles our happy familiarity.

Thirdly, the Saviour appears in great poverty and humility.
This poverty is indeed great. All is wanting, conveniences, joys
and friends, necessaries, everything in this strange and unhome-
like stable. It is a self-chosen poverty, but to all appearance only
brought about by chance. And the obscurity! Outside the town,
at midnight, and unknown to all, Christ comes into the world.
And yet it was for this moment that the Israelite nation, with its
wonderful history, its destinies, guidance, miracles and prophets,
existed; for this moment that the whole human race, with its
long ages of preparation, had lived. How important for Israel
and the whole human race, how important even for the honor of
God, this moment and the knowledge of it was! But it is revealed
to no one, to no king, no priest, no saint; and yet there were saints
in Israel, and how much comfort such a revelation would have
afforded them! No one knows of it. When a royal child is born,
what preparations are made long in advance, and how quickly
the news is spread abroad through the whole kingdom! Here all
is quiet. Only Mary and Joseph form His human court, and the
animals, the cold and darkness of the night, and the rough straw
of the manger, the representatives of the irrational creation, are
His surroundings. It was just as the angel had proclaimed: "This
shall be a sign unto you: you shall find the Infant wrapped in

swaddling-clothes and laid in a manger" (Luke 2:12). We are now familiar with the story of Bethlehem, and this very familiarity dulls our wonder and amazement. Who of us would have planned such a birthplace for the Saviour of the world? But God's ways are not our ways.

Fourthly, in spite of all this, Christ does not appear without glory. His Birth is a virginal one, and that fact is itself a great miracle, long foretold (Isa. 7:14) and long expected; He Himself, content with His swaddling-clothes, decks His angels with the "brightness of God," and sends them to the shepherds to proclaim His arrival. He comes into the world at a time of universal peace, which He Himself, the Prince of Peace, has made (Isa. 9:3 seq.; 11:6 seq.; Ps. 71:3 seq.). True, the world is all astir, but the movement is one of peace and directed by Him. The ancient families awake to the remembrance of their former glory and journey along the highways of the country to get themselves enrolled, and Roman couriers carry the rolls to the Roman metropolis, that the name of the new-born Lord of the world may be deposited on the Capitol, and that He, on His side, may inscribe the whole human race on the muster-rolls of Heaven. The Saviour comes upon earth at the time of an event which influences the whole world, and He is the pivot of this movement and the central figure, in spite of His obscurity. Thus a cloud of darkness and also of wonderful brightness hovers over the Birth of our Saviour.

As to the interior circumstances of His Birth, these lead us into the inner life of the new-born Saviour. Here there is no question of weakness or unconsciousness, but only power and life, magnificent, all-embracing, divine life. This sleep is not without consciousness, for "He That keepeth Israel" does not slumber (Ps. 120:3 seq.); this little hand is the mighty Right Hand of God, which bears up the spheres, and holds the reins of government of the world and of heaven. This breath is mightier than the surging of the sea, it extinguishes the light of life of kings; this closed mouth is judging souls at this moment. His glance assigns to stars and nations their paths; and from this little heart rises the incense-offering of infinite honor and glorification of God. Our Saviour begins His visible life with prayer to His Heavenly Father; it is His morning prayer, His adoration of the eternal majesty, His thanksgiving for the beginning of His earthly day, His offering of His whole being and His day's work as God-Man, the renewal of His vow of sacrifice at the first moment of His Conception: "Behold,

I come" (Ps. 39:8). He takes possession of this earth, in the name
of His Heavenly Father, and vows to Him to build a house and
establish a kingdom in which His glory shall have no end. From
God our Saviour turns His glance towards His Mother. He sees
her dear features for the first time with bodily eyes, and smiles at
her, and surely lifts up His little arms to her, with a love of which
the greatness is incalculable. He looks too at St. Joseph, His dear
foster-father, and then He turns all His thoughts and the cares
of His Heart towards us. Scripture says that Mary wrapped her
"first born" Son in swaddling-clothes, and laid Him in the manger
(Luke 2:7). In truth, He had also later-born brethren, not according to the flesh, but according to the spirit; and we are these
brethren. The thoughts of this first precious moment embraced us
all. How dear to us this circumstance makes the Birth of our
Saviour!

### 3. REASONS FOR THIS MANNER OF APPEARANCE

Why, then, did the Saviour wish to appear and enter the world
in this manner? There are several reasons for it.

First, our Lord wished to appear thus, in order to prove Himself
to be true man. His sleeping, weeping, being nourished at the
breast, and all else that appertains to childhood: are they not so
many proofs of His true and entire human nature, and dear
pledges of the truth that He is very man? Charmed and touched
at this sight, the prophet exclaims: "A Child is born to us, and a
Son is given to us" (Isa. 9:6). And if in spite of such proofs the
reality of His human nature has been denied, what would have
happened had He apepared in the prime of age and strength?
What thanks we owe to our Divine Saviour for this touching
proof of His humanity!

Secondly, it was necessary for the Saviour to appear thus, in
order to prove Himself to be the Redeemer. We needed above all
things the lesson that truth and happiness do not consist in outward pomp and riches, nor in fame and public recognition, or
else our Saviour would not have disdained all these. We needed,
further, the lesson that we must do penance and deny ourselves, in
order to avoid sin and to satisfy for it. His stern surroundings,
the cold, the darkness and the rough, prickly couch of straw,
preach this truth to us. We needed an example of self-denial and
penance, and here we have it. Is it not a thought to move us, that
our Saviour, with so many claims to the honors and goods of this

world, is so poor and forsaken, and that He wills to endure in His tender Body the penance of discomfort, weariness and cold? He thereby places His childhood on a par with His later life. His sojourn in the manger is only a foreshadowing of His thirty-three years, His spirit, His law, and the holiness of His Church. Now He sheds tears; later on, His Blood. The same stern companions (poverty, suffering, and humiliation) stand by His Cross and by His crib. Here as everywhere He is the Redeemer from sin, and by the same means. These three companions accompany Him throughout His earthly life.

Thirdly, our Saviour appears thus in order to prove Himself God. With men, poverty and obscurity are not signs of power and greatness. In our Saviour's case His poverty is by His own will because He has no need of creatures; He possesses absolute freedom, independence and power, and attains the greatest results with the most trifling means, which are really no means at all. In very deed, what has not this manger effected by its poverty, desolation, obscurity and mortification? Like the Cross, it has drawn all to itself; it has transformed the world, Christianized it, brought it happiness and holiness, and civilized it. It has founded the religious orders, in poverty, chastity and obedience; it has brought into the world the spirit of the interior life, of recollection, love of humanity and of obscurity; it has established the equilibrium between high and low, rich and poor; it has comforted innumerable poor and forsaken souls; it has drawn innumerable rich men, princes and kings to embrace voluntary poverty and self-effacement; it has raised childhood out of the state of contempt, and made it sublime and worthy of veneration. It has even given birth to our Christian altar. The Blessed Sacrament has its type in the manger.

Thus the first visible appearance of the Saviour here upon earth was quite in keeping with His Person and the ends for which He came; unfathomably deep, wonderful and significant, full of grace and truth. So He was to come, and not otherwise; as the prophet had beheld Him: "The people that walked in darkness have seen a great light . . . they shall rejoice before Thee, as they that rejoice in the harvest, as conquerors rejoice after taking a prey . . . for a Child is born to us, and a Son is given to us, and the government is upon His shoulders; and His name shall be called Wonderful, Counselor, God, the Mighty, the Father of the world to come, the Prince of peace" (Isa. 9:2–6; Mich. 5:3). Yes, infinite peace, infinite joy and infinite light stream forth from the manger over the earth; infinite honor and glory rise up thence to Heaven, to the throne of the Triune God. Incomprehensible and unbounded was the complacency of the Most Holy Trinity in the new-born Saviour. The three Divine Persons bent joyfully and graciously over the manger; the Father seemed to Himself to be more a father, and in another manner, by the temporal Birth of the Son, and on this Son's account He blessed the earth. The Son experienced a sweet joy in being now, as it were, by His holy Humanity, a part of His visible creation, and never yet had that creation been so beautiful. The Holy Ghost, the exultant love of the Father and the Son, ever old and ever new, gave full vent to His uncreated joy around the manger and Bethlehem, in the apparition and jubilant songs of the angels. The angel world assembled in shining hosts and sang in the midnight sky, in surging, glorious melodies, the song of praise: "Glory to God in the highest, and on earth peace to men of good will!" (Luke 2:14.) This song is the song of praise of the Birth of our Lord, the exultant exposition of its glory; it is at once praise of God, adoration of the new-born Word, and loving congratulation of man, because his nature has been so gloriously honored above that of the angels, and because for him has dawned the day of redemption and eternal salvation. This jubilant song, "Glory to God in the highest, and on earth peace to men of good will," is the most fitting expression of our thoughts and sentiments at the gracious Birth of our Lord.

## THE SHEPHERDS

Luke 2:8. And there were in the same country shepherds watching, and keeping the night-watches over their flock.—9. And behold, an angel of the Lord stood by them, and the brightness of God shone round about them, and they feared with a great fear.—10. And the angel said to them: "Fear not, for behold I bring you good tidings of great joy, that shall be to all the people;—11. For this day is born to you a Saviour, who is Christ the Lord, in the city of David.—12. And this shall be a sign unto you: You shall find the infant wrapped in swaddling-clothes, and laid in a manger."—13. And suddenly there was with the angel a multitude of the heavenly army, praising God and saying:—14. "Glory to God in the highest, and on earth peace to men of good will."—15. And it came to pass, after the angels departed from them into heaven, the shepherds said one to another: "Let us go over to Bethlehem, and let us see this word that is come to pass, which the Lord hath shown to us."—16. And they came with haste; and they found Mary and Joseph, and the infant lying in the manger.—17. And seeing, they understood of the word that had been spoken to them concerning this child.—18.

And all that heard wondered, and at those things that were told them by the shepherds.—19. But Mary kept all these words, pondering them in her heart.—20. And the shepherds returned, glorifying and praising God for all the things they had heard and seen, as it was told unto them.

The signification of this mystery, as of so many of those which follow, is the revelation of the Birth of the Saviour. He had to be made known to us, because He had come for our salvation. But this salvation is gained only by faith in Him, and the object of faith comes through revelation. Who are then the happy men to whom the first revelation is accorded?

### 1. TO WHOM THE BIRTH OF OUR LORD WAS FIRST REVEALED

In the first place, it was to Israelites that the first revelation was accorded, because it was to them that the promise of the Messias had been given. The Saviour comes for them in the first instance.

But to whom among the Israelites was this revelation accorded? Or rather, to whom was it not accorded? Not to the rich and powerful, not to learned men, priests and scribes, not to the relatives of the Messias, and not even to saints, at least not to saints learned in theology and recognized as such.

To whom among the Israelites, then, was the revelation sent? To plain, uneducated, simple and unknown shepherds, who were keeping the night-watch over their flocks near Bethlehem (Luke 2:8). The place of the apparition is a pretty, undulating valley, about half a league east of Bethlehem, covered with fields, pastures, and woods of fig and olive. In the Promised Land the winter rains deck the fields with fresh green, and when the weather is mild, the flocks pass the night in the open air. Here lay the fields and pastures where Ruth once gleaned the ears of corn and David tended his flocks. The Flock Tower (Gen. 35:21), near which the Messias was to appear (Mich. 4:8), lay quite near. There the shepherds watched by their flocks.

### 2. IN WHAT MANNER THE REVELATION TOOK PLACE

The revelation was made through angels. Angels are the messengers of God and of our Saviour. Apparitions of angels were not unknown to the Israelites, as sacred history testifies, and the shepherds were simple men, more susceptible to visible and tangible things than to interior inspirations and spiritual intimations. The Lord Whose arrival they were to proclaim came in a visible form; therefore the angels also appeared visibly.

The manner in which the angels made the revelation to the shepherds has its own features of special grace and joy and grandeur. At first a single angel appeared, glorious in the radiant brightness of God, so that the poor shepherds found themselves in an instant flooded with the heavenly, divine light, and began to be afraid (Luke 2:9). Never had angel appeared in such glory, in "the brightness of God." And he appeared thus, because he announced the arrival of God Himself, because he wished to bring out by contrast with his splendor the poverty and helplessness of the Lord, and to awaken from the very outset belief in the message, that they should find Him as an "infant wrapped in swaddling-clothes, and laid in a manger." This Child, Whose messenger the angel is and in Whose light he clothes himself, is no other than the Lord, the Messias, Jehovah Himself (Luke 2:9, 11). Further, the angel delivers his message in a most friendly and gracious manner. He bids them not to fear (Luke 2:11), for his tidings are joyful ones, not only for them, but for all the people. And then he announces to them the Birth of the "Saviour" of all mankind, the "Christ" (Messias) of God's people; yes, the Birth of "the Lord" (Luke 2:11), as it had been promised. Lastly, he gives them the sign by which they were to know the Messias, viz. "a child in swaddling-clothes . . . in the manger," and thereby invites them to go and seek Him. And they understand the import of the heavenly message.

But this was not yet enough. For the same end—to proclaim the greatness of the new-born Child, and to confirm the words of the first angel—there now appeared a great number of angels, intoning around the shepherds that magnificent song of praise: "Glory to God in the highest, and on earth peace to men of good will," that is, to men who are the object of God's benevolence (Luke 2:13, 14). In this song of praise they extol the results of the Incarnation and Nativity of the Redeemer, viz. the honor which God receives thereby and the happiness of men, which consists chiefly in peace, since this includes in itself the fulness of all good things (Mich. 5:5). The end of longing and supplication was now come. The blessed angels praised God for it, and rejoiced at our happiness; they seemed not to think of themselves. God's honor and our weal were their joy. How beautiful, how powerful and glorious, how entrancing this song, this music, this outburst of heavenly exultation must have been, rolling forth over the hills of Judaea and to the ends of creation! Never had earth heard such melodies. Must not the hearts of the shepherds have melted and throbbed with joy, and their eyes have overflowed at the beauty and majesty of the heavenly hosts?

But something far more beautiful and charming still awaited them, as they went, following the angel's directions, and found everything as it had been told them. Surely they were received by Joseph and Mary with great friendliness, respect and joy, and admitted to behold, adore, and perhaps caress the little Child. Happy shepherds! They saw not merely the holy angels and a ray of the glory of the Lord, but Mary and Joseph and the Lord Himself. They are the happy inheritors of all the promises. What David and Abraham longed to see, that they have, in all its beautiful reality and truth. Who can estimate their happiness?

### 3. WHY THE REVELATION WAS MADE IN THIS MANNER

The primary reason why the first revelation of our Saviour's Nativity was made to the shepherds, and in this manner, is the Will of God. He chooses His instruments according to His wise and holy purposes. As later He chooses the poor Apostles, so now He chooses the shepherds. The advent of the Lord was first to be made known through them. And so it happened. The shepherds, after their return from the manger in the cave, related everywhere what they had seen, and there was much astonishment among the people (Luke 2:17, 18, 19). And with this the shepherds disappear from the Gospel narrative. Before and after the apparition of the angels, nothing is known of them. One ray of the glory of the new-born Saviour fell upon them, and that sufficed to make them famous and memorable for ever, blessed and dear to all Christians. We cannot keep Christmas without them.

The second reason was that this manner of revelation was suited to Christ. The Saviour was poor, and wished to be poor, and therefore He chose for His friends poor men, who could not relieve His wants. He is the Redeemer of all, of the poor and lowly as well as of the rich, indeed of the poor especially. On this account the joyful tidings are first brought to them, as was His own custom later (Luke 4:18, 7:22). Our Saviour Himself is the God of peace, and therefore He will not have violent soldiers and proud scholars around His manger, but such as have grown up in gentle and peaceful occupations, and are themselves gentle, peaceable and humble. He is the God of the patriarchs and shepherds, and is Himself the supreme Shepherd of our souls and the Sacrificial Lamb for our sins. For this reason around His crib we see shepherds, and (as some think) the shepherds of the Temple flocks, which were fed in these districts. Lastly, the Saviour is the teacher of self-denial, and therefore He chooses as His first courtiers simple, patient men, inured to hardship and accustomed to labor, privation and solitude. His first apostles were shepherds; His later ones were fishermen. Both were prompt in responding to God's invitation.

Finally, one reason may also have been the intention of correcting our natural views and principles, according to which we should perhaps have summoned at first relatives or men in power, the rich and the learned. Our Saviour follows other principles. He calls first those whom God wills, and these are the humble, the poor and despised. They are the first members of Christ's kingdom, as the apostle reminds us later: 'See your vocation, brethren, that there are not many wise according to the flesh, not many mighty, not many noble; but the foolish things of the world hath God chosen" (I Cor. 1:26, 27), "lest the Cross of Christ should be made void" (I Cor. 1:17).

This mystery is a charming and beautiful revelation of the spirit of Jesus. He keeps open court. He came for all, He loves all, the poor, the simple and the humble more than any. The shepherds were especially distinguished by their simplicity. That was, as it appears, their holiness, and the preparation for the great honor and happiness of being the first to find and see the Saviour. Simplicity seeks God alone, not itself; it goes to God in the simplest and most artless manner, through what lies nearest and foremost, through the fulfilment of life's duties, through childlike resignation to what God permits and ordains. Simplicity believes all things, accepts all things, and follows without thinking of itself, like the shepherds here. They do not grow proud when the angels address them; they accept the invitation, return just as contentedly to their flocks, and then are heard of no more. Simplicity is a precious disposition of heart, a charming childhood of the soul, full of peace and fresh joyousness. Perhaps there were at this time no such simple saints in Israel as the shepherds, and therefore they were the most fitting hearers of the angelic concert and the most suitable adorers of the humility and simplicity of the Divine Child.

## THE CIRCUMCISION OF OUR LORD

LUKE 2:21. And after eight days were accomplished that the Child should be circumcised, his name was called Jesus, which was called by the angel, before he was conceived in the womb.

Eight days after the Nativity followed the Circumcision.

### 1. SIGNIFICANCE OF THE CIRCUMCISION

The significance of the Circumcision lay first and principally in the fact that it was the sign of the Covenant, the sign of incorporation into the Jewish religion (Gen. 17:9–14) and of separation from other nations. Consequently circumcision signified also the acceptance of the law, the obligation to keep it (Gal. 5:3), and, in case of transgression, the incurring of the curse (Rom. 2:25); as well as the participation in its blessings and promises, especially in the promise of a numerous posterity and of the Messias. Lastly, circumcision was a sign of sinfulness, and of the necessity of mortification, or circumcision of heart (Deut. 10:16; 30:6). The child received its name, too, at its circumcision (Gen. 17:5; 21:3, 4; Luke 1:59). Then it really began its social existence and had a complete life in the civic and religious order. Circumcision, then, held almost the same place as our baptism, which is not merely the deliverance from original sin, but also the entrance into the Church and incorporation with her, together with the obligation of adhering to her faith and moral law. For this reason St. Paul calls it the type of baptism (Col. 2:11; Phil. 3:3).

As regards the outward performance of the ceremony, the circumcision had to take place on the eighth day after birth (Lev. 12:3); but it might be performed at home or at any other place, and by any person. It was usually the head of the family who performed the circumcision and gave the name. To make the ceremony more solemn, relatives and neighbors were invited, ten of whom were to act as witnesses, and one, who held the child, as a kind of godfather.

### 2. REASONS WHY OUR SAVIOUR SUBJECTED HIMSELF TO THE LAW

Christ was not, as a matter of fact, subject to the law of circumcision. As God-Man He was not bound by human or positive law, any more than a prince is bound by the laws which he makes for his subjects as such, e.g. taxation laws. The God-Man was the Lawgiver and Head of the Old Covenant, and as such did not fall under the obligation of His own laws. Indeed, He often vindicated this freedom later on (Matt. 12:8; 17:25). He subjected Himself to this law, only because He wished to do so, and for the following reasons.

First, our Saviour wished by the Circumcision to give another proof of the reality of His human nature. He assumes a human nature, a country, a nationality, and now also a definite form of religion and a name, He, the Author of all men and nations, the Nameless and Ineffable! He also wishes to prove Himself in the most complete sense a descendant of Abraham, who accepted circumcision as a sign of the Covenant and of faith (Gal. 3:7). Otherwise He would in no case have been accepted by the Jews as a true son of Abraham and as the Messias. Our Lord leaves them no excuse for not accepting Him.

Secondly, our Lord permitted Himself to be circumcised in order to sanction the old law, because it was a divine law and the way to Christ. Indeed, He accepted circumcision in order to fulfil the law in the highest sense of the word, i.e., by perfect observance, by fulfilment of the prophecies, and by endurance of the punishment due to the transgressions of men, His brethren. On this account He sheds His Blood today for the first time, and offers Himself as a victim; and these first drops of blood are only a pledge that He will later offer all His Blood and His very life as a sacrifice. This is the real meaning of the Circumcision for our Saviour. This Blood is like a threatening, lurid glow in the dawn of His Childhood (Matt. 16:3; Gal. 3:10, 13).

Thirdly, our Saviour wished by His Circumcision to encourage us to employ all the means which God prescribes and gives us, in order to avoid sin, to practice obedience, penance and mortification, the true circumcision of heart (Matt. 3:15), and to avoid every scandal (Matt. 17:26). Thus a premium is put on obedience, and a rebuke is administered to our spirit of independence and self-sufficiency.

Fourthly and lastly, our Saviour wished by the Circumcision to win His Name of Jesus and the glory attaching to it. This glory consists, in the first place, in its origin. God Himself was the Author of this Name. He communicated it to Mary (Luke 1:31; Isa. 7:14) and to Joseph (Matt. 1:21), who, as legal father, gave it to the Saviour. Further, the glory of this Name consists in its signification. It signifies "God is salvation, the Saviour," and thus expresses fully and forcibly the task of the God-Man. He had been proclaimed by the prophets as a Saviour (Isa. 12:2; 62:1; Mich. 7:7; Zach. 9:9; Hab. 3:18). Jesus, then, is the personal and full name of the God-Man. Finally, the glory of the Name of Jesus consists in its effects and blessings for us and for our Saviour. It is a real sacramental for us. All that our Saviour has become to us, His Name is also: viz. a pledge of the forgiveness of our sins, and of the granting of our prayers and petitions (John 16:23); a pledge of comfort in temptations, in life and in death; indeed a pledge of all blessings (Acts 4:12). And for our Saviour His Name is the instrument of glory and splendor, because all honor comes to Him through it: invocation, trust, reverence, adoration, love, and the glory of the miracles that are wrought in this Name. It is, as it were, the glorious recompense for the labor of Redemption, so that now at this Name every knee should bow, in heaven, on earth, and under the earth (Phil. 2:10). It is indeed a great and glorious Name. The God-Man had many names (Isa. 7:14; 9:6; Zach. 6:12; Dan. 7:13), but none was dearer or more pleasing to Him than this, chiefly because it constantly reminded Him of us. For this reason it resounds everywhere; it is spoken at His crib, and it stands above His Cross.

### 3. CONCLUSIONS

From what has been said it follows, first, that we must love the Divine Saviour, Who thus vouchsafes to be our like and equal in everything, even to belong to a religion, and Who now really assumes the form of the servant, the sinner, and the victim of atonement, and takes a name by which He is to be all in all to us.

Further, it follows from this mystery that we must submit readily and generously to everything that our religion and vocation exact in the shape of duties and sacrifices (Col. 2:11, 12). Our Saviour undertook far harder duties out of love for us, by the Circumcision and the Name that He assumed. He was to die in atonement for our sins. And He has fulfilled everything. He could never see or hear this Name of His without feeling urged to do and suffer all for us. Should it not be thus with us also, out of love for Him?

The last conclusion is that we should honor, glorify and make use of the Name of Jesus. We can honor it by pronouncing it devoutly, with reverence and heartfelt love, such as the angel

felt when he spoke this Name for the first time; like Mary and
Joseph, who so often had it upon their lips; like all good Christians and faithful adherents of Jesus; like all the apostles and
martyrs, who confessed it and uttered it with their last breath.
And we can make use of it by sealing all our undertakings with
it, doing everything in it, invoking it in all dangers and temptations
(Cant. 8:6). Lastly, we glorify it by bearing it, as Christians,
with honor, by extending the knowledge and service of it as far as
we can, and trying to make all subject to it. Each of these ways of
using and of glorifying the Name of Jesus surrounds it with a new
halo of glory in heaven.

### THE PRESENTATION OF JESUS IN THE TEMPLE

LUKE 2:22. And after the days of her purification according to the law of
Moses were accomplished, they carried him to Jerusalem, to present him to the
Lord,—23. As it is written in the law of the Lord: "Every male opening the womb
shall be called holy to the Lord;"—24. And to offer a sacrifice according as it is
written in the law of the Lord, a pair of turtle-doves, or two young pigeons.—25.
And behold there was a man in Jerusalem named Simeon, and this man was just
and devout, waiting for the consolation of Israel, and the Holy Ghost was in him.
—26. And he had received an answer from the Holy Ghost, that he should not
see death before he had seen the Christ of the Lord.—27. And he came by the
Spirit into the Temple. And when his parents brought in the Child Jesus, to do
for him according to the custom of the law;—28. He also took him into his arms,
and blessed God, and said:—29. "Now thou dost dismiss thy servant, O Lord, according to thy word, in peace;—30. Because my eyes have seen thy salvation,—31.
Which thou hast prepared before the face of all peoples.—32. A light to the
revelation of the Gentiles, and the glory of thy people Israel."—33. And his father
and mother were wondering at those things which were spoken concerning him.—
34. And Simeon blessed them, and said to Mary his mother: "Behold this Child
is set for the fall and for the resurrection of many in Israel, and for a sign which
shall be contradicted;—35. And thy own soul a sword shall pierce, that out of
many hearts thoughts may be revealed."—36. And there was one Anna, a prophet-
ess, the daughter of Phanuel, of the tribe of Aser; she was far advanced in years,
and had lived with her husband seven years from her virginity.—37. And she was a
widow until fourscore and four years, who departed not from the Temple, by
fastings and prayers serving night and day.—38. Now she at the same hour coming
in, confessed to the Lord, and spoke of him to all that looked for the redemption
of Israel.—39. And after they had performed all things according to the law of
the Lord, they returned into Galilee, to their city Nazareth.

The Presentation of Jesus in the Temple took place about forty
days after His Birth.

#### 1. THE PRESENTATION OF JESUS

With regard to the Presentation of Jesus in the Temple there
are three things to be noticed.

First, our Saviour is brought into the Temple. He enters the Temple for the first time. This is a very important fact for Him; so important, that it was the subject of several prophecies. Jerusalem is the scene of the revelation of the Messias, and of the glory of His kingdom (Isa. 60). The Angel of the Testament will enter the Temple (Mal. 3:1), and this second Temple is more glorious than the first, precisely because the Messias enters it (Agg. 2:7–10). He was the God of Israel and the Angel of the Testament; the Temple was there on His account. He had dwelt there from days of yore. Now He comes as God-Man and enters the Temple, not, like the other Israelites, merely to adore there, but to take possession of it, to rule therein; not as a servant, like Moses (Hebr. 3:3), but as son, heir and master; He comes to exercise authority there in the name of the Father, and to manifest Himself. Thus He will show Himself in public life. May not these have been the thoughts with which our Saviour saw for the first time the magnificent Temple, the spacious fore-courts, the porticoes, the beautiful gates and the altar of sacrifice? Other thoughts and sentiments of His may perhaps be contained in the 83rd Psalm, which was a hymn for pilgrims.

Secondly, our Lord is revealed in the Temple. The destination of the Temple, to be the place of the revelation of the Messias, was fulfilled at His very first visit. As the parents of our Saviour brought Him into the Temple, Simeon came at once to meet them (Luke 2:27), and revealed His identity. And this revelation is a very brilliant and glorious one; first, on account of the place, which is no other than Jerusalem and the Temple, the place of worship of the Old Covenant. Secondly, it is glorious on account of the people, who were always present in large numbers, and must have been witnesses of it; and also on account of the time, which was probably the hour of the morning sacrifice. Thirdly, the revelation was a brilliant one, on account of the persons through whom it was made. They were Simeon and Anna, persons respected, well-known, and of acknowledged sanctity, who were filled with the spirit of prophecy (Luke 2:25, 26, 36, 37). Lastly, the revelation was glorious on account of the testimonies and statements which were made concerning our Saviour. They embraced the whole significance, greatness and glory of the Messias, for Israel, for the Gentile world, and for the entire human race. Simeon simply calls our Saviour the promised salvation of all nations (Luke 2:30, 31; Gen. 49:18), the glory of the chosen people (Luke 2:32), and the light to the revelation of the Gentiles (Luke 2:32). The Saviour is the real center of all ecclesiastical and secular history. Whoever enters heaven as saved, owes his salvation to Him; whoever perishes, incurs his damnation through sin against Him (Luke 2:34). Thus Israel will show in its relations to Him by what spirit it is inspired, whether by true piety or by hypocritical selfishness (Luke 2:34). And as Israel, so all mankind. Christ is the sign of contradiction and the stone of stumbling. On the Cross war will be enkindled, and will extend over the whole world and all ages. No one is indifferent with regard to Christ; either He is adored and loved, or He is hated. Before Christ, all declare themselves; there the paths of individuals and of nations separate, leading to heaven or to perdition (Luke 2:34; Isa. 8:14; Ps. 117:22; Dan. 2:45). Christ's vocation, to redeem the world by suffering and death, is also prophesied by Simeon. His words are a summary of the entire doctrine concerning the Christ. And we ought to remark that it is the Holy Ghost Himself Who speaks through Simeon and Anna (Luke 2:26, 27, 36). They proclaimed this testimony wherever there was a real longing for the Messias (Luke 2:38). Such a glorious revelation had never yet taken place.

Thirdly, our Saviour is presented to God. The signification of this ceremony was the actual recognition of God's right of possession over the Israelite nation. The blessing of progeny always proceeds from God; but Israel had become His especial property, in consequence of the deliverance of the people from the Egyptian servitude. In order to assert this right of possession, God had chosen, instead of the whole nation, the Levites for His especial and continual service (Num. 8:16, 17); further, the first-born, whether of man or beast, was to be presented to Him. The first-born sons were ransomed with five sicles ($4.00), which reverted to the priests (Ex. 13:1, 2; 34:19, 20; Num. 18:15). The ransom of the first-born son alone was actually enjoined, and was probably paid by the father at the central gate on the south side of the court of the priests, thirty days after the child's birth, or later (I Kings 1:21). If the first-born himself was brought to the Temple, he was handed over to the priset, who, after the payment of the sicles, gave him back to the parents with a blessing and an expression of thanks. And why then did our Lord wish to undergo this ceremony? Not because He was really obliged to do so. No positive law bound Him, and by the union of His human nature with the Second Person of the Godhead He was consecrated to God as no ceremony could consecrate Him. But the mystery of His Divine Nature was not yet known, and so He did not wish to give scandal, but on the contrary an example of humility, obedience, and zeal, to honor God by all the prescribed ceremonies of religion, and to perfect all worship of God by union with His infinite merits. He made use of every opportunity to honor God and to offer Himself to Him for us. And in reality He was not ransomed at all. Finally, how does our Saviour offer Himself to the Father? In the first place, voluntarily; in the second, by the hands of the ancient priesthood; lastly, with great interior devotion. What went on in the Heart of our Saviour as the priest raised Him in his arms and presented Him to God? His customary acts of adoration, thanksgiving and oblation, but with ever new and more ardent love. It was a great and glorious act of sacrifice, and never had a greater or more glorious offering been made to God in this Temple. His glory filled with its rays the Temple and the whole of earth and heaven. Many of us occasionally offer sacrifices to God, usually some small act or practice of mortification. But how many of us are generous enough to offer their whole being, to be consumed in God's service, in complete union with His holy will?

## 2. ACCESSORY CIRCUMSTANCES OF THE PRESENTATION

The accessory circumstances are connected with the persons who were present with our Saviour and assisted Him in this mystery. These persons are the priests of the Covenant, Mary, Simeon and Anna.

The priesthood of the Old Covenant rendered assistance to our Saviour in this mystery. It was the visible, ministering, official hand by which He presented Himself to the Heavenly Father, in accordance with the law.

God Himself had established that priesthood among His chosen people while they were still wandering in the desert. And He saw to it that this priesthood should be perpetuated amid all the vicissitudes through which the Israelites passed. Thus was the sacrifice of the Old Law continued until it was replaced by the infinite and redeeming sacrifice of the Cross, of which it was the figure.

But Mary had a far more intimate share in the mystery of the Presentation. She herself was present at it, and the Saviour appears in the Temple in her arms. It was not necessary that the presentation and ransom of the first-born son should be performed by the mother; but the law of purification was incumbent upon her, according to which, in order to free herself from her legal uncleanness, she had to come to the Temple forty days after her delivery (or later, but in no case earlier), and offer two sacrifices: a lamb as burnt-offering and a pigeon as sin-offering, or in case of poverty two pigeons or turtle-doves (Lev. 12). Mary made this offering, and, like our Saviour, without being bound by the intention of the Lawgiver. She made it also with the same intention as our Saviour, out of reverence and gratitude to God, and in order not to give scandal. Further, it cost her the loss of the prestige and glory of her virginity. Lastly, she made it with proportionately the same devotion as her Son, because a spark of glowing love for God surely sprang from the Saviour's Heart to her own, whilst the priest took the Child and lifted it up, and whilst she assisted at the payment of the offering. The women were purified after childbirth at the gate of Nicanor, which led from the forecourt of the Gentiles into that of the women; then the mother laid the money for the double sacrifice in the offertory-box which was placed in the women's court for this purpose, and betook herself to the place where she could assist at the sacrifice. Mary was rewarded for this participation in the sacrifice of our Saviour by a special participation in the glory of His manifestation. If our Saviour is the sign of contradiction, through which all men attain salvation or incur damnation, He is not alone in this. His Mother stands at His side. The sword that pierces her Son strikes her also, and therefore she has a share in His glory and honor (Luke 2:34, 35). Not only Simeon and Anna call her blessed, but all generations of those who believe in Jesus and adore Him; just as all who revile her Son revile and abuse her also. No one is indifferent with regard to her either. We are told that Mary and Joseph "wondered" at the words of holy Simeon (Luke 2:33). The reason of this astonishment may have been either the continued and increasingly marvelous revelation of the Child by such various witnesses, heavenly and earthly, the angels, the shepherds, Simeon and Anna; or perhaps the new disclosure made by Simeon concerning the life-work and destiny of the Saviour. Although Mary had a general acquaintance with this destiny, still a progressive increase of her knowledge may very well be assumed. That the disclosure itself was made by another, and with such emphasis, must have gone to her mother's heart, and certainly not without sharp pain. One may well assume that the "sword" already pierced her heart, and sank ever deeper during her whole life-time.

The other actors in the scene are Simeon and Anna. They both express the same spirit and possess the same holiness, only in different vocations. Simeon's holiness had three characteristic attributes. He was just, because his piety was practical, and held fast above all things to the commandments and means of salvation prescribed by God. He feared God, and he was holy and well-pleasing in His sight to his inmost soul, not merely by outward service and righteousness of works. Lastly, he "waited for the consolation of Israel" (Luke 2:25; Isa. 40:1). The corruption of his people and of the world in general rankled like a wound in the heart of the holy old man, and he found peace only in his hope of the Redeemer. So he stood upon the watch-tower of Israel, and looked with burning desire for the coming salvation. This love and longing for the Saviour seems to have been the peculiar feature of his holiness, and the Messias the object of his devotion. This longing was increased by the gifts of grace with which he was adorned; for the Holy Ghost was in him, he was a prophet, and had the assurance of seeing the Messias before his death (Luke 2:26). For this reason he loved best to linger in the Temple, because the Messias was to appear there. St. Anna was marked by the same piety, the same fervor in prayer. She was assiduous at the Temple services. She joined to the aforesaid virtues an extraordinary spirit of penance, and desisted not from fasting even in her eighty-fourth year. She was, as it were, the living pillar of the ancient Temple (Luke 2:36, 37).

Such was the preparation of the two Saints, and now their reward came. That which they had both so longingly awaited, and entreated by prayer and penance, was to be granted to them, and in greater measure than they had expected. The Holy Ghost called Simeon at the moment when Mary came into the Temple with her Child to present Him (Luke 2:27). He saw and recognized Mary and the Saviour; he was permitted to take Him in his arms. His eyes gazed into the depths of the Child's eyes, and in them he saw the glorious vision of the future. He saw the Light of the World rise over the far-off islands of the Gentiles in the East and in the West (Isa. 12:1), and at last become a glorious noontide over Israel also (Luke 2:30, 31, 32). He, the expiring lamp, held this Light of the World; his trembling arms raised the Ransom of mankind in the midst of the Temple, and his heart, so weary of life, grew young again in the embrace of the ever young eternity and beauty of God; and so his lips sang that unspeakably beautiful song, the Church's touching evening prayer of thanksgiving for the blessings and joys of the day of Redemption. In the song of praise "Nunc dimittis," Simeon thanks God that he has attained his object in life, which was to see and proclaim the rise of the light of salvation (Luke 1:78); he is at peace now, and asks to be permitted to quit his post on the watch-tower (Luke 2:29). Secondly, he gives expression to the reason of this peace and contentment, viz. the coming of the Saviour, which has brought salvation in all its plenitude for Israel and the whole world (Luke 2:30–32). Thirdly, he foretells a mystery. He appears to have seen that the Gentiles would attain salvation before Israel (Luke 2:31); he saw how this Messias would become for the latter a sign of contradiction and cause of fall (Isa. 53; Zach. 12:10), and only in later times its real glory (Luke 2:32–35; Rom. 11:30–32). St. Anna too was blessed with this revelation (Luke 2:38), and recognized in this Child the Messias and God of Israel. Her pale and worn features bloomed with a new beauty, her body was reanimated with the youthful glow of love and joy, and she broke forth into praise of the Lord. She utilized the last remaining moments of her life to speak, to all who looked for Israel's Redemption, about the Saviour Who had appeared (Luke 2:38). The names of these two holy Israelites are recorded for their honor and glory, and will be commemorated wherever the Gospel is preached.

### 3. SIGNIFICATION OF THE MYSTERY

The signification of the mystery with regard to the Saviour is, in the first place, that it is a revelation, unsurpassed in its import and magnificence; it might even be called an official revelation, because it was foreseen and foretold by the prophets. This revelation is a consequence of our Saviour's obedience and humility, as seen in His fulfilment of the law. He enters the Temple with the intention of honoring His Heavenly Father and offering Himself to Him, and there honor and glory await Him. One does not know which is more beautiful and important, the example of virtue given by our Saviour and His Mother, or their glorification. At all events we see here in very deed the confirmation of the truth which so often recurs in the life of our Saviour, that self-abasement is followed by exaltation.

This mystery is also the first public and solemn meeting with Israel. The whole Israelite nation is represented in the ministers who take part in the mystery. The Saviour appears for the first time before the priesthood of the Old Covenant; He acknowledges it, submits to it, offers it the price of His ransom, allows Himself to be presented by its hand to His Father, and receives its blessing. The meeting is one of peace, and the priests simply discharge their office without any after-thought. It will be otherwise later on. Today they dismiss Him in peace; some years later they will seize Him and lead Him away to death with the cry: "We have a law, and according to the law He ought to die" (John 19:7). "Away with him!" (John 19:15). Today our Saviour has already passed close by Golgotha, on the way from Bethlehem, and has seen and greeted the awful place from His Mother's arms. The people of Israel too are represented at this meeting by Simeon and Anna. They, like Zachary and Elizabeth, are the very expression of the true holiness of the Old Covenant, which consisted in prayer, penance, and longing for the Messias. Their expectation of the Messias is not the carnal desire of the Jews. What they look for is a Redeemer from sin, and therefore a Saviour by suffering and death, and a sign of contradiction even to their own people. They greet the Saviour with faith and holy joy; by their prophecy they stand apart from the unholy section of their nation, and take their stand with the Mother of Sorrows at the foot of the Cross. In the kingdom of Christ, Simeon and Anna are the representatives of those interior souls of whom the world knows nothing, but who by their prayers and secret sacrifices sap the strongholds of evil in this world, and bring about its downfall and the supremacy of good. They work like the invisible powers of nature, and are the medium of our Saviour's manifestation and God's interposition in the world. The preparation of a whole life-time is not too much for such glory and consolation.

Souls that, in a hidden life, merely pray and grow more closely united to God are often His chosen instruments for accomplishing His purposes. "The weak things of the world hath God chosen that He may confound the strong; . . . that no flesh should glory in His sight" (I Cor. 11:27–29).

## THE EPIPHANY OF OUR LORD

MATT. 2:1. When Jesus therefore was born in Bethlehem of Juda, in the days of king Herod, behold there came wise men from the East to Jerusalem,—2. Saying: "Where is he that is born King of the Jews? For we have seen his star in the East, and are come to adore him."—3. And king Herod hearing this, was troubled, and all Jerusalem with him.—4. And assembling together all the chief priests and the scribes of the people, he inquired of them where Christ should be born.—5. But they said to him: "In Bethlehem of Juda. For so it is written by the prophet:—6. 'And thou Bethlehem in the land of Juda art not the least among the princes of Juda: for out of thee shall come forth the captain that shall rule my people Israel.' " —7. Then Herod privately calling the wise men learned diligently of them the time of the star which appeared to them;—8. And sending them into Bethlehem, said: "Go and diligently inquire after the Child; and when you have found him, bring me word again, that I also may come and adore him."—9. Who having heard the king, went their way; and behold the star which they had seen in the East went before them, until it came and stood over where the Child was.—10. And seeing the star they rejoiced with exceeding great joy.—11. And entering into the house, they found the Child with Mary his mother, and falling down they adored him; and opening their treasures, they offered him gifts: gold, frankincense, and myrrh.—12. And having received an answer in sleep that they should not return to Herod, they went back another way into their country.

It seems most in accordance with Holy Scripture (Luke 2:39; Matt. 2:16, 22) to assume that the Magi did not come to pay their homage until a year, or at any rate some months, after the Nativity of our Lord. According to this supposition the Holy Family, having returned to Nazareth after the Presentation in the Temple, removed again to Bethlehem, and only fled thence into Egypt upon the angel's warning, after the adoration of the Magi.

### 1. CIRCUMSTANCES OF THE MYSTERY

The mystery of the Epiphany of our Lord comprises, as regards its exterior circumstances, the manner in which the Magi were called, their obedience to the voice, and the reward of their fidelity.

The Magi or wise men, as they are called, were probably descendants of the priestly families who, in Media and Persia, acted as priests, officials of the crown, and tutors of the kings or princes of the tribes; and who, being the possessors of the religious and philosophical knowledge of their time, experienced in astronomy, exercised great influence over the princes and people. It has not been ascertained whether they came from Persia, Chaldaea or Arabia, but at all events it was from a country situated east of the Promised Land, "from the East" (Matt. 2:1). By the frequent contact of these nations with the Israelite people, extending down to the most recent times, and especially by the captivity in Assyria and Babylon, the Magi may have come into possession of the Holy Scriptures and prophecies, and thus have become acquainted with Balaam's prophecy of the Star of Jacob (Num. 24:17; cf. Dan. 2:47; 3:96; 6:25; 14:40). In addition to this they may probably have received a special revelation, with instructions to go and pay homage to the God-King as soon as a certain star should appear. This star actually did appear at the time of Christ's Birth, whether it was an already existing star or a newly-created one, a comet or other unusual atmospheric phenomenon (Matt. 2:2), which could go before the Magi, disappear and reappear, just as the designs of God required.[1] Assuredly, too, the interior impulse of God's grace worked upon their hearts at the appearance of the star, so that they felt themselves bound to follow it and adore the new-born king. Thus God called the Magi in a manner most appropriate to them, not by angels, but by natural phenomena, to the study of which they were devoted; most appropriate also to Christ, Who is the Light of the World; and lastly, most appropriate to the anticipating, accompanying and crowning grace, of which the wondrous star, by its origin and by the charm, certainty and happy result of its guidance, was a most striking symbol.

This interior and exterior impulse of God's grace was followed by the Magi with holy faith, with all confidence and decision, and also with perseverance through all difficulties and sacrifices. Three of these sacrifices call for special notice. First, the departure from their home. To natural prudence it might almost seem like madness on the part of the wise men, who were very highly respected in their own country (and perhaps already advanced in age), to start off on a long and adventurous journey with no motive save that prompted by their religious feeling, and uncertain whether they would ever return to their country and people again. But for them it was a call, such as had been given to Abraham (Gen. 12:1), and they obeyed it. The second difficulty was that they were obliged to inquire of Herod concerning the birth of the new-born king. Did they not know who Herod was, and how little he would make of killing new-born kings? Did they not see

[1] It is not probable that the star guided the Magi all the way. Nothing is said of this in Scripture, and God does not work miracles unnecessarily.

the startled faces of the people of Jerusalem, who, as it seems, were partisans of Herod, only susceptible to outward splendor, and idle and indifferent to all else? Did they not see that they had fallen into a lion's den? (Matt. 2:3.) And yet they inquire quite fearlessly and without anxiety, where the new-born king of the Jews is (Matt. 2:2). If Herod's cunning had not suggested other thoughts to him, they would certainly have been doomed to death. The third difficulty awaited them in the person of the Saviour Himself. They had naturally expected some signs of princely and royal pomp, at least the court of the chief of a tribe. And what do they find? The very opposite of all this. And is this the great King? They do not listen to the voice of nature, but to that of faith. They adore, and offer their intellect and their hearts as a sacrifice, with the valuable gifts of gold, frankincense and myrrh which they lay at the Child's feet (Matt. 2:11).

And so they were rewarded by God. On the journey they had the great consolation of seeing their star appear once more, to guide them to the crib of the Child (Matt. 2:9, 10). Moreover God sensibly protected them; not only in Jerusalem at the court of bloodthirsty Herod, who in his lust of power had spared neither his own children nor his wives, but also in Bethlehem, where He warned them not to return to him (Matt. 2:12). At our Saviour's crib they made acquaintance with Jesus and Mary and learnt the Christian faith, and returned to their home as believers, confessors and apostles. It is even said that one of them died as a martyr, and now they are great Saints and enjoy the veneration of the Church, as the heads and princes of the Gentile Church. Such is the mystery of the holy Magi.

## 2. SIGNIFICATION OF THE MYSTERY

And what then is the signification of this mystery? Why this glorious transformation? Why this shining star, this gift of gold, this frankincense and these spices, in the obscurity and poverty of the Holy Childhood? The poor lodging of our Saviour has become changed into a royal abode, a Christian cathedral. That is the signification of the mystery; it reveals the whole kingly dignity of Christ and the special characteristics of this kingship.

The whole mystery is a revelation and recognition of Christ's kingly dignity. The Magi themselves proclaim it, when they ask where the new-born "king" of the Jews is housed. It is, then, a homage paid to Christ as the Messias and God-King. The gifts they offer, namely gold, frankincense and myrrh (Matt. 2:11), are symbolic of this homage, and have a deep religious meaning. The gold is for the King, the frankincense for God, and the myrrh for the Redeemer. It is therefore a divine and priestly royalty that they adore in the Child. Herod sees in the Saviour a pretender to the throne, and therefore he trembles and plots to destroy Him. So too the Church understands the meaning of the feast, and in her liturgy weaves into a magnificent song of praise the prophecies concerning Christ's kingship.

The characteristics of Christ's kingship are likewise displayed on a magnificent scale in this mystery. First, its origin. It is not an acquired kingship, gained by purchase or force, or conferred by the subjects, but it is innate, inherent, personal. Christ is a king, because He is the God-Man. He possesses the source and unction of all kingship in Himself and in His being (Apoc. 19:16). In this sense may be interpreted the inquiry of the Magi for the Child "born" King of the Jews. Secondly, the duration and extent of this kingship are revealed. Christ bears in Himself the kingship. He does not rule like other kings, who often do not attain to power until late in life, whose power depends upon the strength and wealth of their subjects, and from whose hand death soon wrests the scepter. His reign begins at once, from the very first moment of His existence; He receives homage in His crib and, weak and helpless though He is, gathers round Him at once vassals and revenues. "And of His kingdom there shall be no end" (Luke 1:32, 33). To His own, Christ does not die. Thirdly, the power of Christ's kingship is manifested. It extends over all men and all things. He is Lord of the material world. To Him belong the gold and treasures of the earth, and the stars obey His nod. He is Lord of men; of His enemies, in the first place, who tremble at the news of His arrival (Matt. 2:3), and who, despite all their resistance, end by serving His plans. He is Lord of His faithful adherents, whom He calls as He wills, and makes capable of every sacrifice; for He is the Lord of grace. Lastly, He is Lord of the Jews and Gentiles, Lord of the whole earth and of the whole human race. Today already the Gentile world, represented by the Magi, pays Him its homage. Fourthly, the benefits and blessings of this kingship are made manifest. Christ is Lord of all, and therefore He loves all and calls all: shepherds and Magi, poor men and kings, just men and sinners, Jews and Gentiles. How generously and magnificently He rewards the Magi, in time and in eternity! If He accepts service and gifts, it is only in order to reward and recompense them with greater things. He is God, and does not need our goods; He is a priest and redeemer, Who gives His life for us and enriches us with the treasures of His Redemption. Fifthly, the destinies of this kingship are here revealed. The mystery of our Lord's Epiphany is, as it were, a luminous and brilliant picture, showing forth not only the present, but also the future splendor of Christ's kingship. It is an unfolding of the destinies of the Old and the New Covenant in connection with this kingship. The Gentiles are called, and by their presence He is made manifest in Israel. By the answer of the Sanhedrim, Israel itself, though it does not approach Him, directs the Gentiles to Bethlehem, to the Messias; and thus the rejection of Israel and the vocation of the Gentile world is prefigured. Christ is the starting-point, center and end of all. The great prophecies which had so gloriously proclaimed Christ as the light and salvation of the Gentile world and the king and Messias of the nations (Isa. 60; Ps. 71) are now fulfilled. Christ's kingship is glorified on all sides, in its redeeming, priestly and divine character, in its nature, its origin, duration and power; and from all sides come acknowledgment and homage, from earth and heaven, from heathenism and Judaism. The mystery hovers over the crib of our Saviour like a sun-lit cloud, diffusing its light all around, the cloud of Thabor over our Lord's Childhood. In the crib, as on the Cross, this kingship glows with a lustrous splendor.

### 3. LESSONS TO BE DRAWN FROM THE MYSTERY

The first lesson is joy in our Saviour and heartfelt congratulation, that on this day He receives so much honor and appreciation, through all the marvels that take place around Him. How He must have rejoiced over the truly kingly hearts of the holy Magi, who gave themselves with their gifts, and rejoiced in their sacrifice! And Mary and Joseph too must have rejoiced at all the honors paid to their Son and Lord. To them also we will offer our heartfelt congratulations.

The second lesson is gratitude. We stand very close to this mystery. In it we see prefigured our own vocation to Christianity. The Magi are the first called, the first-fruits, the princely ancestors of the Gentile Church. In their train the Gentile nations have enlisted under Christ's standard, and we are the last comers. We have entered into the inheritance of the Jews, not through our merits, but through the electing grace of Jesus Christ, Who called us, while we were yet afar off, to the wondrous light of His faith and Church. For this we must thank our Lord with all our hearts today. The proof of this gratitude will be seen in our efforts to do something towards the conversion of the heathen world. How sad it is that the greater part of mankind still sits in the shadow of death! Let us therefore ask the intercession of the holy Magi; implore our Lord, Who is the Light of the Gentiles, to have mercy upon them; and take part in the work of the propagation of the faith. Gratitude for the great grace of faith, compassion for the poor heathens, our brethren, and zeal for the kingdom of Christ, all require this endeavor on our part.

The third lesson is this: If the mystery of today is the manifestation of Christ's kingship, then let us also pay homage to our King, and serve Him with love, generosity and self-sacrifice. Everything in this mystery exhales the spirit of generosity and sacrifice. These gifts that the Magi offer are but the symbols of this spirit of sacrifice; the sacrifice of love, the sacrifice of prayer, and the sacrifice of self-denial. They embrace our whole being and our whole life. The noble-hearted Magi themselves also preach to us this spirit of sacrifice. How many sacrifices they make! Or rather, what sacrifices do they not make? They leave their home and families, they sacrifice their treasures, their repose, they offer their hearts, and almost sacrifice their lives. And how do they make the sacrifice? "We have seen His star in the East and are come" (Matt. 2:2), that is to say, quickly, readily, generously, perseveringly, and with childlike simplicity and humility. And from what motives? At all events we have more, and greater ones. They did not see Christ's kingdom; but we see its greatness, splendor and power, and enjoy all its blessings. Let us not, therefore, allow ourselves to be discouraged in Christ's service by sacrifices and difficulties. Did not God come to the help of the Magi in the difficulties they had to encounter? And what would their journey have been without the difficulties? No more than a pilgrimage such as thousands undertake every year to Mecca. Now they have become apostles, and perhaps martyrs. How foolish and ridiculous, had they turned back with their camels as soon as their home disap-

peared from sight, or as they stood before Jerusalem, or before
the poor lodging of the Saviour! The Person of our Lord also
encourages us to this spirit of sacrifice. We must and will have
a lord and king. Where shall we find one wiser, more powerful,
more gracious and munificent than our Saviour? How magnificently has He rewarded the Magi even here below, and much more
in eternity, for their labor, their confession of Him, and the dangers
they encountered! One little ray of this heavenly glory is the
veneration they enjoy in the Church Militant, the glorious feast
with its solemn octave; the record of their deed immortalized in
paintings, and the altars and churches dedicated to them. For
centuries they have rested from the toil of their journey, and in
return for their homage they are reaping the religious veneration
of the Christian people.

## HEROD AND THE HOLY INNOCENTS

MATT. 2:16. Then Herod, perceiving that he was deluded by the wise men,
was exceeding angry; and sending killed all the men-children that were in Bethlehem, and in all the borders thereof, from two years old and under, according to
the time which he had diligently inquired of the wise men.—17. Then was fulfilled
that which was spoken by Jeremias the prophet, saying:—18. "A voice in Rama
was heard, lamentation and great mourning; Rachel bewailing her children, and
would not be comforted, because they are not."

In order to get the new-born King into his hands, Herod had
charged the Magi to go to Bethlehem, inquire after the Child,
and bring him word as to Its abode. But the wise men received
the warning not to return to Herod, and now that he saw himself
deluded, he gave orders to kill all the male children in Bethlehem
and the surrounding districts who had been born within the last
two years. And so it was done. But meanwhile the Saviour had
fled into Egypt. In this mystery there are three personalities that
claim our particular consideration.

### 1. HEROD

In King Herod we have an instructive example of the nature
and effects of the passions. The lesson may be reduced to two
propositions. The first is: The passions are evil counselors, because
they give us bad advice and make us unhappy.

Our lower passions give us bad advice, because their point of
view is bad. They grasp only what is proximate, temporal and
sensual, and so they set before us as our aim only private interests,

and not the common good; and in our private interests they con-
sult only the sensual and temporal, and themselves. Thus they
cheat us of all higher and nobler aims, suggesting fear where there
is nothing to be afraid of, and giving us false security where we
have need to fear.

In this our evil passions do us harm, and make us unhappy by
their counsel. They begin by rendering us uneasy and discon-
tented. Herod was a slave to the most terrible of all passions, the
love of power. He had laboriously climbed to the throne, and
was guarding it jealously and passionately against all aspirants,
not excepting his children and other relatives. Hence he was fright-
ened now at the news brought by the wise men of the birth of
a new king (Matt. 2:3), and yet there was no ground for his fears.
Christ did not desire a temporal crown; He had other crowns, and
did not hurl kings from their thrones. "Non eripit mortalia, qui
regna dat coelestia." So Herod really fears where there is nothing
to fear, and does not fear where he ought rightly to have done so.
That is the unwise policy of passion. Of what use are his throne
and his crown to him, in all this anxiety and discontent? Secondly, the passions make us unhappy by making criminals of us,
like Herod. Love of power makes him hypocritical. In spite of all
his uneasiness, hostility and impiety, he feigns ease, friendliness
and piety (Matt. 2:8). He promises to make with his Court a
pilgrimage to the new King. At last, when he sees himself deceived
and destitute of all other means, his passion makes him a ruthless
tyrant. He will stifle in blood the new-born King, and he raises
his arm for that terrible stroke which cost the lives of all the male
children up to two years old in Bethlehem and the surrounding
district. As Bethlehem did not number a thousand families (Mich.
5:2), these may have been about twenty little ones. Herod's
atrocious deed, combined with so many others, drew down
upon Herod the abhorrence and curse of the nation and of
all mankind. And all this without any success. What did Herod
wish? To destroy Jesus and all remembrance of Him. And what
is the result? He makes the advent of Christ all the more noted,
by the assembling of the Sanhedrim, by his inquiry as to the birthplace of the Messias, and lastly by the horror of a massacre which
imprinted itself indelibly upon the memory of the people. The
children are slaughtered, but Christ escapes, whilst Herod himself
is claimed by death. A few months after the murder of the Innocents (before the Feast of the Pasch, in the year 750 after the

building of Rome), he succumbed to a hideous and frightful disease. What, then, did he gain by his crime?

The passions, then, are bad counselors; but they are good servants. That is the second lesson that Herod gives us. How he calculates and reckons everything! He leaves no stone unturned, but does all that cunning and craft can suggest. And where that does not suffice, he has recourse to violent measures. Acts impelled by a passion, if they are good in themselves and directed towards a supernatural end, are sometimes found in the lives of the saints. There are no saints who have not a passion for virtue, for Christ's kingdom, and for God.

## 2. THE HOLY INNOCENTS

Looked at from a natural point of view, how sad is the fate of these little children! And yet how enviable is their lot, when considered from a supernatural stand-point!

Let us ask ourselves first what these children would have become, if they had not met with this fate. In all probability, quite ordinary men, common workmen, or at most officials of Herod or the Romans; perhaps profligates, yes, perhaps even enemies of our Saviour, and participators in His murder later on. At all events they would not have gained a crown, and their happiness would not have lasted beyond the ruin which later overtook the whole nation.

Secondly, let us ask ourselves what these children have now become. Saints, and saints too with a special prerogative; for they are said to have received from God special power to help in the hour of death. They are now innocent souls, wearing the crown of virginity in heaven. For this reason the beautiful passage from the Apocalypse, where St. John depicts the happiness and bliss of innocent souls in heaven, is applied to them in the Mass for the feast. They are clad with white robes, in their hands they bear palms, and on their foreheads is written the name of God; they follow the Lamb whithersoever He goes; they form His permanent Court, and in the kingdom of heaven none are so gracious and glorious as they (Apoc. 14:1–5). Add to this that they are holy martyrs. The Church acknowledges them as such, because they lost their lives on account of Christ; and she celebrates their feast with striking solemnity and with a touching mournfulness, even amid the joys of Christmas-tide. They were even the subject of a prophecy, indirectly at least. Jeremias makes Rachel, the ancestress of three of the tribes of Israel, bewail with the same lament the punishment of Israel's being led away into captivity and the final rejection of the nation, which rejection had its beginning in the attempt to slay the Messias in the massacre of the Holy Innocents. "A voice in Rama was heard, lamentation and great mourning; Rachel bewailing her children, and would not be comforted, because they are not" (Jer. 31:15; Matt. 2:17, 18). The fate of the children is linked with that of the whole nation; their destruction is the prophecy and beginning of the ruin of their people.

Thirdly, let us ask ourselves how they attained to their happiness. Very early. "On the threshold of life," as the Church sings of them in her office, they accomplished their task; quickly and without pain, at least without any protracted pain. In a moment, at one blow, all was over. They closed their eyes to the sight of earth and kinsfolk, to open them to the contemplation of God's countenance for ever. Happy children! And who made them so happy?

### 3. THE SAVIOUR

The wailing of the Holy Innocents rings in our ears across the centuries, and recalls the horrors of that scene of bloodshed. The song of the angels proclaiming to us the peace and joy of the holy Christmas night always reminds us also of the tragedy of these little Innocents. But as darkness flees before the light, so grief and terror melt away in joy and glory and loud Alleluias in presence of the Lord of glory, Who steps in and envelops all in light by the sweet revelation of His wisdom, power and goodness.

In the first place, this mystery is a manifestation of the wisdom of our Saviour. The heart-rending anguish, the cries of agony and the blood belong to the majesty of the manger. They are the tribute to the wisdom of Jesus, living symbols of the law of mortification and suffering, and a revelation of the ways of Jesus and of every Christian life. The truth that even innocence must do penance is brought out most clearly. The Holy Innocents typify the Passion of Jesus and the Via Crucis and death of every Christian. As light and warmth radiate from the sun, so suffering radiates from Jesus and surrounds all who approach Him. As the Holy Innocents now fall like sacrificial lambs, so also is the Saviour to die as a sacrificial Lamb, and in a far more terrible manner. So the neighborhood of our Lord's crib is bathed in blood. The swaddling-clothes are only the predecessors of the winding-sheet. Could the truth that we must suffer and do penance be placed before us in a more striking manner than in this mystery?

Further, the mystery is a revelation of the might of Jesus. Under His Hand the most stupendous changes are wrought. Misfortune, death and destruction become by contact with Him salvation, life, joy, and excess of happiness and glory. No one gains more and loses less than he who offers his life and his all for Christ. Our Saviour triumphs by the plots of His enemies and the death of His adherents. The cries and the blood of the Innocents are as an undying voice by which He announces His arrival and existence in Israel. Against the Lord there is no wisdom and no strength (Prov. 21:30).

Lastly, the mystery is a revelation of the bounty of our Lord. We see how He rewards. How dear to us He has made these innocent children! We cannot spare them from the world of Bethlehem. How like they are to the Saviour, in age and form, in grace and lot in life! Their only fault was that they were born with Him in Bethlehem. They are His little fellow-citizens, His apostles and evangelists, yes, and likewise His substitutes in death. They did not die merely for Him, but instead of Him. They preserved the life of our Saviour for us, and to them we owe, so to speak, all that He became to us in the thirty-three years of His life. Because of this sweet relation to our Saviour our holy Mother the Church loves and honors them so much. Mary, too, must have felt the most sympathetic love for the dear little martyrs. Their fate told her what was in store for her beloved Child. The author of the Church's hymn sees in a charming vision the little martyrs in their glory, playing around the Blessed Virgin and her Divine Child, and sings:

Salvete, flores martyrum,  
Quos lucis ipso in limine  
Christi insecutor sustulit,  
Ceu turbo nascentes rosas.

Hail, flowers of martyrdom so bright!  
Scarce born to earth, yet ripe for Heaven;  
As chilling winds the flow'rets blight,  
Your life is spent or ere 'tis given.

Vos, prima Christi victima,  
Grex immolatorum tener,  
Aram sub ipsam simplices  
Palma et coronis luditis.

First offering to our Lord are ye,  
And tender victims for His sake;  
The Martyrs' crown, with childish glee,  
Your sport and plaything you do make.

| Jesu, tibi sit gloria, | All glory, Jesus, be to Thee, |
| Qui natus es de Virgine, | Of Mary born, a Virgin blest; |
| Cum Patre et almo Spiritu | To Father and the Spirit be |
| In sempiterna saecula. | One glory every age confessed. |

## THE FLIGHT INTO EGYPT

MATT. 2:13. And after they were departed, behold an angel of the Lord appeared in sleep to Joseph, saying: "Arise, and take the Child and his mother, and fly into Egypt; and be there until I shall tell thee. For it will come to pass that Herod will seek the Child to destroy him."—14. Who arose, and took the Child and his mother by night, and retired into Egypt.—15. And he was there until the death of Herod; that it might be fulfilled which the Lord spoke by the prophet, saying: "Out of Egypt have I called my Son."—19. But when Herod was dead, behold an angel of the Lord appeared in sleep to Joseph in Egypt,—20. Saying: "Arise, and take the Child and his mother, and go into the land of Israel; for they are dead that sought the life of the Child."—21. Who arose, and took the Child and his mother, and came into the land of Israel.—22. But hearing that Archelaus reigned in Judaea in the room of Herod his father, he was afraid to go thither; and being warned in sleep, retired into the quarters of Galilee.—23. And coming he dwelt in a city called Nazareth; that it might be fulfilled which was said by the prophets: That he shall be called a Nazarene.

After the departure of the Magi (Matt. 2:13), and before Herod had time to strike a blow, the Holy Family had received instructions to flee into Egypt.

### 1. THE FLIGHT

The cause of the flight was, in the first place, the wild passion of Herod, and his ruthless plan of having the children murdered (Matt. 2:13). But the immediate occasion of it was the command and dispensation of God, which was conveyed to St. Joseph in a prophetic dream, by an angel. The message appointed flight as the means of safety; it specified the land of Egypt as the place of refuge; it indicated the duration of the sojourn there: till the angel should come again; and finally, it gave the reason for the flight, viz. persecution on the part of Herod (Matt. 2:13). This dispensation is in accordance with God's rule of leaving to His creatures freedom of action, and of not intervening supernaturally except where and when it is necessary. He lets Herod do as he pleases, and only gives warning of his plans; the actual deliverance is to be accomplished by Joseph and Mary. Egypt had been from the earliest times the refuge of the Jews. Abraham (Gen. 12:10), Jacob (Gen. 46:6), and Joseph (Gen. 37:28) had been there, and later on also the persecuted Jews sought the shelter of Egypt (Isa.

30:2; III Kings 11:40; IV Kings 25:26), especially under the Ptolemies. From Bethlehem, Egypt could be reached in forty hours; as a Roman province it offered perfect security. Besides this, there were other ends of Providence which caused Egypt to be appointed as the place of refuge. The message was far from being pleasant or welcome news to the Holy Family; indeed, it was a hard trial for them. One only needs to consider the words of the angel, one by one, to see this. "Arise." St. Joseph had had many journeys now, and it seemed as if he were never to get any rest since the Saviour had come into his life. "Take the Child and His Mother." To flee alone is feasible, but to take two others with one, and under such circumstances, renders flight considerably more difficult. "Flee into Egypt." Exile, then, is commanded, and that is always hard to bear. "Be there until I shall tell thee." The uncertainty was a new element of suffering. "Herod will seek the Child to destroy Him." As if there were no other means of protecting the life of the Son of God against the tyrant. God had known how to shield His people otherwise against Pharao and Sennacherib. In short, from all points of view the order was a most severe trial.

Yet it was carried out in exact compliance with the angel's words. Joseph arose, took the Child and His Mother by night, and fled into Egypt (Matt. 2:14); that is to say, quickly and with great humility, so that probably none of the objections touched upon even came into his mind, and also with great perseverance. The journey lasted from eight to ten days, and the route led either over Hebron through the desert, or past Eleutheropolis to Gaza, or, according to an old tradition, along the sea-coast over Joppe, for greater security. God sent the Israelites, on their way through the desert, the pillar of cloud, the manna, and the miraculous water from the rock. We do not hear of any such prodigies performed for the sake of the Holy Family. They were spared none of the disagreeable aspects of the journey. What were the motives of this obedience and perseverance on the part of the Holy Family? First, the Will and command of God. God willed it so, and that was enough. He has His plans, and His Providence is wisdom, power, and goodness. Again, love of our Divine Saviour. His life was in danger. What would they not have done and suffered in order to preserve it! Lastly, our Saviour's example taught them humility, resignation, and patience in all adversities.

## 2. THE SOJOURN IN EGYPT

The circumstances of this sojourn are not known to us with certainty. Opinions vary with regard to its duration; it may have lasted from a few months to two, four, or six years, according to the different calculations of time. At all events the flight must have taken place immediately after the departure of the Magi, and the return could have been made in the course of the year following Herod's death, and after his sons had entered upon their inheritance: Archelaus in Judaea, and Herod Antipas in Galilee.

According to a tradition, the abode of the Holy Family was in the neighborhood of Heliopolis, not far from Memphis and the Great Pyramids. The sanctuary which marks their dwelling-place is venerated in a southern suburb of Cairo; and farther north at the edge of the desert, in the village of Matarieh, is shown the immense sycamore-tree [1] beside which a running spring is said to have welled forth while the Holy Family rested there.

As to the other circumstances, the sojourn in Egypt must have been a life of poverty, and all the more so that they were foreigners and new arrivals. Further, it was a life of labor, because St. Joseph was obliged to earn their bread by the work of his hands; a life, then, of earnest labor, but yet full of content and trust in God. Then, too, it was a life of prayer, and assuredly also of many trials. They were in exile, and idolatry in its most degraded forms unveiled its impurity before their eyes; for Heliopolis was one of the chief sites of the sun-worship, and of its priesthood. But these trials were borne without any sentimental indulgence in homesickness, without impatience and without complaint. Lastly, it was likewise assuredly a life of joy. Jewish colonies were to be found in almost all parts of Egypt at that time; near Heliopolis had stood for a century and a half a magnificent temple, the services of which rivaled those of Jerusalem in splendor, and they must certainly have been a great comfort to the exiles. It is most likely that the Holy Family made acquaintance with many a good Jewish family, and it is not less likely that they had friends

---

[1] The tree now shown is not the original sycamore under which the Holy Family is said to have rested, but one planted on the site of this tree after its decay, some 1100 years ago. This second tree is also decaying; the greater part of it lies on the ground, and only one branch still bears leaves. A sapling has been planted behind it, and the whole site is enclosed by a grating. (Translator's Note.)

also among the Gentiles. God blessed the exiles with heavenly consolation, and they had a constant source of joy in our dear Saviour. If their stay lasted for two or three years, it must have been here that He spoke the first words, uttered the first audible prayers, wore the first little coat, tried the first steps, and performed the first little duties, all infinitely sweet and tender domestic joys. The eyes of the little Saviour noticed, too, the marvels of that ancient and wonderful land. He saw the rising of the Nile; surely His glance rested often upon the obelisks of Heliopolis and upon the old pyramids beyond the river, and with how many a lotus-blossom may His little hand have played on the banks of the stream!

### 3. THE RETURN FROM EGYPT

At last the angel came again with the message to return, for Herod and all who sought the life of the Child were dead (Matt. 2:19, 20). Whilst Archelaus was in Rome in order to get his title to the throne confirmed, many of Herod's adherents were killed in an insurrection of the Jews, and perhaps among the number those who had urged him to the murder of the Innocents. God does not forsake His own. He and the Church overcome all their enemies by patient waiting.

How was the message received by the Holy Family? No doubt with joy—that does not offend God—but with a modest, humble joy. All other joy is unseemly in presence of God's Providence.

After the Holy Family had taken a cordial and grateful leave of their acquaintances, they set out on their journey, which led, according to tradition, along the sea-coast by Joppe and Caesarea to Nazareth in Galilee. As it appears, St. Joseph intended to settle in Bethlehem with his family. But on hearing that Archelaus, who was also a very cruel prince (cf. Introduction, p. 9), reigned in Judaea, he decided, out of fear for the Holy Child's life, to take up his abode in Nazareth, and was confirmed therein by a divine communication (Matt. 2:21, 22, 23). As St. Matthew remarks, our Saviour was to receive in consequence of this abode at Nazareth one of those names by which the Messias had been frequently announced by the prophets. "Nazarene" means "delegate," or "one consecrated to God," and also "sprig, bud, flower" (Isa. 4:2; 11:1; 45:8; Jer. 23:5; 33:15; Zach. 3:8; 6:12). So Nazareth became henceforth the home of our Saviour.

#### 4. SIGNIFICATION OF THE MYSTERY

The signification of the mystery of the Flight into Egypt is threefold.

To begin with, this mystery is the first encounter of our Saviour with the government, and in consequence of its unhappy policy the encounter is a hostile one and destined to remain so. This enmity passes from the father to the son, and devolves upon the Roman successors to the political power. Nevertheless it is instructive to see kingdoms and governments under the sway of Divine Providence. Egypt, which in former days had been the enemy of Israel, becomes at a later period its comfort and refuge, and gives shelter to its Messias.

The second signification is a mystical one, and concerns the relation of Egypt to the Messias. In Egypt the family of Jacob increased to a mighty people; there God first called it His "first-born son" (Ex. 4:22; Osee 11:1); there, by freeing it from the Egyptian yoke, he adopted it peculiarly as His own, and there He instituted the Paschal Lamb, the chief type of the Messias. Now, at the Flight into Egypt, the real "first-born Son," the real Paschal Lamb comes, and as the nation went through its probation and was formed to piety and labor, to the mechanical arts and to suffering, in the "iron furnace" of Egypt (Deut. 4:20), so too the Saviour was there to be trained to work and suffering. He saw the pyramids on which Abraham's eyes had gazed; He saw the land of Gessen, and it is even said that He dwelt close to the island in the Nile where Moses was exposed in the basket of bulrushes. This correspondence even as to locality between the type and the reality agrees exactly with the uniform action of Divine Providence. Now was to be fulfilled and accomplished the prophecy of blessing (Isa. 19:19; Deut. 23:7), which had begun with the immigration of the Jews into Egypt (II Mach. 1:1), the translation of the Holy Scriptures, and the erection of the temple near Heliopolis. The idols of Egypt, in particular the image of the sun-god at Heliopolis, are said to have fallen to the ground on our Saviour's arrival (Isa. 19:1). Perhaps too the wonderful growth of Christianity and especially of the monastic life, which took place later in Egypt, was a special blessing due to the sojourn of the Holy Family there.

The third signification of this mystery is a moral one. It was our Saviour's Will to be an object of persecution even in His

Childhood, in order to set us an example of patience and humility in adversity. He too will taste the bread of banishment, for the solace of all future exiles. And what a depth of abasement there is in the Creator thus fleeing before His creature! God respects the freedom of His creatures, and leaves them full play for their actions, without however altering His decrees. On the contrary, these decrees embrace all the creature's freedom of action, and make it fit into His design. Mary and Joseph are there also to give us an example of patience, humility, submission and endurance in all the changes and adversities of life. Through this they grew in virtue and merit, and won a claim to our veneration and gratitude. In very truth our Saviour owes to them His life, for they saved Him from His enemies. The trial passed away, like all things temporal, and God was present all the time with His help and consolation. And after the trial there came again pleasant, quiet days, the happy time at Nazareth.

### THE FINDING IN THE TEMPLE

LUKE 2:41. And his parents went every year to Jerusalem, at the solemn day of the Pasch.—42. And when he was twelve years old, they going up into Jerusalem according to the custom of the feast,—43. And having fulfilled the days, when they returned, the Child Jesus remained in Jerusalem; and his parents knew it not. —44. And thinking that he was in the company, they came a day's journey, and sought him among their kinsfolk and acquaintance.—45. And not finding him, they returned into Jerusalem, seeking him.—46. And it came to pass that after three days they found him in the temple sitting in the midst of the doctors, hearing them and asking them questions.—47. And all that heard him were astonished at his wisdom and his answers.—48. And seeing him, they wondered. And his mother said to him: "Son, why hast thou done so to us? behold thy father and I have sought thee sorrowing."—49. And he said to them: "How is it that you sought me? did you not know that I must be about my Father's business?"—50. And they understood not the word that he spoke unto them.

The only fact in the hidden life of which the circumstances are known with certainty is that Jesus went with His parents to the Feast of the Pasch, remained behind when they left the city, and appeared in public in the Temple.

### 1. NARRATIVE AND EXTERNAL CIRCUMSTANCES OF THE MYSTERY

The first circumstance was the time. The mystery falls about midway in the course of the hidden life. Our Saviour had attained his twelfth year (Luke 2:42), and was now at the age when, as a responsible member of the community and entitled to full rights,

He was subject to the law; or, as the Jews were accustomed to say, He had become "a son of the law." Now the Feast of the Pasch was drawing near, and He wished to celebrate it for the first time in Jerusalem, as in duty bound; since the law commanded all men to make a pilgrimage to the Temple three times in the year, the Pasch being fixed for one of these pilgrimages (Deut. 16:16). The women sometimes accompanied their husbands out of devotion (I Kings 1:3 seq.). So our Saviour went as a pilgrim to Jerusalem, accompanied by His parents, who undertook this Paschal pilgrimage every year (Luke 2:41).

The second circumstance is the feast and the place of its celebration. The Feast of the Pasch was one of the centers, indeed the chief center and focus of Jewish ecclesiastical life. Since the visit to the national sanctuary formed an essential part of the celebration of the Pasch, the concourse of people from all parts of the world was immense, and amounted to hundreds of thousands. No feast of the year had such deep significance as that of the Pasch, the memorial of that divine act which made Israel the chosen people of God and released it from the bonds of Egypt. Lastly, the sacrifice by which this feast was distinguished, the Paschal Lamb, was the original and chief sacrifice of the whole Covenant, and the principal type of the Saviour. All these details have an important bearing on the mystery.

The third circumstance was that our Saviour remained behind in Jerusalem when His parents started on their homeward journey. The Paschal Lamb was eaten on the 14th of Nisan (March), the solemn sacrifice took place on the 15th, and on the 16th the first-fruits of barley were offered; then the pilgrims could set out on their return journey. Perhaps Mary and Joseph did so. But our Saviour did not go with them; He quitted His parents intentionally and with a set purpose—no difficult feat in the vast crowd of pilgrims traveling in separate companies (Luke 2:43, 44). At the first encampment for the night, probably in Beroth or Ophni, His parents discovered His absence, and set out with unspeakable sorrow and anxiety, seeking for Him all the way back to the city and probably also in the city itself, until they found Him at last on the third day in the Temple, sitting in the midst of the doctors (Luke 2:45, 46).

That was the fourth circumstance. Whilst His parents were seeking Him, He had been attending the lectures which were held in the synagogue (a building adjacent to the Temple) or on one of the Temple terraces, by resident or visiting doctors of the law. Everyone could attend them, and might propose his doubts and questions. There, as it appears, our Saviour lingered for the greater part of this time, and excited universal attention and admiration by the insight and wisdom displayed in His questions and answers (Luke 2:47, 48).

Many features of this mystery come upon us as a surprise and a revelation, and are quite at variance with the usual conduct of our Lord: His withdrawal from the supervision and control of His parents, His exposing them to such unspeakable sorrow and anxiety for so long a time, His public appearance in the Temple and His acceptance of the applause excited by the display of His wisdom. All these things were in marked contrast to the character of the hidden life, which was above all things a life of obedience and deepest humility; they were quite contradictory to His usual mode of action; they caused bitter pain not only to His parents, but also to His own Heart, which was filled with such love and respect for them. Indeed, under ordinary circumstances, they would have been a violation of the simplest filial duty; for who does not understand the pain and anxiety endured by His father and Mother during these three days? It was this that occasioned Mary's gentle reproach: "Son, why hast Thou done so to us? behold, Thy father and I have sought Thee sorrowing" (Luke 2:48). There must have been some profound mystery underlying our Saviour's conduct.

### 2. MEANING AND LESSON OF THE MYSTERY

Our Saviour Himself gives us the key to the solution of these problems, in His answer to His Mother: "How is it that you sought Me? Did you not know that I must be about My Father's business?" (Luke 2:49.) What did He mean by this? Evidently that, though He has a Mother and owes her consideration, He has nevertheless a Father also, Who is greater, and Whose Will and command must always take the first place. And what else does the Heavenly Father will and command but the promotion of His honor and the salvation of mankind by the manifestation of His Son? Our Saviour came to fulfil this behest and Will of His Father; that is His life-work, as He often declares later in His public life (John 4:34; 5:30; 6:37–40; 17:3). This staying behind and appearing in the Temple is but a new manifestation of Himself; or more strictly speaking, it is a transient prelude of His public life, and this in a double sense, according to its end and according to the manner of His public ministry.

As regards its end, the public life of our Saviour is a magnificent witness of Himself, a revelation of His coming, His existence and work, by means of miracles and teaching. Here also we have something similar. Why does He appear in public? Why does He allow His wonderful wisdom to shine forth? Why does He attract attention to Himself, and suffer the plaudits of the crowd? If we examine carefully the words of Holy Scripture, we see in all this a new manifestation of our Saviour, full of an importance peculiar to itself. And why? First, because it is the first manifestation of which He Himself is the agent. Hitherto others (Elizabeth, the angels, the shepherds, Simeon and Anna, the Magi) had borne witness to Him, but now He bears witness of Himself. Secondly, the manifestation is important because it is so attractive. What is more lovable and engaging than an intelligent child of this age? It is under this form that our Saviour chooses now to appear before the people. Thirdly, the manifestation is important because it has a splendor of its own, revealing as it does His insight and wisdom, and also His Divinity; for He calls God His Father, although in a mysterious and obscure manner (Luke 2:49). And lastly, it is of consequence on account of the great attention and admiration accorded to Him. We get a glimpse of the wonder He excited by the fact that His parents found Him "sitting in the midst of the doctors," and marveled at the sight (Luke 2:48). It seems, then, that He was not sitting with the other listeners and scholars; but that the doctors, filled with admiring interest, had taken Him into their own circle and were questioning Him. This says a great deal, if we consider how important a position the doctors of the law held at this time, and what respect was paid to them. For this reason some of the holy Fathers call this occurrence a miracle. As Heli once bowed before the supernatural wisdom of little Samuel, and Daniel, when but a youth, pronounced sentence upon the two elders, so now the twelve-year-old Saviour sits among the doctors of the law. It is certainly a remarkable event, and in keeping with the public appearance of Jesus in later years.

Moreover this scene was also a prelude to the public life with regard to the exterior circumstances and the manner in which our Saviour manifested Himself afterwards, by teaching and working miracles. There was the same complete detachment from hearth and home, flesh and blood; the same poverty and separation from His family. As later on He left His Mother and lived on alms, so now He left His parents and depended on the charity of kind people for food and shelter. It is true that His absence is one of three days only; but we must remember how much more trying are the circumstances, through the grief of His parents and their ignorance of His whereabouts. Thus, then, His appearance in the Temple was really a perfect though transient prelude to His public life, a true manifestation of Himself. The answer of Jesus: "Did you not know that I must be about My Father's business?" is the first word that Holy Scripture records as spoken by Him. It is a great and majestic saying, a revelation of the entire Messianic vocation of Jesus, sudden as a gleam of lightning in the midst of the obscurity and domestic quiet of the hidden life. No wonder that Mary and Joseph were perplexed at such an unexpected disclosure (Luke 2:50).

### 3. REASONS UNDERLYING THE MYSTERY

There are three principal reasons why our Saviour thus manifested Himself.

The first reason concerned the Jews. It was very opportune that our Saviour should give some evidence of Himself again, for the last manifestation of Him had been made by the Magi, and the next was not to take place until His Baptism in the Jordan. Since, then, so long a period was to elapse between the two events, it was very fitting that our Saviour should once more recall Himself to the memory of the Jews, as He was about to disappear so completely in the hidden life. The circumstances of time and place (the Paschal feast and the Temple) were very well chosen for this object (Isa. 2:3; Mich. 4:2). That He first revealed Himself in the lecture-hall, and to the doctors of the law, is also significant. He thus declared Himself the teacher even of these teachers of the law, whose task it was to proclaim to the people the coming of the Messias, but with whom He was later to come into such serious and fatal conflict.

The second reason was one that concerned His parents, and especially His holy Mother. Our Saviour evidently wished not only to comfort her and excuse His behavior towards her, by this reference to the Will of His Heavenly Father, but also to instruct her and make her understand more clearly His extraordinary and higher vocation; namely that He was not on earth merely to carry out the duties of family life, but that He stood under a higher power. For this reason our Saviour very fittingly chose as the time of this admonition the expiration of His twelfth year, when the child outgrew the authority of his parents. He wished to prepare His Mother for the future separation, to be made at His entrance upon His office as Teacher. By this separation she was to assist and share in His vocation. She was also to give us an example of readiness and the noblest spirit of renunciation, when the call of God is heard and sacrifice is demanded. Parents have in this mystery a lesson as to their duty in matters concerning the vocation of their children. They see in Mary, on this occasion, not only the noblest patience and readiness to resign herself to what God wills or permits, but also the authority and right of the mother vindicated, as she gently questions our Saviour about the reason of His conduct. Parents have the right to inquire into their children's vocation and to test it, but not to make it impossible and overthrow it. On the contrary, it is their duty to submit in all patience and resignation to the recognized Will of God with regard to their children. The Will of God and nothing else must decide this matter, for the parents as well as for the children. They too must be about the Father's business. Then they have a share in all the good that proceeds from the vocation of the children. Mary is a beautiful example and a powerful help in the difficulties that arise for parents with regard to these matters, and she merited by her heroic virtue special graces for all who have to suffer such trials. Her example shows us what we have to do, and her aid enables us to act according to her example.

The third and last reason applies to ourselves. We needed a great example of obedience to the call of God under all circumstances. This mystery is really one of vocation, and contains for us the important lesson to carry out God's behest, let Him call us when, how, and to what He will. We must follow. On this account also our Saviour offered this lesson during His youth, because it is generally in youth that it becomes our duty to choose a vocation. The whole mystery is arranged in accordance with this intention. Our Saviour's example teaches us in the first place to what, whither, and how we must follow God. In this case the divine call is unusual, when we regard its object; the Saviour is to appear in public and bear witness of Himself in the midst of the hidden life. It is unusual with regard to the circumstances, demanding as it does entire detachment from flesh and blood, and requiring a hard sacrifice. Lastly, it is unusual with regard to the time; for Jesus is still only a boy in His twelfth year. In short, the call tends towards higher things, to the exclusive service of God, to evangelical perfection, to which the apostolic life must essentially conform. Our Saviour teaches us how we are to obey God's call, viz. completely, immediately, courageously and earnestly. He does not temper the hardness of the sacrifice for His parents. He leaves them without any warning; He makes no advances to them; and when at last He is found, He has no tender, caressing excuse to offer, nothing but the earnest and majestic words: "Did you not know that I must be about My Father's business?" Does not our Saviour thrust aside by this example all the difficulties that can oppose a vocation, from whatever source they may come: tender age, consideration for parents, the sacrifices contained in the vocation itself, or the perfect detachment that it entails? There is not a difficulty in any vocation that is not included in this mystery and solution by the example of our Saviour.

There is therefore nothing left for us to do but to follow the call of God, and to put out of our hearts all attachment to created things. What glorious motives, again, this mystery offers us! Above all, God, Who claims over us rights greater than those of even our nearest and dearest; He has indeed a right to all that we have, and especially to our love. But all excessive attachments are opposed to this love, and we may offer anything else we please, it will not satisfy God; for He will have our hearts, not our possessions. We must love God with all our hearts, with all our souls, and with all our strength. The second motive is our Saviour. This mystery gives us for the first time a glimpse into His Heart, into His sentiments of love and boundless reverence for God. In His Heart is God, God alone, and nothing but His Will rules there; every other claim must be silent before this, every feeling, even the holiest and most justifiable. Our Lord's behavior to His Mother and St. Joseph on this occasion passes a stern and trenchant judgment upon our inordinate attachments. What can we urge against it? That our Saviour really sought in all things only the Will and service of God, is seen by the manner in which He submits to be taken home again by His parents, and suffers Himself to disappear for so long in the shadow of the hidden life.

## C. The Hidden Life of Jesus

Luke 2:40. And the Child grew, and waxed strong, full of wisdom, and the grace of God was in Him.—51. And He went down with them, and came to Nazareth; and was subject to them.—52. And Jesus advanced in wisdom and age, and grace with God and men.

We now come to the hidden life. It is a sweet, tranquil time of holy obscurity, a life full of mystery and majesty, prolonged over thirty years.

### 1. THE OCCUPATIONS OF THIS LIFE

The apocryphal writings relate all sorts of wonderful deeds and occurrences as having filled up this period of our Saviour's life. What do the Gospels say? There we have only three features recorded of this life, and if we add two others which are suggested by its very nature, we have five elements which go to make up the whole of the hidden life.

In the first place, the life in Nazareth was certainly one of prayer. The Gospel does not mention this point in so many words, but it is a natural deduction from the history itself, and from the fact that the parents, according to the custom of pious Israelites, went every year to the Feast of the Pasch, and took with them the divine Child from the time that He had attained His twelfth year. Thus we may infer that true and great piety was practised in the Holy Family, and that the practice of prayer was constant, in the private devotions of the family as well as in attendance at divine service in the synagogue. In this matter above all things our Saviour had to set us an example. The spirit of prayer permeated the whole day's work, and sanctified it by the holy purpose and intention with which it was performed. And how often may not the Boy, the Youth, the Man Jesus have read aloud to His listening Mother from the Holy Scriptures!

Secondly, the hidden life was one of obedience. Holy Scripture lays particular stress upon this (Luke 2:51), a sign that His life was above all a life of obedience, and that of the most perfect kind. He was subject to His parents, and fulfilled their commands and wishes in every respect: exteriorly with great punctuality and perseverance, and with such ease, grace and joy, that they had not the slightest hesitation in giving Him an order; and interiorly with complete conformity of will and intellect, out of reverence for God, Whose representatives He saw in His parents. Yes, He practised obedience not merely occasionally, and without ever resisting; but during this period of His life, as the Holy Scripture so clearly shows, His sole aim and desire was obedience and subjection. Obedience to His parents was not only the outward criterion of His life and work, but the aim and endeavor of His thoughts, wishes and plans, the circle in which His interior and exterior life moved. And yet, who were His superiors, and who was He? This view of obedience, and this interior disposition with regard to it, form certainly the most beautiful and wonderful trait in His life of subjection.

Thirdly, the hidden life was one of labor. The people of Nazareth knew Him as the son of Joseph the carpenter (Matt. 13:55), and as a carpenter Himself (Mark 6:3). He worked with His hands, and it was real labor, practical and serious, because by it He earned His bread; it was quite ordinary, exterior work, which was not even immediately directed towards promoting the honor of God, and called for no especial intellectual gifts; it was toil that demanded much exertion, toil in which His sacred, divine hands became hard and rough, and His face was browned by the sun; often too the sweat stood upon His forehead, and His breast heaved with exertion. It is true that manual labor, even the lowliest, was held in honor by the Jews, as is meet and right; so that even the son of the High Priest had to learn thoroughly some handicraft. But still, who can see without emotion the Son of God working thus to earn His bread, working at the humble trade of a carpenter?

Fourthly, the life in Nazareth was one of obscurity and deepest humility. How retired is the life of our Saviour, and how hidden it all is! The choice of the place of His abode favors this obscurity. Nazareth was quite a solitary corner in a ravine of the Galilean highlands, altogether insignificant and of no fame in the Old Covenant (John 1:46). It was distinguished only by its pure air and the beautiful views from its heights. His obscurity is intensified by the parents and relatives whom He chose for His own; for they do not seem to have occupied any public office even in Nazareth. His occupation aided His desire of concealment, because it was one in which no one had ever yet made a name for himself. Lastly, He conceals all that is remarkable in Himself. Who saw anything of the treasures of wisdom and power latent in Him? Who had any suspicion of the holiness that dwelt in Him? All this He conceals. When He made His appearance in

public life, no one knew anything of Him, except that He was
from Nazareth, and the son of Joseph and Mary. Even Nathanael,
who was from Cana, and thus lived only a few leagues off, had
heard nothing of Him. In truth, He "went down" to Nazareth
(Luke 2:51), to the deepest obscurity of humility and concealment. What might He not have done and accomplished during
this time for the glory of God and the salvation of the world? Did
His Heart, so full of love for God and man, never urge this thought
upon Him? And is not this a great mystery, thus to retire and apparently condemn Himself to inactivity in His youth, just when
the desire of action is so strong?

Lastly, the hidden life is one of progress and development. Holy
Scripture mentions this twice (Luke 2:40, 52). But what are we
to understand by this progress? This advance and growth is something external, being the gradual revelation (in harmony with
His growth in age) of the wisdom and holiness inherent in Him.
An internal increase of knowledge can be predicated only of His
natural and experimental knowledge, depending on the development of the faculties. From the first moment of His Conception
our Saviour had the full measure of supernatural knowledge,
grace, holiness and power. In all this He made no advance; He did
not merit for Himself, but only for us. The fulness of supernatural
knowledge and holiness, from the first moment of His life, was due
to Him as the Son of God; it was the endowment befitting His
rank. Further, He enjoyed from the moment of His Conception
the actual contemplation of God, and with this all holiness and
knowledge was given to Him in a still higher manner. Any actual
increase in grace and in the favor of God, if such were possible,
was not adapted to the exercise of His office as Redeemer. On the
contrary, the richer He was in knowledge and holiness, the better
He could fulfil that office. Thus our Saviour advanced ("grew")
only in the sense aforesaid. His body grew in grace and strength,
His powers developed and were exercised upon work suited to
His age, and His wisdom, insight and virtue were outwardly manifested in proportion to His advance in age and to His external
surroundings. Thus His advance and growth were beautiful, as
can be the case only with a child brought up under the most ad-
vantageous circumstances. This then was the manner of His life
until His thirtieth year. No fitter surroundings could be imagined
for such a life than the peace, simplicity and obscurity of Nazareth, utterly devoid of all that suggests the romance of greatness

or the wildness of the desert, but full of a gentle, grave charm. Nazareth is the very picture of an innocent, uneventful life.

### 2. THE DISPOSITIONS OF JESUS AMID THESE OCCUPATIONS

The dispositions in which He thus passed His life at Nazareth were as follows:

First, great interior and exterior peace. He did not go about complaining of His lot in life, brooding and longing for more useful occupation. He was tranquillity and contentment itself, outwardly and inwardly. Our Saviour was wise with that true wisdom which knows that there is only one absolutely necessary being, God; and that God to attain His ends has no need of His creatures, not even, strictly speaking, of the God-Man Himself.

Secondly, His disposition of mind was that of great endurance and courage. Not till He was thirty did God permit Him to enter on His active career; thus He had a long, long period of waiting. Our Saviour remained, therefore, twice as long as other children amid the surroundings of ordinary domestic life, in the position of childlike subjection, dependence and obscurity. Only the smallest part of His life was allotted to His public career as the God-Man.

Thirdly, His dispositions with regard to His daily occupations, so mean apparently in themselves, were those of great reverence and esteem. It was all God's Will, the business of His Heavenly Father, and that was reason enough to do it with holy care, zeal and love. In this respect it was the same thing to Him whether He worked a miracle, instituted the Sacraments, or made a plow-share. All were to Him equally the Will of God, and therefore holy (John 8:29; Ps. 72:23).

Lastly, He did all with a very interior spirit, offering His actions for the glory of God and the great work of Redemption, and crowning them with bright gems of beautiful interior virtues.

### 3. MOTIVES FOR PURSUING THESE OCCUPATIONS

There were two principal motives animating this life.

The first motive was God, submission to God's Will. Our Saviour evidently wished to give us a great and very important lesson. From a natural point of view, we think we are living and working only when we do what pleases us, in other words what corresponds to our passions, our self-will, our ambition, covet-ousness and sensuality. But this is not the right view. The whole scheme of life is that we should do what God wills. To do God's Will is the whole man and the whole life (Eccl. 12:13). This is the great example set us by our Saviour. One needs only to have the spirit of faith, and then the Will of God, be it what it may, is great, holy, wise and beautiful enough, not merely to satisfy us, but also to make us perfectly happy. He who does what God wills, does enough, and he whom God knows, is famous enough. As a matter of fact, many events occurred in the political and religious world during the years of this hidden life. But what procured God more honor, and upon whom did He look with greater complacency than upon His Son amid His simple occupations in the quiet of Nazareth? For this reason we are told that "the grace of God was with Him" (Luke 2:40).

The second motive was consideration for us. Our Divine Saviour gives us in His hidden life the example of an ordinary Christian career, and lays the foundation of all personal and social progress, of all private and public welfare. This foundation consists precisely in the occupations of the hidden life. Our welfare consists in doing the Will of God, which is expressed in the commandments of God and the Church. It consists also in prayer and in the fulfilment of our religious duties towards God, because all blessing, all merit, and all perseverance in the fulfilment of our duties come from prayer. Again, our welfare is based on obedience. By obedience we honor God in His representatives; we bring to Him the most costly of sacrifices, that of our will; we practise the highest and most beautiful virtues, faith, trust, humility, self-abnegation. Obedience is altogether God's ordinance, and he who forsakes obedience forsakes God's ordinance. Thus everything outside God Himself is subject to obedience. It is to make this obedience more meritorious, tolerable and easy, that our Saviour leads for so long a time a life of obedience and subjection. Another foundation of all welfare is work. Work is holy, because it is God's law and sanctified by the example of Christ; it sanctifies, because it atones for sin, prevents sin, and gains us eternal merit for heaven; it has a special saving influence both in the kingdom of Christ and in the world at large, because, by preventing sin, it stays the avenging hand of God, procures well-being and furthers progress, conditions which are necessary to the existence of Christ's kingdom. The example of Christ makes work, even menial and common work, a source of temporal and eternal progress and welfare. Lastly, the foundation of all well-being is humility, which holds in check inordinate striving after greatness and honor. Ambition may be an enemy of all happiness. If unrestrained, it makes us untruthful, unhappy, vain and ridiculous, and ruins our character and virtue. It is in society often the enemy of peace and charity, the cause of swindling, agitation and social disturbances in civic, political and religious circles; in the course of history many revolutions and heresies have proceeded from it.

We understand now why He led for so long a time a life of obscurity, labor and obedience. He had something much more important to do than to hurry through the world and preach the Gospel. He had first Himself to practise the Gospel that He preached later on, and to build up human society from the very basis upon the right foundations. This He does in His hidden life. It is the Gospel of ordinary social life. Because humility is the foundation of every virtue, and because the greater part of mankind passes its life in these circumstances and has to merit heaven in them, our Saviour also, because He is the Redeemer of all, passes His life in these occupations. He did not seek Himself, but the will of God. So this hidden life is not lost. It is an important part of His work of Redemption. He lived not only for God, but also for us. He is here really the "Hidden God and Saviour" (Isa. 45:15). We must thank Him for this with all our hearts, and we must take from it the lesson that one never lives more for the general good than when one serves God and does His Will.

## Mary and the Youthful Life of Jesus

Luke 2:19. But Mary kept all these words, pondering them in her heart.— 51. And his mother kept all these words in her heart.

We cannot quit the youthful life of Jesus without touching upon the position and relations of Mary to it.

### 1. Mary's Relation to the Youthful Life of Jesus

Mary's relation to the youthful life of Jesus was entirely that of a mother, and she spent herself, according to Holy Scripture, in a double service, exterior and interior.

The exterior service consisted in waiting upon, tending and bringing up the Divine Child. Holy Scripture contains only one sentence with regard to this service; namely that Mary wrapped the new-born Child in swaddling-clothes, and laid Him in the manger (Luke 2:7). All the rest is to be read between the lines, and is a matter of course. The Saviour was a true human child, and it was His will to grow up under the same circumstances as we do; and Mary was His true Mother, and therefore did for Him all that a mother does for her child. The life of them both is a true human life like our own, measured according to the standard of time and circumstances. The childhood and youth of Jesus are related in Holy Scripture in few words, but in reality they occupied days, weeks, months and years with their homely office of nursing, tending, feeding, carrying and dressing, just as is the case with us. All this Mary did for the Divine Child; and how? In the first place, with great and untiring care, day and night. No nurse of a royal child could be so devoted to her high-born charge as was Mary. In the next place, she did it with great skill. As her ancestor David once fed and conducted by the skilfulness of his hands the people entrusted to him (Ps. 77:72), so this wise Virgin and Mother nursed and tended the Son of her heart with no less wisdom and judgment. Lastly, she did it with such love and tenderness, and at the same time such reverence, as was due to her Child, her God and Redeemer. It is a beautiful and certainly a true thought, that God put into Mary's heart all the love and tenderness that the human race owed to the Saviour. She regarded herself as the representative of mankind in this royal service, like the priest when he offers sacrifice, and assuredly no priest handles the holy Body of Christ with such reverence and love as Mary did. And there were other circumstances which rendered this attendance upon the Child much more direct and personal. In the first place, the poverty of the family, which scarcely admitted of the service of strange hands; then, too, the various journeys, the discomforts of Bethlehem, and the misery of exile. Thus it came about that Mary was, and had to be, everything to the Child, nurse, waiting-maid, companion; she bore Him in her arms, and pillowed Him on her breast. What a happy, faithful nurse and mother had our Saviour in Mary!

But so far we have dealt only with the outward service. Her interior, spiritual service was far more precious. Twice the Holy Scripture makes a special and emphatic mention of this: "But Mary kept all these words, pondering them in her heart" (Luke 2:19, 51). This service then consisted in the spiritual activity and sympathy with which Mary accompanied the mysteries of our

Saviour's youth. This activity is threefold. First, she observed and followed all these mysteries attentively, and lived them through with Him. Secondly, she imprinted them deep in her heart and mind, and reflected them in her words and actions. Sometimes, when we hear or read a beautiful poem or song, we wish to possess it, copy it and learn it by heart, in order to enjoy it again and take pleasure in it. Mary did something of this sort. Where could these mysteries and events have found a better and safer resting-place or have been preserved in fresher and more vivid remembrance, than in the heart of the mother? What is more susceptible and retentive than a mother's heart? Thirdly, she retained these mysteries only in order to think over and consider them again and again. They were the subject of her meditations in the quiet hours when she gave full play to her thoughts, in prayer, sitting at the Holy Child's crib, or working near the youthful Saviour. She spun continually at the golden thread of these mysteries, and began again and again with new delight; she compared them one with another, tried to comprehend them in their height and breadth and extent, to fathom them in their depth and sublimity, and to follow them out in their wonderful connection.

Mary had before her the living center and expression of her loving thoughts. She saw God's countenance in the face of her Child. She could contemplate it now for years, daily and hourly; she could see it in childhood, in the beauty of boyhood, in the serious cheerfulness of ripening manhood, in the apparent unconsciousness of childish slumber, or lighted up with heartfelt love and heavenly wisdom, in the ecstasy of contemplation. She could gaze upon this countenance till she knew it, so to speak, by heart (Faber). In this countenance all God's mysteries were revealed to her; the Divinity in humanity, infinity and eternity in this span of life, omnipotence and majesty in weakness and helplessness, the unspeakable Word in speechlessness, the joy of the whole creation in sorrow, tears and persecution. She could follow up to her heart's content the beautiful mystery of His growth; she could see how His face grew broader and longer, the features becoming more set and expressive, the cheeks taking on a deeper tinge, His hair darkening; she could see how He passed on ever to more perfect work; how His heavenly wisdom revealed itself more and more, seeming always more lovable when the conversation turned upon God and divine things; and, oh joy for a mother! she could watch how in His every feature and gesture He day by day presented some new and touching resemblance to herself. And how did she accompany these precious observations in her heart? She adored all these manifestations of His Divinity and humanity; she adored everything in Him, and hallowed thus, as it were, all devotions to the God-Man by her participation in them; everything in Him was to her a motive for praise, for admiration, for love, for reverent joy and rapture. She well knew that she represented heaven and earth in her adoration and love, as well as in her outward services. We had our place too in her prayers. Unceasingly she offered herself to Jesus for us, offered us to Jesus, and offered Jesus to His Father for us (Faber). These were the services that Mary rendered our Saviour, and the occupations of the thirty blissful years of peaceful sojourn with Him in Nazareth; occupations of immeasurable depth, unspeakable value and incalculable perfection, and yet they left undisturbed the quiet calm of the life at Nazareth.

## 2. MARY'S USE OF HER OPPORTUNITIES

Mary made use of her unique relation to the Saviour in a twofold manner: first for herself, and then for us.

For herself Mary made use of her intercourse with our Saviour for her own sanctification. It may well be that one reason among others, why our Saviour remained so long at Nazareth, was to perfect His holy Mother. After God, then, the chief fruit of this life of Jesus falls to Mary's share, and rightly. Mary is the highest and most sublime of God's creatures; she stands the nearest to our Saviour. No one understood Him better, or made a more abundant and magnificent return for the time and attention He bestowed upon her. With her the harvest was always a hundredfold. The Childhood of Jesus was for Mary a third and quite extraordinary epoch of grace. The first began with her Immaculate Conception, the second with the Incarnation, the third with the Birth and hidden life of Jesus. Indeed, every glance at the Divine Child was a new revelation of God, all contact with Him an interior sanctification and increase in purity, every word, every gesture, every look of His a new grace. If one glance of Jesus did so much at the calling of the Apostles, and with Peter; if one conversation with Him so often decided the salvation of a soul; if one touch of His healed the sick and raised the dead to life: what a power of sanctification there must have been in living together

with Him for years, in the daily sight of Him, in the sweet conversations with Him, in the thousand little attentions and kind
offices which she, as His Mother, bestowed upon Him, and which
in their reaction deposited new treasures of grace and holiness in
the heart of the Immaculate Mother! Ever as time went on did she
become more enveloped in the holiness of Jesus. She was to Him
a beautiful world in which He was always at work, and where His
graces of redemption and His designs as God and Creator had
the most signal triumphs. Erstwhile the beauty of this Paradise
had enticed Him from the bosom of the Father; how marvelous
must it have been after the work of thirty years! If our Saviour
by His earthly sojourn had accomplished nothing but the sanctification of His Mother, His coming would have been justified and
repaid beyond measure.

But Mary used her privileges on our behalf also: not, it is true,
by proclaiming our Lord's advent, for that was the work of others,
the Apostles; but in thinking of us, recommending us to our
Lord, and offering Him for us; and later on in a special manner,
when the time came to record and set forth in Holy Writ the
material object of our faith. Divine facts are the object of our
faith, and these facts, according to God's ordinance, are confirmed by witnesses and handed down to posterity. The Apostles
and other contemporaries of the public ministry of Jesus were able
to bear witness to many of the deeds and events of His life; but
for the greater part of it, and for the most important facts, there
was but one witness, and that was Mary. Through the long and
studied retirement and obscurity of Jesus, His life had completely
escaped the world's notice. When the Evangelists undertook to
write His life, there were no eyewitnesses of our Lord's Nativity
living except Mary, and absolutely no one save herself could have
given testimony of the Incarnation and the conversation of the
angel with her. And without the knowledge of these facts what
would the life of Jesus be, but a building without foundations, a
stream of which the source is known to no one? Mary, then,
contributed this precious addition to the mysteries of our faith,
and such was the outcome of her exceptional relation to the Childhood of Jesus. We owe to her the knowledge of this Childhood,
just as we owe to her the Child Jesus Himself. St. Luke may very
possibly have sat at her feet, have heard from her lips those touching incidents of the youth of Jesus which he has recorded in his
Gospel. He seems even to avow it, by noting on two occasions

that Mary had kept all these things in her heart, as though he wished thereby to indicate the source of his information.

### 3. CONCLUSIONS

From what has been said it follows, first, that not only must we honor Mary for the holiness which she acquired by her daily intimacy with Jesus, but also thank her with all our hearts for the great services she rendered to our Saviour and to us. For us it was that she brought forth the Saviour, reared Him, offered Him countless times to the Heavenly Father. Pharao's daughter did no more than to adopt the infant Moses as her son, and had him brought up by another; with her own hands Mary nourished, clothed and tended the Saviour. We owe to her the real, true, living Saviour. And to her also we owe in a mystic sense the Saviour as He is portrayed for us in the Holy Scriptures, at least what we know of Him in the charming history of His Childhood. Mary has become not only the Mother but also the Evangelist of our Saviour. We owe to Mary, then, the charming lessons, the sweet consolations and childlike joys that we draw from reading and meditating on this gracious Childhood of Jesus. They come from her. She has preserved and stored away these treasures in her virginal heart; and of her bounty she has distributed them to us. The beginning and source of the apostolic tradition of the life of Jesus has its springs in the heart of Mary. May she ever be thanked and praised for it!

The second conclusion is that we must imitate Mary in the occupations of her hidden life. She had this inestimable advantage, that she lived with the Saviour and, as His Mother, could and was bound to tend Him, so that her interior and exterior life had the Saviour for its direct object. This is a privilege which St. Joseph alone was permitted to share with her. But we too can enjoy this advantage to a certain extent, if we make it our favorite employment to think often and gladly of our Saviour and His life, to picture Him to ourselves in some mystery, to apply it to our day's work, and to conform ourselves to His example, inwardly and outwardly. This is an occupation of great value, peculiarly well-pleasing to God, similar to Mary's occupation, and of the greatest utility to us, either for acquiring the spirit of joy or for laying up treasures of merit. This is the way in which we may keep and ponder in our hearts the mysteries of Jesus. And who knows if it will not be of utility to others also? The mysteries of the Childhood and hidden life are of especial importance, for this very reason that there are found the main elements of our ordinary daily life, in the practice of prayer, work and obedience. Here in very deed we catch the fragrance of the interior life. One cannot approach these mysteries without inhaling their subtle perfume; and we must often return to them in order to be penetrated and sanctified by their spirit.

## II. THE PUBLIC LIFE OF JESUS

### A. Proximate Preparation for the Public Life

#### From the Appearance of John the Baptist Till the First Celebration of the Pasch

The time had now come for the Saviour to leave His retirement and begin His public ministry. But this too was a gradual process, and was not done without preparation.

This preparation was to be marked by two epochs. The instrument for the first epoch had long been ready, and only waited for the call. It was St. John the Baptist, who, chosen and consecrated for this preparation from his mother's womb (Luke 1:17), awaited in the wilderness the signal to begin his mission. This moment had now come. John made his appearance, and worked wonders by his words and virtue. Our Lord Himself marked the second epoch of the preparation, by showing Himself to the Baptist and to His first disciples, revealing and bearing witness of Himself, arousing their faith, confirming it by working for the first time a great miracle, and thus entering upon His public career.

The period from the appearance of St. John till the first celebration of the Pasch is the time of this preparation. It embraces the first preparatory activity of St. John, the Baptism of Jesus, His sojourn in the desert, the first calling of the disciples, and the first public miracle at Cana.

#### Appearance and Preaching of St. John. His First Testimony to Christ

Luke 3:1. Now in the fifteenth year of the reign of Tiberius Caesar, Pontius Pilate being governor of Judaea, and Herod being tetrarch of Galilee, and Philip his brother tetrarch of Ituraea and the country of Trachonitis, and Lysanias tetrarch of Abilina,—2. Under the high priests Annas and Caiphas, the word of the Lord was made unto John the son of Zachary in the desert.—3. And he came into all the country about the Jordan, preaching the baptism of penance for the remission of sins;—4. As it was written in the book of the sayings of Isaias the prophet: "The voice of one crying in the wilderness: Prepare ye the way of the Lord, make straight his path;—5. Every valley shall be filled; and every mountain and hill shall be brought low; and the crooked shall be made straight, and the rough ways plain;— 6. And all flesh shall see the salvation of God."—7. He said therefore to the multitudes that went forth to be baptized by him: "Ye offspring of vipers, who hath shown you to flee from the wrath to come?—8. Bring forth therefore fruits worthy of penance, and do not begin to say: We have Abraham for our father. For I say unto you, that God is able of these stones to raise up children to Abraham.—9. For now the axe is laid to the root of the trees. Every tree therefore that bringeth not forth good fruit, shall be cut down and cast into the fire." 10. And the people asked him, saying: "What then shall we do?"—11. And he answering, said to them: "He that hath two coats, let him give to him that hath none; and he that hath meat, let him do in like manner."—12. And the publicans also came to be baptized, and said to him: "Master, what shall we do?"—13. But he said to them: "Ask nothing more than that which is appointed you."—14. And the soldiers also asked him, saying: "And what shall we do?" And he said to them: "Do violence to no man, neither calumniate any man; and be content with your pay."—15. And as the people was of opinion, and all were thinking in their hearts of John, that perhaps he might be the Christ:—16. John answered, saying unto all: "I indeed baptize you with water; but there shall come one mightier than I, the latchet of whose shoes I am not worthy to loose; he shall baptize you with the Holy Ghost and with fire.—17. Whose fan is in his hand, and he will purge his floor, and will gather the wheat into his barn; but the chaff he will burn with unquenchable fire."—18. And many other things exhorting did he preach to the people.

MARK 1:1. The beginning of the Gospel of Jesus Christ the Son of God.—2. As it is written in Isaias the prophet: "Behold I send my angel before thy face, who shall prepare the way before thee.—3. A voice of one crying in the desert: Prepare ye the way of the Lord, make straight his paths."—4. John was in the desert baptizing, and preaching the baptism of penance unto remission of sins.—5. And there went out to him all the country of Judaea, and all they of Jerusalem, and were baptized by him in the river of Jordan, confessing their sins.—6. And John was clothed with camel's-hair, and a leathern girdle about his loins; and he ate locusts and wild honey. And he preached, saying:—7. "There cometh after me one mightier than I, the latchet of whose shoes I am not worthy to stoop down and loose.—8. I have baptized you with water; but he shall baptize you with the Holy Ghost."

MATT. 3:1. And in those days cometh John the Baptist preaching in the desert of Judaea,—2. And saying: "Do penance; for the kingdom of heaven is at hand." —3. For this is he that was spoken of by Isaias the prophet, saying: "The voice of one crying in the desert: Prepare ye the way of the Lord, make straight his paths."—4. And the same John had his garment of camel's-hair, and a leathern girdle about his loins; and his meat was locusts and wild honey.—5. Then went out to him Jerusalem and all Judaea, and all the country about Jordan;—6. And were baptized by him in the Jordan confessing their sins.—7. And seeing many of the Pharisees and Sadducees coming to his baptism, he said to them: "Ye brood of vipers, who hath shown you to flee from the wrath to come?—8. Bring forth therefore fruit worthy of penance.—9. And think not to say within yourselves: We have Abraham for our father; for I tell you that God is able of these stones to raise up children to Abraham.—10. For now the axe is laid to the root of the trees. Every tree therefore that doth not yield good fruit, shall be cut down, and cast into the fire.—11. I indeed baptize you in water unto penance; but he that shall come after me, is mightier than I, whose shoes I am not worthy to bear; he shall baptize you in the Holy Ghost and fire.—12. Whose fan is in his hand, and he will thoroughly cleanse his floor, and gather his wheat into the barn; but the chaff he will burn with unquenchable fire."

## 1. CIRCUMSTANCES OF JOHN'S APPEARANCE

When St. John the Baptist began his public mission, the Emperor Tiberius had reached the fifteenth year of his reign (i.e. dating the reign of Tiberius from the period of his association with Augustus as joint Emperor, A.D. 12), Pontius Pilate was governor of Judaea and Samaria, while the tetrarchs, Herod (Antipas), Philip and Lysanias, were ruling over the other provinces of Palestine. The High Priests at that time were Annas and Caiphas (Luke 3:1, 2). These circumstances give us at once the key to the political, religious and moral situation. Judaea and Samaria belonged to the Roman Empire, no longer merely as a confederate state, but as an actual Roman province. The world-wide power of Rome was thus brought into immediate contact with the Messias, and had to take up a decisive position with regard to Him, as later events proved. The political differences and divided jurisdiction in the country increased the universal discontent, and thus in one way rendered the ministry of our Saviour more difficult, whilst facilitating it in another. But the climax of the evil was the illegal joint-rule of Annas and Caiphas, who, successively installed and deposed by the Romans, dominated the religious life of the nation in an unworthy alliance (Luke 3:2); the one as head of the priesthood, the other perhaps as president of the Great Council (cf. Introd., p. 11). A yet further evil was the existence of numerous sects and factions, which are seen to take an active part at the very first appearance of John (cf. Introd., p. 11).—It was at this time of general corruption and misery, when everyone was looking with longing eyes for a deliverer, that John appeared as the harbinger of salvation.

The place chosen for his appearance was no town or inhabited district, but the desert, i.e. the wide tract of pasture and prairie land on the banks of the Lower Jordan (cf. Introd., p. 5). John never left the desert. He drew the people out to him there. He needed the water of the Jordan to baptize with, and so he went at God's command to these districts, and began to preach. The rugged aspect of the place and its historical associations lent yet greater power to his words, which were borne far and wide by the travelers on the great road that passed close by. The whole region was full of memories of the past, and called up to the minds of his hearers how their forefathers had crossed the Jordan to enter the Promised Land, how in sadness it had been repeatedly crossed again on their way to captivity and how joyfully on their return. It was from the Jordan, also, that the Messias was to come (Isa. 40:3).

For nearly thirty years John had been preparing himself for his mission in complete isolation, in prayer and austere penance; and now, at the express command of God (Luke 3:2), he entered upon it. Everything in this vocation is divine, time, place and occasion; it has in it nothing of self-will.

## 2. APPEARANCE AND MINISTRY OF ST. JOHN

The object of St. John's ministry was, in general, to prepare for the coming of the Lord (Isa. 40:3; Mal. 3:1; Luke 1:17, 76; John 1:31). But this preparation was to be accomplished in particular by the preaching of penance and of faith in Christ. Such was the scope of his work.

His appearance and ministry corresponded perfectly to this. He preached penance like the prophets (Jer. 3:21–25; Ez. 18:31, 32; Dan. 9:3–5; Mich. 7:9), in the first place by his very exterior and manner of life, which displayed extreme poverty, mortification and austerity (Matt. 3:4; Mark 1:6); indeed, it exhibited all the asceticism of the ancient prophets, and of Elias in particular (IV Kings 1:8). He preached penance secondly by his words (Matt. 3:2; Mark 1:4; Luke 3:3). Moreover, in order to arouse and to give expression to this spirit of penance, he practised an unusual ceremony, namely the baptism of water. This baptism was neither a sacrament nor a sacramental of the Old Covenant, but an unusual rite which John performed at God's command (Luke 3:3; Mark 1:4; Matt. 3:6; John 1:33), and which formed the characteristic feature of his ministry. For this reason he is called simply "the Baptist," and his whole mission "the baptism of John" (John 1:25; Matt. 21:25). That a washing with water denoted a purification from sin was already known to the people from many of the ceremonies of the law; but baptism, or plunging into water, as a sign of purification of the whole man, combined with confession of sins, was quite new, and also humiliating to the Jews. As a motive for penance John gives the coming of the "kingdom of heaven" (Matt. 3:2), the kingdom of God or Messianic

kingdom, which all expected, which the prophets had proclaimed
(Isa. 42:1; Jer. 3:13; Ez. 11:16; Soph. 3:8; Dan. 2:44; 7:13), and
which is really "heavenly" and divine as regards its origin, aim
and means. Sin had destroyed the kingdom of God in men; penance would prepare for and establish it anew in their hearts. The
unprepared state of the people was strikingly typified by the desert
in which John preached, and it is in allusion to its rugged unfitness
to be the road of an approaching king that he exhorts them to
level and make straight the paths (John 1:23).

St. John fitted his preaching to the needs of the various classes
of his hearers. He sternly rebuked the factious Pharisees and
Sadducees (Matt. 3:7; Luke 3:7), who probably only came to
him in order to gain the favor of the people, or with some malicious intent towards himself. "Offspring of vipers," he justly calls
them, thus summing up in a word their whole character and their
spiteful, malicious, insinuating and intolerant spirit, which they
passed on from generation to generation. He thus points out also
their peculiar sin of presumptuous reliance upon their carnal
descent from Abraham. This presumption, refusing every change
of disposition, demanded salvation not as a grace but as its due.
He exhorts them in powerful and striking figures of speech to true
penance, warning them that mere blood-relationship is nothing
before God, and that severe, sure and speedy judgment awaits the
whole nation and each individual, if they let the last moment of
grace pass away unheeded (Luke 3:7-9; Matt. 3:7-10). He had
before him the sects in their last degeneracy (cf. Introd., p. 12).
On the other hand, John treated with great mildness the people,
the publicans and the soldiers, who, pierced to the heart by his
preaching, presented themselves for baptism (Luke 3:10-14). Of
the publicans and soldiers many certainly were heathens. He required of them only works of charity (Luke 3:11), justice (Luke
3:13), mildness and moderation (Luke 3:14); that is to say,
merely the observance of the natural law.

But John also prepares the way for Christ by preaching faith in
Him, belief in His near approach and in the majesty of His Person. The opinion of the people that John himself was the Messias
gave him the immediate occasion for this. He corrects this opinion and bears a threefold testimony to Christ. First, he bears witness to the coming of the Messias (Luke 3:16; Mark 1:7; Matt.
3:11). Secondly, to His greatness and glory, in comparison with
which he humbles himself to the dust. He is not worthy, he de-

clares, to bear the shoes of the Teacher Who is coming (Matt. 3:11), or, kneeling, to loose His shoe-latchet (Mark 1:7). His mission too is far inferior to that of the Messias. John administers only the baptism of water unto penance (Mark 1:4), which of itself bestows no interior sanctity, but acts only like a sacramental, whereas Christ baptizes with fire and with the Holy Ghost; that is to say, His baptism does not merely cleanse exteriorly like water, but like fire changes the very substance, by interior sanctification and by the communication of the Holy Spirit. Perhaps the pictures of Christ's baptism and of the day of Pentecost may have floated before John's mind. Thirdly, he bears witness to Christ's relations to the Old Covenant, and to His Divine Nature; for He is the Judge, indeed the Lord of the "threshing-floor," i.e. the kingdom of God, which embraces not only Israel but the whole world; the wheat is His; He sifts it, and as Judge delivers over the chaff to the "unquenchable fire" (Matt. 13:37, 41); and He is truly God, because He imparts the Holy Ghost (Isa. 44:3; Joel 2:28). Thus, then, John prepared the way for Christ.

### 3. RESULTS OF ST. JOHN'S PREACHING

The results of John's preaching were wonderful indeed, and were evident throughout the whole land, in Judaea (Mark 1:5; Matt. 3:5, 6) as well as in Galilee (Matt. 11:8). All classes alike were influenced by it: priests and people, publicans and soldiers, Gentiles and Israelites. Drawn by the compelling power of his wonderful personality, they went to him, confessed their sins, and received baptism. One sect alone, the Pharisees, held coldly aloof; they had drawn back after John's crushing address to them (Luke 7:30; 20:5). For nearly 400 years no prophet had arisen. Malachias was the last, and he had prophesied concerning John. Thus St. John's appearance influenced the people in a remarkable manner, not in consequence of any miracles worked by him, but by the power of his very appearance, his words and virtues, so that he was even thought to be the Messias.

Regarded under another aspect, the personality and ministry of St. John and the effects produced thereby become a type of Christ and of His whole kingdom. In the Forerunner himself we see the good, healthful tendency of the Old Covenant in its austere virtue and seclusion, its insufficiency in itself and its longing desire of Christ, for Whom it was to prepare the way. But the degeneracy of the Old Covenant is equally apparent. In the Pharisees and Sadducees the cankering wound is laid bare; and in their repellent attitude to the Forerunner and prophet of Christ we see the first beginnings of the opposition to which Christ and the Baptist were both to fall victims, and which would bring about the ruin of these sects themselves, as John foretold to them. Important outlines of the ministry and work of Christ are here likewise apparent. The first is the testimony of His coming and of its significance, His dignity as the Messias, and His Divinity. Secondly, we have the institution of baptism, which is here only a type, but will later on become one of the chief Sacraments of the Church. Lastly, there is in the indulgent reception of sinners, publicans and heathens a touching resemblance between John and Christ, which seems almost a prophecy of the future favors to be granted to the Gentile world. Thus the words of the angel, that John would be great before the Lord, would go before Him and prepare for Him a perfect people (Luke 1:15, 17), were already for the most part fulfilled.

## The Baptism of Jesus

MATT. 3:13. Then cometh Jesus from Galilee to the Jordan unto John, to be baptized by him.—14. But John stayed him, saying: "I ought to be baptized by thee, and comest thou to me?"—15. And Jesus answering, said to him: "Suffer it to be so now; for so it becometh us to fulfil all justice." Then he suffered him.—16. And Jesus being baptized, forthwith came out of the water; and lo, the heavens were opened to him; and he saw the Spirit of God descending as a dove, and coming upon him.—17. And behold a voice from heaven, saying: "This is my beloved Son, in whom I am well pleased."

MARK 1:9. And it came to pass in those days, Jesus came from Nazareth of Galilee, and was baptized by John in the Jordan.—10. And forthwith coming up out of the water, he saw the heavens opened, and the Spirit as a dove descending, and remaining on him.—11. And there came a voice from heaven: "Thou art my beloved Son, in thee I am well pleased."

LUKE 3:21. Now it came to pass, when all the people was baptized, that Jesus also being baptized and praying, heaven was opened:—22. And the Holy Ghost descended in a bodily shape as a dove upon him; and a voice came from heaven: "Thou art my beloved Son, in thee I am well pleased."

### 1. OUR SAVIOUR LEAVES NAZARETH

The movement among the people had made such progress that our Saviour considered it time to reveal Himself to them. He therefore quitted Nazareth.

This parting was naturally no small sacrifice to Him. He left a comfortable home, a regular occupation, simple habits of life; He left His holy Mother, who was so dear and congenial to Him,

and with whom He effected so much. She remained behind alone,
and must have felt the separation deeply. On the other hand, He
was about to enter upon an unsettled and painful mode of life, in
which much of the time would be spent in the company of the
unjust and imperfect.

But He went, not to return. And for what reasons? The apostolic
vocation requires this complete detachment from home and from
ties of flesh and blood, for the sake of example, for the completeness of the sacrifice, and in order to gain strength and freedom of
action. He Himself made grave demands upon His disciples in
this respect later on (Luke 9:59 seq.; 14:33). He wished to set the
example Himself, and at the same time to make our sacrifice meritorious and easy. The Mother had thus a share in the apostolic
work of her Son.

And how did He take leave? Surely after having first prepared
His Mother for it, and after she had made the sacrifice willingly
and generously. The farewell itself was loving, affectionate, sorrowful, and yet so quiet, tempered by humility, unselfishness and
ardent love towards God and men.

So our Lord departed to found His kingdom. No potentate of
this earth ever set out upon such an undertaking, and in such a
manner, without retinue or pomp, alone, poor, and unknown;
He had only His Divinity and Humanity, joined with the power of
poverty, suffering and death. We find His thoughts and feelings
on this departure foreshadowed by Isaias: "The Lord God hath
opened my ear, and I do not resist; I have not gone back. . . .
The Lord God is my helper, therefore am I not confounded;
therefore have I set my face as a most hard rock, and I know that
I shall not be confounded. He is near That justifieth me; Who
will contend with me? . . . Behold the Lord God is my helper
. . . Who is there among you that feareth the Lord . . . that
hath walked in darkness? . . . Let him hope in the name of the
Lord, and lean upon his God" (Isa. 50:5–10).

## 2. OUR SAVIOUR IS BAPTIZED BY JOHN

Our Saviour directed His steps to the Jordan, where John was
baptizing and preaching. According to tradition, it was the spot
beyond the Lower Jordan, not far from Jericho, where the Israelites had crossed the river. Here, under the influence of John, was
manifested a most ardent longing for the coming of the Messias.
It was to this spot, therefore, that Jesus came to be baptized.

And why did our Lord wish to receive baptism from John? First, in order to ratify the whole mission of the Forerunner, and especially his baptism, as a type of Christian baptism (Luke 20:4). It was also in order to sanctify, honor and reward him for his fidelity, zeal, and great unselfishness. John had never come to the Saviour (John 1:31); now our Lord comes to him. Secondly, our Saviour wished on this occasion to be revealed to the people and inaugurated in His ministry by God. Thirdly, He intended to set us an example of humility and childlike readiness to make use of all the means of salvation temporarily ordained by God, even if they are not strictly enjoined. Our Saviour specifies this reason Himself (Matt. 3:15). The baptism of penance was one of these means, and the Will of God, that it should be employed, applied (as a counsel, though not as a strict command) to the whole nation (Luke 3:21; John 1:33). The God-Man had become as one of the people, and had hitherto subjected Himself to the whole law; now He wished also to receive baptism. It is well worthy of note that the first public act of Jesus is an act of un-fathomable humility, self-abasement and penance. Fourthly, our Lord intended thereby to typify in Himself Christian baptism, and so to encourage all men to its reception by His example. Christ could not receive His own baptism, because it was not yet insti-tuted, and because, as the origin of this Sacrament, He already possessed all the graces that it imparts. But He could receive the typical baptism which John administered, because this was only a confession of truth and a means of penance. For Christ stands here as a representative and model of the whole human race doing penance and sanctifying itself. For this reason He had Himself baptized and thereby invites all to receive His baptism.

How then did the baptism take place? Let us picture to our-selves the meeting, the actual baptism, and the dispositions by which it was accompanied on both sides. With John, what reverence! What a childlike joy this austere man felt at seeing the Messias, Whom he foreshadowed! Then his surprise, humility and confusion, that the Saviour comes to him, listens to his preaching, and presents Himself for baptism! It was probably by this humility also that he recognized our Lord. Lastly, we must not overlook the childlike simplicity with which St. John performs the act, since the Saviour wishes it. And on the other hand, what esteem our Saviour must have felt for His great and glorious Fore-runner (Matt. 11:11), what pleasure at his simplicity, and what affection towards this faithful, unselfish heart! Whilst John, trembling with reverence, performs the baptism, our Saviour baptizes his soul with a flood of heavenly graces; and the God-Man Himself pours out before His Heavenly Father acts of all those virtues which such an event would naturally call forth. Therefore we are told that He prayed (Luke 3:21).

### 3. THE SAVIOUR IS REVEALED

As our Saviour came out of the water, visible signs appeared in the heavens above Him. The sky was opened, i.e. some unusual atmospheric phenomenon was seen; the Holy Ghost descended upon Him in the shape of a dove of dazzling whiteness, and a voice was heard saying: "This is My beloved Son, in Whom I am well pleased" (Matt. 3:17; Mark 1:10; Luke 3:21, 22; John 1:32).

The signification of these signs was, first, a revelation of the Saviour, more glorious and solemn than any ever hitherto vouchsafed; for the Most Holy Trinity Itself bore clear testimony to His Divinity before all the people. Secondly, the apparition was a reward of our Saviour's humility, concealment, obedience, and submission at His baptism. One is never nearer exaltation than when being humiliated for God. Thirdly, these heavenly signs are the solemn authorization of Jesus for His public ministry as Prophet, Priest, and King, and the official inauguration of this ministry. All this lies in the solemn declaration that He is the true Son of God. What He teaches, institutes and suffers, is well pleasing to God, and God's Will. For this reason too the Holy Ghost, Who confers and inaugurates every ecclesiastical office, appears. The Saviour baptizes in the Holy Ghost, because the latter proceeds from Him and is the same divine Nature and has been so from all eternity. Lastly, the revelation of Christ, together with His baptism, is also a revelation and foundation of the Sacrament of baptism; and above all it establishes its necessity. Henceforth baptism is to be used as a means of salvation (John 3:5, 22; 4:1; Matt. 28:19). Many even maintain that this baptism of Christ was the institution of the Sacrament of Baptism, at all events as regards the actual ceremony itself. The universal obligation of baptism was imposed later on (Matt. 28:19; Mark 16:15, 16; cf. John 3:5). Further, the essentials of the baptismal rite were here prefigured by the water and the revelation of the Most Holy Trinity, the confession of which is an essential part of the formula of baptism. Finally, the effects of this Sacrament are indicated:

viz. the cleansing from sin, by immersion or washing; the interior sanctification in grace, by the descent of the Holy Ghost; the adoption as children of God with Christ and in Christ, by the voice of the Father; and the title to heaven, by the opening of the heavens. What took place perceptibly in Christ's case, takes place invisibly in the case of everyone who receives baptism, although not in the same manner. Since the world of sanctified souls was to proceed from Christ through baptism, therefore the Holy Ghost descends upon Him at His baptism, as He had once hovered over the waters in order that the beautiful visible world might proceed from them.

Thus the baptism of Christ is a great and sublime mystery. It is the most solemn revelation of His Divinity, in the midst of His humility and abasement. It is the culminating point of John's ministry, the prefiguration of the baptism of the Church and of the whole human race. For this reason the holy Fathers say that Christ submerged the whole world in the Jordan at His baptism, and drew it out again with Himself.

## OUR SAVIOUR IN THE DESERT

MATT. 4:1. Then Jesus was led by the Spirit into the desert, to be tempted by the devil.—2. And when he had fasted forty days and forty nights, afterwards he was hungry.—3. And the tempter coming said to him: "If thou be the Son of God, command that these stones be made bread."—4. Who answered and said: "It is written: Not in bread alone doth man live, but in every word that proceedeth from the mouth of God."—5. Then the devil took him up into the holy city, and set him upon the pinnacle of the Temple,—6. And said to him: "If thou be the Son of God, cast thyself down, for it is written: That he hath given his angels charge over thee, and in their hands shall they bear thee up, lest perhaps thou dash thy foot against a stone."—7. Jesus said to him: "It is written again: Thou shalt not tempt the Lord thy God."—8. Again the devil took him up into a very high mountain, and showed him all the kingdoms of the world and the glory of them,—9. And said to him: "All these will I give thee, if falling down thou wilt adore me." —10. Then Jesus saith to him: "Begone, Satan; for it is written: The Lord thy God shalt thou adore, and him only shalt thou serve."—11. Then the devil left him; and behold angels came and ministered to him.

MARK 1:12. And immediately the Spirit drove him out into the desert.—13. And he was in the desert forty days and forty nights, and was tempted by Satan; and he was with beasts, and the angels ministered to him.

LUKE 4:1. And Jesus being full of the Holy Ghost, returned from the Jordan, and was led by the Spirit into the desert—2. For the space of forty days; and was tempted by the devil. And he ate nothing in those days; and when they were ended, he was hungry.—3. And the devil said to him: "If thou be the Son of God, say to this stone that it be made bread."—4. And Jesus answered him: "It is written, that man liveth not by bread alone, but by every word of God."—5. And the devil led him into a high mountain, and showed him all the kingdoms of the world in a moment of time.—6. And he said to him: "To thee will I give all this power, and the glory of them; for to me they are delivered, and to whom I will, I give them.—7. If thou therefore wilt adore before me, all shall be thine."—8. And Jesus answering said to him: "It is written: Thou shalt adore the Lord thy God, and him only shalt thou serve."—9. And he brought him to Jerusalem, and set him on a pinnacle of the Temple; and he said to him: "If thou be the Son of God, cast thyself from hence.—10. For it is written, that he hath given his angels charge over thee, that they keep thee;—11. And that in their hands they shall bear thee up, lest perhaps thou dash thy foot against a stone."—12. And Jesus answering said to him: "It is said: Thou shalt not tempt the Lord thy God."—13. And all the temptation being ended, the devil departed from him for a time.

### 1. OUR SAVIOUR GOES INTO THE DESERT

After His baptism our Lord retired into the desert which extends from Jericho towards Jerusalem and belongs to the northern part of the Desert of Juda (cf. Introd., p. 5). Who led Him to do this? All three Evangelists who relate this mystery remark that it was the Holy Ghost (Matt. 4:1; Mark 1:12; Luke 4:1). With His visible descent and His inauguration of our Lord in His office as a public teacher, the Holy Ghost assumes, so to speak, the guidance of the God-Man. He first leads Him into solitude. The Holy Ghost directs all towards an end. He leads us to the sanctification of others, to converse with men, to outward activity, but also to the pursuit of our own sanctification, to God, and to the interior life. The natural order of things is first to lay the foundations of the spiritual life in ourselves, and then to guide others into it. If we would lead others to God, we must first be deeply rooted in Him.

And how does our Saviour follow this impulse of the Holy Spirit? As it appears, immediately, without tarrying longer at the Jordan (Luke 4:1), because it was not God's Will that He should remain there now; and perhaps also in order to escape from the admiration of the people. Further, He goes quite readily, allows Himself to be led (Matt. 4:1; Mark 1:12); indeed, He is "full of the Holy Ghost" (Luke 4:1), that is, overflowing with the joy and consolation of the Holy Ghost and borne along by His impulse. This assistance of the Holy Spirit was to be His support in the life upon which He was now about to enter.

The impulse not merely to be exteriorly active, but to recollect oneself interiorly and to pray, certainly comes from the Holy Ghost. We must give ear to it, therefore, and beg of the Holy Spirit not to desist from sending us this impulse, even though we often are deaf to His voice or even resist it. From this cultivation of the interior life comes all merit, all blessings, and all perseverance in spiritual activity. Our Saviour going into the desert is a beautiful example of the way in which we must follow the guidance of the Holy Ghost.

## 2. OUR SAVIOUR'S LIFE IN THE DESERT

We must here consider what was the manner of this life in the desert, and from what motives our Lord led it.

The life in the desert was, first, a life of prayer, for one cannot imagine it to have been otherwise, a life of extraordinary, long, un-interrupted, fervent and perfect prayer.

Further, it was a life of penance; first as regards the place, which was not a pleasant hermitage near Jericho, the district of palms and balsam, but a desert. This mountain, on account of its bar-renness, the depth and number of its precipices, its inaccessibility and sterility, is one of the most desolate places in the world; for which reason it was much frequented later on by hermits, in the spirit of penance. It was further a life of penance as regards the season, probably winter-time, with the discomfort of rain and wind; and lastly on account of the fast, which lasted for forty days and nights without interruption, so that at the end our Saviour "was hungry," that is, He felt the pain, exhaustion and hardship of such an extended fast (Matt. 4:2; Luke 4:2). It must have been owing to a special intervention of the Divinity that He did not feel the effects of the fast before.

Thirdly, the life led by our Saviour in the desert was one of temptation and combat with the Evil One, though not in the sense that our Lord was continually tempted. Holy Scripture re-cords only three temptations, and these at the close of the fast. They are described as follows. Our Lord's exhaustion gave oc-casion to the first. The Evil One tempted Him to satisfy hunger by unlawful means, namely by a miracle of transubstantiation that was quite unnecessary and therefore a tempting of God, since pro-visions were to be had in the neighborhood, or also because God, since He exacted this abstinence from food, could sustain our Saviour's life by other means. Further, the Evil One tempted Him to perform a miracle, which should not only relieve Him of the hard and humiliating penance of fasting, but also reveal His Divinity to the devil, neither of which objects were at present the Will of God; it was to be a miracle, then, performed *suadente diabolo* (Matt. 4:3; Luke 4:3). Our Saviour rejects the proposal by a saying which was meant to encourage us to trust in God in similar temptations: "It is written: Not in bread alone doth man live, but in every word that proceedeth from the mouth of God" (Matt. 4:4; Luke 4:4; Deut. 8:3); that is, God can sustain life not only by food but by other means, if He wills it, and has therefore no need of this miracle. This trust in God is made use of by the Evil One for the second temptation; our Saviour was to be seduced to presumption. The devil sets Him upon a pinnacle of the Temple, from which it was not possible to descend except by jumping down, and proposes that He should venture the leap, trusting in the sure help of God and the holy angels. Possibly it was the intention of the Evil One that our Saviour should announce Himself to the people as the Messias by this sudden coming down to them, as it were, from heaven, which was equally contrary to God's will (Matt. 4:5, 6; Luke 4:9–11). Our Lord rejects this proposal also as a tempting of God (Matt. 4:7; Luke 4:12). Finally, Satan makes trial of all the capacity for passion that can be in a man, by setting before Him in a dazzling light all the riches, sensual pleasures and honors of the world, and promising to give Him all these, if He would pay homage to him (Satan) as prince of the world. That would have been simply apostasy from God (Matt. 4:8–10; Luke 4:5–8). The summit of Mount Quarantine, from which there is a charming view of Jericho, the plains of the Jordan, and far around over Peraea and the shores of the Dead Sea, was certainly peculiarly adapted for this temptation.[1] We see from this how our Saviour was tempted, viz. exteriorly, for an interior temptation was not possible with the God-Man; repeatedly, in manifold ways, first from this side, then from another; under the appearance of good and of evil, openly and covertly, from what was not sinful in itself, the preservation of life, to what was sinful, to presumption and to the most flagrant sin of all, apostasy from God; lastly, He even felt the touch of the Evil One, as He allowed Himself to be borne through the air by Satan. But we see also how our Saviour resists: with great exterior calmness and fearlessness; in the simplest manner, merely repulsing the devil by expressing the opposite principles of

---

[1] The temptation which St. Matthew gives as the second, is placed by St. Luke as the third. The Saviour was to prove Himself, then, upon Satan's temptation, first, Lord of the natural world; secondly, Prince of the kingdom of the world; lastly, Head of the kingdom of God. In both the last cases Satan offers Him his assistance. Thus the temptations follow a natural gradation.

faith and of God's law; further, with great decision of will, not arguing the matter; and lastly, He acts perseveringly and victoriously, so that the Evil One retires vanquished for a time (Luke 4:13).

And why does our Saviour go through all this? First, that He may share in all that belongs to human life, however hard and humiliating it may be, so long as it is not sinful. Our lives must be spent in the practice of prayer, penance and combat. He has undergone all these, and that is our comfort (Hebr. 4:15). Secondly, our Saviour wished to teach us by His example that we must pray, do penance and fight, and especially in what manner we are to do this. He would teach us also that we must be prepared for temptation, manifold and hard, even, and indeed particularly, in the practice of prayer and penance. In all these matters our Saviour's example here is quite unusual and extraordinary, in order that we may at least do what is ordinary. Thirdly, He wished to make satisfaction for us, to repair and atone for the faults we commit in this threefold respect. There was great need for atonement here. By negligence in prayer and penance, and especially by weakness in temptation, the whole human race had gradually fallen into the power of Satan. The fall of Adam, which had ensued upon similar temptations; the repeated falls of Israel, which had yielded to one temptation after another (Deut. 6:16; 8:2; Ex. 17:7) and was now in the very act of falling away from God altogether; and lastly, the falls of all men,—all had to be repaired. Fourthly, our Saviour wished to gain for us grace for the difficult work of prayer, penance and combat. And He has done so. In the dark hours of conflict with the fearful powers of hell, when we feel ourselves alone and forsaken, how comforting is the thought that our good Master is not far from us, but in our hearts, with the grace that He has merited for us (II Cor. 12:9). According to the report of pilgrims, a light now burns again over the cavern in which tradition says that our Lord prayed and was tempted. This light is a symbol of His grace. Let us ask Him for it. It will not fail us. Fifthly, this life in the desert was to be a preparation for the public ministry, for it is fitting and right to begin every important work with prayer, in order to give God the honor and to obtain His blessing upon it. Moses acted in this way (Ex. 24:18; Deut. 9:9). This was exacted too by the work itself which our Saviour had in view. It was a question of the salvation of souls, ransomed only by prayer and penance; and a question of the destruction of the kingdom of Satan in the world. The strong one who held sway over the world as his possession (Luke 4:6) had to be vanquished before he would yield up his prey. Here he felt for the first time the power of One stronger than he. Lastly, it was a question of the foundation of the kingdom of the Church. Christ had to give her inward stability and strength against all hostilities. This inward strength lies in readiness in prayer, penance and combat, and this He established for ever in the Church by His life in the desert. He thus began the forty days of the Lenten fast, that salutary discipline of Christian warfare (*praesidia militiae christianae*), whereby the Church yearly steels herself to fresh spiritual endeavor.

### 3. OUR SAVIOUR LEAVES THE DESERT, VICTORIOUS AND STRENGTHENED

The last temptation was repulsed, and then the scene suddenly changed. The desert became a paradise, and its solitude was peopled with holy angels. After the long privation, they ministered to our Lord with heavenly food; after the ignominy and humiliation of the temptation, they offered Him praise and congratulation upon His victory; and instead of the dominion over the earth which He was to have bought by paying homage to Satan, they offered the adoration of the heavenly host. How wonderfully the words that had been exchanged in the conflict of the temptation were fulfilled: "Man liveth not by bread alone, but by every word of God"; "God hath given His angels charge over Thee, that they keep Thee"; "All these will I give Thee, if falling down Thou wilt adore me." It was a great and glorious victory, a victory for us all. The defeat of Satan had now begun, the defeat accomplished by the lowliness and weakness of Christ. This was the beginning of the war; it was completed by the mighty words: "All power is given to Me in heaven and in earth" (Matt. 28:18). If the exterior inauguration of the teaching office took place at Christ's baptism, the interior was accomplished here. In prayer, penance and combat consists the armor of the strong.

## The Deputation Sent to John. His Second Testimony to Christ

John 1:19. And this is the testimony of John, when the Jews sent from Jerusalem priests and Levites to him, to ask him: "Who art thou?"—20. And he confessed, and did not deny; and he confessed: "I am not the Christ."—21. And they asked him: "What then? Art thou Elias?" And he said: "I am not."—"Art thou the prophet?" And he answered: "No."—22. They said therefore unto him: "Who art thou, that we may give an answer to them that sent us? what sayest thou of thyself?"—23. He said: "I am the voice of one crying in the wilderness: Make straight the way of the Lord, as said the prophet Isaias."—24. And they that were sent were of the Pharisees.—25. And they asked him, and said to him: "Why then dost thou baptize, if thou be not Christ, nor Elias, nor the prophet?"—26. John answered them, saying: "I baptize with water; but there hath stood one in the midst of you, whom you know not.—27. The same is he that shall come after me, who is preferred before me; the latchet of whose shoe I am not worthy to loose."—28. These things were done in Bethania beyond the Jordan, where John was baptizing.

### 1. THE DEPUTATION SENT TO JOHN

The spiritual authorities among the Jews could no longer remain indifferent to the powerful movement brought about by the preaching and baptism of John, and above all by his announcement of the coming Messias. They resolved, therefore, to dispatch a deputation of "priests and Levites" to him from Jerusalem, evidently members of the Sanhedrim (John 1:19, 22) and duly commissioned by the High Priests, to make an official inquiry as to his mission.

The embassy was a lawful one, for it was not only the right of the synagogue but also their duty to take cognizance of the introduction and practice of the new rite, and of the highly important question of the coming of the Messias; and John acknowledges this right by giving them an answer. But the spirit of the deputation does not seem to have been a good one. The Evangelist St. John observes that it was sent "by the Jews" (John 1:19), and he usually denotes by this expression the unbelieving, recreant party, hostile to our Lord (John 2:18; 5:16; 7:1), who were supported by the Sanhedrim, and whose center and nucleus was in Jerusalem and Judaea; it consisted (says this Evangelist) of Pharisees (John 1:24), who stood aloof from the whole movement (Luke 7:30), not only out of a sort of blind zeal in preventing any innovation in the law and tradition, but also from a certain pride, because John dared to propose a baptism of penance to

God's chosen people. The reception they had already met with from John (Matt. 3:7) and the address of the messengers themselves (John 1:19) betray their incredulity, malice, pride and sensitiveness. The issue shows the same thing (Matt. 21:32).

The deputation reached St. John immediately before our Saviour's return from the desert (John 1:29), finding him at Bethania, beyond the Jordan. This "Bethania" may perhaps mean no particular locality, but rather the low-lying land near the Jordan, here probably the Middle Jordan. St. John appears to have repeatedly changed the place of his baptizing. The specification of the site indicates the importance of the occurrence.

The question which the deputation put to John was a double one. First as regarded his person, i.e. his vocation. Without directly naming the Messias, they ask in an indirect manner whether he was himself the Messias, or at any rate Elias or one of the old prophets: the one, namely, who was to herald the coming of the Messias (Mal. 4:5, 6; Deut. 18:15), and whom some thought to be the Messias Himself (John 7:40, 41), whilst others held the contrary (John 6:14). As John replies in the negative, they ask him, secondly, his authority for the new ceremony of baptism that he performs, because the cleansing from sin by baptism was exclusively the office of the Messias (Isa. 44:3; Ez. 36:25; Zach. 13:1; Joel 3:28). The question was contrived with true pharisaical cunning. They thought that if he declared himself to be the Messias or a prophet, he would be obliged to ask credentials and authorization of the Sanhedrim; and if he neglected to do this, they could accuse him of acting unlawfully.

## 2. ST. JOHN'S ANSWER

John's answer is also twofold.

He first replies to the double question put by the deputation. With regard to his person, he denies repeatedly and with decision (John 1:20) that he is the Messias, or Elias, or a prophet in the above-mentioned sense (John 1:21). Pressed by the deputation to give them some information as to who he really is, he answers that he is the "voice of one crying in the desert," of which Isaias had spoken in prophecy (Isa. 40:3; John 1:23); that is to say, he is sent and accredited by God. It was the best answer he could have given, at once true, modest (calling himself, as it were, a mere "voice," and wishing not to be looked at but to be listened to), and yet complete and weighty. John lets God and Holy

Scripture bear witness to him. These were sufficient credentials for conscientious men acquainted with the law. For this reason John adds: "as said the prophet Isaias" (John 1:23). John stands, then, even though he is not the Messias nor one of the prophets, yet in immediate proximity to Him Whom all expected; in other words, the Messianic time has come. With regard to his baptism, he declares that it is not the baptism of the Messias (Matt. 3:11), but only a preparation for it, a baptism with water. Herein also John was our Lord's Forerunner.

Secondly, he joins to the statement concerning himself a glorious testimony to the Messias: first, that He is already there, "in the midst" of them, though they "knew Him not"; hitherto John had only prophesied of Him as about to come; secondly, that He will appear in public and declare Himself; thirdly, that He is of incomparably higher rank, indeed that, though younger in age, He was "before" him (John), that is to say, eternal, and simply God, before Whom the "greatest among those born of women" humbly bows (Luke 7:28; John 1:27). Undaunted before the people, he is also undaunted before the deputation. He delivers his glorious testimony and then dismisses them. They had information now, and perhaps more than they wished for.

### 3. THE IMPORTANCE OF THE EMBASSY AND OF JOHN'S ANSWER

This embassy and the testimony of John are of importance in every respect. In the first place, as regards the Jews; God so disposed it that an entirely official announcement, a divine testimony (John 1:23) of the arrival of the Messias was now given to them. This testimony could not be unknown to the priests and Levites, with their legal learning; and their unbelief is here shown to be sufficiently serious (John 1:26). Why did they not inquire concerning this mysterious personage, whom they "knew not"? Either they did not trouble themselves about Him, or they despised John, His herald. Their incredulity and opposition begin with the announcement of His presence. No one, neither the Precursor of the Messias nor the Messias Himself, may come without their knowledge and consent, or otherwise than they wish. Later on our Saviour Himself appeals to this testimony of the Baptist. Secondly, with regard to the Messias, we gain here the knowledge that He has, according to the general opinion, a great prophet for His herald, and that He is full of high and divine dignity. Thirdly, the fearless and lofty character of John is again disclosed; how faithfully, undauntedly, zealously and unselfishly he fulfils his vocation to proclaim Christ! He declares openly and repeatedly that he is not Christ, and that he is as nothing compared to Him. Humility is always a witness for Christ, for His Person, His doctrine and His graces, and is a necessary condition in His witnesses. John became by this humility a member of Christ, whilst the Jews in their pride fell away from Him and went to their ruin. How our Saviour must have rejoiced at the zeal and humility of His servant!

## John's Third Testimony to Christ

JOHN 1:29. The next day John saw Jesus coming to him, and he saith: "Behold the Lamb of God, behold him who taketh away the sin of the world.—30. This is he of whom I said: After me there cometh a man, who is preferred before me; because he was before me.—31. And I knew him not; but that he may be made manifest in Israel, therefore am I come baptizing with water."—32. And John gave testimony, saying: "I saw the Spirit coming down as a dove from heaven, and he remained upon him.—33. And I knew him not; but he who sent me to baptize with water, said to me: He upon whom thou shalt see the Spirit descending and remaining upon him, he it is that baptizeth with the Holy Ghost.—34. And I saw; and I gave testimony, that this is the Son of God."

### 1. OCCASION OF THE TESTIMONY

While John is still baptizing at the Jordan, our Lord pays him another visit (John 1:29), a short one indeed, but made with a great object. Our Saviour has just returned from the desert, and He desires not only to be further revealed to the people by John, but to choose His first disciples from those of His Forerunner. He seems only to have passed by. He did not linger by John. The latter himself declares this in the words: "I knew him not" (John 1:31). He saw Jesus only three times altogether (Matt. 3:13; John 1:29, 36). But he always maintained a respectful reserve, and never held long intercourse with Him. He acted thus out of humility, as well as on account of the duties of his vocation. Any suspicion of collusion was to be kept far remote from his testimony. The appearance of Jesus and His entrance into public life seem more imposing and effective, when the first impulse to the assembling of His disciples is given by the testimony of John (Schanz).

## 2. THE TESTIMONY

As soon as our Lord appears, John points Him out to those around him and delivers his testimony.

He declares first the vocation of Jesus as Redeemer of the world by His sacrificial death, and then His corresponding attributes. His vocation as Redeemer of the world is briefly and completely expressed in the words: "Behold the Lamb of God, behold Him that taketh away the sin of the world" (John 1:29). The sacrificial death in expiation of the debt of sin is strikingly expressed by the figure of the lamb. The Messias is thus depicted in the prophecies (Isa. 53:4, 7; Jer. 11:19), and is similarly typified in the daily sacrifices by the slaughter of two lambs (Ex. 29:38); in the great annual sacrifice of the Covenant, the Paschal Lamb (Ex. 12); and lastly by the destinies of several saints of the Old Testament, such as Abel and Isaac. In this sense our Saviour may be called "the Lamb which was slain from the beginning of the world" (Apoc. 13:8); and in place of these sacrifices and types He now comes Himself (Ps. 39:8), with the stamp of sacrifice upon His whole life and death. Only thus will He baptize in the Holy Ghost and obtain grace for us. John also points out the attributes of the Messias corresponding to this. They are all comprehended in the figure of "the Lamb of God"; viz. purity and innocence, simplicity, patience and gentleness, and above all His Divinity. The denomination "Lamb of God" is equivalent to "the lamb sent from God," God's property, and God Himself. Besides this, John attests the Divinity of Jesus by His eternity (John 1:30) and by His sending and imparting the Holy Ghost in baptism (John 1:33); and then expressly calls Him the Son of God (John 1:34). Only a divine sacrifice could redeem mankind. In contrast to Jesus, John is merely His Forerunner, who prepares the way for Him. He indicates his own vocation briefly and pithily; he had come baptizing with water, that Jesus might be made manifest in Israel (John 1:31).

John confirms and emphasizes this testimony by indicating that his mission proceeds from God (John 1:33), and avows that he had learnt that Jesus was indeed God and the Messias by no natural means, such as converse with Him, for he had never seen Him before His baptism (John 1:31), but by an interior divine inspiration as our Saviour presented Himself before him, and by an exterior divine token which had previously been given to him and which was fulfilled publicly in presence of the people, viz. the visible descent of the Holy Spirit.

### 3. IMPORTANCE OF THE TESTIMONY

This testimony of John is important, first, on account of the express declaration of the Divinity of Jesus, a declaration based upon His Person and vocation. It is the first express public acknowledgment, and it is withal so beautiful and comprehensive that the Church still employs it constantly as a confession of faith in the Divinity of Jesus before the reception of Holy Communion. Further, the testimony is important on account of the disclosure to the Jews of the vocation of Jesus as Redeemer. In their pride they did not consider themselves to be in need of redemption, and expected merely deliverance from the outward oppression of foreign rule; further, they laid claim to this deliverance for the Israelite nation exclusively; and lastly, they would hear nothing of a suffering Messias. They expected a Messias according to their carnal desires. John, on the contrary, in accordance with the prophets and other holy Israelites (Luke 1:68–79; 2:30–32), announces One Who shall redeem the whole world from sin, and that by His own suffering and death. He proclaims the divine and yet servile form of the Messias. For John was full of the spirit of God, a man deeply in earnest, who understood the need of suffering. In him passion did not extinguish the higher light. He himself went the way of penance and sacrifice, and his path was to become yet more difficult. Thus he needed the comfort of a lofty example. No one understands the necessity and utility of penance and mortification better than one who unites the practice of it with innocence. The indication of the Messianic vocation of Jesus under the figure of "the Lamb of God" is peculiar to St. John the Evangelist, and is employed by him very frequently, especially in the Apocalypse. It is as though this name, under which he first learned to know the Saviour, continually re-echoed in his heart to the end of his life. He had understood his first master well.

## Our Lord's First Disciples

John 1:35. The next day again John stood, and two of his disciples.—36. And beholding Jesus walking, he saith: "Behold the Lamb of God."—37. And the two disciples heard him speak, and they followed Jesus.—38. And Jesus turning, and seeing them following him, said to them: "What seek you?" Who said to him:

"Rabbi (which is to say, being interpreted, Master), where dwellest thou?"—39. He saith to them: "Come and see." They came, and saw where he abode, and they stayed with him that day; now it was about the tenth hour.—40. And Andrew, the brother of Simon Peter, was one of the two who had heard of John, and followed him.—41. He findeth first his brother Simon, and saith to him: "We have found the Messias" (which is, being interpreted, the Christ).—42. And he brought him to Jesus. And Jesus looking upon him said: "Thou art Simon the son of Jona; thou shalt be called Cephas," which is interpreted, Peter.—43. On the following day he would go forth into Galilee, and he findeth Philip. And Jesus saith to him: "Follow me."—44. Now Philip was of Bethsaida, the city of Andrew and Peter.—45. Philip findeth Nathanael, and saith to him: "We have found him of whom Moses in the law, and the prophets did write, Jesus the son of Joseph of Nazareth."—46. And Nathanael said to him: "Can anything of good come from Nazareth?" Philip saith to him: "Come and see."—47. Jesus saw Nathanael coming to him, and he saith to him: "Behold an Israelite indeed, in whom there is no guile."—48. Nathanael said to him: "Whence knowest thou me?" Jesus answered and said to him: "Before that Philip called thee, when thou wast under the fig-tree, I saw thee."—49. Nathanael answered him and said: "Rabbi, thou art the Son of God, thou art the king of Israel."—50. Jesus answered and said to him: "Because I said unto thee, I saw thee under the fig-tree, thou believest; greater things than these shalt thou see."—51. And he saith to him: "Amen, amen I say to you, you shall see the heaven opened and the angels of God ascending and descending upon the Son of man."

## 1. HOW THE DISCIPLES ARE LED TO OUR LORD

Of the causes which helped to lead the disciples to our Lord, the first was the glorious testimony which John the Baptist bore to Him, and which he repeated on the following day in the presence of two of his disciples, assuredly with the intention of inducing them to become His followers. As our Saviour was passing near where he stood with his disciples, he gazed after Him with a look of reverence and unutterable love, and then pointed to Him, with the words: "Behold the Lamb of God" (John 1:35, 36).

Further, as he spoke, the grace of God was at work in their hearts, inspiring them to follow Him of Whom John bore witness.

Thirdly, the disciples themselves had their share in this work by bringing one another to our Lord, as Andrew brought Peter, and Philip brought Nathanael.

Lastly, our Lord's appearance here finally won them over; the marvelous dignity and charm of His Person, and the wise and prudent manner in which He received and treated each individual disciple according to his nature and disposition, were the effective causes in the calling of the first disciples.

## 2. HOW THE DISCIPLES WERE RECEIVED AND WON BY OUR LORD

The disciples who stood beside John were Andrew and (probably) John the Evangelist (John 1:37–40). Urged by the testimony of their master and by grace, they went after our Lord, though probably shyly enough. He turned, full of friendliness and kindness, and asked them: "What seek you?" He then invited them to His dwelling, and kept them with Him the whole day. The conversation and manner of our Saviour must have been most winning; for St. John, in his old age, still remembered the exact hour at which He had met them (John 1:39), a circumstance from which we may conclude that he himself was the happy disciple. And Andrew's joyful exclamation to Simon: "We have found the Messias," proves what a deep impression this conversation had made upon him also. Thus our Lord gained by His friendly manner these two disciples, who (especially John) were particularly susceptible to love and friendship. They had indeed gained in our Lord a most faithful, powerful and tender friend.

Peter was brought to Jesus by his brother Andrew. And how did our Lord win him? Peter's attention and breathless expectation had already been aroused by Andrew's news of having found the Messias, the greatest news that could be announced to a believing Israelite (John 1:40, 41); and now our Saviour appeals at once to the most susceptible part of his nature. He looks significantly at him (John 1:42), calls him immediately by his name and, by telling him that he shall be called Cephas (Peter), mysteriously reveals to him a great future. The change of name denotes in Holy Scripture a special vocation (Gen. 17:5; 32:28). This greatly impressed Peter, who was a thorough Galilean in character, faithful, open, warm-hearted, impulsive and bold. He too found with our Saviour what fitted him; true fame and a position of unequaled power. This is well understood by every visitor to St. Peter's in Rome, when he sees the gigantic dome over the grave of the Prince of the Apostles, and reads in the golden cupola the words: "Thou art Peter, and upon this rock I will build My Church."

On the following day, as our Saviour was about to go into Galilee, He met with Philip, who was from Bethsaida, the home of Peter and Andrew (John 1:43, 44). The two words, "Follow

Me," sufficed to decide him to join our Saviour (John 1:43). He seems to have had a very good, docile, somewhat calculating and reflective character (John 6:7; 12:22).

Nathanael, probably identical with Bartholomew (John 21:2; Matt. 10:3; Mark 3:18; Luke 6:14), a native of Cana in Galilee (John 21:2), appears to have been a truth-seeking, educated and independent man. It was perhaps on this account that Philip gave him such an exact, almost official statement concerning Jesus of Nazareth, the son of Joseph, the Messias of whom Moses and the prophets wrote (John 1:45). Nathanael replies somewhat coldly, almost mockingly, asking if the greatest Good could come from such an out-of-the-way corner as Nazareth; but nevertheless he accepts the invitation to "come and see" (John 1:46). And how does our Saviour receive him? He immediately praises his integrity and sincerity; He shows him that He already knows of his conversation with Philip, and names to him an event of his life that no one but the Searcher of hearts could know. Nothing gives us such power over men, as when we praise them and at the same time show them that we read them through and through. Here our Lord even allowed a ray of His supernatural knowledge to shine forth, and thus revealed His Divinity to the disciples for the first time, though with some reserve. He proves to Nathanael that He is the Lord of his conscience and sees through his whole soul. Nathanael, overpowered, yields at once and responds by a solemn profession of his faith, in which he acknowledges our Saviour as Teacher, Son of God, and Messias, at least as the Messias who was to rule over Israel (John 1:47–50). Nathanael also has found with our Saviour what he sought; the Messias of Whom he was in quest, the Master Who inspired him with reverence by His superior wisdom, the Lord and Judge of his conscience, and the Author of his eternal salvation.

### 3. HOW OUR LORD CONFIRMED THE DISCIPLES IN THEIR ALLEGIANCE TO HIM

Lastly, our Lord confirmed Nathanael and the other disciples in their devotion to Him by the hint and prediction that they would later on be witnesses of still greater and more solemn proofs of His Divinity. They should "see the heaven opened and the angels of God ascending and descending upon the Son of Man"; i.e. they should recognize Him as Lord of heaven, as Mediator of grace and reconciliation, for the actual bestowal of which He employs the angels (John 1:50, 51). Our Lord probably alluded here, in connection with the words of Nathanael: "Thou art the king of Israel," to the vision of Jacob (Gen. 28:12), who, as the ancestor of the tribes of Israel and intermediary of the blessing of the Covenant, enjoyed special intercourse with the angels (Gen. 31:11; 48:16) and was a type of Christ. In Christ the type was fulfilled. Our Saviour calls Himself the "Son of Man" here for the first time, and very often later on. This is the name given by the prophets to the Messias (Dan. 7:13, 14); and it forcibly expresses His human nature and at the same time His relationship to the entire human race as its head and representative.

There are three important and very interesting points in this mystery. In the first place, we see John at the climax of his vocation. Here he not only bears testimony to Christ and points Him out, but he leads his disciples to Him, supplies the material for the foundation of the Church, and thus forms the link between the Old and New Covenant. Thus the foundation-stones of the Church are taken from the temple of the Old Law. In the confessions of Andrew, Philip and Nathanael we hear the echo of John's testimony. Nathanael's confession, "Thou art the Son of God" (John 1:49), answers to the testimony of John: "This is the Son of God" (John 1:34). Secondly, we see here already the first beginnings and essential outlines of the Church, in the calling of the Apostles and their commencing to believe in the Divinity of Jesus. The Saviour had scarcely gained two disciples, when Peter was already called to be, as it were, the head of the little college. It is perhaps not without special significance that we are told: "Andrew findeth first his brother Simon" (John 1:41). Andrew and John both had brothers, who seem to have been in the vicinity, viz., Peter and James. Before John had introduced his brother James to our Lord, Andrew had already brought Peter to Him. Then, too, the words with which Christ received Simon remind us spontaneously of the promise of the primacy (Matt. 16:18). Finally, our Saviour manifests Himself here in a manner full of sweetness and majesty. One needs only to see Him and make His acquaintance, in order to love and follow Him (John 1:39, 46). How true the words are already proved to be, that He is "the Light which enlighteneth every man" (John 1:9), and on the other hand, that "he that doth truth, cometh to the Light, that his works may be made manifest, because they are

THE MARRIAGE-FEAST AT CANA

done in God" (John 3:21)! These first conquests of the faith are the type of the conquest of the whole world by the word of faith.

## THE MARRIAGE-FEAST AT CANA

JOHN 2:1. And the third day there was a marriage in Cana of Galilee; and the mother of Jesus was there.—2. And Jesus also was invited, and his disciples, to the marriage.—3. And the wine failing, the mother of Jesus saith to him: "They have no wine."—4. And Jesus saith to her: "Woman, what is it to me and to thee? my hour is not yet come."—5. His mother saith to the waiters: "Whatsoever he shall say to you, do ye."—6. Now there were set there six water-pots of stone, according to the manner of the purifying of the Jews, containing two or three measures apiece.—7. Jesus saith to them: "Fill the water-pots with water." And they filled them up to the brim.—8. And Jesus saith to them: "Draw out now, and carry to the chief steward of the feast." And they carried it.—9. And when the chief steward had tasted the water made wine, and knew not whence it was, but the waiters knew who had drawn the water; the chief steward calleth the bridegroom,—10. And saith to him: "Every man at first setteth forth good wine, and when men have well drunk, then that which is worse; but thou hast kept the good wine until now."—11. This beginning of miracles did Jesus in Cana of Galilee, and manifested his glory; and his disciples believed in him.

Our Saviour was now on the way with His new disciples from the Jordan to Capharnaum in Galilee. On the third day of the journey He stopped at Cana, where His holy Mother was present on the occasion of a marriage, and there worked the miracle of the changing of water into wine. Cana is a village of some importance, between Nazareth and Tiberias, in a hilly, fertile district. It is built in terraces and situated on the slope of a hill. Indian fig-trees border the heights in irregular lines, and in the valley beneath, at a spot surrounded by cactus shrubs and hedges, is the only spring in the district, from which therefore the water for the miracle must have been obtained.

### 1. THE MIRACLE

The miracle in itself is a great and glorious one. In the first place, because it is our Saviour's first public miracle; as St. John says, the "beginning of miracles" (John 2:11).

Secondly, it is in its character a miracle of the first rank; indeed, St. John records only absolute miracles. That at Cana was not merely an alteration, but a real substantial change of water into wine. Our Lord hereby proved that He is the absolute Lord of creation and can control it at will.

Thirdly, the miracle is remarkable for the quiet and unobtrusive manner in which it was performed, as well as for its great opportuneness. The occasion of it was most simple, the manner of effecting it was without any ceremonial that could attract the senses; it was based upon something already existing and close at hand, namely water, and was effected without exterior means. On the other hand, the miracle is attested by the most irrefutable circumstances. It was worked on a public occasion, before many witnesses who were above suspicion (the servants, the chief steward and the bridegroom) so that it can in no case be denied.

Fourthly, the miracle is rendered very beautiful by its mystic signification. The holy Fathers see in this marriage-feast and in the gift of the wonderful wine an emblem of the espousals of Christ with the Church. This union, of which matrimony is a symbol (Eph. 5:32), effected here and in heaven, appears in Holy Scripture as a magnificent marriage-feast, at which the Bridegroom gives us to drink of the marvelously transubstantiated wine of His Blood and, in heaven, of the "new" chalice (Matt. 26:29) of eternal bliss. And now, at the very beginning of His public ministry, when the apostolic college has just been founded, He celebrates the commencement of these espousals, and fittingly expresses the joy of His Heart by assisting at a marriage and performing a miracle which so strikingly typifies His union with the Church in the Holy Eucharist and in heaven.

## 2. OCCASION OF THE MIRACLE

The miracle gains a special charm from the circumstances which gave rise to it.

The first circumstance was the marriage itself and the presence of the Mother of Jesus (John 2:1), who was probably there as a sympathetic acquaintance and friend, advising, arranging and helping, and who most likely suggested to the bride and bridegroom the invitation of our Saviour and His disciples (John 2:2). The worthiness of the spouses is implied by the fact that they invited our Saviour, and that He accepted the invitation.

The second circumstance was the embarrassment caused by the failing of the wine (John 2:3). Perhaps the acceptance of the invitation on the part of our Saviour and His disciples, and the consequent considerable increase in the number of guests at table, was also one of the causes of this deficiency, and thus it was fitting that our Saviour should render assistance in the difficulty.

But the proximate occasion and the cause of the miracle was the Mother of Jesus and her request (John 2:3). Our Lord granted this request, first, in consideration of her faith, which, without having seen any miracles hitherto, was firmly convinced of her Son's omnipotence; secondly, in consideration of the modesty and delicacy with which the request was made (John 2:3); thirdly, in consideration of her motherly care, attention and kindness, which had immediately discovered the want of wine (or perhaps her attention had been called to it); and lastly, in consideration of her firm confidence. During the hidden life of our Lord she would certainly not have asked for a public miracle. Now He was revealed and had begun His public life, so she considered the request well-timed. She did not desire anything that was not conformable to God's Will, and so she could be sure of having her petition granted.

### 3. THE EFFECT OF THE MIRACLE

The effect of the miracle is stated in the words: "Jesus . . . manifested His glory, and His disciples believed in Him" (John 2:11). His disciples believed, that is to say, were wonderfully strengthened in the faith to which they had already attained at the first meeting with Jesus, by His disclosure of things that He could only know by divine wisdom. That was a miracle in the purely spiritual sphere; now they had a miracle within the province of visible things, as a confirmation of the promise of "greater" things which they were to see (John 1:50), and their faith must have been greatly increased thereby. This was probably the principal intention of our Saviour, and the disciples needed this strengthening in faith also, in view of the future events in Jerusalem. But this miracle without doubt also spread the faith in Him as a messenger of God, or even in His Divinity itself, beyond the circle of the disciples, among the acquaintances and relatives of our Lord, many of whom were probably present at the marriage. That is the "glory" which was to be manifested by all miracles, and also by this one.

The miracle is not only a manifestation of His Divinity, but also of the sweetness and beauty of His natural character. How kind it is of Him to accept the invitation and be present at the marriage of comparatively poor people! He despises nothing that belongs to good and honorable earthly customs, and hallows them all by His presence and the bright example of His virtue. The holy Fathers see in His acceptance of the invitation a ratification of legitimate matrimony. It is not without significance that our loving Lord celebrates His departure from the quiet family life in which He had spent so long a time by His first great miracle, and He performs it at the establishment of a new family life, and for the joy and comfort of the new couple. The miracle is, as it were, the solemn leave-taking of His family, and His royal thanks for all the good He has enjoyed in its bosom. How beautifully the generosity and munificence of our Saviour are manifested here, by His working so great a miracle and bestowing excellent wine in such abundant measure (John 2:10) [1] on account of a domestic embarrassment, unimportant in itself. This abundance of miraculous wine is at the same time a prophetic symbol of the fulness of blessing that our Saviour will bestow upon the world by His Church. Lastly, this miracle proves our Lord's high esteem and love for His holy Mother. There is no slight nor repulse implied in the words: "Woman, what is it to Me and to thee?" This somewhat rough Hebrew manner of speech signifies, as employed in Holy Scripture, nothing more than that something comes awkwardly or inopportunely, or that it is impracticable (Matt. 8:29; 27:19; Luke 8:28; IV Kings 3:13; 9:18, 19; Jos. 12:24; Judg. 11:12; II Kings 16:10; III Kings 17:18). Neither is there anything derogatory in the term "woman"; it is rather one of respect, the Hebrew word being equivalent to "Lady" (John 19:26). Our Lord means to say: Whether miracles are to be worked or not depends on My will and upon that of My Heavenly Father, since I am no longer subject to your authority. When the hour is come in which I am to reveal Myself, I will do as you wish. Apparently His words were thus understood by His Mother, and her direction to the servants: "Whatsoever He shall say to you, do ye" (John 2:5), well agrees with this. The power of Mary's intercession is gloriously manifested here. It is certainly not without great significance that our Saviour, at this important turning-point of His life, made the strengthening in faith of His disciples and the manifestation of His Divinity dependent upon the intercession of His Mother. This is the revelation of the disposition of God, that in Christ's kingdom everything goes through the hand and heart of His Mother, the communication of justification as well as of faith (John 2:11). Thus our Lord really revealed His glory, that glory full of grace and truth.

In the development and connection of the mysteries of our

---

[1] The six waterpots of stone, containing two or three measures apiece, are calculated to have held about 50 gallons in English measure.

Saviour, this miracle is the glorious close of the immediate prep-aration for the public ministry; the brilliant transit from the obscurity of private life into the bright light of the most magnifi-cent manifestations of His Divinity by miracles; the impressive confirmation and strengthening of the newly-awakened faith of the disciples; and the revelation of the position of power held by the Mother of God in the development of God's kingdom here below. As her prayer brings about the advent and birth of the Sun of Justice, so also her request decides the rise and shining of this Sun in public action.

## B. The Public Life from the First to the Second Paschal Feast

This period of the public life of Jesus contains His first appear-ance in Jerusalem and His ministry in the country districts of Judaea; the imprisonment of the Baptist; the expulsion of Jesus from Judaea and the removal of His sphere of action to Galilee; the brief revelation of Himself in Samaria; the beginnings of His ministry in Galilee and the hostility on the part of the Pharisees; and the last calling of disciples.

### First Feast of the Pasch. The Purification of the Temple

John 2:12. After this he went down to Capharnaum, he and his mother, and his brethren, and his disciples; and they remained there not many days.—13. And the Pasch of the Jews was at hand, and Jesus went up to Jerusalem.—14. And he found in the Temple them that sold oxen and sheep and doves, and the changers of money sitting.—15. And when he had made as it were a scourge of little cords, he drove them all out of the Temple, the sheep also and the oxen, and the money of the changers he poured out, and the tables he overthrew.—16. And to them that sold doves he said: "Take these things hence, and make not the house of my Father a house of traffic."—17. And his disciples remembered that it was written: The zeal of thy house hath eaten me up.—18. The Jews therefore answered and said to him: "What sign dost thou show unto us, seeing thou dost these things?" —19. Jesus answered and said to them: "Destroy this temple, and in three days I will raise it up."—20. The Jews then said: "Six and forty years was this Temple in building, and wilt thou raise it up in three days?"—21. But he spoke of the temple of his body.—22. When therefore he was risen again from the dead, his disciples remembered that he had said this, and they believed the scripture and the word that Jesus had said.—23. Now when he was at Jerusalem at the Pasch, upon the festival day, many believed in his name, seeing his signs which he did.— 24. But Jesus did not trust himself unto them, for that he knew all men,—25. And because he needed not that any should give testimony of man; for he knew what was in man.

### 1. OUR SAVIOUR GOES TO JERUSALEM FOR THE FEAST
### OF THE PASCH

After a stay of a few days at Capharnaum, whither our Lord had gone from Cana (or from Nazareth) with His holy Mother, His brethren (i.e. His cousins: James the Less, Judas, Joseph and Simon) and His disciples, the Feast of the Pasch drew near, and He went to keep it at Jerusalem, which was now to be the chief scene of His ministry. On this occasion our Saviour showed Himself for the first time in public as the Messias, and the circumstances of time and place are of considerable importance.

St. John apparently wishes to lay stress upon the fact that the announcement of the message of salvation, and the open manifestation of the Messias as Teacher of the law, went out from Judaea and in particular from Jerusalem (John 2:13). The prophecies point to Jerusalem (Mal. 3:1). John the Baptist had promised the arrival of the Messias in Judaea; there He must be made manifest. Lastly, Judaea and especially Jerusalem was the true center of the religious life of the nation (John 4:20; Matt. 22:34, 37).

The Feast of the Pasch was especially chosen by our Saviour, because it was the great feast of the Covenant, on which the nation presented itself "before God," and because the sacrifice of the Paschal Lamb, the most perfect type of the sacrificial Death of Jesus, stood in such close relationship to Him as Priest and Victim. It was the time and place best adapted for revealing Himself and commencing His public teaching and work of reform. There incredulity could pronounce itself, as opposed to the progressive revelation of Jesus as Son of God, could gather strength and lead to a decision. At this Feast of the Pasch our Saviour first reveals Himself as the Messias by a great and significant action; on the third following Paschal feast He ends His life as the true Paschal Lamb, and this as the consequent development of the movement which had begun with His action on this first feast. The Paschal feasts in our Lord's life are turning-points in the development of His destiny. The prophetic words "Destroy this temple" (John 2:19) link the first and last Paschal feasts essentially one to the other.

## 2. OUR SAVIOUR PURIFIES THE TEMPLE

As is evident from the sequel, it was at his Feast of the Pasch that our Saviour made His first appearance as teacher of the law and also worked miracles (John 2:23; 3:2); but what rendered it chiefly remarkable was the purification of the Temple. On entering the sacred edifice our Saviour perceived a great disorder. In the fore-court of the Gentiles (cf. Introd., p. 6) cattle, flour, oil, and other necessaries for the Paschal services were being sold; and at the exchange tables foreign money was being changed for coin of the country and Temple sicles (John 2:14). Our Lord wished to put a stop to this flagrant abuse.

What, then, did He wish to abolish? Not the traffic itself, which was necessary, but its taking place in the fore-court of the Temple (John 2:16). It was a humiliation and an annoyance for the Gentiles that their place of worship should be thus misused, and a great misconception of God's merciful intentions towards them (III Kings 8:41). It was further an indignity and a profanation for the House of God to be turned into a market-hall, and surely also a disturbance to devotion and to the divine service, especially at festival times, when there was a great throng of pilgrims. It was even forbidden by the Temple laws to enter the building with baggage or a purse. Lastly, it was also an occasion of fraud and usury, and perhaps of disgraceful avarice on the part of the priests and rulers of the Temple, who derived pecuniary profit from it. At all events it was a scandalous neglect of their duty to care for the beauty and honor of the House of God, for which they displayed, in other respects, a superstitious reverence (Jer. 7:4). We hereby gain a glimpse of the decay of true piety, at least among the leaders of the people. Assuredly these "sons of Levi" stood in need of being "purified" by the Messias (Mal. 2; 3:3), and of His cleansing and renovating intervention in religious matters.

And how does our Saviour set about the purification of the Temple? In the first place, with great moderation. Perhaps He had seen the abuse before this, and with sorrow; but He had not interfered, because it was not the business of a private individual, and He had not yet entered upon His public ministry. Further, one can scarcely think otherwise than that our Saviour first tried milder measures with the market-people, or at least did not fail to remonstrate with and threaten them. He showed no less modera-

tion in the actual work of purification. Whilst He drove the oxen
and sheep and the market-people before Him out of the Temple
and overturned the tables of the money-changers, He bade the
dealers in doves carry the cages away (John 2:16); thus showing
great consideration for the vendors, whose wares would otherwise have flown away, and also for the poor, because these birds
were the offerings of poor women after childbirth (Luke 2:24).
But in the second place, our Lord acted with courage and decision, with boldness and energy, with terrifying zeal and sternness,
and with a majesty and power that drove all before Him and filled
them with terror (John 2:15). He twisted cords into a scourge,
because it was not permitted to set foot upon the Temple hill
with a stick. Moreover the scourge was a symbol of the mysterious
power and majesty of His Godhead, which inspired all around
Him with supernatural fear. He Himself declares in what capacity
He here appears and acts: "Make not the House of My Father
a house of traffic" (John 2:16). It is not merely the prophet, the
Messias, but the Son of the God of Israel, Who claims reverence
for His Temple and His Father. In truth it was a glorious deed,
a miracle in the accompanying circumstances, a revelation in word
and deed of His Messianic vocation and His Divinity.

### 3. OUR SAVIOUR IS CALLED TO ACCOUNT BY THE PRIESTS

This purification of the holy Temple led to a protest on the
part of the Jews. Whilst the disciples saw in it the fulfilment of
a Messianic prophecy (Ps. 68:10) and therefore a revelation of
the Messias (John 2:17), the Jews, i.e. the priests who belonged
to the sect of the Pharisees or of the Sadducees, the governors
of the Temple, and the members of the Sanhedrim, saw nothing
supernatural in it, but regarded it on the contrary as presumption,
as an interference with their rights, an attack upon their authority,
a public and grave condemnation of their forgetfulness of duty
and disrespect for the Temple and for God. Full of vexation, envy
and unbelief, they sought to nullify the effect of the deed by
calling our Lord to account and requiring a miracle in proof of
His divine authority (John 2:18); and this all the more, because
they had perhaps also received information of the words He had
spoken whilst driving out the dealers. Their intention was evidently insincere, and sprang from resistance to truth and conscience and, in its very source, from unbelief. They followed the
same policy again later on (Matt. 12:38; 16:1). It is an easy means

of escaping from the obligation to believe, to take one's stand upon an exterior miracle, the reality of which, if granted, can afterwards be disputed. Later on, after the multiplication of bread, the Jews also asked: "What sign dost Thou show?" (John 6:30.) This bold act of our Saviour was a telling appeal to the conscience of the people, and a powerful stirring of the stagnant waters of hypocrisy and unbelief. He roused these dispositions and brought them to light, and so forced the dominant party to a decision concerning the Messias. In order to crush this audacious man, from Whom they evidently had everything to fear, and to get Him out of the way, they demand of Him a miracle.

Our Saviour's answer was suited to this disposition of mind: "Destroy this temple, and in three days I will raise it up" (John 2:19). The answer was, first, an equivocal one, because they would not have believed even if He had given them a direct answer, or worked a miracle. The words might mean the material Temple or the temple of His Body, and they denoted in the latter case the true and supreme sanctuary of God, the God-Man Himself (Matt. 12:6). It is a just punishment of the insincerity of this people, that our Saviour holds the truth before them under a veil and as in an enigma. This will often be the case again during His public life (Matt. 13:13). But He expressed Himself more clearly with regard to His Resurrection later on (Matt. 12:39). In the second place, the answer was nevertheless a sufficiently clear one, inasmuch as it made plain to them that He had at command a higher, divine authority, whereby He was ready and powerful enough to do still greater and more marvelous things. Lastly, the answer is prophetic. By the "temple" our Saviour meant His Body (John 2:21). He prophesied hereby His Death and Resurrection, and gave them a twofold miracle; that of His Resurrection, which is the greatest and most conclusive proof of His Divinity, and the miracle of its prediction. He saw in spirit how the antipathy and unbelief which had been aroused by this deed would pass into mortal hatred, and how no miracle but the Resurrection would overcome this incredulity. He saw, so to speak, the end in the beginning, and therefore He held out to them the prospect of His Resurrection, as a sign of His power and authority. So these words were like a flash of lightning, illuminating His public life from its rise until its setting. In their perplexity, ignorance, or malice, the Jews referred all this to the material Temple, and scornfully asked how it would be possible for Him to accom-

plish in three days what had been done only by the laborious work
of forty-six years (John 2:20; cf. Introd., p. 6). They might have
seen from the testimony of the Baptist and the purification of the
Temple, that He was the One with the winnowing-fan (Matt.
3:12) Who had been predicted, and that He needed no miracle
to prove His authority. But as He promised an eventual miracle,
they could not say that He rejected their demand. Their reference
to the material Temple was merely an evasion to which they
resorted in their embarrassment (Matt. 21:25; 22:19). But they
took no active steps against our Lord at that time.

With the people, the effect of the purification of the Temple
and the other miracles that He performed on this occasion (John
2:23) was that many believed in Him and His divine mission.
But our Lord recognized by virtue of His omniscience the defec-
tive and fickle nature of their faith, and "did not trust Himself"
(i.e. the more profound doctrine with regard to the mystery of
His mission and His nature) "unto them" (John 2:24, 25). For
this reason He received no one here into the number of His disciples.

Such is the first appearance of our Saviour in Jerusalem before
the priesthood and people, and it is one of the highest significance. It is the opening scene of the new revelation. It shows the
Saviour in His essential character as Messias and Son of God,
in word and deed. He shows Himself here as the "Angel of the
Testament" prophesied by Malachias (Mal. 3:1); He calls the
Lord of the Temple His Father, works a true miracle in the purification of the Temple, and thus unfolds the entire authoritative
power of the Messias; He simply exercises in the Temple the authority of Lord over His own House. Secondly, it shows our
Saviour fulfilling His mission, repairing the honor of His Father
by the purification of the Temple and of religion in general. Indeed, it is significant that He celebrates the beginning and the end
of His ministry by a cleansing of the Temple (Matt. 21:12). It
shows us, thirdly, what was the chief motive power of our
Saviour's life, namely a consuming zeal for God's glory, a zeal
infinitely greater than that of the priest Phinees (Num. 25). The
words of Scripture: "The zeal of Thy house hath eaten me up"
(Ps. 68:10), are an epitome of His interior dispositions, the soul
of His inner life, the true cause of His death. Finally, this first
public appearance shows us the part He had to play in life, namely
to be the leader of a little band of believers and weak disciples, in

intercourse with a fickle, untrustworthy people, in conflict with the unbelief of a depraved priesthood, succumbing to and yet vanquishing this unbelief by His Death and Resurrection. Such is the vista which His public life opens out. He begins it today, commences the combat, and prophesies His Death and Resurrection. It is also significant that His words, "Destroy this temple," were made use of to introduce the final process against Him; and from these very words the falsity of the accusation is evident. St. John thus supplements the other Evangelists (Matt. 26:61; cf. Acts 6:14). Thus all the germs of the subsequent development are contained in this mystery. It is, so to speak, the program and public prediction of His destiny in life (cf. Ps. 68).

## NICODEMUS

JOHN 3:1. And there was a man of the Pharisees, named Nicodemus, a ruler of the Jews.—2. This man came to Jesus by night and said to him: "Rabbi, we know that thou art come a teacher from God; for no man can do these signs which thou dost, unless God be with him."—3. Jesus answered and said to him: "Amen, amen I say to thee, unless a man be born again, he cannot see the kingdom of God."—4. Nicodemus saith to him: "How can a man be born when he is old? can he enter a second time into his mother's womb, and be born again?"—5. Jesus answered: "Amen, amen I say to thee, unless a man be born again of water and the Holy Ghost, he cannot enter into the kingdom of God.—6. That which is born of the flesh, is flesh; and that which is born of the Spirit, is spirit.—7. Wonder not that I said to thee: You must be born again.—8. The Spirit breatheth where he will, and thou hearest his voice, but thou knowest not whence he cometh or whither he goeth: so is every one that is born of the Spirit."—9. Nicodemus answered and said to him: "How can these things be done?"—10. Jesus answered and said to him: "Art thou a master in Israel, and knowest not these things?—11. Amen, amen I say to thee, that we speak what we know, and we testify what we have seen, and you receive not our testimony.—12. If I have spoken to you earthly things, and you believe not; how will you believe if I shall speak to you heavenly things?—13. And no man hath ascended into heaven, but he that descended from heaven, the Son of Man who is in heaven.—14. And as Moses lifted up the serpent in the desert, so must the Son of Man be lifted up;—15. That whosoever believeth in him may not perish, but may have life everlasting.—16. For God so loved the world as to give his only-begotten Son; that whosoever believeth in him may not perish, but may have life everlasting.—17. For God sent not his Son into the world to judge the world, but that the world may be saved by him.—18. He that believeth in him is not judged; but he that doth not believe is already judged, because he believeth not in the name of the only-begotten Son of God.—19. And this is the judgment: because the light is come into the world, and men loved darkness rather than the light; for their works were evil.—20. For every one that doth evil hateth the light, and cometh not to the light, that his works may not be reproved;—21. But he that doth truth, cometh to the light, that his works may be made manifest, because they are done in God."

### 1. HOW NICODEMUS COMES TO OUR SAVIOUR

During our Saviour's stay in Jerusalem Nicodemus came to speak with Him. Who was Nicodemus? A man much looked up to by the Jews (John 3:1), a member of the Sanhedrim (John 7:50), an eminent teacher of the law (John 3:10), and a Pharisee. As may be seen from all that is related of him, he was full of Jewish and pharisaical prejudices with regard to the manner and object of the coming of the Messias, the nature of His kingdom, and the conditions of participation in it; but he was honorable, sincere, inquiring, humble, and full of eagerness to find salvation (John 3:2).

When does he come? Immediately, at the very first public appearance of Jesus, and by night (John 3:2), perhaps in order to speak with our Lord without interruption, perhaps because he did not wish to be seen receiving instruction from another master, perhaps for fear of the Pharisees (John 7:50; 19:38, 39) or out of consideration for our Saviour.

What attracted Nicodemus? Above all, the miracles which our Lord worked in Jerusalem on this occasion (John 3:2); also His doctrine (John 3:2) and the conviction which had been formed in his mind and in the minds of other Pharisees that our Saviour had a special mission from God and was a prophet, perhaps even the Messias.

And what did he want of our Saviour? As may be guessed from his words of greeting (John 3:2), Nicodemus had a presentiment that our Saviour was the Messias. He wished, then, to learn if this was really the case and what would be the nature of His kingdom, a share in which every Pharisee claimed as his right. It may well have been a sacrifice for Nicodemus to make up his mind to visit our Saviour, but the result showed how important it was for him to follow the invitation of grace.

### 2. HOW OUR SAVIOUR INSTRUCTS NICODEMUS

Our Saviour knew the thoughts of Nicodemus, and instructed him in everything, the nature of His Person and kingdom, the "kingdom of God" (John 3:3), by revealing to him two means necessary for participation in it, which contained all that he wished to know.

The first means is baptism; that is, an entirely new and spiritual existence through the Sacrament of Baptism. Our Saviour tells him four things concerning this Sacrament. First, He defines with precision its essentials; water and the Holy Ghost (John 3:5). Secondly, He defines its effect, which, in contrast to the Jewish view that carnal descent from Abraham sufficed for participation in the kingdom of God, is represented as a true spiritual regeneration by the Holy Ghost (3:3, 7). Thirdly, our Saviour declares the absolute necessity of baptism for salvation, and emphasizes this necessity by the repeated affirmation: "Amen, amen I say to thee" (John 3:5), and then by demonstration: God is a Spirit and therefore His kingdom also is immaterial, spiritual and supernatural. But nothing natural, such as the natural birth of the flesh, can suffice for the supernatural effect of making us children of God and heirs of the kingdom of heaven; a spiritual birth by the power of the Holy Ghost must take place (John 3:6). Fourthly, as a necessary consequence, our Saviour represents this effect of the Sacrament, the regeneration by the Holy Ghost, as most sublime, mysterious and inexplicable with regard to its origin, nature and aim; and He points out that our not understanding it is no reason for not believing in it. As a proof of this our Saviour employs the deep and significant comparison of the wind, the most incorporeal of material things; its source, progress and destination are unknown to us, and yet we are convinced of its existence, because we perceive it with our senses (John 3:7, 8). "Wind" and "spirit" are denoted in several languages by the same word, and the wind is a symbol of the Holy Ghost, and typifies His origin in the breathing of the love of Father and Son and in His effects upon the creature. The efficacy of baptism has its origin in the love of God, i.e. in the Holy Ghost, and communicates the Holy Ghost Himself and His life. What a different being, how truly celestial is a man thus spiritually born, in comparison with the carnal son of Abraham! Our Saviour does but confirm here what John had prophesied of Him, namely that He would baptize with the Holy Ghost (Matt. 3:11; Mark 1:8; Luke 3:6; John 1:33).

The second means of salvation is faith. Because Nicodemus, like all his sect, regarded the kingdom of the Messias merely as one of natural and sensual happiness, he cannot comprehend the mystery of spiritual regeneration (John 3:4, 9); and therefore our Saviour takes occasion to establish the necessity of faith, as the only means of comprehending supernatural truths and the hidden decrees of God, and thus of becoming participators in the kingdom of the Messias. If he does not understand the mystery of regeneration, which was to be accomplished here below, how much less then will he comprehend other divine purposes fulfilled above (John 3:12), which are connected with this spiritual regeneration by the Holy Ghost as its preliminaries or developments, and which belong to the very essence of the kingdom of the Messias. And herewith our Saviour reveals to him the deepest supernatural mysteries, namely the incomprehensible love of God in the fact and nature of the Incarnation and in its object, the redemption of mankind by the Death on the Cross. Moreover our Saviour gives powerful motives for accepting and assenting to these truths. The first motive is His testimony as the Son of God, who, because He is in heaven, knows and has seen all this (John 3:11, 13) either by His eternal omniscience or by His knowledge as God-Man, and has become Man in order to bear witness to it; the second is the great manifestation of the love of God in the Incarnation, the Redemption by the Death on the Cross (John 3:14, 16), and the blessings and benefits of eternal life (John 3:15, 16, 17), which God had already caused to be illustrated in the Old Covenant by types, as a reward of faith (John 3:14); the third motive for belief is the punishment to be inflicted upon unbelief at the judgment, not that this is the object of God's coming among mankind, but rather the incidental and natural consequence of unbelief (John 3:17, 18, 19); fourthly, the truth that the real cause of unbelief is insincerity of heart and moral corruption (John 3:19, 20, 21), which hides itself from the light of truth on false pretexts. "And men loved darkness rather than the light. For their works were evil."

Our Saviour left nothing unanswered. For the instruction of this erudite and sincere Pharisee, He took occasion to speak of the greatness and glory of the kingdom of the Messias, of which His Heart was full. In connection with this idea He unfolds and reveals the most profound mysteries of religion. Therefore He unrolls before Nicodemus in magnificent outlines the whole nature of this kingdom. Its nature is interior, immaterial, spiritual and supernatural (Luke 17:20); its Author and Head is a human and yet Divine Being; its character is not triumph, but redemption through ignominy and death; its operation is not an external judgment, the exaltation of the Jews and overthrow of the Gentiles, but an interior judgment, by which men will be ranked according to their faith or unbelief: all sharp contrasts to the carnal views and expectations of the Jews with regard to the kingdom of the Messias.

### 3. HOW OUR SAVIOUR WINS NICODEMUS

The result showed that Nicodemus was gained for our Lord. And how had He succeeded in this? First by His great gentleness and kindness. He does not upbraid Nicodemus for his Jewish prejudices, but seeks to correct them. He disregards his reserve and his fear of the Pharisees, which may have induced him to seek our Lord only by night. Our Saviour looks only at his goodwill and longing for the truth.

Secondly, our Lord wins Nicodemus by His intellectual superiority, which He allows him to feel, though with great delicacy (John 3:10, 11, 12). He lets him see how superficial and insufficient is the wisdom of his school in matters concerning salvation and the kingdom of the Messias, so that it does not even know the necessary conditions of participation in the same; and yet the baptism with the Spirit by the Messias had been foretold often enough in the Scriptures (Jer. 31:33; Ez. 36:25; Zach. 13:1).

Thirdly, our Lord wins Nicodemus by praise, not expressed by flattery but implied in encouragement, telling him that He expects other steps from his sincerity and probity (John 3:21). But it needs the sight of the Cross to induce Nicodemus to take the final and decisive step; the Cross, the prospect of which is here mysteriously held out to him in the figure of the brazen serpent.

Fourthly and lastly, our Lord displays towards Nicodemus unusual confidence, and reveals to him without reserve the greatest and most profound mysteries: His Divinity, His Incarnation, His office of Redeemer and Judge, whereas He did not trust Himself to anyone else in Jerusalem (John 2:24). So Nicodemus must surely have quitted our Lord full of faith, gratitude and devotion. And though he does not immediately declare himself openly as one of His adherents, yet the foundation for such a declaration is laid, and he will complete it in due time (John 19:39). It is worthy of note that this Nicodemus appears upon the scenes of the first and fourth Paschal feasts. On the first of these feasts our Lord prophesies His death, on the fourth He accomplishes it. How different is the part taken by Nicodemus in the destinies of our Lord on these two decisive occasions! Our Lord's kindness and indulgence have brought about this wonderful spiritual development.

We have here an example of a familiar conversation of our Saviour with His friends and faithful followers. Several points deserve consideration; in the first place, this conversation gives us a glimpse of the public feeling of the time, and of the power of prejudice over even the best men of pharisaical tendency, and shows the irritation of this party even at the very first appearance of the Saviour. Nicodemus only dares (as we may well assume, from fear) to visit our Lord by night. On the other hand, it is also consoling to see how, even with this party, love of justice, probity, good-will and sincere desire of truth can overcome prejudice by the grace of God. It is almost touching to see how this aged and celebrated teacher of the law sinks down at our Saviour's feet, willing to be taught. Further, we have here a good opportunity of becoming acquainted with the wonderful character and personality of our Saviour; the beauty of His mind, the superiority of His intellect, the depth and ingenuity of His speech and method of teaching (John 3:8); then His prudence and dexterity in the treatment of different people, and above all His kindness, condescension, openness and straightforwardness, wherever He finds good-will and a receptive mind. He grants everything to sincerity and good-will. Lastly, the conversation is exceedingly important as regards faith. Our Saviour reveals and confirms here the following truths: the necessity and essential character of baptism, and the necessity of faith, just as He teaches them later on (Mark 16:16; Matt. 28:19); then the mystery of the Most Holy Trinity; the mystery of the Incarnation, together with its object, the Redemption and its accomplishment by the Death on the Cross; the beatific vision enjoyed by the God-Man, and His power over all things (Matt. 11:27). The Lamb of God appears in all He says. Thus the conversation with Nicodemus is a true and complete self-manifestation; and that in Judaea, in Jerusalem, and to a member of the Great Council and a teacher of the law.

### Dispute of John's Disciples with the Jews

#### John's Fourth Testimony to Christ

JOHN 3:22. After these things Jesus and his disciples came into the land of Judaea; and there he abode with them and baptized.—23. And John also was baptizing in Ennon near Salim, because there was much water there; and they came and were baptized.—24. For John was not yet cast into prison.—25. And there arose a question between some of John's disciples and the Jews concerning purification;—26. And they came to John, and said to him: "Rabbi, he that was with thee beyond the Jordan, to whom thou gavest testimony, behold he baptizeth, and all men come to him."—27. John answered and said: "A man cannot receive anything, unless it be given him from heaven.—28. You yourselves do bear me witness, that I said: I am not Christ; but that I am sent before him.—29. He that hath the bride is the bridegroom; but the friend of the bridegroom, who standeth and heareth him, rejoiceth with joy because of the bridegroom's voice. This my joy therefore is fulfilled.—30. He must increase, but I must decrease.—31. He that cometh from above is above all. He that is of the earth, of the earth he is, and of the earth he speaketh. He that cometh from heaven is above all.—32. And what he hath seen and heard, that he testifieth; and no man receiveth his testimony. —33. He that hath received his testimony, hath set to his seal that God is true.— 34. For he whom God hath sent, speaketh the words of God; for God doth not give the spirit by measure.—35. The Father loveth the Son; and he hath given all things into his hand.—36. He that believeth in the Son, hath life everlasting; but he that believeth not the Son, shall not see life, but the wrath of God abideth on him."

## 1. OUR SAVIOUR WORKS IN JUDAEA

After the Feast of the Pasch our Saviour went with His disciples into the country districts of Judaea, and worked there. In this He was guided by the same reasons as prompted Him to exercise His ministry in Jerusalem; the rather perhaps, now that He had met with little response in the city, at any rate from those in power. In any case Judaea was the scene of the chief events of sacred history. The ministry of Jesus is now for the first time particularly specified as that of baptism (John 3:22; 4:1). He proceeds, as a matter of fact, according to the doctrine He had placed before Nicodemus, and thus fulfils the sign of the Messias which John had foretold of Him (Matt. 3:11).

As regards the manner of this baptismal ministry we are told, first, that our Saviour Himself did not baptize, but His disciples (John 4:2). The baptism of Jesus is thus at once proved to be a different one from that of John, and superior to his. John authorized no one to baptize in his name; our Saviour imparts to His disciples this authority, and this baptism was probably administered "in the name of Jesus," that is, in the name of the Messias, Who had come and was present. As regards its effect, some interpreters of Scripture think that it imparted grace and the Holy Ghost, in contrast to the baptism of John; others however are not of this opinion. At all events it was an extraordinary anticipation of the Sacrament of Baptism, and a preparation of the people for the same by awakening in them the spirit of penance. Probably this was the reason why our Saviour did not baptize in person. The same thing may be true of the unction administered by the disciples (Mark 6:13), in relation to the Sacrament of Extreme

Unction. Secondly, we are given to understand that this baptismal ministry was on the one hand very great and important, indeed greater than that of John (John 3:26; 4:1); but on the other hand without lasting and real fruit of faith, for the people did not receive the testimony of Jesus (John 3:32). On the contrary, His baptism was the occasion of dispute.

### 2. JOHN'S DISCIPLES FALL INTO A DISPUTE WITH THE JEWS

The first occasion of this dispute was the baptismal ministry of Jesus. John was not yet imprisoned, and he also continued to baptize, for he had not received any divine command to cease doing so after the coming of Jesus, and moreover he had thereby opportunities of calling the attention of his disciples and of the people who flocked to him to our Saviour, and of leading them to Him. He had only withdrawn (out of reverence and as though to give place to our Lord) from the lowlands of the Jordan to Ennon, near Salim, which is situated not far from Sichem in Samaria, and near the border of Galilee.

The second occasion of the dispute was certain Jews, who, coming perhaps from the baptism of the disciples of Jesus, fell into an argument with John's disciples, either about legal purifications or about baptism itself (John 3:25); it may be that they irritated these disciples by unwise exaggeration of the success of Jesus, or with the intention of raising a dispute.

The final occasion was the blind and exaggerated zeal with which John's disciples were attached to their master, so that they even resisted, whether from partiality or from selfishness, his own statements and instructions; they came to John and complained that the man to whom he had borne testimony, and who therefore owed his influence to him (John), was now presuming to baptize also, which John alone was authorized to do, and that all men were thronging to Him (John 3:26). These words imply no little envy and, while they cast a slight upon Jesus, over-estimate the person of the Baptist. The disciples seem to have adopted only the outward austerity of their master, but not his lofty spirit, his interior virtue, his humility and unselfishness.

### 3. JOHN BEARS TESTIMONY TO JESUS

John gives a threefold answer, corresponding to the complaint. He first answers it in a general way. The success of Jesus came from God and was His gift, therefore it must not cause them astonishment or vexation (John 3:27). This was a true and reasonable answer, and sufficient to satisfy reasonable men.

Secondly, John turns the very words of his disciples against themselves, for they admitted that he had borne testimony to Jesus; and he declares once more that he is not Christ, but merely His Forerunner, as their own words testified (John 3:28). He then indicates further his relation to Christ by comparing himself to a bridegroom's friend or supporter, whose office it is to ask the hand of the bride for his friend, to be the intermediary between the bethrothed couple, and to superintend the wedding festivity. The friend does not appropriate the bride for himself, he is not envious when the bride and bridegroom meet; on the contrary, he stands at a respectful distance, and rejoices when he has to give place to the bridegroom (John 3:29). Such is the position of St. John. His influence and even his life must decline; he must disappear, but Jesus must increase in the esteem of men (John 3:30). His joy is fulfilled thereby (John 3:29). Thus the disciples had an answer to their complaint that all were thronging to Jesus. This comparison with the "friend of the bridegroom" is significant. In Holy Scripture the covenant with God is often represented as a marriage-bond (Isa. 50:1; 54:6; Jer. 2:2; Osee 2:19; Ps. 44). Jehovah Himself had appeared in the person of the Messias. How tender, noble, and full of meaning is John's simile! It is the expression and picture of a truly apostolic laborer. He is only the "friend of the bridegroom," nothing more.

Thirdly, St. John profits by this occasion to bear a new and glorious testimony to Christ. In order to extol Him, he leaves the comparison with himself and other men. We are all of earthly origin, and therefore earthly and retricted in our being, our knowledge and our faculties. With us everything is a grace of God, and even that is restricted (John 3:31). But Christ is of heavenly origin, and therefore superior to all (John 3:31); He is God's eyewitness and envoy (John 3:32, 34), simply the Son of God (John 3:35, 36). Therefore the Father loves Him, and has given to Him the Spirit without measure, more than to all the prophets (John 3:34); the fulness of divine knowledge (John 3:32, 34) and power, all this He has given into His hand (John 3:35). He is the Source of all knowledge, revelation and salvation. From this John infers the obligation of believing in Him and attaching oneself to Him, and gives beautiful reasons for so doing. First, faith in Jesus is a testimony to the truth of God Himself, just as unbelief, on the other hand, taxes God with untruthfulness (John 3:33). The second motive is the reward and punishment: "He that believeth in the Son hath life everlasting; but he that believeth not the Son shall not see life, but the wrath of God abideth on him" (John 3:36). He sorrowfully adds: "No man receiveth His (i.e. Jesus') testimony" (John 3:22).

Such is the ministry of Jesus in the rural districts of Judaea, and it is not unlike the ministry in the city in its results. There was a great deal of sensation and crowding to Him, but little conversion of heart; plenty of dispute, but no readiness to believe. The most beautiful and sublime thing here is the testimony of St. John. It is his last and loftiest word about Jesus, and his last earnest exhortation to the Jews and to his disciples. It is his farewell address. Henceforth he disappears. One feels in his closing words how painful to him is the misconception of the object of his ministry, of his testimony and of the self-manifestation of Jesus in Judaea. He cannot divest the people of their Jewish stubbornness and hardness of heart. He bears witness to the unbelief of Judaea, laments it with deep sorrow, and threatens it with the anger of God. Indeed, his words sound like an echo of the closing words of the last prophet: "Behold, I will send you Elias the prophet, before the coming of the great and dreadful day of the Lord. And he shall turn the heart of the fathers to the children, and the heart of the children to their fathers: lest I come and strike the earth with anathema" (Mal. 4:5, 6). They sound like a prophecy and an exclamation of despair of the salvation of his people, upon whom the wrath of God will rest on account of their unbelief. But his last words are not merely a sigh and a lamentation. His grief makes him rise to a sublime and glorious testimony of Christ, and he declares also that Christ has found His bride and will conclude the alliance in spite of all unbelief and resistance. How noble and strong is the character of John, and yet how tempered by delicacy! How earnestly, unselfishly and heroically he sums up in word and deed his relation to Christ! Like the morning star, he precedes the Sun of Justice, shines in splendor, and sinks with joy before the glory of His rising.

### ARREST AND IMPRISONMENT OF JOHN THE BAPTIST

JOHN 4:1. When Jesus therefore understood that the Pharisees had heard that Jesus maketh more disciples and baptizeth more than John,—2. (Though Jesus himself did not baptize, but his disciples,)—3. He left Judaea and went again into Galilee.

LUKE 3:19. But Herod the tetrarch, when he was reproved by him (John) for Herodias, his brother's wife, and for all the evils which Herod had done,—20. He added this also above all, and shut up John in prison.

MARK 1:14. And after that John was delivered up, Jesus came into Galilee, preaching the Gospel of the kingdom of God.

MARK 6:17. For Herod himself had sent and apprehended John, and bound him in prison for the sake of Herodias, the wife of Philip his brother, because he had married her.—18. For John said to Herod: "It is not lawful for thee to have thy brother's wife."

MATT. 4:12. And when Jesus had heard that John was delivered up, he retired into Galilee.

MATT. 14:3. For Herod had apprehended John and bound him, and put him into prison, because of Herodias, his brother's wife.—4. For John said to him: "It is not lawful for thee to have her."—5. And having a mind to put him to death, he feared the people; because they esteemed him as a prophet.

### 1. OCCASION OF JOHN'S ARREST

The remote cause of the arrest of St. John was the crime of Herod and Herodias. Herod carried off Herodias, the wife of his half-brother Philip (not the prince of Ituraea, but a private citizen), and lived openly with her. It was a disgraceful deed and a public scandal, brought about on the one hand by the lust of Herod and on the other by the ambition of Herodias, who wished to become a princess. Public morality was seriously injured by this example of persons in such high position.

The occasion was the apostolic candor and fearlessness of St. John. Publicly, since the scandal was a public one, he rebuked Herod for the incest (Mark 6:18; Matt. 14:3, 4), as well as for many other evil deeds (Luke 3:19); and this at the risk of the displeasure and revenge of the powerful sinners, and to the danger of his liberty and his life. But John was a man of inflexible determination and a lover of justice. He feared nothing and no one but God, and was therefore feared and respected even by his enemies.

The Pharisees appear to have been instrumental, inasmuch as they "delivered up" John to Herod. Two Evangelists make use of this expression (Mark 1:14; Matt. 4:12), and it states not only that John was consigned to prison, but also how and through whom; namely, by treachery on the part of the Pharisees. More hidden reasons also argue for this assumption. John was for the Pharisees an extremely unpleasant monitor, and was also dangerous on account of his influence. He rebuked them unmercifully and publicly for their unbelief (John 1:26; 3:32), pride and carnal confidence (Matt. 3:7). His extraordinary mission (John 1:24,

25) and austere manner of life (Matt. 11:18) probably irritated them no less, and above all his open and resolute support of our Saviour as the true Messias. Our Saviour Himself seems to allude to this treachery later on (Matt. 17:12; Luke 13:33). They profited then by Herod's exasperation, delivered John up, and thus got rid of their dangerous monitor without making themselves obnoxious to the people, who revered him as a prophet.

## 2. ARREST AND IMPRISONMENT OF JOHN

With regard to John's arrest no particulars are recorded. But we may assume with good reason that he yielded to force in a noble, dignified and willing manner, although he possibly knew of the project and could have protected himself by his influence with the people. As we are told by tradition, he was brought to the Castle of Machaerus, on the east coast of the Dead Sea, to be kept in custody there (cf. Introd., p. 2). This took place late in the autumn following the first Feast of the Pasch.

Here John hallowed his prison by prayer, to which he could now devote himself as he had formerly done in the desert; he hallowed it by patience, suffering, and willing endurance of captivity; indeed, he even sanctified his imprisonment by zeal for souls. As it appears, Herod mitigated by degrees the strictness of his captivity and permitted him some intercourse with his disciples (Matt. 11:2). Herod respected the great man, heard him repeatedly, and followed his advice in many respects (Mark 6:20). How touching and edifying is this prison life of St. John! The great and holy man lies in a deep dungeon, guarded by fox and hyena— Herod and Herodias; a short time before sought after and highly honored by all the people, now solitary and forsaken; hitherto so powerful in word and deed before the whole nation, now his voice has died away in a prison; his hands, which have baptized thousands, even the Messias, and bestowed incalculable blessings, are bound and loaded with chains; his glorious ministry, after scarcely a year's duration, is violently put an end to by the cruel caprice of the most disgraceful passions. How sad all this is from a natural point of view! But his spirit is unbroken. With a noble joy in suffering he bears his captivity, and thus promotes the work of our Lord. "He must increase, but I must decrease." How often may he have been present in thought on the other side of the Jordan, beside his Lord! How his heart must have throbbed with holy longing, love, and desire to see Him acknowledged by the whole nation, when from the heights of his inaccessible castle-dungeon he accompanied Him in spirit on His way!

### 3. CONSEQUENCES FOR OUR LORD

The arrest of John caused our Lord to leave Judaea with His disciples and to remove the scene of His ministry to Galilee. St. Mark relates that Jesus came into Galilee after John had been delivered up (Mark 1:14); and St. Matthew says that Jesus retired into Galilee after He had heard that John was delivered up (Matt. 4:12). St. John adds that Jesus left Judaea because He had "understood that the Pharisees had heard that Jesus maketh more disciples and baptizeth more than John" (John 4:1, 3). These texts supplement and throw light upon each other. Our Saviour evidently foresaw that the Pharisees would take measures against Him, because they remarked that His appearance was accompanied by a still more powerful effect upon the people than that of John. The Pharisees could very easily, in order to get rid of Him also, inform against Him as a disciple and partisan of John, and propose His arrest. In far-off Galilee the ministry of Jesus did not strike the attention of the Pharisees so much, and irritated them less. Their influence was not so powerful there. The Pharisees, rather than Herod, were the real enemies of our Saviour. Besides, they afterwards attempted steps against our Lord similar to those against John, in Galilee (Mark 3:6) and Peraea (Luke 13:31). For these reasons our Saviour preferred to go into Galilee, after having worked in Judaea, as it seems, during the spring, summer and autumn (John 4:35).

Thus the Pharisees forcibly drove away salvation from Judaea, and under their influence the opposition grew more and more serious. "He came unto His own, and His own received Him not" (John 1:11). John in bonds and Jesus driven away,—such is the state of affairs about a year after our Saviour's first appearance at the Jordan.

## OUR SAVIOUR IN SAMARIA

JOHN 4:4. And Jesus was of necessity to pass through Samaria.—5. He cometh therefore to a city of Samaria which is called Sichar, near the land which Jacob gave to his son Joseph.—6. Now Jacob's well was there. Jesus therefore being wearied with his journey, sat thus on the well. It was about the sixth hour.—7. There cometh a woman of Samaria to draw water. Jesus saith to her: "Give me to drink." —8. (For his disciples were gone into the city to buy meats.)—9. Then that Samaritan woman saith to him: "How dost thou, being a Jew, ask of me to drink, who am a Samaritan woman?" For the Jews do not communicate with the Samaritans.—10. Jesus answered and said to her: "If thou didst know the gift of God, and who he is that saith to thee, Give me to drink; thou perhaps wouldst have asked of him, and he would have given thee l:ving water."—11. The woman saith to him: "Sir, thou hast nothing wherein to draw, and the well is deep; from whence then hast thou living water?—12. Art thou greater than our father Jacob, who gave us the well, and drank thereof himself, and his children, and his cattle?" —13. Jesus answered and said to her: "Whosoever drinketh of this water, shall thirst again; but he that shall drink of the water that I will give him, shall not thirst for ever.—14. But the water that I will give him shall become in him a fountain of water springing up into life everlasting."—15. The woman saith to him: "Sir, give me this water, that I may not thirst, nor come hither to draw."—16. Jesus saith to her: "Go, call thy husband, and come hither."—17. The woman answered and said: "I have no husband." Jesus saith to her: "Thou hast said well, I have no husband;—18. For thou hast had five husbands, and he whom thou now hast, is not thy husband; this thou hast said truly."—19. The woman saith to him: "Sir, I perceive that thou art a prophet.—20. Our fathers adored on this mountain, and you say that at Jerusalem is the place where men must adore."—21. Jesus saith to her: "Woman, believe me, that the hour cometh, when you shall neither on this mountain nor in Jerusalem adore the Father.—22. You adore that which you know not; we adore that which we know; for salvation is of the Jews.—23. But the hour cometh, and now is, when the true adorers shall adore the Father in spirit and in truth. For the Father also seeketh such to adore him.—24. God is a spirit; and they that adore him, must adore him in spirit and in truth."—25. The woman saith to him: "I know that the Messias cometh (who is called Christ); therefore when he is come, he will tell us all things."—26. Jesus saith to her: "I am he, who am speaking with thee."—27. And immediately his disciples came; and they wondered that he talked with the woman. Yet no man said: What seekest thou, or why talkest thou with her?—28. The woman therefore left her water-pot, and went her way into the city, and saith to the men there:—29. "Come, and see a man who has told me all things whatsoever I have done. Is not he the Christ?" —30. They went therefore out of the city, and came unto him.—31. In the meantime the disciples prayed him, saying: "Rabbi, eat."—32. But he said to them: "I have meat to eat which you know not."—33. The disciples therefore said one to another: "Hath any man brought him to eat?"—34. Jesus saith to them: "My meat is to do the will of him that sent me, that I may perfect his work.—35. Do not you say, there are yet four months, and then the harvest cometh? Behold I say to you, Lift up your eyes, and see the countries, for they are white already to harvest.—36. And he that reapeth, receiveth wages, and gathereth fruit unto life everlasting; that both he that soweth and he that reapeth may rejoice together.— 37. For in this is the saying true: that it is one man that soweth, and it is another that reapeth.—38. I have sent you to reap that in which you did not labor; others have labored, and you have entered into their labors."—39. Now of that city many of the Samaritans believed in him, for the word of the woman giving testimony: "He told me all things whatsoever I have done."—40. So when the Samaritans were come to him, they desired him that he would tarry there. And he abode there two days.—41. And many more believed in him because of his own word.—42. And they said to the woman: "We now believe, not for thy saying; for we ourselves have heard him, and know that this is indeed the Saviour of the world."

### 1. OUR SAVIOUR RESTS AT THE WELL OF JACOB, NEAR SICHAR

On His way through the interior from Judaea to Galilee our Saviour came to Sichar, at the foot of Mt. Garizim, and sat down

at the well of Jacob whilst His disciples went to buy food in the
city. He sits there quite simply, as though He had nothing in view
but to rest from His weariness. But everything points to a mystery
of mercy and a profound and gracious intention of our Saviour.
The ruling party had driven Him out of Judaea, and so He directs
His labors to Galilee, where another part of Israel dwelt, which
had remained faithful. But why does He take the road through
Samaria to Galilee, and not along by the Jordan through Peraea?
Why does He take His mid-day rest here?

Evidently He wishes to bestow here the blessing of a revelation
of Himself, as is shown in the course of the mystery. And why?
It is a sacred ground upon which He rests, full of great, touching,
and holy reminiscences; of Abraham, who first built an altar here
(Gen. 12:6, 7); of Jacob, who bought the piece of land, erected
an altar, and dug the well upon which our Saviour sits (Gen.
33:18, 20); of Joseph, who was buried here (Gen. 47:22; Jos.
24:32); and lastly of the stone of testimony and the altar which
Moses ordered to be erected (Deut. 28:4, 8). Here the tribe of
Ephraim had formerly dwelt, and hence, unhappily, the revolt
of the ten tribes had proceeded (III Kings 12:6), which brought
about the Assyrian captivity. The poor, degenerate, abandoned
Samaritans lived there now (cf. Introd., pp. 4 f.). Perhaps a milder
treatment and overtures on the part of Israel might have brought
about a change for the better. But no advances were made, until
our Saviour came to comfort the poor, forsaken and "foolish people" of Sichem (Eccli. 50:28), the nation of "strangers" in the
Promised Land, and this only in passing by; He did not remain
with them, because His mission was to the chosen people of God.
He Himself calls them strangers (Luke 17:18), and also forbids
His disciples to preach to them during His lifetime (Matt. 10:5).
He evidently wished merely to prepare the Samaritans for the
preaching of the Apostles after His Ascension (Acts 1:8). On the
lips of a Jew the epithet "Samaritan" was a term of opprobrium.
This insult they later cast upon our Lord (John 8:48). But this
was a matter of indifference to Him. Such may well have been
His thoughts and intentions, as He sat there on the well, in sight
of the city on Mt. Garizim.

## 2. OUR SAVIOUR REVEALS HIMSELF TO THE SAMARITAN WOMAN

At this moment a woman, probably a native of Samaria, came
out of the city to draw water from the well. The poor woman—

in many respects the type of her people—was living in error (John 4:17, 18), but not entirely depraved (John 4:17, 19), not irreligious (John 4:12, 20, 25), frank and outspoken (John 4:19, 29), and not without curiosity.

And how does our Saviour act in order to win her? With great knowledge of human nature, with liberty of spirit and with magnanimity. He approaches her first, and asks, contrary to all custom of His countrymen, for a drink of water, so that the woman herself wonders, since she immediately recognizes Him as a Jew by His speech and dress (John 4:7, 9). It is often the best means of winning people, to ask a small service of them, because this both shows and awakens confidence, and is a good way of making the first overtures. He then excites her curiosity by the mysterious hints concerning His Person and His gift of "living water," better than that of Jacob, indeed of miraculous effect, so that it quenches thirst for ever, and springs up, as it were, into heaven (John 4:10, 13, 14). This water is not merely natural, but supernatural, and signifies Christ Himself (John 7:37; I Cor. 10:4) and the Holy Ghost, with all the supernatural gifts that lead to everlasting life; those namely of doctrine and grace. Since the woman does not or will not understand this, and takes His words in a natural sense (John 4:11, 12, 15), He convinces her, thirdly, by a revelation of the state of her conscience and her sinful life; but He makes this revelation very considerately and briefly, and introduces it very skilfully, by bidding her call her husband, that He may speak with him of His doctrine; for the Jewish teachers of the law scorned to instruct women in public (John 4:27). In any case this turn of the conversation influenced the woman more strongly and quickly than mere instruction. It was a proof of higher knowledge, and led her to look back upon her past life, while at the same time it awakened the spirit of penance and contrition. Fourthly, He wins the woman by the moderation and candor with which He discusses, from a higher stand-point, the principal point of controversy between the Jews and the Samaritans (John 4:21–24). He consoles her by saying that the dispute was now to come to an end, for a new religion was beginning, which, in accordance with the spiritual being of God, was not exclusively attached to place and nationality; but its adherents would adore God, "the Father," "in spirit and in truth," i.e. in the spirit of adoption as God's children and of the faith which Christ had brought. Nevertheless He does not compromise the truth in the least, but declares that the religion of her countrymen was not true, since they had separated themselves from revelation by their rejection of the prophets, but that "salvation," the Messias, was to come from the Jews. Finally, as soon as she has expressed her firm hope of the Messias, He completes the work of grace by the plain statement that He Himself is the Messias (John 4:26). One can imagine the joyful surprise of the woman at this moment.

In this mystery our Saviour makes use of something close at hand, the well of water, to awaken in the untaught woman a consciousness of her need of salvation and heaven; He deepens this feeling by revealing to her the state of her conscience, and by the promise of a religion which, though proceeding from Judaism, does not wound the national feeling of the Samaritan woman, and which offers her all that she wishes; He crowns the instruction by the revelation of His rank as the Messias, the only profound supernatural truth which He at present vouchsafes to His catechumen. Under this wise treatment she gradually draws nearer to our Saviour. At first she calls Him "a Jew" (John 4:9), then "Sir" (John 4:11), immediately after "a prophet" (John 4:19), and finally "Christ" (John 4:29). That our Lord chose this obscure and apparently unworthy woman to be the recipient of His revelation, should make us admire and adore the hidden ways of Providence.

### 3. OUR SAVIOUR WINS THE SICHEMITES

The direct means which our Saviour employed in order to gain the Sichemites was the woman to whom He had just revealed Himself. In her joyful emotion she forgets the water-pot (John 4:28), hurries eagerly into the city, and with self-forgetful zeal (John 4:29) induces the inhabitants to come out to our Saviour.

The indirect means was our Saviour's zeal for souls, which is so intense and insatiable that it consumes Him more than bodily hunger (John 4:32); and which, enlightened and full of supernatural wisdom, has only the Will of God for its rule and rejoices unselfishly at its accomplishment. He has labored, the Apostles reap, here in Sichar as already in Judaea, and later on in the whole world (John 4:36–38).

Thus did Sichar receive the gift of salvation. The Sichemites themselves invited our Saviour to stay with them (John 4:30, 40); they believed with touching simplicity, without a profuse display of miracles and signs (John 4:39, 41), and acknowledged and

greeted Him with joy as "the Saviour of the world" (John 4:42).
Beautiful indeed is the faith shown by these poor people, who
yield at a word, on the first appearance of the Messias, without
miracles and signs; it is a striking accusation and condemnation
of Israel, which does not believe at the testimony of the Baptist
or even after so many signs of our Saviour, but repulses Him. Assuredly the faith of the Sichemites was a great honor and joy to
our Saviour. In the exultation of His Heart He scorns bodily
nourishment, rejoices at the wonderful counsels of God, the first
operation of which He hails in the approaching Sichemites, while
He already beholds in spirit their more perfect fulfilment by the
Apostles (Acts 8:5). Whilst the corn in the fields needs four
months longer to ripen, He sees the harvest of souls already
golden; the Sichemites are the first-fruits, and away beyond them
the whole great harvest-field of the Gentile Church is awaiting
Him (John 4:35).

Such was the appearance of our Lord in unhappy Samaria.
The mystery is full of important lessons and deep significance.
It is, in the first place, a kind of prelude and prophecy of the whole
ministry of Jesus and of the fate of Israel. Our Saviour departs
from Israel, coerced and driven away; but His mission is not frus-
trated on that account. He turns to the nations outside Israel, and
finds joyful faith, even without miracles, at a mere word. But He
only prepares them for their conversion by a passing visit, by His
labor and Death. The disciples will reap the harvest in these nations; He Himself is sent only to the sheep of the House of Jacob.
But the disciples have learnt that not in Israel alone, but also beyond its limits they may expect ready response to their teaching
in faith and in the fear of God. Further, this mystery is a revelation of God's mysterious counsels in the distribution of grace
(John 1:9, 12, 13), and also a brilliant revelation of the great and
glorious character of the Church and of Christianity. The Samaritans are the "foolish" nation, which venerates what it does
not know; Judaism is a true religion, salvation and the Messias
proceed from it; but it is degenerate, and remains even in its true
form limited to one nation and one country, whilst Christianity
knows no bounds, and possesses and arouses the true spirit of the
worship of God. Lastly, we have here another beautiful revelation of the character and personality of Jesus, above all of His infinite goodness and compassion for this poor, forsaken people,
for whose conversion He chooses to employ this misguided soul,

in order to reveal Himself clearly and plainly to her and to the Sichemites, as He never did to the Jewish people. How gloriously, further, does His prudence and delicate consideration in the treatment of men and their souls manifest itself! How He contrives to lead them where He wishes, and how well He understands the way to unravel gently and skilfully the tangled skein of their consciences! How far He stands above the spirit of prejudice, and with what liberty of spirit He acts! But it is our Saviour's zeal for souls in the intrinsic beauty of its character that is especially revealed to us in this mystery. We see here its lofty motive, which is no other than the Will of His Heavenly Father; its supernatural wisdom, which wins by gentleness and tact what had been lost for hundreds of years. So ardent is this zeal that it sets aside the need of bodily food and occupies His whole being, His thoughts and endeavors. So unselfish is it that it claims for itself only the work of preparing and sowing, and leaves for the disciples the gain, honor and joy of the harvest (John 4:36). Lastly we see here His zeal for souls in its divine and unassuming modesty, which rejoices only at the honor of God and the salvation of men. The conversation with the Samaritan woman and the Apostles opens out to us a precious glimpse of the interior life, the thoughts and endeavors of that Sacred Heart of our Saviour, so infinitely worthy of all our love.

## OUR SAVIOUR COMES INTO GALILEE

JOHN 4:43. Now after two days he departed thence and went into Galilee.—44. For Jesus himself gave testimony that a prophet hath no honor in his own country.—45. And when he was come into Galilee, the Galileans received him, having seen all the things he had done at Jerusalem on the festival day; for they also went to the festival day.

LUKE 4:14. And Jesus returned in the power of the Spirit into Galilee, and the fame of him went out through the whole country.—15. And he taught in their synagogues, and was magnified by all.

MARK 1:14. And after that John was delivered up, Jesus came into Galilee, preaching the gospel of the kingdom of God.

MATT. 4:12. And when Jesus had heard that John was delivered up, he retired into Galilee.

### 1. CAUSE OF THE JOURNEY INTO GALILEE

After a stay of two days in Sichar our Saviour proceeded on His journey and entered Galilee, in order to work there permanently. He was induced to do this, first, because He had been driven out of Judaea by the Pharisees, who, as it seems, would have used force if He had not gone away. St. John himself remarks that our Saviour confirmed by word and experience the proverb that a prophet has no honor in His own country. Judaea was his real home (Matt. 2:22). Secondly, it had been prophesied that the Messias would first work in Galilee, and this is also mentioned by St. Matthew (Isa. 9:1; Matt. 4:14–16). This is all the more important, because the Jews later urged against Him that the Messias was not to come from Galilee (John 7:41, 52). Thirdly, one reason lay (as may be seen from Isa. 9:1, 3) in the moral state of the Galilean people. They had fallen into religious tepidity, partly on account of their distance from Jerusalem, the place of worship and focus of religious life, which they only visited at festival seasons and with difficulty; partly also on account of their frequent intercourse with the Gentiles, who had been from the remotest times numerous in Galilee (Judg. 4:2; III Kings 9:11), which they brought under their sway sooner than Judaea (III Kings 15:20; IV Kings 15:29). It is for this reason that Upper Galilee was also called "Galilee of the Gentiles" (Isa. 9:1). Another motive which induced our Saviour to devote Himself especially to the Galileans was the contempt and neglect which they met with from the inhabitants of Judaea, because the latter did not regard them as pure-blooded Jews (Matt. 9:36). Fourthly, our Saviour found thereby an opportunity for intercourse with the Gentiles, and thus of becoming gradually known among them also (John 12:21). Lastly, Galilee had been His home in youth, and He must offer salvation to His countrymen. Such were the reasons which induced Him to remove henceforth the scene of His labors to Galilee.

## 2. OUR SAVIOUR'S RECEPTION BY THE GALILEANS

The Galileans responded heartily to the advances of our Saviour, and showed Him honor. They received Him joyfully and enthusiastically, because they had been witnesses of His miracles at the last Feast of the Pasch in Jerusalem (John 4:45), and saw in their glorious countryman a prophet (Luke 4:14, 15). It often happens that an illustrious person is persecuted in his native place, but when he quits it and does great deeds elsewhere, his countrymen boast of him as one of themselves. The Galileans subsequently showed this disposition towards Him. They believed in Him, thronged to Him, and were attached to Him. They had a very open and susceptible character, and it was easy to inspire them with enthusiasm. Their distance from Jerusalem and the circumstance that they had Herod for their governor prevented the Pharisees from exerting so much power and influence over them. They never drove our Saviour away. To be sure, unbelief showed itself in Galilee also, but, as it appears, only locally (Luke 4:29; 10:13); and if our Lord met with contradiction and opposition, it proceeded chiefly from the Pharisees of the metropolis (John 6:41; Luke 5:17; Matt. 15:1, 12; Mark 3:22; 7:1).

### 3. RESULTS OF THE SOJOURN IN GALILEE FOR THE MINISTRY OF OUR SAVIOUR

This peaceable and friendly disposition of the Galileans afforded our Saviour time and opportunity to begin, establish and develop His work by teaching and miracles, and especially by the establishment and organization of the Church. Henceforth He appears in Jerusalem only at festival seasons, manifests His Divinity and His rank as Messias by miracles and progressive revelations, but meets only with unbelief and dies there. But in Galilee He unfolds His doctrine on all sides, and founds and perfects His Church by calling, instructing and sending out His Apostles and disciples. The Apostles at all events were all Galileans, except perhaps Judas Iscariot. Thus the ministry of Christ had gained a firm and peaceable footing. This was our Saviour's intention in entering Galilee. For this reason St. Luke says of Him that He came into Galilee "in the power of the Spirit" (Luke 4:14), i.e. armed not only with power, but also with the wish and resolution of founding His kingdom by teaching, miracles, and the institution of ecclesiastical authority.

The Jews and the ruling party in Judaea forcibly reject salvation. Apart from this force, it may have been already the intention of Jesus, in His merciful and wise zeal for souls, to turn His ministry towards a people so poor and in such need of salvation as the Galileans, because it was there so necessary and successful. The mysterious action of Divine Providence is also manifested here; it employs for its plans what is insignificant and despised, and causes what is haughtily rejected by one to turn to the welfare of another. Such is the signification of this mystery.

## HEALING OF THE RULER'S SON

JOHN 4:46. He came again therefore into Cana of Galilee, where he made the water wine. And there was a certain ruler whose son was sick at Capharnaum.— 47. He having heard that Jesus was come from Judaea into Galilee, went to him, and prayed him to come down and heal his son; for he was at the point of death. —48. Jesus therefore said to him: "Unless you see signs and wonders, you believe not."—49. The ruler saith to him: "Lord, come down before that my son die." —50. Jesus saith to him: "Go thy way, thy son liveth." The man believed the word which Jesus said to him, and went his way.—51. And as he was going down, his servants met him; and they brought word, saying that his son lived.—52. He asked therefore of them the hour wherein he grew better. And they said to him: "Yesterday at the seventh hour the fever left him."—The father therefore knew that it was at the same hour that Jesus said to him: "Thy son liveth;" and himself believed and his whole house.—54. This is again the second miracle that Jesus did, when he was come out of Judaea into Galilee.

This is the first miracle that our Saviour works in Galilee after His return from Judaea, and it again takes place in Cana. There are three circumstances worthy of note in connection with it.

### 1. THE OCCASION OF THE MIRACLE

A ruler from Capharnaum was the occasion of this miracle. He is the first who personally seeks help from our Lord in a temporal necessity. He held a superior post as royal (Herodian) official (John 4:46), and seems to have been rich, for his household is twice spoken of (John 4:51, 53); he had also heard of Jesus already, or had perhaps himself witnessed the miracles in Jerusalem. It was distress and trouble that drove him to our Lord; his son was dying (John 4:47).

### 2. THE CONDITION MADE BY OUR SAVIOUR FOR THE CURE

The condition our Saviour requires for the miracle is faith, faith for all in general and for the ruler in particular, in order that his son may be healed. Our Saviour exclaims immediately, on hearing the ruler's request: "Unless you see signs and wonders, you believe not" (John 4:48). The Jews ought to have followed the example of the Samaritans and ought to have believed the testimony of John and that of our Saviour Himself, even without miracles. But they were desirous of such signs; and since they did not in most cases request them with a bad intention like the Pharisees (John 2:18; Matt. 12:38), but out of distress and necessity, our Saviour in His goodness worked them. He indicates here the signification and object of miracles, viz. to awaken and strengthen faith. If the words contain a reproof, it is meant for the Jews; but for the ruler they are a test of faith and an encouragement to believe. The condition required of him was that he should go home without being accompanied by our Saviour, believing and trusting on His word alone, that his son lived and was healed. Our Saviour shows His wisdom and goodness in that He not only does good to the body of the sick child by working the miracle, but also to the soul of the father by awakening his faith and trust.

### 3. MANNER IN WHICH THE MIRACLE TAKES PLACE

The healing of this child is one of the few miracles that our Saviour worked without being present in person; an absolute miracle, therefore, that well proves His divine omnipotence, which can work everywhere and under all circumstances. It is also attested as such by the news brought by the servants, who inform their master that the cure had taken place at one o'clock in the afternoon, that is, at the same time as our Saviour had assured him that the boy had recovered. Cana is about eight leagues distant from Capharnaum. The word "yesterday" is therefore to be understood either in our ordinary sense, or (since the reckoning of the day began for the Jews with the preceding evening) of the same day on which the ruler had spoken with our Lord.

This cure is in any case a significant and important miracle, first because the circumstances are a proof of the reputation which our Saviour enjoyed at this time; secondly on account of the way in which it was worked, namely, without personal presence at the place where it occurred; thirdly on account of the position of the ruler; and lastly on account of its effect, which was to make the whole family believe in Christ (John 4:53). This example and also rumor of the miracle surely led others to our Saviour.

The value and advantage of temporal adversities are here, as well as in many subsequent events and miracles, very clearly manifested. They make us think of God and seek Him. In temporal happiness one is apt to forget God. Further, misfortunes make us energetic and humble. The ruler goes himself to our Saviour, and entreats Him humbly and repeatedly. They also make us disposed to believe and trust. Although the ruler's faith is not perfect, since he thinks our Saviour's presence necessary for the cure of his child, yet he readily yields to the condition of going away, in good faith that his son was or would be healed. Lastly, adversities make us grateful and zealous for souls. The good man gained over his whole family for our Saviour, and thus the affliction tended also to the honor and service of God.

## Our Saviour in Nazareth [1]

Luke 4:16. And he came to Nazareth where he was brought up; and he went into the synagogue according to his custom on the Sabbath-day; and he rose up to read,—17. And the book of Isaias the prophet was delivered unto him. And as he unfolded the book, he found the place where it was written:—18. "The Spirit of the Lord is upon me, wherefore he hath anointed me, to preach the gospel to the poor he hath sent me, to heal the contrite of heart;—19. To preach deliverance to the captives and sight to the blind; to set at liberty them that are bruised; to preach the acceptable year of the Lord, and the day of reward."—20. And when he had folded the book, he restored it to the minister, and sat down. And the eyes of all in the synagogue were fixed on him.—21. And he began to say to them: "This day is fulfilled this scripture in your ears."—22. And all gave testimony to him; and they wondered at the words of grace that proceeded from his mouth, and they said: "Is not this the son of Joseph?"—23. And he said to them: "Doubtless you will say to me this similitude: Physician, heal thyself; as great things as we have heard done in Capharnaum, do also here in thy own country."—24. And he said: "Amen I say to you, that no prophet is accepted in his own country.—25. In truth I say to you, there were many widows in the days of Elias in Israel, when heaven was shut up three years and six months, when there was a great famine throughout all the earth;—26. And to none of them was Elias sent, but to Sarepta of Sidon, to a widow woman.—27. And there were many lepers in Israel in the time of Eliseus the prophet; and none of them was cleansed, but Naaman the Syrian."—28. And all they in the synagogue, hearing these things, were filled with anger.—29. And they rose up and thrust him out of the city; and they brought him to the brow of the hill, whereon their city was built, that they might cast him down headlong.—30. But he passing through the midst of them, went his way.—31. And he went down into Capharnaum, a city of Galilee; and there he taught them on the Sabbath-days.

Matt. 13:54. And coming into his own country, he taught them in their synagogues, so that they wondered and said: "How came this man by this wisdom and miracles?—55. Is not this the carpenter's son? Is not his mother called Mary, and his brethren James, and Joseph, and Simon, and Jude;—56. And his sisters, are they not all with us? Whence therefore hath he all these things?"—57. And they were scandalized in his regard. But Jesus said to them: "A prophet is not without honor, save in his own country and in his own house."—58. And he wrought not many miracles there, because of their unbelief.

Mark 6:1. And going out from thence, he went into his own country; and his disciples followed him.—2. And when the Sabbath was come he began to teach in the synagogue; and many hearing him were in admiration at his doctrine, saying: "How came this man by all these things? and what wisdom is this that is given to him, and such mighty works as are wrought by his hands?—3. Is not this the carpenter, the Son of Mary, the brother of James, and Joseph, and Jude, and Simon? are not also his sisters here with us?" And they were scandalized in regard of him.—4. And Jesus said to them: "A prophet is not without honor, but in his own country, and in his own house, and among his own kindred."—5. And he could not do

---

1 Some writers assume, not without probability, two visits of our Saviour to Nazareth, the second of which falls in the second year of His public ministry, a few days after the raising of Jairus' daughter.

any miracles there, only that he cured a few that were sick, laying his hands upon them.—6. And he wondered because of their unbelief, and he went through the villages round about teaching.

## 1. OUR SAVIOUR'S VISIT TO NAZARETH

At the beginning of His public ministry our Saviour goes to Nazareth, the home of His youth. It may have been immediately before His visit to Cana or while taking a circuitous route through other places. And with what intentions does He go thither? Assuredly not from merely human motives, such as attachment to home and kindred, curiosity, or vanity, as is often the case with men, but from higher considerations. It was above all a rightly ordered charity that led Him thither, according to which we must first do good to our relatives and fellow-citizens, unless there be some reason for giving preference to strangers. Our Saviour wished, then, to proclaim the tidings of salvation first to them, and thus to show them His gratitude for all the good that He had enjoyed in their midst from His youth up, as St. Luke seems to remark (Luke 4:16). This is the fourth time that we see our Lord satisfy the claims of kinship and friendship in the revelation of Himself. It was the case with the miracle in Cana, and also with His visits to Judaea and to Galilee. Our Saviour does not let Himself be governed by ties of flesh and blood, but still He does not fail to give them their due. He also wished to give for our instruction and consolation an example of an unsuccessful apostolic undertaking, and precisely where failure was not to have been expected. He foresaw this failure, but that did not prevent Him from taking His disciples with Him (Mark 6:1).

## 2. OUR SAVIOUR'S MINISTRY AT NAZARETH

Four of our Saviour's actions at Nazareth are related in the Gospel.

First, he assisted at divine worship in the synagogue on the Sabbath, in accordance with His custom (Luke 4:15, 16) and His piety. We have here a vivid picture of such a solemnity. A synagogue was built by preference on rising ground, at a street-corner, or near a gate-way. It contained, after the model of the Temple in Jerusalem, first the part for the worshipers, the women being kept separate, either in a space partitioned off or in an upper room or kind of gallery, with a grating; then there was a place where the eight-branched candlestick, the lectern, the pulpit and the seats of the teachers of the law stood; lastly, raised a few steps higher, was a curtained niche with the rolls of Scripture. The Sabbath celebration itself was a constant reminder of God's rest after the Creation (Gen. 2:3; Ex. 20:11), and a repetition of the Feast of the Phase, in remembrance of the deliverance out of Egypt (Ex. 31:13; Deut. 5:12 seq.) and for the reanimation of the hope of the Messias. It was spent in prayers imploring the coming of the Messias, and in the reading and interpretation of the law and the prophets by native teachers or such as were passing through the town on a journey.

Secondly, our Saviour rose of His own accord (Luke 4:16) to read and interpret the prophets (viz. Isaias, which was the one appointed for the day), though it was the custom for the superintendent or ruler of the synagogue to name those who were to read. Everyone's attention was aroused, because they must have heard already in Nazareth of the teaching and miracles of Jesus (Luke 4:20, 23). He read and explained a prophecy (Isa. 61:1, 2) acknowledged as Messianic, concerning the mission and task of the Messias as the deliverer of the people. He spoke with such depth, grace and eloquence that all were astonished and showed their approbation (Luke 4:21, 22; Mark 6:2; Matt. 13:54).

Thirdly, He profited by this public occasion to reveal Himself as the Messias of whom the prophet spoke (Luke 4:21), and this in such plain terms as He seldom used. He declared clearly and definitely that with Him the fulfilment of the Messianic prophecies had begun.

Fourthly, our Saviour would work no miracle in Nazareth, since the Nazarenes did not believe, and either openly or covertly wished to see miracles as a proof of His being the Messias, according to the proverb: "Physician, heal thyself," i.e. procure for yourself the recognition of your rank as Messias, and for us the belief in it, by miracles similar to the one you have just worked upon the ruler's son at Capharnaum (Luke 4:23). As a matter of fact He did not work any miracle there, at all events upon one of His two visits (Matt. 13:58), and on the other He only healed a few sick people by laying His hands upon them (Mark 6:6). On the contrary, He rebuked the Nazarenes for their unbelief and for the proposal that He should work miracles among them because they were His fellow-citizens, saying that no prophet found in his native land appreciation and faith. Elias and Eliseus also had found credence and been able to work miracles only among foreigners

(Luke 4:24–27). The Israelites of that period preferred rather to perish in their temporal misery than to apply with faith to the prophets for help. So it was now and even in Nazareth; God did not distribute His gifts out of regard for flesh and blood.

### 3. THE RESULT OF THIS MINISTRY

The result was very lamentable. The approbation and admiration which the Nazarenes could not repress soon disappeared. Instead of seeing in the depth and beauty of His doctrine (which, as they well knew, did not come from natural sources) a testimony to His high authority and mission, they soon passed on to envy (Matt. 13:54, 55, 56), and as He revealed Himself as the Messias and would not attest His mission by miracles, to opposition and unbelief (Mark 6:3; Matt. 13:57). The great happiness and honor they had had of living for years in constant intercourse with our Saviour, and of having concealed the mystery of His divine origin from the world until the day of revelation; the carnal ideas they entertained with regard to the Messias and His origin, power and honor; and on the other hand the sight and presence of His poor family and His ordinary handicraft, and especially the announcement that He had come to save the poor and sinners (Luke 4:18, 19, 22; Mark 6:3), all this was a stumbling-block to them. And as our Saviour began to censure their unbelief, and to compare their moral condition with the worst that had ever been in Israel, with the times of Elias and Eliseus, they grew incensed and, burning with resentment and rage, laid hands upon Him, expelled Him from the synagogue, and brought Him, in all probability with insults and with rough handling, to a steep precipice of the hill on which Nazareth is built, and would have cast Him down headlong (Luke 4:28, 29). But He "passed through their midst," either by making Himself invisible or by paralyzing them with fear by the revelation of His majesty (Luke 4:30). This was the miracle granted to the Nazarenes. One can well imagine what His Heart felt as He saw Himself treated thus, seized and led away to death through the streets of His native town by those who were His fellow-citizens and companions in youth, and to whom He had surely shown much kindness and done much good.

Thus ended His apostolate in Nazareth. We have here again a clear, open and public declaration that He is the Messias, and then the verification of the saying that a prophet and apostle must not expect much from his native place. But in this mystery our

Saviour manifests many virtues: His faithful love for His fellow-citizens; His humility, which does not recoil from failure; and the courage with which He reveals Himself before His fellow-townsmen as the Messias, and reproves their unbelief at the risk of offending them and incurring their antipathy. We must also notice His wisdom and goodness in not working miracles before unbelievers, in order not to increase their responsibility, and in requiring faith before He works them, since faith without miracles is more meritorious (Mark 6:5). In the passage read from the prophet Isaias there is unfolded to us a true, beautiful and attractive picture of the mission and character of the Messias, and we see it fulfilled in our Saviour, trait for trait. The occurrence in Nazareth, strange as it is, is by no means isolated or unlooked-for. It is a typical one, prophetic of future events as well as similar to those of the past. They wish for miracles, and do not believe. The circumstance of their living together with the Messias and being akin to Him is the cause of their ruin. So it had always been with the prophets in Israel, and so it will be with the Messias. Already the seeds of envy, hatred and persecution are springing up in the hearts of His own people; they will bring forth at last the bitter fruit of His Death.

## SETTLEMENT IN CAPHARNAUM AND BEGINNING OF THE MESSIANIC PREACHING

MATT. 4:13. And leaving the city Nazareth, he came and dwelt in Capharnaum on the sea-coast, in the borders of Zabulon and of Nephthalim;—14. That it might be fulfilled which was said by Isaias the prophet:—15. "Land of Zabulon and land of Nephthalim, the way of the sea beyond the Jordan, Galilee of the Gentiles;—16. The people that sat in darkness hath seen great light; and to them that sat in the region of the shadow of death, light is sprung up."—17. From that time Jesus began to preach, and to say: "Do penance, for the kingdom of heaven is at hand." . . . —23. And Jesus went about all Galilee, teaching in their synagogues, and preaching the gospel of the kingdom; and healing all manner of sickness and every infirmity among the people.

LUKE 4:31. And he went down into Capharnaum, a city of Galilee; and there he taught them on the Sabbath-days.—32. And they were astonished at his doctrine; for his speech was with power.

MARK 1:21. And they entered into Capharnaum, and forthwith upon the Sabbath-days, going into the synagogue, he taught them.—22. And they were astonished at his doctrine; for he was teaching them as one having power, and not as the scribes.

### 1. OUR SAVIOUR SETTLES IN CAPHARNAUM

From Nazareth our Saviour betook Himself to Capharnaum, with the intention of taking up His permanent residence there. Capharnaum became His second home (Matt. 9:1), the town of His adoption; there He paid the taxes (Matt. 17:26), and there He had a fixed abode, probably Peter's house (Matt. 13:1, 36; Mark 2:2); there He exercised every form of His apostolic ministry, which consisted in journeys, preaching, working of miracles, and the acquisition of disciples. Thence He started upon His journeys into the surrounding district, and thither He always returned (Mark 1:38; 2:1; John 6:17). There He preached in the synagogue (Mark 1:21; 3:1; John 6:6), on the sea-shore (Mark 2:13; Luke 5:1), or on the surrounding mountains (Matt. 5:1). There He worked so many glorious miracles, and chose the chief among His disciples. How much Capharnaum and the surrounding district are to be envied, which were hallowed by so long a stay of our Lord, and by such glorious works!

### 2. WHY OUR LORD CHOSE CAPHARNAUM AS HIS PERMANENT RESIDENCE

The chief reasons for this choice were first the Will of God and the prophecy of Isaias (Isa. 9:1 seq.), in which, by the "way of the sea beyond Jordan" and the "Galilee of the Gentiles," precisely the north-east, east and north-west environs of the lake, or in other words Upper Galilee, were specified. Secondly, Nazareth, the home of our Saviour in His youth, had itself rejected this happiness, by driving our Saviour out of the town. Thirdly, Capharnaum was much better suited for the purpose of spreading the Gospel than the little inland town of Nazareth. Capharnaum, situated on the north-west coast of the lake, and not far from the beautiful little plain of Genesareth, seems to have been an important and flourishing place (Matt. 12:23), and as the frontier-town it possessed a custom-house (Mark 2:14) and a garrison (Matt. 8:5), on account of the traffic between Damascus and Acre (Ptolemais). Besides this, the mild climate, the salubrious and verdant surroundings, and the numerous medicinal springs near Tiberias attracted visitors and strangers from all directions (cf. Introd., p. 3). Thus our Saviour had opportunities of doing much good, temporal and spiritual, and of spreading His Gospel abroad in the whole world, among Gentiles as well as Jews. The vicinity of the lake, too, made it an easy matter to get to any place, and also to escape pursuit if necessary. Lastly, Capharnaum and the neighborhood was the home of many of the disciples. Thus our Saviour found there a very convenient and safe home, and could devote Himself entirely to the people. We see thus how every step taken by our Lord is guided by the highest wisdom and goodness.

### 3. HOW OUR SAVIOUR BEGINS TO WORK IN CAPHARNAUM AND ITS ENVIRONS

The apostolic ministry of Jesus consisted of two things: He preached the Gospel and healed all kinds of diseases (Matt. 4:23).

Teaching is the first mark of apostolic zeal, and our Lord began this immediately in the synagogues of Capharnaum and the surrounding district, especially on the Sabbath-days (Luke 4:31, 32, 43, 44; Mark 1:21, 39; Matt. 4:17). And what was the tenor of His preaching? First, He exhorted the people to penance, as John the Baptist had done. Penance is always the first step in the right direction; especially was it so in that voluptuous, worldly district, and among the people that "sat in darkness." How could they become participators in God's kingdom, without turning away from sin? He thereby opposed the first prejudice of the Jews, that they needed no Redeemer from sin, and that it sufficed for salvation to be a descendant of Abraham (Matt. 3:9). Secondly, our Lord proclaimed that the time was accomplished and the "kingdom of heaven" near, i.e. that the fulness of time had come, that the kingdom of the Messias, which all were expecting, the blessing of Abraham, the fruit of the revelations and mercies of God, the fruit of all expectations, prayers and hopes, and of all the labors and sacrifices of the Old Covenant, was now no longer a thing of the future, but really there present, as John the Baptist had said; not, however, as a kingdom of earthly pleasure and honor, but as a "kingdom of heaven," a supernatural kingdom. By this teaching a blow is struck at the other prejudice of the Jews, the expectation of an earthly, material Messianic kingdom. Our Lord exhorted the people, therefore, to believe and accept "the Gospel," the joyful tidings and proclamation of the kingdom of the Messias (Matt. 4:17; Mark 1:15).

And how did our Saviour preach? With power and authority, accompanying His words by miracles (Luke 4:32; Mark 1:22; Matt. 7:28, 29). The people felt at once the difference between the method of the scribes, to which they had hitherto been accustomed, and that of our Saviour. The former generally rested their teaching upon merely human principles and the tenets of various schools, lost themselves in absurd trivialities and sophistries, and deprived themselves of all due prestige by their dissensions and by the contrast which their lives presented to their doctrine. Our Saviour, on the contrary, propounded necessary and elevating truths, with the authority of a lawgiver, with convincing power, and with the help of grace in the hearts of His hearers. It was indeed "the voice of the Lord in power, the voice of the Lord in magnificence" (Ps. 28:4).

The effect of His words is correspondingly great. All are struck with astonishment at the power of His teaching (Mark 1:22; Luke 4:32). And thus the glorious prophecy is fulfilled: "At the first time the land of Zabulon and the land of Nephthali was in shame; and at the last the way of the sea beyond the Jordan of the Galilee of the Gentiles was honored.[1] . . . The people that walked in darkness have seen a great light. . . . They shall rejoice before thee, as they that rejoice in the harvest, as conquerors rejoice after taking a prey, when they divide the spoils. . . . For the yoke of their burden . . . thou hast overcome as in the day of Madian. . . . A Child is born to us . . . the government is upon his shoulder; and his name shall be called Wonderful, Counselor, God, the Mighty, the Father of the world to come, the Prince of peace" (Isa. 9:1 seq.). The doctrine of Jesus, His miracles and holy life are a great light, and the poor, forsaken land suns itself in its rays; the sign of the conqueror of Madian, the dew upon Gedeon's fleece, is fulfilled for the second time in Galilee: once at the virginal conception of our Lord at Nazareth, and again now that the dew of divine doctrine and grace falls so abundantly upon the favored land. How sweetly our Lord shows Himself, in the choice of His dwelling-place, as the Man of compassion for the poor and forsaken, as the Man of God, Who allows Himself to be guided solely by consideration for the greater glory of God and the salvation of souls.

[1] Thus the Hebrew text. The Douay version has "The land of Nephthali was *lightly touched*, and . . . the way of the sea . . . was *heavily loaded*." (Translator's Note.)

### THE HEALING OF THE DEMONIAC IN THE SYNAGOGUE

LUKE 4:33. And in the synagogue there was a man who had an unclean devil, and he cried out with a loud voice,—34. Saying: "Let us alone, what have we to do with thee, Jesus of Nazareth? art thou come to destroy us? I know thee who thou art, the Holy One of God."—35. And Jesus rebuked him, saying: "Hold thy peace, and go out of him." And when the devil had thrown him into the midst, he went out of him, and hurt him not at all.—36. And there came fear upon all, and they talked among themselves, saying: "What word is this, for with authority and power he commandeth the unclean spirits, and they go out?"—37. And the fame of him was published into every place of the country.

MARK 1:23. And there was in their synagogue a man with an unclean spirit; and he cried out,—24. Saying: "What have we to do with thee, Jesus of Nazareth? art thou come to destroy us? I know who thou art, the Holy One of God."—25. And Jesus threatened him, saying: "Speak no more and go out of the man."—26. And the unclean spirit tearing him, and crying out with a loud voice, went out of him.—27. And they were all amazed, insomuch that they questioned among themselves, saying: "What thing is this? what is this new doctrine? for with power he commandeth even the unclean spirits, and they obey him."—28. And the fame of him was spread forthwith into all the country of Galilee.

#### 1. OUR SAVIOUR'S ENCOUNTER WITH THE DEMONIAC

Our Lord confirmed His preaching by miracles. In the synagogue at Capharnaum He met with a demoniac. This encounter is not without importance. Our Saviour stands for the first time face to face with this visible sign of Satan's dominion over the human race, and He stands there as the assailant and conqueror, as the Strong One Who is come to destroy the works of Satan (I John 3:8). In consequence of original as well as actual sin, Satan ruled over our race, not merely through sin and the passions, heathenism and death, but also, by God's permission, with or without fault of man, by actual occupation of the human body and arbitrary employment of it for extraordinary works.

As grace has its mysticism, so also sin and hell have theirs. The fact of possession by the devil rests upon the statements of Holy Scripture, the experience of almost all nations, and of the Church herself. With the Jews possession and its remedy, exorcism, were recognized facts, and our Saviour also confirms them by conflict with this phase of Satan's kingdom (Matt. 12:24, 27 seq.).

Our Saviour is very often to be seen engaged in this contest, and thus it may be asked why possession so often occurred at the time of Christ. Assuredly the personal approach and intervention of God by the Incarnation had for its consequence a special counteraction on the part of hell. Further, the existence of the spirit world was denied by some among the Gentiles, and even by Jews (especially by the Sadducees), and so God manifested it in a fitting manner by the fact of possession. It had to be clearly shown whom heathenism really served, how low the human race had fallen, and that it had become subject not only to human oppressors, but even to the tyranny of evil spirits. For this reason, probably, more demoniacs were found in Galilee, where the Gentiles were numerous, than in Judaea. Besides, the prospect of spiritual deliverance from the yoke of Satan had to be held out and indicated by the bodily deliverance. Lastly, the Divinity of Christ could not be more convincingly proved than by His power over the Evil One who had taken possession of the whole world. It was a time of conflict. The "Stronger" comes to take away the spoil from the "strong man" (Luke 11:22). Thus the expulsion of the devil from the demoniac was the dawn of the victory over sin, death and hell.

## 2. THE BEHAVIOR OF OUR SAVIOUR AND OF THE DEMONIAC

It is very instructive to study the behavior of our Saviour and on the other hand that of the demoniac.

The evil spirit, who was a spirit of uncleanness, i.e. of unholiness and impiety (Mark 1:23; Luke 4:33), immediately becomes very excited and uneasy, even without being attacked, at the mere sight and presence of Jesus, or perhaps on hearing His doctrine. Then he is seized with terror and weakness. He complains that our Saviour's presence is untimely; he trembles and howls, and cries out that the end of his sway has now come. At least he acknowledges our Saviour to be God. He probably conjectured from all that had happened previously that Jesus was the Messias, and so his confession is a cry of distress at the violence done him, a sign of terror and weakness in presence of our Lord. Lastly, since the Evil One finds no mercy, he makes his last futile attempt to ruin his victim; he tears the demoniac and throws him down, but without being able to injure him. Such is the behavior of the evil spirit (Mark 1:23, 24, 26; Luke 4:33, 34, 35).

In our Saviour we see in the first place great tranquillity; secondly, a sublime majesty. He heeds neither the acknowledgment nor the menaces of the evil spirit. On the contrary, He bids him be silent. He scorns to receive recognition or be revealed by such unclean lips. To proclaim Christ is the glory of the Apostles. Then, too, He wishes to teach us by His example not to parley with the

Evil One, who only seeks to deceive and injure us by truth as well as by lies. Lastly, He speaks with authority to the evil spirit, as to the most wretched, contemptible slave, and expels him with a word (Mark 1:25, 26; Luke 4:35).

### 3. EFFECT OF THE EXPULSION OF THE DEVIL

If the people of Capharnaum had been struck with astonishment at the teaching of our Saviour, they were filled with reverence and fear at this power over the evil spirits. They asked one another what word and what new manner of teaching this was, that He had power and authority over the evil spirits (Mark 1:27; Luke 4:36). It is precisely the wonderful and powerful word of the Lord, which breaks the cedars of Libanus and shakes the desert (Ps. 28:5, 8). The peculiarity of the miracle is that our Lord's power does not work without resistance, as in the case of the miracles wrought upon the powers of nature, but that another power is opposed to His, viz. that of hell, and that this power is subdued by a word. The report of the miracle was immediately spread throughout the whole district (Luke 4:37; Mark 1:28).

There is scarcely anything that throws into stronger relief the power of the God-Man than the behavior of the Evil One in His presence, and his terrified and unwilling testimony to our Saviour. One can understand the universal astonishment. Nothing like this had taken place before. It throws a clear light upon the nature of the evil spirits, who are so strong and at the same time so weak, so sagacious on the one hand, and on the other unwise enough to promote God's cause whilst hating and opposing it. The behavior of our Saviour towards them is also most striking. He, Who is otherwise all goodness and mercy, has for them nothing but sternness, severity and contempt. His words sound like a declaration of war against all the powers of hell. The evil spirits must go out of the world. So it must be. They are condemned, incorrigible enemies of God and of the human race. All the ruin of poor humanity begins with them. On the other hand, with what compassion our Lord received the pitiable victims of their hatred and malice, after He had rescued them from the jaws of hell! The Church imitates our Saviour in her attitude towards the evil spirits, especially in her exorcisms.

## FURTHER ACTIVITY AND SUCCESS OF JESUS IN CAPHARNAUM. HEALING OF ST. PETER'S WIFE'S MOTHER, AND OTHER MIRACULOUS CURES

LUKE 4:38. And Jesus rising up out of the synagogue, went into Simon's house. And Simon's wife's mother was taken with a great fever; and they besought him for her.—39. And standing over her, he commmanded the fever, and it left her. And immediately rising, she ministered to them.—40. And when the sun was down, all they that had any sick with divers diseases brought them to him. And he laying his hands on everyone of them, healed them.—41. And devils went out from many, crying out and saying: "Thou art the Son of God." And rebuking them, he suffered them not to speak; for they knew that he was Christ.—42. And when it was day, going out he went into a desert place; and the multitudes sought him and came unto him; and they stayed him that he should not depart from them.— 43. To whom he said: "To other cities also I must preach the kingdom of God; for therefore am I sent."—44. And he was preaching in the synagogues of Galilee. MARK 1:29. And immediately going out of the synagogue, they came into the house of Simon and Andrew, with James and John.—30. And Simon's wife's mother lay in a fit of a fever; and forthwith they tell him of her.—31. And coming to her he lifted her up, taking her by the hand; and immediately the fever left her, and she ministered unto them.—32. And when it was evening after sunset, they brought to him all that were ill and that were possessed with devils.—33. And all the city was gathered together at the door.—34. And he healed many that were troubled with divers diseases; and he cast out many devils, and he suffered them not to speak, because they knew him.—35. And rising very early, going out he went into a desert place; and there he prayed.—36. And Simon and they that were with him followed after him.—37. And when they had found him, they said to him: "All seek for thee."—38. And he saith to them: "Let us go into the neighboring towns and cities, that I may preach there also; for to this purpose am I come."— 39. And he was preaching in their synagogues and in all Galilee, and casting out devils. MATT. 8:14. And when Jesus was come into Peter's house, he saw his wife's mother lying, and sick of a fever.—15. And he touched her hand, and the fever left her, and she arose and ministered to them.—16. And when evening was come, they brought to him many that were possessed with devils; and he cast out the spirits with his word; and all that were sick he healed.—17. That it might be fulfilled which was spoken by the prophet Isaias, saying: "He took our infirmities and bore our diseases."

The results of our Lord's ministry at Capharnaum may be considered in three occurrences.

### 1. OUR SAVIOUR HEALS PETER'S WIFE'S MOTHER

From the synagogue our Saviour betook Himself with James and John to the house of Peter (Matt. 8:14; Luke 4:38; Mark 1:29). Peter and Andrew were natives of Bethsaida (John 1:44), which was probably situated south of Capharnaum in the plain of Genesareth, on a small creek of the lake. Peter's wife's mother lay sick of a violent fever in a house in Capharnaum, which these two disciples seem to have shared with her, perhaps for reasons connected with business. The miraculous cure was brought about in response to the entreaties of her domestics and relatives, among whom Peter was surely the foremost (Mark 1:30; Luke 4:38). The great confidence and high esteem which our Saviour had already acquired by His miracles are here made manifest.

Our Saviour shows His great goodness and graciousness by the way in which He approves of the sympathy of the household for their mother, and receives their petitions on her behalf. Love and sympathy are pleasing to Him, and He often permits something to happen in order to give us an opportunity to exercise it. He shows it, secondly, by going in person to the sick woman, and there taking her kindly by the hand, raising her up and freeing her from the fever (Luke 4:39; Mark 1:31; Matt. 8:15). Thirdly, in working this miracle He probably intended to confirm Peter in his resolve of following Him. Thus by this benefit our Saviour prepared a still greater one for Peter and the whole family.

As regards the mother, we must observe her active and thoughtful gratitude. She rose at once, and in her joy she could not make haste enough to wait upon our Saviour and the disciples at table (Mark 1:31; Luke 4:39; Matt. 8:15). To labor at once for the glory of God is the best thanksgiving for restored health.

## 2. OUR SAVIOUR HEALS MANY OTHERS

When the sun had set and night was drawing in, the people brought many, indeed all who were sick of various diseases, together with those who were possessed with devils, so that the whole town was assembled before the house; evidently a new sign of the people's increased esteem and confidence in our Saviour (Mark 1:32, 33; Luke 4:40; Matt. 8:16). He must cure them all now. Our Lord probably needed rest, and now, at night, His work was about to begin. The people had let the Sabbath pass by, and were unwilling to wait longer. So it may often happen. Men cannot always come at times that are convenient to us, and God permits the inconvenience in order to try our patience. Besides, we do the same thing ourselves when we are in distress, and are glad if we are kindly received.

And what does our Saviour do? He does not send them away or put them off till morning. He is not vexed at their want of consideration. He might have healed them all at once by a general benediction, and so have dismissed them. But He does not do this; He goes to each one, lays His hands upon each, and heals each separately. He overflows with kindness for all. Only towards the evil spirits, who, in the persons of the possessed, now proclaim Him as the Messias, does He show sternness, as He commands them to be silent. Their recognition of His Divinity was probably an assured one; but they proclaim it with the malicious intention of embittering the Pharisees or the people against our Saviour by a premature announcement of it, and so of finally bringing about His destruction.

This scene gives us a vivid picture of the effect of the appearance of Jesus in the world. It was night, the sun had set; all were infirm, ill and wretched, under the ban of sin and of the temporal curse, and the power of hell prevailed everywhere. And then our Saviour comes, the Light of the world, tender, consoling; before His healing words and the blessings imparted by His hand, sin and hell and the host of temporal misfortunes take flight. In the mystery of the weakness and humiliation of atoning suffering lay the power to accomplish the extirpation of sin and all unhappiness, as the prophets had foretold (Isa. 53:2 seq.; Matt. 8:17).

### 3. OUR SAVIOUR LEAVES CAPHARNAUM FOR A TIME

After the exertions of the night our Saviour leaves Capharnaum very early, in order to pray in a solitary place and then to visit the surrounding country (Mark 1:35; Luke 4:42). As soon as His absence was noticed in Capharnaum the people and disciples, with Peter at their head, followed Him and told Him that all were seeking Him, and begged Him not to leave them (Mark 1:36, 37; Luke 4:42). But our Saviour told them that He must also bring the good tidings to other cities, that it was for this purpose that He had come (Luke 4:43; Mark 1:38); and He actually did go into the surrounding district and preached there (Luke 4:44; Mark 1:39)

From these occurrences it is plainly to be seen how our Saviour gradually gains esteem and popularity, and especially how Peter and the disciples, under the influence of His miracles, gradually detach themselves more from the people, and draw near to our Saviour in the quality of Apostles and pillars of the Church. Peter appears here already as the leader and spokesman of the people and the disciples. In our Saviour all the features of the apostolic spirit are manifested: kindness and compassion for all without distinction; unwearied activity by day and by night; fervor in prayer, in order to give God the glory of the success already granted by Him, and to obtain success in future; lastly, pure unselfish zeal for the glory of God and the salvation of souls, which does not seek satisfaction or rest in what has already been attained, but always goes on to new toils. It is characteristic of apostolic men to brook no delay, but ever to press on to fresh fields of labor.

## THE MIRACULOUS DRAUGHT OF FISHES

LUKE 5:1. And it came to pass that when the multitudes pressed upon him to hear the word of God, he stood by the lake of Genesareth,—2. And saw two ships standing by the lake; but the fishermen were gone out of them and were washing their nets.—3. And going up into one of the ships that was Simon's, he desired him to draw back a little from the land. And sitting, he taught the multitudes out of the ship.—4. Now when he had ceased to speak, he said to Simon: "Launch out into the deep, and let down your nets for a draught."—5. And Simon answering, said to him: "Master, we have labored all the night, and have taken nothing; but at thy word I will let down the net."—6. And when they had done this, they enclosed a very great multitude of fishes, and their net broke.—7. And they beckoned to their partners that were in the other ship, that they should come and help them. And they came, and filled both the ships, so that they were almost sinking.—8. Which when Simon Peter saw, he fell down at Jesus' knees, saying: "Depart from me, for I am a sinful man, O Lord."—9. For he was wholly astonished, and all that were with him, at the draught of the fishes which they had taken.—10. And so were also James and John the sons of Zebedee, who were Simon's partners. And Jesus said to Simon: "Fear not; from henceforth thou shalt catch men."—11. And having brought their ships to land, leaving all things, they followed him.

MATT. 4:18. And Jesus walking by the sea of Galilee, saw two brethren, Simon who is called Peter, and Andrew his brother, casting a net into the sea (for they were fishers).—19. And he saith to them: "Come ye after me, and I will make you to be fishers of men."—20. And they immediately leaving their nets, followed him.—21. And going on from thence, he saw other two brethren, James the son of Zebedee and John his brother, in a ship with Zebedee their father, mending their nets; and he called them.—22. And they forthwith left their nets and father, and followed him.

MARK 1:16. And passing by the sea of Galilee, he saw Simon and Andrew his brother, casting nets into the sea (for they were fishermen).—17. And Jesus said to them: "Come after me, and I will make you to become fishers of men."—18. And immediately leaving their nets, they followed him.—19. And going on from thence a little farther, he saw James the son of Zebedee and John his brother, who also were mending their nets in the ship;—20. And forthwith he called them. And leaving their father Zebedee in the ship with his hired men, they followed him.

### 1. OCCASION OF THE MIRACLE

As our Saviour stood by the lake-side, the people thronged around Him, begging Him to teach them (Luke 5:1). He saw Peter's little boat, moored near that of Zebedee, and getting into it, He pushed off a little from the shore in order to address the people more easily. Such were the circumstances which led to the miracle which He afterwards worked (Luke 5:2; Mark 1:16, 19; Matt. 4:18, 21). Whether the scene was Bethsaida, Capharnaum, or a place on the coast between the two, cannot be ascertained. The little creek in which Bethsaida is said to have lain was very well adapted for such an occasion.

But the real motive of the miracle was our Saviour's intention of deciding Peter and the other three disciples, Andrew, James and John, to join Him finally and completely, renouncing their family and occupation. Hitherto, though they had become disciples, they had continued to follow their calling as fishermen. Peter and the sons of Zebedee seem to have been partners in business (Luke 5:10). The miraculous draught of fishes is one of the miracles which our Lord performed solely for the purpose of instructing and confirming the disciples in their apostolic vocation. He here intended to lead them to a further step. The three mysteries already mentioned—the first meeting (John 1:42), the miracle at Cana, and the healing of Peter's mother-in-law—all had the same end in view.

We see here incidentally our Lord's zeal for gaining souls; His resourcefulness in all difficulties; the humility with which He requests Peter to place the boat at His disposal; and lastly the wisdom and care with which He gently guides all to the end He desires.

## 2. THE MIRACLE

The miracle is remarkable in three respects.

First, as regards the circumstances, which were most unfavorable; for the miracle took place in broad daylight and near the shore, whereas fish are more easily caught by night and in deep water. Further, the nets were filled very quickly, although the disciples had labored all night in vain (Luke 5:5); and in such abundance that Peter's net broke and both ships were filled to the verge of sinking (Luke 5:6, 7). Lastly, the miracle occurred before many witnesses, in the presence of the crews of both ships (Luke 5:7).

Secondly, the miracle shows our Saviour's gracious condescension and kindness, and is a sort of compensation to Peter for the night uselessly spent, a reward for the service he had rendered our Lord by placing the ship at His disposal, and a return for the faith and confidence with which he let down the net at our Lord's word, though naturally there was no hope of success (Luke 5:4, 5).

Thirdly, the miracle is very aptly and suitably chosen for the object of removing Peter's last doubt and hesitation as to his apostolic vocation, by a striking proof of the Godhead and divine power of Christ. For this reason our Lord chooses a miracle within Peter's sphere of action, in order that it might be better appreciated and make more impression upon him; a miracle, too, which so strikingly typified his future vocation. He was destined later on to gather men out from the depths of a life of sin into the net of the Church, and to bring them as God's adopted children to the shore of eternal happiness, just as he now draws the fishes to the bank in his net. Our Saviour Himself points out the parallel with the words: "From henceforth thou shalt catch men" (Luke 5:10; Mark 1:17; Matt. 4:19; 13:47; John 21:6; cf. Ez. 47:10; Jer. 16:16).

### 3. EFFECT OF THE MIRACLE

The effect of the miracle was precisely what our Saviour had intended: viz. to induce Peter by a clear sign of His Divinity to follow Him permanently.

The first impression that the sight of the miracle produced in the souls of St. Peter and the other disciples was a reverential awe at seeing themselves so near to the Godhead (Luke 5:9).

The second (with Peter especially) was a lively feeling of humility and unworthiness at coming into contact with the Divinity. He cast himself at our Saviour's feet and begged Him to depart from him, since he was such a sinful man (Luke 5:8). Peter had probably been made conscious by the miracle that he had not as yet had a high enough esteem for our Lord, Who here proved Himself so evidently to be God.

Thirdly, at our Saviour's words: "Fear not; from henceforth thou shalt catch men" (Luke 5:10), St. Peter's soul was filled with great confidence. Perhaps he had hitherto had considerable hesitation to enter upon his vocation, either out of solicitude for his family, or anxiety at the great and unaccustomed duties it involved, for which he did not consider himself fitted. All this fades away before our Lord's words and the proof of His power afforded by the miracle, in which He held out to Peter a pledge of His divine assistance for all the consequences of the step that he was invited to take.

The final effect of the miracle was that Peter and the other three disciples resolved to leave their ships, trade, and families immediately, and to follow our Saviour (Luke 5:11; Mark 1:18, 20; Matt. 4:20, 22).

It was indeed an important draught of fishes that Peter took on this day; never had there been one so great on the Galilean lake, or on the sea of the whole world. It meant much more than if Peter had fished up the ancient crown of David from the bottom of the lake and re-established the kingdom of Israel. It was the last, decisive call of Peter to the apostolic office, and it surpasses in significance and importance the calling of Abraham or Moses. These founded by their ready obedience only the Old Covenant; the Apostles, by their decision to follow our Lord, founded the Church. Indeed, this mystery symbolizes the Church in her chief features. Our Saviour is the Master of the draught of fishes; He occasions it, bestows the blessing and the success. Peter leads and accomplishes the work; our Lord's commission is addressed to him, and for him the miracle is chiefly worked; his little ship is the Church, in which Christ is, teaches, catches fish and works miracles. The object of the Church and of Peter's ship is the catching of fish, which, according to our Saviour's words, is a symbol of the salvation of souls. Success is sure, and has for its pledge the divine assistance, given here in the miracle and the words of our Lord. This assistance was fully granted on the first Feast of Pentecost, and has ever remained with the Church in her subsequent history. The condition of success, however, is humble confidence. Thus we have here the whole Church prefigured, in her constitution, her end, her means and her success.

## THE HEALING OF THE LEPER

LUKE 5:12. And it came to pass, when he was in a certain city, behold a man full of leprosy, who seeing Jesus, and falling on his face, besought him, saying: "Lord, if thou wilt, thou canst make me clean."—13. And stretching forth his hand he touched him, saying: "I will; be thou cleansed." And immediately the leprosy departed from him.—14. And he charged him that he should tell no man, but: "Go, show thyself to the priest, and offer for thy cleansing according as Moses commanded, for a testimony to them."—15. But the fame of him went abroad the more, and great multitudes came together to hear, and to be healed by him of their infirmities.—16. And he retired into the desert and prayed.

MARK 1:40. And there came a leper to him, beseeching him, and kneeling down, said to him: "If thou wilt, thou canst make me clean."—41. And Jesus having compassion on him, stretched forth his hand; and touching him, saith to him: "I will. Be thou made clean."—42. And when he had spoken, immediately the leprosy departed from him, and he was made clean.—43. And he strictly charged him, and forthwith sent him away.—44. And he saith to him: "See thou tell no one, but go, show thyself to the high priest, and offer for thy cleansing the things that Moses commanded, for a testimony to them."—45. But he being gone out, began to publish and to blaze abroad the word; so that he could not openly go into the city, but was without in desert places, and they flocked to him from all sides.

MATT. 8:2. And behold a leper came and adored him, saying: "Lord, if thou wilt, thou canst make me clean."—3. And Jesus stretching forth his hand, touched him, saying: "I will, be thou made clean." And forthwith his leprosy was cleansed. —4. And Jesus saith to him: "See thou tell no man; but go, show thyself to the priest, and offer the gift which Moses commanded for a testimony unto them."

## 1. OF THE WRETCHED STATE OF THE LEPER

At a certain place, probably in the vicinity of Capharnaum (Luke 5:12), a leper presented himself to our Saviour and begged to be cured.

Leprosy was a terrible disease. In the first place, it disfigured its victims and made them hideous. The skin became discolored, the limbs swollen; wounds and ulcers set in; a discharge exuded from the eyes; the voice sounded hoarse; the nails fell off; the whole body decayed and its members gradually fell away. The leper was scarcely more than a walking corpse.

Secondly, the disease was very painful, because of the irritation and twitching experienced in all the limbs; and to the physical pains were added the mental sufferings of melancholy, uneasiness, and a morbid longing for death.

Thirdly, leprosy was degrading, because it entailed Levitical uncleanness. Its treatment and the recognition of its outbreak or of deliverance from it were incumbent upon the priests, and had thence a religious character. The leper was considered incapacitated for approaching the sanctuary or having intercourse with his brethren; he had to depart from the midst of the people, and to wear conspicuous clothing to warn them not to touch him; he had to go bare-headed and with muffled chin, and to fetch his food from an appointed place where it was set for him, as though for a wild beast. To complete the misery, there was always connected with the disease the thought of moral impurity, of sin and punishment (Lev. 13:46; Num. 12:9 seq.; Deut. 24:8, 9; II Par. 26:19).

Lastly, leprosy was incurable and was considered very contagious. In short, the condition of the leper was one of extreme abandonment and misery. Such was the wretched state of the sick man in question; indeed, it seems that with him the disease had already assumed all its loathsomeness, for it is recorded of him that he was "full of leprosy" (Luke 5:12).

## 2. HOW THE LEPER IS HEALED

Apart from his wretched condition, which must have inspired everyone with compassion, it was surely the leper's disposition of soul which conduced to his cure. He had probably heard of the goodness and miraculous power of Jesus, and so he took courage and suddenly pushed his way to our Lord, though such an act was forbidden by the law, as St. Luke seems to imply by saying: "Behold a man full of leprosy, who seeing Jesus, and falling on his face, besought him . . ." (Luke 5:12). "A leper came and adored him, saying: 'Lord, if Thou wilt, Thou canst make me clean'" (Matt. 8:2; Mark 1:40; Luke 5:12). His whole behavior showed not only great respect, but also an extraordinary degree of faith and confidence in the power and goodness of Jesus. He probably regarded our Saviour not merely as a worker of miracles, but as the Messias. How forcibly this is expressed in the simple words: "If Thou wilt, Thou canst make me clean"!

On the part of our Saviour it was, in the first place, compassion for the poor leper that induced Him to work the miracle, as St. Mark (1:41) expressly observes. He gave a special sign of this compassion and benevolence by touching the loathsome sufferer with His hand, and thus effecting the cure. Secondly, we may attribute it also to our Lord's satisfaction and joy at the faith and trust of the sick man. This appears from the words with which He heals him: "I will, be thou made clean" (Matt. 8:3). Thirdly, we see here a marvelous proof of the power of Jesus, which, independent of any other cause, effects the cure by a mere touch and a word. Moses had to pray and call upon God on behalf of his sister Mary, who was afflicted with leprosy (Num. 12:13). Christ is more powerful than Moses, more powerful than the law itself, which could only judge of leprosy and prevent it, but not cure it.

### 3. CONDITIONS IMPOSED BY OUR LORD UPON THE HEALED MAN

Our Lord imposed two conditions on the cleansed leper.

The first was that he should fulfil the law, present himself to the priests in Jerusalem, offer the sacrifice and get himself declared clean (Lev. 14:1 seq.). The ceremony required by the law was as follows. Outside the town a sparrow was killed; a second sparrow was dipped in water mixed with the blood of the first one, and then allowed to fly away. In the Temple the cleansed man had to offer a lamb, and was himself sprinkled with its blood and anointed with oil, as a sign of his recovery of the priestly character imparted to the Israelite in circumcision, but which he had lost by the uncleanness of leprosy. And why did our Saviour require this? The sudden cure might easily have led the man to disregard the legal regulations, and so have aroused the resentment of the priesthood, as though our Saviour wished to abolish the law. The treatment of leprosy was, according to the law, the peculiar duty of the priests. There seems to lie in this command an indication of the guarded manner in which our Lord dealt with the unbelieving priesthood. For this reason He says: "For a testimony to them" (Luke 5:14; Mark 1:44; Matt. 8:4). Also, our Saviour intended to give the priests in the Temple further information concerning Himself, in order to cleanse them from the far worse leprosy of unbelief. The words "for a testimony to them" may have this meaning. Lastly, we may rightly see in the healing of the leper a type of the cleansing from sin in the Sacrament of Penance, because leprosy bears a strong resemblance to sin in many points —in its nature, consequences and treatment. For this and the above reasons our Saviour sends all the lepers whom He heals to the priests (Luke 17:14). Considered thus, the Old Testament ceremony of declaring the leper cleansed acquires a new and striking meaning, since it symbolizes the purification from sin by the Sacrament of Penance.

The second condition laid upon him was the strict charge not to remain any longer at the place of the cure, nor to say anything about the miracle (Mark 1:43, 44; Luke 5:14). This prohibition is repeated on other occasions, and therefore its motives must be considered here. In the first place, our Saviour wished to give a lesson in humility to His disciples and also to us. Good is never to be done for the purpose of obtaining honor, nor ought we to procure ourselves honor from it. The Jewish party-leaders sought to obtain adherents by sensational means; our Saviour, on the contrary, by the convincing power of His doctrine and miracles, while He avoided all unnecessary sensation (Schanz). Secondly, our Saviour chose as a rule to be made known only by the preaching of the Apostles. They are His appointed witnesses. Thirdly, it is better for the man himself to withdraw into solitude and, instead of attracting attention to himself as a marvel, to think over the benefit he has received and give thanks to God for it.

Lastly, our Saviour wished to avoid unnecessary excitement among the people and among His enemies. In this case such appears to have been His chief motive. For, as the man published the miracle far and wide (we may well believe, with a good intention and out of enthusiastic gratitude), there seems to have been general excitement, and everyone flocked to our Lord to be healed, so that He could not let Himself be seen in public in the towns without causing great sensation. For this reason, we are told, He withdrew from the people and gave Himself to prayer (Luke 5:15, 16; Mark 1:45). We have here already displayed a slight sign of the hostility towards Jesus. All these reasons throw fresh light upon the virtues and noble character of our Saviour.

## THE HEALING OF THE PARALYTIC

LUKE 5:17. And it came to pass on a certain day, as he sat teaching, that there were also Pharisees and doctors of the law sitting by, that were come out of every town of Galilee and Judaea and Jerusalem; and the power of the Lord was to heal them.—18. And behold men brought in a bed a man who had the palsy; and they sought means to bring him in and to lay him before him.—19. And when they could not find by what way they might bring him in, because of the multitude, they went up upon the roof and let him down through the tiles with his bed into the midst before Jesus.—20. Whose faith when he saw, he said: "Man, thy sins are forgiven thee."—21. And the scribes and Pharisees began to think, saying: "Who is this who speaketh blasphemies? Who can forgive sins, but God alone?"—22. And when Jesus knew their thoughts, answering he said to them: "What is it you think in your hearts?—23. Which is easier to say, Thy sins are forgiven thee: or to say, Arise and walk?—24. But that you may know that the Son of Man hath power on earth to forgive sins (he saith to the sick of the palsy), I say to thee, Arise, take up thy bed, and go into thy house."—25. And immediately rising up before them, he took up the bed on which he lay; and he went away to his own house, glorifying God.—26. And all were astonished; and they glorified God. And they were filled with fear, saying: "We have seen wonderful things today."

MARK 2:1. And again he entered into Capharnaum after some days.—2. And it was heard that he was in the house, and many came together, so that there was no room, no not even at the door; and he spoke to them the word.—3. And they came to him bringing one sick of the palsy, who was carried by four.—4. And when they could not offer him unto him for the multitude, they uncovered the roof where he was; and opening it they let down the bed wherein the man sick of the palsy lay.—5. And when Jesus had seen their faith, he saith to the sick of the palsy: "Son, thy sins are forgiven thee."—6. And there were some of the scribes sitting there, and thinking in their hearts:—7. "Why doth this man speak thus? he blasphemeth. Who can forgive sins but God only?"—8. Which Jesus presently knowing in his spirit, that they so thought within themselves, saith to them: "Why think you these things in your hearts?—9. Which is easier, to say to the sick of the palsy: Thy sins are forgiven thee; or to say: Arise, take up thy bed, and walk?—10. But that you may know that the Son of Man hath power on earth to forgive sins (he saith to the sick of the palsy),—11. I say to thee, Arise, take up thy bed, and go into thy house."—12. And immediately he arose;

and taking up his bed, went his way in the sight of all, so that all wondered and glorified God, saying: "We never saw the like."

MATT. 9:1. And entering into a boat, he passed over the water and came into his own city.—2. And behold they brought to him one sick of the palsy, lying in a bed. And Jesus seeing their faith, said to the man sick of the palsy: "Be of good heart, son, thy sins are forgiven thee."—3. And behold some of the scribes said within themselves: "He blasphemeth."—4. And Jesus seeing their thoughts, said: "Why do you think evil in your hearts?—5. Whether is easier, to say, Thy sins are forgiven thee; or to say, Arise and walk?—6. But that you may know that the Son of Man hath power on earth to forgive sins (then said he to the man sick of the palsy), Arise, take up thy bed, and go into thy house."—7. And he arose, and went into his house.—8. And the multitude seeing it, feared, and glorified God that gave such power to men.

### 1. INTRODUCTORY CIRCUMSTANCES OF THE MIRACLE

Our Saviour was again at Capharnaum (Matt. 9:1; Mark 2:1) and teaching, probably in Peter's house, before such a throng of people that there was not even standing-room at the door (Mark 2:2; Luke 5:19).

A peculiar circumstance was the presence of numerous scribes and Pharisees, who had come not only from all the towns of Galilee, but also from Judaea and Jerusalem (Luke 5:17), a sign that the rumor of the teaching and miracles of Jesus had spread beyond Galilee in all directions and again attracted attention to Him in the metropolis. This was perhaps owing to the testimony of the leper, given a short time before. They wished, then, to acquire certain knowledge of the events, actually to observe the doings and teaching of Jesus; assuredly not with the intention of profiting by them like the people, who were so desirous to learn and to obtain salvation, but in order to carp and cavil at everything in an indifferent, proud and incredulous spirit, to pick up something against our Saviour and to intimidate Him. They were intent on making even our Saviour's deeds of mercy an object of pharisaical attack. It was with these dispositions that the numerous Pharisees surrounded our Saviour as He taught the people.

Whilst He was thus teaching, a sick man was suddenly let down in a litter by means of ropes, in the midst of the assemblage. It was a poor paralytic. Four men had compassionately carried him thither, but since they could not bring him in on account of the overcrowding of the house, they had mounted with their burden upon the roof, either by an outside staircase or over the roof of the neighboring house. Then they let him down into the midst of the astonished assembly, where the poor sufferer, in close proximity to his Deliverer, doubtless implored His help with great earnestness. All these circumstances—the immense concourse of people standing round, the presence of so many Pharisees, the impetuosity of faith and love with which the four men had accomplished the act of charity, the entreaties of the sick man—all these prepared the way for the miracle and brought it about. They gave a character of unusual solemnity to the occasion, as the Evangelist remarks (Luke 5:17): "The power of the Lord was (there) to heal them."

## 2. THE MIRACLE ITSELF

The way in which our Saviour performs the miracle is deserving of notice. His intention in working it was not merely to heal the sick man, but to profit by this solemn occasion to reveal Himself to the people and the Pharisees, by His power of forgiving sins, as the Messias and the Son of God.

He made this revelation, first, by asserting that He had power to forgive sins, and then by exercising this power. Instead of immediately curing the bodily disease of the sick man, He remits his sins (Luke 5:20; Mark 2:5; Matt. 9:2). The words express the actual remission of sins, as is the case in similar passages (Luke 7:47, 48; John 20:23). And the Pharisees so understand them. Our Saviour remits the man's sins first, because it was His chief object here to reveal this power, and because sin in itself is a much worse evil than bodily sickness, and in this case moreover, may have been the cause of the paralysis. This treatment certainly suited the dispositions and thoughts of the sick man, who, at the sight of Jesus, remembered his sins with shame and contrition. Our Saviour was able thus to exert upon the sufferer His power to remit sins, because the faith, confidence and love of the bearers had obtained for him the grace of contrition and interior conversion (Luke 5:20; Mark 2:5; Matt. 9:2).

Secondly, our Saviour vindicates His implied assertion that He possessed this power, and removes the doubts concerning it, stigmatizing as "evil" the secret thoughts of the Pharisees (known to Him, as the Searcher of hearts), who considered His words "blasphemous" (Matt. 9:4; Luke 5:21).

Thirdly, our Lord substantiates His power to forgive sins by the miracle of the cure, in fact He works this miracle expressly for this purpose (Luke 5:23, 24, 25; Mark 2:9–12; Matt. 9:5, 6, 7). It is the power which belongs to Him as the Messias. So it had been prophesied (Isa. 53:11; 54:5; Dan. 9:24; Luke 1:77; Matt. 1:21; John 1:29). And He takes away sin not merely by suffering in the stead of sinners, but also by simply remitting it. Our Saviour lays particular stress upon this, that He, while sojourning on earth, has power to remit sins (Luke 5:24; Matt. 9:6; Mark 2:10). This is a proof of His Divinity, as the Pharisees themselves recognized (Luke 5:21; Mark 2:7; Matt. 9:3), and for its substantiation He works the miracle. For man to forgive sins and to work miraculous cures are in themselves equally difficult and in fact impossible, but for God the one is as easy as the other. But the miraculous cure carries stronger conviction, because it appeals to the senses, whilst the forgiveness of sins is accomplished invisibly. On this account our Saviour works the one as a firm assurance of the other. The miracle itself was worked suddenly, by a word, and was rendered irrefutable by the fact that the paralytic immediately stood up at our Saviour's command, took up his own bed, and carried it home before all the people (Luke 5:24, 25; Mark 2:11, 12; Matt. 9:6, 7).

### 3. EFFECT OF THE MIRACLE

The effect produced by the miracle upon the paralytic was naturally joy and heartfelt gratitude, to which he gave vent in loud praises of God (Luke 5:25). In the people it aroused astonishment and reverential awe (Matt. 9:8; Mark 2:12), admiration and expressions of gratitude to God. Some cried: "We never saw the like" (Mark 2:12), others: "We have seen wonderful things today" (Luke 5:26). And what was the effect on the Pharisees? The "power of the Lord to heal them" was indeed there. Our Lord worked no less than three miracles before their eyes, and yet they persisted in their unbelief. Henceforth blasphemy remained their constant accusation against our Lord, whenever He forgave sins (Luke 7:49); indeed, it would appear that this miracle was, so to speak, the signal for them to begin to persecute our Saviour openly. By this mystery He had in very deed taken an important step in the revelation of Himself.

How many thanks we owe Him for demonstrating so solemnly His power to forgive sins; for asserting it with such constancy before His enemies, confirming it by miracles, and thus giving a double proof of His Divinity; for afterwards imparting this His power to men, to His Church, and confirming their power in advance by the miracle of the cure of the paralytic man! This miracle is a type of the forgiveness of sins in the New Covenant;

first because our Saviour Himself links the cure with the forgiveness of sins, and because of this paralysis, whether it was the result of a stroke or of acute rheumatism, is a vivid picture of the effects of sin. In this sense the words of the Evangelist, "The multitudes . . . glorified God that gave such power to men" (Matt. 9:8), first acquire their full significance. We have here too an example of our Lord's custom of sometimes confirming an important point of His doctrine by a corresponding miracle.

## The Call of St. Matthew

Luke 5:27. And after these things he went forth, and saw a publican named Levi sitting at the receipt of custom; and he said to him: "Follow me."—28. And leaving all things, he rose up and followed him.—29. And Levi made him a great feast in his own house; and there was a great company of publicans and of others, that were at table with him.—30. But the Pharisees and scribes murmured, saying to his disciples: "Why do you eat and drink with publicans and sinners?"—31. And Jesus answering, said to them: "They that are whole need not the physician; but they that are sick.—32. I came not to call the just, but sinners to penance."

Mark 2:13. And he went forth again to the sea-side; and all the multitude came to him, and he taught them.—14. And when he was passing by, he saw Levi the son of Alpheus sitting at the receipt of custom; and he saith to him: "Follow me." And rising up he followed him.—15. And it came to pass that as he sat at meat in his house, many publicans and sinners sat down together with Jesus and his disciples. For they were many, who also followed him.—16. And the scribes and Pharisees, seeing that he ate with publicans and sinners, said to his disciples: "Why doth your master eat and drink with publicans and sinners?"—17. Jesus hearing this, saith to them: "They that are well have no need of a physician, but they that are sick. For I came not to call the just, but sinners."

Matt. 9:9. And when Jesus passed on from thence, he saw a man sitting in the custom-house, named Matthew; and he saith to him: "Follow me." And he arose up and followed him.—10. And it came to pass as he was sitting at meat in the house, behold many publicans and sinners came and sat down with Jesus and his disciples.—11. And the Pharisees seeing it, said to his disciples: "Why doth your master eat with publicans and sinners?"—12. But Jesus hearing it, said: "They that are in health need not a physician, but they that are ill.—13. Go then and learn what this meaneth: I will have mercy, and not sacrifice. For I am not come to call the just, but sinners."

### 1. ST. MATTHEW BEFORE HIS CALL

From the house in which the paralytic had been healed our Saviour betook Himself to the sea-shore, where He taught the people; thence probably going northwards, He came to one of the custom-houses, of which there were most likely several on the high-road between Damascus and Acre. Here He met with the publican Levi, the son of a certain Alpheus, who must not however be confused with the father of the two apostles James and Jude, who also bore this name (Mark 2:14). Matthew, then, belonged to the detested class of tax-gatherers, or publicans (Matt. 10:3).

These publicans held a lease of the lesser taxes from the Roman chief tax-gatherers, and were held in extreme abhorrence by the Jews, partly because they were regarded as tools of the foreign rulers, partly on account of their violence and injustice in the exercise of their office (Luke 3:13). If they were Jews, they were considered traitors to their country, and were avoided on principle by the zealous Jews, who placed them on a par with heathens and public sinners (Matt. 9:10, 11; 18:17; 21:31; Mark 2:15, 16; Luke 3:13; 5:30). Nevertheless there were many among them who did not deserve this evil reputation, and of these the Evangelist relates that many followed our Saviour and became His adherents (Mark 2:15).

Matthew was probably one of these. He had most likely learned to know our Saviour through His sermons and miracles in Capharnaum, and had formed a high opinion of Him; it may be that he had even come to believe Him to be the Messias. Nevertheless he belonged to a class branded by the people, and was a worldling by business and calling. This was the man whom our Lord was now seeking for an Apostle.

## 2. HOW MATTHEW WAS CALLED

Our Saviour found Matthew in the midst of his occupation (Luke 5:27; Mark 2:14; Matt. 9:9). As all the Evangelists remark, our Lord looked at him. It must have been a significant glance, full both of majesty and kindness; a glance that pierced to his inmost soul. It was a glance of God's eternal predestination, that brought with it a whole world of grace; a look of the divine omnipotence which calls into existence what does not yet exist, and in one moment both scatters the seed and ripens and matures the fruit. At the same time our Lord called him, and said: "Follow Me." These words made it clear to him immediately that he must forsake house, business, family, income, everything, and join Christ, like the other disciples. But he receives in return for all this the honor and joy of the friendship and close companionship of Jesus, the glory of the Apostolate, and the fame of an Evangelist. How glorious is the exchange: the seat of a judge of Israel for a place in the custom-house, labor for immortal souls instead of earthly goods, heaven as a reward instead of silver and gold, the Gospel for bills of merchandise!

### 3. HOW MATTHEW FOLLOWS THE CALL

The manner in which Matthew followed the call of Jesus bears every mark of generosity. In the first place, he followed immediately, as all the Evangelists remark. Secondly, he left everything, house, family and business (Luke 5:28). Thirdly, he followed with great joy and gratitude. In remembrance of this hour of grace he changed, as it seems,[1] his name of Levi into Matthew (God's grace or gift), as though he only now began to live. Then he prepared a great banquet, and invited all his fellow tax-gatherers to it, as well as our Saviour and His disciples (Luke 5:29; Mark 2:15; Matt. 9:10). Here we have a series of great and even heroic actions, showing that good and noble hearts were to be found even among the despised publicans.

St. Matthew's intention in giving this joyful feast was not only to show his gratitude to our Saviour and to celebrate the close of his previous life and the beginning of a new one, but probably also to bring his fellow-publicans into contact with our Lord and make them acquainted with Him. So he begins at once to work as an Apostle. Our Saviour accepted the invitation, and the publicans came also in large numbers. It is their feast. How the hearts of these poor men melt under the love and friendliness of our Saviour! How joyous and frank they are, now that they have found a heart that goes out to them! The Pharisees saw this, either because they had been lurking around to spy out everything, or because their attention had been attracted by the publicity and rejoicing of the banquet. But they were vexed instead of being glad, and though they probably feared to be worsted in an encounter with our Saviour Himself, they were not ashamed to attack the disciples, who were at this time already numerous (Mark 2:15), on the point of their eating with publicans and sinners (Luke 5:30; Mark 2:16; Matt. 9:11). Our Saviour in His answer not only defended His actions but also condemned the Pharisees on these heads. First, He replied by a common proverb, that the physician was for the sick and not for the healthy; according to their opinion the publicans were the sick, and they themselves the healthy, holy people, who did not require a physi-

---

[1] Double names of the same person occur, however, often enough in other cases (Acts 1:23; 4:36).

cian (Luke 5:31; Mark 2:17; Matt. 9:12). Perhaps there lay in these words a touch of irony. Secondly, our Saviour declared (Matt. 9:13) that the law and the prophets nowhere forbade compassion and indulgence towards sinners; that, on the contrary, they required not merely the service of outward sacrifices, but far more charity towards one's neighbor, according to the words of the prophets (Osee 6:6; Zach. 7:9), who had reproached their forefathers already with having nothing of the spirit of the law, but only the empty exterior observance, and had foretold that they would be punished by God on this account. It was thus that they acted now, misunderstanding the object of the whole law, which demanded recognition of one's own sins (Rom. 3:20) and pitying compassion for one's neighbor; therefore punishment would not fail to fall upon them. Thirdly, He declared plainly that His vocation and task in life was to save what was lost and to receive in mercy and pardon all who came to Him contrite and believing. He is before all things the Messias of sinners (Luke 5:32; Mark 2:17).

In this answer lies the key to this mystery and to a long series of lessons and occurrences in the life of Jesus. They show us why He approached the forsaken publicans, defended them, received them, and even chose an Apostle from amongst them. It is His protest against the national prejudice of the Jews and Pharisees as to their own righteousness, which led them to despise not only the Gentiles, but even that part of their nation which did not do homage in word and deed to their phantom of a national Saviour. Our Lord here continues the opposition which had been already begun by John the Baptist; and after our Saviour's Death the Apostles will continue to carry it on. Christianity and Judaism are on this point irreconcilable, and the latter perishes in her contradiction.

This mystery is a continuation and development of the previous one. There the Pharisees silently denied the power of the Messias to forgive sins; now they oppose its use and application to publicans and public sinners. They show here for the first time open hostility to our Lord, and it is worthy of note that it is provoked by the call of Matthew, a publican, to the apostolate, and by the overtures made by Jesus to this class of men. Thus the call of St. Matthew is really the beginning of a new series of complications in the life of our Saviour.

The mystery teaches us that we should never despair of anyone, and that God can make use of all in His kingdom. It shows us further the importance of a kind word and a friendly glance, and also that it must be the rule of an enlightened director of souls to begin at the point where it is most necessary.

## DISCUSSION ABOUT FASTING

LUKE 5:33. And they (the Pharisees and scribes) said to him (Jesus): "Why do the disciples of John fast often and make prayers, and the disciples of the Pharisees in like manner; but thine eat and drink?"—34. To whom he said: "Can you make the children of the bridegroom fast, whilst the bridegroom is with them? —35. But the days will come when the bridegroom shall be taken away from them; then shall they fast in those days."—36. And he spoke also a similitude to them: that "no man putteth a piece from a new garment upon an old garment; otherwise he both rendeth the new, and the piece taken from the new agreeth not with the old.—37. And no man putteth new wine into old bottles; otherwise the new wine will break the bottles, and it will be spilled and the bottles will be lost.—38. But new wine must be put into new bottles; and both are preserved.— 39. And no man drinking old, hath presently a mind to new; for he saith, the old is better."

MARK 2:18. And the disciples of John and the Pharisees used to fast; and they come and say to him: "Why do the disciples of John and of the Pharisees fast, but thy disciples do not fast?"—19. And Jesus saith to them: "Can the children of the marriage fast, as long as the bridegroom is with them? As long as they have the bridegroom with them, they cannot fast.—20. But the days will come when the bridegroom shall be taken away from them; and then they shall fast in those days.—21. No man seweth a piece of raw cloth to an old garment; otherwise the new piecing taketh away from the old, and there is made a greater rent.—22. And no man putteth new wine into old bottles; otherwise the wine will burst the bottles, and both the wine will be spilled, and the bottles will be lost. But new wine must be put into new bottles."

MATT. 9:14. Then came to him the disciples of John, saying: "Why do we and the Pharisees fast often, but thy disciples do not fast?"—15. And Jesus said to them: "Can the children of the bridegroom mourn, as long as the bridegroom is with them? But the days will come when the bridegroom shall be taken away from them, and then they shall fast.—16. And nobody putteth a piece of raw cloth unto an old garment. For it taketh away the fulness thereof from the garment, and there is made a greater rent.—17. Neither do they put new wine into old bottles. Otherwise the bottles break, and the wine runneth out, and the bottles perish. But new wine they put into new bottles; and both are preserved."

### 1. THE ACCUSERS

It may have been the feast given by Matthew which led to this accusation and discussion. The accusers this time were not only the Pharisees, but leagued with them were the disciples of John (Matt. 9:14; Mark 2:18). John's disciples (or at any rate some of them) seem not to have liked the ministry of Jesus (John 3:26). As long as John was with them he held their opposition in check; but after his arrest his disciples dispersed, and biased as they were by Jewish views and full of zeal for ritualistic precepts, they joined with the Pharisees against our Saviour. They did not understand our Lord's character, and watched the course of His ministry with distrust and dissatisfaction. Thus it may have come about that the Pharisees and the disciples of John were keeping one of the fasts which they observed two or three times a week, when our Saviour and His disciples took part in Matthew's banquet. Both parties then united for an attack, in which John's disciples were the speakers.

## 2. THE ACCUSATION

The accusation consisted in the reproach that our Lord did not urge His disciples to the practice of fasting and prayer, as John had done and the Pharisees did, but that He led an ordinary life and was even seen at feasts (Mark 2:18; Matt. 9:14). Herein is plainly shown the narrow-minded, onesided, intolerant spirit so inherent in sects.

In the first place they set value only upon exterior things. Prayer and fasting, although practices of the spiritual life, are but the exterior, or so to speak the bodily part of it. In spite of much prayer and fasting one can still be very far from interior perfection, like John's disciples and the Pharisees in the present instance. After all, this praying (at any rate with the Pharisees) was mere hypocrisy, convinced as they were of their own sanctity (Luke 18:11); and their fasting was mere display, partly religious, partly political. Just as public fasts were held at times of great catastrophes as a sign of sorrow and mourning (Judg. 20:26; II Kings 1:12; I Mach. 3:47), so also the Pharisees, as thorough patriots, made use of fasting to display their sorrow over the subjection of the country under foreign rule and over the long tarrying of the Messias. They acted the part of mourners over the bride of Sion (Bar. 4:12; 5:9), and would not enjoy life until the deliverer came. So their doings in this respect were but a sour product of the passions (Zach. 7:4 seq.).

Secondly, the Pharisees reckoned as a proof of true holiness only what they had themselves invented. It was not a question here of prescribed fasting and prayers, but of free and self-imposed observances (Luke 18:12). The law prescribed fasting on the Day of Atonement (Lev. 16:29), and a few fast-days were afterwards added in consequence of tragic events (IV Kings 25:8). Pious Israelites imposed fasts upon themselves (Num. 30:14; Luke 2:37).

So also John the Baptist (Matt. 11:18), his disciples, and the Pharisees (Luke 18:12). Whoever did not do so was wanting, in their opinion, in true sanctity.

Thirdly, not content to go their own way, they exalted themselves above others, condemned them, and were vexed at their behavior, as one plainly sees in the words of John's disciples, when they lay stress upon the pretended lack of piety by the disciples of Jesus (Luke 5:33). And they raise this accusation openly, and directly against the Person of our Saviour.

### 3. THE ANSWER OF JESUS

The answer contains three parts.

In the first place, our Saviour does not despise or reject fasting in itself. On the contrary, He will not neglect to give commands with regard to it, and the disciples will obey them, following the example which He Himself has already set. This is implied in the words: "They shall fast" (Luke 5:35; Matt. 9:15; 17:20; Mark 2:20; 9:28; Acts 13:2; II Cor. 6:5; 11:27).

Secondly, our Saviour replies that it is not the time now to give commands concerning this, and that it is a matter dependent upon circumstances, because fasting and prayer are not the aim, but only the means in the spiritual life, and means must be adapted to circumstances of time and the dispositions of men. He illustrates both these kinds of circumstances by similitudes or little parables. With regard to the time, He observes, it would be very unseemly if the friends and guests of the bridegroom were to fast at the marriage-feast of their friend out of love for austerity (Luke 5:34; Mark 2:19; Matt. 9:15). So it is now. Our Saviour, as the Messias, woos the Church and mankind, and since the disciples are the arrangers of the espousals and participators in the bridal festivities, it is fitting that they should rejoice. Mourning would simply be a declaration that the Messias, the Bridegroom of Israel, had not yet come. The similitude must have been familiar to the Pharisees from various passages of the Scriptures. John had made use of it in speaking to his disciples (John 3:29). They could not misunderstand it. With regard to the dispositions of men, our Saviour says that it is not good nor indeed possible to amalgamate the New Law with the Old. The spirit of each was so different. He illustrates this by the similitudes of the wine and the bottles, and of the patch of unshrunk cloth on an old garment (Luke 5:36–38; Mark 2:21, 22; Matt. 9:16, 17). The new garment would be spoilt by having the piece taken out of it, and the new piece would not match the old [1] (cf. Gal. 4:1; Col. 2:17; Rom. 8:15; Hebr. 8:9; 9:9). Later on they will fast, and for better reasons than the Pharisees (Luke 17:22; John 16:12); not for the sake of display, but from religious motives (amongst others, heartfelt sorrow at the violent removal of the bridegroom). With these mysterious words our Saviour here announces for the first time His Death, and that the Jews will give the disciples this cause for fasting.

Thirdly, our Saviour explains the annoyance of the disciples of John in particular, by their not understanding the Gospel and finding it strange, because they had grown old in the observance of the ancient law; everyone who is accustomed to old wine finds new unpalatable, even when the latter is better (Luke 5:39). Here He gives them and all observers of law a warning to beware of the force of long habit, and not immediately to reject as bad everything that is new. The remark applied also to our Lord's own disciples, whose training proceeded slowly, but yet more quickly than the reinstruction of the divines of the old school, precisely because the former were not prejudiced. Perhaps it was for this reason that our Lord did not choose His disciples from among the educated classes.

The mystery is yet a further beautiful delineation of the character of Jesus. In the first place, how well His magnificent intellect is shown in the striking and tender figures in which He clothes His thoughts! Secondly is revealed the moderation, solidity and good sense of His teaching, and of His manner of treating and guiding men. In these few sentences He enunciates the only correct principles with regard to the employment and practice of outward austerities in the spiritual life. And they stand out all the more sharply in contrast to the unenlightened asceticism of the Pharisees and of John's disciples. Thirdly, how refreshing is the calmness, patience, and mildness of our Lord in the face of such a tactless and offensive accusation! He employs no sharp, satirical words in His defence. He instructs, explains, and even excuses the ill-humor and annoyance from which the accusation proceeded. What a beautiful example of controversy is here given us!

[1] So St. Luke. The other Evangelists say much the same thing in rather different words; that the unshrunk cloth, when it got wet, would tear the old garment upon which it had been sewn.

## C. The Public Life of Jesus from the Second to the Third Paschal Feast

In this period the following points are of special importance. The formation of the Apostolic College; the training of the Apostles by the great doctrinal sermons, by a rapid succession of extraordinary miracles, and by the practical experiment of an apostolic mission; the beheading of John the Baptist; and, in the controversies with the Pharisees, the enunciation of the doctrine concerning the observance of the Sabbath, and the announcement of the Holy Eucharist. The promise of the Holy Eucharist carries contradiction and dissension even into the midst of the disciples, and decides the issue of the ministry in Galilee.

### The Healing of the Man Who Had Been Infirm for Thirty-eight Years

John 5:1. After these things was a festival day of the Jews, and Jesus went up to Jerusalem.—2. Now there is at Jerusalem a pond, called Probatica, which in Hebrew is named Bethsaida, having five porches.—3. In these lay a great multitude of sick, of blind, of lame, of withered, waiting for the moving of the water.—4. And an angel of the Lord descended at certain times into the pond; and the water was moved. And he that went down first into the pond after the motion of the water, was made whole of whatsoever infirmity he lay under.—5. And there was a certain man there, that had been eight and thirty years under his infirmity.—6. Him when Jesus had seen lying, and knew that he had been now a long time, he saith to him: "Wilt thou be made whole?"—7. The infirm man answered him: "Sir, I have no man, when the water is troubled, to put me into the pond. For whilst I am coming, another goeth down before me."—8. Jesus saith to him: "Arise, take up thy bed, and walk."—9. And immediately the man was made whole; and he took up his bed and walked. And it was the Sabbath that day.—10. The Jews therefore said to him that was healed: "It is the Sabbath, it is not lawful for thee to take up thy bed."—11. He answered them: "He that made me whole, he said to me: Take up thy bed, and walk."—12. They asked him therefore: "Who is that man who said to thee: Take up thy bed, and walk?"—13. But he who was healed, knew not who it was. For Jesus went aside from the multitude standing in the place.—14. Afterwards Jesus findeth him in the Temple, and saith to him: "Behold thou art made whole; sin no more, lest some worse thing happen to thee."—15. And the man went his way, and told the Jews that it was Jesus who had made him whole.—16. Therefore did the Jews persecute Jesus, because he did these things on the Sabbath.

It is the Feast of the Pasch (John 5:1), and our Saviour must not fail to appear in Jerusalem, in order to manifest Himself in opposition to the unbelief of the Jews, and to bring about by degrees the completion of His sacrifice. At this Paschal feast also He takes a further important step towards this end. The occasion of this was afforded by the miraculous cure of the man who had been infirm for thirty-eight years.

### 1. HOW JUSTIFIABLE THIS MIRACLE WAS

There was in Jerusalem a pond called Probatica (sheep-pond), near which stood a kind of hospital called Bethsaida, a charitable foundation, which, according to the most ancient tradition, was probably situated in the vicinity of the famous Pool of Siloë. Four side-porches and a middle porch surrounded the double pond. The waters of this pond possessed a miraculous quality, that when set in motion from time to time by the hand of an angel, they undulated powerfully, and healed whoever first descended into them of whatever infirmity he lay under. This fact, in connection with others related in Holy Scripture (I Par. 21:12 seq.; Tob. 3:25; 12:15; Ps. 77:25; Dan. 10:13; Apoc. 9:15), affords us a glimpse of the beneficent action of God in the material world through the holy angels. In the porches, corridors and chambers of this hospital was a great throng of all kinds of sufferers, lame, blind, withered, who all longingly awaited the moving of the water (John 5:2, 3).

Our Saviour, then, visited this hospital during the crowded and joyous days of the feast, probably to comfort the poor sufferers. He found there a man in a most pitiable condition. He was infirm in body and soul, and presented a picture of the most extreme helplessness and abandonment, though in the midst of many people and hard by the healing pool. He had been ill for thirty-eight years, and who knows how long he had already lain there on the brink of the healing water! How often it had been set in motion! But because he had no one to help him, someone else had always got before him, and so he remained lying there in his misery (John 5:7).

To this man, then, our Saviour came, and being filled with compassion for his corporal and spiritual misery, He resolved to heal him. Could His assistance be anywhere more needed?

### 2. THE MODESTY AND RESERVE WITH WHICH OUR LORD WORKS THE MIRACLE

This reserve is especially shown in three circumstances.

First, our Saviour does not expressly require of the sick man faith and confidence that He is able to heal him, as He does in other instances. He only asks, out of sympathy and compassion, if he desires to be healed. Our Saviour was unknown to the sick man, and did not wish to be known at the outset (John 5:6). But without doubt this kindly question drew the poor man out of his state of dejection, and perhaps excited him under the influence of grace even to faith and confidence in Jesus, Who approached him so sympathetically. At all events the sick man expressed very forcibly, though tacitly, his desire and request for help, by the statement of his pitiable condition (John 5:7).

Secondly, our Lord heals the paralyzed man very quietly and without attracting attention, by saying that he was to arise, take up his bed and walk (John 5:8). By the words "Arise, take up thy bed and walk," our Saviour merely intended to substantiate the miracle. He often commands something of this kind to estab- lish the fact of a miracle (Luke 5:24; Mark 5:43; John 2:8).

Thirdly, our Saviour immediately disappears in the crowd (John 5:13). He thereby intended, first, to avoid any commotion amongst the people on account of the miracle; secondly, to let the miracle itself be made known to the Pharisees by the paralytic; and thirdly, to let a discussion arise concerning the command of Sabbath observance, in consequence of the man's carrying away his bed. From these circumstances it may be seen that He did not wish to give occasion for persecution, and in nowise im- prudently or inopportunely challenged unbelief.

### 3. HOW THE MIRACLE BECAME KNOWN

The miracle became known and attracted attention first be- cause the healed man, whether out of joyful excitement or because he had thus understood our Lord's words, carried away his bed, and perhaps even through the streets (John 5:9). Secondly, the miracle came to light in consequence of the interference of the Pharisees, who stopped him and forbade him to carry his bed on the Sabbath (John 5:10); but wrongly, for the law (Ex. 20:8 ff.) only forbade noisy carrying of burdens for the sake of gain. Even if our Lord had commanded the carrying of the bed, He did this in order to substantiate the miracle, and the execution of the command was just as permissible as any action in connection with the Temple service (Matt. 12:5, 8). The answer of the man might have taught the Jews that He Who has power over life and death can command nothing contrary to the law; that one may and must obey Him with simplicity; indeed that He is Lord of the Sabbath

(John 5:11; Matt. 12:8). As such He was not bound by the law concerning the Sabbath, and if He did not observe it on this occasion, it was with the purpose of teaching the Jews a lesson; for the violation of the Sabbath was merely a pretext of theirs for persecuting our Lord. In this sense the command is simply a prediction of the end of their religion (Schanz). But the Jews would hear nothing of the miracle, and only inquired maliciously for the name of the man who had permitted the paralytic to carry his bed on the Sabbath. However, the latter himself did not know the name of his deliverer (John 5:13). Thirdly, our Saviour revealed Himself to the paralytic in the Temple, where they met, and this self-manifestation was justified by its manner, which had nothing conspicuous in it, and by its object, which was no other than to restore the man to health of soul as well as of body, and to preserve him from future misery (John 5:14). Fourthly and lastly, the man himself pointed out the miracle-worker to the Jews, but as it seems with a good intention, to bear testimony to our Saviour and to show his gratitude (John 5:15), or simply because he had been asked.

Thus the whole course of the miracle bears a peculiar stamp of opportuneness and reserve; indeed, the entire behavior of our Lord at this Paschal feast forms somewhat of a contrast, in this respect, to His appearance at the first one. He evidently did not wish to irritate His enemies. Nevertheless the occurrence filled the Jews with vexation, anger and rage, so that they persecuted Him and even sought to compass His death (John 5:16, 18). In fact, this miracle gave rise to the first open breach with the Jews, as is plainly shown in the following mystery and will also be seen later on (John 7:21). The hostile Jews, in their wicked design to destroy Jesus, seize upon every incident to further their malicious plan.

Besides the beautiful example of wise and charitable moderation and great mercy, we have in the mystery another striking type of the Sacrament of Penance. Indeed, the miraculous cure of paralysis and gout appears everywhere in the Gospels as a type of the Sacrament of Penance. As was the case with the paralytic man at Capharnaum, so here too the sickness is not merely the figure, but also the result of sin. As in the former case of the paralytic at Capharnaum, here the bodily disease is connected with the disease of the soul (sin), and the cure of body and soul is accomplished by the same act of divine power (Luke 5:24; John 5:8). Moreover both the healed men are commanded, as a confirmation of the miraculous cure, to take up their beds and walk; and this is precisely the effect of the Sacrament of Penance, that it restores life to us by remission of sin, and the use of this life by grace (Luke 5:25; John 5:9). Here is added, besides, the exterior circumstance of the medicinal poor of Bethsaida, which, with its marvelous healing power, represents the Church, because in the Chuch alone is to be found the salutary means of penance appointed by God. Lastly, the whole course of the mystery is a striking picture of the coming and working of our Saviour in order to heal mankind of sin. The unhappy condition of the world and the human race is excellently depicted in the inmates of the Bethsaida hospital, and especially in this poor sufferer. Nothing can help him, neither healing waters nor angels; he would have died with the remedy close at hand. Then our Saviour comes, full of compassion and power, first offers and then effects his cure; yes, He establishes in virtue of His sacrificial Death, which is also to be consummated on a Paschal feast, a "charitable foundation" of grace, a new and more magnificent home of healing, which stands open to all and at all times, as had been prophesied of Him (Zach. 12:10; 13:1); and the foundation of this home falls likewise upon a Paschal feast (John 20:23).

## Discourse on the Second Feast of the Pasch

John 5:16. Therefore did the Jews persecute Jesus, because he did these things on the Sabbath.—17. But Jesus answered them: "My Father worketh until now, and I work."—18. Hereupon therefore the Jews sought the more to kill him, because he did not only break the Sabbath, but also said God was his Father, making himself equal to God. Then Jesus answered and said to them:—19. "Amen, amen, I say unto you: the Son cannot do anything of himself, but what he seeth the Father doing; for what things soever he doth, these the Son also doth in like manner.—20. For the Father loveth the Son, and showeth him all things which himself doth; and greater works than these will he show him, that you may wonder.—21. For as the Father raiseth up the dead, and giveth life; so the Son also giveth life to whom he will.—22. For neither doth the Father judge any man; but hath given all judgment to the Son.—23. That all men may honor the Son, as they honor the Father. He who honoreth not the Son, honoreth not the Father who hath sent him.—24. Amen, amen, I say unto you, that he who heareth my word, and believeth him that sent me, hath life everlasting, and cometh not into judgment, but is passed from death to life.—25. Amen, amen I say unto you, that the hour cometh and now is, when the dead shall hear the voice of the Son of God, and they that hear shall live.—26. For as the Father hath life in himself, so he hath given to the Son also to have life in himself;—27. And

he hath given him power to do judgment, because he is the Son of man.—
28. Wonder not at this, for the hour cometh wherein all that are in the graves
shall hear the voice of the Son of God.—29. And they that have done good things,
shall come forth unto the resurrection of life; but they that have done evil, unto
the resurrection of judgment.—30. I cannot of myself do anything. As I hear,
so I judge; and my judgment is just; because I seek not my own will, but the will
of him that sent me.—31. If I bear witness of myself, my witness is not true.—
32. There is another that beareth witness of me; and I know that the witness
which he witnesseth of me is true.—33. You sent to John, and he gave testimony
to the truth.—34. But I receive not testimony from man; but I say these things
that you may be saved.—35. He was a burning and a shining light. And you were
willing for a time to rejoice in his light.—36. But I have a greater testimony than
that of John. For the works which the Father hath given me to perfect, the
works themselves which I do, give testimony of me, that the Father hath sent
me.—37. And the Father himself who hath sent me, hath given testimony of me;
neither have you heard his voice at any time, nor seen his shape.—38. And you
have not his word abiding in you; for whom he hath sent, him you believe not.—
39. Search the scriptures, for you think in them to have life everlasting; and the
same are they that give testimony of me;—40. And you will not come to me that
you may have life.—41. I receive not glory from men.—42. But I know you, that
you have not the love of God in you.—43. I am come in the name of my Father,
and you receive me not; if another shall come in his own name, him you will
receive.—44. How can you believe, who receive glory one from another, and the
glory which is from God alone, you do not seek?—45. Think not that I will accuse
you to the Father; there is one that accuseth you, Moses, in whom you trust.—
46. For if you did believe Moses, you would perhaps believe me also; for he
wrote of me.—47. But if you do not believe his writings; how will you believe
my words?"

### 1. REPROACHES OF THE JEWS AGAINST OUR SAVIOUR

The Jews persecuted our Saviour on account of the healing of
the paralytic (John 5:16). We are not told the nature of this
persecution, unless we may gather that they were already plotting
against His life (John 5:18). They probably began to dispute with
our Saviour publicly in the Temple, and cast at Him a twofold
reproach. The first was profanation of the Sabbath, either because, as they said, He had commanded the paralytic to carry his
bed, or in general because He worked miracles and healed the sick
on the Sabbath-day (John 5:16). As our Saviour responded that
He profaned the Sabbath rest (Gen. 2:2; Ex. 20:9, 10) no more
than did God, "His Father," when He performed exterior works
(John 5:17), the Jews charged Him secondly with blasphemy
(Lev. 24:16) in calling God His Father and putting Himself on
an equality with Him (John 5:18).

### 2. OUR SAVIOUR'S REPLY

Our Lord gives a twofold reply to this accusation.
In the first place, He does not retract the assertion that His

works are the works of the Father, but maintains it, and proves it by His consubstantiality with the Father, or in other words His Divinity. This is the foundation of the proof. His working is not a mere imitation of the working of the Father, but is actually identical with it. The Jews understood the Sabbath rest of God, which was the model and reason of their own, in a wrong sense, and condemned God and men alike to absolute repose. But such is not the case. God still continues to work, even after the creation of the world, by preservation and manifestation in the natural and supernatural orders. And if the Father works, then the Son works with Him, by virtue of His consubstantiality with the Father. Our Saviour proves this by intrinsic reasons and also by external evidence.

The intrinsic reasoning consists in this, that He says His works are really the works of His Heavenly Father, because they both have the same nature, the same life, the same knowledge, the same will and action; the Father without any communication from another Person, but He through communication from the Father. He expresses all this figuratively (John 5:19, 20, 30). The Father shows Him everything, the Son sees, hears everything, because He is the Image begotten by the Father, the expression and comprehension of all that the Father knows and does exteriorly. Thus the knowledge and will of the Father is for Him not merely the model, but also the principle of His knowledge, will and work, in consequence namely of the communication of the Divine Nature; for in God seeing and hearing are the same thing as knowing, and knowledge is the same as nature, which is in the Son with the same sovereignty and freedom of action as in the Father (John 5:26). Such works, still more glorious than those our Saviour had already accomplished (John 5:20), are: the raising to life of those spiritually or corporeally dead, according to His own choice (John 5:21); especially the reanimation of the spiritually dead, by faith, to the life of grace and glory (John 5:24, 25, 26); then (because the acceptance of grace is free) the prerogative of exercising absolute judgment, and that in the quality of Son of Man (John 5:22, 27); lastly, the raising to life of all corporeally dead, to the final decision at the Last Judgment (John 5:28, 29). Since these works of Christ are divine, there can therefore be no question of either error or presumption, profanation of the Sabbath or blasphemy (John 5:30), when He heals on the Sabbath-day or declares Himself to be God. As external evidence that He really is the Son of God, He cites various witnesses. He passes over His own testimony by word of mouth (John 5:31). The first witnesses, then, are His miraculous works and divine actions (John 5:36). The second testimony is that of John the Baptist (John 5:33), which, although He does not need it (John 5:34), is nevertheless quite reliable (John 5:35), but unfortunately fruitless, because the Jews did not profit by it (John 5:35). The third testimony is that of the Father (John 5:32, 37, 38), through the Holy Scriptures and through Moses (John 5:39, 46, 47; Deut. 18:18). But the Jews have not understood this evidence, and since they will neither see God's face nor hear His voice in a personal revelation as formerly, they only have the revelation existing outwardly in the Scriptures, but not abiding in themselves; therefore they do not believe in Jesus (John 5:40).

Upon these grounds our Saviour, secondly, lays claim to equal honor (John 5:23) and the same readiness of belief as are due to the Father (John 5:24, 38, 43); but He does not make this claim out of ambition (John 5:41). He promises eternal life as a reward for this readiness of belief (John 5:40). On the other hand, He threatens them with punishment for their incredulity, viz. the temporal misery which is involved in believing in false Messiahs and being seduced by them (John 5:43), instead of believing in Him, the promised prophet (Deut. 18:15–19); and He warns them of the judgment, in which Moses himself will appear as accuser against them (John 5:45, 46, 47). Our Saviour also mentions the causes of this incredulity, viz. a bad will and ill-feeling against Himself (John 5:40); secondly, want of love of God (John 5:42); and lastly, ambition and human respect (John 5:44). Thus the discourse of Jesus ends with an open reproof of the Jews, which lays bare all their moral corruption. They accuse Him of transgressing the law by profanation of the Sabbath and blasphemy, whilst they themselves have fallen away from the law, and on that account do not believe.

### 3. RESULT OF THE SECOND FEAST OF THE PASCH

The result is twofold.

With regard to our Saviour, this Paschal feast shows important steps taken in the revelation concerning His Person and life-work. On the first Feast of the Pasch He only touched lightly in public upon His Divinity, by saying that the Jews made the House of His

Father a place of traffic and a market-hall (John 2:16). Now He speaks more plainly, and proves it by the identity of His being, life and work with that of the Father, and also by His supreme power in the natural and the supernatural order, because He has in Himself the source and support of life. The doctrine He puts forth now is confirmed later on in the words: "I and the Father are one" (John 10:30). Our Saviour unfolds in this discourse the whole wealth and depth of His interior consciousness of His Divinity, the whole sphere of His power and activity, and the whole majesty of the God-like Figure which shines forth from the pages of Holy Scripture. And He utters this in Jerusalem, publicly, before the people and the members of the Sanhedrim, His enemies. We have here an express statement made by Jesus, that Moses had written of Him (Gen. 3:15; 49:10; Num. 24:17; Deut. 18:15 seq.). With regard to His task of purifying religion, we here find our Saviour about to remove a very serious abuse; viz. as regards the observance of the Sabbath, which the Pharisees had degraded into a caricature by arbitrary regulations and reversal of its object. This dispute, which runs through almost the entire public life of our Saviour, began upon this Feast of the Pasch.

There is also to be remarked a great increase of hostility to our Saviour on the part of the Jews. On the first Paschal feast it did not result in their taking any actual measures against Him, in spite of the formal protest made against His forcible purging of the Temple, and in spite also of their great displeasure and the strained situation; now they openly persecute Him, and are already occupied with the plan of getting Him out of the way by violence. Almost more important still is the fact that this dispute about the Sabbath reveals the inmost hearts of these men, and lays bare the deep wound from which they suffer. This wound is insensibility and incapacity for any divine revelation, falling away from the Scriptures and from Moses, and the pitiable error of an almost fanatical adherence to the latter in word, whilst they denied him in deed. The spirit of the Old Covenant has completely died away in them. They are no longer true Israelites, and therefore they cannot be Christ's disciples either, because Moses and the law are guides to Christ. Thus, after a year of public work, the situation has become very serious.

## The Plucking of the Ears of Corn on the Sabbath

Luke 6:1. And it came to pass on the second first Sabbath, that as he went through the corn-fields his disciples plucked the ears and did eat, rubbing them in their hands.—2. And some of the Pharisees said to them: "Why do you that which is not lawful on the Sabbath-days?"—3. And Jesus answering them, said: "Have you not read so much as this, what David did, when himself was hungry and they that were with him;—4. How he went into the house of God, and took and ate the bread of proposition, and gave to them that were with him; which is not lawful to eat, but only for the priests?"—5. And he said to them: "The Son of man is Lord also of the Sabbath."

Mark 2:23. And it came to pass again, as the Lord walked through the corn-fields on the Sabbath, that his disciples began to go forward and to pluck the ears of corn.—24. And the Pharisees said to him: "Behold, why do they on the Sabbath-day that which is not lawful?"—25. And he said to them: "Have you never read what David did, when he had need, and was hungry himself, and they that were with him?—26. How he went into the house of God under Abiathar the high priest, and did eat the loaves of proposition which was not lawful to eat but for the priests, and gave to them who were with him?"—27. And he said to them: "The Sabbath was made for man, not man for the Sabbath.—28. Therefore the Son of man is Lord of the Sabbath also."

Matt. 12:1. At that time Jesus went through the corn on the Sabbath; and his disciples being hungry began to pluck the ears and to eat.—2. And the Pharisees seeing them, said to him: "Behold, thy disciples do that which is not lawful to do on the Sabbath-days."—3. But he said to them: "Have you not read what David did when he was hungry, and they that were with him;—4. How he entered into the house of God, and did eat the loaves of proposition, which it was not lawful for him to eat, nor for them that were with him, but for the priests only?—5. Or have ye not read in the law, that on the Sabbath-days the priests in the Temple break the Sabbath and are without blame?—6. But I tell you that there is here a greater than the Temple.—7. And if you knew what this meaneth: I will have mercy, and not sacrifice; you would never have condemned the innocent.—8. For the Son of man is Lord even of the Sabbath."

### 1. THE DISCIPLES PLUCK EARS OF CORN ON THE SABBATH

Our Saviour had returned into Galilee after the Feast of the Pasch. On a certain Sabbath (Matt. 12:1; Mark 2:23; Luke 6:1), which is called by St. Luke the "second first," He walked with His disciples through the fields. The words "second first" may indicate the first Sabbath in the second month, or the first after the second day of the Pasch, or the Sabbath second in importance, viz. the one before Pentecost, but in any case it was after the second day of the Pasch, on which the first sheaf was offered (Lev. 22:9 seq.), and whilst the harvest was ripe. The disciples had nothing to eat, and were hungry (Matt. 12:1). They began to pluck the ears of corn (wheat), rubbed them in their hands, and satisfied thus the craving of their appetite. The field in which this is said to have taken place is still pointed out, not far from Cana, on the road to Tiberias.

As it would appear, our Saviour did not Himself participate in the meal; but in His indulgent kindness He allowed it to take place. Here we may well meditate upon the great poverty, unassuming habits and self-forgetfulness of our Lord and His disciples. They take nothing with them, and have not even the barest necessaries. They have only the hard, dusty road, with the burning sky above, no tent, no spring, nothing around them but waving corn-fields which do not belong to them. Such are the surroundings of the Lord of heaven and earth, and of His envoys. How simple, poor, and hard for nature to bear! And yet the Apostles were satisfied, and did not wish to be better off than their Lord and Master. What a beautiful example of apostolic poverty and cheerfulness!

### 2. THE PHARISEES ATTACK OUR SAVIOUR ON ACCOUNT OF THE DISCIPLES

Our Saviour is rebuked by the Pharisees (Matt. 12:2; Mark 2:24; Luke 6:2) on account of the innocent means whereby His disciples appease their hunger.

There are many very disagreeable features in the behavior of the Pharisees. First, they watch our Lord and steal after Him everywhere, without any authority to do so, and with the intention of doing Him injury. Perhaps they had instructions from Jerusalem to this effect. Secondly, they charged our Saviour, as all the Evangelists say (Matt. 12:2; Mark 2:24; Luke 6:2), with an unlawful deed; not, indeed, with committing theft upon the property of others, for the plucking of ears of corn was permitted (Deut. 23:25), but with profaning the Sabbath by plucking and rubbing the ears. In their arbitrary interpretation and distortion of the law, they regarded plucking as reaping, and rubbing as threshing. The law only forbade menial and unnecessary labor (Ex. 34:21; 35:2; Lev. 23:3; Num. 15:32; Jer. 17:21; Amos 8:5; Nehem. 10:31; 13:15, 19). It was therefore a false accusation and a rash judgment, as though the Apostles had wantonly profaned the Sabbath (Matt. 12:7). Lastly, they did this in a harsh, unfeeling and inconsiderate manner, not taking into consideration the straits of hunger to which the disciples were reduced.

### 3. OUR SAVIOUR DEFENDS HIS DISCIPLES

Our Saviour defends His disciples by showing that they have not transgressed against the sacredness of the Sabbath, and rejects the accusation as contrary to charity.

He proves that the plucking and rubbing of the ears of corn was not against the law of the Sabbath; and shows, first, that the object of these regulations is no other than the welfare of man. The Sabbath is made for man, and not man for the Sabbath. The Sabbath laws must not destroy man, either in body or soul, otherwise they are no longer obligatory (Mark 2:27). Our Lord illustrates this by two examples. First, that of David (I Kings 21:1), to whom the priest Achimelech (or Abiathar, I Kings 2:11–20; Mark 2:26) gave the loaves of proposition to eat in his need; though this was much more contrary to the law than the action of the disciples (Lev. 24:5 seq.), because these loaves were consecrated bread, and might only be eaten by the priests in the holy place (Lev. 24:9). Nevertheless the High Priest did not consider the regulations binding in this case (Mark 2:26). Our Saviour further illustrates His principle by the example of the priests, who performed all the heavy work in the Temple on the Sabbath-day (Num. 28:9), and yet did not thereby transgress against the Sabbath (Matt. 12:5). One may, then, supersede the regulations concerning the Sabbath, for reasons of charity and for the divine service. The latter case is here all the more to the point, since the journeying of the Apostles with our Saviour and their service of Him is far superior to the Temple service. For "here is a greater than the Temple," namely Christ Himself, the God-Man. Secondly, our Saviour proves by appealing to His own power and authority that the Apostles' behavior did not in any case violate the Sabbath. He saw what the Apostles did, and He suffered and permitted it, therefore it is no longer against the Sabbath observance; "for the Son of Man is Lord of the Sabbath" (Matt. 12:8; Mark 2:28; Luke 6:5). He hereby declares that He is not only holier than the most holy thing in the Old Covenant, namely the Temple, but absolute Lord of His laws and institutions; and that He consequently has power to grant dispensations and make alterations at His own good pleasure.

In the second place, our Saviour rejects the accusation because it offended against the true spirit of the law, which was the spirit of charity and due compassion (Matt. 12:7). The accusation proceeded from animosity, antipathy, and love of carping, and was made under circumstances which betrayed harshness and want of feeling. For this reason our Saviour repeats His reproach and the exhortation of the prophet Osee (Matt. 12:7; cf. Matt. 9:13; Osee 6:6).

As we see, the same controversy about the celebration of the Sabbath, which was the result of the preceding mystery, is here continued. The Pharisees seem to have issued instructions to watch and persecute our Saviour with regard to this point. The mystery contains an important disclosure concerning the nature and spirit of the divine laws, especially those which are positive. Precise and definite as they are, they are nevertheless broad in spirit, considerate and adaptable to the various conditions of mankind. Charity, that is, the good of our neighbor in every respect, is their object and principle, as our Saviour very plainly shows. Thus the laws, in the intention and hand of God, are true benefits, not mere coercive measures. And these principles have passed on from our Saviour to the Church. On the other hand, we see what the divine laws become when men's passions seize upon them and arbitrarily administer them.

Further, the character of our Saviour as Lord and Legislator is here again beautifully revealed, with His clear foresight of time and circumstances, His kind, generous heart and divine authority. Especially in the latter respect the mystery is an important step in the revelation of the nature and power of the God-Man. He does not attempt to evade the question in dispute, nor does He make any concession to His enemies; He decides it against them, on the strength of His full sway over the Temple, the law and the entire Covenant. He is more than the Temple; He is its Lord, and the Lawgiver and God of the Old Covenant. He had never yet expressed Himself so clearly upon this point.

## THE HEALING OF THE WITHERED HAND

LUKE 6:6. And it came to pass also on another Sabbath, that he entered into the synagogue and taught. And there was a man whose right hand was withered.— 7. And the scribes and Pharisees watched if he would heal on the Sabbath, that they might find an accusation against him.—8. But he knew their thoughts, and said to the man who had the withered hand: "Arise, and stand forth in the midst." And rising, he stood forth.—9. Then Jesus said to them: "I ask you, if it be lawful on the Sabbath-days to do good or to do evil; to save life, or to destroy?"— 10. And looking round about on them all, he said to the man: "Stretch forth thy hand." And he stretched it forth; and his hand was restored.—11. And they were

filled with madness; and they talked one with another, what they might do to
Jesus.

MARK 3:1. And he entered again into the synagogue; and there was a man
there who had a withered hand.—2. And they watched him whether he would
heal on the Sabbath-days, that they might accuse him.—3. And he said to the
man who had the withered hand: "Stand up in the midst."—4. And he saith
to them: "Is it lawful to do good on the Sabbath-days, or to do evil? To save life,
or to destroy?" But they held their peace.—5. And looking round about on them
with anger, being grieved for the blindness of their hearts, he saith to the man:
"Stretch forth thy hand." And he stretched it forth; and his hand was restored
unto him.—6. And the Pharisees going out immediately made a consultation with
the Herodians against him, how they might destroy him.

MATT. 12:9. And when he had passed from thence, he came into their synagogue.—10. And behold there was a man who had a withered hand, and they
asked him, saying: "Is it lawful to heal on the Sabbath-days?" that they might
accuse him.—11. But he said to them: "What man shall there be among you,
that hath one sheep, and if the same fall into a pit on the Sabbath-day, will he
not take hold on it and lift it up?—12. How much better is a man than a sheep?
Therefore it is lawful to do a good deed on the Sabbath-days."—13. Then he saith
to the man: "Stretch forth thy hand." And he stretched it forth, and it was
restored to health even as the other.—14. And the Pharisees going out made a
consultation against him, how they might destroy him.—15. But Jesus knowing
it, retired from thence; and many followed him, and he healed them all.—16. And
he charged them that they should not make him known.—17. That it might
be fulfilled which was spoken by Isaias the prophet, saying:—18. "Behold my
servant whom I have chosen, my beloved in whom my soul hath been well pleased.
I will put my Spirit upon him, and he shall show judgment to the Gentiles.—
19. He shall not contend, nor cry out, neither shall any man hear his voice in the
streets.—20. The bruised reed he shall not break, and smoking flax he shall not
extinguish; till he send forth judgment unto victory.—21. And in his name the
Gentiles shall hope."

## 1. THE DEVICE OF THE PHARISEES

On another Sabbath our Saviour went again into the synagogue and taught (Luke 6:6). A man was there who had a withered hand. Thereupon the Pharisees formed new plans, full of
craft, malice and insincerity.

They showed their craft by watching our Saviour (Mark 3:2;
Luke 6:7) to see if He would heal the man; perhaps they had
even pushed him forward, confident that our Lord would take
compassion on the poor sufferer. They showed it further when,
as our Saviour read their thoughts and bade him stand forth in the
midst, they interfered and asked Him if it was lawful to heal on
the Sabbath-day (Matt. 12:10). They did this publicly in the
synagogue, before many people, in order to remind Him of the
Sabbath and thus make it impossible for Him to excuse Himself
by forgetfulness. Their plan was full of malice, because they had
the intention of accusing Him (Matt. 12:10; Luke 6:7) and even

(as the sequel showed) of endangering His life (Matt. 12:14). Lastly, they acted with great insincerity in keeping silence and not answering, when our Saviour in His turn asked them if it was permitted to heal on the Sabbath, to do evil and not rather good (Mark 3:4).

### 2. OUR SAVIOUR DEFEATS THE PLAN BY HIS RESPONSE AND HEALS THE SUFFERER

Our Saviour answers the Pharisees by a counter-question, asking whether it was lawful for a man, if his sheep fell into a pit on the Sabbath-day, to pull it out (Matt. 12:11). This was permitted even by the casuists of the Pharisaic school. He asked, further, what was more admissible on the Sabbath-day, to do good or to do evil, namely to save or to destroy and allow to perish (Mark 3:4; Luke 6:9). They would not give any answer to this, thereby declaring that a sheep and the profit to be gained by it was of more consequence to them than the welfare of a man, and that it was better to leave him in a suffering state, incapable of earning his bread, than to heal him on the Sabbath. We see everywhere the same hard, unfeeling and selfish spirit of Pharisaism.

At their silence, our Saviour looked at them with just indignation and also with sorrow at their blindness (Mark 3:5; Luke 6:10), and commanded the sufferer to stretch out his withered hand; and it immediately became as sound and healthy as the other (Matt. 12:13).

### 3. THE EFFECT PRODUCED BY THE MIRACLE

This unanswerable question and the humiliating defeat before all the people, together with the glorious miracle, aroused in the Pharisees a mad fury (Luke 6:11). They withdrew, went to the Herodians, and took counsel with them as to what they could do to our Lord and how they could destroy Him (Luke 6:11; Mark 3:6; Matt. 12:14). Thus they make an alliance with their enemies, and with the enemies of their nation, against the Saviour.

In consequence of this excitement of His enemies, our Lord withdrew from the town to the sea-coast (Mark 3:7; Matt. 12:15). All the people thronged after Him. They brought the sick and such as were possessed with devils, and He healed them and forbade the evil spirits to reveal Him (Mark 3:12). He did this out of consideration and forbearance towards His enemies, in order not to irritate them further.

So it is always the same hostile spirit which continues to manifest itself on the part of the Pharisees. Now it is the question of the Sabbath that they are pursuing, and through which they wish to destroy our Saviour. Even the simple act of curing by a word is to them profanation of the Sabbath, and they ally themselves for the first time with the detested Herodians against Jesus. With regard to our Lord Himself, the might of His intellect is above all conspicuous here. How telling is the simile of the sheep, which He takes from the casuistry of His enemies, and how it puts them to confusion, demonstrating that they have more pity for an animal than for a man! In what a withering manner He turns the question of the Pharisees (as to whether it was lawful to heal on the Sabbath) against themselves, by asking which was more seemly on the Sabbath, to do evil or to do good, to save a life or to allow it to perish! Indeed, we should never refuse help when it is in our power to give it and there is no reason to the contrary, as in the present case. This mystery serves to reveal yet more gloriously our Lord's generosity, moderation and gentleness towards His enemies. In truth, this unceasing persecution and spying, this craft and insincerity might have aroused the wrath of any heart, and yet our Lord, even in His indignation, does not forget His compassion. He always answers, always instructs, and if He works the miracle in this case it is not in order to irritate them, on the contrary He avoids this, withdraws in order to work His miracles out of their sight, and does not suffer the evil spirits to speak. St. Matthew rightly quotes here (Matt. 12:18–21) a passage from the magnificent character-sketch of the Messias drawn by Isaias. The prophet points out, besides the qualities of the Messias, His divine mission, His endowment with the Holy Ghost, and His vocation of proclaiming the law of God; and especially the manner in which He will exercise this vocation, viz. with great outward moderation, calmness and gentleness in word and deed. He will not, therefore, "contend nor cry out," neither will He completely break and tread down what is near destruction, but will raise it up and reanimate it (Isa. 42:1–4). This our Saviour does, not only with regard to the sick in body and to penitent sinners, but also to His enemies, by not upbraiding and annihilating them, but with forbearance retiring before them and lightening their judgment by the moderation of His behavior.

## THE CHOICE OF THE APOSTLES

LUKE 6:12. And it came to pass in those days that he went out into a mountain to pray, and he passed the whole night in the prayer of God.—13. And when day was come he called unto him his disciples; and he chose twelve of them (whom also he named Apostles) :—14. Simon whom he surnamed Peter, and Andrew his brother, James and John, Philip and Bartholomew,—15. Matthew and Thomas, James the son of Alpheus, and Simon who is called Zelotes,—16. And Jude the brother of James, and Judas Iscariot who was the traitor.

MARK 3:13. And going up into a mountain, he called unto him whom he would himself; and they came to him.—14. And he made that twelve should be with him, and that he might send them to preach.—15. And he gave them power to heal sicknesses and to cast out devils.—16. And to Simon he gave the name Peter.—17. And James the son of Zebedee, and John the brother of James; and he named them Boanerges, which is the sons of thunder.—18. And Andrew and Philip, and Bartholomew and Matthew, and Thomas and James of Alpheus, and Thaddeus, and Simon the Cananean,—19. And Judas Iscariot, who also betrayed him.

MATT. 10:1. And having called his twelve disciples together he gave them power over unclean spirits, to cast them out, and to heal all manner of diseases and all manner of infirmities.—2. And the names of the twelve Apostles are these: The first, Simon, who is called Peter, and Andrew his brother.—3. James the son of Zebedee, and John his brother, Philip and Bartholomew, Thomas and Matthew the publican, and James the son of Alpheus, and Thaddeus;—4. Simeon the Cananean, and Judas Iscariot, who also betrayed him.

### 1. PREPARATION FOR THE CHOICE

Our Saviour was in the neighborhood of Capharnaum, not far from the sea (Matt. 3:7). One evening He went up a mountain apart and passed the night in prayer; this prayer was the proximate preparation for the choice of the Apostles.

It was in the first place an extraordinary prayer, like that during the sojourn in the desert, because our Lord was now again contemplating something of unusual importance. Secondly, it was very fitting that He should offer special prayer, in order to give God the glory and begin the work with Him. Lastly, this prayer was very fervent and devout, truly divine and yet human. And what, then, was its subject? We may reverently suppose that our Saviour reflected and prayed as to the choice of the Apostles which He intended to make on the following morning. This choice was nothing less than the foundation of His kingdom and His Church, the foundation of the hierarchy. The vague, floating elements of His following were now to be sorted, collected and arranged, and out of those who had hitherto followed Him the foundation-stones were to be chosen and laid together, and thus the constitution of the Church was to be traced. Our Saviour rejoiced over this great work, which unfolded such a glorious plan of wisdom and goodness. God vouchsafed to let Himself be represented bv men. This kingdom of God on earth, which was for men, was likewise to rest upon men for its preservation, extension and defence. Thereby God elevated men, granted them a large share in His own power and authority, and united them among themselves and with heaven in one great divine family and kingdom. Our Saviour rejoiced at this, and thanked His Heavenly Father for all the glory that this work would bring Him, and for all the advantages which men would derive from it. He was Man, and regarded all the honor that fell to our lot as shown to Himself. Our Saviour further took counsel with His Heavenly Father in this prayer concerning the choice of the Apostles and their successors. The Father appointed them and gave them to Him (John 17:6, 11, 24; 18:9), and He received them from His Father's hand. Lastly, our Saviour entreated most earnestly in this prayer for all graces of holiness, protection, and efficiency for the hierarchy of the Church (John 17:9–20). The future of the Church was here decided. Thus this prayer was the truest preparation for the choice of the Apostles.

### 2. THE CHOICE OF THE APOSTLES

On the morning after this prayer our Lord proceeded to choose the Apostles.

Why did He call these twelve? Not from necessity. Our Lord did not need any external assistance, nor could the Apostles, naturally speaking, offer any qualities suited for the end for which He called them. They were mostly of the working classes, and only one or two of them may perhaps have received a good education. The work of God was not to rest upon anything natural (I Cor. 1:17, 18, 27, 28). They were not even saints in the usual sense of the word. The only consideration that guided Him was the good pleasure of God, as it is recorded: "He called whom He would" (Mark 3:13). It was simply a mystery of divine love and benevolence (John 15:16).

To what did our Lord call the Apostles? First, to the greatest happiness, to friendship, to the most familiar intercourse with Himself, to be His companions in life and the members of His household. They were henceforth to be with Him, witnesses of His life, His virtues, doctrine and miracles; they were to be His especial family, as we are told: "that they should be with Him"

(Mark 3:14; John 15:15). Our Saviour Himself twice calls them "blessed" on account of this preference (Matt. 13:16; Luke 10:23). He called them, secondly, to the highest honor; for they were to be His messengers, His "Apostles" (Luke 6:13), His ambassadors and representatives with men. Thirdly, He called them to the highest power (Mark 3:14, 15; Matt. 10:1, 5), to participation in the plenitude of His own power (John 17:18; 20:21; Matt. 16:19; II Cor. 5:20). He chose them to hold His own office of teacher, priest and pastor; to be the foundation and the rulers of His Church (Matt. 16:18; 18:17) and the assessors of His future judgment (Matt. 19:28). Like the twelve patriarchs in the Old Covenant, the Apostles were to be the recipients of the revelation and of all graces and blessings. Fourthly, our Saviour called the Apostles to the highest sanctity, a sanctity resembling His own, because they were to represent Him, and to represent Him worthily (John 17:6, 8, 17). Lastly, He called them to the same destiny in life, to apostolic labor, to the working of miracles, to persecutions and a bloody death, and finally to participation in His glory (Luke 21:12; 22:29; John 15:20; 17:14). The Apostolate is assuredly the greatest and most glorious gift that can be bestowed by God upon any man.

And how did our Saviour perform the consecration of the Apostles? "When day was come, He called unto him His disciples; and He chose twelve of them" (Luke 6:13; Mark 3:13; Matt. 10:1). What a sublime and magnificent scene! We seem to see the mountains and the sea-coast radiant with morning light, and the numerous, expectant throng; our Saviour stands a little above them, with a look of majesty, transfigured by holy joy and devotion; before Him is the band of disciples in reverential awe and expectation. And now our Saviour calls them singly by name and appoints them as Apostles (Luke 6:13). Who is not here reminded of a great and solemn ordination of priests in a cathedral church? How similar are all the features: the listening, praying people, the young clerics, with their hearts full of longing and throbbing with impatience; the Bishop, in full canonicals and surrounded by the assisting clergy, calls the name of each one separately and confers upon him the imposition of hands and the holy unction. It is always a magnificent sight. But never yet did any ordination surpass in sublimity the scene of the choice of the Apostles.

### 3. THE READY COMPLIANCE OF THE APOSTLES

The Apostles "came" (Mark 3:13), and we can imagine with what dispositions and sentiments of joy, gratitude, devotion and love they approached our Saviour and were received and blessed by Him. First came Simon—faithful, courageous, impetuous Simon. Our Lord looked on him with complacency, and gave him the name of Peter as a sign of superiority over the other Apostles (Gen. 49:8). Then, also among the first, the pure-hearted, child-like John. How our Saviour must have rejoiced at the sight of him! (Deut. 33:12.) And then came the other Apostles, one after another. Each one received his special blessing, like the sons of Jacob and the tribes of Israel, and our Lord rejoiced as He thought what each in particular was to be to Him. Besides the precedence of St. Peter, there seems to have been a certain interdependence and systematic arrangement among the other Apostles. We also see amongst them two or three of our Lord's cousins: James the Less (the future Bishop of Jerusalem), Judas Thaddaeus, and probably also Simon the Cananean. Only Judas, the traitor, seems to have been from Judaea; the others were natives of Galilee.

But the Apostles not only followed the call of our Lord; they remained with Him, "continued" with Him (Luke 22:28), and responded to the honor they had received by their fidelity and zeal, by their high estem of their vocation and the capability they showed for their office. Almost all of them sealed their Apostolate, after unspeakable labors and sufferings, by a glorious martyrdom.

Such was the choice of the Apostles, a mystery of the greatest importance. It is the laying of the foundation of the Church; it is the erection of the hierarchy, and the beginning of the kingdom of God and of Christ here below; and at the same time it is the commencement of the rejection of the Synagogue. It must be clearly understood that Christ does not make His Church and its government grow out of the Church of the Old Covenant, and does not simply let the latter pass into the former. He puts new things in the place of old; He erects a new temple, Church and hierarchy side by side with those of the Old Law. The reason is simple: the old institution cannot be remodeled. And if the old order of things does not adapt itself to the new, it will become reprobate.

The conclusions to be drawn from this are, first, that we should show our Lord very great gratitude for the organization of the

Church by the call of the Apostles and the establishment of the ecclesiastical hierarchy, to which our Saviour, full of graciousness and condescension, calls not only the Apostles but so many of us, as their successors. There is nothing greater, more awe-inspiring, more powerful and beneficial in the world and for the world than this hierarchy. The second lesson we may learn is confidence, because in the choice of the Apostles and in the fitness for their office which, in spite of their natural insufficiency, they yet showed, we see the power of the divine election, which does not call because it finds fitness, but creates fitness as it calls. Lastly, a lesson which is brought home to us by the fate of the unhappy Judas is the need of fear of God, humility, distrust of ourselves and a zealous use of the grace offered to us. It may be wondered at that he too was called. This is a mystery of the wisdom and justice of God. The vocation was a great grace from God, but this grace does not annul the freedom of man and the possibility of abuse of grace. Judas probably had faith and a good will at this time; but instead of cooperating with grace, he gradually gave way more and more to the temptation of the devil and the prompting of his evil passions, and thus became, to his own ruin, the unhappy instrument of the Passion and Death of Jesus. What may our Saviour have thought and felt at the sight of him, as He pronounced his name and Judas stepped forth? (Ps. 108:8.) The unhappy man and his fate are, so to speak, a prophecy that the hierarchy would also be disfigured by unworthy members; to their own ruin, it is true (Luke 14:35), but yet to the glory of our Lord's power, which in spite of human frailty yet preserves the divine hierarchy in its existence, activity and immortal honor. And this power proceeds from the prayer with which Christ began the choice of the Apostles. There is no prayer more full of honor for God, more useful to the Church and the world than intercession for the ecclesiastical hierarchy, after the example of our Saviour.

## The Sermon on the Mount

### 1. SIGNIFICATION OF THE SERMON ON THE MOUNT

The so-called Sermon on the Mount, as it is given by St. Matthew, is probably a collection and abridgment of the chief truths and principles of the moral teaching of the kingdom of God, which our Saviour propounded to the people on this and probably other occasions, in His discourses in Galilee and elsewhere.

St. Matthew, in accordance with the aim he had in view, considers more the Jews and the ancient law, and very often arranges his material according to its purport; whilst St. Luke, writing for those without the bounds of Judaism, keeps to a more general method and maintains throughout his Gospel the historical order of events.

## 2. CIRCUMSTANCES OF THE SERMON ON THE MOUNT

Our Saviour had completed the choice of the Apostles, and now descended, accompanied by the chosen twelve and other disciples, to the people, in order to instruct and heal them. It is the whole Church in its organized form and with its mission to the world which now descends from the mountain. Thus the Sermon on the Mount took place upon that mountain upon which our Saviour had passed the night in prayer and made the choice of the Apostles (Matt. 8:1; Luke 6:17). Tradition points out as the mountain of the beatitudes a height westwards of Capharnaum, called the Horns of Hattin, because it has a deep depression in the middle with summits on either side, being shaped somewhat like a saddle with its two pommels. Our Saviour is said to have sat upon the eastern point, whilst the people had settled themselves in the depression or on a little plateau below. The prospect from this height is a most beautiful one, comprising the fertile plain of Zabulon, the sea-shore, and the surrounding mountains with their castles and towns. The audience was large and mixed, consisting of the Apostles and disciples (Luke 6:17; Matt. 5:1, 2), an innumerable multitude of people from Galilee, the East Jordan districts and Decapolis, Judaea, Jerusalem, amongst them being Jews of every class of life and shade of thought; and finally Gentiles from Tyre and Sidon (Luke 6:17; Matt. 4:25). Thus the human race was represented more completely and by larger numbers than at the giving of the law on Mt. Sinai, or at the administration of the oath of the Covenant to the people on Mt. Hebal. It is the new elect people of God. Our Saviour sits upon elevated ground, proclaiming His New Law with the dignity of a prophet and lawgiver, and yet with the gentleness and mildness of the Incarnate Wisdom of God.

## 3. DIVISION OF THE SERMON ON THE MOUNT

Our Saviour first propounds the eight beatitudes (Luke 6:20–26; Matt. 5:3–12). He makes a statement regarding the task and position of the Apostles towards Israel and the world (Matt. 5:14-16). Thirdly, He specifies His relation to the Old Law in itself (Matt. 5:17-30, 33-48), and to its corruption by the Pharisees, or as He terms it the "justice of the Pharisees" (Matt. 5:20; 6:1-6, 16-18). Fourthly, He lays especial stress upon the preeminent law of love of one's neighbor (Luke 6:27-38, 42; Matt. 7:1-5, 12). Lastly follow a few more important rules of moral life for the Apostles and the faithful (Luke 6:39, 40, 43-49; Matt. 7:13-29).

## THE EIGHT BEATITUDES

MATT. 5:1. And Jesus seeing the multitudes, went up into a mountain; and when he was set down, his disciples came unto him.—2. And opening his mouth he taught them, saying: 3. "Blessed are the poor in spirit: for theirs is the kingdom of heaven.—4. Blessed are the meek: for they shall possess the land.—5. Blessed are they that mourn: for they shall be comforted.—6. Blessed are they that hunger and thirst after justice: for they shall have their fill.—7. Blessed are the merciful: for they shall obtain mercy.—8. Blessed are the clean of heart: for they shall see God.—9. Blessed are the peace-makers: for they shall be called the children of God.—10. Blessed are they that suffer persecution for justice' sake: for theirs is the kingdom of heaven.—11. Blessed are ye when they shall revile you, and persecute you, and speak all that is evil against you, untruly, for my sake;—12. Be glad and rejoice, for your reward is very great in heaven; for so they persecuted the prophets that were before you."

LUKE 6:20. And Jesus lifting up his eyes on his disciples, said: "Blessed are ye poor: for yours is the kingdom of God.—21. Blessed are ye that hunger now: for you shall be filled. Blessed are ye that weep now: for you shall laugh.—22. Blessed shall you be when men shall hate you, and when they shall separate you, and shall reproach you, and cast out your name as evil, for the Son of Man's sake.—23. Be glad in that day and rejoice; for behold, your reward is great in heaven. For according to these things did their fathers to the prophets.—24. But woe to you that are rich: for you have your consolation.—25. Woe to you that are filled: for you shall hunger. Woe to you that now laugh: for you shall mourn and weep.—26. Woe to you when men shall bless you: for according to these things did their fathers to the false prophets."

### 1. SIGNIFICATION OF THE EIGHT BEATITUDES

The eight beatitudes are general principles of Christian morality and perfection, the moral principles of the kingdom of Christ, as opposed to the false theories of the world and in particular to the mistaken ideas of the Jews with regard to the kingdom of the Messias.

Moral theology must before all things determine the last end of life, propose it as our aim, and point out means to attain to it. This last end is no other than eternal blessedness, and the means to it are virtuous actions or practices of virtue. Both of these are presented by the eight beatitudes. They first point out the way, the steps towards the end, in the various virtues which they prescribe for its attainment; and they hold out the end itself as a corresponding reward for each virtue. For this reason the word "blessed," or on the contrary "woe" is everywhere employed. The eight beatitudes, then, are the royal highway of Christ, the golden ladder to eternal bliss, or the beatification and canonization of the Christian virtues. Thus the New Law may already be distinguished, by the mild and winning manner of its proclamation, as the law of grace and love, in contrast to the fear and terror of the ancient law.

The eight beatitudes, with which the Sermon on the Mount commences, may be considered as a summary of the entire discourse, since the latter part of it repeatedly returns to the subjects of these beatitudes and enlarges upon them.

## 2. DIVISION OF THE EIGHT BEATITUDES

The beatitudes are practices of the principal virtues, by which we prepare ourselves in daily life for eternal bliss. This preparation is first a negative one, and consists in the removal of hindrances; and secondly a positive one, which is occupied with the practice of works which immediately further our progress on the way to perfection. Thus the first three beatitudes—poverty, meekness and mourning—prepare us negatively for our end, because they check the inclination to riches, anger, and love of pleasure; but we are positively disposed to good by mercy and peaceableness as regards our neighbor, and by hunger and thirst after righteousness ("justice"), purity of heart and love of suffering as regards ourselves. Eternal bliss is promised to each of these virtues in a corresponding form.

## THE FIRST BEATITUDE

"Blessed are the poor in spirit: for theirs is the kingdom of heaven."
(MATT. 5:3; LUKE 6:20)

### 1. MEANING AND SIGNIFICATION OF THIS BEATITUDE

Poverty "in spirit" or "according to the spirit" signifies the spirit of poverty as well as actual poverty, either chosen by inspiration of the Holy Ghost or endured for reasons of the supernatural life. The passage of St. Luke (6:20), especially the "woe" pronounced against the rich (6:24), scarcely admits of any other interpretation than exterior, material possessions as the subject of this beatitude. What our Saviour wishes to inculcate by this first beatitude is above all spiritual poverty, i.e. a wise estimation of earthly, material possessions, detachment of heart, freedom from any irregular eagerness for them, whether we possess them or not. If we do not possess them, we must not be unhappy on that account, nor strive after them inordinately. If on the other hand we have material possessions, we must not be too much attached to them, esteem them too highly, or seek immoderately to retain and increase them; but on the contrary content ourselves with little, and even renounce temporal goods and embrace actual poverty, if higher, supernatural reasons require it. In any case, to be poor in spirit is to keep one's heart free and not to suffer it to grow attached to material goods.

This is the first fundamental law of our Saviour's kingdom, as opposed to the world, which aims mainly at temporal riches and outward power, and puts its confidence in these; and as opposed to the Jews, who also dreamed only of an outward, political glory. in the kingdom of the Messias.

## 2. MOTIVES TO BE DRAWN FROM THE PROMISE OF REWARD

As a reward of poverty in spirit our Saviour promises heaven as a "kingdom," that it, a possession incomparably greater, more beautiful, glorious and lasting than any that can be renounced here.

And this kingdom is sure, promised by a divine utterance; therefore we are told that "theirs *is* the kingdom of heaven." The renunciation of earthly things from supernatural considerations is like a purchase, by which heaven is delivered over to us as a matter of justice. Our Saviour afterwards repeats this promise still more expressly and solemnly, with regard to the poverty of the Apostles (Matt. 19:29). The certainty of the possession of heaven is also already given in another sense, since by the renunciation of material goods one avoids the greatest danger of losing it, because covetousness is the root of sin and money the means to sin (I Tim. 6:9). For this reason our Saviour pronounces the "woe" upon the rich, because riches procure them all kinds of comforts and lead them to think that they can be happy without heaven.

Even here below poverty in spirit is a foretaste and anticipation of heaven, because it frees us from certain temporal cares, bestows facility and inclination for intercourse with God in prayer, and freedom and aptitude for much good.

### 3. CONCLUSION

What gratitude we owe to our Saviour for this glorious utterance! How much that is good and great it has effected in the world! How many it has comforted in poverty! How many it has drawn away from earthly things and led to real poverty! From how many rich has it wrested their crowns and scepters! These words laid the first stone of the monastic life. It is indeed a true beatitude.

Whosoever desires to have the spirit of Jesus knows what he has to do. This is the first counsel that Christ gives us, and the first step to salvation and perfection, just as the first endeavor of the world is directed towards possessions and riches, because it can do and effect nothing without them.

### The Second Beatitude

"Blessed are the meek: for they shall possess the land."
(MATT. 5:4)

#### 1. WHAT MEEKNESS IS

Meekness is the virtue which curbs inordinate anger and unrestrained desire of revenge, and in general checks the inclination to obtain our rights and punish wrongs by outward violence or taking the law into our own hands. Without doubt our Saviour means here not merely abstaining from unlawful vengeance, but also the refraining from forcible or violent means in the assertion and maintenance of rights, and lays down as a characteristic feature of His kingdom Christian mildness and gentleness, which does not strive after and obtain its end by outward force, but rather by humble endurance.

The signification of the beatitude becomes clearer to us by our considering the violence upon which heathendom, the kingdom of the world, leaned, which appealed to might instead of right, thus involving itself in almost endless wars. From Judaism also the beatitude receives its explanation; inasmuch as the Jews fancied that the kingdom of the Messias, the "land of promise" of their fathers, could only be obtained by force and the power of arms, and inasmuch as they burned with an indomitable desire of revenge upon their oppressors.

## 2. THE MOTIVES WHICH INDUCE US TO PRACTISE THIS MEEKNESS

In the first place, heaven is promised to the meek under the figure of the "land of promise," which is no other than the kingdom of the Messias in the Church here below and in heaven (cf. Ps. 36:9, 11, 22, 28, 29, 34). Only those who practise the meekness spoken of will conquer and possess this land for themselves and for others, because our Lord will not found and establish His kingdom by outward force and armed attack and resistance, but by humble suffering for justice and truth. This is the characteristic of Jesus, His kingdom and His Church, and also the means to obtain possession of the kingdom and belong to it.

Secondly, there is nothing that wins us the esteem and love of men and the favor of God so much as gentleness. In this Christian gentleness lies a great majesty, a great ascendancy of intellect, an extraordinary command over one's will, and a great proof of kindness, patience, submission and humility. All this inclines to us not only the hearts of men, but also the Heart of God. So the meek will "possess the land" in this sense also. They are the favorites and rulers of earth and heaven.

From this follows, thirdly, the importance of this spirit for the apostolic ministry. The very nature of gentleness is winning, and to this is added the blessing which belongs to humility and endurance. So the Church has conquered the world not by the sword, but by patience and gentleness, whilst other conquerors are the terror and abomination of the earth.

All that has been said should lead us to form the resolution to subdue in our hearts, in accordance with the spirit of Jesus, anger and revengefulness even in little matters of everyday life, and to train ourselves to the virtue of meekness.

## THE THIRD BEATITUDE

"Blessed are they that mourn: for they shall be comforted."
(MATT. 5:5; LUKE 6:21–25.)

### 1. WHAT THIS MOURNING IS

This mourning is not melancholy, sentimentality or ill-humor, nor yet the natural sorrow and simple grief occasioned by the loss of a temporal blessing; neither is it the fanatical and hypocritical grief of which the Pharisees made a show, when they lamented over the humiliation of Jerusalem and the whole nation before the world under a foreign yoke. All this is by no means virtue.

The mourning which our Saviour calls "blessed" is rather a certain spirit of earnestness, which excludes before all things the pursuit of earthly joys and blind devotion to temporal pleasure and love of amusement; an earnestness which also directs its attention to what is likely to inspire us with grief in this temporal life, and which imposes moderation and restraint in the enjoyment of temporal pleasures.

This beatitude, then, is the direct opposite of the pleasure-seeking of the world, which not merely wishes to hold a perpetual carnival, but makes the gratification of earthly desires its sole object in life (Wisd. 2:1–9). "Woe to you that now laugh!" (Luke 6:25) are the solemn words of our Saviour with regard to this self-indulgence.

## 2. REASON OF THIS MOURNING

This mourning is founded first upon the nature of man, who acknowledges as his aim something higher than the gratification of the pursuit of sensual pleasure. It is founded still more upon the essential character of Christianity, which proposes to man an aim beyond this world, entirely supernatural and far beyond his nature, and which therefore imposes upon him the obligation of wise moderation in the seeking of earthly enjoyments, for the sake of higher considerations. But this eternal aim is such that its attainment repays man for all the sacrifices of renunciation here below and fills his whole nature with bliss, as is indicated in the reward promised. "They shall be comforted" in proportion as they have mourned here below; and God Himself will be their consolation and their Comforter (Apoc. 7:17; 21:4). They "shall laugh" (Luke 6:21), and of their joy shall be no end (John 16:22). Israel also will be comforted by its Messias (Isa. 61:1–3; Luke 2:25), but not according to carnal ideas and not completely here upon earth, but in heaven after the second advent of Jesus (cf. Isa. 40:1, 11; 66:10–14; Soph. 3:14–18).

Secondly, a further motive for this mourning lies in its great advantages. This noble sorrow, besides keeping our hearts constantly directed towards God and things eternal, preserving us from sin and folly, enriching us with merits for eternity and affording us the most solid consolation here below, also opens our eyes to the great dangers and evils which this life holds for us and for our fellow-men, and makes our hearts susceptible and disposed to remedy them. And how great these evils are, temporal and spiritual: those which affect ourselves, our fellow-men, the Church, and the whole human race! Whoever reflects earnestly upon all these evils can never, properly speaking, thoroughly rejoice here upon earth.

A third reason for this Christian mourning lies in the unhappy results of its antithesis, earthly pleasure. This vain joy in earthly things plunges us into frivolity, indifference to things eternal and supernatural, forgetfulness of God and all its evil consequences. This is but too well proved by ancient and modern heathenism, with its perpetual feasts and its worship outwardly full of sensual beauty and pleasure, but within full of moral degeneracy and corruption, of temporal and eternal unhappiness. Temporal consolation vanishes at death. Worldlings find in God no comforter, but a Judge, and eternal mourning and weeping begins (Luke 6:25). This mourning, on the contrary, is a true distinguishing mark of Christ, the Church, and all the Saints.

## THE FOURTH BEATITUDE

"Blessed are they that hunger and thirst after justice: for they shall have their fill."
(MATT. 5:6; LUKE 6:21)

### 1. WHAT IS TO BE UNDERSTOOD BY THIS HUNGER AND THIRST

Some understand this hunger and thirst in the literal sense, of temporal privation and want suffered for justice' sake; others again think that it consists in the vain strife for right and justice in earthly law-courts; others, finally, in zeal for the honor of God.

But usually, and we think more correctly, by this hunger and thirst is understood an active desire and endeavor after virtue, perfection and holiness, by the employment of all the means which religion offers us; in a word, the thirst for the kingdom of the Messias, which is always represented as a kingdom of justice and holiness (Isa. 4:3; 11:4; Jer. 23:5; 30:9; Ez. 11:19; Dan. 9:24; Osee 2:19; Ps. 44:3). This beatitude, then, denotes the true striving after the supernatural blessings of the soul and of heaven, as opposed to the endeavors of the world, which are directed only towards sensual and earthly things, and as opposed to the sensual, carnal views of Judaism with regard to the kingdom of the Messias, which they did not regard as a kingdom of supernatural justice and virtue, but as an overflowing abundance of earthly felicity.

### 2. THE REASONS WHICH ENCOURAGE US TO THIS ENDEAVOR

First, the consideration that the kingdom of Christ is before all things a kingdom of supernatural justice and holiness. Its end is heaven, and its means, institutions and success consist solely in freeing us from sin and enabling us to acquire virtue and supernatural merits, in order that we may gain the bliss of heaven in the fullest possible measure. The kingdom of Christ and the Church are the supernatural means instituted for our salvation, and they direct our whole being to things eternal (Luke 1:75; Ps. 71:3, 7 seq.; 84:11; Rom. 14-17).

Secondly, virtue, perfection and holiness are blessings which lie within man's power, and which can be certainly gained by him, with the grace of God. This truth is indicated by the promise: "They shall have their fill." In Christ we find all; deliverance from sin and death (Rom. 8:2), grace (Rom. 8:4), and eternal life (John 4:13, 14). And nothing is more pleasing to God than this desire and striving for supernatural holiness, and for no end does He give more abundant grace. This ardent desire itself is the best means of attaining to holiness. It makes all efforts easy. Hunger gives to everything a good savor.

### 3. THE NATURE OF THIS DESIRE

According to our Saviour's words, this desire must be earnest, strong and active, dominating our whole being, thoughts and endeavors; a desire to which even temporal aims are subordinate and which they must subserve; a desire and a purpose that may even be made the sole object of life, as is the case in holy religion.

## The Fifth Beatitude

"Blessed are the merciful: for they shall obtain mercy."
(MATT. 5:7)

### 1. NATURE OF MERCY

Mercy is compassion for the evils of our fellow-men and willingness to remedy them. There are two kinds of evils, corporal and spiritual. Therefore there are also corporal and spiritual works of mercy; and this virtue may be practised in thought, disposition, word and works.

## 2. MOTIVES

The first motive is the sublime nature of mercy. It springs from love of one's neighbor, and is therefore, as regards its nature, one of the highest virtues. It gives us a special likeness to God, all Whose ways are mercy and truth (Ps. 24:10; James 2:13; II Cor. 1:3; Luke 6:36). For this reason the Messianic kingdom must bear this divine mark, as opposed to the hard-heartedness and uncharitableness of heathenism and Judaism (Rom. 1:31; Matt. 9:13; 12:7). Indeed, the Church is God's home of refuge for the spiritual and corporal misery of mankind (Isa. 40:11; Luke 1:54, 72).

The second motive is the peculiar fitness of this virtue, because there are so many evils and miseries of every kind in the world, and because we ourselves have received and still receive so much mercy from God and men. We are entirely dependent upon the mercy of God and men, and cannot subsist without it.

The blessings that it brings us are the third motive. "They shall obtain mercy." We shall, above all, find in God a merciful Judge. For how many is the practice of mercy the indirect means of reaching eternal happiness! And we shall not be without the blessings of mercy in our prayers and interior life. God will visit us with comforting thoughts, will gladly grant our petitions and constantly give us new encouragement and inclination for good works (Isa. 58:7–12).

## THE SIXTH BEATITUDE

"Blessed are the clean of heart: for they shall see God."
(MATT. 5:8)

### 1. MEANING OF THIS BEATITUDE

By this "cleanness of heart" is understood freedom from sin, especially from the sin of the flesh; and also that purity of the senses, the heart, thoughts and intentions, that simplicity and sincerity which, unlike the intriguing and dishonorable spirit of the Jewish sects of that period, seeks God sincerely and without guile. This purity arises from the purging and stripping off of selfishness, and from the entire direction of our whole being towards God. It only attains its perfect splendor by union with God, as crystal only sparkles in its full brightness when the sun shines through it. Purity, then, consists negatively in freedom from sin, positively in the union of our intentions with God. How far remote from the perfection of this purity was the hypocrisy of the Pharisees! (Matt. 15:19, 20; 23:25.)

## 2. MOTIVES

The motives for this virtue lie in the subjoined promise, "They shall see God"; and this promise will be completely fulfilled in eternity by the communication of the direct contemplation of God. They will see the Face of God unveiled; and what does this not mean and imply—to behold the face of infinite truth, beauty and goodness! What an honor! What a happiness! What a joy! The greater and more perfect our purity was upon earth, the more intimate will be the union and the more familiar the intercourse. According to St. John the virginal souls are the most glorious band among the citizens of heaven, and form the privileged train of the Lamb (Apoc. 14:1 seq.).

Pure souls have a foretaste of this distinction even here below, since God communicates Himself to them in a special manner, in treasures of knowledge, love and joy. Purity is in itself a store of virtue, because one cannot acquire it without contempt of the world, self-conquest, prayer and humility. God beholds in the mirror of purity the reflection of His own purity and beauty, and inclines towards it full of complacency. Thus pure hearts are here and in eternity the familiar friends of God and, in a way, behold His face. The figure of speech seems to be taken from the customs of the Oriental princes, who seldom show themselves to the people and only hold intercourse with their court.

It was necessary to proclaim this beatitude, and to raise to a law of Christ's kingdom that virtue in which the honor, strength and beauty of man consist. For even the religion of heathenism was, in part at least, the most depraved prostitution. And Judaism did not attain to that flower of purity, the virginal state, but needed on the contrary to be emended and perfected in many respects with regard to this virtue. Christianity alone ventures to set up virginity as a counsel, because Christianity alone has and gives the strength to will and to keep it.

## The Seventh Beatitude

"Blessed are the peace-makers: for they shall be called the children of God."
(MATT. 5:9.)

### 1. WHAT PEACEABLENESS IS

There is a peace with ourselves and a peace with our neighbor, an inward and an otuward peace. Peace with ourselves consists in directing our chief endeavor towards one object, namely God, in subjecting this endeavor to His Will, and in persevering and remaining in it in spite of interior or exterior hindrances. Outward peace, or peace with our neighbor, consists in wishing and striving for what our neighbor wishes and strives for, provided that such is not contrary to the Will of God. This inward and outward peace is an effect of love. Through the love of God we love Him above all things, refer all our endeavors to Him, and make them subordinate to Him. Through love of our neighbor we love him as ourselves and therefore wish for him the good things we rightly wish for ourselves.

The endeavor to preserve this inward and outward peace is peaceableness, and its perfection consists in not merely keeping this peace within ourselves, but also seeking to establish it in the heart of our neighbor; that is, in being peace-makers between God and men and between men and their fellow-men. Such is the perfection of this beatitude.

### 2. WHY WE SHOULD PRACTISE THIS PEACEABLENESS

This peaceableness is, in the first place, a beautiful feature of love for God, because it makes us resemble Him. God is the God of peace, because He is blessedness and love in Himself and towards His creatures, and wishes to make them partakers of His bliss (Rom. 15:33; I Cor. 14:33; II Cor. 13:11). He wishes nothing more ardently than that His peace may be in them (Jer. 29:11; Ps. 124:5; II Thess. 3:16). This peaceableness also makes us resemble our Saviour, Who is the Prince of Peace (Isa. 9:6, 7) and peace itself (Mich. 5:5); the victorious effort of Whose life is no other than the mediation of this peace (Eph. 2:14 seq.), as the angels proclaimed at His Birth (Luke 2:14), as He Himself so often said (Luke 24:36; John 14:27) and the prophets foretold (Ps. 71:7; Isa. 2:4; 11:6 seq.; Mich. 4:3; Agg. 2:10; Luke 1:79). The Holy Ghost also recognizes in this peace a trace in us of His own attributes (Rom. 14:17; Gal. 5:22), and the holy angels see in us their companions. So the kingdom of Christ, the Church, must also be a kingdom of this divine peace, her Gospel a message of peace (Eph. 6:15), the salutation of her Apostles a greeting of peace (Matt. 10:12), and her preaching a proclamation of peace (Isa. 52:7). This peace imparts to us a resemblance to all that is Godlike; it makes us children of God, as the promise of this beatitude declares, by establishing God's supremacy in us (Col. 1:20; Phil. 4:7). On the contrary, enmity with God and man, discord and strife are the distinctive character of Satan and his world-kingdom, heathenism; and unfortunately Judaism also showed a trace of this dissension in those desires of revenge which the Jews imagined the Messias would entertain.

Secondly, the establishing of this peace is a work of charity toward our neighbor. Peace, as we have described it, is the greatest blessing here below, the plenitude of all graces and blessings, the pledge of temporal and eternal happiness, and the foretaste of heaven. How happy men would be if they possessed this peace! Those who bring it about are the greatest benefactors of the world; they make peace without war.

Thirdly, our true holiness consists in the possession of this peace, because peace is love (I Thess. 5:13, 23), and to establish it is to increase God's kingdom upon earth. Nothing merits for us the favor of God so much as this.

## THE EIGHTH BEATITUDE

MATT. 5:10. Blessed are they that suffer persecution for justice' sake: for theirs is the kingdom of heaven.—11. Blessed are ye when they shall revile you, and persecute you, and speak all that is evil against you untruly for my sake.—12. Be glad and rejoice, for your reward is very great in heaven; for so they persecuted the prophets that were before you.

LUKE 6:22. Blessed shall you be when men shall hate you, and when they shall separate you, and shall reproach you, and cast out your name as evil, for the Son of man's sake.—23. Be glad in that day and rejoice; for behold, your reward is great in heaven. For according to these things did their fathers to the prophets.— 26. Woe to you when men shall bless you; for according to these things did their fathers to the false prophets.

### 1. WHAT KIND OF PERSECUTION IS HERE MEANT

By persecution our Saviour means every hostility in thought, word and deed, as He Himself explains it: "when men shall hate you" (Luke 6:22); when they spread abroad slanderous, defaming, calumnious reports against you, so that your name is branded (Matt. 5:11; Luke 6:22); when they proceed to acts of violence, even to murder, as they did to the prophets, whom they persecuted, banished and killed (Matt. 5:12; Luke 6:23). Every form of persecution is included, even the most extreme.

But this hostility must be undeserved on the part of the servants of Christ, unjust on the part of the persecutors; it must be inflicted upon the former on account of justice, Christian virtue, the faith which they practise and defend, or for the sake of the Name of Jesus, the Son of Man (Luke 6:22; Matt. 5:10, 11). A natural reason does not suffice to entitle to a claim upon this beatitude, much less a fault on the part of those persecuted (I Peter 4:15).

## 2. HOW WE MUST SUFFER PERSECUTION

Though we need not seek persecution and expose ourselves to it unnecessarily, we must at least suffer it, accept it, and not avoid it when this cannot be done without violation of duty. We must bear it with patience, without hatred or desire of being revenged upon our persecutors, and without rebellion against God, Who permits it; but on the contrary, in the spirit of faith and due humility. Secondly, we must endeavor to accept persecution with gladness and rejoicing, as a great happiness. So our Saviour Himself teaches (Matt. 5:12; Luke 6:23). Thirdly and lastly, we must persevere in bearing it, because otherwise all suffering and all magnanimity in suffering is of no use and does not attain its end.

## 3. WHY WE MUST SUFFER PERSECUTION

From our Saviour's words may be gathered that a great good, a great happiness and a great honor lies in the persecution mentioned. This results first from the reason of the persecution, since we suffer for justice and for the sake of our Saviour Himself. It is a great honor for a man to stand up as a witness for virtue, for the faith, for the truth of Christianity, for eternal bliss and for God Himself. God and the world need this testimony, and the world believes the testimony of blood more readily than it does any other.

Secondly, there lies a great good in the endurance of persecution, on account of the virtues which are necessarily practised in it; namely, detachment from things temporal, courage and generosity. Only heroes in virtue can stand the test of this conflict.

For this reason our Saviour calls attention to the example of the prophets, the Apostles of the Old Covenant, who so courageously overcame in it (Matt. 5:12; Luke 6:23). Indeed, He goes still further, and pronounces the "woe" upon those who are praised and loved by the world, saying that this is a sign that they belong to the false prophets (Luke 6:26), with whom the world is at peace. This is a proof that there has always been persecution, and that it arises naturally from the contrast between righteousness and the world.

Thirdly, persecution is a great good on account of the reward it merits. This reward is the kingdom of heaven, not in an ordinary measure, but to overflowing (Matt. 5:12; Luke 6:23). The confessors and martyrs do not buy heaven with the riches of this earth, but with their blood and life; they take it by storm, so to speak, sword in hand. Our Saviour encourages His champions to be glad and rejoice in every affliction and temporal distress, however great it may be. How great and glorious, then, must be the reward that is awaiting them in heaven! In the light of this glory all the darkness of their earthly combat is brightened (I Peter 4:14). This beatitude is in reality like a prophecy, a flash of light thrown upon the future of the disciples, the Church, and our Saviour Himself: on the one hand bloody persecutions by the Jews, on the other the certainty and glory of the victory of the witnesses of Jesus.

## The Task of the Apostles and the Faithful, in Two Similitudes

MATT. 5:13. You are the salt of the earth. But if the salt lose its savor, wherewith shall it be salted? It is good for nothing any more but to be cast out and to be trodden on by men.—14. You are the light of the world. A city seated on a mountain cannot be hid.—15. Neither do men light a candle and put it under a bushel, but upon a candlestick, that it may shine to all that are in the house.—16. So let your light shine before men, that they may see your good works, and glorify your Father who is in heaven.

Our Saviour, after having stated the chief principles of practical Christian morality, addresses Himself chiefly to the Apostles, whom the Sermon on the Mount primarily concerns, and points out in two similitudes first their task in the world, and secondly the duty of accomplishing it. But these similitudes of salt and light apply secondarily to all the faithful (Luke 14:34; Phil. 2:15; Eph. 5:8; I Thess. 5:5; I Peter 2:9).

### 1. FIRST SIMILITUDE: "YOU ARE THE SALT OF THE EARTH"

Salt preserves and stimulates life, imparts savor to tasteless things, removes decay, purifies, and sanctifies sacrifices. It effects these results unnoticed, quietly, and by the dissolution of itself. Various usages have given to salt a quite religious significance. In the Old Covenant it was mixed with all sacrifices, and is therefore called the salt of the covenant (Lev. 2:13); even in the New Covenant it is the symbol of supernatural wisdom, innocence and purity, and is placed upon the tongue of the catechumen in baptism with this signification (Mark 9:49; Col. 4:5, 6).

The task of the apostolate is similar to this. It must, in the spiritual world, awaken and stimulate what is dead, season what is tasteless and insipid, cleanse or preserve from sin, make of man a holy sacrifice, well-pleasing to God, and lastly transfigure and spiritualize all flesh by the resurrection. All this it is able to accomplish, and does accomplish, in union with and by virtue of the great sacrifice of Christ, by the preaching of the Gospel and the moral law. By imbibing and becoming penetrated with the doctrine of Christ, by preaching it in word and life and by offering himself as a sacrifice, the Apostle fills himself with the power and grace of the sacrifice of Jesus, and thus becomes the salt of Christ, to purify the world from sin, fill it with divine wisdom, and prepare it to become a sacrifice well-pleasing to God. Without this apostolic salt the spiritual life of mankind would be without savor and seasoning.

The duty of accomplishing this task is shown in the punishment of those who neglect it and allow the apostolic salt to lose its savor. This takes place when, in the life and preaching of the Apostle, the supernatural part of the teaching of faith and morals is weakened by being mixed with the natural and worldly spirit; when, through cowardice, he no longer emphasizes and lays stress upon the supernatural character of faith, and does not bring into prominence, in his life and teaching, the sharpness and savor of the moral law, which consists in complete self-denial, renunciation, detachment and sacrifice. The first punishment is uselessness, and that absolute. What is salt worth, when it no longer seasons? The second punishment is the impossibility of finding a remedy, at all events in the ordinary course of things, because the Apostle holds the highest position and has no one above him who might be able to correct him; just as salt cannot be restored to savor by anything else. The third punishment is disgrace and scorn. The insipid salt, since it is of no use for anything, is thrown out into the street and trodden in the mud (Matt. 5:13).

## 2. SECOND SIMILITUDE: "YOU ARE THE LIGHT OF THE WORLD"

Light illumines, brightens, beautifies and fertilizes everything. So is it also with the Apostolate. As our Saviour Himself is the Light of the world (John 9:5) by His holy doctrine and example, so too in his degree is the Apostle, when he has imbibed the doctrine of Christ and gives it forth by word and example (Matt. 5:14, 16).

From this follows the obligation to let this light shine, and our Saviour adds beautiful motives for this. First, the office and the work of the Apostle require it. As our Saviour and His life are the light of men (John 1:4), so also the Apostle is not merely the bearer of light, but is himself light, and as such he lives and exists. This thought is illustrated by our Saviour in another simile, that of the city upon a high mountain (such as Saphet, for example, which could be seen from the place of the Sermon on the Mount). It is not possible for a city in such a position to remain unseen. So it is with the Apostle and the Church (Matt. 5:14). Secondly, it is God's intention that the Apostles should shine. As a candle is only placed upon a candlestick in order that it may serve as a light to all in the house, so the Apostle is raised by God to his lofty position in order that all may receive light from him. The ancients, on account of the difficulty they had in kindling fire afresh, kept a light burning day and night in the house, under a shade (bushel) or in a dark place; when it was needed, as in the reception-room, the lamp was placed upon a high stand or sconce. Our Saviour here alludes to this custom (Matt. 5:15). Thirdly, the welfare of men and the honor of God may require this manifestation of our light. At the sight of good works men praise God, from Whom all good comes, and Who bestows so many benefits upon them by means of the Apostolate; and they feel themselves incited to imitate the good example of the Apostles by the practice of good works, for by it they see that virtue is possible.

Such is the position and significance of the Apostolate, the Church, and all the faithful, as revealed by our Saviour with regard to Judaism and the whole world. How great and important is the work! The Apostles are in the hands of God the chief means of kindling and awakening supernatural light and life in the world, and the representatives and living tables of the moral law which our Saviour has just proclaimed. They are the greatest benefactors of the human race, and for these benefits the world owes its gratitude to them, as well as to God Himself. It is an encouragement to the Apostles to perform their high office with zeal and care, and to let their light shine; but also a warning not to let their salt "lose its savor," lest they incur the terrible penalty. This warning applies to all the faithful, in greater or less degree.

## RELATIONS OF OUR SAVIOUR TO THE OLD LAW

MATT. 5:17. Do not think that I am come to destroy the law or the prophets: I am not come to destroy, but to fulfil.—18. For amen I say unto you, until heaven and earth pass, one jot or one tittle shall not pass of the law, till all be fulfilled.—19. He therefore that shall break one of these least commandments, and shall so teach men, shall be called the least in the kingdom of heaven. But he that shall do and teach, he shall be called great in the kingdom of heaven.—20. For I tell you, that unless your justice abound more than that of the scribes and Pharisees, you shall not enter into the kingdom of heaven.

### 1. WHY OUR SAVIOUR MAKES THIS STATEMENT WITH REGARD TO HIS RELATIONS TO THE OLD LAW

Our Saviour first touches in general upon His relations to the Old Law; and He was obliged to do this, for the following reasons. The law existed, as an obligatory expression of the Will of God and an epitome of the true way of salvation in respect of faith, morality and the means of grace. Our Saviour could not therefore ignore it. Besides this, the people's respect and zeal for the law had in later years greatly increased; indeed it had become unduly and unwholesomely exaggerated, owing to the Pharisaic interpretation of the law, which had encircled every detail of life as by a thick and stifling hedge (cf. Introd., p. 11). Lastly, several of the utterances of our Saviour (John 4:23; Luke 5:21, 24; 6:5), wrongly interpreted, had already often aroused suspicion and had caused Him to be accused of despising and wishing to abolish the law; and this gained greater weight from the fact that He was proclaimed to be the Messias, of whom it had been prophesied that he would be a lawgiver and the founder of a New Covenant (Jer. 31:31). Our Saviour must necessarily, therefore, declare His true relation to the law before the disciples, the people, and His enemies.

## 2. HOW OUR SAVIOUR DESCRIBES HIS RELATIONS TO THE OLD LAW

In the first place, our Saviour says that He is not come to destroy and abolish "the law and the prophets," i.e. the Old Law (Matt. 5:17). As a matter of fact, He altered nothing of the old moral law. The Ten Commandments form the basis of the New Law as of the Old, and our Saviour has only added a few commands which the circumstances made necessary, such as to join the new Church, to submit to her superiors, to make use of the new Sacraments. But the Ten Commandments are the practical expression of the eternal law, and point out to the creature the way towards its eternal end, which can only be one and remain one, as long as the same creation exists. Our Saviour therefore protests solemnly and energetically (Matt. 5:18) that nothing in these Commandments may be altered, not even "one jot or one tittle"; sooner will heaven and earth pass away. Indeed, He threatens with the punishment of exclusion from the kingdom of heaven [1] (Matt. 5:19, 20) whoever should despise and teach others to despise even a single one of the apparently unimportant Commandments (one of the "least"). On the other hand He promises a special reward in heaven to those who observe these Commandments and teach men to observe them. As regards the ritual law, our Saviour always observed it, and never forbade its observance during His ministry "until all was fulfilled" (Matt. 5:18), i.e. until His Death and until the Descent of the Holy Ghost and the proclamation of the New Law. Then, indeed, the observance of the Jewish ritual became useless and pernicious, and the new order of things took its place. The law and the prophets had their end in Christ (Rom. 10:4); they were only guides to Him (Gal. 3:24), a foreshadowing of Him and of His future coming (Col. 2:16, 17), and they themselves declared that they were only temporary and transient and would give place to another order. The Old and the New Law were not two entirely different codes. They pursued the same end, and differed only in their degree of perfection; the one had its root in the other, and the New Law was the flower and final development of the pre-

---

[1] According to others, one who despises or teaches to despise small points of the law as worthless and useless, will lose the title of teacher and receive the last place in the kingdom of the Messias, even if he obtains part in it at all (cf. I Cor. 3:11, 15).

ceding one. To bring about this development was not to abolish the Old Law; on the contrary, it would have been altered and abolished if the development had not taken place.

Secondly, our Saviour says that He will not merely not destroy the law, but will rather fulfil it, i.e. bring it to perfection, and that in more senses than one. He has perfected the moral law by restoring and teaching its true sense in a clear and comprehensible manner; by emphasizing not merely the letter but also the spirit of the law, bringing its end and aim, love for God and for one's neighbor, into prominence, and expanding it still farther by setting forth the perfection of the law in the counsels. He extended the matter of faith by revealing the Christian truths, which were not clearly expressed in the Old Covenant. He perfected the ritual law by setting the reality of the Sacrifice and Sacraments of the New Covenant in the place of the types, and adding (by means of the former) such powerful graces to the whole order of salvation, that the observance of the law became easy and pleasant. He perfected the whole economy of salvation by the erection of a new ecclesiastical hierarchy. In this sense He also fulfilled the prophecies, as far as they concerned Himself and His kingdom.

Thirdly, our Saviour solemnly protests against the "justice of the Pharisees," i.e. against that interpretation and practice of the law of the Old Covenant which the Pharisees had devised and introduced. He does not recognize this "justice" as sufficient for salvation, because it mutilated the sense of the law in many respects by false and arbitrary interpretation; because its professors only laid stress upon the exterior, the letter of the law, but disregarded the spirit, the real virtue; and because they multiplied the regulations to a ridiculous and intolerable extent, and gave them out for divine precepts.

### 3. CONCLUSIONS TO BE DRAWN FROM THIS

In the first place, our Saviour's conception of the double Law is beautiful and worthy of our admiration. He regards it as one law, the expression of God's Will, differing according to grades and states of perfection; one tree, with root, trunk and branches, and, like everything else that proceeds from God, living and capable of development. The law is to Him holy, and therefore He recognizes and respects it, purifies it from the parasitic plants of human additions and disfigurements, and perfects without destroying it, for God cannot contradict Himself.

From this it follows, secondly, that every one of God's laws has a claim to our respect, veneration, and observance. This is most certainly according to the spirit of God and of our Saviour.

Thirdly, it is the glory of the Apostolate not merely to observe the law, but to proclaim it to the world and to foster regard and veneration for it, as well as to teach its observance. Our Saviour promises to the Apostolate a special reward and distinction in the kingdom of heaven, in return for this. "He that shall do and teach (these commandments) shall be called great in the kingdom of heaven" (Matt. 5:19). Theologians understand by these words the special reward in heaven of the teachers of the Christian law.

## The Law of Charity, or Love of One's Neighbor

Our Saviour now passes on to a few definite points, in which He explains and perfects the Old Law. We place here all the precepts given by our Lord in the Sermon on the Mount with regard to charity, arranging them according to their subject-matter; taking first the negative precepts of refraining from anger, implacability, hatred of enemies, and unjust judgments, and secondly the positive precepts of generous love of one's neighbor.

### 1. a) REFRAINING FROM ANGER: OR GENTLENESS IN THOUGHT, WORD AND DEED

MATT. 5:21. You have heard that it was said to them of old: Thou shalt not kill; and whosoever shall kill, shall be in danger of the judgment.—22. But I say to you, that whosoever is angry with his brother, shall be in danger of the judgment. And whosoever shall say to his brother, Raca, shall be in danger of the council. And whosoever shall say, Thou fool, shall be in danger of hell fire.—23. If therefore thou offer thy gift at the altar, and there thou remember that thy brother hath anything against thee;—24. Leave there thy offering before the altar, and go first to be reconciled to thy brother, and then coming thou shalt offer thy gift.—25. Be at agreement with thy adversary betimes, whilst thou art in the way with him; lest perhaps the adversary deliver thee to the judge, and the judge deliver thee to the officer, and thou be cast into prison.—26. Amen I say to thee, thou shalt not go out from thence till thou repay the last farthing.

Our Saviour first supplements, completes and perfects the Old Law, which according to its literal meaning forbade only murder and manslaughter (Ex. 20:13; 21:12; Lev. 24:17; Num. 35:11, 16; Deut. 17:8; 19:12). He teaches that there are, besides ill-treatment of our neighbor, other and grievous sins against the Fifth Commandment; interior sins, such as anger and the wish to do an injury, and exterior ones, such as insult—"Raca," "Thou fool" (Matt. 5:22); and these He strictly forbids. The gravity of such transgressions is seen at once in the punishments which He imposes for them. These punishments are such as were inflicted by the local tribunal for serious offences (Deut. 16:18), or even by the supreme court of justice, which decided cases of crimes against religion. Nay, He even mentions the most unusual punishments, such as death by fire in the terrible valley of Gehenna, where the notorious worship of Moloch had once been celebrated (Jos. 18:16; Jer. 19:2 seq.); where, at the time of Christ, all refuse was burnt; and where the people therefore always had before their eyes a living picture of hell (Matt. 10:28; Luke 12:5). These sins, then, are such as to deserve the punishment of hell, and the gravity of the respective offences evidently corresponds to the gradation of the punishments: simple execution, extraordinary capital punishment such as stoning or hanging, and lastly execution followed by the consignment of the sinner to hell (Schanz).

Our Saviour next gives motives for the practice of charity. The first and chief motive lies in the grave importance which He attaches to all sins against charity, as is evident from the punishment threatened and also from the relation borne by these lesser offences to murder and manslaughter, which were already forbidden by the Old Law. It is these very offences which lead to the more grievous sins. From inward anger arise insulting words and acts of violence. But a perfect law must also remove the sources and occasions of gross sins and regulate the entire man, both in his interior and exterior life. Thus we see in what consists the perfection added by our Saviour to the Old Law. The second motive is that charity and love of peace are of so great importance that even the highest practices of religion, such as sacrifice, cannot be pleasing to God without them. For this reason our Saviour says that if our neighbor entertains anger and resentment against us, justly or unjustly, we should rather let the sacrifice wait, and first seek to be reconciled to him. This is the first thing God requires of us, and the necessary condition upon which He will accept our sacrifice with complacency (Matt. 5:23).

As a means of escaping the punishments imposed upon offences against charity, our Saviour desires that we should be reconciled with our neighbor during this life. Reconciliation is a divine compromise, which anticipates the judgment in eternity. If this reconciliation is not accomplished during life, the eternal judgment

takes place with all severity (Matt. 5:25). Our Saviour draws
the comparison from the judicial proceedings of the world.

### b) REFRAINING FROM SEVERITY IN THE REQUIREMENT
#### OF RESTITUTION

MATT. 5:38. You have heard that it hath been said: An eye for an eye, and
a tooth for a tooth.—39. But I say to you not to resist evil; but if one strike thee
on thy right cheek, turn to him also the other;—40. And if a man will contend
with thee in judgment and take away thy coat, let go thy cloak also unto him.—
41. And whosoever will force thee one mile, go with him other two.—42. Give
to him that asketh of thee, and from him that would borrow of thee turn not away.
LUKE 6:29. And to him that striketh thee on the one cheek, offer also the other.
And him that taketh away from thee thy cloak, forbid not to take thy coat also.—
30. Give to everyone that asketh thee, and of him that taketh away thy goods,
ask them not again.

Our Saviour does not altogether forbid us to have recourse to
the law in order to obtain restitution or inflict a penalty, provided
that this be done without any inward ill-feeling or malicious
pleasure (Ex. 21:24; Lev. 24:20; Deut. 19:21). But He places
beside this the ideal of Christian patience and magnanimity,
which repays the evil-doing of a malicious adversary by redoubled
charity (Matt. 5:39). He illustrates this by practical examples,
such as not merely giving and lending to those who ask, and that
without requiring interest (Matt. 5:42; Luke 6:34, 35), but also
much harder things, such as presenting the left cheek when one
has been struck on the right (Matt. 5:39; Luke 6:29); accompanying a person two miles when one has been obliged (according to the Oriental custom at that time) to go one (Matt. 5:41);
and even making considerable sacrifices, such as yielding up one's
cloak when one has already been robbed of a coat (Matt. 5:40;
Luke 6:29), and yet a cloak is considered so necessary in the East
that the possession of it was ensured by a special law (Ex. 22:26;
Deut. 24:13). Of course most of these cases are only counsels
and matters of perfection, and they could only become strict
obligations under very unusual circumstances; for example, if it
were a question of necessary confession of the truth of the Christian law, or avoidance of a serious scandal. Our Saviour Himself
did not present the other cheek when He was struck in the court
of justice, but defended Himself (John 18:23); and St. Paul did
likewise (Acts 22:25).

The motives for so acting lie first in the beauty of this ideal and
in the rarity of such greatness of mind and soul; secondly, in the
example of so many Saints in the Church, who often obeyed

our Saviour's words literally; lastly, in the character of the legislation of the Church, which has mitigated the severity and terror of the ancient law throughout, in accordance with the spirit of these words.

### c) REFRAINING FROM HATRED OF ENEMIES

MATT. 5:43. You have heard that it hath been said: Thou shalt love thy neighbor, and hate thy enemy.—44. But I say to you: Love your enemies, do good to them that hate you, and pray for them that persecute and calumniate you;—45. That you may be the children of your Father who is in heaven, who maketh his sun to rise upon the good and bad, and raineth upon the just and the unjust.—46. For if you love them that love you, what reward shall you have? Do not even the publicans this?—47. And if you salute your brethren only, what do you more? Do not also the heathens this?—48. Be you therefore perfect, as also your heavenly Father is perfect.
    LUKE 6:27. But I say to you that hear: Love your enemies, do good to them that hate you.—28. Bless them that curse you, and pray for them that calumniate you.—32. And if you love them that love you, what thanks are to you? For sinners also love those that love them.—33. And if you do good to them who do good to you, what thanks are to you? For sinners also do this.—34. And if you lend to them of whom you hope to receive, what thanks are to you? For sinners also lend to sinners, for to receive as much.—35. But love ye your enemies; do good and lend, hoping for nothing thereby; and your reward shall be great, and you shall be the sons of the Highest; for he is kind to the unthankful and to the evil.—36. Be ye therefore merciful, as your Father also is merciful.

The ancient law commanded love only to one's "citizens" (Lev. 19:18), i.e. the members of the tribes of Israel and also the proselytes, even when personal enmity co-existed with outward marks of charity (Ex. 23:4, 5; Deut. 22:1 seq.). Of alien races the Law says nothing expressly. Herein, then, it was evidently deficient, and left room for natural weaknesses; all the more so that the Gentiles were the enemies of God (Ex. 17:14; 23:30; Num. 25:17; Deut. 7:2; 23:6, 19; 25:19). The Pharisees are said to have gone still farther, and to have commanded the people to hate the Gentiles. Our Saviour, on the contrary, commands us to love our enemies also, whoever they may be, and to love them in deed. By this command it is strictly forbidden, under pain of sin, to hate an enemy and offender inwardly and deliberately, to wish him ill, or to exclude him from the ordinary marks of kindness which are practised towards all. To give special tokens of love, such as our Saviour mentions here, is not a command, but a counsel and a matter of perfection.

The first motive adduced by our Saviour is the example of God Himself (Matt. 5:45; Luke 6:35, 36), Who bestows sunshine and rain and all temporal blessings upon the wicked and ungrateful as well as on the good, without any distinction, and Whose chief attribute is mercy and fatherly love. We shall resemble this great and good God, as children resemble their father, if we are merciful to our enemies. It is by this mark that He recognizes us, and we gain by it His love and affection. As a second motive our Saviour points out the loftiness and rarity of this spirit. It is far above all natural inclinations and selfishness. To be kind to those who are kind to us; to salute and do good to those who salute and do good to us; to lend to those who pay us interest: all this is of common occurrence, even the heathens and publicans (Matt. 5:46, 47) and sinners (Luke 6:32, 33, 34) act thus. But to do good to our enemies is something far higher, and belongs to the practice of true perfection. The third motive is the extraordinary reward in heaven (Luke 6:35).

#### d) REFRAINING FROM RASH JUDGMENT

MATT. 7:1. Judge not, that you may not be judged.—2. For with what judgment you judge, you shall be judged; and with what measure you mete, it shall be measured to you again.—3. And why seest thou the mote that is in thy brother's eye, and seest not the beam that is in thy own eye?—4. Or how sayest thou to thy brother: Let me cast the mote out of thy eye; and behold a beam is in thy own eye?—5. Thou hypocrite, cast out first the beam out of thy own eye, and then shalt thou see to cast out the mote out of thy brother's eye.

LUKE 6:37. Judge not, and you shall not be judged. Condemn not, and you shall not be condemned. Forgive, and you shall be forgiven.

Our Saviour does not forbid just legal judgment, nor yet well-founded private judgment in notorious matters, but only unauthorized private judging (Luke 6:37), to which we may be led by uncharitableness or by having too good an opinion of ourselves. The Israelite nation, as the chosen people of God, was in especial danger of despising and condemning all outsiders without regard for their circumstances; and in giving this precept our Saviour may have had the Pharisees especially in view.

As a motive for avoiding this sin He warns us of the retribution of an equally severe judgment upon ourselves. This motive is very strongly emphasized in His words as recorded by St. Matthew. An equal judgment and an equal measure of severity will fall upon anyone who so judges (Matt. 7:2). Another reason against rash judgment is that we have no authority to judge. We are not appointed by God as judges, and thus we arrogate to ourselves His judgment-seat, which as yet stands vacant. Insight and sanctity are also as a rule wanting to us. In any case, by so acting we commit a fault equal to, or even worse than that for which we condemn our neighbor. Thus the similitude of the mote and the beam, which St. Matthew places here, is very applicable to those who form rash judgments (Matt. 7:3–5).

## 2. POSITIVE PRINCIPLES OF CHARITY

MATT. 7:12. All things therefore whatsoever ye would that men should do to you, do you also to them. For this is the law and the prophets.

LUKE 6:31. And as you would that men should do to you, do you also to them in like manner.—38. Give, and it shall be given to you; good measure and pressed down and shaken together and running over shall they give into your bosom. For with the same measure that you shall mete withal it shall be measured to you again.

Our Saviour adds a few positive precepts with regard to charity, and above all lays down the general principle that we must render to others the services that we wish and expect from them, and treat others as we ourselves wish to be treated (Matt. 7:12; Luke 6:31). He elucidates this principle still further as regards liberality towards our neighbor. We must not merely give our neighbor as much as he asks (Matt. 5:42; Luke 6:30), but rather an abundant measure, generously exceeding his request; "good measure, pressed down and shaken together and running over" (Luke 6:38).

As a motive our Saviour points out the meaning, significance and extent of the command of charity; that to practise it is to fulfil the whole law, because the object of the various commandments is only the perfect fulfilment of love of one's neighbor and thereby also love of God, since the one is included in the other (Matt. 7:12). In such an abundant fulfilment of the law there is certainly nothing wanting. The second motive is the recompense; God and men will treat us in the same manner (Luke 6:38).

What especially strikes our attention in this passage is the loftiness of sentiment, the unselfishness and magnanimity towards one's neighbor, be he friend or foe, which it inculcates. This is the royal, divine law, the law of perfection, which not merely does not yield to the base passions of nature, but exerts an improving and ennobling influence upon them; which not merely restrains and prevents evil, but makes evil almost impossible, so to speak, by a noble striving after what is best and highest; which does not merely prescribe what is of obligation, but opens out higher paths to zeal for good. This is without doubt the wisest and most thorough manner of making men good. And to what a height of perfection does not this law raise man! To realize this we have only to consider the precepts and instructions of our Saviour with regard to charitable deeds and love of our enemies. The following is a summary of them: 1. not to do evil; 2. not to render evil for evil; 3. not to revenge oneself in any way; 4. to offer to endure an injury; 5. to grant more than is unjustly desired of us; 6. not to hate those who injure us; 7. to love them, even; 8. to do good to them; 9. to pray to God for them (Schanz). Whoever acts thus is in truth a living image of God (Matt. 5:48).

## Duties towards Ourselves

The preceding instructions concern our relations to our fellow-men. With regard to ourselves our Saviour lays stress, in the Sermon on the Mount, upon three points: chastity, simplicity in speech, and humility.

### 1. CHASTITY

MATT. 5:27. You have heard that it was said to them of old: Thou shalt not commit adultery.—28. But I say to you, that whosoever shall look on a woman to lust after her, hath already committed adultery with her in his heart.—29. And if thy right eye scandalize thee, pluck it out and cast it from thee; for it is expedient for thee that one of thy members should perish, rather than thy whole body be cast into hell.—30. And if thy right hand scandalize thee, cut it off, and cast it from thee; for it is expedient for thee that one of thy members should perish, rather than that the whole body go into hell.

The ancient law aimed in the first place at the protection of the marriage-bond, by forbidding adultery (Ex. 20:14) and the desire to commit it (Deut. 5:21). But it was very deficient in precepts of chastity, especially with regard to unmarried persons. In order to perfect the law, our Saviour now forbids expressly even an unchaste glance proceeding from lust, and thereby also any other outward sign of it which can be given, and in general every form of impurity (Matt. 5:28). And He forbids everything of the kind so strictly, that we must be ready to sacrifice what is nearest, dearest, and most necessary to us, such as an eye, a hand, a foot, if it is a proximate occasion for us of such sins. Indeed, He even forbids it under threat of Gehenna, hell (Matt. 5:29, 30).

### 2. SIMPLICITY IN SPEECH, BY AVOIDANCE OF SWEARING

MATT. 5:33. Again you have heard that it was said to them of old, Thou shalt not forswear thyself; but thou shalt perform thy oaths to the Lord.—34. But I say to you not to swear at all, neither by heaven, for it is the throne of God;—35.

Nor by the earth, for it is his footstool; nor by Jerusalem, for it is the city of the great king.—36. Neither shalt thou swear by thy head, because thou canst not make one hair white or black.—37. But let your speech be yea, yea; no, no; and that which is over and above this is of evil.

Our Saviour does not forbid an oath taken with truth, reverently and in a case of necessity. It is good in itself, and a glorification of the Name of God (Deut. 6:13; Ex. 20:7; Lev. 19:12). God Himself swears (Hebr. 6:13 seq.; 7:21), and our Saviour declares that one must keep an oath (Matt. 5:33) taken according to the law (Ex. 20:7; Lev. 19:12). What He requires is that we should not, as a rule, swear by God at all, either directly or indirectly (Matt. 5:34–36), in order that no false or in any way sinful oath may be taken. The Pharisees had caused no little confusion and harm by making a distinction between formulas of swearing which did or did not bind the speaker (Matt. 23:16 seq.). Our Saviour rejects this distinction, and now desires that we should as a rule merely give our word, "yes" or "no," in all truth and simplicity (Matt. 5:37).

He gives as a reason for this that everything beyond the simple statement of the truth "is of evil" (Matt. 5:37). To go beyond simple affirmation and negation is only a sign that untruthfulness and lying are possible among men and actually do occur, so that one must have recourse to the invocation of God in order to be sure of the truth. Even God's oaths presuppose distrust upon our side. As a second motive it may be added that in swearing, and especially in frequent swearing, one easily falls into sin, into "evil," by swearing either without necessity or without reverence. How much it is to be wished that our Saviour's precept were universally followed, and that oaths were not necessary! This would indeed establish a kingdom of truth, fear of God, and charity. This precept is certainly the reason why the Church places such restrictions upon the taking of oaths, and causes her priests especially to refrain from it.

### 3. HUMILITY

MATT. 6:1. Take heed that you do not your justice before men, to be seen by them; otherwise you shall not have a reward of your Father who is in heaven.— 2. Therefore when thou dost an alms-deed, sound not a trumpet before thee, as the hypocrites do in the synagogues and in the streets, that they may be honored by men. Amen I say to you, they have received their reward.—3. But when thou dost alms, let not thy left hand know what thy right hand doth;—4. That thy alms may be in secret, and thy Father who seeth in secret will repay thee.—5. And when ye pray, you shall not be as the hypocrites, that love to stand and pray in the synagogues and corners of the streets, that they may be seen by men; Amen I say to you, they have received their reward.—6. But thou when thou shalt pray, enter into thy chamber, and having shut the door, pray to thy Father in secret; and thy Father who seeth in secret will repay thee. . . .—16. And when you fast, be not as the hypocrites, sad. For they disfigure their faces, that they may appear unto men to fast. Amen I say to you, they have received their reward.— 17. But thou, when thou fastest, anoint thy head, and wash thy face,—18. That thou appear not to men to fast, but to thy Father who is in secret; and thy Father who seeth in secret will repay thee.

Our Saviour first warns us in general terms not to do our good works ("justice") for the sake of human praise, that is, publicly and out of human respect (Matt. 6:1). He does not forbid this publicity in itself, which is often obligatory, and is even recommended by Him under certain circumstances (Matt. 5:16); but it is the vain intention that He condemns. To wish to be seen is no sin, but to wish to be seen for the sake of being praised is a sin. Our Saviour then passes on to particular good works, viz. prayer, almsgiving and fasting, in which almost the whole law, with its relations to God, our neighbor and ourselves, is contained. He points out the defects in the example set by the Pharisees in each of these relations, but without naming those in fault. They liked to collect alms, and distributed them publicly in the synagogues; they sought out conspicuous places for prayer in the streets and synagogues; they fasted twice a week, and went about unwashed at the hours for meals, to show that they were fasting. Our Saviour condemns all this, and advises us on the contrary to keep as secret as possible all that does not belong to the public and universal practice of religion, and to conceal it from others with a holy ingenuity, as is very beautifully and clearly brought out in St. Matthew's Gospel (Matt. 6:3, 6, 18).

To urge us to follow this teaching our Saviour points out, first, that if we act otherwise we are not merely very superficial in performing our duties, but we actually commit a sin, the sin of hypocrisy. In three places He calls those who act thus "hypocrites" (Matt. 6:2, 5, 16). They put on an appearance of glorifying God by virtue and good works, whilst in reality they are seeking their own glory by this outward show of piety. The second motive is the uselessness of such deeds for eternity. "They have received their reward" (Matt. 6:2, 5, 16) upon earth, because they have obtained what they wish for; they have nothing more to hope for in eternity. The third motive is the reward bestowed by God for humility. The Father sees all things, even the most secret, and rewards them (Matt. 6:4, 16, 18); and the purer and more loving the intention with which they are done, the greater is their reward.

It is the spirit of simplicity and truthfulness, of interior and exterior purity and sincerity which is especially emphasized here, that beautiful virtue which is so true a mark of the spirit of Jesus as opposed to the lax interpretation of the law and the hypocritical character of the Pharisees. Our Saviour thus enlarges upon the sixth beatitude.

## WARNING AGAINST FALSE TEACHERS

MATT. 7:3. And why seest thou the mote that is in thy brother's eye, and seest not the beam that is in thy own eye?—4. Or how sayest thou to thy brother: Let me cast the mote out of thy eye; and behold a beam is in thy own eye?—5. Thou hypocrite, cast out first the beam out of thy own eye, and then shalt thou see to cast out the mote out of thy brother's eye.—6. Give not that which is holy to dogs; neither cast ye your pearls before swine, lest perhaps they trample them under their feet, and turning upon you, they tear you. . . . —13. Enter ye in at the narrow gate: for wide is the gate, and broad is the way that leadeth to destruction, and many there are who go in thereat.—14. How narrow is the gate, and strait is the way that leadeth to life, and few there are that find it.—15. Beware of false prophets, who come to you in the clothing of sheep, but inwardly they are ravening wolves.—16. By their fruits you shall know them. Do men gather grapes of thorns, or figs of thistles?—17. Even so every good tree bringeth forth good fruit, and the evil tree bringeth forth evil fruit.—18. A good tree cannot bring forth evil fruit, neither can an evil tree bring forth good fruit.—19. Every tree that bringeth not forth good fruit shall be cut down, and shall be cast into the fire.—20. Wherefore by their fruits you shall know them.—21. Not everyone that saith to me, Lord, Lord, shall enter into the kingdom of heaven; but he that doth the will of my Father who is in heaven, he shall enter into the kingdom of heaven.—22. Many will say to me in that day: Lord, Lord, have not we prophesied in thy name, and cast out devils in thy name, and done many miracles in thy name?—23. And then will I profess unto them, I never knew you; depart from me, you that work iniquity.

LUKE 6:39. And he spoke also to them a similitude: Can the blind lead the blind? Do they not both fall into the ditch?—40. The disciple is not above his master; but everyone shall be perfect, if he be as his master.—41. And why seest thou the mote in thy brother's eye, but the beam that is in thy own eye thou considerest not?—42. Or how canst thou say to thy brother: Brother, let me pull the mote out of thy eye, when thou thyself seest not the beam in thy own eye? Hypocrite, cast first the beam out of thy own eye, and then shalt thou see clearly to take out the mote from thy brother's eye.—43. For there is no good tree that bringeth forth evil fruit; nor an evil tree that bringeth forth good fruit.—44. For every tree is known by its fruit. For men do not gather figs from thorns; nor from a bramble bush do they gather the grape.—45. A good man out of the good treasure of his heart bringeth forth that which is good; and an evil man out of the evil treasure bringeth forth that which is evil. For out of the abundance of the heart the mouth speaketh.—46. And why call you me Lord, Lord, and do not the things which I say?

Our Saviour here gives a warning to the Apostles and all the
people against false teachers. St. Matthew records the similitudes
of the beam in the eye and the good and evil trees in connection
with this warning; St. Luke adds the similitude of the blind leader,
but does not point out the connection. The warning applies to the
Church at all times, but at this period especially on account of
the relations between the Jewish people and the Pharisees, who
domineered over all, even the lawyers, priests and scribes. The
people were dependent upon these teachers, and therefore had
all the more need of being warned against the harm which the
bad example of the pharisaical "justice" must necessarily do
amongst them. This warning consists of three parts.

### 1. OUR SAVIOUR WARNS US AGAINST FOLLOWING INCOMPETENT TEACHERS

Our Saviour shows that it is intellectual incapacity as well
as fanaticism which constitutes this incompetency to teach (Luke
6:39), together with pride and self-exaltation, which, unconscious
of its own insufficiency, thinks itself able and authorized to instruct and correct everyone else (Luke 6:41; Matt. 7:3, 4; cf.
also Matt. 15:14; 23:15). This exactly describes the state of the
Pharisees.

He enforces this warning by grave considerations. First, He
says that following such guidance will only result in the fall of
both master and disciple into the ditch and cause their ruin, as in
fact had been the case (Luke 6:39). At best, our Saviour remarks
secondly, the disciple will be no better than his master; that is to
say, he will share the blind infatuation of the latter (Luke 6:40).
Thirdly, the unhappy guide is warned by our Saviour to turn
his attention to his own improvement before all else, because
he is sunk much deeper in spiritual misery than his pupil, since
he can scarcely be exempt from the sin of hypocrisy (Matt. 7:5;
Luke 6:42). He cannot possibly be sincere in his proceedings, and
cloaks his dishonesty with the pretence of zeal and clear insight
(Matt. 7:5; 23:16 seq.).

### 2. OUR SAVIOUR WARNS US AGAINST IMPRUDENCE IN IMPARTING THE MYSTERIES OF THE FAITH TO OTHERS

Our Saviour makes use, for this warning, of a figure taken from
Oriental town-life, where all refuse is thrown out of the houses
into the street, so that it often happens that lost treasures, such

as pearls, may be accidentally thrown out with the rubbish. In the streets there are always a number of dogs and pigs roaming about, which are very vicious if interfered with. Our Lord compares to such pearls, which have fallen among the dogs and pigs, the mysteries of the faith which come to the knowledge of enemies of the Church by the want of caution of her children (Matt. 7:6).

He gives three motives as a warning against this. First, it is useless and vain to make such communications. What are pigs and dogs, which only care to satisfy their hunger, to do with pearls? Secondly, these mysteries of the faith are only disfigured and profaned by the enemies of the Church, as pearls are trodden in the mud by unclean animals. Thirdly, if anyone attempts to protect and defend such mysteries, he is attacked and defamed by these enemies, as those who try to save pearls from dogs are only beset by them in return (Matt. 7:6). Who does not here think involuntarily of the mysteries taught by the Church to the Jews and heathens, and of the devotions and practices of the Church as opposed to those of other creeds? What have the latter made of them? How have they treated those who defended them?

### 3. OUR SAVIOUR GIVES THE MARKS BY WHICH FALSE TEACHERS MAY BE RECOGNIZED

Our Saviour first warns against deceitful appearances, against the "sheep's clothing"; namely a suave manner, smooth words, pious speeches, specious doctrines of public welfare, virtue and liberty (Matt. 7:15; Luke 6:46). All this does not exclude the possibility of such teachers being "ravening wolves" inwardly. A sure mark by which we may distinguish between good teachers and false ones is their manner of life, their "works," which must be in harmony with the Will of God (Matt. 7:21). These show what a man really is. Our Saviour illustrates and corroborates this by the similitude of the tree. Its goodness or worthlessness is recognized by its fruits (Matt. 7:16; Luke 6:43); and He says that a bad man can no more bring forth good works from the bad treasure of his heart, or a good man bad works from the good treasure of his heart, than a bramble bush can produce figs and grapes (Luke 6:45). At any rate this is the general rule. Life and works, if they are to be consistent with the Gospel, must bear the stamp of earnestness and self-denial. This earnestness of life is compared by our Saviour to walking along a narrow path and passing through a strait gate (Matt. 7:13). The restriction and limitation of our natural desires is a mark of the true religion, and one of her fundamental laws. These laws do not favor corrupt nature. One need only cast a glance over the precepts of the Sermon on the Mount to be convinced of this. The unflinching mortification of carnal lusts (Matt. 7:14) is therefore the mark of adherents of the true religion, and especially of her teachers. If they have not this mark, they are not genuine.

As a deterrent for the false teachers themselves our Saviour adds the threat of reprobation in the Judgment. Honorable relations with Himself, such as having been bearers of His teaching authority and miraculous power, will not be taken into consideration (Matt. 7:22); their hypocrisy and dishonesty will be unmasked, and they will be rejected from the kingdom of heaven (Matt. 7:23). Not to be "known" by God, to be repulsed by God, is terrible; it means, in other words, damnation. It is to be remarked that our Saviour now for the first time announces Himself as Judge.

## Conclusion of the Sermon on the Mount

MATT. 7:24. Everyone therefore that heareth these my words and doth them, shall be likened to a wise man that built his house upon a rock.—25. And the rain fell, and the floods came, and the winds blew, and they beat upon that house; and it fell not, for it was founded on a rock.—26. And everyone that heareth these my words and doth them not, shall be like a foolish man that built his house upon the sand.—27. And the rain fell, and the floods came, and the winds blew, and they beat upon that house, and it fell, and great was the fall thereof.—28. And it came to pass, when Jesus had fully ended these words, the people were in admiration at his doctrine.—29. For he was teaching them as one having power, and not as their scribes and Pharisees.

LUKE 6:47. Everyone that cometh to me, and heareth my words and doth them, I will show you to whom he is like.—48. He is like to a man building a house, who digged deep, and laid the foundation upon a rock. And when a flood came, the stream beat vehemently upon that house, and it could not shake it; for it was founded on a rock.—49. But he that heareth and doth not, is like to a man building his house upon the earth without a foundation; against which the stream beat vehemently, and immediately it fell, and the ruin of that house was great.

In the conclusion of the Sermon on the Mount our Saviour invites all, first, to come to Him, i.e. to adhere to Him by desire of their soul's welfare, by trust, faith and devotion; secondly, to hear His doctrine and become familiar with it; and thirdly, to put it into practice (Luke 6:47; Matt. 7:24). Whoever practises what he sees in our Saviour and hears from Him, is a true and perfect disciple. Our Saviour wishes then, above all things, that our lives should be consistent with what we know and believe.

He encourages us to form this resolution by the following motives. First, it is true wisdom; it makes us like "the wise man" of the Gospel (Matt. 7:24; Luke 6:48) the man, that is to say, with whom intellect and will, knowledge and life have become one. Otherwise there is within us nothing but dissension and contradiction. And for what do we possess knowledge, if not in order to live up to it? Secondly, this alone gives stability and a firm purpose to all we do. Herein alone are found all the conditions of perseverance. Our Saviour here again employs a similitude, viz. the comparison of a building which has deep foundations and stands upon a rock, forming as it were a part of it. No deluge of rain, such as is common in some parts of the East in winter-time, and no flood caused by this rain, will be able to harm such a house. So it will be with a wise man. The foundation is no other than Christ (I Cor. 3:11), and the rock also is Christ (Eph. 2:20; I Cor. 10:4). The wise man with his intellect and will, his whole life, aims and actions, is so to speak built into Him by means of the Church, of faith and of grace. He is organically united to Christ in his entire life. The gale may blow, the rain pour, and the floods roll onwards; he stands firm against all the dangers and storms of the passions, temptations, and persecutions of life (Rom. 8:35); even in the Judgment he will suffer no harm. But the opposite of this is also true. Whoever merely hears the words of Christ, but does not carry them out in practice, whose life is at variance with his knowledge, is a foolish man, who builds his house upon sand. It will have no stability in the unavoidable storms of life, and much less in the Judgment of our Lord. Its fall will be great and complete (Matt. 7:27; Luke 6:49). With this earnest warning to the disciples, to the people and to us also, our Saviour concludes His Sermon on the Mount. It sounds like an opening chord of the prophecies of destruction uttered by Him when entering the city in His triumph on Palm Sunday (Luke 19:42 seq.). It is not enough to know the precepts of our Lord; we must also put them into practice.

The effect of this sermon upon the people was, in the first place, admiration and astonishment at the truth, clearness, certainty, novelty, depth, beauty and sublimity of the doctrine; further, it brought the conviction that here not merely a teacher and interpreter of the law, but the Lawgiver and Judge Himself, the Shepherd and Teacher promised by the prophets (Joel 2:23) had spoken. This teaching power of our Lord stood out still more gloriously in contrast to the manner in which the Pharisaical teachers of the law gave their instructions; these, in spite of all their pretended holiness and hypocritical practices, were not "as one having power."

## The Centurion of Capharnaum

Luke 7:1. And when he had finished all his words in the hearing of the people, he entered into Capharnaum.—2. And the servant of a certain centurion, who was dear to him, being sick, was ready to die.—3. And when he had heard of Jesus, he sent unto him the ancients of the Jews, desiring him to come and heal his servant.—4. And when they came to Jesus, they besought him earnestly, saying to him: "He is worthy that thou shouldst do this for him;—5. For he loveth our nation; and he hath built us a synagogue."—6. And Jesus went with them. And when he was now not far from the house, the centurion sent his friends to him, saying: "Lord, trouble not thyself; for I am not worthy that thou shouldst enter under my roof.—7. For which cause neither did I think myself worthy to come to thee; but say the word, and my servant shall be healed.—8. For I also am a man subject to authority, having under me soldiers; and I say to one, Go, and he goeth; and to another, Come, and he cometh; and to my servant, Do this, and he doeth it."—9. Which Jesus hearing, marveled; and turning about to the multitude that followed him, he said: "Amen I say to you, I have not found so great faith even in Israel."—10. And they who were sent being returned to the house, found the servant whole who had been sick.

Matt. 8:5. And when he had entered into Capharnaum, there came to him a centurion, beseeching him,—6. And saying: "Lord, my servant lieth at home sick of the palsy, and is grievously tormented."—7. And Jesus saith to him: "I will come and heal him."—8. And the centurion making answer said: "Lord, I am not worthy that thou shouldst enter under my roof; but only say the word, and my servant shall be healed.—9. For I also am a man subject to authority, having under me soldiers; and I say to this, Go, and he goeth; and to another, Come, and he cometh; and to my servant, Do this, and he doeth it."—10. And Jesus hearing this, marveled; and said to them that followed him: "Amen I say to you, I have not found so great faith in Israel."

From the place where He had preached the Sermon our Saviour betook Himself to Capharnaum, accompanied by a great multitude of people (Matt. 8:1, 5; Luke 7:1). Capharnaum, as an important post and probably also the frontier town on the road to Ituraea, had a garrison (probably Herodian) with a centurion at its head. This centurion had a sick servant. Having heard the rumors of our Saviour's miracles (Luke 7:3), he sent and begged Him to heal his servant.

## 1. THE CENTURION

The centurion manifests in his conduct qualities and virtues which render him truly worthy of miraculous assistance.

First, he shows a kind heart. The sick servant was "dear to him" (Luke 7:2). This makes it clear that they stood in the best mutual relations. The servant seems to have been very devoted to his master, and the master loved him like a member of his family. The danger of the servant touches the master sensibly, and he takes trouble on his behalf and does all that he can for him. Such is the right relationship between masters and servants (Eccli. 7:23).

Secondly, the centurion is truly religious. The elders of the city, who present his petition to our Saviour, say of him that he loved the Jewish nation and had built for them the synagogue in Capharnaum (Luke 7:4, 5); the very one, perhaps, in which our Lord so often preached. The centurion was probably a Roman, but in the service of Herod, and (as it seems) a "proselyte of the gate." [1] It was rare indeed for Romans and soldiers to show such care for religion, or to become attached to foreigners, especially Jews. But this good disposition brought him a rich reward.

Thirdly, we see in the centurion unusual modesty and humility. He does not dare to come himself, to ask on his own account (Luke 7:7), but sends to the elders of the town, that they may do it in his name (Luke 7:3). The Jews, however, had apparently gone farther in their zeal than he intended; for it had not been his intention to induce our Saviour to come to him (Luke 7:3, 6). And as he sees that our Lord is really approaching, he considers himself altogether too impure and unworthy to receive so high a guest into his house, and begs Him in all humility (again through messengers) not to come (Luke 7:6, 7).

Lastly, the centurion shows himself to be a man of entire and perfect faith. All that he had heard of our Saviour and perhaps himself witnessed in Capharnaum, where our Lord had worked so many and such glorious miracles, had given him a high opinion of Jesus and a sublime faith in Him. He was convinced that the presence of our Lord was not necessary for the cure of his servant;

---

[1] There were two classes of proselytes; the so-called "proselytes of the gate" merely took part in the divine services of the Temple and synagogues, without receiving circumcision or embracing the entire ritual law, as those of the stricter class did.

one word and one act of His Will would suffice. He expresses this conviction very forcibly in his soldierly way. He as much as says: "I am only a man, a subordinate officer, and yet I am obeyed at a word; how much more, then, He who has no one above Him."

Such was the disposition of the centurion. He was indeed a great and noble-hearted man, and showed himself worthy of having his wish fulfilled by our Saviour (Luke 7:4). How great is the benevolence and religious feeling, how sincere the humility which we find in this man, and yet he was a Gentile, a Roman and a soldier! There could scarcely be a more beautiful and striking confession of the poverty of a creature, of consciousness of sin, and of faith in the divine power of Jesus than the words of the centurion. For this reason the Church has chosen them to be the constant expression of our sentiments when we approach our Saviour in Holy Communion. What a model this centurion is for priests and for all Christians!

### 2. OUR SAVIOUR

There are three points to be observed in our Saviour's conduct.

First, He complies most readily with the centurion's request (Luke 7:6). He sets out on the way to him immediately. He is not deterred by His personal relations to the elders of the city, which were perhaps not of the most friendly character, but considers only the request itself. That it was not His object to enter into personal intimacy with a man of high position, may be seen from the fact that He did not enter the centurion's house, as the latter declined His visit. He never forced Himself upon great men. He sought only to do good, not to receive it.

Secondly, our Saviour praises the faith of the centurion publicly, before all the people (Luke 7:9); He expresses His admiration of it simply, as any onlooker might have done who was struck by such virtue, and because this faith was indeed extraordinary under such circumstances. He wishes thereby to encourage all to have faith. On this account He ascribes the miracle and the manner of it to the faith of the centurion (Matt. 8:13). This is another instance of a miracle worked by our Lord from a distance; He did so in this case, in order to fulfil exactly the desire of the centurion (Luke 7:7, 10).

Thirdly, our Saviour gently reproves the unbelief of Israel, with the same intention of awakening faith (Luke 7:9; Matt. 8:10). He says that He has not, as a rule, perceived any such strong and earnest marks of faith. The elders themselves did not show such enlightened faith, since they asked our Saviour to come in person. Indeed, this faith and especially this humility are not to be found in the behavior of the Jews towards Him. Our Saviour does not seem to have carried His reproof farther. What St. Matthew here adds (Matt. 8:11, 12) is recorded by St. Luke later, on another occasion (Luke 13:29).

### 3. SIGNIFICANCE OF THE MYSTERY

The significance of the mystery, apart from the miracle, lies in its being the first public meeting of our Saviour with heathenism, a meeting brought about by the mediation of Judaism; and as such it prefigures their respective relations to our Saviour and His kingdom. The chief actors are true types and prophets of things to come. Israel brings about the approach of our Saviour and the miracle, in the person of the elders of the city, who petition for the Gentile. Otherwise perhaps, to judge from other occurrences, our Lord would not have worked a miracle so publicly upon a Gentile (Mark 7:24). Heathenism, represented by the centurion, approaches with wonderful faith and touching humility, whilst Israel remains far behind in these respects. It does not feel, like the Gentiles, all its need of redemption, but receives God's benefits almost as its due. On account of the nation's unbelief, therefore, the kingdom of God will pass over from it to the Gentiles. Thus the conclusion is a confirmation of the last lesson of the Sermon on the Mount, that knowledge alone does not lead to salvation, but faith and good works.

## THE RAISING TO LIFE OF THE YOUNG MAN OF NAIM

LUKE 7:11. And it came to pass afterwards that he went into a city that is called Naim; and there went with him his disciples and a great multitude.—12. And when he came nigh to the gate of the city, behold a dead man was carried out, the only son of his mother, and she was a widow; and a great multitude of the city was with her.—13. Whom when the Lord had seen, being moved with mercy towards her, he said to her "Weep not."—14. And he came near and touched the bier. (And they that carried it stood still.) And he said: "Young man, I say to thee, arise."—15. And he that was dead sat up, and began to speak. And he gave him to his mother.—16. And there came a fear on them all; and they glorified God, saying: "A great prophet is risen up among us; and God hath visited his people."—17. And this rumor of him went forth throughout all Judaea, and throughout all the country round about.

## 1. ACCESSORY CIRCUMSTANCES OF THE MIRACLE

After working the miracle upon the centurion's servant our Saviour left Capharnaum (Luke 7:11), journeyed inland towards the south-west, along the road which opens out into the plain of Esdrelon, between Mt. Thabor and Little Hermon, and arrived at the city of Naim. It must have been towards evening that He approached the city, since funerals generally took place after sunset.

The city itself lies at the foot of Little Hermon. The plain of Esdrelon stretches beyond it, Thabor is close at hand, and far away to the north are seen the partially snow-capped peaks of Great Hermon; in the neighborhood is situated on one side Endor, where the unfortunate king Saul had consulted the soothsaying woman before the battle of Gelboe (I Kings 28:7), and on the other side Sunam, where Eliseus had raised a dead child to life (IV Kings 4:36)—all events which recalled dark times of decline and decay of faith and morals, in which neither great miracles nor heavy afflictions could lead the people to amend their lives (Eccli. 48:16).

Our Saviour proceeded with His disciples and a multitude of people (Luke 7:11) along the road to the town, teaching them as He went, probably, deep lessons of penance and amendment, in keeping with the dark reminiscences of the surrounding district. The miracle He was about to work was to be a still more earnest admonition. Thus they came to the city. It had gates (Luke 7:12), and must have been a not unimportant place, to conclude from the ruins of great walls still to be seen and the many sepulchers in the rocks hard by. Here, then, at the gate, our Saviour met a funeral procession coming out of the city, accompanied by a great number of people. At the head of the procession went the mourning women, the flutists and cymbal-players; then came a woman, weeping quietly; behind her the bier, which consisted merely of a flat board without cover or lid, and was carried by four men. Upon this lay the dead youth, wrapped in a shroud, but so that the face remained uncovered. The procession was closed by the throng of friends, neighbors and other people. The dead man who was to be buried was the son of the woman who walked before the bier, and who appears to have been much respected. The people who were accompanying our Saviour joined the funeral procession, thus forming a great crowd of spectators. Thus all the circumstances—the evening hour, the place and surroundings, the many people on both sides, and the solemn occasion of the funeral—all combined to make the miracle a most impressive one.

## 2. THE PECULIAR FEATURES OF THE MIRACLE

Our Saviour made use of these circumstances in working the miracle. It has three remarkable features. The first is the nature of the miracle itself. It is a resuscitation of a dead person. Only three such miracles are recorded in the Gospels; this is the first of them. By raising the dead to life our Saviour proves Himself to be the absolute Lord of life. It is, then, a miracle of the first rank.

The second peculiarity of the miracle consists in the motive from which our Lord worked it; namely, compassion, which was spontaneously aroused. He who is carried to the grave is the young son, the only child of his mother, who is a widow (Luke 7:12). This is indeed a great sorrow, and only too real a cause for grief. Our Saviour permits the sight of this hallowed grief to work upon His Heart; perhaps He thinks of His own Mother, and of a distant time when she too will accompany Him to His grave, and so He is moved with lively and heartfelt compassion (Luke 7:13). But our Lord does not rest content with this. He passes at once from compassion to active assistance. He goes up to the mother and comforts her: "Weep not!" It was easy to say this, and it had perhaps been said to her already by others. But when our Saviour says it, He knows how to give effect to the words in His own way. He approaches the bier, bids the bearers stand still (Luke 7:14), and raises the dead youth to life.

The manner in which the miracle is accomplished forms the third peculiarity. Other great prophets and workers of miracles have also raised the dead to life; but they did not do so without many accompanying actions. They prayed, entreated, cast themselves upon the dead persons, and sought, as it were, to excite life again by symbolic ceremonies. Thus Elias (III Kings 17:20), Eliseus (IV Kings 4:34), Peter (Acts 9:39), and Paul (Acts 20:10). But our Saviour has in Himself the power to restore life; He is Life itself, and therefore He only speaks the words: "Young man, I say to thee, arise" (Luke 7:14). And the youth awakes, sits up, and begins to speak (Luke 7:15). How mighty our Lord is! But also how tender-hearted! He gives the mother her son (Luke 7:15). He had claims upon this life, but He does not press them; He honors the mother's right, as He had honored her sorrow. He leads the youth to her arms, and we can well imagine with what joyful feelings He gave the precious gift, and with what touching gratitude it was received. What must have been the feelings entertained by mother and son for our Saviour henceforth!

### 3. THE EFFECT OF THE MIRACLE

One may well imagine what a thrilling effect the miracle had upon all the people under these circumstances. St. Luke lays particularly stress upon this. "There came a fear on them all" at the overwhelming sight, and on account of the presence of divine power. "They glorified God, saying: A great prophet is risen up among us, and God hath visited His people" (Luke 7:16). "And this rumor of Him went forth throughout all Judaea, and throughout all the country round about" (Luke 7:17). This is the natural expression of the effect of the extraordinary and divine deed which the people had just seen, and by which our Lord had proved Himself to be sent by God.

This was our Saviour's intention in working this miracle. He wished thereby to give a powerful impulse to faith in His divine mission and His own Divinity, and to deprive unbelief of all foothold. God gives such signs only in times of great decline of faith and important crises. This miracle was also the first actual confirmation of our Lord's solemn announcement in the Temple on the preceding Paschal feast, that He would raise the dead to life in proof of the truth of His Divinity (John 5:21, 25). At the same time we see a most touching revelation of the kind, compassionate and tender Heart of our Saviour.

## THE MESSENGERS OF JOHN THE BAPTIST

LUKE 7:18. And John's disciples told him of all these things.—19. And John called to him two of his disciples, and sent them to Jesus, saying: "Art thou he that art to come, or look we for another?"—20. And when the men were come unto him, they said: "John the Baptist hath sent us to thee, saying: Art thou he that art to come, or look we for another?"—21. (And in that same hour, he cured many of their diseases and hurts, and evil spirits; and to many that were blind he gave sight.)—22. And answering, he said to them: "Go and relate to John what you have heard and seen: The blind see, the lame walk, the lepers are made clean, the deaf hear, the dead rise again, to the poor the Gospel is preached;—23. And blessed is he whosoever shall not be scandalized in me."—24. And when the messengers of John were departed, he began to speak to the multitudes concerning

John. "What went you out into the desert to see? A reed shaken with the wind? —25. But what went you out to see? A man clothed in soft garments? Behold they that are in costly apparel and live delicately, are in the houses of kings.—26. But what went you out to see? A prophet? Yea, I say to you, and more than a prophet; —27. This is he of whom it is written: Behold I send my angel before thy face, who shall prepare thy way before thee.—28. For I say to you: Amongst those that are born of women, there is not a greater prophet than John the Baptist. But he that is the lesser in the kingdom of God, is greater than he."—29. And all the people hearing and the publicans justified God, being baptized with John's baptism. —30. But the Pharisees and the lawyers despised the counsel of God against themselves, being not baptized by him.—31. And the Lord said: "Whereunto then shall I liken the men of this generation? and to what are they like?—32. They are like to children sitting in the market-place, and speaking one to another, and saying: We have piped to you, and you have not danced; we have mourned, and you have not wept.—33. For John the Baptist came neither eating bread nor drinking wine; and you say: He hath a devil.—34. The Son of Man is come eating and drinking; and you say: Behold a man that is a glutton and a drinker of wine, a friend of publicans and sinners.—35. And wisdom is justified by all her children."

MATT. 11:2. Now when John had heard in prison the works of Christ, sending two of his disciples,—3. He said to him: "Art thou he that art to come, or look we for another?"—4. And Jesus making answer said to them: "Go and relate to John what you have heard and seen.—5. The blind see, the lame walk, the lepers are cleansed, the deaf hear, the dead rise again, the poor have the Gospel preached to them;—6. And blessed is he that shall not be scandalized in me."—7. And when they went their way, Jesus began to say to the multitudes concerning John: "What went you out into the desert to see? A reed shaken with the wind?—8. But what went you out to see? A man clothed in soft garments? Behold they that are clothed in soft garments are in the houses of kings.—9. But what went you out to see? A prophet? Yea, I tell you, and more than a prophet—10. For this is he of whom it is written: Behold I send my angel before thy face, who shall prepare thy way before thee.—11. Amen I say to you, there hath not risen among them that are born of women a greater than John the Baptist; yet he that is the lesser in the kingdom of heaven is greater than he.—12. And from the days of John the Baptist until now the kingdom of heaven suffereth violence, and the violent bear it away.— 13. For all the prophets and the law prophesied until John;—14. And if you will receive it, he is Elias that is to come.—15. He that hath ears to hear, let him hear. —16. But whereunto shall I esteem this generation to be like? It is like to children sitting in the market-place, who, crying to their companions,—17. Say: We have piped to you, and you have not danced, we have lamented, and you have not mourned.—18. For John came neither eating nor drinking, and they say: He hath a devil.—19. The Son of Man came eating and drinking, and they say: Behold a man that is a glutton and a wine-drinker, a friend of publicans and sinners. And wisdom is justified by her children."

The rumor of our Saviour's great miracles was brought also to John in his prison, by his disciples (Luke 7:18; Matt. 11:2), who, as it seems, were allowed to have some intercourse with him. He sent, then, two of his disciples to our Saviour, with the inquiry whether He were the Messias who was to come, or if they were to expect another.

### 1. JOHN'S MESSAGE

John's intention in sending this message was not to inquire on his own account if Jesus were the Messias; he had expressed his faith and conviction often enough in his various testimonies to our Saviour. But he made this inquiry for the sake of his disciples, who in their arrogance and obstinacy would not become our Lord's adherents, and also for the sake of all the people. He wished to lead all to believe in the divine mission of our Saviour, and this through the latter's own testimony. Our Lord Himself should bear witness of His rank as the Messias, and thereby confirm and seal John's testimony. This was what the Baptist wished to bring about by this question; indeed, he wished to force our Saviour to give an answer, for he was burning with desire to see Him acknowledged by all Israel, and now it seemed to him that the moment had come.

With this intention, then, John contrived the circumstances of the message. It was to be a most solemn one. With this end in view he put the question in his own name, in his capacity as forerunner of the Messias, not merely in the name of his disciples (Matt. 11:3; Luke 7:19, 20); for this reason he sent the legal number of witnesses (John 8:17), and let them make their appearance and put their question in the presence of all the people (Matt. 11:7); it was for this also that he chose the well-known title of the Messias: "Art thou He that art to come?" (Gen. 49:10; Ez. 21:27; Ps. 39:8; 117:26); and for this reason, finally, he gave the message the form of a question. He thought thus to induce our Saviour to give an answer. Everything is planned with a view to a solemn, decisive self-declaration on the part of our Lord.

### 2. THE ANSWER OF JESUS TO JOHN'S MESSAGE

Our Saviour's answer to John's inquiry contains two parts.

In the first place, He answers John's question. The disciples of the latter arrived just as our Saviour was working a great number of the most various miracles, healing the blind and expelling evil spirits (Luke 7:21). As an answer, He points out to them those who had been healed: "Go and relate to John what you have heard and seen: the blind see, the lame walk, the lepers are made clean, the deaf hear, the dead rise again, to the poor the Gospel is preached" (Luke 7:22; Matt. 11:5). The answer was in the first place complete and satisfactory; it consisted in deeds and miracles which of themselves sufficiently proved Him to be the Messias and Redeemer. They typified the twofold redemption of soul and body of the human race by the Messias. Secondly, the answer was a dogmatic and official one. Our Saviour replies to John as the latter himself had once replied to the messengers of the Jews, when they asked him if he were the Messias; namely, by a prophetic passage of Scripture, in which the answer was contained. Our Lord evidently cites here the prophecy of Isaias, which is now word for word fulfilled (Isa. 35:5; 61:1). Thirdly, the answer was very modest and prudent. Our Saviour did not consider it time yet to speak out openly and clearly to the people with regard to His being the Messias. Much that had been written of Him had first to be fulfilled. Indeed, He always proceeds slowly, and does not hurry the course of events. He allows everyone, those of good will also, time to seek and find Him.

In the second place, our Saviour points out what must be the necessary conclusion from His answer, for the disciples of John, for the Pharisees and the people, and for all men (Luke 7:23; Matt. 11:6). If He was the true Messias, then they should take care not to be scandalized at Him; i.e. they should beware lest He should be to them a cause of stumbling, if they failed to adhere to Him on account of the unassuming manner of His appearance, so little in accordance with their national ideas, and especially on account of His subsequent Passion and Death. Christ is, alas, a stumbling-block; to those, namely, who suffer themselves to be deterred from joining and following Him by the difficulties which this adherence presents, and by His doctrine and example. Unhappily the people as a whole were in the end thus scandalized in Christ (Isa. 8:13, 14). With this answer our Lord dismissed John's disciples.

### 3. CHRIST'S COUNTER-TESTIMONY WITH REGARD TO JOHN

After John's disciples had departed, our Saviour bore a glorious testimony to the Baptist, before all the people. This testimony contained three points.

He first testifies to John's exceptional greatness, proving it in the first place from his virtues and sanctity, and secondly from his office. Amongst his virtues, our Saviour lays especial stress upon his austere manner of life, in contrast to that of his royal persecutors (Matt. 11:8; Luke 7:25); then upon his firmness of character and intrepidity, in contrast to the time-serving character of so many parties amongst the Jews. He compares the latter to a reed, which bows to every wind (Matt. 11:7; Luke 7:24). But John's office is ranked by our Saviour higher than that of a prophet, since he is the Elias prophesied, and thus the immediate forerunner, the preparer of the way for the Messias (Luke 7:26, 27; Matt. 11:9, 14). So John himself was the subject of prophetic prediction (Mal. 3:1; Isa. 40:3). Finally our Lord sums up the entire greatness of John in a few words, saying that among those born of women there is no one greater than he as regards his office (Luke 7:28), so that, though others may equal, none surpass him, at any rate in the Old Covenant; for with the New Covenant, on account of its exalted position with regard to our Saviour, no comparison could be made (at all events with regard to office), since the lesser in this kingdom is greater (as regards office and vocation) than John (Matt. 11:11; Luke 7:28). The reason why our Saviour bore this testimony to John was to honor and reward him for the zeal and unselfishness with which he also had borne testimony to our Lord; further, to guard him from any suspicion of wavering in his personal faith in the mission of Jesus or in the fulfilment of his own vocation; and lastly, to ratify and confirm his statements concerning the Messias, and to induce the people to accept them. With regard to this last purpose, the forcible and striking terms in which He expresses His testimony to John's holiness are especially worthy of note. Why did you go out to the Jordan? Merely to see a shaking reed, or an effeminate man from whom you could learn no good, and of whom you see enough at court? No, you wished to see a fearless and austere prophet, and to hear the truth from him. Believe then his words. It is also to be remarked that our Saviour does not bear testimony to John in the presence of his disciples, because He will not praise indiscreetly, even when the praise is true and well merited.

The second point in the testimony concerning John is a conclusion from what our Saviour has stated with regard to him. He draws attention to a very important mystery well worthy of reflection, which He introduces with the words: "He that hath ears to hear, let him hear" (Matt. 11:15). The mystery is as follows: John is by his office the crowning stone of the Old Covenant, which was merely a preparation in its law and prophets (Matt. 11:13); now, since the days of John, a transition period has set in (Matt. 11:12). One must now no longer, as in the Old Covenant, await and expect, but lay hold of the kingdom of God; carnal descent is no longer valid for its attainment, but violence, and only the violent bear it away.[1] It is now, so to speak, the beginning of the judgment, and Israel is called upon to make its final decision. For John is, in one sense, Elias (Matt. 11:14); first and chiefly with regard to his office, as forerunner of the first advent of the Messias, whilst Elias will precede the second advent; and secondly also as regards his spirit and his lot in life, and his relations towards the princes and people (Mark 9:11, 12). Our Saviour here says plainly that the Messias has come.

In the third point our Saviour throws light upon the spirit of the people, with reference to the earnestness of this period. The people and the publicans, the inferior and despised class of the nation, "fulfilled justice" towards God (Matt. 3:15), i.e. they employed the means of salvation which He appointed, and allowed themselves to be baptized by John; but the Pharisees and scribes despised the Will of God, and would not receive baptism (Luke 7:29, 30). In their obstinacy they resembled perverse, capricious children at their games in the market-place, who will not come to play either at a funeral or a wedding game, if it is against their inclination (Matt. 11:16–19; Luke 7:31–34). So also these Pharisees and scribes. God sends them the austere John and the gentle, humble Son of Man, and they revile and are angry with both. Nevertheless the counsel of God is not hindered nor changed; on the contrary, Divine Providence ("wisdom") is justified by her children, i.e. by the good (Luke 7:35; Matt. 11:19).

This mystery contains John's last effort in favor of our Saviour. Even in prison he cannot rest without working for Him. He cannot wait till our Lord is universally acknowledged, and since he himself can no longer bear witness for Him, he sends his disciples and causes our Saviour Himself to give testimony of His divine mission. In our Saviour we again meet with His great prudence and wise reserve with regard to Himself, and also with His love and gratitude towards His faithful servant John. What more

---

[1] If, indeed, Matt. 11:12 belongs here at all. St. Luke gives these words in a later mystery (Luke 16:16). Here certainly as well as there the words of St. Matthew, as translated by some, are very appropriate: "From the days of John the kingdom of God suffers violence, and the violent tear it away from the people." In these words is expressed the not merely repellent but also directly hostile attitude of the Pharisees towards the kingdom of God, which they began to persecute by delivering up John the Baptist and restraining the people from accepting the Gospel (Luke 11:52).

glorious praise could be bestowed upon John than our Saviour's testimony of him? It is a summary of all his greatness, an incomparable panegyric and a true canonization from the lips of God Himself. On the other hand, how telling and earnest is the manner in which our Lord points out and censures, in all its perversity, obstinacy and stubbornness, the spirit of the Pharisees towards John and towards His own ministry.

## THE PUBLIC SINNER

LUKE 7:36. And one of the Pharisees desired Jesus to eat with him. And he went into the house of the Pharisee, and sat down to meat.—37. And behold a woman that was in the city, a sinner, when she knew that he sat at meat in the Pharisee's house, brought an alabaster box of ointment;—38. And standing behind at his feet, she began to wash his feet with tears, and wiped them with the hairs of her head, and kissed his feet and anointed them with the ointment.—39. And the Pharisee who had invited him, seeing it, spoke within himself, saying: "This man, if he were a prophet, would know surely who and what manner of woman this is that toucheth him; that she is a sinner."—40. And Jesus answering, said to him: "Simon, I have somewhat to say to thee." But he said: "Master, say it."—41. "A certain creditor had two debtors: the one owed five hundred pence, and the other fifty.—42. And whereas they had not wherewith to pay, he forgave them both. Which therefore of the two loveth him most?"—43. Simon answering said: "I suppose that he, to whom he forgave most." And he said to him: "Thou hast judged rightly."—44. And turning to the woman, he said unto Simon: "Dost thou see this woman? I entered into thy house, thou gavest me no water for my feet; but she with tears hath washed my feet, and with her hairs hath wiped them. —45. Thou gavest me no kiss; but she, since she came in, hath not ceased to kiss my feet.—46. My head with oil thou didst not anoint; but she with ointment hath anointed my feet.—47. Wherefore I say to thee: Many sins are forgiven her, because she hath loved much. But to whom less is forgiven, he loveth less."—48. And he said to her: "Thy sins are forgiven thee."—49. And they that sat at meat with him began to say within themselves: "Who is this that forgiveth sins also?" —50. And he said to the woman: "Thy faith hath made thee safe; go in peace."

### 1. A PHARISEE INVITES OUR SAVIOUR TO EAT WITH HIM

Why the Pharisee invited our Saviour to eat in his house, it is not easy to see, unless it was on account of the honor in which hospitality is held in the East (Luke 7:36). Probably it was the custom to invite to table teachers of the law who, in traveling, passed through the town and taught in the synagogue. The invitation might therefore be given as a mere point of etiquette, or from curiosity, or even from a malicious motive. At all events the Pharisee was a true type of his sect. He treated our Saviour coldly, and displayed great want of consideration for Him. He showed Him no marks of friendship and politeness, such as are customary in the East towards persons who are held in respect or who are on terms of intimacy with the host. He did not greet Him with a kiss, did not cause His feet to be washed or His head anointed (Luke 7:44, 45, 46). This behavior corresponded to the relations between our Saviour and the Pharisees at that time.

Our Saviour knew his host very well; but nevertheless He accepts the invitation, and does not appear to notice all this want of respect. He accepts it, in His condescension and unselfishness. He is waiting for the sinner, and can do good.

### 2. THE SINNER APPEARS AT THE BANQUET

During the banquet, at which probably a very stiff and formal spirit prevailed, a woman suddenly approached from behind the divan on which our Saviour was reclining with His feet freed from their sandals. To judge from the costly alabaster box that she carried (Luke 7:37), she was rich, generous and strong-willed, both for good and for evil. Evil was there, and if not of the basest kind, yet bad enough to produce much scandal, on account of its notoriety. It probably consisted of excesses committed with others of her own rank, as may happen in the upper as well as in the lower classes. So, though naturally possessed of a noble heart, she had yet erred greatly, and was like a pearl in the mire of sin and passion.

But she repaired these errors now by her conversion and heroic virtue; above all, by her sublime faith (Luke 7:50). This faith was the beginning of her conversion. She was probably touched, melted and won by the doctrine and miracles of Jesus, and by His lofty and winning personality, His gravity, majesty and gentleness. Her whole behavior at the banquet shows that she saw in our Saviour more than a prophet and messenger of God, even God Himself, Whom she had offended, and from Whom she hoped to obtain forgiveness. Our Saviour's words: "She hath loved much" (Luke 7:47), cannot refer to a merely human love. What secondly distinguishes her conversion is her deep humility. She is clearly sensible Who He is and who she is herself; namely, one deeply in debt and unable to pay what she owes (Luke 7:41, 42). She does not shrink from openly confessing herself as such; she enters the banquet-chamber, casts herself at Jesus' feet, bathes them with her tears, and with her own hair wipes these tears away, as if they were unworthy to touch and remain upon the feet of Jesus. Truly a touching humility in a proud and worldly woman! (Luke 7:38.) With the Jews, it was one of the greatest humiliations for a woman to appear with hair unbound. But the most precious thing about her conversion was her love, as our Saviour Himself points out (Luke 7:47). It is a love of contrition for her errors, and for her wandering away from the Supreme Good. But now she has found this Good, and she submits to it and embraces it with her whole heart. It is a love of the most heartfelt gratitude for the gracious reception which held out to her the prospect of forgiveness of her sins, or for other benefits, such as deliverance from the power of the devil; for the penitent sinner is probably Mary Magdalen, out of whom our Lord cast seven devils (Luke 8:2; Mark 16:9). Although her sins were perhaps already forgiven, she wished once more to offer reparation to her great Benefactor and Supreme Good, to show Him her gratitude and hear the words of forgiveness expressly from His lips. Lastly, it may also be a love of zeal for our Lord's honor. It is very possible that she had come with others into the banquet-hall and, standing at a distance, had been present at the meal (as in the East uninvited persons, especially neighbors, often make their appearance as spectators at the entertainment of strangers); and thus she may have noticed with what a want of consideration our Lord was treated by the Pharisee. Her noble heart could not endure this, and it was to her only a stronger reason to perform her act of penance. It was to be at the same time a public satisfaction for the neglect of the honors due to a guest. For this reason, perhaps, our Saviour may have reckoned up so carefully all the marks of honor that she paid Him, contrasting them with the inconsiderate behavior of the Pharisee (Luke 7:44–46). In a word, it is a true, perfect and heroic love, such as is due to God (Luke 7:47). And who would not be touched at this display of faith, love, and humble contrition?

But how does the Pharisee regard this scene? With invincible incredulity. He does not even regard our Saviour as a prophet. With the prophetic office was combined, according to the general opinion, the knowledge of hearts; and our Saviour had repeatedly given proof of this knowledge. And yet, in the Pharisee's opinion, He does not know who this woman is (Luke 7:39). Further, the Pharisee, in his consciousness of his own righteousness, regards the scene with disdain and contempt, for our Saviour as well as for the sinner. She is deeply culpable, an abandoned creature, not worthy of a glance. He himself is incomparably better; he is no debtor, even for the amount of fifty pence (Luke 7:41). On the

contrary, our Saviour is indebted to him for the honor of the
invitation, and the sinner for admittance into his house. Perhaps
he is even angry with the latter for having put to shame his inconsiderate behavior and exercised in his house the hospitality
which he himself had neglected.

### 3. OUR SAVIOUR JUSTIFIES HIMSELF AND THE SINNER

Our Saviour does not leave this harsh behavior of the Pharisee
without a reply. In this reply He does three things.

First, our Lord justifies Himself, and shows Himself to be a
prophet by proving His knowledge of hearts, minutely detailing
to the Pharisee his own thoughts (Luke 7:40 seq.), and showing
him how far more worthy of His indulgence this penitent is than
he himself.

Secondly, our Saviour reproves the Pharisee for his self-conceit
and contempt of others; and this He does with great delicacy and
acumen, with dignity and earnestness, but also with indulgence
and mildness, letting the Pharisee pronounce judgment upon
himself by proposing to him a parable and a question, apparently
not at all compromising (Luke 7:41–43). He tells him that this
poor woman has certainly sinned much, but that she now gives
Him true and unequivocal proofs of great love, whilst he (Simon)
is most inconsiderate towards Him; and finally that her sins are
remitted in consequence of her great love, and that she now stands
higher in His esteem than the Pharisee, on account of the latter's
want of faith and love (Luke 44–47). Although our Saviour can
endure with condescension and humility a want of respect and
esteem for Himself, He is nevertheless fully conscious of His
dignity, and knows how to vindicate His rights at the proper time
against pride and presumption. He is deeply sensible, therefore,
of the want of all love and gratitude on Simon's part. It is only
the heart's love that can satisfy Him. He cares little for the feast
so grudgingly served by the Pharisee.

Thirdly, our Lord abundantly justifies the sinner, and shows
that she is, on account of her faith and great love, well worthy of
forgiveness; far more worthy indeed than the Pharisee. He accepts with pleasure the proofs of this love; He knows them all,
and enumerates them with care (Luke 7:44–46). Then He forgives her sins, in return for her love. It is touching and instructive
to note how He speaks of love, and in what relation He places it
to justification. He repeatedly assures her of the pardon of her

sins (Luke 7:47, 48). The measure of love is the disposing cause and the measure of the forgiveness (Luke 7:47); and the forgiveness itself is again the motive and impulse of new love (Luke 7:47). Finally, He bestows upon the sinner His own love in return for hers. One feels from His words that this soul is dear to Him, that He loves, defends and protects her as His own property, even at the risk of being accused as a blasphemer because He has assured her of the forgiveness of her sins (Luke 7:49). He dismisses her with the assurance of peace; and peace with Jesus is the pledge of all blessings (Luke 7:50).

Such is the touching incident between our Lord and the penitent sinner. Its significance consists above all in this, that the actors are the members and representatives of schools of thought and classes of life in Israel. The Pharisee is a true representative of his class, and characterizes the whole sect by his spirit and manner of action. But the sinner represents the faithful and contrite Jew or heathen, who is known by his spirit of faith and humility. The whole event casts a side-light on many other incidents (Luke 7:30; Matt. 21:31), and is especially a touching illustration and confirmation of the words of the preceding mystery: "And wisdom is justified by all her children" (Luke 7:35). This mystery is also very precious to us on account of the light which it throws on the character of our Saviour, revealing as it does so clearly His wonderful tact, dignity and intrepidity, and especially His touching kindness and mercy towards sincere, contrite sinners. How kindly and graciously He receives the poor sinner! He regards only her heart and her present dispositions. He forgives and forgets all else in return for her sincere love. Here also He confirms openly and solemnly His power to forgive sins; indeed, He plainly reveals Himself as the omniscient, just and merciful God and Judge. Lastly, the process by which a soul is justified is clearly placed before us in this mystery. Faith begins the work; contrition, confession and love on the one hand and the mercy of God on the other complete it. The reciprocal action of love and forgiveness of sins is here beautifully revealed. Love prepares the way for the pardon of sins (Luke 7:47), but loving contrition is also principally excited by the greatness of the debt of sin, and the forgiveness of this debt becomes in its turn the impulse to new and greater love (Luke 7:42, 47), so that a sinful past is no hindrance to a close union of love. How wonderfully this is shown in the history of this sinner, if, as is the general opinion, she is

Mary Magdalen! Yes, a loving and fervent life after great transgressions is more pleasing to God than an innocent life dragged out in idle security.

## Three Characteristics of the Teaching of Jesus

Luke 8:1. And it came to pass afterwards that he traveled through the cities and towns, preaching and evangelizing the kingdom of God; and the twelve with him,—2. And certain women who had been healed of evil spirits and infirmities: Mary who is called Magdalen, out of whom seven devils were gone forth,—3. And Joanna the wife of Chusa, Herod's steward, and Susanna, and many others who ministered unto him of their substance.—4. And when a very great multitude was gathered together and hastened out of the cities unto him, he spoke by a similitude. . . .—9. And his disciples asked him what this parable might be.—10. To whom he said: "To you it is given to know the mystery of the kingdom of God, but to the rest in parables; that seeing they may not see, and hearing may not understand." . . .—16. "Now no man lighting a candle covereth it with a vessel, or putteth it under a bed; but setteth it upon a candlestick, that they who come in may see the light.—17. For there is not any thing secret, that shall not be made manifest; nor hidden, that shall not be known and come abroad.—18. Take heed therefore how you hear. For whosoever hath, to him shall be given; and whosoever hath not, that also which he thinketh he hath, shall be taken away from him."

Matt. 13:1. The same day Jesus going out of the house, sat by the sea-side.—2. And great multitudes were gathered together unto him, so that he went up into a boat and sat; and all the multitude stood on the shore.—3. And he spoke to them many things in parables. . . .—10. And his disciples came and said to him: "Why speakest thou to them in parables?"—11. Who answered and said to them: "Because to you it is given to know the mysteries of the kingdom of heaven; but to them it is not given.—12. For he that hath, to him shall be given, and he shall abound; but he that hath not, from him shall be taken away that also which he hath.—13. Therefore do I speak to them in parables; because seeing they see not, and hearing they hear not, neither do they understand:—14. And the prophecy of Isaias is fulfilled in them, who saith: By hearing you shall hear, and shall not understand; and seeing you shall see, and shall not perceive.—15. For the heart of this people is grown gross, and with their ears they have been dull of hearing, and their eyes they have shut; lest at any time they should see with their eyes, and hear with their ears, and understand with their heart, and be converted, and I should heal them.—16. But blessed are your eyes, because they see, and your ears, because they hear.—17. For Amen I say to you, many prophets and just men have desired to see the things that you see, and have not seen them; and to hear the things that you hear, and have not heard them." . . .—34. All these things Jesus spoke in parables to the multitudes, and without parables he did not speak to them;—35. That it might be fulfilled which was spoken by the prophet, saying: I will open my mouth in parables, I will utter things hidden from the foundation of the world.

Mark 4:1. And again he began to teach by the sea-side; and a great multitude was gathered together unto him, so that he went up into a ship and sat in the sea, and all the multitude was upon the land by the sea-side.—2. And he taught them many things in parables. . . .—10. And when he was alone, the twelve that were with him asked him the parable.—11. And he said to them: "To you it is given to know the mystery of the kingdom of God, but to them that are without all things are done in parables;—12. That seeing they may see, and not perceive; and hearing they may hear, and not understand: lest at any time they should be converted and their sins should be forgiven them."—13. And he saith to them: "Are you ignorant of this parable? And how shall you know all parables?" . . .—21. And he said to them: "Doth a candle come in to be put under a bushel, or under a bed, and not to be set on a candlestick?—22. For there is nothing hid, which shall not be made manifest; neither was it made secret, but that it may come abroad.—23. If any man have ears to hear, let him hear."—24. And he said to them: "Take heed what you hear. In what measure you shall mete, it shall be measured to you again, and more shall be given to you.—25. For he that hath, to him shall be given; and he that hath not, that also which he hath shall be taken away from him." . . .—33. And with many such parables he spoke to them the word, according as they were able to hear.—34. And without parable he did not speak unto them; but apart, he explained all things to his disciples.

### 1. SUBJECT AND PURPORT OF THIS TEACHING

Our Saviour journeyed through all Galilee, preaching in the cities and towns (Matt. 4:23; 9:35), in the synagogues, on mountains, and on the sea-shore (Matt. 13:1; Mark 4:1). The subject and purport of these addresses were the good tidings of the kingdom of God (Luke 8:1), i.e. the coming of the Messianic kingdom, its nature, its aim, laws and rewards, and the conditions of participation in it. This was certainly "good tidings," in its very subject-matter. It was the beautiful message of peace between heaven and earth and among men themselves; the fulfilment of all the promises and expectations of the Old Testament, the pledge of temporal and eternal welfare. It was also "good tidings" as regards the manner in which our Saviour proclaimed it; a manner namely which expanded the heart, elevated, strengthened and worked beneficially upon all. What, indeed, does poor mankind need more than encouragement? And what can offer it more solid and abundant comfort than the "good tidings" of Christ's kingdom?

### 2. PECULIARITY OF CHRIST'S METHOD OF TEACHING

A peculiarity of Christ's method of teaching was His frequent use of parables. It is interesting and instructive to study somewhat more deeply this mode of instruction.

What is a parable? It is a figure taken from some actual object or occurrence of the visible world, cited in order to explain abstract and spiritual things and to render them clearer and more comprehensible. These parables are sometimes similitudes taken from nature or occurrences of human life, i.e. real allegories fully worked out; sometimes only figures of speech, short allusions or maxims, which nevertheless contain a whole story, e.g.: "Physician, heal thyself" (Luke 4:23), "Cast first the beam out of thy own eye" (Luke 6:41 seq.).

And why did our Saviour teach in this way? First, to speak in parables belongs essentially to the Oriental method of teaching; indeed it is a peculiarity of all Oriental spoken wisdom, after the example of Solomon and the ancients (III Kings 4:32; 10:1 seq.; Eccli. 39:1–3; Bar. 3:23). If our Saviour wished to be considered a great master, He must also give evidence of proficiency in this mode of instruction. Secondly, this had also been prophesied of Him (Ps. 77:2; Matt. 13:35). The Psalmist foretold, in the figure of the rejection of the tribe of Ephraim (Ps. 77:67) and in the desertion of the ten tribes from the house of David, the future falling away of Israel from the Son of David and the rejection of the nation. This rejection is brought about in the first place through the people's own fault, but also partly through the circumstance that our Saviour proposed His doctrine in parables (Luke 8:10; Mark 4:12; Matt. 13:13, 14). This circumstance was a true judgment upon Israel. Thirdly, the mode of teaching in parables offered many advantages, for the speaker as well as for the hearers. It was very well adapted to the mental capacity of any audience. Allegoric wisdom is suited to the learned and the unlearned alike, because it is very simple and popular, and at the same time very attractive and easily remembered, appealing as it does both to the intellect and the imagination. It was likewise suited to the moral condition of the hearers. It stimulated to reflection those who were good and lovers of truth; but for inattentive, idle, ill-disposed and unbelieving hearers it was a judgment, as our Saviour Himself hints: "that seeing they may see, and not perceive; and hearing they may hear, and not understand," i.e. they see enough to be urged to inquire further, but remain in their unbelief and sin (Mark 4:12), because they scorn to search into the half-revealed truth and to submit to it (Luke 8:10; Mark 4:11, 12; Matt. 13:10, 11, 12, 15). Parables in general are very well adapted to bring home things that one cannot or does not wish to say openly. Thus our Lord, later on, very often announced the rejection of the nation in the form of a parable (Luke 13:28; 19:27; 20:16). There lay in this method of teaching, too, a tender and merciful consideration for the Gentiles, many of whom attended our Saviour's addresses, and who might easily have been repelled by an open statement of the doctrines of faith and morals, or perhaps would not have understood them at all.

Yet our Saviour did not always speak in parables, even in Galilee, as in the Sermon on the Mount; but only when it was better suited to the disposition of His audience, and as long as they obviously would not depart from their wrong view of the Messianic kingdom (Matt. 13:34; Mark 4:33, 34). Thus the parable was useful to all, to those "without" and those "within" (Mark 4:11). Things temporal and visible are, according to God's intention, a reflection of things eternal and invisible, and suited to reveal "things hidden from the foundation of the world" (Matt. 13:35) and the "mysteries of the kingdom of heaven" (Matt. 13:11) in their development in this world and the next. Further, parables are not merely figures of speech containing moral precepts, but also prophecies concerning the kingdom of God, the Church, her destinies, institutions and nature, in general and in detail. In the Catholic Church alone all these features are realized. For our divine Saviour Himself the method of teaching in parables had this advantage, that His glorious intellect could reveal itself in all its depth, clearness, delicacy and grace, together with its power of reaching the minds of the people. And He made very frequent use of this method. He propounded many parables, objective and historical, long and short, new and old (Matt. 13:52). He repeatedly made use of the same parables, but always in a new form, as regarded either their aim and application or their development. Thus He advanced in the esteem and favor not only of the people but also of the teachers of the law, so that He could with truth say in this respect also: "More than Solomon is here" (Luke 11:31).

### 3. OUR SAVIOUR'S ESCORT DURING HIS MINISTRY

Our Saviour had a threefold escort on His apostolic journeys.

The Apostles were His constant, official and closest companions (Luke 8:1). Our Lord's addresses and teachings were primarily for them. They were to listen to them and imprint them upon their memory; they were initiated in a special manner into their meaning (Luke 8:10; Mark 4:10, 34; Matt. 13:11, 18); they were, lastly, to preach and communicate to others the lessons they had learned (Matt. 13:52). Our Saviour urges beautiful motives for this transmission of His doctrine or evangelization. First, this is His chief intention in delivering His addresses, and especially in the private explanation of them. He exhorts the Apostles, therefore, to be attentive and grasp their meaning (Luke 8:18; Mark

4:13; 23:24). He further declares this to be His intention by saying that, in reception-rooms and assemblies, the light is not placed under a shade (bushel) or under the divan, where it would give only a very dim light, if any; but upon a high candlestick (Luke 8:16; Mark 4:21). What He says to them in secret, therefore, they are to publish abroad (Matt. 10:27; Luke 12:3). Secondly, our Saviour urges as a motive for proclamation of His doctrine the reward which awaits the Apostles. The measure of their zeal in preaching will also be the measure of their reward (Mark 4:24), not only in eternity but even here below, since he who employs his talent well ("hath" is here equivalent to "employs") will receive for so doing richer gifts of grace (Mark 4:25; Matt. 13:12; Luke 8:18). As a third motive our Saviour points out the honor and preference which the Apostles have before all the Saints of the Old Testament, of being eye-witnesses of the works of Christ and hearing His teaching (Matt. 13:16, 17; Luke 8:10). The position of honor which our Lord here accords to the Apostles is reflected in their pre-eminent place in all Christian tradition.

The companions of our Lord were secondly the holy women. This escort was not of an official character. The women moved in a more distant circle than the Apostles, but yet nearer than the multitudes who came and went. Their companionship was constant in this sense, that probably there was always one or other of the women at hand to help and assist with regard to temporal needs: food, lodging and clothing (Luke 8:2, 3). They filled the purse from which the wants of the Apostles (John 13:29) and the alms for the poor (John 12:6) were supplied. Only three of these holy women are mentioned here: Mary Magdalen, Joanna the wife of Chusa (one of Herod's officials), and Susanna; probably because they were the best known and most influential, and also contributed the most to the temporal support of our Lord and the Apostles. Salome and Mary of Cleophas, the kinswomen or friends of the Apostles, are not named, nor yet the Mother of Jesus, probably because she could not do so much in this way, and because our Saviour would not have her constantly with Him, in order to set us an example of perfect detachment of heart.

The motives from which the holy women thus attached themselves to our Saviour, and for which He permitted them to do this, were: first, gratitude for great benefits to body and soul which He had bestowed upon them (Luke 8:2), by freeing them from sickness, sins, and possession by evil spirits. Secondly, they did this out of love and a spirit of self-sacrifice for our Saviour and His kingdom. They could take part in the spreading of this kingdom in no other way than by receiving it into their hearts, and by offering their money and labor for the temporal needs of those whose task it was to extend and defend it by their apostolic labors. Our Saviour was poor, and wished to be poor, in order to set us the example of poverty and to give to many an opportunity of cooperating in the foundation of His kingdom by their temporal support. It is a great condescension and kindness on the part of our Lord thus to grant to the holy women the honor of supplying the want of temporal goods in His kingdom. How could they have made a better use of their money, time, and all their powers, than by working, giving and collecting alms for our Saviour and the Apostles? In this way, too, the holy women prefigured the various orders and states of the future Church, which devote themselves in a special manner to the service of the Gospel, whether in the secular or in the religious state.

Our Lord's third escort was formed by the people who continually came and went. Taken individually, they were better or worse disposed towards His teaching, according to their individual characters, as is described in the following parables; but as a whole they were eager for salvation and attached to our Saviour, following Him in great crowds, but always under the evil influence of the ruling Pharisaism. They prefigured the Church at large, hearing and learning the Word.

Such is the portait of our Saviour as a teacher. All these traits are employed for the one end, and are well adapted for the successful accomplishment of the salvation of men. The tenor of His teaching is consoling and elevating; His method attractive and alluring by its intellectual power, its clearness, depth and beauty; the example of His life beyond all doubt sublime, edifying, holy and sanctifying. His relations with the women, especially, are very instructive. He heals their infirmities, frees them from the power of the devil, remits their sins and allows them the honor, joy and merit of working for His kingdom in a more remote sphere of action. This our Lord offers to them; but no more. All Apostolic men may learn from this lesson. Women have in this mystery an example of how they may take part in the extension of Christ's kingdom. What a wonderful spectacle it is to see the Messias, as

He wanders from place to place, teaching the multitude! Strange, certainly, to the carnal eye, that He should live on alms; but glorious to the eye of faith! The Son of God lives on the charity of those to whom His charity gives life. How glorious an exchange of benefits between heaven and earth is brought about by the Personality of our Lord!

## THE PARABLE OF THE SOWER AND THE SEED

MATT. 13:1. The same day Jesus going out of the house, sat by the sea-side.— 2. And great multitudes were gathered together unto him, so that he went up into a boat and sat; and all the multitude stood on the shore.—3. And he spoke to them many things in parables, saying: "Behold the sower went forth to sow.— 4. And whilst he soweth, some fell by the wayside, and the birds of the air came and ate them up.—5. And other some fell upon stony ground, where they had not much earth; and they sprang up immediately, because they had no deepness of earth;—6. And when the sun was up, they were scorched; and because they had not root, they withered away.—7. And others fell among thorns; and the thorns grew up and choked them.—8. And others fell upon good ground; and they brought forth fruit, some an hundredfold, some sixtyfold, and some thirtyfold.—9. He that hath ears to hear, let him hear. . . .—18. Hear you therefore the parable of the sower.—19. When any one heareth the word of the kingdom, and understandeth it not, there cometh the wicked one, and catcheth away that which was sown in his heart; this is he that received the seed by the wayside.—20. And he that received the seed upon stony ground: this is he that heareth the word, and immediately receiveth it with joy;—21. Yet hath he not root in himself, but is only for a time; and when there ariseth tribulation and persecution because of the word, he is presently scandalized.—22. And he that received the seed among thorns, is he that heareth the word, and the care of this world and the deceitfulness of riches choketh up the word, and he becometh fruitless.—23. But he that received the seed upon good ground, this is he that heareth the word, and understandeth, and beareth fruit, and yieldeth the one an hundredfold, and another sixty, and another thirty."

MARK 4:1. And again he began to teach by the sea-side; and a great multitude was gathered together unto him, so that he went up into a ship and sat in the sea, and all the multitude was upon the land by the sea-side.—2. And he taught them many things in parables, and said unto them in his doctrine:—3. "Hear ye: Behold, the sower went out to sow.—4. And whilst he soweth, some fell by the wayside, and the birds of the air came, and ate it up.—5. And other some fell upon stony ground where it had not much earth; and it shot up immediately, because it had no depth of earth;—6. And when the sun was risen, it was scorched, and because it had no root, it withered away.—7. And some fell among thorns; and the thorns grew up, and choked it, and it yielded no fruit.—8. And some fell upon good ground; and brought forth fruit that grew up, and increased, and yielded, one thirty, another sixty, and another a hundred."—9. And he said: "He that hath ears to hear, let him hear.—. . . 14. He that soweth, soweth the word.—15. And these are they by the wayside, where the word is sown, and as soon as they have heard, immediately Satan cometh, and taketh away the word that was sown in their hearts.—16. And these likewise are they that are sown on the stony ground: who when they have heard the word, immediately receive it with joy;—17. And they have no root in themselves, but are only for a time; and then when tribulation and persecution arise for the word, they are presently scandalized.—18.

And others there are who are sown among thorns: these are they that hear the word,—19. And the cares of the world, and the deceitfulness of riches, and the lusts after other things entering in choke the word, and it is made fruitless.—20. And these are they who are sown upon the good ground, who hear the word, and receive it, and yield fruit, the one thirty, another sixty, and another a hundred."

LUKE 8:4. And when a very great multitude was gathered together and hastened out of the cities unto him, he spoke by a similitude:—5. "The sower went out to sow his seed; and as he sowed, some fell by the wayside, and it was trodden down, and the fowls of the air devoured it.—6. And other some fell upon a rock; and as soon as it was sprung up, it withered away, because it had no moisture.—7. And other some fell among thorns, and the thorns growing up with it, choked it.—8. And other some fell upon good ground; and being sprung up, yielded fruit a hundredfold." Saying these things, he cried out: "He that hath ears to hear, let him hear.—. . . 11. Now the parable is this: The seed is the word of God.—12. And they by the wayside are they that hear; then the devil cometh, and taketh the word out of their heart, lest believing they should be saved.—13. Now they upon the rock are they who, when they hear, receive the word with joy; and these have no roots; for they believe for a while, and in time of temptation they fall away.—14. And that which fell among thorns are they who have heard, and going their way, are choked with the cares and riches and pleasures of this life, and yield no fruit.—15. But that on the good ground are they who in a good and very good heart, hearing the word, keep it and bring forth fruit in patience."

Here follow several parables. Probably all of them (especially those here recorded by St. Matthew and St. Mark) were not propounded in succession, nor on the same occasion. It is evident from a few details given by the Evangelists (Matt. 13:10, 36; Mark 4:10) that there were at any rate pauses between them and changes of place. The first parable, however, seems to have been delivered under the circumstances so vividly described by St. Matthew (13:1, 2) and St. Mark (4:1). It must have been given either at Capharnaum or Bethsaida. The disciples and crowds of people stood or sat along the sea-shore, and our Saviour taught them from a boat. The locality was very well adapted for this. Capharnaum (probably the Tell Hum of today) presented a flat, rocky coast; and Bethsaida (probably Khan Minich) formed with its semicircular valley (a depression between the mountains) a sort of background which caught the sound of the voice and made it easy for the listeners to understand. In the clear air of Palestine, especially on the lake, the voice is heard very plainly at a long distance. The parable of the sower, too, is introduced in such an abrupt manner—"Behold, the sower" (Matt. 13:3; Mark 4:3)— that one is tempted to assume that our Lord here pointed to a sower who was sowing his field in the vicinity of the coast. Indeed, the scenery of the coast around might offer Him suggestions for almost all the following parables, and especially for the first. The slope of the land forms various terraces of cultivable ground; in the plain below the soil is deep, higher up there is only a thin layer upon rocks. Paths run alongside the fields and between them.

## 1. AIM OF THE PARABLE

The aim of the parable of the seed is to represent the varied success of the Word and the kingdom of God which results from the various dispositions of the souls and minds of men. The parable teaches how the kingdom of God is received in various ways, in consequence of the various difficulties which it encounters in men's hearts; and exhorts at the same time to remove these difficulties and prepare the heart for the reception of the kingdom. The parable concerns all, Jews and Gentiles, sinners and just, according to the disposition of each one, and according as each has to advance from unbelief to faith, from faith to the state of grace, or from the state of grace to perfection.

## 2. DEVELOPMENT AND APPLICATION OF THE PARABLE

The seed is the Word of God, the Word of revelation and faith (Mark 4:14; Luke 8:11); but it also signifies the whole economy of grace, the kingdom of God (Matt. 13:19), the Church with all her supernatural means of salvation (faith, prayer, grace, the Sacraments), even Christ Himself, Who often compares Himself to a grain of corn (John 12:24). The field is the world, man, and the heart of man. Especial stress is laid upon this by St. Matthew (13:19) and St. Mark (4:15–20), who say that men are sown. The sower is God, Christ, and also all those who are commissioned by Him to preach the Word to men. The act of sowing signifies preaching and the administration of the means of grace.

In consequence of interior and exterior hindrances and of the different manner in which these hindrances are treated, the fate of the seed is twofold: it remains unfruitful, or it brings forth fruit.

The seed remains unfruitful and is wasted under three circumstances, and with three classes of men. First, when it falls upon the road or by the roadside. The road, as regards the nature of its soil, is hard and unprepared, and thus unfitted for the reception of seed. The latter therefore remains upon the surface, and is either trodden under foot by the passers-by (Luke 8:5) or eaten by birds (Matt. 13:4; Mark 4:4). There are then two causes of unfruitfulness: an interior, the hardness of the soil; and an exterior, the passers-by and the birds. By the figure of the hard soil of the road are signified people who, on account of their hardness of heart, dissipation, worldliness and earthly views, are insensible and unsusceptible to things supernatural, altogether materially disposed and worldly people. They "hear the Word" but "understand it not" (Matt. 13:19), on account of the hardness of their hearts. In addition to this, worldly distractions and the Evil One come and steal away the Word of faith out of their hearts and minds. Another circumstance under which the seed perishes is its falling upon a superficial layer of earth over rocks. The seed is received, to be sure, and shoots up; but since it cannot find sufficient soil, it does not take deep root, has not the necessary moisture (Luke 8:6) to bear the heat of the sun (Matt. 13:5, 6; Mark 4:5, 6), and so it withers away. Here also there is a double cause of unfruitfulness; the interior cause is the shallowness of the earth, and the exterior the heat of the sun. This figure typifies those who have too little stability, endurance and courage to preserve the life of faith and grace which they have received, in spite of outward difficulties. Imaginative and impulsive people are especially meant here. They receive the Word with joy and enthusiasm, but it does not take firm hold of their will, only of their feelings, which are inconstant and determined by outward influences. So they believe only for a time (Luke 8:13; Mark 4:17; Matt. 13:21); but when any opposition or persecution of the Word breaks out, they are scandalized (Matt. 13:21; Mark 4:17) and fall away (Luke 8:13). Lastly, there is another circumstance under which the seed remains unfruitful; namely, when the soil is good for planting, but encumbered with weeds, thistles and underwood. The weeds grow up with the seed, and even more quickly than it does. They deprive it of moisture and light, and choke it. Here, then, there is only one cause, viz. encumbrance of the ground. By this comparison are meant those who allow their hearts to be occupied with temporal cares, the deceitfulness of riches (Matt. 13:22) and other concupiscences (Mark 4:19) and lusts of life. These stifle and check every higher growth of grace.

But the seed has also a better fate. In the hearts of many it springs up, grows, and bears fruit, in the one thirty, in another sixty, and in a third a hundredfold, fruit of faith, grace, merit and perfection. The cause of this fruitfulness is the goodness of the soil (Luke 8:8; Mark 4:8; Matt. 13:8), which consists in the exact opposite of the qualities which hinder the fruitfulness of the seed in other hearts. A man must hear the Word and receive it into his heart, and this heart must be soft and susceptible, capable of deep feeling, firm and enduring (Luke 8:15), must be free from evil and from earthly desires and endeavors; then it will bear with God's grace thirty, sixty, and even a hundredfold of fruit, as was the case in favored Galilee (Gen. 26:12).

### 3. CONCLUSION TO BE DRAWN FROM THE PARABLE

The lesson we are to draw from this parable, then, will be that we must remove all hindrances which prevent the Word of God from bearing fruit in our hearts, in order that it may bring forth the desired harvest. For this reason our Saviour adds to the parable the significant words: "He that hath ears to hear, let him hear" (Mark 4:9; Matt. 13:9). There are many and beautiful motives for this to be found in the parable.

The first motive lies in the condition of the field, i.e. of our hearts. We can bear fruit, if we will. Therein lies the difference between a piece of arable land and our hearts. We have the latter in our power, but not the former, at least not entirely. Grace is not wanting to us, as is shown by the amplification in St. Mark (4:26–29). If even the poor fields can be made productive by pains and labor, how much more then our hearts! Let us till them, therefore, deepen their soil and remove the weeds.

The second motive lies in the value of the seed. It is exceedingly precious, first, in its intrinsic worth, on account of its origin and nature. It is supernatural and divine. The whole creation with all its natural powers is not able to produce, obtain or merit even one single degree of grace. Secondly, the seed is precious on account of its fruitfulness and the gain it can bring us. Great as the fruitfulness of a grain of wheat can be under the most favorable circumstances, it can nevertheless not equal the fruitfulness of one grace. The latter is infinite and eternal, by its recompense in heaven. But proportionately great and deplorable is the loss of grace through our miserable passions, such as idleness, inconstancy, lust and avarice.

The third motive lies in the sower. The sower is God and our Divine Saviour. How much it has cost Him to puchase the seed, bring it to us and scatter it abroad! How liberally He scatters this seed in the world and in our hearts! How earnestly He desires that it should bring forth fruit in these hearts! No sower has such an ardent longing to reap the harvest of his seed as He has. He wishes this for our sakes; He wishes it for the sake of the teaching Church, which He has commissioned to scatter the seed abroad, as well as of the Church in general, which gains in riches, merit, power, and favor with God by the blessing of an abundant harvest in our hearts; He wishes it, lastly, for His own sake. He is the originator, cultivator and Lord of the great harvest.

## The Parable of the Cockle

MATT. 13:24. Another parable he proposed to them, saying: "The kingdom of heaven is likened to a man that sowed good seed in his field;—25. But while men were asleep, his enemy came and oversowed cockle among the wheat, and went his way.—26. And when the blade was sprung up and had brought forth fruit, then appeared also the cockle.—27. And the servants of the goodman of the house coming said to him: Sir, didst thou not sow good seed in thy field? Whence then hath it cockle?—28. And he said to them: An enemy hath done this. And the servants said to him: Wilt thou that we go and gather it up?—29. And he said: No; lest perhaps gathering up the cockle, you root up the wheat also together with it.—30. Suffer both to grow until the harvest, and in the time of the harvest I will say to the reapers: Gather up first the cockle, and bind it into bundles to burn, but the wheat gather ye into my barn."—. . . 36. Then having sent away the multitudes, he came into the house; and his disciples came to him, saying: "Expound to us the parable of the cockle of the field."—37. Who made answer and said to them: "He that soweth the good seed is the Son of Man.—38. And the field is the world; and the good seed are the children of the kingdom. And the cockle are the children of the wicked one.—39. And the enemy that sowed them is the devil. But the harvest is the end of the world. And the reapers are the angels.—40. Even as cockle therefore is gathered up, and burnt with fire: so shall it be at the end of the world.—41. The Son of Man shall send his angels, and they shall gather out of his kingdom all scandals, and them that work iniquity; —42. And shall cast them into the furnace of fire; there shall be weeping and gnashing of teeth.—43. Then shall the just shine as the sun, in the kingdom of their Father. He that hath ears to hear, let him hear."

The parable of the cockle, as St. Matthew's words seem to imply, was also first propounded to the people and afterwards explained to the disciples in private (Matt. 13:36). It contains a prophecy concerning the future of the Church, viz. that there will always be cockle in its fields (Matt. 13:38). The application of the parable to the circumstances under which our Saviour proposed it is nevertheless not excluded. The parable contains three parts.

### 1. THAT THERE WILL ALWAYS BE COCKLE IN THE CHURCH

By this "cockle" our Divine Saviour means wicked men, i.e. the heterodox, heretics, hypocrites, secret sinners (Matt. 13:38). He calls these "cockle," or more strictly "darnel," which is a common weed in Palestine, very similar to wheat, and not easily distinguishable from it (Matt. 13:26).

Such weeds will always be found in the Church. Our Saviour prophesies it, and thereby refutes the Novatians, the Montanists, and especially the Donatists; perhaps also in a certain sense the Pharisees. But the Church will not consist entirely of weeds. This is shown just as clearly by the parable (Matt. 13:29, 30, 43); and thus is overthrown the assertion of the Protestants, that the whole Church was once corrupt in faith and morals, until their sects arose.

### 2. WHENCE THE COCKLE PROCEEDS

The originator of the cockle is not God, nor the Church. It arises in her, but not from her. Her doctrines of faith and morals may be the occasion, but not the cause of it. The evil does not come from the observance of her precepts, but from departure from them. The Church has never recognized the cockle as her fruit, but always tried to hinder its growth. The Protestant system of tolerating all sects in the Church is hereby refuted. If they are found in the Church, it can only, at most, be because her pastors sleep (Matt. 13:25) and are negligent, which is a concomitant cause of the evil.

The originator of the cockle is always the Evil One, who makes use of the mutability and the faults of men (Matt. 13:25, 39). Our Saviour's words, that a wicked and hostile man has sown the cockle, are often a literal fact in the East. One man, out of revenge and ill-will, sows weeds in the field of another, thus rendering a good crop impossible for years. The Roman law even had provided for the case. It is thus that the Evil One does in the Church, which is the kingdom of God. Our Saviour sows only good seed, and He sows it openly, with care and labor; but the Evil One sows by night, quickly, and out of jealousy and envy. Evil is often quicker and more active than good.

### 3. WHAT THE FATE OF THE COCKLE WILL BE

It is very instructive to learn how men act with regard to the cockle, and what God does. Men, good men, the servants of the Master, see the cockle, wonder at it, will not tolerate it or suffer it to continue to grow, but wish to root it out immediately (Matt. 13:28). This is imprudent zeal, because such rooting out does more harm than good; it is impatience, which frets at the inconvenience and loss of tranquillity which living in company with evil involves; lastly, it is short-sightedness, which looks only at what lies nearest, only at itself and its immediate surroundings, and does not take a wide view nor look at God and the final end.

God acts otherwise. He does not like cockle, i.e. evil, He abhors it; yet He does not root it out immediately, but lets it grow up with the good seed. And why? First, for the sake of the cockle, the wicked. God has created man free, and free he shall remain. So He prefers to permit evil, the abuse of freedom, rather than abrogate this liberty. Further, the wicked can be converted, as long as this life lasts, and we do not know if their conversion will not yet take place, nor when. Secondly, God spares the cockle for the sake of the wheat, i.e. good men. These can gain by living together with the wicked, through patience, humility, and trust in God's Providence, and are thus proved and tried in every way. Life among the wicked is an excellent means to this end. Thirdly, God treats the wicked with such forbearance on His own account. His great world-plan is not overturned, altered or obstructed by their life and conduct. They are included in it like a dark woof, and only serve His Will. Thus the wisdom, the mercy and the power of God are at once revealed and glorified. God can bring good out of evil and thus justifies His tolerance of evil, even of heinous sin.

When the time of mercy has expired, God intervenes. The rooting out at the end of the world will indeed certainly come, the sifting by the angels will be exact and infallible, and the punishment terrible (Matt. 13:30, 39–42). The wicked will be gathered up like stalks by the reapers, bound in bundles and cast into the furnace of fire, where unspeakable anguish will be their portion, so that "weeping and gnashing of teeth" is but a mild term to express their misery and despair. On the other hand, the just will also receive their reward, and it will be a glorious one. As chosen sheaves of fine wheat they will be gathered by the holy angels, with reverence, care and joy, into the barns of the Heavenly Father (Matt. 13:30); and they will shine more gloriously than suns in the kingdom of God (Matt. 13:43).

The importance and significance of this parable consists, first, in its clear manifestation of the truth that the endeavors of the good will never succeed in creating a world which shall contain only what is good, a state of undisturbed peace and the rule of justice here below. There will always be cockle, i.e. scandal and contradiction. So it has always been, and so it always will be, for the above-named reasons. Secondly, the machinations of hell and of wicked men will succeed just as little in entirely rooting out the good from the Church and bringing about the sole sway of evil. Just as surely will good fruit always be found. This also is prophesied here. Lastly, all contrasts and apparent contradictions disappear in the one great end, the universal Judgment, with which this parable concludes. This is the first time that our Saviour gives us details as to the Last Judgment and the triumphant commencement of His eternal kingdom, the great end of all things. He first indicates the purpose of the Last Judgment for society at large, namely, to solve the enigma of the "scandals of His kingdom" (Matt. 13:41) and put an end to them for ever. Then He sketches in a few masterly outlines the course of this Judgment. All concomitant causes are mentioned, and the final result powerfully delineated. Whilst the burning bundles of the unhappy reprobate cast by their lurid glare a weird and terrible light upon the awful gulfs and dark pits of hell, filling them with dense vapors, and whilst their cries of rage rise from the abyss, the transfigured forms of the blessed enter above, shining like glorious suns, through the open gate of the eternal kingdom. In this parable we have the key to all the great disorders and scandals of the world and the Church, and light and consolation in all public afflictions.

### The Parable of the Fishing-net

MATT. 13:47. Again the kingdom of heaven is like to a net cast into the sea, and gathering together of all kinds of fishes.—48. Which, when it was filled, they drew out, and sitting by the shore they chose out the good into vessels, but the bad they cast forth.—49. So shall it be at the end of the world; the angels shall go out, and shall separate the wicked from among the just.—50. And shall cast them into the furnace of fire; there shall be weeping and gnashing of teeth.

The parable of the fishing-net has the same object as that of the cockle. For this reason it is placed immediately after the latter, from which it differs only in a few incidental circumstances, which shall be indicated here.

1. The kingdom of heaven, the Church, is here compared to a draw-net (Matt. 13:47), in which fish in great numbers and of various kinds are caught and drawn to land. The comparison is a good one, for three reasons. First, it is quite in keeping with the surroundings in which our Saviour found Himself at the time.

Probably He propounded this parable also on the sea-shore, and perhaps the listeners had before them the spectacle of just such a draught of fishes. Secondly, the comparison was also adapted to the previous calling of the Apostles, of whom several were fishers, as well as to their future vocation, according to which they were to be fishers of souls (Matt. 4:19). Thirdly, it is very well in keeping with the nature of the Church, which is a social union composed of all races and peoples, who, united by the same faith, the same Sacraments and the same governing power, together make for the shore of eternal happiness. The net signifies the comprehensiveness of faith and the Sacraments, especially Baptism, and is drawn and guided by the rulers of the Church.

2. In this society, then, there are good and bad members, just as there are good and bad fishes in the net (Matt. 13:48). The net is large and deep, catches and holds many, indeed the entire human race. There will be many indifferent, many who are dead in faith and morals, many hypocrites, who are rotten inwardly, but do not outwardly separate from the Church. The Church cannot look into the depths of the soul; she contents herself with requiring, as a condition of membership with her body, the sign, the name and the works of a Christian.

Attention is here called, then, to the existence of bad members. This is simply prophesied, as in the preceding parable; only with the difference that wrong and evil are not represented here as being introduced and caused by an exterior power, by Satan, but as arising from the frailty of our own nature. The evil here alluded to is interior decay.

3. The sorting and separation of the bad from the good is, however, as in the preceding parable, certain, and their lot final, bad for the wicked and full of honor for the good (Matt. 13:48–50). When the net is full, i.e. when the number of those called to the Church is completed, then the angels will draw the net to the shore and the sorting will begin. No one can deceive the eyes of the apparitors of divine justice. The fate of the wicked is delineated in the powerful metaphor of rotting fish, cast out, and fit only for the fire which finally consumes them. So a real Gehenna will be the portion of the wicked (Matt. 5:22). But the good will be kept for the joys of the heavenly banquet.

From this parable three powerful truths may be deduced for special reflection. First: God wishes to save all men. For this reason the net is so large and capacious; it takes in all who come within its range, and guides them with gentle force along the way of salvation. Secondly, the existence of bad members in the bosom of the Church is here emphasized. Everyone, therefore, must pay heed to himself. No one may content himself with mere outward communion with the Church. That does not suffice for salvation. Thirdly, however, it is nowhere said that the number of the wicked will be greater than that of the good.

With regard to our Saviour and His method of teaching, this very parable shows how He makes use of exterior and present circumstances for the basis of His lessons, and how He proposes the same truth in different figures and enlarges upon it by new features and additions. Herein are revealed the beauty and riches of His intellect and the practical and popular character of His mode of teaching.

## The Parable of the Treasure in the Field

Matt. 13:44. The kingdom of heaven is like unto a treasure hidden in a field; which a man having found, hid it, and for joy thereof goeth, and selleth all that he hath, and buyeth that field.

### 1. AIM OF THE PARABLE

The preceding parables contained prophecies concerning the characteristics and destiny of the Church. The two following show on the one hand the value of the Church and of her means of grace, and on the other the sentiments which all should entertain towards this treasure, which is likened to a jewel. Our Saviour first develops this in the parable of the treasure found in another man's field.

### 2. DEVELOPMENT OF THIS AIM IN THE PARABLE

There are three things of importance in the parable. The first is the treasure. According to the description it is a very valuable treasure, which makes the finder and possessor an exceedingly rich and happy man. This treasure denotes the Gospel and its aim (eternal bliss), with the means to attain it (faith and grace), in short all the great and glorious blessings which it offers us for time and eternity. This is certainly a great and glorious treasure, all the more precious that everything about it is supernatural, indiscoverable and unattainable by all the efforts of nature. In this sense the treasure is really hidden. God alone can put us upon its track, by His grace.

Secondly, there is the field in which it is buried. According to an ancient right, hidden treasure belongs to the proprietor of the place in which it is found. Whoever therefore wishes legally to acquire it, must purchase the ground in which it lies. Now the treasure of the Gospel, of faith, grace and the true Sacraments, is only to be found in the Church. Whoever therefore would possess it, must "purchase" the Church, that is, join the Church and become one of her members. But this is often just the difficulty.

On this account our Saviour adds an important point, viz. how the treasure is to be acquired. Before all things, with speed. The finder of the treasure "goes," our Lord says, for a delay, even a short one, might prevent him from obtaining the field and the treasure. The Church and all that she offers us is a grace, and life is short and uncertain. Further, the field must be acquired with determination, eagerness and generosity. "He selleth all that he hath" for the field and the treasure. It is worth all this, and more. Lastly, the field is bought joyfully. All trouble and all sacrifices for the prize are abundantly rewarded by the greatness and value of the treasure.

### 3. APPLICATION OF THE PARABLE

The application is obvious. Whoever wishes to possess the treasure of the Gospel, the comfort of its truths, the fruit of the Sacraments and the right to hope for eternal life, must become a member of the Catholic Church, in which Christ has deposited all this. She alone is the saving Church, because she alone offers us the means of salvation.

This may under certain circumstances involve a great sacrifice, and cost not only possessions and position, but even life itself. Yet even at this price the field must be acquired. The treasure is great and glorious enough to indemnify us for all this. It brings us honor, enriches us, comforts us, and offers us all that we can wish for our happiness here below and in eternity. How many have lost the treasure through indecision and delay! The Jews learnt from our Saviour and the Apostles the greatness of its worth; they were offered it, but delayed to take possession of it, and lo! the Gentiles came and took it away first.

Let him who already possesses this treasure guard it, rejoice, thank God with all his heart, and utilize it to merit eternal life.

## The Parable of the Pearl of Great Price

MATT. 13:45. Again the kingdom of heaven is like to a merchant seeking good pearls.—46. Who, when he had found one pearl of great price, went his way, and sold all that he had, and bought it.

The meaning of this parable is the same as that of the preceding one. The pearl signifies the Gospel and what it offers, especially grace, truth and Christian perfection, and that we may gain these our Saviour incites us to seek this precious possession and make it our own. There are however a few points which distinguish this parable from the former, and which are especially applicable to the religious state. We will therefore develop this application of the parable, with reference to the essential character of this state, its acquirement and the use we make of it.

### 1. VALUE AND COSTLINESS OF THE PEARL

The value and costliness of a pearl depend, first, upon the pure and unblemished quality of its substance and the entirety of its form; secondly, upon its beauty and luster, which delight those who gaze at it; lastly, upon the ease and convenience of keeping it and upon its value to the possessor for use or ornament.

In all this the excellence of the religious state is beautifully delineated. This excellence consists in evangelical perfection, the acquirement of which is the object, essence and result of the religious state. But perfection is something pure and unblemished, to which nothing is wanting. This perfection is to be found abundantly in this state, which embraces all that is contained in the Gospel, precepts and counsels, matters which are of obligation and those which are of choice. It is the entire Gospel, with all its stages of development. Perfection means, secondly, luster and beauty, because it excludes the state of sin and includes the splendor of grace and virtues, particularly love, in which perfection especially consists; perfect love, the love of supererogation, because it does more than it is obliged to do, not contenting itself with obeying the commandments, but passes on to the observance of the counsels. Thus the religious state is resplendent with the luster and beauty of love, and love is the perfection of Christian wisdom. Lastly, perfection may be borne easily and without trouble, because it is a spiritual possession; because it presupposes love, the noblest and freest flight of the will; and because it frees life from all earthly possessions and burdensome cares concerning them. As the possession of a precious pearl often represents a whole fortune, and this pearl is yet easy to carry, so the religious has his whole fortune in his poverty; it clothes, feeds, and provides for him for time and eternity better than any perishable riches. Thus the religious state is really a pearl in its value, beauty and convenience; yes, it is the real evangelical pearl, because it includes in itself all that is most beautiful and sublime in the Gospel.

## 2. THE ACQUISITION OF THE PEARL

What our Saviour says of the acquisition of the pearl is also especially applicable to the choice and embracing of the religious state. In the former parable we are not told how the finder arrived at the discovery of the treasure; but here our Saviour observes that the merchant went out to "seek" precious pearls. It is easier to estimate the value of a treasure of glittering coins than to judge of pearls. So also more divine enlightenment and supernatural discrimination is requisite to estimate the value of the pearl of evangelical perfection in the religious state than to know the Church and the Gospel in general; and more determination and strength of will is needed to bind oneself to the observance of the counsels than to keep the commandments, because the former are optional and require a higher degree of striving after virtue. For this reason our Saviour says in another passage: "If thou *wilt* be perfect" (Matt. 19:21). To embrace perfection is the work of a high mind, a decided and courageous will, and a wise estimation of the things of earth and of heaven.

Further, our Saviour says that the merchant, when he had found the good pearl, gave all that he had to buy it (Matt. 13:46). This is true in an especial sense of the embracing of the religious state. The condition is the renunciation of all that we have: our exterior goods by poverty, the interior and intellectual by obedience, and bodily pleasures by chastity.

## 3. THE USE OF THE PEARL

One must be willing to sacrifice much, indeed everything, in order to acquire the pearl. But the possession of it repays all, by the use which may be made of it for pleasure, ornament and support. The religious state brings unalloyed joy and happiness in life; it offers the greatest advantages for the acquisition of virtues and merits; and finally it provides for us not only in time, but also in eternity. Heaven itself is promised as the reward, with its special privileges, honors and joys (Matt. 19:29).

Blessed is the man, therefore, who is in possession of this pearl. Let him not regret the price he has paid for it. Let him rather thank God for having inspired him with the thought of beginning to seek the pearl. This very desire is a great and gratuitous grace. Our Saviour has given us the knowledge of this jewel and made it possible for us to acquire it. Let everyone then who has this treasure rejoice in its possession, and make use of it for his own benefit and for the glory of God.

## OUR LORD'S RELATIVES SEEK HIM AND ARE TURNED AWAY

MARK 3:20. And they come to a house; and the multitude cometh together again, so that they could not so much as eat bread.—21. And when his friends had heard of it, they went out to lay hold on him; for they said: "He is become mad."—. . . 31. And his mother and his brethren came, and standing without sent unto him calling him.—32. And the multitude sat about him; and they say to him: "Behold thy mother and thy brethren without seek for thee."—33. And answering them, he said: "Who is my mother and my brethren?"—34. And looking round about on them who sat about him, he saith: "Behold my mother and my brethren.—35. For whosoever shall do the will of God, he is my brother and my sister and mother."

MATT. 12:46. As he was yet speaking to the multitudes, behold his mother and his brethren stood without, seeking to speak to him.—47. And one said unto him: "Behold thy mother and thy brethren stand without, seeking thee."—48. But he answering him that told him, said: "Who is my mother, and who are my brethren?" —49. And stretching forth his hand towards his disciples, he said: "Behold my mother and my brethren.—50. For whosoever shall do the will of my Father that is in heaven, he is my brother, and sister, and mother."

LUKE 8:19. And his mother and brethren came unto him; and they could not come at him for the crowd.—20. And it was told him: "Thy mother and thy brethren stand without, desiring to see thee."—21. Who answering, said to them: "My mother and my brethren are they who hear the word of God, and do it."

Our Saviour was again in Capharnaum, in His (or rather Peter's) own house, and was one day teaching in the midst of such a concourse of people that all the entries to the house were blocked up, and no one could approach Him (Mark 3:20). While He was speaking, the Mother of Jesus and His "brethren" (probably cousins or other relatives on His Mother's or St. Joseph's side) appeared at the house and desired to speak with Him.

### 1. INTENTION OF THE RELATIVES IN PAYING HIM THIS VISIT

According to St. Mark (3:20) these relatives or friends did not come with a good intention or for the honor of our Saviour. They came in order to lay hold on Him, because (as they said) He was "mad." If this was really meant in earnest, they did not believe in Him, as St. John later on remarks of them or of other relatives (John 7:5); and in spite of all the many and great miracles which He now worked, their former familiar intercourse with Jesus and the obscurity under which He had veiled His Divinity became a stumbling-block to them. Faith is a grace. But perhaps this reason for their proceeding was only a pretext to put Him and themselves in security against the enmity of the Pharisees, who, according to St. Mark (3:22), were pressing upon Him with cruel energy. It is very possible also that the Pharisees intimidated His relatives and friends, and threatened them with punishment if they did not take measures to withdraw Him from public life. Or perhaps the relatives themselves feared lest our Lord should allow Himself to be led into some fatal step by the enthusiastic crowd; perhaps, too, they did not like to see Him leave His Mother thus alone, and therefore wished to recall Him to His duty towards her. At all events these relatives were actuated by very paltry, selfish, worldly and unworthy thoughts and intentions.

We need scarcely say that nothing of this kind applies to our Saviour's holy Mother. She was probably compelled by the other relatives to accompany them, in order to give more effect to their words. Perhaps, also, she did so with the intention of acting as mediator and restraining them from violent measures; or perhaps she wished to speak with our Lord once more after a long absence. It is indeed very doubtful whether those relatives of whom St. Mark speaks in verse 21 are the same as those mentioned in verse 31. Probably these are two separate incidents, which have here been combined into one.

However that may be, the behavior of these relatives must have been both painful and humiliating to our Lord, and should serve to excite our compassion for Him under this annoyance.

### 2. OUR SAVIOUR'S REPLY TO THE PROPOSAL OF HIS RELATIVES

On account of the multitude of people who surrounded our Saviour and crowded the house, His relatives could not approach Him. They sent, therefore, asking Him to come out to them (Mark 3:31, 32; Matt. 12:47). And what does our Saviour do?

Perhaps those who brought Him the message thought it would give Him great pleasure. But our Lord does not at first pay the slightest attention to the announcement, and continues His address, so that those around Him had to remind Him again that His Mother and relatives were standing before the house and wished to speak to Him (Mark 3:32).

As our Lord's attention is again called to the fact, fully conscious though He is of the unworthy motives of His relatives, He shows no anger at their baseness, which must have seemed so despicable to Him, and caused much pain to His Heart.

Thirdly, being pressed to give a reply, He rejects their proposal in an infinitely dignified and touching manner, saying: "Who is My Mother, and who are My brethren?" He looked, in saying this, at those who sat near Him (Mark 3:34), and stretched out His hand towards His disciples, saying: "Behold My mother and My brethren" (Matt. 12:49). Whoever hears the Word of God, and does it (Luke 8:21), and whoever does "the Will of My Father, that is in heaven, he is My brother, and sister, and mother" (Matt. 12:50; Mark 3:35). By this declaration our Saviour certainly does not deny His blood-relationship with His kinsfolk. He only solemnly affirms, first, that His closest relationship is that with His Father in heaven, and that the Will of this Heavenly Father is His rule and guide in all things; secondly, that He is bound next to those with whom, according to His Father's Will, He has to occupy Himself, viz. His disciples and the souls of men, and that no consideration for mere blood-relationship can be a reason to desist from apostolic work for souls, after He has once in accordance with the Will of His Father devoted Himself to it; thirdly, that He even regards as His kinsfolk those who are near and dear to His Father on account of their fulfilment of His Will, which consists in hearing and doing the Word of God. It is almost the same reply as He once gave to His earthly parents, when they sought Him and found Him in the Temple (Luke 2:49), and as that which He gave later on to the woman who called Mary "blessed" on account of her blood-relationship to Him (Luke 11:28). He means to say that a mere connection by blood, without spiritual relationship through faith and holiness, will not avail to obtain the salvation He has come to give and for which He is laboring.

### 3. IMPORTANCE AND SIGNIFICANCE OF THE ANSWER

The answer of our Lord has a twofold importance and significance. In the first place our Saviour gives us some important lessons. He shows us that we must be ready to endure all kinds of unpleasantnesses, misunderstandings and injuries, even from those who are near and dear to us. Who could have expected that our Lord would be considered by His relatives to be overwrought, deranged in mind, and in need of being recalled to reason and moderation? And yet He includes this also in the plan of His sufferings. Further, the proverb is again confirmed, that an apostle meets with the least success among His own people. Lastly, our Saviour teaches us how earnestly we must adhere to God, serve Him, and prefer His Will to all else. The words here spoken by Jesus once more afford us a glimpse of His Divine Heart, of His boundless reverence and love for God, and show us how all things, even the tenderest and dearest ties, give place and vanish before this love. With these words, also, He again bears witness to His Divinity.

Secondly, our Saviour offers us in this mystery a great consolation and encouragement. He shows us the way to draw close to His Heart and become truly dear to Him, namely, by loving God above all else and accepting and obeying His Will, especially in the apostolic vocation. He looked at the Apostles first, and pointed to them. They are now His nearest and dearest family. And how did Mary take these words? Certainly she was not hurt at them. On the contrary, she well understood them. She was still the nearest to Him, because no one obeyed God's Will so perfectly as she, and she rejoiced with all her heart that means of being near to our Lord and sharing in her joy and honor were offered to us also. We must thank our Saviour with all our hearts for this beautiful and important lesson. It reveals to us the true and deep-rooted attachment and gratitude of His Heart to the souls who faithfully obey God and entirely submit to Him. How dear, then, these words ought to be to us! What must we not do and be ready to do, in order to be numbered among our Lord's beloved relatives! And now that He has made the condition so simple and easy, who would not gladly do his utmost in order to obtain this honor?

## THE STILLING OF THE STORM ON THE LAKE

LUKE 8:22. And it came to pass on a certain day that he went into a little ship with his disciples, and he said to them: "Let us go over to the other side of the lake." And they launched forth.—23. And when they were sailing, he slept; and there came down a storm of wind upon the lake, and they were filled, and were in danger.—24. And they came and awaked him, saying: "Master, we perish."

But he arising, rebuked the wind and the rage of the water, and it ceased; and there was a calm.—25. And he said to them: "Where is your faith?" Who being afraid, wondered, saying one to another: "Who is this (think you), that he commandeth both the winds and the sea, and they obey him?"

MATT. 8:23. And when he entered into the boat, his disciples followed him; —24. And behold a great tempest arose in the sea, so that the boat was covered with waves, but he was asleep.—25. And his disciples came to him and awaked him, saying: "Lord, save us, we perish."—26. And Jesus saith to them: "Why are you fearful, O ye of little faith?" Then rising up, he commanded the winds and the sea, and there came a great calm.—27. But the men wondered, saying: "What manner of man is this, for the winds and the sea obey him?"

MARK 4:35. And he saith to them that day, when evening was come: "Let us pass over to the other side."—36. And sending away the multitude, they take him even as he was in the ship; and there were other ships with him.—37. And there arose a great storm of wind, and the waves beat into the ship, so that the ship was filled.—38. And he was in the hinder part of the ship, sleeping upon a pillow: and they awake him, and say to him: "Master, doth it not concern thee that we perish?"—39. And rising up he rebuked the wind, and said to the sea: "Peace, be still." And the wind ceased; and there was made a great calm.—40. And he said to them: "Why are you fearful? have you not faith yet?" And they feared exceedingly, and they said one to another: "Who is this, thinkest thou, that both wind and sea obey him?"

## 1. MOTIVE OF THE PASSAGE ACROSS THE LAKE

It seems to have been on this occasion that our Saviour, late in the evening, ordered the Apostles to cross over to the east shore of the lake (Mark 4:35; Luke 8:22). And why? All the Evangelists remark that an unusually great multitude of people had been gathered round our Saviour during the day. But He avoided leaving His disciples long at the same place, in the company of a crowd of people. Thus caution and prudence seem to have been the first motives of this order. Further, as the sequel of the mystery shows, He may perhaps have been tired and in need of rest. A passage by night across the lake would give an opportunity for taking some rest, and would have the further advantage of gaining time. In the morning He could begin His work again on the opposite coast. Lastly, our Saviour wishes to accustom His Apostles to work much and hard, to try their faith by the storm, and to form and train them in their vocation by the miracle. The stilling of the storm is the second of the so-called "miracles of the sea," which are worked principally for the sake of the Apostles. Such may probably have been the reasons of His order to cross over.

The Apostles obeyed this order promptly and willingly (Luke 8:22; Matt. 8:23), although it must have been a disagreeable one for several reasons, since it was after a hard day's work and at the approach of night, and especially if they could see the approach of the storm. Our Lord's little ship was accompanied by other vessels (Mark 4:36). During the passage He rested and slept, leaning His head upon a pillow (Mark 4:38), probably in a kind of little cabin in the stern of the ship. This sleep of our Lord's was quite a natural one, probably the effect of His weariness, and it is a proof of the reality of His human nature.

## 2. THE STORM AND THE WONDERFUL MANNER IN WHICH IT WAS STILLED

During the passage a violent storm arose. We need not reject the assumption that this storm may have had a supernatural origin, yet such an explanation is not necessary. The lake lies, as is well-known, below the level of the Mediterranean Sea, and the heat in its basin is very great in summer. On the east coast the lake is surrounded by steep heights, cleft by deep ravines, through which (especially in the evening after a hot day) wild hurricanes often burst over the lake, from the plateau behind and from the north side. Our Saviour, therefore, may have permitted a storm of this kind to arise in quite a natural manner; and the tempest must have been a violent one, for the waves broke over the little ship (Matt. 8:24), it was filling with water (Mark 4:37), and they were in real danger (Luke 8:23) of either sinking or being dashed upon the coast.

And how did the Apostles behave? Of course they did everything in their power to keep their little ship afloat. But as the danger became more and more threatening, they lost courage and thought there was only one expedient, viz. to wake our Saviour. This then they did in great agitation, crying: "Master, doth it not concern Thee that we perish?" (Mark 4:38.) "Save us, we perish!" (Matt. 8:25; Luke 8:24.) The imperfection of this conduct did not consist exactly in their trembling and thinking that they could not weather the storm in the natural course of things, but in thinking that our Lord could help them only if He were awake. In this lay a want of lively and perfect faith; indeed, there is almost a tone of distrust or petulance in their query, if it did not concern Him that they were perishing.

And what, on the other hand, is our Saviour's behavior? He sleeps quietly on, even in the midst of the violent storm (Matt. 8:24). He was perfect master of His natural senses, and could make them really sleep even in the midst of the noise of the storm.

This, as it appears, He did in this case, and for a good reason. But as the Apostles awaken Him, He rises and reproves them, not for their anxiety, which was involuntary and well-founded, but for their faint-heartedness and want of faith. "Why are you fearful, O ye of little faith?" (Matt. 8:26.) "Where is your faith?" (Luke 8:25.) "Have you not faith yet?" (Mark 4:40.) This, then, was their fault. Nevertheless our Lord looked out upon the storm and the waves, and said: "Peace, be still" (Mark 4:39). He rebuked the wind and the waves, and there was a great calm in the atmosphere and on the lake (Matt. 8:26; Luke 8:24). By this one command He did two things: He stilled the wind, and brought a sudden smoothness and calm upon the water, which ordinarily would remain agitated for several hours after the wind ceased.

### 3. EFFECT OF THE MIRACLE

This great miracle filled all present with wonder and astonishment (Matt. 8:27; Luke 8:25), and above all with awe at the nearness of the Godhead. This vivid perception of God's nearness is forcibly expressed in the words of the Apostles and the crew of the ship: "Who is this, that He commandeth both the winds and the sea, and they obey Him?" (Matt. 8:27; Mark 4:40; Luke 8:25.) This seems like an allusion to the passages in the Psalms (Ps. 88:10; 106:25–29) in which God's omnipotence is portrayed in the description of His rule over the sea. The words are equivalent to an acknowledgment of Christ's Divinity.

This was the result that our Saviour desired to effect by the miracle: to confirm and perfect the faith of the Apostles in His Divinity, and through this faith to strengthen them against the exterior difficulties of their vocation. By the miracle of the draught of fishes our Lord strengthened St. Peter and the other Apostles against distrust and despondency in the interior difficulties of this vocation, difficulties which arose from the realization of their own insufficiency and impotence, in face of the greatness and importance of the Apostolic office. Here He arms them against the exterior difficulties, which consist in persecutions from without. For this reason the holy Fathers usually interpret this mystery with reference to the persecutions of the Church, which is the bark of Peter.

Taking this interpretation we may learn the two following lessons. First: persecutions will never be lacking to the Church and the Apostles. The reasons are as follows. In the first place, the natural contrast of the Christian doctrine will always excite the hatred of the world. Further, the Church must show herself to be the work of God by standing the test of difficulties. Then also persecutions are foretold in the prophecies, and by the destiny of Christ Himself. Lastly, they have as a matter of fact never been lacking to the Church. There will always be persecutions. Secondly: these persecutions do no harm and are overcome, whether Christ sleeps or wakes and stills the storm, i.e. whether He helps the Church by imperceptible or by perceptible intervention; He will help and save her. As little as a God could perish in the inland lake of Genesareth, just as little will the Church of God be overpowered by outward persecutions.

These lessons are applicable in their due degree to everyone. Individuals also must suffer storms and persecutions, and for the same reasons. But these storms may be overcome under the same conditions. We must before all things have our Saviour in the ship, sleeping or waking; i.e. we must be in the Church and in the state of grace, and we must steer with the helm of obedience or of Divine Providence; we must further be active, bestir ourselves and do what we can to keep afloat in the storm; lastly, we must place firm confidence in our Lord. Thus it will come about that no storm will hurt us. For persons who are in the state of grace all storms and tempests are but opportunities to prove their trust in God.

## OUR SAVIOUR IN GERASA

MARK 5:1. And they came over the strait of the sea into the country of the Gerasens.—2. And as he went out of the ship, immediately there met him out of the monuments a man with an unclean spirit,—3. Who had his dwelling in the tombs, and no man now could bind him even with chains;—4. For having been often bound with fetters and chains, he had burst the chains and broken the fetters in pieces, and no one could tame him.—5. And he was always day and night in the monuments and in the mountains, crying and cutting himself with stones. —6. And seeing Jesus afar off, he ran and adored him;—7. And crying with a loud voice, he said: "What have I to do with thee, Jesus, the Son of the most high God? I adjure thee by God that thou torment me not."—8. For he said unto him: "Go out of the man, thou unclean spirit."—9. And he asked him: "What is thy name?" And he saith to him: "My name is Legion, for we are many."—10. And he besought him much, that he would not drive him away out of the country. —11. And there was near the mountain a great herd of swine feeding.—12. And the spirits besought him, saying: "Send us into the swine, that we may enter into them."—13. And Jesus immediately gave them leave. And the unclean spirits going out entered into the swine; and the herd with great violence was carried headlong into the sea, being about two thousand, and were stifled in the sea.—14.

And they that fed them fled, and told it in the city and in the fields. And they went out to see what was done;—15. And they come to Jesus, and they see him that was troubled with the devil, sitting clothed and well in his wits, and they were afraid.—16. And they that had seen it, told them in what manner he had been dealt with who had the devil, and concerning the swine.—17. And they began to pray him that he would depart from their coasts.

LUKE 8:26. And they sailed to the country of the Gerasens, which is over against Galilee.—27. And when he was come forth to the land, there met him a certain man who had a devil now a very long time, and he wore no clothes, neither did he abide in a house, but in the sepulchers.—28. And when he saw Jesus, he fell down before him; and crying out with a loud voice, he said: "What have I to do with thee, Jesus, Son of the most high God? I beseech thee, do not torment me."—29. For he commanded the unclean spirit to go out of the man. For many times it seized him, and he was bound with chains, and kept in fetters; and breaking the bonds he was driven by the devil into the deserts.—30. And Jesus asked him, saying: "What is thy name?" But he said: "Legion"; because many devils were entered into him.—31. And they besought him that he would not command them to go into the abyss.—32. And there was a herd of many swine feeding on the mountain; and they besought him that he would suffer them to enter into them. And he suffered them.—33. The devils therefore went out of the man and entered into the swine; and the herd ran violently down a steep place into the lake, and was stifled. —34. Which when they that fed them saw done, they fled, and told it in the city and in the villages.—35. And they went out to see what was done, and they came to Jesus; and found the man out of whom the devils were departed sitting at his feet, clothed and in his right mind, and they were afraid.—36. And they also that had seen told them how he had been healed from the legion;—37. And all the multitude of the country of the Gerasens besought him to depart from them; for they were taken with great fear. And he going up into the ship, returned back again.—38. Now the man, out of whom the devils were departed, besought him that he might be with him. But Jesus sent him away, saying:—39. "Return to thy house, and tell how great things God hath done to thee." And he went through the whole city, publishing how great things Jesus had done to him.

MATT. 8:28. And when he was come on the other side of the water, into the country of the Gerasens, there met him two that were possessed with devils, coming out of the sepulchers, exceeding fierce, so that no one could pass by that way. —29. And behold they cried out, saying: "What have we to do with thee, Jesus, Son of God? Art thou come hither to torment us before the time?"—30. And there was not far from them a herd of many swine feeding.—31. And the devils besought him, saying: "If thou cast us out hence, send us into the herd of swine." —32. And he said to them: "Go." But they going out went into the swine, and behold the whole herd ran violently down a steep place into the sea; and they perished in the waters.—33. And they that kept them fled; and coming into the city, told everything, and concerning them that had been possessed by the devils.—34. And behold the whole city went out to meet Jesus; and when they saw him, they besought him that he would depart from their coasts.

After the lake had grown calm, the little ship steered straight for the country of the Gerasens (Luke 8:26). In the neighborhood of ancient Gamala, in the little plain which lies between the lake and the heights beyond, there are still to be seen the ruins of a town called Kersa, where there is a very steep slope down to the lake on the south side. The district belonged to the so-called

Decapolis (cf. Introd., p. 2), the population of which chiefly consisted of Gentiles. Immediately upon our Saviour's landing, and probably in a kind of narrow defile or ravine between the rocks, in which sepulchers were hewn (Matt. 8:28; Mark 5:2), two demoniacs ran to meet Him. St. Matthew mentions two, SS. Mark and Luke only one, probably because this was the fiercer and more notorious of the two, and because he afterwards wished to follow our Saviour (Mark 5:18; Luke 8:38).

### 1. OUR SAVIOUR'S BEHAVIOR TOWARDS THE EVIL SPIRITS

In this meeting with the demoniacs we see very truly revealed the spirit of the demons on the one hand, and the character of our Saviour on the other.

Our Saviour sets foot for the first time upon real heathen territory, which is in a special sense the kingdom of Satan, the prince of this world. No wonder that the spirit of darkness exerts his terrible despotism here especially, and fully displays his malignity in the demoniacs. The evil spirits manifest above all things their weird, dark, and unclean character. They are unclean spirits (Mark 5:2), they love the solitary places among the sepulchers (Matt. 8:28; Mark 5:3), for death and the grave are the stronghold of Satan; they leave the demoniacs no clothes (Luke 8:27). Secondly, they manifest here their number and power. They are present by thousands, a legion (Luke 8:30; Mark 5:9, 13); and they actually take possession subsequently of two thousand swine. Their power shows itself in terrible manifestations. Nothing can control the demoniacs; they break their fetters in pieces, rave, cut themselves with stones, and make the whole district dangerous, so that no one ventures to pass by (Matt. 8:28; Luke 8:29; Mark 5:3, 4, 5); they destroy a whole herd in a few moments (Matt. 8:32; Mark 5:13; Luke 8:33).[1] The malice also of the fallen spirits is shown in the demoniacs. They are in truth evil spirits, and can only do evil and effect injury. If they cannot do harm to men, they go to the animals, and very probably their intention in so doing is to make our Lord odious to the Gerasens, and thus to render His intended ministry among them impossible (Luke 8:31, 32; Mark 5:10, 12; Matt. 8:31). Their falsehood and untruthfulness is also manifested, that is if they did not know with

---

[1] Others are of opinion that the swine rushed into the abyss of their own accord, because otherwise the devils would have been depriving themselves of their own new dwelling.

certainty that He was the Son of God. They call Him so (Matt. 8:29; Mark 5:7; Luke 8:28), in order that He may not compel them to go out of the demoniacs and quit the district (Mark 5:10) and, indeed, this earth (Luke 8:31). Lastly, the devils display all their weakness and impotence. Instead of obstructing our Lord's path and threatening Him, they approach, cast themselves at His feet, whine like beaten dogs, and entreat and adjure Him "by God" (Mark 5:7) not to send them "into the abyss" (Luke 8:31) or "torment" them (Matt. 8:29; Luke 8:28). As it appears, the fallen spirits have more freedom here on earth than in hell, whither they will be banished after the Judgment (II Peter 2:4; Jude 6), and where they are grievously oppressed by Lucifer. What sad and awful glimpses all this affords us of the nature, the doings, and the unspeakable misery of the Satanic kingdom!

On the other hand, how magnificently and gloriously the majesty and power of our Saviour are revealed! He enters Satan's kingdom, and His mere appearance overcomes the resistance and disarms the power of the evil spirits. By their trembling fear and abject entreaties, they acknowledge Him to be their absolute Lord and Judge. He questions them (Luke 8:30; Mark 5:9), decides their fate, and expels them with a word. They beg and pray only for a less severe sentence. And it is not one devil here, but thousands of them, as they themselves acknowledge.

## 2. OUR SAVIOUR'S BEHAVIOR TOWARDS THE GERASENS

Our Saviour granted the request of the evil spirits to be allowed to enter into the swine belonging to the Gerasens, which were feeding upon the heights close by in great herds (Mark 5:11, 12, 13; Luke 8:32, 33). The devils then immediately took possession of the swine, and the animals rushed in wild precipitation down the slope into the lake, where about 2,000 of them were drowned. Why did our Saviour allow this? There can be no question of wrong if the swine ran into the water of their own accord; and if not, we must remember that the God-Man is also Lord of the visible creation. But He seldom made use of this right. In this case, at all events, the deliverance of a human being from the bondage of Satan was worth more than the lives of these animals and the loss which their destruction entailed. Our Lord reveals here, therefore, the value of a soul. Perhaps the granting of the request of the evil spirits was a punishment upon the Gerasens, whether these latter were Jews or Gentiles. If they were Jews, they were not allowed to eat of these animals, and therefore not to keep them; if Gentiles, they were probably a cause of offence and a scandal to the Jews; and, as it seems, they needed to be roused from their undue care for temporal goods, and admonished to think of what is spiritual and supernatural.

And how do the Gerasens behave? Called to the spot by the drovers of the herds, who fled in haste to the town and all over the district with the news, they came in great crowds, and convinced themselves of the wonderful fact by the evidence of their own eyes and the narration of those who had witnessed it (Matt. 8:34; Mark 5:14–17; Luke 8:34–37). Instead of either taking up a hostile attitude to our Lord, or else on the other hand submitting to Him in faith and receiving Him, they are seized by terror and fear, and beg Him to leave their district. It was neither a childlike nor yet a slavish fear which led them to act thus, but rather the thoroughly worldly spirit which only knows, esteems and loves temporal goods, and feels nothing but fear and dismay when it comes in contact with anything higher and supernatural, which would disturb it in its quiet enjoyment of what is earthly. Our Lord seemed to them full of mystery, and they feared still greater temporal injury. On this account they declined His further sojourn with them. And our Lord went away and took ship again.

### 3. OUR SAVIOUR'S BEHAVIOR TOWARDS ONE OF THE DEMONIACS

It is a beautiful and touching sight to see, as the terrified Gerasens draw near, the one demoniac (as it appears, the more infuriated of the two) sitting at the feet of Jesus, quiet, reasonable, clothed, and freed from his horrible guest (Mark 5:15; Luke 8:35). This is the picture of the rescued lamb in the arms of the Good Shepherd. What a change from a few hours ago! Who does not think of the words: "Come to Me, all you that labor and are burdened . . . and you shall find rest. . . . My yoke is sweet and My burden light" (Matt. 11:28–30)? How incomparably lighter is the yoke of Jesus than that of Satan! The poor man begs our Lord now, at His departure, to take him with Him and allow him to remain with Him (Mark 5:18; Luke 8:38). It is better to be with our Lord than in the dwellings of sinners (Ps. 83:11).

But our Saviour did not allow this (Mark 5:19; Luke 8:39),

probably because the man was a Gentile, and our Lord's mission was to the "sheep of Israel" (Matt. 15:24); then, too, the demoniac's conversion was too recent, and his past life by no means calculated to fit him for the Apostolate. The Jews would have scorned him and made a scandal out of the fact of our Lord's constant intercourse with him. But our Saviour commissioned the healed man to be His apostle in Decapolis, and to proclaim to all what great things He had done to him (Luke 8:39; Mark 5:19). And the former demoniac faithfully fulfilled the charge (Mark 5:20).

Our Saviour evidently wished by this manifestation of divine power to give His disciples a new and convincing proof that He was God and the absolute Lord of the earth and the lower world. This proof was, as it were, the powerful answer to the question of the Apostles at the stilling of the storm,—who this was who commanded the wind and waves. It is instructive to observe this first appearance of our Saviour upon heathen territory. By the very fact of His setting foot upon it, He announces Himself at once as the Heir and Redeemer of all nations, the heathens included, and as the Master of the prince of the world. It is, as it were, a first blow at heathenism and an act of violence done to it, since He overpowers and passes sentence upon its lord. Hell cannot maintain its dominion against Him. It does homage to Him and confesses His power in a most striking manner. Our Lord so disposes matters that His appearance takes the form of a glorious proclamation of His power and Divinity, through the assertion of the evil spirits, their expulsion, the destruction of the herds, the great crowd of witnesses, and the confession of the freed men. Thus our Saviour announces Himself in person in the land of the Gentiles. Heathenism itself does not here act in a manner hostile to Him; it only draws back, embarrassed and perplexed. Our Lord does not exercise any compulsion upon it. He contents Himself for the present with rousing and frightening the people out of their thoughtlessness and their slavery to earthly desires, and out of the bondage of hell. He then retires, but does not forsake them. He calls and appoints for them an apostle from out their own midst, and comes again later on with renewed proofs of His divine power (Mark 7:31).

## The Woman Who Had an Issue of Blood

LUKE 8:40. And it came to pass that when Jesus was returned, the multitude received him; for they were all waiting for him.—41. And behold there came a man whose name was Jairus, and he was a ruler of the synagogue; and he fell down at the feet of Jesus, beseeching him that he would come into his house.—42. For he had an only daughter almost twelve years old, and she was dying. And it happened as he went that he was thronged by the multitudes.—43. And there was a certain woman having an issue of blood twelve years, who had bestowed all her substance on physicians, and could not be healed by any;—44. She came behind him and touched the hem of his garment; and immediately the issue of her blood stopped.—45. And Jesus said: "Who is it that touched me?" And all denying, Peter and they that were with him said: "Master, the multitudes throng and press thee, and dost thou say: Who touched me?"—46. And Jesus said: "Somebody hath touched me; for I know that virtue is gone out from me."—47. And the woman seeing that she was not hid, came trembling and fell down before his feet; and declared before all the people for what cause she had touched him, and how she was immediately healed.—48. But he said to her: "Daughter, thy faith hath made thee whole; go thy way in peace."

MARK 5:21. And when Jesus had passed again in the ship over the strait, a great multitude assembled together unto him, and he was nigh unto the sea.—22. And there cometh one of the rulers of the synagogue named Jairus; and seeing him, falleth down at his feet.—23. And he besought him much, saying: "My daughter is at the point of death; come, lay thy hand upon her, that she may be safe and may live."—24. And he went with him; and a great multitude followed him, and they thronged him.—25. And a woman who was under an issue of blood twelve years,—26. And had suffered many things from many physicians, and had spent all that she had, and was nothing the better, but rather worse;—27. When she had heard of Jesus, came in the crowd behind him, and touched his garment;—28. For she said: "If I shall touch but his garment, I shall be whole."—29. And forthwith the fountain of her blood was dried up; and she felt in her body that she was healed of the evil.—30. And immediately Jesus knowing in himself the virtue that had proceeded from him, turning to the multitude, said: "Who hath touched my garments?"—31. And his disciples said to him: "Thou seest the multitude thronging thee, and sayest thou: Who hath touched me?"—32. And he looked about to see her who had done this.—33. But the woman fearing and trembling, knowing what was done in her, came and fell down before him, and told him all the truth.—34. And he said to her: "Daughter, thy faith hath made thee whole; go in peace, and be thou whole of thy disease."

MATT. 9:18. As he was speaking these things unto them, behold a certain ruler came up and adored him, saying: "Lord, my daughter is even now dead; but come, lay thy hand upon her, and she shall live."—19. And Jesus rising up followed him, with his disciples.—20. And behold a woman who was troubled with an issue of blood twelve years, came behind him and touched the hem of his garment.—21. For she said within herself: "If I shall touch only his garment, I shall be healed."—22. But Jesus turning and seeing her, said: "Be of good heart, daughter, thy faith hath made thee whole." And the woman was made whole from that hour.

### 1. CIRCUMSTANCES LEADING UP TO THE MIRACLE

Having returned from the east coast of the lake, our Lord landed again in the vicinity of Capharnaum, where a multitude of people already awaited Him (perhaps the same who had been there on the previous day); and, as it seems, He at once began to teach (Mark 5:21; Luke 8:40).

While He was speaking, a man named Jairus, one of the three rulers who had to superintend the arrangements of the synagogue and to appoint and supervise the order of divine worship, came to our Saviour with the earnest entreaty that He would come to his little dying daughter, lay His hands upon her and heal her. At this request our Lord at once set out towards the town, and the walk thither led to the miracle which He worked upon the woman who had an issue of blood.

Such a dense crowd of people accompanied our Saviour that they closely thronged and pressed upon Him. This circumstance afforded the poor woman an opportunity to carry out her plan (Mark 5:24–31; Luke 8:42–45) of approaching Him unnoticed, in order to obtain help and healing. It is certainly touching to see how attached the people are to our Lord, whether it is on account of their need of instruction and cure, or out of respect and love. This shows again how high His prestige with them stood. By the presence of this crowd, too, the miracle becomes all the more significant, and its authenticity the more indubitable. Nevertheless this attachment of the people was a source of inconvenience to our Lord, as may well be imagined.

## 2. THE MIRACLE ITSELF

Two series of causes concurred to bring about this miracle.

On the part of the woman, the first cause was her pitiable condition. She had suffered for twelve years already from an issue of blood, a disease in itself odious, from the Israelite standpoint legally unclean, and (on account of various regulations) very troublesome and inconvenient (Lev. 15:25 seq.). She had had much to suffer from physicians, who, as it seems, employed most barbarous remedies against this disease; but in vain. In this manner too she had lost all her fortune, and nothing save death could help her and free her from her suffering (Mark 5:25, 26; Luke 8:43). Another cause on the woman's side was her modesty and humility. According to the opinion of some ecclesiastical writers and holy Fathers, she was a Gentile.[1] For this reason, and on account of her unclean disease, she did not dare to apply

---

[1] Others think her to have been a Jewess.

openly to our Lord for healing, but hoped now to approach Him unnoticed in the throng of people, and be healed by the touch of His garment. A third cause was the lively faith and touching confidence of the woman. She had heard of our Saviour (Mark 5:27), she saw and listened to Him, believed and, buoyed up by happy confidence, thought: "If I touch but His garment, I shall be whole" (Matt. 9:21; Mark 5:28). The sequel was brought about by her longing desire and her courage. All this marks the character of the poor woman.

The other causes were on our Saviour's side. Before all, His omniscience. He knows exactly the distress and the excellent dispositions of the woman, her secret act, and the moment of her cure. Further, the goodness of our Lord is another cause, which induces Him graciously to take into consideration the embarrassment, modesty and natural shyness of the woman, and relieve her distress. A last cause is His power, which acts quietly and instantaneously, yet thoroughly (Mark 5:29; Luke 8:44), and in quite a new manner, viz. by the mere contact with the hem of His upper garment (Mark 5:27; Luke 8:44). This is the first time that He works a miracle by means of exterior objects, and imparts miraculous virtue to His garment. This occurred repeatedly later on (Matt. 14:36).

### 3. THE REVELATION OF THE MIRACLE

At the same instant that the miracle took place, our Lord turned to the people and asked who had touched Him. St. Peter and the other disciples replied that the people around were pressing upon Him; how then could He ask such a question? He responded that He knew with certainty that someone had touched Him, and that a healing power had gone out from Him; and He looked around Him to see where the woman was. She saw herself discovered, came up, fell at our Lord's feet, and confessed everything before all the people (Mark 5:30–33; Luke 8:45–47).

And why did our Saviour act thus? First, in order to substantiate the healing as a miracle, and to complete it. By asking who had touched Him, and assuring the by-standers that a healing virtue had gone out from Him, He proved that the miracle was a work of His power, of which He was fully conscious; and also gave evidence at once of His omniscience and omnipotence. Indeed, the circumstances—our Lord's question, the answer of the disciples, the confession of the woman, the presence of so many people—make the scene a brilliant manifestation of our Saviour's Divinity. Secondly, He revealed the miracle in this manner in order to encourage Jairus in particular to lively faith and confidence. His faith and trust were not as great as this woman's. In order to raise him to a higher spiritual level, our Saviour permitted this incident to occur. The example of the lively faith of the woman, and its reward in the miracle, were especially for his benefit. This is the mutual relationship of these two miracles. The one occasioned and led to the other. Lastly, our Saviour wished to comfort the good woman, to reward her and increase her faith. Trembling and confused, she approached, fearing our Lord's displeasure, because she, a heathen woman and unclean, had ventured to draw near Him amidst the throng, and thus as it were surreptitiously obtained the benefit. He speaks therefore most reassuringly to her, bidding her "go in peace." He assures her of the completeness of her cure, praises her faith, and even ascribes the miracle to it, thus precluding its explanation by any magical power. Indeed, He even addresses her with the gracious name of "daughter," and shows her thus the way to attain to the adoption of God's children by faith in His Son and attachment to Him, the Redeemer of all men (Mark 5:34; Luke 8:48). In fact, the holy Fathers see in the woman with the issue of blood a type of heathendom in its spiritual and temporal misery, its uncleanness, poverty, desolation and helplessness, but also in its humility and believing trust. Thus our Saviour benefited her heart and soul as well as her body. According to historical tradition, she was a native of Caesarea Philippi (Paneas), and after her return thither, as a mark of her gratitude, she caused a bronze statue to be erected before her house, representing our Saviour in the act of giving His hand to a woman kneeling before Him, and raising her to her feet. Between the two figures, at the hem of our Saviour's garment, a medicinal herb was growing.

Among other things we have in this mystery a prototype of the miraculous cures wrought through the relics of our Saviour and of His Saints.

## The Raising to Life of Jairus' Daughter

Luke 8:41. And behold there came a man whose name was Jairus, and he was a ruler of the synagogue; and he fell down at the feet of Jesus, beseeching him that he would come into his house.—42. For he had an only daughter almost twelve years old, and she was dying.—. . . 49. As he was yet speaking, there cometh one to the ruler of the synagogue, saying to him: "Thy daughter is dead; trouble him not."—50. And Jesus hearing this word, answered the father of the maid: "Fear not; believe only, and she shall be safe."—51. And when he was come to the house, he suffered not any man to go in with him but Peter, and James, and John, and the father and mother of the maiden.—52. And all wept and mourned for her. But he said: "Weep not; the maid is not dead, but sleepeth."—53. And they laughed him to scorn, knowing that she was dead.—54. But he taking her by the hand, cried out, saying: "Maid, arise."—55. And her spirit returned, and she rose immediately. And he bid them give her to eat.—56. And her parents were astonished; whom he charged to tell no man what was done.

MARK 5:22. And there cometh one of the rulers of the synagogue named Jairus; and seeing him, falleth down at his feet.—23. And he besought him much, saying: "My daughter is at the point of death; come, lay thy hand upon her, that she may be safe and may live."—24. And he went with him; and a great multitude followed him, and they thronged him.—. . . 35. While he was yet speaking, some come from the ruler of the synagogue's house, saying: "Thy daughter is dead; why dost thou trouble the Master any farther?"—36. But Jesus having heard the word that was spoken, saith to the ruler of the synagogue: "Fear not; only believe."—37. And he admitted not any man to follow him, but Peter, and James, and John the brother of James.—38. And they come to the house of the ruler of the synagogue, and he seeth a tumult, and people weeping and wailing much.—39. And going in, he saith to them: "Why make you this ado, and weep? The damsel is not dead, but sleepeth."—40. And they laughed him to scorn. But he having put them all out, taketh the father and the mother of the damsel, and them that were with him, and entereth in where the damsel was lying.—41. And taking the damsel by the hand, he saith to her: "Talitha cumi," which is, being interpreted, "Damsel (I say to thee), arise."—42. And immediately the damsel rose up and walked; and she was twelve years old; and they were astonished with a great astonishment.—43. And he charged them strictly that no man should know it; and commanded that something should be given her to eat.

MATT. 9:18. As he was speaking these things unto them, behold a certain ruler came up and adored him, saying: "Lord, my daughter is even now dead; but come, lay thy hand upon her, and she shall live."—19. And Jesus rising up followed him, with his disciples.—. . . 23. And when Jesus was come into the house of the ruler, and saw the minstrels and the multitude making a rout, he said:—24. "Give place; for the girl is not dead, but sleepeth." And they laughed him to scorn.—25. And when the multitude was put forth, he went in and took her by the hand. And the maid arose.—26. And the fame hereof went abroad into all that country.

## 1. THE MIRACLE

Scarcely was the woman with the issue of blood healed when news was brought to Jairus that his little daughter had just breathed her last. Our Saviour therefore encourages the father to have faith, proceeds on the way with him, and raises the little maiden to life. This is one of the most important miracles; first on account of its nature, since it is the raising to life of a dead person, and thus proves the absolute sway of our Lord over life in this world and the next. Led by His hand, so to speak, and at His word, the spirit of the dead child returns (Luke 8:55). Secondly, it was important because of its connection with the preceding miracle, which served as a preparation for it. Lastly, on account of the extraordinary circumstances which led up to it. Jairus, a well-known and influential man, comes to our Saviour before a multitude of people, and beseeches Him openly and with most earnest entreaty to come to his house and lay His hand upon his little daughter, that she may not die; for if He does so, she will surely live (Matt. 9:18; Mark 5:22, 23; Luke 8:41, 42). Thus all were waiting in intense expectation to see what would happen. The goodness of Jesus, His merciful Heart, and His zeal for the glory of God were all equally appealed to. The miracle, wrought in favor of such an influential family, was naturally calculated to be of powerful assistance to our Saviour and His work.

### 2. MANNER IN WHICH THE MIRACLE WAS PERFORMED

The accomplishment of the miracle is remarkable in two ways.

First, our Saviour displays great readiness, solicitude, and even a certain tenacity of purpose in carrying it out. He immediately complies with the ruler's entreaty, and goes with him; He encourages him to faith by the miracle wrought upon the woman and sustains his confidence as the news of his daughter's death is brought to him, by the encouraging words that he is not to fear, only to believe firmly, and the child will be saved (Luke 8:49, 50; Mark 5:35, 36). He is evidently determined not to abandon him. Our Saviour overlooks defects which might otherwise have repelled Him, such as the imperfection of the ruler's faith in contrast to that of the woman He had just healed (Mark 5:23; Luke 8:41), and the circumstance that the man had probably only been driven to Him by his distress. The family seems to have been rather cold and worldly-minded; our Lord was "laughed to scorn" in the house, and little is said of the gratitude of the parents. Perhaps the ruler did not wish to break with the Pharisees. Besides this, our Saviour displays the most delicate consideration for Jairus. He does not let the people enter the house, does not even take all the Apostles with Him, because this would have been troublesome and unpleasant for the family; moreover He seems to wish to depreciate the great benefit He is about to confer, saying that the maiden was only sleeping; lastly, He charges them to make no stir about the miracle, probably in order that the family might not become obnoxious to the Pharisees (Mark 5:43; Luke 8:56), or in order to teach the people not to ask of Him the miracle of raising the dead to life as easily as that of healing the sick. In short, He acts with the greatest consideration.

On the other hand, however, our Saviour takes care to afford no ground for doubting the reality of the miracle. He takes the three chief of His disciples and the dead maiden's parents with Him into the room where she lay (Mark 5:40; Luke 8:51). By saying that the child was only sleeping, He arouses the most decided contradiction from the people of the house; and therein lies a proof of her actual death (Mark 5:38–40; Luke 8:52, 53) and at the same time a declaration of the miracle. Our Saviour repeatedly makes use of this expression when speaking of death, especially with regard to those whom He is about to raise to life again (John 11:11), and in general to indicate that death, especially a good death, is merely sleep, not cessation of life for ever. Further, He takes the hand of the maiden and says: "Maid, arise" (Mark 5:41; Luke 8:54), as a proof that the event takes place through miraculous power. Lastly, He bids them give the child something to eat, in order to substantiate the truth and reality of her raising to life (Mark 5:43; Luke 8:55).

### 3. THE EFFECT OF THE MIRACLE

The miracle had a threefold effect. As regards the parents, we are told that they "were astonished" (Luke 8:56) "with a great astonishment" (Mark 5:42) as they saw the reanimated child begin to walk about. There is nothing else recorded about their gratitude or attachment to our Lord, as was the case with so many who published our Saviour's benefits abroad and extolled them everywhere, in spite of His prohibition.

On the other hand, the effect produced upon the people was even greater than usual. The report of the miracle went through the whole district (Matt. 9:26). It could not be otherwise, on account of the publicity and striking character of the event and its attendant circumstances.

The disciples were as deeply impressed as the people. The miracle seems to have been intended for them in particular, since they alone, with the child's parents, were admitted to witness it. Altogether it is remarkable in this period of our Saviour's life how He endeavors to perfect the faith of the Apostles in His Divinity by such extraordinary miracles, so various in character, and following each other in such quick succession. He scarcely leaves them time to recover from the impression made by one miracle before surprising them with another.

For an apostolic laborer this mystery contains a valuable lesson as to how he should deal with persons of high position. He should not seek them himself, but let them seek him; he must be ready for everything and show towards them kind feeling and supernatural love; when he has once won them for God, he must not easily let them go again; he must not make much of what he does; must overlook a great deal in their behavior and that of their household; and lastly, he must be disinterested enough to expect no thanks. Let this, together with admiration for the Person of Jesus and love to Him, be the effect of this mystery upon us.

The holy Fathers see in this double miracle types of heathenism and Judaism, and of their relations to our Saviour and the Church. The woman with the issue of blood typifies heathenism; the daughter of Jairus, Judaism. And there is a good foundation for this interpretation. The little girl has lived twelve years, and is growing into the bloom of maidenhood; and the poor woman has been suffering from her disease an equal length of time. So also heathenism has lived in uncleanness and helplessness during the whole time that Judaism, since its election in the person of Abraham, has been maturing for our Saviour. Both meet before the Messias, but with very different dispositions. Heathenism, by its faith, humility and trust, gains admittance into the Church of Jesus. Judaism dies, and only obtains a place in the Church after heathenism and through its endeavors, according to St. Paul's prophecy (Rom. 11:25). If Jairus had had such perfect faith as the woman with the issue of blood, his little daughter would perhaps have been healed immediately, like the son of the ruler at Capharnaum (John 4:50). As it is, she dies, and is raised to life only after the woman has been healed through her faith, and the father, encouraged by this example, has also become firm in faith. On our Saviour's side also the comparison holds good. Whilst making no particular advances to the woman, but rather letting Himself be sought by her, He shows extraordinary complaisance towards the father of the little maiden, and even employs loving force in order to confer the great benefit upon them both. Just in the same way He behaves towards Israel and towards heathenism, and with the same result (Rom. 10:20).

## The Two Blind Men of Capharnaum

Matt. 9:27. And as Jesus passed from thence, there followed him two blind men, crying out and saying: "Have mercy on us, O Son of David."—28. And when he was come to the house, the blind men came to him. And Jesus saith to them: "Do you believe that I can do this unto you?" They say to him: "Yea, Lord."—29. Then he touched their eyes, saying: "According to your faith be it done unto you."—30. And their eyes were opened; and Jesus strictly charged them, saying: "See that no man know this."—31. But they going out spread his fame abroad in all that country.

### 1. THE FAITH OF THE BLIND MEN

As it appears, the miracle wrought upon the blind men followed immediately upon the preceding one (Matt. 9:27). As our Saviour went away from the house of the ruler of the synagogue, two blind men followed Him, calling upon Him with most fervent faith to heal them. This faith had doubtless been awakened by His many extraordinary miracles, the report of which had spread throughout the whole country. Capharnaum had just been the scene of two great miracles. Under the influence of grace and of this powerful impression, the blind men had undoubtedly formed a high and exalted idea of our Saviour, and were filled with lively faith, strong desire and great confidence that He would heal them.

They now give very energetic expression to this faith and confidence, by crying out after Him: "Have mercy on us, O Son of David!" (Matt. 9:27.) This, from an Israelite, was equivalent to a confession of the dignity of Jesus as the Messias. Except the Apostles, no one had yet uttered this in such plain terms. The utmost any had dared to say was that "a great prophet is risen up among us" (Luke 7:16). And they confess this faith simply, openly, vigorously, fearlessly, in the open street, in spite of the Pharisees and scribes who were lurking everywhere.

### 2. TRIAL OF THIS FAITH

Our Saviour tried the faith of the two blind men in the first place by appearing not to notice them and letting them follow Him and cry out, without troubling Himself about them. But they do not let themselves grow discouraged; they continue to cry out, and follow our Saviour until He enters a house. They follow Him into the house also, go up to Him and beg Him to heal them. But this was not yet enough. Our Saviour asks them if they really believe that He can do what they ask of Him. With decision and a renewed protestation of their respect, calling Him "Lord," they answer that they do believe (Matt. 9:28).

The reason why our Saviour treated them thus was to prepare them the better, by patience, submission, humility and perseverance. They were to cooperate with grace and thus in some measure merit the miracle, as our Saviour expressly says: "According to your faith be it done unto you" (Matt. 9:29). The reason for His not paying attention, whilst outside the house, to the request or to the loud confession of His dignity as the Messias, was probably prudence and wise reserve, in order not to irritate His enemies by accepting this title of honor, and not to anticipate the course of events.

### 3. THE REWARD OF THIS FAITH

After the blind men had stood the test, our Saviour touched their eyes and they received sight (Matt. 9:30). By this act He typified baptism, the essential character of which consists in its being the Sacrament of faith and of supernatural life, and the ceremonies of which, as performed upon the senses of the catechumen, have the same symbolical meaning.

Modesty and consideration for His enemies may also have caused our Saviour to forbid the healed men to spread abroad the report of the miracle (Matt. 9:30), or rather of their faith in Him as the Messias (Matt. 9:27). But they, in their deep and generous gratitude, did not obey the prohibition, but spoke of the miracle everywhere (Matt. 9:31).

This is the first cure of blindness that is related in detail. In this mystery also we see revealed the same beautiful traits of the character of Jesus, His prudence and wisdom, goodness and divine power. From the blind men we may learn the lesson that nothing can resist faith, trust and perseverance. The public recognition of our Saviour's dignity as Messias, by the Jewish dogmatic title "Son of David," is given to Him for the first time by the lips of the people.

## THE SENDING FORTH OF THE APOSTLES

LUKE 9:1. Then calling together the twelve apostles, he gave them power and authority over all devils, and to cure diseases.—2. And he sent them to preach the kingdom of God, and to heal the sick.—3. And he said to them: "Take nothing for your journey, neither staff nor scrip, nor bread, nor money, neither have two coats.—4. And whatsoever house you shall enter into, abide there, and depart not from thence.—5. And whosoever will not receive you, when ye go out of that city, shake off even the dust of your feet for a testimony against them."—6. And going out they went about through the towns, preaching the gospel and healing everywhere.

MARK 6:7. And he called the twelve, and began to send them two and two, and gave them power over unclean spirits.—8. And he commanded them that they should take nothing for the way, but a staff only; no scrip, no bread, nor money in their purse,—9. But to be shod with sandals, and that they should not put on two coats.—10. And he said to them: "Wheresoever you shall enter into a house, there abide till you depart from that place.—11. And whosoever shall not receive you, nor hear you; going forth from thence, shake off the dust from your feet for a testimony to them."—12. And going forth they preached that men should do penance;—13. And they cast out many devils, and anointed with oil many that were sick, and healed them.

MATT. 10:1. And having called his twelve disciples together, he gave them power over unclean spirits, to cast them out, and to heal all manner of diseases, and all manner of infirmities.—2. And the names of the twelve apostles are these: The first, Simon, who is called Peter, and Andrew his brother,—3. James the son of Zebedee, and John his brother, Philip and Bartholomew, Thomas and Matthew the publican, and James the son of Alpheus, and Thaddeus,—4. Simon the Cananean, and Judas Iscariot, who also betrayed him.—5. These twelve Jesus sent; commanding them, saying: "Go ye not into the way of the Gentiles, and into the cities of the Samaritans enter ye not;—6. But go ye rather to the lost sheep of the house of Israel.—7. And going preach, saying: The kingdom of heaven is at hand.—8. Heal the sick, raise the dead, cleanse the lepers, cast out devils; freely have you received, freely give.—9. Do not possess gold, nor silver, nor money in your purses;—10. No scrip for your journey, nor two coats, nor shoes, nor a staff; for the workman is worthy of his meat.—11. And into whatsoever city or town you shall enter, inquire who in it is worthy; and there abide till you go thence. —12. And when you come into the house, salute it, saying: Peace be to this house.—13. And if that house be worthy, your peace shall come upon it; but if it be not worthy, your peace shall return to you.—14. And whosoever shall not receive you, nor hear your words; going forth out of that house or city, shake off the dust from your feet.—15. Amen I say to you, it shall be more tolerable for the land of Sodom and Gomorrha in the day of judgment, than for that city."

### 1. WHY OUR SAVIOUR SENDS OUT THE APOSTLES

Our Saviour probably had in view three objects in sending out His Apostles.

First, He wished to prove before the whole nation and the whole world that He was in full possession of all apostolic authority, that He had its source within Himself, and could impart and exercise it as He pleased, in His own Person or through others. He now makes use of this plenary power even during His lifetime, by not merely preaching and working miracles Himself, but also authorizing others to do so. For this reason He sends the Apostles in His name and with His authority and power. He multiplied Himself, so to speak, in His Apostles.

Secondly, our Saviour also wished to make known to the

Israelite nation the fact that He had founded a new economy of grace, through new instruments. On this account He does not content Himself with having appointed and selected these instruments by the choice of the Apostles, but He wills that they should also assert themselves in all earnest and in a manner calculated to impress the people. This delegation is only an anticipation of the future sending out of the Apostles from the mountain in Galilee, after His Resurrection (Matt. 28:19).

Thirdly, our Saviour intended to let the Apostles gain practical experience in their future vocation. Hitherto they had always been with Him, had listened to His addresses, and probably helped a little also. But to act or speak oneself is a very different thing from standing by and watching others. Now they had to try their own powers. By such an experiment one enters into the spirit of one's vocation, gains a practical idea of it, acquires readiness in it, and lastly, which is best of all, one learns to love it. It was for these reasons that our Lord sent out the Apostles.

## 2. HOW OUR SAVIOUR SENDS THE APOSTLES

In sending out the Apostles our Saviour shows them every possible consideration, prepares them by previous instruction and arms them with power.

This tender consideration is manifested in His sending them during His lifetime, in order that the thought of His nearness may inspire them with confidence; and also in order to be able to instruct, correct and train them Himself, upon their return. Then He sends them "two and two" (Mark 6:7), for mutual assistance, comfort and supervision, and in order to confirm and give weight to their testimony (Deut. 19:15), as He also bore testimony of Himself (John 8:17, 18, 19). Lastly, He does not send them to the Gentiles and Samaritans, but rather to the House of Israel (Matt. 10:5, 6), and this in order that they may not incur the hostility of the Jews, who were jealous, and who moreover had the first claim to the Gospel (Acts 13:46; Rom. 1:16; 11:17; 15:8). He Himself observed the same rule during His lifetime (Matt. 15:24), and only authorized the Apostles to a universal mission after He had broken the bonds of Judaism by His death. Besides, they might have fared ill among the Samaritans and Gentiles. They were only novices as yet, and so He spared them and accustomed them by degrees to labor and adversity.

Secondly, our Lord prepared the Apostles by instruction. He

taught them first what was the object of their mission. They were to proclaim the joyful tidings that the kingdom of heaven was at hand (Matt. 10:7), to preach the kingdom of God (Luke 9:2) with its aims, means, and promises. At the same time they were to do good to men in regard to their bodily needs, to heal the sick (Luke 9:2), in short, to comfort and benefit them in soul and body, to wish them peace, i.e. the fulness of all temporal and eternal happiness, whether the wish was accepted or remained devoid of all effect through the fault of those who rejected it (Matt. 10:12, 13). Further, He gave them instructions with regard to their behavior. He recommends to them the practice of poverty. They are to take no money and no scrip with them, nor a change of clothing, nor a staff carried either for the sake of appearance or for defence; but simply bare necessaries, such as sandals, or a staff if they require one for support (Matt. 10:9, 10; Mark 6:8, 9; Luke 9:3). They are to go as they are, without procuring themselves any conveniences, not even a staff if they have not one already (Mark 6:8). He bids them be modest in their requirements and edifying in their conduct. They are not to go from one house to another, in order not to grieve their host (Matt. 10:11; Mark 6:10; Luke 9:4); they are to choose worthy persons as their hosts and entertainers (Matt. 10:11). Lastly, our Saviour teaches them to be disinterested. They are to accept nothing for their services. They have received freely the gift of doing good, freely they are to impart it (Matt. 10:8). He recommends them all this on account of the nature of the benefits they are about to bestow, which are spiritual and may not be given in exchange for temporal goods; secondly, for the instruction and edification of the people, to whom it was necessary to preach by example as well as by word of mouth; lastly, for the Apostles themselves, who would otherwise be in great danger of giving way to self-interest, exacting habits, and inconsiderateness. Moreover it was fitting that they should not appear otherwise than He Himself, Whose will it was to found the kingdom of God in the servile form of poverty and humility, not in power and honor. If the Apostle does his duty, God and those to whom the Apostle does good, to whose spiritual welfare he devotes his full time, whom he serves with no thought of earthly reward, will provide for him. The workman is worthy of his meat (Matt. 10:10).

Thirdly, our Saviour endowed the Apostles for the exercise of the apostolic office with full authority and power. He authorizes

them to preach in His Name (Matt. 10:7; Luke 9:2), and in ratification of this He gives first the power of working miracles—healing the sick, raising the dead to life, expelling evil spirits (Matt.
10:8; Mark 6:7; Luke 9:2)—as He Himself did; and secondly, He
lays upon the hearers the duty of listening to the Apostles and
accepting their words. If they are not received in any place, they
are to depart, and to shake off the dust from their feet as a sign
that they renounce all fellowship with such an unclean place, and
in announcement of a severe judgment upon it; the judgment
upon such a town will be worse than that upon Sodom (Matt.
10:14, 15; Mark 6:11; Luke 9:5). It must not be overlooked that
our Saviour here only gently hints at failures and persecution.
The Apostles could not bear more as yet. This is a part of His
wisdom in training them. So He dismisses them, equipped with
the plentitude of apostolic power, armed and protected on all
sides.

### 3. HOW OUR SAVIOUR CAUSES THE MISSION TO SUCCEED

Our Saviour provided, lastly, for their success. The Apostles'
mission after the descent of the Holy Ghost did not run so
smoothly; but here He protected them from outward troubles
and persecutions, gave grace to their words and confirmed them
by the promised miracles. "They went about through the towns,
preaching the Gospel and healing everywhere" (Luke 9:6); "they
cast out many devils, and anointed with oil many that were sick
and healed them" (Mark 6:13). This anointing was a foreshadowing of the Sacrament of Extreme Unction.

Thus our Saviour attained His object in sending out the Apostles. They returned after the lapse of a few days, surely with increased love for their vocation, with a much higher idea of our
Lord and much more perfect faith in Him and His divine power,
now that they saw He could also effect through them what He
performed Himself, and that His power was not limited by any
conditions. And the people must have shared this conviction. On
their return the Apostles related to our Saviour all that they had
done and taught (Mark 6:30; Luke 9:10). Here we have a touching example of their childlike candor and desire to learn and be
trained in their vocation. And we may be sure that our Saviour
on His side did not fail to give them sympathy, encouragement
and instruction, and to fill them with joy. Thus we have here again
a beautiful manifestation of the spirit of Jesus, of His love for the

Apostles, His care for their training, His wise indulgence and mildness in their education, and lastly of the apostolic virtues which He wishes to inculcate upon them. Truly in this mystery His might as God and Head of the Church shines forth with a new radiance, as He imparts His power to the Apostles and manifests it through them. We see here the Church herself, not only in her organization, but also in her activity, aim and means, her spirit and gifts of grace; even the priestly power is already foreshadowed, in the anointing of the sick. The pastoral instruction given to the Apostles, which, as we see, embraces the entire apostolic ministry, its aim and means, and the lot which awaits it, is of especial importance for all members of the hierarchy. It is indeed calculated to inspire love and enthusiasm for the apostolic vocation, since the aim is so beautiful and sublime, the means (poverty, frugality, disinterestedness) so blameless and so noble, and the result (making other men happy and advancing in merit oneself) so glorious. The special protection and assistance under which we see the Apostles here on their first mission must also incite us to courage and confidence.

## THE BEHEADING OF ST. JOHN

MATT. 14:1. At that time Herod the tetrarch heard the fame of Jesus;—2. And he said to his servants: "This is John the Baptist; he is risen from the dead, and therefore mighty works show forth themselves in him."—3. For Herod had apprehended John and bound him, and put him into prison because of Herodias, his brother's wife.—4. For John said to him: "It is not lawful for thee to have her."—5. And having a mind to put him to death, he feared the people; because they esteemed him as a prophet.—6. But on Herod's birthday the daughter of Herodias danced before them, and pleased Herod.—7. Whereupon he promised with an oath to give her whatsoever she would ask of him.—8. But she being instructed before by her mother, said: "Give me here in a dish the head of John the Baptist." —9. And the king was struck sad; yet because of his oath, and for them that sat with him at table, he commanded it to be given.—10. And he sent and beheaded John in the prison.—11. And his head was brought in a dish, and it was given to the damsel, and she brought it to her mother.—12. And his disciples came and took the body, and buried it; and came and told Jesus.

MARK 6:14. And king Herod heard (for his name was made manifest); and he said: "John the Baptist is risen again from the dead; and therefore mighty works show forth themselves in him."—15. And others said: "It is Elias." But others said: "It is a prophet, as one of the prophets."—16. Which Herod hearing, said: "John whom I beheaded, he is risen again from the dead."—17. For Herod himself had sent and apprehended John, and bound him in prison for the sake of Herodias, the wife of Philip his brother, because he had married her.—18. For John said to Herod: "It is not lawful for thee to have thy brother's wife."—19. Now Herodias laid snares for him; and was desirous to put him to death and could not.— 20. For Herod feared John, knowing him to be a just and holy man; and kept

him, and when he heard him did many things; and he heard him willingly.—
21. And when a convenient day was come, Herod made a supper for his birthday,
for the princes, and tribunes, and chief men of Galilee;—22. And when the daughter
of the same Herodias had come in, and had danced, and pleased Herod, and them
that were at table with him; the king said to the damsel: "Ask of me what thou
wilt, and I will give it thee."—23. And he swore to her: "Whatsoever thou shalt
ask I will give thee, though it be the half of my kingdom."—24. Who when she
was gone out, said to her mother: "What shall I ask?" But she said: "The head
of John the Baptist."—25. And when she was come in immediately with haste
to the king, she asked, saying: "I will that forthwith thou give me in a dish the
head of John the Baptist."—26. And the king was struck sad; yet because of his
oath, and because of them that were with him at table, he would not displease
her;—27. But sending an executioner, he commanded that his head should be
brought in a dish. And he beheaded him in the prison,—28. And brought his
head in a dish; and gave it to the damsel, and the damsel gave it to her mother.
—29. Which his disciples hearing, came and took his body; and laid it in a tomb.

Luke 9:7. Now Herod the tetrarch heard of all things that were done by him;
and he was in a doubt, because it was said—8. By some, that John was risen from
the dead; but by other some, that Elias hath appeared; and by others, that one of
the old prophets was risen again.—9. And Herod said: "John I have beheaded;
but who is this of whom I hear such things?" And he sought to see him.

## 1. IMMEDIATE CAUSES OF THE EXECUTION

The execution of John took place before the Apostles had returned to our Saviour at the close of their mission. The immediate
causes which brought about this sad event were, on the part of
Herodias, her hatred and constant dread of St. John. Herod feared
and respected him (Mark 6:20; Matt. 14:5), and thus Herodias
was not sure of her throne as long as he lived. She therefore formed
a plot to murder him, and watched for a favorable opportunity to
carry it out (Mark 6:19). This opportunity presented itself on
Herod's birthday, which he celebrated according to heathen custom (Gen. 40:20; II Mach. 6:7) by a State banquet with the
great men of his court, the military commanders and chief men
of Galilee, probably at the Castle of Machaerus, in a dungeon of
which John was imprisoned. As was the custom, the pleasures of
the table were enhanced by performances of dancers; and Salome,
the daughter of Herodias by her first marriage, led the dance and
fascinated Herod and the whole company at table. Perhaps the
whole performance was a cunning plot of Herodias, by which she
intended to entangle Herod and ruin John; at all events when, in
consequence of the dance, Herod afforded her an opportunity of
carrying out her murderous plan, she seized upon it with great
resolution (Mark 6:24; Matt. 14:8).

On Herod's part the cause, in the first instance, was his imprudence in binding himself by an oath (Mark 6:24; Matt. 14:7).

The oath might have cost him the half of his kingdom; as it was, it led to the beheading of John, and made him the murderer of a prophet. A further cause was Herod's weakness and human respect. When the girl at Herodias' instigation requested the head of John (Mark 6:25; Matt. 14:8), Herod was grieved and sorry; but on account of the company at table and of having pledged his royal word (Matt. 14:9; Mark 6:26), he complied with the disgraceful demand. Perhaps it may also have been supported by the Galilean notabilities present. So the execution was ordered. Thus debauch, devilish hatred, imprudence and weakness were the causes of the murder of St. John.

## 2. THE EXECUTION OF ST. JOHN

Herod now sent someone (a soldier, probably) to the dungeon below, and he immediately performed the execution (Matt. 14:10; Mark 6:27). How shall we picture the last moments of the Saint? Death surely did not take him unawares. He accepted it without fear, undauntedly, with touching humility, simplicity and dignity, without indignation or vindictive feeling against his murderers; and lastly, with devotion and joy. Why should he stay longer in this world, where all things holy were persecuted and Christ was not recognized? He had accomplished his mission; his death effected more for Christ's kingdom now than his life. Our Saviour was certainly his last thought, and he rejoiced to be able to assimilate his death to the sacrificial Death of the Lamb of God whom he had proclaimed. Perhaps he spoke for the last time, in his touching humility and love, the words: "He must increase, but I must decrease" (John 3:30). So his head fell, and his holy soul soared away from this earth, which he had hallowed by his virtues, into the hand of his Saviour and Judge. Not quite three years had elapsed since his first appearance in public, and he had spent nearly two of them in prison. His head was immediately brought to Herodias (Matt. 14:11; Mark 6:28), who is said to have flouted it and then thrown it into a hole in the earth. The body was taken away by his disciples and buried in a tomb (Matt. 14:12; Mark 6:29). Later his grave was venerated in Samaria; his head, or at all events a part of it, was brought to Rome, and the shroud is preserved at Aix-la-Chapelle.

Such was the death of St. John the Baptist. How pitiable it is, and how inexpressibly lamentable it is in all its circumstances! He is put to death in the midst of universal public rejoicing, on the birthday of the monarch, through the malice of a king's mistress and a dancing-girl. He is slain in a wretched dungeon, quickly and unceremoniously, without any ado, as though his death were of no account. Short work does the world make with the servants of God, and past them it goes on its way to the pleasures of life. The end of St. Peter and St. Paul had at least something great and glorious in it, but in St. John's death there is nothing but bitterest poverty and abandonment. Even heaven seems unsympathetic. Our Saviour is near, He knows everything; John dies for Him, and He does not move in the matter; sends no angel, as He did to Peter; does not appear to him, as to Stephen, at least Scripture does not say so; He simply allows him to perish. St. John was to taste beforehand of the abandonment of Golgotha.

### 3. THE EFFECT OF THE EXECUTION

The effect of the execution upon the people, when the deed became known, must have been tremendous; to what an extent the minds of the people were swayed by terror is shown at the subsequent activity, preaching and miracles of the Apostles and our Saviour. Whilst some thought: "Elias hath appeared . . . one of the old prophets is risen again," others openly said that John was risen from the dead (Luke 9:8), and that it was his power that worked in our Saviour. These sayings were reported to Herod, and he wavered anxiously, wondering if it could possibly be John, whom he had put to death, or not (Luke 9:9; Matt. 14:2; Mark 6:14, 16). And he wished to see Jesus, from motives of fear and curiosity as to whether He really were John or not. But he was only to see Him a year later, and to treat Him shamefully, as he had treated John.

We have here a true picture of the life of this world. Such is the way of the world. The more unworthy part of humanity lives, revels, rules and triumphs by cunning, violence and wickedness. For all that is right and holy, there seems to be no place; these meet only with persecution, defeat and destruction. So it has always been, and so it will continue to be. How happy will be the world to come, which corrects this terrible contradiction and discord! How glorious the reward which compensates for this injustice! Blessed are they who participate in this reward. We catch a glimpse of this divine order even here below, in the insufficiency of outward success for the victor, in his remorse of conscience and fear of the coming judgment, and in the veneration and glory which falls to the lot of the victims, even in this life. This is the important lesson which the death of the great St. John affords us.

## THE FIRST MULTIPLICATION OF BREAD

JOHN 6:1. After these things Jesus went over the sea of Galilee, which is that of Tiberias;—2. And a great multitude followed him, because they saw the miracles which he did on them that were diseased.—3. Jesus therefore went up into a mountain; and there he sat with his disciples.—4. Now the Pasch, the festival day of the Jews, was near at hand.—5. When Jesus therefore had lifted up his eyes, and seen that a very great multitude cometh to him, he said to Philip: "Whence shall we buy bread, that these may eat?"—6. And this he said to try him; for he himself knew what he would do.—7. Philip answered him: "Two hundred pennyworth of bread is not sufficient for them, that everyone may take a little."—8. One of his disciples, Andrew, the brother of Simon Peter, saith to him:—9. "There is a boy here that hath five barley loaves and two fishes; but what are these among so many?"—10. Then Jesus said: "Make the men sit down." Now there was much grass in the place. The men therefore sat down, in number about five thousand.—11. And Jesus took the loaves; and when he had given thanks, he distributed to them that were sat down. In like manner also of the fishes as much as they would.—12. And when they were filled, he said to his disciples: "Gather up the fragments that remain, lest they be lost."—13. They gathered up therefore, and filled twelve baskets with the fragments of the five barley loaves, which remained over and above to them that had eaten.—14. Now those men, when they had seen what a miracle Jesus had done, said: "This is of a truth the prophet that is to come into the world."—15. Jesus therefore, when he knew that they would come to take him by force and make him king, fled again into the mountain, himself alone.—16. And when evening was come, his disciples went down to the sea.

LUKE 9:10. And the apostles, when they were returned, told him all they had done; and taking them he went aside into a desert place apart, which belongeth to Bethsaida.—11. Which when the people knew, they followed him; and he received them, and spoke to them of the kingdom of God, and healed them who had need of healing.—12. Now the day began to decline. And the twelve came and said to him: "Send away the multitude, that going into the towns and villages round about, they may lodge and get victuals; for we are here in a desert place."—13. But he said to them: "Give you them to eat." And they said: "We have no more than five loaves and two fishes; unless perhaps we should go and buy food for all this multitude."—14. Now there were about five thousand men. And he said to his disciples: "Make them sit down by fifties in a company."—15. And they did so, and made them all sit down.—16. And taking the five loaves and the two fishes, he looked up to heaven, and blessed them; and he broke, and distributed to his disciples, to set before the multitude.—17. And they did all eat, and were filled. And there were taken up of fragments that remained to them, twelve baskets.

MARK 6:31. And he said to them: "Come apart into a desert place, and rest a little." For there were many coming and going; and they had not so much as time to eat.—32. And going up into a ship, they went into a desert place apart.—33. And they saw them going away, and many knew; and they ran flocking thither on foot from all the cities, and were there before them.—34. And Jesus going out saw a great multitude; and he had compassion on them, because they were as sheep not having a shepherd, and he began to teach them many things.—35. And when the day was now far spent, his disciples came to him, saying:

"This is a desert place, and the hour is now past;—36. Send them away, that going into the next villages and towns, they may buy themselves meat to eat."— 37. And he answering said to them: "Give you them to eat." And they said to him: "Let us go and buy bread for two hundred pence, and we will give them to eat."— 38. And he saith to them: "How many loaves have you? Go and see." And when they knew, they say: "Five, and two fishes."—39. And he commanded them that they should make them all sit down by companies upon the green grass.— 40. And they sat down in ranks, by hundreds and by fifties.—41. And when he had taken the five loaves and the two fishes, looking up to heaven, he blessed, and broke the loaves, and gave to his disciples to set before them; and the two fishes he divided among them all.—42. And they all did eat, and had their fill.—43. And they took up the leavings, twelve full baskets of fragments, and of the fishes.—44. And they that did eat, were five thousand men.—45. And immediately he obliged his disciples to go up into the ship, that they might go before him over the water to Bethsaida; whilst he dismissed the people.—46. And when he had dismissed them, he went up to the mountain to pray.

MATT. 14:13. Which when Jesus had heard, he retired from thence by boat, into a desert place apart; and the multitudes having heard of it, followed him on foot out of the cities.—14. And he coming forth saw a great multitude, and had compassion on them, and healed their sick.—15. And when it was evening, his disciples came to him, saying: "This is a desert place, and the hour is now past; send away the multitudes, that going into the towns, they may buy themselves victuals."—16. But Jesus said to them: "They have no need to go; give you them to eat."—17. They answered him: "We have not here, but five loaves and two fishes."—18. Who said to them: "Bring them hither to me."—19. And when he had commanded the multitudes to sit down upon the grass, he took the five loaves and the two fishes, and looking up to heaven he blessed, and brake, and gave the loaves to his disciples, and the disciples to the multitudes.—20. And they did all eat, and were filled. And they took up what remained, twelve full baskets of fragments.—21. And the number of them that did eat was five thousand men, besides women and children.—22. And forthwith Jesus obliged his disciples to go up into the boat, and to go before him over the water, till he dismissed the people.

## 1. CIRCUMSTANCES LEADING UP TO THE MIRACLE

There were three principal circumstances which led to the miracle.

In the first place our Saviour, after the return of the Apostles, crosses over with them to the north-east shore of the Sea of Galilee. There was a double reason for this. On the one hand, the miracles wrought by Jesus and the Apostles had attracted the attention of the Herodian Court, and it was to be feared that some measures might be taken against our Lord. It was therefore advisable for Him to withdraw and choose another scene for the miracle of the multiplication of the loaves (Luke 9:9; Matt. 14:13); for the Herodians and the Pharisees now made common cause against Him (Mark 3:6; 8:15). On the other hand, He wished to let the tired Apostles rest in a solitary place, because they had been overworked and were fatigued (Mark 6:31; Luke 9:10; Matt. 14:13). This place was near Bethsaida (Julias, Introd.

p. 2), at the north-east end of the lake, beyond the Jordan, in the territory of Philip the tetrarch, where the heights of Galaad begin, stretching behind a little plain along the coast.

The second circumstance was that the people, who saw Him steering towards the shore of Bethsaida, followed Him by the inland route across the Jordan and sought Him in His solitude in great numbers, bringing with them sick and maimed; for since it was the time of the Pasch (John 6:4) and everyone was afoot, probably many out of the places through which they passed on their way had joined them (Mark 6:33; Luke 9:11; Matt. 14:13; John 6:2). When our Saviour on coming out of His solitude saw the people, He forgot rest and refreshment and, touched at their good will and at seeing them so forsaken by their pastors, received them, began to heal their sick and to teach them many things concerning the kingdom of God. This He continued to do all day long until evening (Mark 6:34; Luke 9:11; Matt. 14:14). The people remained with Him in spite of their weariness and want of food. The distance from Capharnaum round the lake to Bethsaida was about two leagues. Among the thousands were certainly many women and children, and probably many had forgotten in their haste to take provisions with them.

A third circumstance was the representation made by the Apostles, who called our Saviour's attention to the advanced hour and the loneliness of the place, and asked Him to dismiss the people, that they might obtain provisions in the neighboring towns and villages (Matt. 14:15; Mark 6:35, 36; Luke 9:12). Such, then, were the circumstances which led up to the miracle.

### 2. THE MIRACLE ITSELF

There are three things to be considered with regard to this miracle.

The first is the actual cause which led to it. This was solely our Lord's own will and desire, His kindness and charity, and His intention of strengthening the faith of His Apostles and the people. This is clearly shown in the consultation which our Lord held with the Apostles, as they begged Him to dismiss the people in order that they might find something to eat. "Why then dismiss them? Do not send them away. Give them something to eat." "Shall we go into the villages and buy bread for them?" answer the Apostles. Turning to Philip, our Lord asks: "Whence (for how much) shall we buy enough bread?" Philip thinks 200 denarii (about $30) would not suffice to buy even a little piece for each. "How many loaves have you?" responds our Saviour; "go and see." Andrew reports that a boy has five barley loaves and two fishes (perhaps as a gift for our Saviour, or for sale, or for his own use). "But what are these among so many?" (John 6:5–9; Luke 9:12, 13; Mark 6:37, 38; Matt. 14:16, 17.) Our Saviour evidently intends by this conversation with His Apostles to show the impossibility of providing a meal by natural means, and thereby to set the greatness of the miracle in a clear light; and on the other hand to test them in order to see if their faith in His Divinity would not suggest the means, and if they would not also cooperate in the miracle by this very faith, and thus themselves bring it about (John 6:6).

The miracle itself is the second thing to be considered. It is one of the greatest and most important, because by its very nature it affects the substance of things, since it causes an increase of them; further, because it was not worked upon one man, but (one may say) as often and upon as many thousand men as received and ate of the bread; and lastly, because it was performed so surely and irrefutably, publicly and solemnly, before so many thousand witnesses, and produced such a great effect. Our Saviour intended by this miracle to confirm the faith of the Apostles and the people by a mighty act.

Thirdly, the manner in which our Lord works the miracle must be considered. All is done with great order and calm. He makes the Apostles separate the people into companies of fifty or a hundred, and bids them sit down on the grass (Matt. 14:19; Mark 6:39; Luke 9:14, 15; John 6:10). The Apostles, already full of faith and accustomed to managing the people, carry out His orders without loss of time, and it is a pleasing sight to see the people, divided into groups, sitting on the grass-grown hill-side; behind them the rising heights, and before them the little plain stretching away to the lake, crossed by brooks, on the banks of which the oleander woods are beginning to bloom, for it is spring-time. Further, our Saviour performs the miracle with great piety. He takes the loaves and fishes, raises His eyes to heaven, blesses and breaks the food, and gives it to the Apostles to set before the people (Matt. 14:19; Mark 6:41; Luke 9:16; John 6:11). Who is not here reminded of a father beginning to celebrate the Paschal feast with his family? Our Saviour celebrates here, as it were, His Pasch. We see the same trait of piety in His care for the remains of the miraculous meal (John 6:12). Thirdly, He showed great kindness and consideration for the Apostles, since He let them take part in the miracle, whether the loaves increased only in His hands and the Apostles merely distributed them, or that the bread increased only in their hands, or that the increase began in the hands of Jesus and continued in those of the Apostles (Matt. 14:19; Mark 6:41; Luke 9:16; John 6:11). Lastly, our Saviour worked the miracle with generosity and great munificence. He gave so much bread that all had enough (Matt. 14:20; Mark 6:42; Luke 9:17; John 6:12), indeed as much as they desired (John 6:11), and in such abundance that twelve baskets full of fragments could be collected (Matt. 14:20; Mark 6:43; Luke 9:17; John 6:13); thus He showed a truly royal munificence. Five thousand men alone ate, without reckoning the women and children (Matt. 14:21; Mark 6:44; Luke 9:14; John 6:10). It was the custom with the Jews to take with them in baskets what they needed on a journey; hence the baskets for the fragments. The quantity of food which remained over attests not merely the bounty and munificence of our Lord, but also His wisdom. The remains, much greater than the original provision, are an irrefutable proof of the miracle. Such was the outward accomplishment of the miracle. Incomparably more beautiful and precious, in themselves and in the eyes of God, were the interior dispositions—the kindness, benevolence, love, joy, and gratitude towards God—with which our Lord did everything.

### 3. THE EFFECTS OF THE MIRACLE

The effect must naturally have been very remarkable, since the miracle lasted a considerable time and was renewed upon each participator. Under the powerful impression produced by this marvel (which very naturally recalled the miraculous feeding of the people in the wilderness under Moses) and the influence of the solemn Paschal season, it is not surprising that voices began to ask if our Saviour were not the promised great prophet who was to come, i.e. the Messias, and that the impulsive Galileans began to form the plan of taking Him with them to Jerusalem by force, and there, on the Feast of the Pasch, proclaiming Him the king of Israel (John 6:14). The gratitude, enthusiasm, and conviction that Jesus was the Messias, which prompted this resolution, were certainly commendable, but they were wrong in thinking that His kingdom was to be a material and earthly one.

Thus good and evil, faith and unbelief, gratitude and egotism mingled together in this resolve.

Our Saviour saw their thoughts, and in order to anticipate and prevent their plan He ordered the disciples to embark at once and row back to Capharnaum, on the west coast. He could thus dismiss the people more easily. They saw from this that He would not remain here, and dispersed. Jesus Himself disappeared, and went up to the mountain from which He had descended to the people, in order to pray (John 6:15, 16; Matt. 14:22, 23; Mark 6:45, 46). This special prayer is a sign that something important is again impending.

Such was the first multiplication of the loaves, and it is a beautiful and significant mystery. It is above all very important and full of meaning as regards the Person and character of Jesus. The zeal for souls with which His Heart was burning is here strikingly revealed; at the sight of the poor people He forgets all His own wants, receives them kindly, and is never weary of instructing them. He shows also His kindness of heart, immediately falls in with the suggestion of the Apostles, and had indeed already intended to work the miracle. Further, He manifests His piety, beginning everything with God and by prayer. We see too His magnanimity; the Apostles themselves are to feed the people who have deprived them of their repose, to share their provisions with them, and for this very purpose He bestows abundance of bread and fish. Lastly, we see the wisdom of His Sacred Heart in the care He takes that the miracle shall be irrefutably established, while His humility and unselfishness are revealed in the quiet, unobtrusive manner in which He performs it, in His acceptance of the assistance of the Apostles, and again in His refusing to let the people make Him king, in their gratitude. Here indeed is depicted the character of a king. And what prospects He opens out to faith by this miracle, in entirely new spheres of His divine power! What a vista it opens of new types of divine things, taking us back to Moses and the manna, and onwards to His own destiny, to the fourth Paschal feast which He will celebrate in Jerusalem a year later, and still farther on into His Eucharistic life in the Church! For the Apostles too and for the Church the mystery is of great significance. To the Apostles this miracle of the multiplication of the loaves must have brought a great increase of faith and love, since they saw the Divinity of our Saviour so gloriously confirmed and themselves so honored. They are the official intermediaries between our Saviour and the people. They represent to Him the wants of the latter, and He holds a familiar consultation with them as to how these wants may be satisfied. The Apostles here appear for the first time as taking an active part in a miracle of our Saviour, as His instruments, so to speak, and thus prefigure their glorious vocation and office with regard to the Holy Eucharist, which is the soul of the Catholic Church. Lastly, the mystery affords a fresh evidence of the worldly and carnal ideas of the Jews concerning the Messianic kingdom, and therein lies the germ of their own future fate.

## Our Saviour Walks upon the Water

John 6:17. And when they had gone up into a ship, they went over the sea to Capharnaum; and it was now dark, and Jesus was not come unto them.—18. And the sea arose, by reason of a great wind that blew.—19. When they had rowed therefore about five and twenty or thirty furlongs, they see Jesus walking upon the sea, and drawing nigh to the ship, and they were afraid.—20. But he saith to them: "It is I, be not afraid."—21. They were willing therefore to take him into the ship; and presently the ship was at the land, to which they were going.

Mark 6:47. And when it was late, the ship was in the midst of the sea, and himself alone on the land.—48. And seeing them laboring in rowing (for the wind was against them), and about the fourth watch of the night, he cometh to them, walking upon the sea; and he would have passed by them.—49. But they seeing him walking upon the sea, thought it was an apparition, and they cried out.—50. For they all saw him, and were troubled. And immediately he spoke with them, and said to them: "Have a good heart, it is I, fear ye not."—51. And he went up to them into the ship, and the wind ceased; and they were far more astonished within themselves:—52. For they understood not concerning the loaves; for their heart was blinded.

Matt. 14:24. But the boat in the midst of the sea was tossed with the waves; for the wind was contrary.—25. And in the fourth watch of the night he came to them, walking upon the sea.—26. And they seeing him walking upon the sea were troubled, saying: "It is an apparition." And they cried out for fear.—27. And immediately Jesus spoke to them, saying: "Be of good heart: It is I, fear ye not."—28. And Peter making answer, said: "Lord, if it be thou, bid me come to thee upon the waters."—29. And he said: "Come." And Peter going down out of the boat, walked upon the water to come to Jesus.—30. But seeing the wind strong, he was afraid; and when he began to sink, he cried out, saying: "Lord, save me."—31. And immediately Jesus stretching forth his hand took hold of him, and said to him: "O thou of little faith, why didst thou doubt?"—32. And when they were come up into the boat, the wind ceased.—33. And they that were in the boat came and adored him, saying: "Indeed thou art the Son of God."

The miracles performed on or in connection with the sea have, as has already been observed, their special signification for the Apostles, for Peter in particular, and in and through them for the whole Church. So also our Saviour's walking upon the water.

### 1. THE SIGNIFICANCE OF THE MIRACLE FOR THE APOSTLES

Hard indeed for the Apostles was the order to embark, and the passage itself no easy one. It was already evening, and dark (Matt. 14:23; Mark 6:47; John 6:17); there was a very strong and contrary wind, the sea ran high, the little boat was tossed about by the waves, and it was almost in vain that the Apostles wearied themselves with rowing, in order to make progress (Matt. 14:24; Mark 6:48; John 6:18). Indeed, from evening until about three or four o'clock in the morning they had only made from 25 to 30 furlongs (John 6:19), about two-thirds of the distance, which was nearly 40 furlongs, or five miles; and they were quite alone and left to their own resources (Mark 6:47; John 6:17). It was certainly a very unpleasant situation. But our Saviour, in prayer upon the heights near the coast, did not forget them. He saw how they strove against wind and waves, had compassion on them, and came to them at last, at the fourth watch (from three to six o'clock in the morning), walking upon the water, in order to comfort and help them (Matt. 14:25; Mark 6:48; John 6:19). They thought it was a spirit, and cried out for fear; but He reassured them, told them who He was, entered the boat, stilled the storm, and they suddenly saw themselves at the shore (Matt. 14:26, 27, 32; Mark 6:49, 50, 51; John 6:19, 20, 21). This, then, was our Saviour's first intention in walking upon the water; He wished to comfort His disciples by His presence and to help them out of their difficulty.

His second intention was to strengthen and increase the faith of the Apostles by a new and extraordinary proof of His divine power over the elements and the laws of nature. The exceeding fear of the Apostles, and the doubt of St. Peter implied by the words: "Lord, if it be Thou, bid me come to Thee upon the waters" (Matt. 14:28), sufficiently show that even the miracle of the loaves had not yet made their faith universal and unhesitating. For this reason St. Mark observes that "they understood not concerning the loaves; for their heart was blinded" (Mark 6:51, 52). In their utter surprise at the miracle, they knew not what to think of it. It was probably on this account that our Saviour made as though He would pass by (Mark 6:48). The Apostles also needed to be strengthened in faith in preparation for the promise of the Holy Eucharist, which He was now about to make to them. With this intention our Saviour adds miracle to miracle, passing through the air, walking upon the water, stilling the storm, and bringing the boat suddenly to land. In this passage through the air and walking upon the water, our Saviour works a miracle which is especially calculated to prepare them to believe in the real presence of His Body in the Holy Eucharist. This is a miracle wrought upon His own Body; it attests His power over the same, and is a foreshadowing of the Transfiguration on Thabor and of the glorious state of His Body and its miraculous presence in the Blessed Sacrament of the Altar. It is the practical explanation of the words they are soon to hear: "The spirit quickeneth, the flesh profiteth nothing" (John 6:64). The events in the synagogue at Capharnaum are so important that our Saviour must leave nothing undone in order to bring about the right dispositions in the minds of the Apostles. For this reason He has been working, during this period which immediately precedes it, one astounding miracle after another before their eyes, in order to make their faith in His Divinity clear, conscious and steadfast. The effect of this miracle upon the Apostles, then, was in this case also an express acknowledgment of His Divinity (Matt. 14:33). The people too had a certain share in this miracle and its effect, inasmuch as they became conscious in Capharnaum that our Saviour must have come across the lake by miraculous means (John 6:22, 25).

## 2. SIGNIFICANCE OF THE MIRACLE FOR ST. PETER

The latter part of the miracle had a special significance for St. Peter, who begged our Saviour, as a sign that it was really He who was walking upon the water, to allow him to come to Him. Our Saviour permitted it; Peter really walked, like our Lord Himself, upon the water, but on his beginning to doubt immediately began also to sink, when Jesus took him by the hand, reproving him for his doubt, and both came up into the boat together. St. Peter receives here a valuable lesson with regard to his characteristic fault, and also instruction for his future office as head of the Church, while at the same time that office is here prefigured.

Although there may have been some indiscretion and misplaced zeal in the desire of St. Peter to walk upon the water (Matt. 14:28), it yet proves his faith, love and attachment to our Saviour. He was always a thought, a word and a deed ahead of the others. In order to give him a lesson our Saviour let him fall into the usual consequences of this fault, namely faint-heartedness and discouragement. He began to be afraid of the powerful wind and tumultuous waves, and sank. In his distress, but yet full of faith, he cried out, and our Lord caught him by the hand with the reproof: "O thou of little faith, why didst thou doubt?" (Matt. 14:30, 31.) Supported by our Saviour's hand, he now walked firmly and safely to the boat (Matt. 14:32). Thus the goodness of our Lord and Peter's believing prayer for help repaired the fault, but it taught him a useful lesson. Peter is the master of the ship; he alone claims a share in the miraculous walking of our Lord, and obtains it; he is not supported by the boat, but by his faith and our Lord's hand; he may, therefore, begin to sink, but is not submerged and does not perish, so long as he believes and trusts to our Lord's hand. Such is the Papal Infallibility in its distinguishing characteristics: sustained by God's unfailing hand. This new miracle, that Peter also walked upon the waves through the power of Christ, must surely have powerfully increased the faith and love of Peter himself and of the other Apostles.

### 3. SIGNIFICATION OF THE MIRACLE FOR THE CHURCH

The following interpretation of the miracle relates not only to the Church in general, but also to each individual member of the Church.

This miracle is before all things a revelation of Christ's government and divine protection of His Church. Even if He sends her out into the darkness, through fearful storms, over menacing waves, and if she seems to be sailing alone and unaided, our Lord is yet thinking of her in His divine yet human prayer on the shore. He sees her; He loves and pities her. He follows her, accompanies her, recognized or unrecognized, often even in a strange, inexplicable form. Now He is at her side, now in advance, showing her the way and smoothing the waves. He encourages her, repairs her faults, guides, protects and speeds her on her way, not only in His own Person, but also through the Pope, her head. It is a beautiful and touching picture of the Papal Infallibility and power; Christ and Peter walking hand in hand, this alliance of the visible and the invisible, the Divine and the human Head of the Church. They hold one another fast; the Hand of the One is power, that of the other trust. Thus united they enter into the common ship; both together still the storm; both together bring about a calm, offer security and a quick, happy passage. This helping and guiding presence of our Lord is evident in many critical periods of Church history.

This interpretation of the miracle is in a manner repeated in every member of the Church. It teaches each one of us, first, to have confidence, whatever may happen. God, our Saviour, is with us by His Providence; that is, with His wisdom, goodness and power. We must not fear, however terrible things may seem to us. Secondly, we must beware of presumption, which is sometimes followed by the opposite fault and makes us responsible for the consequences. Thirdly and lastly, we must not despair even if this should be the case, but call for help. Our Lord's hand is near. Through prayer we may seize it.

### JESUS IN THE SYNAGOGUE AT CAPHARNAUM. OUR SAVIOUR THE BREAD OF LIFE

JOHN 6:22. The next day the multitude that stood on the other side of the sea saw that there was no other ship there but one, and that Jesus had not entered into the ship with his disciples, but that his disciples were gone away alone;—23. But other ships came in from Tiberias, nigh unto the place where they had eaten bread, the Lord giving thanks.—24. When therefore the multitude saw that Jesus was not there, nor his disciples, they took shipping, and came to Capharnaum seeking for Jesus.—25. And when they had found him on the other side of the sea, they said to him: "Rabbi, when camest thou hither?"—26. Jesus answered them and said: "Amen, amen I say to you: you seek me not because you have seen miracles, but because you did eat of the loaves and were filled.—27. Labor not for the meat which perisheth, but for that which endureth unto life everlasting, which the Son of Man will give you. For him hath God the Father sealed."—28. They said therefore unto him: "What shall we do that we may work the works of God?"—29. Jesus answered and said to them: "This is the work of God, that you believe in him whom he hath sent."—30. They said therefore to him: "What sign therefore dost thou show that we may see, and may believe thee? What dost thou work?—31. Our fathers did eat manna in the desert, as it is written: He gave them bread from heaven to eat."—32. Then Jesus said to them: "Amen, amen I say to you, Moses gave you not bread from heaven, but my Father giveth you the true bread from heaven.—33. For the bread of God is that which cometh down from heaven, and giveth life to the world."—34. They said therefore unto him: "Lord, give us always this bread."—35. And Jesus said to them: "I am the bread of life; he that cometh to me shall not hunger, and he that believeth in me shall never thirst.—36. But I said unto you, that you also have seen me, and you believe not.—37. All that the Father giveth me, shall come to me; and him that cometh to me, I will not cast out;—38. Because I came down from heaven, not to do my own will, but the will of him that sent me.—39. Now this is the will of the Father who sent me: that of all that he hath given me, I should lose nothing, but should raise it up again in the last day.—40. And this is the will of my Father that sent me: that everyone who seeth the Son, and believeth in him, may have life everlasting, and I will raise him up in the last day."—41. The Jews therefore murmured at him, because he had said: "I am the living bread which came down from heaven."—42. And they said: "Is not this Jesus the son of Joseph, whose father and mother we know? How then saith he: I came down from heaven?"—43. Jesus therefore answered and said to them: "Murmur not among yourselves.—44. No man can come to me, except the

Father, who hath sent me, draw him; and I will raise him up in the last day.—
45. It is written in the prophets: And they shall all be taught of God. Everyone
that hath heard of the Father, and hath learned, cometh to me.—46. Not that
any man hath seen the Father, but he who is of God, he hath seen the Father.—
47. Amen, amen I say unto you: He that believeth in me hath everlasting life.—
48. I am the bread of life.—49. Your fathers did eat manna in the desert, and
are dead.—50. This is the bread which cometh down from heaven; that if any
man eat of it, he may not die.—51. I am the living bread, which came
down from heaven.—52. If any man eat of this bread, he shall live for ever;
and the bread that I will give is my flesh for the life of the world."—53. The
Jews therefore strove among themselves, saying: "How can this man give us his
flesh to eat?"—54. Then Jesus said to them: "Amen, amen I say unto you: Except
you eat the flesh of the Son of Man, and drink his blood, you shall not have life in
you.—55. He that eateth my flesh, and drinketh my blood, hath everlasting life;
and I will raise him up in the last day.—56. For my flesh is meat indeed; and
my blood is drink indeed;—57. He that eateth my flesh and drinketh my blood,
abideth in me, and I in him.—58. As the living Father hath sent me, and I live by
the Father; so he that eateth me, the same also shall live by me.—59. This is the
bread that came down from heaven. Not as your fathers did eat manna, and are
dead. He that eateth this bread shall live for ever."—60. These things he said
teaching in the synagogue in Capharnaum.—61. Many therefore of his disciples
hearing it, said: "This saying is hard, and who can hear it?"—62. But Jesus knowing in himself that his disciples murmured at this, said to them: "Doth this
scandalize you?—63. If then you shall see the Son of Man ascend up where he
was before?—64. It is the spirit that quickeneth; the flesh profiteth nothing. The
words that I have spoken to you are spirit and life.—65. But there are some of
you that believe not." For Jesus knew from the beginning who they were that did
not believe, and who he was that would betray him.—66. And he said: "Therefore did I say to you, that no man can come to me, unless it be given him by
my Father."—67. After this many of his disciples went back, and walked no more
with him.—68. Then Jesus said to the twelve: "Will you also go away?"—69. And
Simon Peter answered him: "Lord, to whom shall we go? Thou hast the words
of eternal life.—70. And we have believed and have known that thou art the
Christ, the Son of God."—71. Jesus answered them: "Have not I chosen you
twelve, and one of you is a devil?"—72. Now he meant Judas Iscariot, the son
of Simon; for this same was about to betray him, whereas he was one of the twelve.

## 1. CIRCUMSTANCES OF THE DISCOURSE

This important discourse was held by our Saviour at the time
of the Paschal feast (John 6:4), a fact in itself of great significance with regard to events both past and future, as will be shown
in the mystery itself. Moreover it was probably delivered on a
Sabbath-day (John 6:60), which is considered a sort of Paschal
celebration.

The place was not the lonely wilderness, but Capharnum (John
6:24, 25), one of the most populous and important cities of
Galilee; and further it was in the synagogue of Capharnaum.
These circumstances gave a deeper meaning to every particular:
the certainty and importance of the revelation, the promise, and

the sorrow of our Lord at the apostasy of many. The audience was large, on account of the time and place as well as of the previous miracles. It consisted chiefly of the crowds of people who had been witnesses of the multiplication of the loaves. They were very much astonished, on the morning after the miracle, not to find our Saviour at the place where it had been performed, since the only boat that was there at the time (viz. that belonging to the Apostles) had gone off without Him. They made use of some ships which had just come over from Tiberias, to seek our Saviour in Capharnaum, and found Him there (John 6:22–25) or at some place near (Matt. 14:34; Mark 6:53), from which He followed them to Capharnaum. They received no answer to their question as to how He had come across the lake (John 6:26); but still they must have had some suspicion of a new miracle. They were therefore greatly excited, but yet, with all their enthusiasm, full of Jewish ideas, anxious only for what was earthly and material; for our Saviour Himself reproaches them (John 6:26) for seeking only temporal blessings in Him and His miracles (John 6:34). Besides these, there were also Jews in the synagogue (John 6:41, 53), i.e. such as had either been sent hither from Judaea by the Pharisees, or at all events held with their party; without faith (John 6:36), and full of prejudice against our Saviour. As often as His words rise above material things, they reject them, murmur and fall away. These Jews and the people, together with the Apostles and a number of disciples (John 6:61), constituted His hearers; thus the larger part of His audience was by no means spiritually-minded.

### 2. THE DISCOURSE

The entire address consists of an introduction and one principal proposition divided into two parts.

The introduction takes the form of the following colloquy. The people seek Jesus in Capharnaum, and our Saviour thus reproaches them: "You seek, even in My miracles, only material bread; strive rather to obtain the bread of eternal life, the spiritual bread which the Son of Man will give you: for the Father has marked Him out and attested the truth of His words by the seal of miracles" (John 6:26, 27). "What then shall we do, in order to obtain this bread?" the people ask (John 6:28). "Believe in the Son of Man, whom God has sent," is the answer of Jesus (John 6:29). "Moses gave our fathers, the whole nation, heavenly manna during many years. What special, greater sign will You do, in order that we may believe in You?" reply the Jews, who will be satisfied with no other wonder, in order to acknowledge Him as the Messias, than that of His allowing Himself to be made king by them (John 6:30, 31). "Moses did not give you the true bread (but merely the type of it)," our Lord answers; "the Father gives you the true bread, which really comes down from heaven and gives life to the world" (John 6:32, 33). "Give us this bread now (that we may believe in You)," say the Jews (John 6:34). "I am the (this) bread of life," is our Saviour's answer (John 6:35).

"I am the bread of life": this, then, is the great proposition which our Lord wishes to place before them. All is in beautiful sequence: He works the miracle of the loaves, the people desire material bread, and expect that the Messias will work a greater miracle than that of the manna had been, in order to nourish them; therefore our Saviour represents Himself as the true Bread of Life, in His Person, His Incarnation and quality of God-Man and Messias, and in the Holy Eucharist. This double quality of our Saviour corresponds to a double requirement on His side and a double duty on ours, in order to obtain Him as the Bread of Life (John 6:28).

The first requirement and duty is faith in Jesus, as the Son of God and His Messenger. So the Jews understood our Saviour, and therefore they murmured, because He ascribed to Himself a divine origin (John 6:41, 42). In this quality our Saviour is the Bread of Life through faith. He treats of this in verses 35–51, giving beautiful motives for this duty of faith. On His own side the motives are as follows: He is "sealed" by the Father, indeed by virtue of His generation by the Father He is essentially His seal and image, authenticated by miracles (John 6:27); He alone sees the Father, whilst all others only hear Him through grace (John 6:46). On our side the motives of faith are its glorious advantages and rewards. "He that believeth shall never thirst" (John 6:35); our Saviour will not cast out the believer nor suffer him to be lost, but will raise him up at the last day and give him everlasting life (John 6:37, 39, 40, 44, 47), and this in accordance with the decree and will of the Father, which He is come to fulfil (John 6:38, 39). On the contrary, whoever does not accept the invitation of grace to believe in Jesus, resists this Will of the Father, falls into unbelief and becomes reprobate; he does not belong to the

Messias, for this grace of being "given," "taught" and "drawn" is the work of the Father (John 6:37, 39, 44, 45).

The second requirement and duty towards our Saviour as the Eucharistic Bread is actually to partake of It with faith. Our Saviour expressly declares and treats of this in verses 52–59, in which He reveals the whole mystery of the Holy Eucharist. He first promises to institute It (John 6:52). Secondly, He reveals Its substance, viz. His Flesh and Blood, Divinity and Humanity, under the appearances of bread and wine (John 6:52, 56, 57, 63, 64); It is to be really consumed (John 6:54, 55, 57). He also gives sufficient proofs of this truth. The first thing that confirms it is the ordinary sense of the words, which cannot reasonably be understood otherwise, especially when compared with the subsequent institution of the Sacrament (Luke 22:19). Further, our Saviour promises this giving of Himself for food as something new, which has not been before (John 6:52); He compares it to the manna, which was really eaten (John 6:49, 59). Then again the disciples and the Jews understood it thus, and He acquiesces in this, nay, protests its truth and insists upon it, at the risk of the apostasy of the Jews, His disciples and Apostles, even of the whole world (John 6:54, 62, 68). Finally, He explains this miracle by appealing to other and greater ones: to His Divinity, which can make of His tangible, mortal body a glorified and spiritual one, such as He had at His Ascension (John 6:63, 64). Thirdly, He speaks of the Holy Eucharist as a Sacrament, prescribing Its consumption as a condition of eternal life (John 6:54, 55); and as a sacrifice, especially in verse 52, which, according to the words of Scripture, expresses the sacrificial character of the Body and Blood of Christ in the sacrifice of the Cross as well as in that of Holy Mass, which are both real sacrifices (Luke 22:19; I Cor. 11:24). By this sacrificial character the Holy Eucharist fulfils the type of the Paschal Lamb, the consecrated and sacrificed flesh of which was at once a sacrifice and a sacrificial meal. Fourthly, our Saviour lays stress upon the effects of the Holy Eucharist. It is the Sacrament of life, the preservation of life, the protection of life (of soul as well as of body) against death; It is the increase of life, corresponding exactly to the effect produced by the food under the appearances of which It is administered (John 6:50, 52, 54, 55, 59). The Holy Eucharist unites us really to Christ; in the first place physically, as the food consumed unites itself to our body, and out of this union arises the moral union also, by a spiritual transformation into Christ (John 6:57), which reaches its highest perfection in an entirely God-like life, resembling that of the God-Man. As the Son of God He is generated by the Father and sent by Him, and has in Himself, through this union of life with the Father, the divine life of the latter; so also will he who receives (consumes) the Body of Christ participate, by virtue of the union with Him, in His divinely-human life (John 6:58). Our Saviour ends His address as He had begun it, with the words: "This is the bread that came down from heaven" (John 6:33, 35, 41, 59).

### 3. CONSEQUENCES AND EFFECTS OF THE DISCOURSE

The results of this discourse showed themselves in the people, the disciples and the Apostles, and differed in each case.

The people, however well-disposed and enthusiastic they seem to be, always reject the words of our Lord whenever what He requires rises above things sensible and material. If He requires faith (John 6:29), they demand miracles, always miracles. Now again, as He promises a more excellent bread than Moses had given (John 6:30, 31), and as He terms Himself the Bread of Life and ascribes to Himself a divine origin, they murmur, led away by the Pharisaic party; they speak of His origin with contempt (John 6:41, 42), and dispute amongst themselves over the possibility of His giving them His flesh to eat, but do not ask for an explanation (John 6:53). The fact is, they do not believe, as our Saviour Himself reproachfully declares, although they have seen miracles (John 6:36). And He also gives the explanation of this unbelief: it is because they have not the special attraction of grace and enlightenment which the Father gives or withholds as He wills; and because they resist the ordinary and sufficient grace (John 6:44). So, with them, it all ends. In Galilee the people do not seek to kill our Saviour, they merely forsake Him.

The disciples are scandalized at the mystery of the Holy Eucharist (John 6:61). Our Saviour tries to lighten their difficulty, first by the revelation of His wisdom, telling them their secret thoughts (John 6:62); secondly, by hinting at His glorious Ascension, which presupposes a spiritualized Body, such as they were here to represent to themselves, not a Body such as He now has (John 6:63); and thirdly, by appealing to His Divinity, which can effect everything, whilst His Humanity alone cannot do so; the Divinity alone produces all the supernatural effects which He predicts of His Body (John 6:64). But they persist in their re-

sistance (John 6:65), and, with His deep insight, He recognizes
the cause of this unbelief in their want of special enlightenment,
as was the case with the Jews (John 6:66). Many of His disciples
openly break with Him, give up their faith in Him, and hold no
further intercourse with Him. How this desertion must have
pained His Heart!

In His grief and in His love for the Apostles, He turns to these,
asking if they also will forsake Him (John 6:68). Peter, full as
ever of faith and zeal, impetuously replies, in the name of all:
"Lord, to whom shall we go? (We know no one to whom we
would rather go, or who is more necessary to us.) Thou alone
hast the saving doctrine. For we have believed in Thee, and know
(as we have seen by Thy miracles) that Thou art the Son of God"
(John 6:69, 70). A glorious confession of faith, made publicly,
before all the people and in the face of the angry contradictions
of our Lord's enemies. What consolation this full and courageous
confession must have given Him! But even this joy was not un-
mixed. Peter had thought he could speak in the name and from
the hearts of all the Apostles. And yet our Lord answered: "Have
not I chosen you twelve, and one of you is a devil?" (John 6:71.)
An enemy, even among such a small number, an opponent, envious and antagonistic to the death! He meant Judas, who was to
betray Him, although he was one of the twelve. It would appear,
therefore, that Judas was already in bad dispositions, or that his
faith in the Divinity of Jesus suffered shipwreck on this occasion
(John 6:65), and he now entered upon the fatal path which ended
with the betrayal of our Lord and Judas' own suicide.

Such was the memorable day at Capharnaum. It is infinite in
the range of its influence with regard to the Person of our Saviour
as well as to the entire system of our holy religion. How gloriously
the character of Jesus is revealed here! How well His magnificent
intellect understands the art of linking the most profound instructions to the circumstances of the moment! In connection
with the word "bread" He unfolds the most sublime revelations
concerning His nature, His task in life, His influence in the human
race, His future existence in the Eucharistic Life, and the tremendous efficacy of the latter. It is always the same idea, but with
what a multiplicity, variety and wealth of truths He surrounds it!
At the same time the purity and disinterestedness of His Will
are manifested. He loves truth, and will have no half-hearted
followers. He does not fear, therefore, to try their spirit by clear,

sharply defined truths, and to call upon them to make their decision. He retracts nothing, though the whole world should forsake Him. "Will you also go away?" He says to the Apostles. One feels in these words all the gravity of the situation, and the pain and sadness of His sacred, human Heart. Lastly, the day is of importance with regard to the destiny of our Saviour. It is the third Feast of the Pasch (John 6:4). The revelation of Himself which He had made upon the second Paschal feast, in Jerusalem, is here carried considerably farther, and therefore the plot against Him is yet more fully developed; the fourth Paschal feast is prefigured in every respect, and the way for it paved. Indeed, the three mysteries which fall about this period of the third Paschal feast— the miracle of the loaves, the walking upon the water, and the promise of the Holy Eucharist—make up a fairly perfect picture of the fourth Paschal feast, upon which our Saviour instituted the Blessed Sacrament, was betrayed by an Apostle (John 6:65, 71), grieved by the pusillanimity and faint-heartedness of Peter and the unbelief and desertion of the people, and brought to the Cross by the hatred of His enemies. All these sorrowful events have here their types and foreshadowings. His position is already so critical that He cannot celebrate the Feast of the Pasch in Jerusalem, because the Jews seek to kill Him (John 7:1). It is beyond all doubt that a decisive turn was given to affairs by this mystery, and that dissension and disruption were introduced even amongst the disciples (John 6:67).

With regard to faith and doctrine, the new evidences given here of the Divinity of Christ are of special importance. He Himself ascribes divine attributes to His own Person. He is the Son of God (John 6:32, 40); He sees the Father (John 6:46); He has the same life as the Father (John 6:58); He is the Searcher of hearts (John 6:62, 65, 71); the Source of supernatural life (John 6:33, 35, 47, 52, 55); the Lord of life and death (John 6:39, 40). And in addition to all this we have the testimony of St. Peter. Secondly, the mystery of the Holy Eucharist is revealed in every respect, as regards Its nature, use and effects, and also Its history. Here we have not only the preparation for It by types, such as the manna, but also Its history in Christendom; Its veneration and the contradiction It meets with are prefigured here. On the one hand Peter and the Apostles foreshadow the adorers of the Blessed Sacrament, whilst the disciples and the Jews represent those who outrage and deny It. Lastly, the mystery contains a testimony to the necessity and efficacy of the preventing grace of God, which yet does no violence to the freedom of man. No one comes to Christ except by the inspiration and drawing of the Father (John 6:44, 45, 66–69). A glimpse is here afforded us of the manner in which divine predestination is carried out and put into effect. How significant and important is this attraction towards our Divine Saviour in the spiritual life! It is simply election, predestination. How important also is prayer to our Heavenly Father, that He may reveal His Son to us, draw us and give us to Him! Faith and the Blessed Sacrament are the chief means of union with Christ.

## D. The Public Life from the Third Feast of the Pasch to the Feast of Tabernacles

During this period our Saviour continues to reveal Himself by miracles. The culminating points of this revelation of Himself to the Apostles are His answer to Peter's confession of His Divinity, and the Transfiguration. Our Lord then begins to predict His Passion. The constitution of the Church receives an important amplification in the promise of the Primacy to Peter, and in the choice and sending forth of the seventy disciples. This period contains repeated instances of labor upon ground where heathenism was strong, namely in Tyre, Sidon, Ituraea and the Decapolis, and ends with the close of the ministry in Galilee.

### The Dispute Concerning Tradition

MATT. 14:34. And having passed the water, they came into the country of Genesar.—35. And when the men of that place had knowledge of him, they sent into all that country and brought to him all that were diseased;—36. And they besought him that they might touch but the hem of his garment. And as many as touched, were made whole.—15:1. Then came to him from Jerusalem scribes and Pharisees, saying:—2. "Why do thy disciples transgress the tradition of the ancients? For they wash not their hands when they eat bread."—3. But he answering, said to them: "Why do you also transgress the commandment of God for your tradition? For God said:—4. Honor thy father and mother; and: He that shall curse father or mother, let him die the death.—5. But you say: Whosover shall say to father or mother, The gift whatsoever proceedeth from me, shall profit thee;—6. And he shall not honor his father or his mother: and you have made void the commandment of God for your tradition.—7. Hypocrites, well hath Isaias prophesied of you, saying:—8. This people honoreth me with their lips; but their heart is far from me.—9. And in vain do they worship me, teaching doctrines and commandments of men."—10. And having called together the multitudes unto him, he said to them: "Hear ye and understand.—11. Not that which goeth into the mouth, defileth a man; but what cometh out of the mouth, this defileth a man."—12. Then came his disciples, and said to him: "Dost thou know that the Pharisees, when they heard this word, were scandalized?"—

13. But he answering said: "Every plant which my heavenly Father hath not planted, shall be rooted up.—14. Let them alone; they are blind, and leaders of the blind; and if the blind lead the blind, both fall into the pit."—15. And Peter answering said to him: "Expound to us this parable."—16. But he said: "Are you also yet without understanding?—17. Do you not understand, that whatsoever entereth into the mouth, goeth into the belly, and is cast out into the privy?—18. But the things which proceed out of the mouth, come forth from the heart, and those things defile a man.—19. For from the heart come forth evil thoughts, murders, adulteries, fornications, thefts, false testimonies, blasphemies;—20. These are the things that defile a man. But to eat with unwashed hands doth not defile a man."

MARK 6:53. And when they had passed over, they came into the land of Genesareth, and set to the shore.—54. And when they were gone out of the ship, immediately they knew him;—55. And running through that whole country, they began to carry about in beds those that were sick, where they heard he was.—56. And whithersoever he entered, into towns or into villages or into cities, they laid the sick in the streets, and besought him that they might touch but the hem of his garment; and as many as touched him were made whole.—7:1. And there assembled together unto him the Pharisees and some of the scribes, coming from Jerusalem.—2. And when they had seen some of his disciples eat bread with common, that is, with unwashed hands, they found fault.—3. For the Pharisees and all the Jews eat not without often washing their hands, holding the tradition of the ancients;—4. And when they come from the market, unless they be washed, they eat not; and many other things there are that have been delivered to them to observe, the washings of cups and of pots, and of brazen vessels and of beds.—5. And the Pharisees and scribes asked him: "Why do not thy disciples walk according to the tradition of the ancients, but they eat bread with common hands?"—6. But he answering, said to them: "Well did Isaias prophesy of you hypocrites, as it is written: This people honoreth me with their lips, but their heart is far from me.—7. And in vain do they worship me, teaching doctrines and precepts of men.—8. For leaving the commandment of God, you hold the tradition of men, the washings of pots and of cups; and many other things you do like to these."—9. And he said to them: "Well do you make void the commandment of God, that you may keep your own tradition.—10. For Moses said: Honor thy father and thy mother; and: He that shall curse father or mother, dying let him die.—11. But you say: If a man shall say to his father or mother, Corban (which is a gift), whatsoever is from me, shall profit thee;—12. And farther you suffer him not to do anything for his father or mother,—13. Making void the word of God by your own tradition, which you have given forth. And many other such like things you do."—14. And calling again the multitude unto him, he said to them: "Hear ye me all and understand.—15. There is nothing from without a man that entering into him, can defile him, but the things which come from a man, those are they that defile a man.—16. If any man have ears to hear, let him hear."—17. And when he was come into the house from the multitude, his disciples asked him the parable.—18. And he saith to them: "So are you also without knowledge? Understand you not that everything from without, entering into a man, cannot defile him;—19. Because it entereth not into his heart, but goeth into the belly, and goeth out into the privy, purging all meats?"—20. But he said that "the things which come out from a man, they defile a man.—21. For from within out of the heart of men proceed evil thoughts, adulteries, fornications, murders,—22. Thefts, covetousness, wickedness, deceit, lasciviousness, an evil eye, blasphemy, pride, foolishness.—23. All these evil things come from within, and defile a man."

JOHN 7:1. After these things Jesus walked in Galilee, for he would not walk in Judaea; because the Jews sought to kill him.

### 1. OUR SAVIOUR IS ATTACKED AND ACCUSED BY THE PHARISEES

Immediately upon His landing, on His return from the eastern shore of the lake, the rumor of our Lord's arrival was bruited abroad. And as He did not go into Judaea for the Feast of the Pasch, on account of the danger from the Jews, but remained in Galilee (John 7:1) and chiefly in Genesareth (Matt. 14:34; Mark 6:53), in the beautiful plain along the shore of the lake between Magdala and Bethsaida, all the people flocked thither to Him. They brought the sick, with the entreaty that they might be allowed merely to touch the hem of His garment. And all these sufferers were healed (Matt. 14:35, 36; Mark 6:55, 56). Probably it was this circumstance together with other recent events, which attracted the attention of the Pharisees and other enemies of our Blessed Lord.

It was the Pharisees and scribes who made the attack and accusation, and, amongst others, certain of them who had come from Jerusalem, who may have been sent officially, or perhaps had only come by chance. The teachers of the law traveled about the country a good deal, taught the law and exercised their vigilance over matters of doctrine, naturally according to the views of the Pharisees, if they belonged to that sect. Thus they were spying on our Lord, and found that some of the disciples ate without having previously washed their hands. They made out of this an accusation against our Saviour (Mark 7:5; Matt. 15:2).

And how did they bring the accusation against Him? Publicly, before all the people, attacking the Master instead of the disciples, in order to gain material for a new accusation from His answer; and without having previously called the disciples to account, they condemned and reviled their conduct, and with them their Master also (Mark 7:2).

What, then, was the actual subject of the accusation? Not a transgression of the law itself, but a violation of the "tradition of the ancients," and by this were meant not real precepts, but merely the interpretation of the law handed down from ancient masters who had made out of a few legal regulations (Lev. 15:11; Num. 19:22) a whole system of the most meaningless and tiresome ceremonies (observation of washings and purifications etc.) from a vain fear of contracting impurity by touching legally unclean objects, persons, and articles of food; as St. Mark indicates

(7:3, 4, 7) by the words "many other things." It was only a question, therefore, of human precepts, or "commandments of men" (Matt. 15:9; Mark 7:7). And they attached as much importance to these human precepts as to the actual law; indeed they placed them above it, thus destroying the law itself and its spirit by arbitrary, meaningless forms. A teacher was more to them than a prophet; his word, more than miracles. Such, then, was the accusation, full of malice and without foundation.

### 2. OUR SAVIOUR REPUDIATES THE ACCUSATION

Our Saviour repudiates the accusation very wisely. He does not enter into a discussion about the precepts and their authorization, nor does He deny the latter. This would only have injured His cause and furnished His enemies with a weapon against Him. Still less does He annul the dogmatic and ecclesiastical traditions. He does nothing of this kind.

He only opposes the precepts of the schools and sects. He attacks these latter unanswerably, on their weakest point, by an *argumentum ad hominem,* showing them in a practical, very well chosen matter how their precepts annul and set aside the commandments of God Himself, e.g. the Fourth Commandment. According to their teaching a man might say to his parents: "What could profit you of my property (or in order that it may profit you) is a gift to God," i.e. he paid a certain sum to the Temple and the priests, and then was not bound to trouble himself any further about the support of his parents (Matt. 15:5; Mark 7:11). In denunciation of this custom our Saviour very earnestly cites the law and the curse which was incurred by its violation (Ex. 20:12; 21:17; Deut. 5:16; Lev. 20:9), and emphasizes very strongly the "commandment of God" as opposed to the "precepts of man" (Mark 7:7, 8, 13; Matt. 15:3, 6, 9). "And," He remarks, "many other such like things you do" (Mark 7:13).

The answer becomes crushing when He quotes the prophetic passage from Isaias (29:13), in which he upbraids the people with the inveterate vices of inward degeneracy, lifelessness and torpidity, with the contradiction between their interior vices and outward profession, and the universal moral blindness of high and low, and finally announces the judgment. In truth, Pharisaism was nothing but the last development of this spirit, which the prophet censured even in his time, and the final destruction of the city and its Temple was nothing but the fulfilment of the measure of punishment of which the chastisement through the Assyrians and Babylonians had been only a part. Our Saviour rightly calls them "hypocrites," who worship God "in vain," without any foundation upon law and reason, without any moral value or result, in a meaningless and ignorant manner (Matt. 15:7; Mark 6:6, 7). He does not expressly announce to them the coming chastisement, but they could read it in the Book of Isaias.

### 3. OUR SAVIOUR PROFITS BY THE ACCUSATION TO GIVE A POSITIVE INSTRUCTION

As soon as the Pharisees were repulsed our Saviour called back the people, who, it appears, had made way out of respect for the teachers of the law; and He profited by the opportunity to instruct them as to what really constituted cleanness or uncleanness with regard to the laws concerning food (Gen. 7:8; Lev. 11), which were very wisely observed in the Old Covenant in order to separate and protect the people from heathenism. Uncleanness does not consist in the nature of the things themselves, but in the moral impurity which is contracted by partaking of what is forbidden, and which comes from the heart. Thus it is not really what goes into a man that defiles him, but what goes out from him, disobedience and all other sinful desires (Matt. 15:10, 11; Mark 6:14–16). So our Saviour explains it later on more fully, to His disciples in private (Matt. 15:15–20; Mark 7:17–23).

At the same time He sets at rest the fear of His disciples that the Pharisees had been scandalized by His words and would revenge themselves. To the first of these points He answers merely in an evasive manner, that they should "let them alone"; the scandal was a thoroughly Pharisaic one, i.e. one for which they had no other reason or occasion than their own perversity and malice, and He would give no answer to it, because it was not necessary and would be of no use. Otherwise He willingly gave explanations, as He did on this occasion to the Apostles (Matt. 15:15–20). Further, they were not to be afraid either of the Pharisees or of the misguided people. Every plant, i.e. every doctrine, which did not come from His Father would be rooted up by Him, together with its inventors and adherents. They would all perish, and that through their own doing, like a blind man and his blind guide (Matt. 11:12–14). Our Lord here utters a veiled prophecy of the judgment to come upon the people and their leaders.

We have here another beautiful example of our Saviour's method of teaching, showing how He makes use of every opportunity to give instruction and to build up the spiritual edifice of His Church; an example, also, of His clear and solid intellect, of the wisdom and prudence of His answers, and of His love of truth. Nothing is more repugnant to Him than untruth and hypocrisy. He rightly points out this as being the very essence of Pharisaism, and predicts the anger and chastisement of God upon it. On the other hand, our Lord here explains the authority and value of outward observances. He by no means rejects dogmatic and ecclesiastical traditions. He merely opposes purely human precepts which are proclaimed as the law of God, and this with evasion and to the detriment of the commandments of God and of believing reason. But the commandments of our holy Church are not mere human precepts, and do not derogate from reason and God's commandments, but rather to the contrary.

## THE CANAANITE WOMAN

MATT. 15:21. And Jesus went from thence, and retired into the coasts of Tyre and Sidon.—22. And behold a woman of Canaan who came out of those coasts, crying out, said to him: "Have mercy on me, O Lord, thou son of David; my daughter is grievously troubled by a devil."—23. Who answered her not a word. And his disciples came and besought him, saying: "Send her away; for she crieth after us."—24. And he answering, said: "I was not sent but to the sheep that are lost of the house of Israel."—25. But she came and adored him, saying: "Lord, help me."—26. Who answering said: "It is not good to take the bread of the children, and to cast it to the dogs."—27. But she said: "Yea, Lord; for the whelps also eat of the crumbs that fall from the table of their masters."—28. Then Jesus answering, said to her: "O woman, great is thy faith; be it done to thee as thou wilt." And her daughter was cured from that hour.

MARK 7:24. And rising from thence he went into the coast of Tyre and Sidon; and entering into a house, he would that no man should know it, and he could not be hid.—25. For a woman as soon as she heard of him, whose daughter had an unclean spirit, came in and fell down at his feet.—26. For the woman was a Gentile, a Syrophenician born. And she besought him that he would cast forth the devil out of her daughter.—27. Who said to her: "Suffer first the children to be filled; for it is not good to take the bread of the children and cast it to the dogs."—28. But she answered, and said to him: "Yea, Lord; for the whelps also eat under the table of the crumbs of the children."—29. And he said to her: "For this saying go thy way, the devil is gone out of thy daughter."—30. And when she was come into her house, she found the girl lying upon the bed, and that the devil was gone out.

### 1. OUR SAVIOUR

Our Saviour now undertook with His disciples a journey into the districts of Tyre and Sidon, which probably lasted about four or five days (cf. Introd., p. 4). The reason for this was probably His wish to escape from His enemies, or to bring comfort and instruction to the Israelites who dwelt there; but in any case He did not intend to exercise a public ministry there. It was Gentile land, the former "land of Canaan," and He "would that no man should know it" (Mark 7:24). But that was not possible. Immediately there came to Him a woman, a Gentile and Syrophenician (Mark 7:26), well educated (as it seems) and of the upper class, and followed Him, imploring Him to deliver her daughter, who was possessed by a devil and "grievously troubled" (Matt. 15:22). Our Lord would have nothing to do with her, paid no heed to her entreaties, and answered the Apostles, as they interceded for her, that He was only "sent to the sheep that were lost of the house of Israel" (Matt. 15:23, 24). He only granted her request at last after having previously given her a second and very hard rebuff.

In this occurrence we have three beautiful traits of character to admire in our Lord. First, His touching fidelity, sincerity and prudence with regard to His vocation. He is sent only to Israel. Such is the dispensation and ordinance of God. How it restricts His sphere of action! And yet how faithfully He abides by it, in word and deed! He scarcely ever goes beyond its limits, and when this does occur, still He does nothing officially, but merely as it were in passing, and because pressed by circumstances; and He acknowledges the right of Israel openly and in plain terms, setting the Gentiles aside, until Israel itself rejects Him. His Apostles are the first to go to the Gentile nations. But what a faithless flock this Israel was! How little it repaid His touching care! (Rom. 10:21.) And how much this cost His Sacred Heart, which saw and loved Its sheep amongst the Gentile nations also! (John 10:16; 11:52.) Nevertheless prudence willed it so; had He acted otherwise, the Jews would have reproached Him with it (John 7:35). Probably it was on this account that He at first rejected the intercession of the Apostles in this case.

Secondly, we must admire the wisdom of our Lord, as seen in His treatment of the woman. On the road He simply does not listen to her, and vouchsafes her neither a word nor a glance, because this was the most considerate manner of not granting her request. As she follows Him into the house (Mark 7:25), He replies very harshly that it is not good to cast the children's bread to the dogs, the children must first be satisfied (Matt. 15:26; Mark 7:27). He addresses her as a Gentile, a dog, certainly no honorable reception. And why does He do this? First on the woman's account, and on ours. In truth nothing better can befall us than to be given an opportunity to practise perseverance, to cooperate earnestly with grace, and to be purified, tried and humbled. In this manner we prepare ourselves best for the reception of great graces. This was the case here with this woman. Secondly, our Saviour acted thus on account of the matter in question. The Gentiles, full of unbelief and of the impurity of idolatry, stood infinitely below Israel, however degenerate the latter might be. In contrast to the children of the house, the dog is the type of uncleanness, of one who has no rights. For this reason our Saviour thus speaks to her, employing the ordinary form of speech. It was always opportune to establish this truth and recall it to remembrance. The very fact of her daughter's possession might sufficiently tell the mother to what an unclean and shameful master she and the whole of heathendom had fallen a prey, and it is not without reason that our Saviour, on His second entrance into Gentile land, immediately meets with a case of possession.

But we also see, thirdly, the power and goodness of our Lord. The Canaanite woman had stood the test well. He can no longer resist her confidence, perseverance and humility. He works the miracle from a distance, immediately frees her daughter (Mark 7:30), praises her faith and ascribes the miracle to it (Mark 7:29; Matt. 15:28).

### 2. THE APOSTLES

The Apostles appear here in the sublime and beautiful rôle of mediators. Quite unasked, they intercede (Matt. 15:23), and for a Gentile, whether from pity or because they were weary of hearing the poor woman begging and crying so loudly behind them. We see here an advance in their consciousness of their office as mediators, and since they go so far as to ask (indirectly) a miracle of our Lord, we may also hail with joy a considerable advance in their spirit of faith. The reason our Lord gave for not granting their request was calculated to give them an insight into their position, office and relations to Israel and to the Gentile nations; further, to inspire them with confidence and with love for their own nation, since it was so dear to God; and lastly, to increase their love for our Saviour, Who, in spite of all contradiction, remained so faithful to His vocation.

### 3. THE CANAANITE WOMAN

There are in this woman many beautiful and most touching qualities, well worthy of meditation. In the first place, her great love for her child. She sees it the victim of such a fearful and tyrannical power, and is helpless against the evil, as indeed all heathendom was. She feels the terrible misfortune as if it were her own. For this reason she begs our Saviour to have mercy on *her* (Matt. 15:22). It is this love which makes her so quick to devise an answer, so persevering and tenacious of her purpose, and which helps her to overcome all the bitterness of her errand and reception.

Further, the woman shows extraordinary faith, great confidence, and great perseverance. She calls our Saviour "Lord" and "Son of David" (Matt. 15:22). And with this she says everything. Natives of Tyre and Sidon had been present at the Sermon on the Mount, and since then the rumor of His miracles had spread everywhere. Thus she had arrived, by the grace of God, at the faith which so many Jews lacked and even opposed. As the prophet Elias had been obliged to come into this district, to Sarepta, in order to find faith, so also our Saviour. And no trials are able to make the woman waver in her confidence.

But the most touching thing of all is her humility. Our Saviour never put anyone else to such a hard test in this respect. First He lets her follow and entreat Him all along the street, without vouchsafing her so much as a glance; on the contrary, He even repulses her intercessors. Nevertheless she hurries after Him into the house, and falls at His feet (Mark 7:25; Matt. 15:25); and here she receives an extremely harsh rebuff. And what does the rich, probably aristocratic Gentile woman do? She is convinced of her unworthiness, acknowledges it, but contrives to reply to our Saviour's hard words in such an ingenious and touching manner that He is disarmed. He had said: "It is not good to take the bread of the children and cast it to the dogs." "Yea, Lord," she answers, "for the whelps also eat under the table of the crumbs of the children, their masters" (Mat. 15:27; Mark 7:28). In these words lie such ingenuity and beauty of thought, such touching humility and nobility of sentiment, that they are unanswerable. How our Saviour must have rejoiced over this soul! He answered: "For this saying go thy way, the devil is gone out of thy daughter" (Mark 7:29). We may conclude from the last words of the woman that she was of the upper class and well educated. They reveal extraordinary quickness and versatility of intellect. She actually found everything as our Saviour had said. Her daughter lay upon the bed, freed from the evil spirit (Mark 7:30).

It is evident that our Saviour intended, by His visit to the land of Canaan and this miracle of the deliverance of a Canaanite girl from the power of the devil, to reveal God's merciful intention of gradually removing the curse of Cham from his descendants, but only after and through Israel. For this reason our Lord marks out so sharply, by word and deed, the relations between Israel and heathendom. Only after the former has disdained salvation are the Apostles to go to the Gentiles (Acts 13:46). Our Saviour also shows very strikingly in this mystery what a believing, persevering, and especially a humble prayer can effect (Mark 7:29). Lastly, we may learn here neither to spare wise humiliations, nor to take them amiss when we receive them.

## THE CURE OF THE DEAF-MUTE

MARK 7:31. And again going out of the coasts of Tyre, he came by Sidon to the sea of Galilee, through the midst of the coasts of Decapolis.—32. And they bring to him one deaf and dumb; and they besought him that he would lay his hand upon him.—33. And taking him from the multitude apart, he put his fingers into his ears, and spitting, he touched his tongue;—34. And looking up to heaven, he groaned, and said to him: "Ephpheta," which is: Be thou opened.—35. And immediately his ears were opened, and the string of his tongue was loosed, and he spoke right.—36. And he charged them that they should tell no man. But the more he charged them, so much the more a great deal did they publish it;—37. And so much the more did they wonder, saying: "He hath done all things well; he hath made both the deaf to hear and the dumb to speak."

From Tyre our Saviour betook Himself to Sidon, and thence, probably, in a south-easterly direction back along the road that runs through the valley between the southern spurs of Libanus, across the Upper Jordan, southwards through the midst of Decapolis (Mark 7:31). Here in the district of Decapolis (i.e. the ten cities) a deaf-mute was brought to Him, and He healed him (Mark 7:32). Our Lord was already known here, chiefly through the miracle in Gerasa and the multiplication of the loaves.

### 1. PECULIARITIES OF THIS MIRACLE

There are three principal peculiarities of this miracle recorded by the Evangelist. First, our Lord led the deaf-mute aside from the people. Secondly, He made us of several outward ceremonies in the cure: He placed His fingers in the man's ears, touched his tongue with saliva, groaned and said: "Ephpheta," "Be thou opened" (Mark 7:33, 34). Thirdly, He forbade the man to make known the miracle of his cure (Mark 7:36).

## 2. REASONS OF THESE PECULIARITIES

The reason of the first and third peculiarities was the circumstance that our Saviour was in the midst of Decapolis, where the Gentiles were predominant. It is owing to this that He does not work there publicly and officially, but only incidentally, and without wishing to attract attention; generally, too, when urged by circumstances, as here He is constrained by the entreaties of the poor man (Mark 7:32).

He allowed the man whom He had healed at Gerasa to publish abroad the benefit He had bestowed upon him, because He was just about to leave that locality; but here He was in the midst of the district, and therefore did not wish the miracle to make a stir.

The first and proximate reason for the use of ceremonies was to prepare the deaf-mute for his cure. Being deaf and dumb, he could have no knowledge of our Saviour or of the intention with which he had been brought to Him. Our Lord therefore had to make use of signs which might indicate all this to him. As a matter of fact, He chose precisely those which were calculated to inspire the sufferer with the thought of the cure of his deafness and dumbness, and to arouse in Him the wish for this cure and cooperation with it. Perhaps the deaf-mute was a Gentile.

The second reason for the ceremonies was a mystical one. Many cures are evidently types and prophecies of future Sacraments of the Church. The cures of dumbness, blindness and deafness usually typify the Sacrament of Baptism. The cure in question especially corresponds with this Sacrament in three particulars. First in the nature of the evil removed and in the positive good imparted. Blindness, deafness and dumbness generally (or at any rate very often) appear as inborn evils (John 9:1), often even in combination with possession (Matt. 9:33; 12:22; Mark 9:16, 24; Luke 11:14), and are a kind of paralysis of nature, especially of the functions of intellectual life. By the miraculous cure the use of life is restored to the sufferer. In baptism the inborn original sin, the supernatural death, is removed by the bestowal of

supernatural life, in sanctifying grace; and this sanctifying grace brings with it all the corresponding faculties for the exercise of supernatural life, or life of faith, i.e. the power to hear, see and utter supernatural truth. For this reason baptism is also called the Sacrament of faith, because it bestows, so to speak, the senses of the life of faith. Secondly, the cure in this case corresponds to baptism as regards the Author and Finisher of this miraculous life. Here it is our Saviour Who, by means of mysterious signs which symbolize the Holy Ghost (e.g. His sighing or groaning), re-establishes perfect life; in baptism it is also our Saviour and the Holy Ghost Who are symbolized in the salt of wisdom, the touch of the finger, the breath and saliva. Thirdly, the ceremonies at this cure bear a striking resemblance to those employed at baptism. As in this case other people bring the deaf-mute and ask our Saviour on his behalf to lay His hands upon him, so also the sponsors bring the child to be baptized, and respond in his name to the question of the priest, what he asks of the Church, "Faith." The candidate for baptism also is taken aside, as it were, from the world, and led into the Church. At his baptism there follow almost the same ceremonies: the imposition of hands, the breathing upon him, touching him with saliva, and laying the fingers in his ears; and all this to indicate that the senses stand in need of healing and participate in the cure, in order that they may behold and understand the beauty of the mysteries of faith and of the moral law, impart them to others, and praise God in a new life. Baptism effects in a spiritual manner all that the miraculous cure effected upon the poor deaf-mute, and more. "The string of his tongue was loosed, and he spoke right" (Mark 7:35).

### 3. EFFECT OF THE MIRACLE

Although our Saviour forbade any stir to be made about the miracle (Mark 7:36), it was not possible to prevent this. The people, the quondam deaf-mute and those who had brought him to our Lord published it everywhere. All said with astonishment: "He hath done all things well: He hath made both the deaf to hear, and the dumb to speak" (Mark 7:37). It sounds like a confirmation of the prophetic passage: "Say to the faint-hearted: Take courage and fear not; behold your God will bring the revenge of recompense; God Himself will come, and will save you. Then shall the eyes of the blind be opened, and the ears of the deaf shall be unstopped; then shall the lame man leap as a hart, and the tongue of the dumb shall be free" (Isa. 35:4–6).

Thus the land beyond Jordan beheld again the glory of the Lord. His first appearance had been terrifying; now He comes in mildness, working interiorly, and bringing the daylight of faith to those who walk in darkness and in the shadow of death. The miracle is like the rosy dawn of holy baptism. How many have had their senses opened to the perception of the supernatural by this holy Sacrament! How joyfully surprised and how strong must this poor Gentile have felt, who was thus, as it were, born afresh to a new and glorious life! We all, too, have had our ears, tongues and mouths touched by our gracious Lord in holy baptism, through the Holy Ghost, and He has breathed into us the supernatural life. Oh that He would awaken, promote and perfect this life in us, that we may hear, see and speak supernaturally, and lead a life well-pleasing to God!

## THE SECOND MULTIPLICATION OF LOAVES

MATT. 15:29. And when Jesus had passed away from thence, he came nigh the sea of Galilee; and going up into a mountain, he sat there.—30. And there came to him great multitudes, having with them the dumb, the blind, the lame, the maimed, and many others; and they cast them down at his feet, and he healed them;—31. So that the multitudes marveled, seeing the dumb speak, the lame walk, the blind see; and they glorified the God of Israel.—32. And Jesus called together his disciples, and said: "I have compassion on the multitude, because they continue with me now three days, and have not what to eat; and I will not send them away fasting, lest they faint in the way."—33. And the disciples say unto him: "Whence then should we have so many loaves in the desert, as to fill so great a multitude?"—34. And Jesus said to them: "How many loaves have you?" But they said: "Seven, and a few little fishes."—35. And he commanded the multitude to sit down upon the ground.—36. And taking the seven loaves and the fishes, and giving thanks, he brake, and gave to his disciples, and the disciples gave to the people.—37. And they did all eat, and had their fill. And they took up seven baskets full of what remained of the fragments.—38. And they that did eat were four thousand men, besides children and women.—39. And having dismissed the multitude he went up into a boat, and came into the coasts of Magedan.

MARK 8:1. In those days again when there was a great multitude, and had nothing to eat; calling his disciples together, he saith to them:—2. "I have compassion on the multitude; for behold they have now been with me three days, and have nothing to eat;—3. And if I shall send them away fasting to their home, they will faint in the way; for some of them came from afar off."—4. And his disciples answered him: "From whence can anyone fill them here with bread in the wilderness?"—5. And he asked them: "How many loaves have ye?" Who said: "Seven." —6. And he commanded the multitude to sit down upon the ground. And taking the seven loaves, giving thanks he broke, and gave to his disciples for to set before them, and they set them before the people.—7. And they had a few little fishes;

and he blessed them, and commanded them to be set before them.—8. And they did eat and were filled, and they took up that which was left of the fragments, seven baskets.—9. And they that had eaten were about four thousand; and he sent them away.

Our Saviour now gradually directed His steps once more towards the Lake of Genesareth. He probably came to the little plain between the lake and the Galilean heights, near Bethsaida (Julias), where He had already worked the first miracle of multiplication of loaves (Mark 15:29).[1] At His approach, and probably even on the road thither, great multitudes again flocked to Him with innumerable sick and infirm persons of all descriptions, dumb, blind and lame. Jesus was seated on one of the heights. They merely cast the sick down at His feet either from their excessive weariness or being forced to this haste on account of the thronging crowd. And He healed them all. The people were beside themselves with astonishment and gratitude to God, as they saw those whom He had healed thus walking in their midst (Matt. 15:30, 31). Thus the wilderness had become an encampment, and He continued for several days to cure the sick and instruct the people (Matt. 15:32; Mark 8:2). Naturally a want of provisions now began to be felt, because their store was already exhausted (Mark 8:1; Matt. 15:32). Our Lord then worked the second miraculous multiplication of loaves.

Why did our Saviour work this great miracle *twice?* In the first place, no doubt, because the immediate need arose twice. But other and very likely reasons may certainly be adduced for it. Our Lord probably intended to prove Himself a prophet in nowise inferior to Moses; for this reason He worked the miracle repeatedly, and under similar circumstances to those of Moses in the wilderness, thereby preparing the way for the institution of the Holy Eucharist, of which this multiplication of bread, as well as the manna, was a type. In this meditation we shall endeavor to see wherein the Holy Eucharist corresponds with these two types. The conformity will be found to be threefold: in motive, nature, and effects.

## 1. THE MOTIVE

The motive of the gift of manna, the multiplication of loaves, and the institution of the Holy Eucharist is the mercy, goodness and love of God. Israel "in the great and terrible wilderness"

[1] According to another tradition, the place was on the western shore the lake.

(Deut. 8:15, 16) without bread, and the people here in the lonely tract of land along the lake without food, with the many lame, blind, maimed, weary and hungry (Matt. 15:30), are types of the Church and of the whole human race in this world. The food "that perisheth" (John 6:27), or (as in this case) fails, can never satisfy the wants of the soul. If our Lord does not help us, we shall "faint in the way," for we all "come from afar," and all have far to go. Therefore our Lord has compassion on the people (Matt. 15:32; Mark 8:2). It is before all things, then, a preventing goodness and mercy on the part of our Lord; secondly, an omniscient goodness, for He knows exactly how long each one has been with Him and how far each has to go; further, an all-embracing love, which bears in mind both body and soul, and which, though considering in the first place the temporal welfare (in the case of the manna as well as in that of the multiplication of loaves), yet does not forget the spiritual; for our Lord intended by both miracles to strengthen the people spiritually, to excite them to faith, draw them to Himself, keep them in dependence upon Him, and put them to the test (Ex. 16:4). The Holy Eucharist especially is the supernatural nourishment of the soul, as our Saviour says when promising It; as regards the body, It merely conduces to its future glory, confers a title to this glory, and is a pledge of it. But the Holy Eucharist is not merely the work of mercy and goodness, but also of the most boundless love; It is the very Sacrament of love.

## 2. THE NATURE OF THE BREAD, AND THE MANNER IN WHICH IT IS PRODUCED

The bread is in both cases miraculous, the effect of a miracle. For this reason it is called manna, "bread of heaven," "bread of angels" (Ps. 78:24, 25; Wisd. 16:20; Ex. 16:4). And it was renewed daily in a miraculous manner (Num. 11:9). Just as miraculous also was the bread here in the wilderness. The same seven loaves were eaten, not additional ones, because no others were created. The Holy Eucharist is assuredly not less miraculous. Though eaten, It is not consumed (i.e. exhausted). It is always the same bread, not by multiplication or increase, but by transubstantiation. It is the Body of Christ Himself, not merely made present by a miracle, but a compendium of many continuous miracles united in His Eucharistic Presence.

The manner of producing the bread was likewise very simple

in both cases: in the wilderness by a rain of manna, on the shore of the lake by a simple blessing, which is outwardly not unlike the Eucharistic form of consecration (Matt. 15:36; Mark 8:6). Further, we see the miracle accomplished in all cases by the mediation and with the cooperation of men; in the wilderness through Moses, on the shore of the lake through the Apostles, in the Holy Eucharist through the priest. Thirdly, the miracle is worked for all; the bread is given to all who wish to receive it, in great abundance, for a long time and repeatedly. The manna was eaten during fully forty years. Here, in the case of the multiplication of loaves, as many baskets of fragments remain as there were loaves originally, namely seven (Matt. 15:37; Mark 8:8). The Eucharistic Bread, above all, surpasses all types in the abundance and munificence with which It is given.

### 3. THE EFFECTS

The results of the miracle in each case are similar in every respect. All have their fill; some are grateful whereas others despise the bread (Num. 21:5), murmur, do not believe (Ex. 16:20, 27), and fall away. As in the wilderness, so by the lake. The Holy Eucharist is, with regard to Its effects, the spiritual food of the soul; It satiates, strengthens and elevates. What material nourishment does for the body, Holy Communion does for the soul. Its special effect is love for our Divine Saviour. Nevertheless indifference, unbelief, contempt and profanation, abuse even, are not wanting in this case either.

We see even the preparation for the worthy and fruitful reception of the Holy Eucharist prefigured in the well-disposed who were present at this multiplication of loaves. They had a great esteem for the blessings which our Saviour offered them, and a great attachment for Him. They had already been with Him for three days, forgetting every temporal consideration, even food and drink. This is the right preparation for Holy Communion: desire for spiritual blessings, high esteem of the Blessed Sacrament, and great longing for It.

Thus our Saviour prepares the minds of the people (and especially of the Apostles) for the actual institution of the Blessed Sacrament in manifold ways: by instruction, by promise, and by the twice repeated miracle of the loaves. Indeed, the answer of the disciples to our Lord's question, how many loaves they have, sounds less doubtful and desponding here than on the former occasion (Matt. 15:33; Mark 8:4). This is a sign that they have gained in readiness of belief, in full trust in our Lord's word. The Divine Wisdom "reacheth from end to end mightily and ordereth all things sweetly" (Wisd. 8:1).

## WARNING AGAINST THE LEAVEN OF THE PHARISEES AND HERODIANS

MATT. 16:1. And there came to him the Pharisees and Sadducees tempting; and they asked him to show them a sign from heaven.—2. But he answered and said to them: "When it is evening, you say: It will be fair weather, for the sky is red.—3. And in the morning: Today there will be a storm, for the sky is red and lowering.—4. You know then how to discern the face of the sky; and can you not know the signs of the times? A wicked and adulterous generation seeketh after a sign; and a sign shall not be given it, but the sign of Jonas the prophet." And he left them and went away.—5. And when his disciples were come over the water, they had forgotten to take bread.—6. Who said to them: "Take heed and beware of the leaven of the Pharisees and Sadducees."—7. But they thought within themselves, saying: "Because we have taken no bread."—8. And Jesus knowing it, said: "Why do you think within yourselves, O ye of little faith, for that you have no bread?—9. Do you not yet understand, neither do you remember the five loaves among five thousand men, and how many baskets you took up?—10. Nor the seven loaves among four thousand men, and how many baskets you took up?—11. Why do you not understand that it was not concerning bread I said to you: Beware of the leaven of the Pharisees and Sadducees?"—12. Then they understood that he said not that they should beware of the leaven of bread, but of the doctrine of the Pharisees and Sadducees.

MARK 8:10. And immediately going up into a ship with his disciples, he came into the parts of Dalmanutha.—11. And the Pharisees came forth, and began to question with him, asking him a sign from heaven, tempting him.—12. And sighing deeply in spirit, he saith: "Why doth this generation ask a sign? Amen I say to you, If a sign shall be given to this generation."—13. And leaving them, he went up again into the ship, and passed to the other side of the water.—14. And they forgot to take bread; and they had but one loaf with them in the ship.—15. And he charged them saying: "Take heed and beware of the leaven of the Pharisees, and of the leaven of Herod."—16. And they reasoned among themselves, saying: "Because we have no bread."—17. Which Jesus knowing, saith to them: "Why do you reason, beca[...] you have no bread? Do you not yet know nor understand? Have you still y[...]d?—18. Having eyes see you not? And having ears hear you n[...]member,—19. When I broke the five loaves among five th[...]ull of fragments took you up?" They say to him: "Twe[...]en loaves among four thousand, how many baskets [...] they say to him: "Seven."—21. And he said to th[...]erstand?"

After our Saviour had fed th[...]d them immediately, embarked with the Apostles in a boa[...] and crossed over to the western shore of the lake, to the district of Magedan (Magdala) or Dalmanutha (Mark 8:10; Matt. 15:39). There the Pharisees came to dispute with Him.

Scarcely had our Lord begun to work in this district, when the
Pharisees attacked Him. They even went out of the towns to seek
Him (Mark 8:11), and came up to Him (Matt. 16:1). And here
again the Pharisees were joined by the Sadducees (probably
Herodians) against Him. They began to "question" or dispute
with Him (Mark 8:11), probably concerning the signs by which
the advent of the Messias might be recognized. Perhaps they
maintained that His arrival must be accompanied and announced
by signs from heaven (Joel 2:30; Isa. 7:11), as Moses had given
bread from heaven and the sign of miraculous darkness, or as
Elias had obtained fire from heaven by his prayer (III Kings
18:38); if He were the Messias, therefore, He also must work
signs from heaven. The proposal was very unnecessary, because
He had even recently worked enough miracles of every description to enable them to believe if they had been willing to do so.
But they were unbelieving enough to deny those already worked
as well as the fresh ones they desired Him to perform. Further,
the proposal was made with a malicious intention. They only
wished to tempt Him (Mark 8:11). Whatever form His answer
might take, they were resolved to turn it against Him.

And how does our Saviour behave towards them? He does not
work a sign as they desire (Matt. 16:4; Mark 8:12), for the above
reasons, because it would have been simply a display. Further, He
gives them a beautiful answer, earnest and to the point. As it
appears, the learned men of the Jews were occupied somewhat
with astronomy and meteorology. Hence He tells them that they
know very well how to interpret the signs of the zodiac and prog-
nosticate the weather, e.g. to foretell rain in the evening when
the morning sky is red and lowering, and fine weather for the
following day when the sun sets in floods of rosy light; but they
do not know how to judge of the signs of the times, i.e. of the
advent of the Messias, of salvation for the nation in general and
for each individual in particular. So they are ignorant of what is
of most importance (Matt. 16:2-4). And yet He has worked
miracles enough to enable them to conclude from these, with far
more certainty, that the Messias has come. All the prophecies
concerning Christ that have already been fulfilled are "signs of
the times": the star at His Birth, the voice and heavenly vision

at the Jordan, His own miracles. Lastly, He emphatically declares with regard to this excessive desire for miracles: "A wicked and adulterous generation seeketh after a sign" (Matt. 16:4). Our Lord thereby strikes a blow at the interior corruption and apostasy of the people, whose union with God often appears in the language of the prophets under the figure of a marriage-bond (Jer. 3:8). And the present adultery is far more criminal than the former, since Israel's Bridegroom is now visibly present, and they wish to kill Him and follow after false Messiases. With this answer He leaves the Pharisees standing there, goes away and embarks for the north-eastern shore of the lake (Mark 8:13), but with deep sorrow in His Heart, to which He gives vent by sighing deeply (Mark 8:12).

### 2. OUR LORD WARNS THE APOSTLES AGAINST THE LEAVEN OF THE PHARISEES

On the passage across the lake or upon their landing on the east coast (Matt. 16:5), our Saviour said to the Apostles: "Take heed and beware of the leaven of the Pharisees and Sadducees," or of Herod and the Herodians, who, on account either of their frivolous life or of their political intrigues, were congenial in spirit to the Sadducees, and often took proceedings against Jesus in company with the Pharisees (Matt. 16:6; Mark 8:15).

Two things gave occasion to this warning. In the first place, the malice and perversity of the Pharisees and Sadducees, who made common cause against Him and were now actively antagonistic. Our Saviour seems to have been occupied in thought, during the passage, with their sad state, and full of sorrow and compassion for their blindness and the mischief they did among the people. He rightly calls their doings and their spirit "leaven," i.e. a spiritual ferment, here certainly calculated to do harm, not good, and which, proceeding from the Pharisees and Sadducees, agitated the people and the whole life of Israel, exciting them not to sound culture, but to hatred and perversity. On another occasion He calls this leaven simply "hypocrisy" (Luke 12:1). The warning was thus a conclusion, as it were, drawn from His inward thoughts and uttered aloud to the Apostles, full of apprehension as He was lest any of them might be affected by the contagion. The second occasion was the circumstance that the disciples, on leaving the western shore, had forgotten to buy bread, so that there was now only one loaf in the boat (Mark 8:14). The disciples thought that the warning referred to this, that they were not to use the bread of the Pharisees, and became uneasy. Our Saviour had foreseen this, and wished to test and instruct them by means of this warning.

### 3. OUR SAVIOUR EXPLAINS THE MISUNDERSTANDING AND REPROVES THE APOSTLES FOR IT

In this misunderstanding lay at once an error and a fault.

The error lay in that the Apostles thought they might not in future buy bread from the Pharisees, nor eat with them or in their presence. And yet they did not see how they could avoid it. Thence arose the fault of uneasiness, perplexity and distrust, because they did not see how they could then continue to live amongst their fellow-citizens or in fact obtain sustenance at all, especially in this chiefly Gentile district; for they were not allowed to buy bread from the Gentiles either. On this account our Saviour calls them "of little faith" (Matt. 16:7, 8; Mark 8:17).

Our Lord now does two things. First, He explains the error, saying that it was not a question of the leaven of bread, but of the leaven in their heart and in the dispositions of the Pharisees (Matt. 16:11, 12). Secondly, He reproves the Apostles for their distrust and pusillanimity, appealing to their experience in the two miracles of the multiplication of the loaves, in order to convince them of His power to help in every difficulty which arises in fulfilling His commands. With this intention He questions them catechetically regarding the two miracles of the increase of loaves, and how many baskets full of fragments they had collected (Mark 8:19, 20; Matt. 16:9, 10). He then draws from these two miracles the practical lesson they contain for the Apostles, namely confidence in His power and goodness under all circumstances. Indeed, the tone in which He speaks on this occasion shows clearly His disapproval of anxiety and uneasiness about temporal affairs, arising from want of trust (Mark 8:17, 18, 21). If He had satisfied five thousand, and at another time four thousand people with a few loaves, how much more will He be able, in case of extremity, to feed His twelve Apostles with one loaf!

This mystery shows us how greatly the persecution on the part of His enemies increases, and how He sees fit to avoid them by fleeing from one side of the lake to the other. Secondly, it shows us how painfully sensitive His Heart is to the malicious and crafty spirit of persecution, how sorrowful it makes Him, and how He sighs over it (Mark 8:12). Lastly, we see how He wishes us to bear in our hearts the deeds He has performed, and to use them as our guides in daily life. The two multiplications of bread were to fill the Apostles not only with faith in His Divinity, but especially also with unshakable confidence in His Providence.

### THE BLIND MAN OF BETHSAIDA

MARK 8:22. And they came to Bethsaida; and they bring to him a blind man, and they besought him that he would touch him.—23. And taking the blind man by the hand, he led him out of the town; and spitting upon his eyes, laying his hands on him, he asked him if he saw anything.—24. And looking up, he said: "I see men, as it were trees, walking."—25. After that again he laid his hands upon his eyes; and he began to see, and was restored, so that he saw all things clearly.—26. And he sent him into his house, saying: "Go into thy house; and if thou enter into the town, tell nobody."

Having landed, our Saviour betook Himself to Bethsaida (Julias), one of the chief towns of the principality of Philip (Trachonitis), near the spot where the Jordan flows into the Lake of Genesareth. Here a blind man was brought to Him, and He was entreated to lay His hands upon him (Mark 8:22). He performed the miracle in much the same manner as in the case of the cure of the deaf-mute. There are, however, in this case a few peculiarities to be observed.

#### 1. OUR SAVIOUR LEADS THE BLIND MAN OUT OF THE TOWN

It is uncertain whether the place where the blind man was brought to Jesus was Bethsaida itself, a suburb, or a village near. The reason why our Lord will not work the miracle in the town itself is probably that it is in a district where the Gentile element is predominant, and He is always very sparing of miracles in such parts. It is a touching incident that our Lord Himself should lead the poor blind man. Perhaps He wished to predispose him favorably by this sign of love (Mark 8:23).

#### 2. OUR LORD HEALS THE BLIND MAN GRADUALLY

Outside the town our Saviour touched the eyes of the blind man with saliva, laid His hands upon him, and asked him if he could now see. The blind man answered that he saw people, like trees, walking, i.e. in an indistinct and shadowy manner, not clearly. But when our Lord had laid his hands upon him for the second time, he saw very plainly (Mark 8:25).

And why does our Saviour heal the blind man gradually, rather than instantaneously? Probably the faith and confidence of the sufferer were not very great; he had been brought by others, who besought our Lord on his behalf. But at our Lord's touch his faith, trust and desire to be healed grew stronger. For this reason he joyfully cried out that he could already see people walking. It would seem from this that he had become blind by some unfortunate accident. Our Saviour also proves here that His power is not dependent upon fixed exterior conditions. Probably He took into consideration, in His manner of treatment, the constitution of the sufferer upon whom He worked the miracle.

### 3. OUR SAVIOUR FORBIDS WITH ESPECIAL STRICTNESS THE PUBLICATION OF THE MIRACLE

After the cure our Saviour immediately sent the blind man home; he was not to say a word about the miracle, even in the town itself (Mark 8:26). The reason was probably the one above alluded to, that our Lord was in a Gentile district, and perhaps did not wish to make any new enemies. One is almost led to think, in this case, that our Saviour ordered the healed man to go home on his own account also, in order that he might reflect upon the benefit in quiet recollection and retirement, thank God for it, and not employ it for selfish purposes.

We have here another instance of our Lord's using the healing of the blind to prefigure the Sacrament of Baptism in its mystical ceremonies and effect.

## CONFESSION OF ST. PETER AND PROMISE OF THE PRIMACY

MATT. 16:13. And Jesus came into the quarters of Caesarea Philippi; and he asked his disciples, saying: "Who do men say that the Son of Man is?"—14. But they said: "Some John the Baptist, and other some Elias, and others Jeremias, or one of the prophets."—15. Jesus saith to them: "But who do you say that I am?"—16. Simon Peter answered and said: "Thou art Christ, the Son of the Living God."—17. And Jesus answering, said to him: "Blessed art thou, Simon Bar-Jona; because flesh and blood hath not revealed it to thee, but my Father who is in heaven.—18. And I say to thee: That thou art Peter, and upon this rock I will build my church, and the gates of hell shall not prevail against it.—19. And I will give to thee the keys of the kingdom of heaven. And whatsoever thou shalt bind upon earth, it shall be bound also in heaven; and whatsoever thou shalt loose on earth, it shall be loosed also in heaven."—20. Then he commanded his disciples that they should tell no one that he was Jesus the Christ.

MARK 8:27. And Jesus went out, and his disciples, into the towns of Caesarea Philippi; and in the way he asked his disciples, saying to them: "Who do men say that I am?"—28. Who answered him, saying: "John the Baptist; but some

Elias, and others as one of the prophets."—29. Then he saith to them: "But who do you say that I am?" Peter answering said to him: "Thou art the Christ."—30. And he strictly charged them that they should not tell any man of him.

LUKE 9:18. And it came to pass as he was alone praying, his disciples also were with him; and he asked them, saying: "Who do the people say that I am?"—19. But they answered, and said: "John the Baptist; but some say Elias, and others say that one of the former prophets is risen again."—20. And he said to them: "But who do you say that I am?" Simon Peter answering, said: "The Christ of God."—21. But he strictly charging them, commanded they should tell this to no man.

From Bethsaida our Saviour proceeded northwards with the Apostles a good day's journey, past Lake Merom into the districts of Caesarea Philippi, also called Paneas (Matt. 16:13; Mark 8:27). There He asked them whom they thought Him to be, received the confession of Peter, and promised him the Primacy.

### 1. OUR SAVIOUR'S QUESTION TO THE APOSTLES

We must here consider the circumstances under which our Saviour addresses this question to the Apostles, and also the question itself.

As regards the time, this incident occurred late in His public ministry, more than two years after its commencement, after the prophecies were already (for the greater part) fulfilled and the Apostles sufficiently instructed; now He was nearing His Passion, and must reveal it, in order to strengthen and prepare the disciples for it. The place was in the vicinity of Caesarea Philippi, to the north of which lay a magnificent mountain district at the foot of Great Hermon (cf. Introd., p. 1). Further, our Saviour addressed this question to the Apostles after special prayer, during which they were near Him, perhaps praying also (Luke 9:18). Thus the question was one of great importance, and had been made the subject of prayer before God. Lastly, it took place in the presence of the Apostles alone, and of no others. The fact that He immediately afterwards forbade them to tell the people that He was the Messias is another argument in favor of accepting these circumstances (Luke 9:21; Mark 8:30; Matt. 16:20). But the Apostles themselves were all assembled (Luke 9:18); it was a solemn moment, and of great significance.

The question itself had two parts. Our Saviour first asked the Apostles what other people said of Him (Matt. 16:13; Mark 8:27; Luke 9:18); then, whom they themselves held Him to be (Matt. 16:15; Mark 8:29; Luke 9:18, 20). He desires an open and clear confession of their belief concerning Himself. He first asks about the opinion of the people, in order to prepare the disciples for their own answer, and also to throw it into clearer light by the contrast.

## 2. THE ANSWER OF THE APOSTLES AND OF ST. PETER

The answer is also twofold.

The Apostles first answer the question as to what the people said of our Saviour: that some thought Him to be Elias (Mal. 4:5; Eccli. 48:10; Matt. 11:14); others, John the Baptist (Mark 6:14); others, Jeremias (probably with reference to the fact that he had concealed the Ark of the Covenant and was the people's special intercessor, II Mach. 2:5; 15:14), or some other one of the old prophets (Luke 9:19). It was the popular belief that the advent of the Messias would be preceded by the appearance of ancient prophets, a well-founded belief with respect to Elias. All that the people said shows that they regarded our Saviour as a pledge and herald of the Messianic kingdom, and as one sent from God (Matt. 16:14; Mark 8:28; Luke 9:19).

To the second question, as to whom they, the Apostles, held Him to be, St. Peter answered: "Thou art Christ, the Son of the Living God" (Matt. 16:16; Mark 8:29; Luke 9:20). It is the magnificence of this confession which is so striking here. It is both great and complete. It is almost a summary of Christian revelation with regard to the God-Man. First we have the confession of the Incarnation: "Thou," Jesus of Nazareth, who standest before me in the flesh; then the confession of the task and offices of His Humanity: "Thou art Christ," the Anointed, the Messias, that is Priest, Prophet and King; lastly, the confession of His true Divinity: "Thou art . . . the Son of the Living God," of Jehovah; Thou art, therefore, the Lord, end and heir of all revelation. This confession embraces the entire Trinity, the Father, the Son, and (at least in the anointing of Christ as Priest, Prophet and King) the Holy Ghost. We must notice also the manner in which this confession was made. Peter is the first to speak, and though probably the rest agree with him, he acts independently and not merely as their spokesman. He speaks for himself, of himself, and as the organ of divine revelation, as our Saviour's answer plainly declares (Matt. 16:17). Further, St. Peter bears his testimony with firmness, enthusiasm and full consciousness of the gravity of his words. We can easily picture him as he steps forward from the midst of the disciples, his right hand raised, his eyes bright, his whole being filled with the fire of the Holy Ghost, and makes his confession of faith in clear, decided tones. One can scarcely conceive of a Pope even pronouncing a dogmatical decision *ex cathedra* in more enthusiastic and sublime a manner.

### 3. THE REWARD OF ST. PETER'S CONFESSION

First, our Saviour confirms the confession of Peter, declaring it to be the effect of a supernatural inspiration, not of natural perception; that not flesh and blood, but the Heavenly Father had revealed this to him (Matt. 16:17; cf. also John 44:46).

Secondly, He calls St. Peter blessed: "Blessed art thou, Simon Bar-Jona" (Matt. 16:17), blessed on account of this faith in Christ's Divinity and of the glorious results and effects which will ensue from the confession of it: viz. the intimate relations to our Saviour and His kingdom through the Primacy, the future holiness, the martyr's death, and the special glory in heaven. Perhaps it is on account of this utterance of our Saviour that the Pope to this day still bears the title of "Beatissimus Pater."

Thirdly, our Lord promises St. Peter the Primacy. Thou callest me Christ, the Son of the Living God; and I call thee Peter, and make thee the foundation of the Church, for upon thee I will build My Church (Matt. 16:18). He also calls him by his original name, in order to indicate beyond a doubt the person who is to be the bearer of the Primacy: Simon, the son of Jonas, who has just spoken. And with the change of name He promises him also a change in his position, promises him a high vocation, as had been the case with Abraham (Gen. 17:5) and Jacob (Gen. 32:28), when God made them the progenitors of the tribes of the people and bearers of the hereditary blessing.

Our Saviour now explains and defines this vocation and office more particularly. With regard to its nature, it is essentially concerned with the Church, and is in fact the Primacy. Our Lord first describes the nature of this Primacy, and then its operation, outward and inward. Its essential character consists in its being the foundation of the Church. The Church is, so to speak, an edifice, and the firmness of an edifice depends upon its foundation. The foundation is most intimately connected with the building, since it supports it. So it is with the Primacy. The Church is a society; and the foundation of a society is the governing power. If, therefore, Peter is to support and bear up the Church as a foundation does the building, he must have full ecclesiastical power. Thus the whole Church, the teaching as well as the hearing body, rests upon him, stands and falls with him. Still more: doctrine, Sacraments and pastoral faculties all come from him, and proceed from him. He is a living foundation. Our Saviour also indicates the outward operation of the Primacy, in the power of resistance and unshakable firmness which He confers upon the whole Church against exterior violence, whether it come from the world of men or of spirits, whether the attack consist in falsehood (heresy and unbelief), hatred (schism), death (sin), curse (sacrilege and execration), or outward persecution. All these hostile powers are the gates, the city, the kingdom of hell, but their united strength will avail nothing against this foundation, and hence also nothing against the Church herself. By this, infallibility in official (*ex cathedra*) declaration regarding faith and morals is undoubtedly to be understood, for the Church is before all things a society of members united in one faith, and the foundation of the faith is infallibility, the official infallibility of the Head, upon which all else depends (Matt. 16:18). The exercise and operation of the Primacy within the Church consists, according to the words of our Saviour, in the absolute power of the keys, or power to bind and to loose (Matt. 16:19), by declaration of doctrine with regard to faith and morals, by the imposition or abolition of commands or prohibitions and ecclesiastical punishments, and lastly by absolution from sin and the punishments due to sin. The power of the keys and the power to bind and to loose (Job 12:14; Isa. 22:22; Apoc. 3:7) are one and the same, namely the absolute power over the Church; absolute or unlimited as far as its subject and matter are concerned, naturally within the prescribed bounds, and unlimited with regard to the extent of the Church, which embraces the whole earth. "Whatsoever thou shalt bind upon earth, it shall be bound also in heaven; and whatsoever thou shalt loose on earth, it shall be loosed also in heaven" (Matt. 16:19). It is a divine, yet human power, similar to that of our Saviour. The foundation of this power and the invisible Head of the Church is Christ; the visible head, Peter. The foundation of his power is faith, not as a merely personal supernatural conviction, but as official infallibility.

This mystery has also its own significance with regard to the character of our Saviour, inasmuch as in it may be seen another beautiful manifestation of His calmness and wisdom in the regulation and arrangement of the revelations of the faith, and in the establishment of the Church; and also His great humility and unselfishness. How long He waits before expressly requiring the confession, with what modest words and under what humble circumstances He at last asks it! "Who do men say that the Son of Man is?" (Matt. 16:13.) He receives the confession in the presence of the disciples alone, and forbids them to proclaim Him to the people as the Messias (Matt. 16:20; Mark 8:30; Luke 9:21), because it was as yet useless to do so, since the prophecies were only in part fulfilled, and the mystery could not be clearly expounded as long as the doctrines of the Trinity and the Incarnation of God had not been proclaimed; and also because it was to be feared that there would be a tumult among the carnally-minded people at the news of the arrival of the Messias (John 6:15).

As regards doctrines of faith, this mystery contains two very important points. First, St. Peter's express acknowledgment of the Godhead of Christ, a testimony much clearer and more comprehensive than any previous one. Our Saviour accepts this acknowledgment, and confirms it as being an inspiration and the result of divine revelation. St. Peter is a beautiful example of lively, strong, ready and enthusiastic faith. This faith brought him the Primacy as its reward. This Primacy, which is here definitely promised and its nature and extent most clearly expressed, is the second point of importance with regard to faith. How faithfully, brilliantly and gloriously this promise, made in the presence of a few Apostles on foreign and heathen soil, has been fulfilled! It has moved the whole earth, endured through all ages, and found even in our own days a solemn ratification by a General Council of the Church and a joyful echo in all Catholic hearts; it has become the sign of the times. It is as though our Saviour had chosen, as the scene of this mystery, the imposing yet beautiful and fertile district near Mount Hermon, in order to illustrate the greatness, splendor and durability of the Ecclesiastical Primacy, its countless victories and abundant blessings. Here, in the shadow of the great temple of Pan and Augustus, was planted as it were the tender sapling of the power by which all the princes and gods of this world were to be conquered, through the instrumentality of the poor Galilean fisherman. How dear and full of importance to us children of the Catholic Church this mystery must be, which amplifies the promise of the Church, promises her a head in the person of Peter, and lays the foundation of her Unity, Apostolicity, Catholicity, and Holiness! On the other hand, our Lord openly and actually declares by this promise that the Old Ceremonial and Judicial Law is abolished, that with the New Covenant a new Church will begin to exist; yes (since the promise of the Primacy is given outside of Judaea and Galilee), even that the kingdom of the Messias will pass over from the Jews to the Gentiles.

## PREDICTION OF THE PASSION. THE DOCTRINE OF THE CROSS

MARK 8:31. And he began to teach them that the Son of Man must suffer many things, and be rejected by the ancients and by the high priests and the scribes, and be killed; and after three days rise again.—32. And he spoke the word openly. And Peter taking him, began to rebuke him.—33. Who turning about and seeing his disciples, threatened Peter, saying: "Go behind me, Satan, because thou savorest not the things that are of God, but that are of men."—34. And calling the multitude together with his disciples, he said to them: "If any man will follow me, let him deny himself and take up his cross, and follow me.—35. For whosoever will save his life, shall lose it; and whosoever shall lose his life for my sake and the Gospel, shall save it.—36. For what shall it profit a man, if he gain the whole world, and suffer the loss of his soul?—37. Or what shall a man give in exchange for his soul?—38. For he that shall be ashamed of me and of my words in this adulterous and sinful generation, the Son of Man also will be ashamed of him, when he shall come in the glory of his Father with the holy angels."—39. And he said to them: "Amen I say to you, that there are some of them that stand here, who shall not taste death, till they see the kingdom of God coming in power."

MATT. 16:21. From that time Jesus began to show to his disciples that he must go to Jerusalem, and suffer many things from the ancients and scribes and chief priests, and be put to death, and the third day rise again.—22. And Peter taking him, began to rebuke him, saying: "Lord, be it far from thee; this shall not be unto thee."—23. Who turning, said to Peter: "Go behind me, Satan, thou art a scandal unto me; because thou savorest not the things that are of God, but the things that are of men."—24. Then Jesus said to his disciples: "If any man will come after me, let him deny himself, and take up his cross, and follow me.—25. For he that will save his life, shall lose it; and he that shall lose his life for my sake, shall find it.—26. For what doth it profit a man, if he gain the whole world, and suffer the loss of his own soul? Or what exchange shall a man give for his soul?—27. For the Son of Man shall come in the glory of his Father with his angels; and then will he render to every man according to his works.—28. Amen I say to you, there are some of them that stand here, that shall not taste death, till they see the Son of Man coming in his kingdom."

LUKE 9:22. "The Son of Man must suffer many things, and be rejected by the ancients and chief priests and scribes, and be killed and the third day rise again."—23. And he said to all: "If any man will come after me, let him deny himself, and take up his cross daily, and follow me.—24. For whosoever will save his life, shall lose it; for he that shall lose his life for my sake, shall save it.—25. For what is a man advantaged, if he gain the whole world, and lose himself, and cast away himself?—26. For he that shall be ashamed of me and of my words, of him the Son of Man shall be ashamed, when he shall come in his majesty, and that of his Father, and of the holy angels.—27. But I tell you of a truth There are some standing here, that shall not taste death, till they see the kingdom of God."

Our Saviour had probably returned from the dominion of Philip the Tetrarch and re-entered Galilee, when He predicted His Passion and propounded the doctrine of the Cross. He would scarcely have done this before Gentile hearers.

### 1. OUR SAVIOUR PREDICTS HIS PASSION

The time of the prediction is very suitable and well chosen. Our Saviour did not speak openly of His Passion sooner, because His disciples could not have borne it; but now they were strengthened by His many miracles and by their own repeated confession of faith in His Divinity. But neither did He wait longer, because time was necessary to accustom the Apostles to the thought, and to enable them to grasp its meaning. There were now about ten months to elapse before the last Feast of the Pasch.

The first prediction of the Passion was complete in its outlines. Our Lord informed the Apostles of the place at which it would occur, viz. Jerusalem (Matt. 16:21), the very city which had been predicted by the prophets as the scene of the revelation and glory of the Messias (Ps. 2:6; Isa. 60), especially the Temple (Agg. 2:7–10), the bloody sacrifices of which were a constant prophecy of the sacrificial Death of Jesus. Secondly, our Saviour also foretold at whose hands He would have to suffer, viz. from the people, represented by the holders of ecclesiastical power, the high priests, scribes and ancients (Matt. 16:21; Mark 8:31; Luke 9:22). Lastly, He spoke of what He was to suffer: "many things," public rejection (Luke 9:22) and death; and then foretold also His Resurrection from the dead. The manner in which our Saviour made this prediction was quite open (Mark 8:32), whilst He had hitherto only intimated His Passion in figures and hints (John 2:19; 6:52). Henceforth He spoke of it often. Our Saviour's intention in so doing was gradually to prepare the disciples for the mystery of the Cross, to make them familiar with the thought of His Passion and Death, and especially to instruct them concerning His readiness to suffer, and to comfort them by the glorious motives which He had for it. In all this are shown again the wisdom, prudence, and humility of our Saviour.

## 2. OUR SAVIOUR REJECTS THE PROPOSAL OF ST. PETER TO RENOUNCE HIS INTENTION OF SUFFERING

It may well be imagined how the prediction of the Passion must have overthrown all the hopes and expectations of the Apostles. The very words "Jerusalem," "the priests," "suffer," "die," were to them as claps of thunder. St. Peter as usual immediately gives utterance to their thoughts.

He went up to our Lord, probably on the journey, as He was walking ahead of the disciples, and earnestly tried to dissuade Him from permitting such a thing to happen and going voluntarily to suc ha shameful death. God forbid—"Be it far from Thee" (Matt. 16:22; Mark 8:32). Peter did this unasked, and also secretly (Matt. 16:22; Mark 8:32), perhaps because he would not admonish our Lord before the others, perhaps also with the not altogether praiseworthy intention of obtaining His special favor. The motive of this representation was certainly the special affection and love of St. Peter for our Lord, but it was unenlightened and imperfect love, as our Saviour Himself tells him. It may be also that a little selfishness on Peter's part crept in; for it was not pleasant to be the representative of a suffering Saviour. His preference before all the others may also have encouraged him to take this step. "Flesh and blood" speaks out in all this, natural repugnance for suffering and the Cross, mingled with Jewish conceptions of the Messias. It may be, however, that Peter spoke in the name of the rest as well as for himself, since our Saviour arranges that the reproof should be heard by the other Apostles also (Mark 8:33). Our Saviour rejects his proposal with decision, in an answer both stern and grave (Matt. 16:23; Mark 8:33). He turns away from Peter, and designates as "Satan" him, whom He had just before called "blessed" and indicated as His representative and the foundation of the Church, thus classing him as an opponent of God's decrees of salvation, and therefore a "scandal," because he wishes to prevent Him from fulfilling the Will of God (that He should suffer). The reason for the sharpness of the reproof was not so much the greatness of Peter's fault (for our Lord immediately excuses him, saying that he had acted in ignorance of the plans and thoughts of God, and prompted by merely natural feeling) as the spirit which he had unconsciously followed. Our Lord strongly condemns this spirit in Peter, in the Apostles and in all of us. He wished to give us an impressive warning, once for all, not to follow this bent of nature, which becomes in Satan's hand a means of temptation to resist the Will of God. One may call this step of Peter's the second temptation of our Lord on the part of the devil; his third was directed against Him during the Passion itself.

### 3. OUR SAVIOUR PROPOUNDS FOR THE FIRST TIME THE DOCTRINE OF THE CROSS

Our Saviour now profited by the opportunity to confirm His prediction and to propose it to all as the doctrine of the Cross. This doctrine comprises three points.

Our Saviour first explains what is to be understood by a "cross." Under the term "cross" He includes every contradiction and difficulty, whether interior or exterior, mental, moral or physical. He specifies this "cross" now as "self-denial," mortification of evil passions in order to obey His Law (Matt. 16:24; Mark 8:34; Luke 9:23), now as the loss of the life of the body (Matt. 16:25; Mark 8:35; Luke 9:24) in consequence of courageous confession of the faith and the Gospel amidst an unbelieving people (Mark 8:35); that is to say, perfect following after Jesus along the path of the commandments and the Apostolic life, following of Him till death, in spite of all the trials and adversities which this may entail, some for one person, others for another. Our Saviour alludes by the word "cross" to the custom of obliging criminals to carry their cross to the place of execution.

Secondly, our Saviour brings forward motives for carrying the cross and for suffering. In the first place, the necessity of it. This necessity exists for all without exception. The expressions used are quite general: "If any man will come after me, let him take up his cross." For this reason our Saviour called all to be present when He spoke these words, the people as well as the disciples, and propounded the doctrine to all (Matt. 16:24; Mark 8:34; Luke 9:23). This universal obligation of carrying the cross is founded by Him upon three considerations. In the first place, it is a necessary condition of being a disciple of Jesus (Matt. 16:24; Mark 8:34; Luke 9:23). There is neither inward nor outward conformity with the life, spirit and destiny of Jesus without it. How powerfully this motive incites us, when we compare the cross we are asked to take up with that which He Himself is to carry, and upon which (according to His prediction) He is to die! The cross, or a kind of gallows, was in use with the Jews as one of the appurtenances of execution, and was regarded as the very synonym of shame and disgrace (Deut. 21:23). Further, the carrying of the cross is a necessary condition of the salvation of the soul (Matt. 16:25, 26; Mark 8:35–37; Luke 9:24, 25). Our soul and its salvation are our greatest blessings, to which the possession of the whole world is not to be compared; blessings, the loss of which cannot be repaired, any more than the loss of our life (Matt. 16:26; Mark 8:36; Luke 9:25). It is in allusion to this that our Saviour plays upon the words "soul" and "life," in a manner full of meaning. We cannot save this soul if we are not ready to sacrifice our temporal life. Whoever saves this life by denying Christ, loses the life of the soul; but whoever offers his temporal life for Christ, gains the life and salvation of the soul (Matt. 16:25; Mark 8:35; Luke 9:24). Lastly, the carrying of the cross is a necessary condition of participation in the kingdom and glory of Christ. This glory is sure, and some of those present will live to see the beginning of it, in the judgment upon Jerusalem (Matt. 16:28; Mark 8:39; Luke 9:27); but the final accomplishment of it will be at the Last Judgment. This glory is great and marvelous. It will reveal our Saviour as the Son of God and Lord of heaven; for He will come in His glory, in the glory of the Father and of the holy angels (Matt. 16:27; Mark 8:38; Luke 9:26). Everyone will participate in this glory according to his works (Matt. 16:27). Whoever has been ashamed of the Son of Man before sinful men, of him the Son of Man will also be ashamed in His glory (Mark 8:38; Luke 9:26).

It is the first time that our Saviour propounds the doctrine of the Cross to the people, but it was necessary now, on account of the increase of persecution on the part of His enemies. He does it with great prudence and caution, and (before the people) in a manner quite different from that in which He had spoken of it to His disciples. He says nothing to the people of His Passion, because they could not have borne it, and because He would not Himself bring about His Passion. But He lets the disciples look deeper. In all that He says to them and to Peter, as well as in what He says to the people, we have a comprehensive revelation of the doctrine of the Cross; namely, what it is and in what it consists, what sentiments we are to entertain and what to avoid with respect to it, as we see in the colloquy of St. Peter with our Lord, and lastly why we must manifest these sentiments. The motives are concisely summed up, and consist in the necessity of saving one's soul, the honor and advantage of being a disciple of Jesus, and the example of Jesus Himself in sentiments and action. It must be particularly noticed what stress our Saviour lays upon the reward, thus indicating that suffering is not our last end, but only a means to it, a period of transition.

## THE TRANSFIGURATION

LUKE 9:28. And it came to pass about eight days after these words, that he took Peter and James and John, and went up into a mountain to pray.—29. And whilst he prayed, the shape of his countenance was altered; and his raiment became white and glittering.—30. And behold two men were talking with him. And they were Moses and Elias,—31. Appearing in majesty. And they spoke of his decease that he should accomplish in Jerusalem.—32. But Peter and they that were with him were heavy with sleep. And awaking, they saw his glory, and the two men that stood with him.—33. And it came to pass that as they were departing from him, Peter saith to Jesus: "Master, it is good for us to be here; and let us make three tabernacles, one for thee, and one for Moses, and one for Elias:" not knowing what he said.—34. And as he spoke these things, there came a cloud and overshadowed them; and they were afraid when they entered into the cloud.—35. And a voice came out of the cloud, saying: "This is my beloved Son, hear him."—36. And whilst the voice was uttered, Jesus was found alone. And they held their peace, and told no man in those days any of these things which they had seen.

MARK 9:1. And after six days Jesus taketh with him Peter and James and John, and leadeth them up into a high mountain apart by themselves, and was transfigured before them.—2. And his garments became shining, and exceeding white as snow, so as no fuller upon earth can make white.—3. And there appeared to them Elias with Moses; and they were talking with Jesus.—4. And Peter answering, said to Jesus: "Rabbi, it is good for us to be here; and let us make three tabernacles, one for thee, and one for Moses, and one for Elias."—5. For he knew not what he said; for they were struck with fear.—6. And there was a cloud overshadowing them, and a voice came out of the cloud, saying: "This is my most beloved Son; hear ye him."—7. And immediately looking about, they saw no man any more but Jesus only with them.—8. And as they came down from the mountain, he charged them not to tell any man what things they had seen, till the Son of Man shall be risen again from the dead.—9. And they kept the word to themselves, questioning together what that should mean: When he shall be risen from the dead.—10. And they asked him, saying: "Why then do the Pharisees and scribes say that Elias must come first?"—11. Who answering, said to them: "Elias when he shall come first, shall restore all things; and as it is written of the Son of Man, that he must suffer many things and be despised.—12. But I say to you, that Elias also is come (and they have done to him whatsoever they would), as it is written of him."

MATT. 17:1. And after six days Jesus taketh unto him Peter and James, and John his brother, and bringeth them up into a high mountain apart;—2. And he was transfigured before them. And his face did shine as the sun; and his garments became white as snow.—3. And behold there appeared to them Moses and Elias talking with him.—4. And Peter answering, said to Jesus: "Lord, it is good for us to be here; if thou wilt, let us make here three tabernacles, one for thee, and one for Moses, and one for Elias."—5. And as he was yet speaking, behold a bright cloud overshaded them. And lo a voice out of the cloud, saying: "This is my beloved Son, in whom I am well pleased; hear ye him."—6. And the disciples hearing, fell upon their face; and were very much afraid.—7. And Jesus came and touched them, and said to them: "Arise and fear not."—8. And they lifting up their eyes, saw no one, but only Jesus.—9. And as they came down from the mountain, Jesus charged them, saying: "Tell the vision to no man, till the Son of Man be risen from the dead."—10. And his disciples asked him, saying: "Why then do the scribes say that Elias must come first?"—11. But he answering, said to them: "Elias indeed shall come, and restore all things;—12. But I say to you, that Elias is already come, and they knew him not, but have done unto him whatsoever they had a mind. So also the Son of Man shall suffer from them."—13. Then the disciples understood that he had spoken to them of John the Baptist.

## 1. CIRCUMSTANCES LEADING UP TO THE TRANSFIGURATION: ITS OBJECT

As regards the time, it was "six days" (Matt. 17:1; Mark 9:1), or according to St. Luke, "about eight days" (Luke 9:28) after the prediction of the Passion, that our Saviour accomplished this important mystery. Its importance, as well as its connection with the preceding mystery, may be seen from this exact statement of the date, as well as from the circumstance that no less than three Evangelists relate the facts.

Both probability and tradition point to Mount Thabor in Galilee as the site of the Transfiguration. In six days our Lord could easily make the journey of about 20 leagues' distance from Caesarea to the vicinity of Thabor. In the mystery which follows it, scribes reappear, a sign that the occurrence took place in Galilee. Mount Thabor was in every way suited to be the scene of the Transfiguration: naturally, by its open position next the plain of Esdrelon, and by its majestic and beautiful form, like a huge, flat-topped pyramid, with its magnificent view over the Mediterranean Sea, the Lake of Galilee, and the whole scene of the ministry of Jesus; and also historically, by the memories it recalled of Barac's victory over the Canaanite kings and Debbora's song of triumph.

As witnesses our Lord called three disciples, Peter, James and John; He would not choose fewer, since three was the legal number, nor more, lest the event should become more widely known than was necessary. They are the same three Apostles who were to be present at His Agony in the Garden of Gethsemani. In order to strengthen the others, they must first be specially strengthened themselves. Here also may be noticed a certain subordination among the Apostles.

Our Saviour gave as a reason for taking the three disciples up the mountain with Him that He was going "to pray" (Luke 9:28). He actually did pray on the mountain (Luke 9:29), and this again shows that He had something important in design. But prayer was not His only intention. He only gave this motive in order to keep the matter secret, and not to excite the envy and dissatisfaction of the other Apostles. The three willingly followed His invitation, and we may learn thence never to decline a suggestion of this kind. We do not know what such a refusal may deprive us of. Our Saviour's real intention was to strengthen the Apostles by His Transfiguration, that they might rightly accept the truths He had just revealed of His future glory, His coming Passion, and His true Divinity. He wished to confirm their faith in these three truths, and to lead them to a deeper comprehension of them. With this intention, then, our Saviour took the three Apostles with Him, and we may imagine how pleasant the ascent must have been in the evening, under the shady oaks, elms, and pistachio-trees with which the mountain is wooded. Arrived at the summit, our Saviour betook Himself to prayer, and likewise the Apostles. But as this prayer was of long duration, they fell asleep (Luke 9:32) and only awoke as our Lord, already transfigured, stood before them.

### 2. THE TRANSFIGURATION ITSELF

The three principal features of the mystery were extremely well calculated to realize our Saviour's intentions. First, the Transfiguration itself confirmed His statement concerning His future majesty as Judge and King, and allowed a ray of the latent divine glory to shine through the "form of a servant" (Phil. 2:6–8; Col. 2:9). The Transfiguration did not consist in a complete transformation of the Body of Christ into its glorious state, such as it assumed after His Resurrection, but only in a transfigured appearance, an outward brightness and glory; and perhaps also in His being raised from the ground. Thus we read in the Gospels that "He was transfigured before them" (Matt. 17:2; Mark 9:1); "the shape of His countenance was altered" (Luke 9:29); "His face did shine," "His raiment became white and glittering" (Matt. 17:2; Luke 9:29). How great the splendor must have been appears from the further description: "His face did shine as the sun," "His garments became shining and exceeding white as snow, so as no fuller upon earth can make white" (Matt. 17:2; Mark 9:2). Moses and Elias also "appeared in majesty" (Luke

9:31). We may further estimate the splendor of the vision by the effects which it produced upon the Apostles. What they saw was so beautiful, and what they felt so delightful, the effulgence so soft and grateful, that they were either dumb in a rapture of awe (Mark 9:5) or, like Peter, spoke confusedly, as in a dream (Luke 9:33). "Lord," cried Peter, "it is good for us to be here; let us make three tabernacles, one for Thee, and one for Moses, and one for Elias" (Matt. 17:4; Mark 9:4). A heavenly joy is expressed by these words.

The second feature in the Transfiguration was the appearance of Moses and Elias. The latter appeared in his own body, because he has not yet died; the former, perhaps, with the appearance of a body, or in his own raised to life; both of them in glory similar to that of our Saviour. And why did they appear? They came, in the first place, to do homage to our Lord and adore Him. There is then no dissension between the Old Covenant and the New. On the contrary, Moses and Elias are pledges of the advent and future coming of the kingdom of Christ; the law and the prophets are His servants, He is their Lord and goal. They came, further, to hear how He would accomplish the redemption of Israel, namely by His Passion and Death (Luke 9:31). This revelation of His Passion was also to confirm the prediction He had made to His disciples concerning it, and to teach them that it was not unforeseen, but a divine, premeditated plan; not a hopeless wreck, but the fulfilment of the eternal decrees of God. Since Christ's Passion had the blood-guiltiness and reprobation of Israel as its consequence, these Saints of the Old Covenant might well intercede also for their unhappy nation.

The third thing to be considered in the mystery is the shining cloud which, after the words of St. Peter: "It is good for us to be here," descended upon and enveloped our Saviour and the Apostles; further, the loud voice: "This is My Beloved Son, in Whom I am well pleased; hear ye Him" (Matt. 17:5; Mark 9:6; Luke 9:34, 35). This was evidently the express and solemn confirmation of Christ's Divinity and of His office as Prophet and Priest. The appearance of a bright cloud is always, in the Scriptures, the sign of the immediate proximity and presence of God (Ex. 40:32; III Kings 8:10), and the words which were heard from out the cloud testify this plainly enough. Thus also Moses (Ex. 24:15; 34:5) and Elias (III Kings 19:9 etc.) were drawn into mysterious proximity to God, and Abraham (Gen. 15:1 etc.), Isaac (Gen.

26:2) and Jacob (Gen. 28:14) received the ratification of the Covenant from God under similar circumstances. The impression made by this appearance and revelation in the bright cloud was so powerful that the Apostles, overcome by fear and terror, fell upon their faces and remained thus prostrate until our Saviour approached, touched them, and bade them rise and lay aside all fear (Matt. 17:6–8; Mark 9:7; Luke 9:36).

### 3. SUBSEQUENT INCIDENTS

When the Apostles arose, all the glory had vanished, and no one stood beside them but our Lord, in His ordinary form and appearance. As they descended the mountain He bade them say nothing of what had taken place until His Resurrection, and the Apostles obeyed (Matt. 17:8, 9; Mark 9:7–9; Luke 9:36). To act otherwise could have done no good. The more marvelous things were said of our Saviour, the more would unbelief be scandalized by His subsequent Passion. Perhaps, too, the other Apostles might not have been able to bear and understand it. Here also the one was to learn from and be strengthened by the other. So the ordinary work-a-day life began again, in silence and humility, and with the Cross in sight.

The conversation during the descent turned first upon the signification of our Saviour's Resurrection from the dead, because He had told them to let nothing transpire of the vision until His Resurrection (Mark 9:9). Secondly, the Apostles asked our Saviour how it was that, according to the saying of the scribes, Elias must come before the beginning of the Messianic kingdom, or before the advent of the Messias (Matt. 17:10; Mark 9:20). This tradition of the scribes was founded upon the prophets (Mal. 4:5; Eccli. 48:10). The Apostles now asked how this was to be reconciled, that Elias was to appear (according to the scribes) before the Messias, and now he had appeared after Him; or (as others think) why Elias had gone away, since the glory of the Resurrection was immediately impending; and, if he was to return directly, why they might not speak of it. Our Saviour replied that these points might be very easily reconciled. Elias was to come before the Messias and "restore all things," i.e. convert Israel to Him, and Elias had already come; both were true. The prophet Malachias speaks of a twofold advent of the Messias: the one for the Last Judgment, which Elias precedes (Mal. 4:5), the other for the redemption of the world, and this is preceded by

John the Baptist (Mal. 3:1). But the latter had already appeared; and they (the scribes) had not recognized him, but had done to him "whatsoever they had a mind" (Matt. 17:11, 12; 11:14), and so also the Son of Man would have to suffer from them. Similar in sense, but with a slight difference of expression, is the answer as recorded by St. Mark (9:11, 12). Elias will come and restore all things. But how is this to be reconciled with what is written of the Son of Man, that He is to suffer many things and be despised? When Elias has converted the Jews, they will certainly not persecute the Messias. Elias, the prophet, cannot therefore come before His first advent (Mark 9:11, 12). Nevertheless an Elias, namely John, has already appeared, and they have done to him all that they had a mind, as it is written of Elias, i.e. similarly to what is recorded in the life of Elias the Thesbite (Mark 9:12). As Elias was persecuted by Jezabel (III Kings 19:2), so also John by Herodias.

In this mystery there lies a deep wisdom, and it is wonderfully adapted to the end in view. In order to convince the Apostles of the promised glory, He not only lets them behold a ray of it manifested in Himself and in the two prophets, but allows them also to taste and enjoy it in the exceeding consolation they experienced. This Transfiguration is the aurora of future glory and the dawn of Christian mysticism. All the supernatural states of favored Saints are, as it were, rays of light emanating from Thabor, and we see already in this dawn of the future glory of Jesus how great the sacrifice was that He made, when He deprived Himself of it and took the "form of a servant" here below. For this we must thank Him with all our hearts. The Divinity of our Lord is here gloriously confirmed, and so impressively that St. Peter, long years after, could not forget its splendor, but bore it with him in all the labors and crusades of his earthly pilgrimage, like a light in a dark place (II Peter 1:16–19).

The Transfiguration is one of the great occasions on which the Father bore witness to His Son in divine power and glory, as at His Baptism and afterwards in the Temple, immediately before His Passion. Lastly, the Cross is justified as the wondrous plan of God which shall accomplish everything, and lead to glory the Author of our faith and those who are heirs of glory (Hebr. 2:9, 10). The suffering Messias is the true Messias; such is the truth established by the conversation of Jesus with the two ancient prophets. The nearer men stand to Jesus and His work, the more they are initiated into the mystery of the Cross. We see this here exemplified in the two forerunners of our Lord. The Cross embraces the Old Covenant as well as the New. This is a truth which not only reconciles us to the Cross, but also enables us to carry it bravely and joyfully, to seek and to love it (I Peter 2:21; 4:13) for the sake of Christ and in the hope of future glory; therefore He desires that the Apostles should proclaim the glory of the Transfiguration after His Death (Matt. 17:9; Mark 9:8). The glory of the Cross is the same glory that we see in our Lord upon Thabor.

## THE HEALING OF THE DUMB MAN

LUKE 9:37. And it came to pass the day following, when they came down from the mountain, there met them a great multitude.—38. And behold a man among the crowd cried out, saying: "Master, I beseech thee, look upon my son, because he is my only one.—39. And lo, a spirit seizeth him, and he suddenly crieth out, and he throweth him down and teareth him so that he foameth, and bruising him he hardly departeth from him.—40. And I desired thy disciples to cast him out, and they could not."—41. And Jesus answering, said: "O faithless and perverse generation, how long shall I be with you and suffer you? Bring hither thy son."—42. And as he was coming to him, the devil threw him down and tore him.—43. And Jesus rebuked the unclean spirit, and cured the boy, and restored him to his father.

MARK 9:13. And coming to his disciples, he saw a great multitude about them, and the scribes disputing with them.—14. And presently all the people seeing Jesus, were astonished and struck with fear; and running to him, they saluted him.—15. And he asked them: "What do you question about among you?"—16. And one of the multitude answering, said: "Master, I have brought my son to thee having a dumb spirit,—17. Who, wheresoever he taketh him, dasheth him, and he foameth, and gnasheth with the teeth, and pineth away; and I spoke to thy disciples to cast him out, and they could not."—18. Who answering them, said: "O incredulous generation, how long shall I be with you? How long shall I suffer you? Bring him unto me."—19. And they brought him. And when he had seen him, immediately the spirit troubled him; and being thrown down upon the ground, he rolled about foaming.—20. And he asked his father: "How long time is it since this hath happened unto him?" But he said: "From his infancy.—21. And oftentimes hath he cast him into the fire and into waters, to destroy him; but if thou canst do anything, help us, having compassion on us."—22. And Jesus saith to him: "If thou canst believe, all things are possible to him that believeth."—23. And immediately the father of the boy crying out, with tears said: "I do believe, Lord; help my unbelief."—24. And when Jesus saw the multitude running together, he threatened the unclean spirit, saying to him: "Deaf and dumb spirit, I command thee, go out of him; and enter not any more into him."—25. And crying out, and greatly tearing him, he went out of him, and he became as dead, so that many said: "He is dead."—26. But Jesus taking him by the hand, lifted him up, and he arose.—27. And when he was come into the house, his disciples secretly asked him: "Why could not we cast him out?"—28. And he said to them: "This kind can go out by nothing but by prayer and fasting."

MATT: 16:14. And when he was come to the multitude, there came to him a man falling down on his knees before him, saying: "Lord, have pity on my son, for he is a lunatic, and suffereth much; for he falleth often into the fire, and often into the water;—15. And I brought him to thy disciples, and they could not cure him."—16. Then Jesus answered and said: "O unbelieving and perverse generation, how long shall I be with you? How long shall I suffer you? Bring him hither to me."—17. And Jesus rebuked him, and the devil went out of him, and the child was cured from that hour.—18. Then came the disciples to Jesus secretly. and said: "Why could not we cast him out?"—19. Jesus said to them: "Because of your unbelief. For amen I say to you, if you have faith as a grain of mustard-seed, you shall say to this mountain, Remove from hence thither, and it shall remove, and nothing shall be impossible to you.—20. But this kind is not cast out but by prayer and fasting."

Having descended from the Mount of Transfiguration, our Lord healed the dumb lunatic boy who was possessed by a devil. The circumstances of the cure were as follows.

### 1. OUR SAVIOUR REPROVES UNBELIEF

On reaching the foot of the mountain our Saviour found a great multitude assembled, and His disciples disputing with the scribes (Mark 9:13). The dispute probably turned upon the case of possession in question, and the reason why the disciples could render no assistance with respect to it (Mark 9:17). The scribes seem to have been fond of engaging in dispute with them in the absence of their Master, and the disciples probably could not avoid their attacks. When our Saviour appeared, all the people were astonished and struck with reverential fear, whether because of IIis unexpected intervention, or because they had taken too lively a part in the discussion (and not in favor of the Apostles), and now wondered what He Himself would do. All arose, and going respectfully to meet Him, saluted Him (Mark 9:14). Upon our Saviour's asking what was the cause of their dispute, a man stepped forward, and casting himself at His feet, besought Him to look upon his son and take pity upon him, for the boy was a lunatic and dumb, the effect of possession; an evil spirit often seized him and threw him down, and he then cried out, foaming, gnashing his teeth and rolling about as though the devil would tear him to pieces. He declared that he himself had begged the disciples to expel the evil spirit, but they had not been able to do so (Mark 9:16, 17; Luke 9:38–40; Matt. 17:14, 15). This failure of the disciples was a painful circumstance, and by no means tended to the honor of our Saviour Himself, since He had given the disciples power over evil spirits. So they stood abashed and confused before Him. But a short time before transfigured and glorious, our Saviour now finds Himself surrounded by the trying embarrassments of daily life; just before flooded with the joy of divine conversation, He now finds Himself confronted with the horrible sight of diabolical possession.

The reproof given by our Saviour under these circumstances is directed against their want of faith. "O faithless and perverse generation, how long shall I be with you and suffer you?" (Luke 9:41; Mark 9:18; Matt. 17:16.) The reproof applied to all, in a greater or less degree, according as they deserved it. It applied to the disciples, because they were disheartened at their first failure (Matt. 17:19); and also to the man and the other people standing round with the scribes, because they were wanting in faith and confidence (Mark 9:22). Our Saviour's intention was to awaken these two virtues, the want of which had grieved Him.

### 2. OUR SAVIOUR AWAKENS THE FAITH OF THE FATHER OF THE DEMONIAC, AND WORKS THE MIRACLE

In order to induce the father to believe, our Saviour employed three means. First, He allowed the evil spirit to exercise his power upon the possessed child, as soon as the latter was brought to Him. "Being thrown down upon the ground, he rolled about foaming" (Mark 9:19; Luke 9:42). The evil spirit thereby manifested his fear and impotence against our Saviour, and excited anew in the father the desire for the deliverance of his son. Secondly, our Saviour showed great sympathy with the father, questioning him with regard to the details of the disease and possession. The father answered that the evil spirit had tormented his son from his infancy, had often thrown him into fire and water in order to destroy him (Mark 9:21). The sympathy comforted the father, and emboldened him to add the earnest entreaty: "If Thou canst do anything, help us, having compassion on us" (Mark 9:21). The request is certainly couched in words which show a very imperfect faith. Thirdly, our Saviour expressly encourages the father to believe, and holds out to him the prospect of complete success. "If thou canst believe; all things are possible to him that believeth" (Mark 9:22). Thereupon the father, weeping, breaks out into the words: "I do believe, Lord; help my unbelief" (i.e. imperfect faith—Mark 9:23). With this good will to believe he fulfils the measure of faith required, and his confidence increases so much that he not only asks the cure of his child, but also aid for himself.

Such being the disposition of the father, and the throng of people increasing, our Saviour worked the miracle, saying authoritatively to the evil spirit: "Deaf and dumb spirit, I command thee, go out of him and enter not any more into him." With a loud cry and wild gestures, so that the boy lay upon the ground as one dead (indeed many said that he was dead), the devil went out of him. Jesus then took the boy's hand, raised him to his feet and gave him to his father (Mark 9:24–26; Luke 9:43; Matt. 17:17). We see our Saviour, here as elsewhere, manifesting His power and majesty against the fallen spirits, but showing only the tenderest consideration and kindness towards men.

### 3. OUR SAVIOUR INSTRUCTS HIS DISCIPLES CONCERNING THE SECRET POWER OF EXPELLING DEVILS

After our Lord had entered a house, the Apostles asked Him privately why they had not been able to expel the evil spirit (Mark 9:27; Matt. 17:18). This inquiry manifests not only their eagerness to learn and be trained in their vocation, but also their humility and simplicity.

Our Saviour in His answer informs the Apostles of the means, in so far as these are dependent upon themselves and lie in their disposition of soul. The actual power to cast out devils consists, of course, in the gift granted by God and in the grace and power of His Name (Luke 9:1). Nevertheless God makes the success of this power dependent also upon the holder of it. The first thing requisite is to have faith. Our Saviour reproaches the disciples with not having been able to cast out the evil spirit on account of their want of faith, and adds that they would be able even to remove mountains, and that nothing would be impossible to them, if they had only faith as great as a grain of mustard-seed (Matt. 17:19). By this faith is meant the so-called miraculous faith, i.e. a faith which possesses such confidence and assurance that a miracle ensues from it. This firm faith was wanting to the Apostles in this case. Others, like St. Gregory Thaumaturgus, have actually performed the miracle mentioned—that of moving mountains—by their faith. The second means is prayer and fasting. "This (particularly malignant) kind (of devils) is not cast out but by prayer and fasting" (Matt. 17:20; Mark 9:28). By fasting man frees himself from the fetters and power of unbridled nature and the baser passions, in which the diabolical power in part consists; and by prayer he unites himself to God and obtains divine strength.

Evidently all this is intended to teach us faith and confidence. In the utterance with regard to fasting and prayer there lies an important hint for the entire spiritual life. Prayer and self-conquest give us the mysterious strength which makes us invincible and terrible to the Evil One.

## NEW PREDICTION OF THE PASSION

LUKE 9:44. And all were astonished at the mighty power of God; but while all wondered at the things he did, he said to his disciples: "Lay you up in your hearts these words; for it shall come to pass that the Son of Man shall be delivered into the hands of men."—45. But they understood not this word, and it was hid from them, so that they perceived it not; and they were afraid to ask him concerning this word.

MARK 9:29. And departing from thence they passed through Galilee; and he would not that any man should know it.—30. And he taught his disciples, and said to them: "The Son of Man shall be betrayed into the hands of men, and they shall kill him, and after that he is killed, he shall rise again the third day."—31. But they understood not the word; and they were afraid to ask him.

MATT. 17:21. And when they abode together in Galilee, Jesus said to them: "The Son of Man shall be betrayed into the hands of men;—22. And they shall kill him, and the third day he shall rise again." And they were troubled exceedingly.

### 1. CIRCUMSTANCES OF THE PREDICTION

The scene of the prediction was either in Galilee or in the districts through which our Saviour passed on His way thither, from the Mount of Transfiguration (Mark 9:29; Matt. 17:21).

It appears to have been made on the journey, if we may judge from the details given. The way led through quiet places, for our Saviour did not wish to excite attention (Mark 4:29), probably because the recent great miracle of the expulsion of the devil had filled the people with new astonishment at the "mighty power of God," with admiration and enthusiasm (Luke 9:44). So He avoided increasing this excitement. Nay, He even chose this period of popular favor in order to speak of His Passion.

### 2. PREDICTION OF THE PASSION

The prediction itself is not so detailed as the first one; but still it contains the chief points, His Death and Resurrection, with a new feature, viz. the betrayal and deliverance of the "Son of

Man . . . into the hands of men," though it does not point to the traitor himself (Luke 9:44; Mark 9:30; Matt. 17:21, 22).

It is moreover very earnest and impressive. A deep and painful antithesis lies in the words chosen, that the "Son of Man," the noblest scion, the ornament and head of the human race, is to be killed by the very men for whose salvation He has come. Our Saviour appears, too, to have impressed His words upon His disciples very earnestly and emphatically, for He said: "Lay you up in your hearts these words" (Luke 9:44), i.e. hear and remark well what men now say of Me on account of the miracles that I work, for the time will come when they will be quite otherwise disposed towards Me.

Our Saviour's intention in making this disclosure was evidently to direct the thoughts of the Apostles more and more to His Passion, and not to let them lose sight of it, especially now that, on the one hand, the flood of enthusiasm for Him rolled high, and on the other the Passion itself was ever drawing nearer. This is a touching proof of the caution and humility of our Lord, and it affords us at the same time a glimpse of His thoughts and of His Sacred Heart, over which the Cross was casting ever deeper shadows and, we may feel sure, at the same time increasing His anxiety and apprehension, in so far as and because He willed it to be so.

### 3. EFFECT OF THE PREDICTION UPON THE APOSTLES

It is very instructive to note how the Apostles received the renewed prediction of the Passion. The Evangelists record three points with regard to it.

First, the Apostles did not understand our Lord's words. It seemed to them unintelligible and inexplicable (Luke 9:45; Mark 9:31) that the Saviour, the Messias, God, could die a violent death and end His life in such a shameful manner. They interpreted the words in any other sense rather than the one in which they were spoken, and in which our Lord intended them to be understood; and this partly on account of their rooted idea of a glorious Messias, partly out of fear and repugnance for the matter itself.

The second point mentioned by the Evangelists is that the Apostles became troubled and sorrowful (Matt. 17:22), as anyone naturally would be at the presage of a great evil which is to befall him and others whom he loves.

Thirdly, we are told, the Apostles feared to ask an explanation, in spite of their apprehension and sadness (Luke 9:45; Mark 9:31). It is so natural to a man to turn his thoughts away from misfortune and crosses, and avoid every reminder and unpleasant explanation. Our Saviour let the matter rest there, and did not express Himself further, that they might not know everything and be too much discouraged by it (Luke 9:45). In the Apostles we see delineated feature for feature the disposition and behavior of the natural man towards crosses and sufferings. So we all think, feel and act under such circumstances, unless we have been transformed by grace. But in our Saviour the operations of grace only are manifested. He thinks often, constantly even of His Passion, speaks of it, goes to meet it courageously and with unchanging purpose. Oh that our gracious Lord would take us all into the school of His cross-loving Heart!

## THE TEMPLE TRIBUTE

MATT. 17:23. And when they were come to Capharnaum, they that received the didrachma came to Peter, and said to him: "Doth not your master pay the didrachma?"—24. He said: "Yes." And when he was come into the house, Jesus prevented him, saying: "What is thy opinion, Simon? The kings of the earth, of whom do they receive tribute or custom? Of their own children, or of stangers?"—25. And he said: "Of strangers." Jesus said to him: "Then the children are free.—26. But that we may not scandalize them, go to the sea, and cast in a hook; and that fish which shall first come up, take; and when thou hast opened its mouth, thou shalt find a stater; take that, and give it to them for me and thee."

In the course of His wanderings our Saviour came again to Capharnaum (Matt. 17:23). There the collectors of the Temple tribute came to Peter.

### 1. THE QUESTION PUT TO PETER BY THE TEMPLE TAX-GATHERERS

The tribute which the tax-gatherers were collecting was a sum which every Israelite, from his twentieth year upwards, had to pay towards the expenses of the Temple service. It was therefore a tribute paid to God. The tax amounted to half a sicle (two drachmas or denarii = forty cents), and was paid at the end of the last month in the year; that is to say, before (or sometimes after) the Paschal month, and at the place of residence (not necessarily birthplace) of each person. The priests and probably also the Levites and Rabbis were exempt from the tax (II Esdr. 10:33 etc.). The zeal of the tax-gatherers for their duty is very evident from the manner in which they exercise their office. Further, they display great politeness and consideration in their conduct. They ask if the Master did not also pay the tax, or in other words if He had perhaps already paid it elsewhere, or if He paid it at all. They do not address themselves to our Saviour Himself, but to Peter, out of respect and consideration for our Lord, or perhaps because Peter was the owner of the house at which He was staying (Matt. 17:23).

## 2. peter's answer

St. Peter immediately answers in the affirmative, without further reflection or reserve. It is so like Peter to act thus. It did not occur to him that he had recognized in Jesus the Son of God; he thought it a matter of course that his Master would pay the tribute like everyone else. Probably, too, our Saviour had hitherto actually done so. These may have been the reasons which occasioned his answer (Matt. 17:24).

## 3. our saviour's rectification of peter's answer

As Peter went into the house, either to fetch the money or to inform our Saviour of the incident, our Lord anticipated him with the question in parable form, in which He repudiates, as Son of God, any obligation to pay a tribute to His Father; but still He complies with the demand from motives of charity and humility, sends Peter to the lake and works the well-known miracle (Matt. 17:24–26).

There are here many beautiful traits to be considered in our Saviour.

In the first place, His great poverty. He has not even half a sicle in His possession, and must either have recourse to the charity of others or work a miracle, in order to pay the tax.

Further, our Saviour here manifests His dignity and prerogative as the Son of God. He protests against the action of Peter, who had overlooked this. But the protest is very skilfully worded, goes straight to the point, and is most kindly put. He merely hints it by a question, asking in the form of an allegory if kings draw tribute from their children or from their subjects. The answer was evident. By this protest our Saviour asserts and expresses His dignity as the Son of God, and also proves it afresh by the omniscience through which He reveals to Peter his conversation with the tax-gatherers and by the subsequent miracle, as

He creates a sicle of gold in the mouth of the fish (unless it be assumed that He knew of its being there, and thus again manifested His omniscience).

Thirdly, we may notice the great prudence, modesty and charity of our Lord. In order not to give scandal and excite sensation, displeasure and opposition, as though He despised the Temple, our Saviour willingly subjects Himself to pay to God a tribute to which He, as Son of God, was not subject. He will do or omit nothing at the expense of charity.

Lastly, our Saviour shows His esteem and love for St. Peter, by (probably) excepting him also from the obligation to pay the tax (Matt. 17:26), but then bidding him pay for himself at the same time, and giving him a share in the performance of the miracle.

The signification of this mystery is, first, that Peter is to be confirmed in his faith in the Divinity of Jesus (in His Divine Sonship) by this manifestation of divine omniscience and power, and to be led to exercise this faith practically, in thought, judgment and deed. Further, our Saviour wished by thus condescendingly placing Peter on a level with Himself, bidding him pay the tax for them both and miraculously procuring the coin for it, to prefigure the Church and especially the Primacy in its essential character, attributes, and relations to the world and the times. Christ and Peter are, in a certain respect, one. The same authority and power work in them; the same elevation of position raises them above certain temporal claims; they enjoy the same freedom from obligations to which others are subject; they bear the same relation towards the needs and requirements of life and of the times; their authority and power were instituted, developed and maintained in the same manner, viz. by the concurrence of divine and human, earthly and supernatural causes, as we see for example in the origin of the States of the Church; and lastly, they show the same gracious and affable condescension to the course of affairs and the requirements of the times. We see here again, therefore, so exactly our Saviour Himself in all His majesty, gentleness and condescension.

### DISPUTE OF THE APOSTLES CONCERNING PRECEDENCE

LUKE 9:46. And there entered a thought into them, which of them should be greater.—47. But Jesus seeing the thoughts of their heart, took a child and set him by him,—48. And said to them: "Whosoever shall receive this child in my name, receiveth me; and whosoever shall receive me, receiveth him that sent me. For he that is the lesser among you all, he is the greater."

MARK 9:32. And they came to Capharnaum. And when they were in the house, he asked them: "What did you treat of in the way?"—33. But they held their peace; for in the way they had disputed among themselves, which of them should be the greatest.—34. And sitting down, he called the twelve, and saith to them: "If any man desire to be first, he shall be the last of all, and the minister of all."—35. And taking a child, he set him in the midst of them. Whom when he had embraced, he saith to them:—36. "Whosoever shall receive one such child as this in my name, receiveth me; and whosoever shall receive me, receiveth not me, but him that sent me."

MATT. 18:1. At that hour the disciples came to Jesus, saying: "Who, thinkest thou, is the greater in the kingdom of heaven?"—2. And Jesus calling unto him a little child, set him in the midst of them,—3. And said: "Amen I say to you, unless you be converted, and become as little children, you shall not enter into the kingdom of heaven.—4. Whosoever therefore shall humble himself as this little child, he is the greater in the kingdom of heaven.—5. And he that shall receive one such little child in my name, receiveth me."

Upon one of the wanderings in the neighborhood of Capharnaum (Mark 9:32), the Apostles fell into a dispute amongst themselves concerning precedence in the Messianic kingdom.

### 1. THE APOSTLES' DISPUTE CONCERNING PRECEDENCE

The prediction of the Resurrection of Jesus and the manifestation of His kingdom may have given rise to the dispute; perhaps also the distinction which had repeatedly fallen to the lot of the three disciples, especially Peter.

As it seems, the discussion had been somewhat animated, and had been carried on during the walk to Capharnaum, whilst our Saviour, perhaps lost in prayer or reflection, walked behind or in advance of them. On reaching the house, our Saviour called them to account as to what had passed between them on the way. They were silent at first from embarrassment, but at length, perceiving that He had penetrated their thoughts, they laid before Him the question under dispute, viz. who would be the greatest in the "kingdom of heaven," i.e. the earthly kingdom of the Messias (Mark 9:32, 33; Luke 9:46; Matt. 18:1).

We may here remark how foolish and wrong this discussion was. In the first place, it was useless, because it did no one any good. Secondly, it was absurd. What reason could any of them imagine or bring forward? What did our Lord think of it? "What hast thou that thou hast not received?" (I Cor. 4:7.) Thirdly, the discussion was harmful, because it proceeded from envy, jealousy, ambition, and false conceptions of the Messianic kingdom, and could only provoke disagreement and contention. This was the reason why the Apostles were ashamed to answer when our Lord called them to account.

## 2. OUR LORD'S REPROOF

Our Lord now sat down in the midst of the Apostles and reproved them for their conduct. We are struck first by the care He shows in their training. He lets no fault pass uncensured.

Further, we must consider the manner in which He gave the reproof. In the first place, it was given kindly. He does not inveigh against the Apostles by a single word. Secondly, He rebukes their ambition not only by word, but by an action calculated to impress them deeply. He calls a little child to Him, embraces it and sets it before Him in the midst of them, saying: "Unless you . . . become as little children, you shall not enter into the kingdom of heaven" (Matt. 18:3). In the child, our Lord sets before the Apostles the most charming and striking picture of disinterestedness, humility and subjection. Thirdly, the reproof raises them to higher thoughts and encourages them. Our Lord does not put a veto upon all seeking after greatness and distinction. He turns their thoughts away from the strife for posts of honor in an earthly kingdom of the Messias, directs them towards the right aim of ambition, viz. to be great in God's eyes, and puts them upon the right path towards it, that of humility and self-abasement: "If any man desire to be the first, he shall be the last of all and the minister of all" (Mark 9:34; Luke 9:48). And in order that the Apostles may not be discouraged at the greatness of the humility required of them, our Saviour begins to extol the child, and represents it in its humility as something most sublime and worthy of reverence: "Whosoever therefore shall humble himself as this little child, he is the greater in the kingdom of heaven" (Matt. 18:4). Not ambition, but childlike humility entitles to the first place in God's estimation, and consequently in heaven also. The degree of childlike humility attained will be the degree of greatness in heaven. "Whosoever shall receive one such child as this in My name, receiveth Me; and whosoever shall receive Me, receiveth not Me, but him that sent Me" (Mark 9:36; Luke 9:48). The child is the image of Christ's humility, and therefore the object of the Father's preference; and for this reason our Saviour recommends it to our esteem, love and care and its humility to our imitation.

### 3. THE CONCLUSION

From the reasons just given we see how this mystery teaches us, on the one hand, to avoid ambition, especially as it creeps in even among those who are near to our Saviour; and on the other hand, how desirable is a childlike, humble spirit, as the three following reasons show.

In the first place, humility is necessary to all, and in a certain sense even necessary for salvation and participation in God's kingdom. Without a certain degree of this humility we cannot enter the Church or the kingdom of heaven, or remain in the Church after having entered it.

Secondly, this humility is the object of the love and affection of God and men. We see the child, the representative of this humility, drawn close to our Saviour in the most gracious manner, caressed, honored and blessed by Him (Luke 9:47; Mark 9:35).

Thirdly, there lies in this humility something very sublime and majestic, a living resemblance to our Saviour and a reflection of the Divine Sonship and the purity and holiness of God. It means death to egotism, and the absorption of oneself in God (Mark 9:36; Luke 9:48). This childlike spirit of simplicity, humility and innocence is the pungent salt which destroys all that is unholy in us, and with which everyone must be salted who wishes to escape the salting of hell-fire (Mark 9:48).

## MIRACULOUS GIFTS AND THE APOSTOLIC COLLEGE

LUKE 9:49. And John answering, said: "Master, we saw a certain man casting out devils in thy name, and we forbade him, because he followeth not with us."—50. And Jesus said to him: "Forbid him not; for he that is not against you, is for you."

MARK 9:37. John answered him, saying: "Master, we saw one casting out devils in thy name, who followeth not us, and we forbade him."—38. But Jesus said: "Do not forbid him; for there is no man that doth a miracle in my name, and can soon speak ill of me.—39. For he that is not against you, is for you.—40. For whosoever shall give you to drink a cup of water in my name, because you belong to Christ; Amen I say to you, he shall not lose his reward."

St. John profited by the interval of silence which probably ensued amongst the Apostles after the reproof, to inquire if it was permissible for others also, who did not belong to the Apostolic College, to cast out devils in the Name of Jesus; they had found someone doing this, and had forbidden him to continue.

## 1. OCCASION OF THE QUESTION

Various causes may have given rise to this question, but probably it was chiefly due to the embarrassment which the reproof for their ambition had produced in the Apostles. It is but natural under such circumstances to wish to change the topic. It may be, also, that our Saviour's previous words: "Whosoever shall receive one such child as this in My Name, receiveth Me. And whosoever shall receive Me, receiveth not Me, but Him that sent Me" (Mark 9:36; Luke 9:48), gave rise to the question, St. John thinking that whoever received Jesus must also join Him outwardly and belong to the Apostolic College like themselves, otherwise he might not employ the Name of Jesus to work miracles. Lastly, it may also have been the sudden remembrance of the man who had ventured to do such a thing.

## 2. ERRONEOUS SUPPOSITION IN THIS QUESTION

The question appears to proceed principally from the supposition that the employment of this miraculous gift was an essential part of the Apostolic office. Our Saviour had, it is true, given this power to the Apostles also; but it was merely incidental, not essential. The essentials of the Apostolic office consisted in the possession of the threefold power, priestly, prophetic and pastoral. St. John does not seem to have perceived this distinction; hence the importance which he attached to the matter. Another erroneous supposition was that these miraculous gifts were exclusively attached to the Apostolic College; for this reason the Apostles forbade the man to exercise them (Luke 9:49; Mark 9:37). A still deeper cause was most probably a certain narrow-mindedness on the part of the Apostles, mingled with zeal for their Master's honor.

## 3. OUR SAVIOUR'S CORRECTION OF THE ERROR

Our Saviour now does two things.

First, He reproves the Apostles for what they had done, saying that they had acted wrongly. "Forbid him not" (Luke 9:50; Mark 9:38).

Secondly, He gives three reasons for this. One reason concerns Himself. Whoever works miracles in the Name of Jesus evidently believes in Him, and therefore does not oppose Him and will say no evil of Him, even though he may not belong to the

Apostolic College (Mark 9:38). Also, greater glory accrues to our Saviour, when many have this gift of miracles in His Name and through His power. This shows His might, freedom and independence. As a matter of fact, such miraculous gifts are often granted to simple laymen, to indemnify them, as it were, for not enjoying the privileges of the official exercise of the apostolic and priestly office. A similar reason is urged by our Saviour with regard to the Apostles themselves. "He that is not against you, is for you" (Mark 9:39; Luke 9:50). That is to say, a person is not your enemy simply because he does not belong to your number; he may be a believer, and thus also friendly and well-disposed. Our Lord takes the third reason from the doings of the man in question. He says, if even the smallest service (such as the giving of a cup of water to the Apostles) rendered for Christ's sake is good and meritorious, how much better and more meritorious is the work of casting out devils in the Name of Jesus (Mark 9:40).

From this occurrence we learn above all how envy creeps in even among religious persons, and how greatly we must be on our guard against it. Envy is a certain sadness at the well-being of our neighbor, inasmuch as this is derogatory to our own. It is therefore a breach of charity, and arises from a kind of pettiness and narrowness of mind, and especially also from pride. In this respect this instruction is a continuation of the preceding lesson on humility. The effects of envy are very often discontent and aversion towards God and our neighbor, joy at the ill-success and sadness at the well-being of the latter, and depreciation of him. These considerations give us motives enough for driving this spirit out of our hearts, since it is so entirely repugnant to our Saviour and so opposed to His whole nature. Moses and St. Paul also showed a similar and beautiful mark of large-heartedness (Num. 11:29; Phil. 1:18). This incident shows us the mildness and considerate delicacy of our Saviour; the candor and sincerity with which He everywhere speaks and teaches the truth; and lastly His noble broad-mindedness, which is so wise and has such a beneficent influence, and which we must manifest not only in our personal relations to others, but also in the affairs of the state of life to which we belong. The maxim: "He that is not against us, is for us," will allay many a pang of jealousy. The success of others is not prejudicial to us; on the contrary, they labor for the same cause and serve the one Lord of all. If only He is glorified, it must be a matter of indifference to us through whom the glory comes.

## OF SCANDAL

MARK 9:41. "And whosoever shall scandalize one of these little ones that believe in me, it were better for him that a millstone were hanged about his neck, and he were cast into the sea.—42. And if thy hand scandalize thee, cut it off; it is better for thee to enter into life maimed, than having two hands to go into hell, into unquenchable fire;—43. Where their worm dieth not, and the fire is not extinguished.—44. And if thy foot scandalize thee, cut it off; it is better for thee to enter lame into life everlasting, than having two feet to be cast into the hell of unquenchable fire,—45. Where their worm dieth not, and the fire is not extinguished.—46. And if thy eye scandalize thee, pluck it out; it is better for thee with one eye to enter into the kingdom of God, than having two eyes to be cast into the hell of fire;—47. Where their worm dieth not, and the fire is not extinguished.—48. For everyone shall be salted with fire, and every victim shall be salted with salt.—49. Salt is good. But if the salt become unsavory, wherewith will you season it? Have salt in you, and have peace among you."

MATT 18:6. "But he that shall scandalize one of these little ones that believe in me, it were better for him that a millstone should be hanged about his neck, and that he should be drowned in the depth of the sea.—7. Woe to the world because of scandals. For it must needs be that scandals come; but nevertheless woe to that man by whom the scandal cometh.—8. And if thy hand or thy foot scandalize thee, cut it off, and cast it from thee; it is better for thee to go into life maimed or lame, than having two hands or two feet to be cast into everlasting fire.—9. And if thy eye scandalize thee, pluck it out, and cast it from thee; it is better for thee having one eye to enter into life, than having two eyes to be cast into hell fire.—10. See that you despise not one of these little ones; for I say to you, that their angels in heaven always see the face of my Father, who is in heaven.—11. For the Son of Man is come to save that which was lost.—12. What think you? If a man have a hundred sheep, and one of them should go astray; doth he not leave the ninety-nine in the mountains, and go to seek that which is gone astray?—13. And if it so be that he find it; Amen I say to you, he rejoiceth more for that, than for the ninety-nine that went not astray.—14. Even so it is not the will of your Father, who is in heaven, that one of these little ones should perish."

After the digression considered in the last meditation our Saviour reverts once more to the subject of the child, and adds to the promise of reward for kindness to one of these little ones (Mark 9:36; Matt. 18:5), also the warning against giving scandal to such as these.

### 1. NATURE OF SCANDAL

Scandal is any word or deed by which we become an occasion of sin to others; just as, on the other hand, the "receiving" of a child (Matt. 18:5; Mark 9:36) signifies the bestowing of any benefit, and especially spiritual aid. By "others," "one's neighbor," are understood all men, especially the faithful, and more particularly still children and weak souls, who are more exposed to the pernicious influence of scandal on account of their lack of moral strength (Matt. 18:6; Mark 9:41).

## 2. REALITY AND ACTUAL EXISTENCE OF SCANDAL

Our Saviour, in His warning against giving scandal, not only indicates the possibility of it, but also states as a matter of fact that there will always be scandals, indeed that there must always be scandals in the world, in the natural course of things (Matt. 18:7); not of necessity, but owing to the action of free causes. These causes are: the permission of God, the temptation of the Evil One, and the malice and weakness of men. Thus the whole world is, as a matter of fact, one terrible system of giving and taking scandal.

## 3. GRAVITY OF SCANDAL

The gravity of scandal is sufficiently evident from the fact that our Saviour pronounces "woe" upon the world on account of the unhappiness and evil which it occasions. This reiterated "woe" is an expression of pity for those who are exposed to scandal, and also of warning and menace for the one who gives the scandal, on account of the punishments he incurs (Matt. 18:7). In particular, the serious nature of scandal is evident from the greatness of the evils which we should be ready to suffer, rather than to give or take it.

Our Saviour illustrates this first, with regard to the scandal-giver, by the punishment of being drowned in the sea by means of a millstone hung round the neck, i.e. by a sure, severe and shameful punishment. It is nevertheless more tolerable for the sufferer than the evil of giving scandal, because this latter is a sin in itself and has fatal consequences for him and for others. It is sufficiently evident from the punishment named that the scandal-giver is such a pest to society that one cannot remove him too far or too securely (Matt. 18:6; Mark 9:41). Secondly, our Lord sets forth the gravity of giving scandal by contrasting it with the efforts of the holy angels, who, by virtue of their nearness to God and enjoyment of the beatific vision of His glory, are the eminent and mighty protectors of little ones, and do not consider it beneath their dignity to guide them carefully towards their last end (Matt. 18:10). He contrasts this vice also with the labors of the God-Man Himself, Whose life-work it is to save and bring in the lost, Whose pastoral solicitude, labor and joy are so touchingly described in the parable of the sheep lost and found (Matt. 18:11–13). Lastly, He contrasts it with the eternal decree of the

Father, Who wills the eternal welfare of these little ones (Matt.
18:14), moves heaven and earth for them, and makes the whole
creation subserve their salvation. Men and angels and even the
Son of God Himself draw from this decree, as though from the
countenance of God, encouragement, light, and strength to work
for the salvation of souls. He who gives scandal opposes all this
work, frustrates and destroys it in souls. Thus scandal is the very
work of the devil, and the scandal-giver a true accomplice of Satan;
indeed, he is himself a very Satan, an antagonist of all God's plans
and arrangements. It follows from this as a necessary consequence
what a fate awaits the scandal-giver, against whom the holy angels
and God's cause itself are witnesses, accusers and avengers.

Our Saviour then proceeds to illustrate the evil of taking scandal, by the greatness of the sacrifices which we must be willing to
make rather than expose ourselves to it. We must sacrifice hand,
foot, or even eye, if it becomes an occasion of scandal to us (Matt.
18:8, 9), i.e. renounce the dearest and most necessary things rather
than let ourselves be led into sin (Matt. 5:29). And our Saviour
also tells us the reason, namely that all these evils are not to be
compared with hell, which is the penalty of mortal sin. Hell itself
is very vividly and forcibly represented, as a terrible punishment
by fire in a shameful and wicked place (Matt. 18:8, 9; 5:22), such
as is the valley of Gehenna; and also as a punishment eternal in
its duration, for St. Mark twice calls this fire "unquenchable," and
adds thrice: "Where their worm dieth not, and the fire is not
extinguished" (Mark 9:42, 43, 44, 45, 47; Isa. 30:33; 66:24; Eccli.
17:19). The picture of the punishment gains still more in awful-
ness (according to the interpretation of some commentators)
by the words of our Saviour, as recorded by St. Mark: "For every
one shall be salted with fire, and every victim shall be salted with
salt" (Mark 9:48). By virtue of its purifying, seasoning and preserving power, salt is a sign of the Covenant (Lev. 2:13), and
every sacrifice had to be "salted with salt" as a sign that it belonged to God. So it is also in a spiritual sense with every human
being. In the case of the Saints, the spiritual salt of purity and
suffering has already done its cleansing and seasoning work here
below, and in heaven exercises only its preserving virtue, in the
beatific state; but since the scandal-givers and scandal-takers did
not let themselves be salted during life with the salt of purity and
innocence, and would not become a sacrifice of God's clemency,
they are now salted with the salt of hell-fire as a sacrifice of His

justice. According to the view of Holy Scripture the damned are also victims of God's justice (Jer. 46:10; Ez. 21:10; 39:17). In this picture of being salted with fire we perceive the idea of an all-penetrating, scorching and painful punishment; and also the idea of eternity, because salt is preservative, and does not consume, but keeps from decay.[1]

Our Divine Saviour concludes the lesson upon scandal, according to St. Mark, by saying (in continuation of the words about being salted with fire): "Salt is good. But if the salt become unsavory, wherewith will you season it? Have salt in you, and have peace among you" (Mark 9:49). He hereby alludes to the cause from which the dispute as to precedence had arisen, viz. ambition, or the want of a childlike spirit, and names as the remedy for it this very childlike spirit of humility and peace. Salt is the symbol of this spirit, being the sign of wisdom and of peace with God. Ambition, on the contrary, destroys this peace and wisdom. It is all the more necessary that the Apostles should have this salt, since it is their vocation to remedy the evils of the world by means of it. But how can they impart it to others, if they do not possess it themselves?

With regard to doctrines of faith, this mystery is of twofold importance: viz. on account of the express and irrefutable teaching of the eternity of the punishment of hell, and also on account of the foundation it affords for the doctrine of the existence of guardian angels. As regards morals, it teaches us especially the gravity of scandal, a subject here fully developed and illustrated. Lastly, with regard to the Person of our Saviour, we see especially displayed His goodness and love for men, which orders all things, heaven and earth and all His works, His coming, and His efforts for the salvation of men. We have here too an example of the powerful eloquence and wisdom of Jesus. How wonderfully, how touchingly He sets forth the motives against giving scandal, and also those which should incite us to loving care for the welfare of men, even of little ones and weaklings!

[1] Others understand the passage as referring to the good. As every sacrifice becomes agreeable to God through the salt of the Covenant, so must everyone, in order to become pleasing to Him, permit himself to be salted with the salt of purity, mortification and suffering.

## Of Fraternal Correction

Matt. 18:15. "But if thy brother shall offend against thee, go and rebuke him between thee and him alone; if he shall hear thee, thou shalt gain thy brother.—16. And if he will not hear thee, take with thee one or two more, that in the mouth of two or three witnesses every word may stand.—17. And if he will not hear them, tell the church; and if he will not hear the church, let him be to thee as the heathen and publican.—18. Amen I say to you, whatsoever you shall bind upon earth, shall be bound also in heaven; and whatsoever you shall loose upon earth, shall be loosed also in heaven.—19. Again I say to you, that if two of you shall consent upon earth, concerning anything whatsoever they shall ask, it shall be done to them by my Father who is in heaven.—20. For where there are two or three gathered together in my name, there am I in the midst of them."

From the subject of scandal our Saviour takes occasion to speak of fraternal correction.

### 1. WHAT FRATERNAL CORRECTION IS

The matter of fraternal correction is sin (Matt. 18:15), not merely inasmuch as it offends and injures us, but sin as such, and inasmuch as it is always a scandal, if an exterior action. The motive in giving it is not, then, personal satisfaction for the one offended or injured, but our neighbor's amendment and the welfare of his soul, as our Saviour says: "If he shall hear thee, thou shalt gain thy brother" (Matt. 18:15). To "rebuke" signifies here to make representations to him, in order to bring him to acknowledge his fault and amend it. By this fraternal correction, therefore, our Lord does not mean accusation before a court of justice.

### 2. MOTIVES FOR THE EXERCISE OF FRATERNAL CORRECTION

The first motive is Christ, God, His words and example. Our Saviour gives a commandment which binds every one, the faithful in general as well as the Apostles, and the obligation may even be grave under certain circumstances. It is certainly not a grave one, however, if prudence tells us that the reproof will avail nothing, but only make the matter worse; that the person who gives the reproof will suffer great injury by doing so; or that another can give it better. Christ's example is set forth in His teaching on scandal, and in the efforts of God and of our Saviour to save the sinner. As He seeks to save the erring one, who is at the same time an offender against Himself, so should we also do, whether the sinner has committed a fault against us or not.

The second motive is our neighbor. We "gain our brother," a brother, our brother and Christ's. Who would not rejoice to guide one who has gone astray into the right path, to rescue one who has fallen into a pit? Sin is the most fatal error, the greatest evil that can befall our neighbor. Fraternal correction is therefore a great act of charity.

We ourselves are the third motive; either our punishment, since our Lord will require of us the soul of our neighbor, whom we could have saved, and yet allowed to perish (Ez. 3:18); or our profit, because fraternal correction is such a beautiful work of mercy and of love for God, often so easy, too.

From all this it is evident that fraternal correction stands to scandal in the position of a remedy to an evil. What scandal injures, fraternal correction seeks to repair.

### 3. HOW FRATERNAL CORRECTION MUST BE EXERCISED

Our Saviour gives together with the obligation, instructions as to the manner in which fraternal correction must be exercised. He distinguishes a triple gradation by which the correction is to proceed in order to bring about a real amendment, and the observance of this gradation is, as a rule, just as binding as the correction itself, partly on account of charity and partly on account of justice.

The first step is to reprove the offending brother in private (Matt. 18:15). If that is of no use, we must proceed to the second, and take one or two witnesses with us, partly in order to make him ashamed and produce a greater impression upon him, partly in order to be able to prove before the Supreme Judge that the correction has taken place (Matt. 18:15; Deut. 19:15). As a last resource we must bring the matter before the Church, i.e. an ecclesiastical superior; not before a secular judge, because it is usually a question of the offender's amendment, not of his exterior chastisement. The Church is officially charged with the cure of souls. If he does not hear the Church either, he is to be regarded as a heathen and publican, i.e. as one who is expelled from the Church, does not belong to her any more, and must be avoided, as the Jews held aloof from the heathens and publicans (Matt. 18:17).

From this it is clear that the obligation of submitting to the judgment of the Church is incumbent upon us, and also that she has the right to exclude from her communion, and therefore to declare this exclusion, or in other words to inflict excommunication, the motive of which, however, is desire for the amendment of the offender and solicitude for her other members. This is here clearly shown by our Saviour, and He also proves the power of the Church, first by saying: "Whatsoever you shall bind upon earth shall be bound also in heaven; and whatsoever you shall loose upon earth shall be loosed also in heaven" (Matt. 18:18). It is the same power which is promised to Peter, but it is always exercised by the Church in subordination to him; it is divine, and includes in itself the sacramental and the exterior judicial power of making obligatory laws, punishing, and dispensing from obligations and punishments, not only for this world, but also for the next. Our Saviour proves this power of the Church, secondly, by telling us that as He is present with His efficacy and authority at every little private assembly of the faithful held in His Name (i.e. in union with Him), merely for the purpose of obtaining something by prayer, so much the more will He be present when the Church speaks and commands in the exercise of her pastoral and judicial office, whether at councils or otherwise (Matt. 18:20).

With respect to moral doctrine we see explained in this mystery the duty of fraternal correction, accompanied by consideration for the good name of the offender; further, the divine power of united, believing prayer. With respect to faith the mystery is of great importance, on account of Christ's statement concerning the authority and power of the Church. She is the supreme judge and the supreme court of appeal in matters of faith and morals, and her decisions with regard to binding and loosing have force here below and in eternity. All things good come to us from our union with her; separation from her makes everything fruitless and frustrates even the power of prayer. But this judicial office of the Church also presupposes that she is visible, for of what use can an invisible court of justice be, here on earth? It is also significant that our Saviour here imparts the power which He had previously given to Peter alone (Matt. 16:19) to the entire Apostolic College, indeed to all ecclesiastical superiors, though in dependence upon Peter. Thus He here carries on the building-up of the Church and her hierarchy. As regards the character of our Saviour, we see here an important additional feature in His mild, indulgent love for sinners, as displayed in this mystery. He leaves no stone unturned to save them, employing to this end even men, as the devil also makes use of their aid in the giving of scandal. Men are to restrain the terrible devastations of scandal, by means of fraternal correction.

## MAGNANIMITY IN FORGIVING INJURIES. THE PARABLE OF THE KING AND HIS TWO SERVANTS

MATT. 18:21. Then came Peter unto him, and said: "Lord, how often shall my brother offend against me, and I forgive him? Till seven times?"—22. Jesus saith to him: "I say not to thee, till seven times; but till seventy times seven times.—23. Therefore is the kingdom of heaven likened to a king, who would take an account of his servants.—24. And when he had begun to take the account, one was brought to him, that owed him ten thousand talents.—25. And as he had not wherewith to pay it, his lord commanded that he should be sold, and his wife and children, and all that he had, and payment to be made.—26. But that servant falling down, besought him, saying: Have patience with me, and I will pay thee all.—27. And the lord of that servant being moved with pity, let him go and forgave him the debt.—28. But when that servant was gone out, he found one of his fellow-servants that owed him an hundred pence; and laying hold of him, he throttled him, saying: Pay what thou owest.—29. And his fellow-servant, falling down, besought him, saying: Have patience with me, and I will pay thee all.—30. And he would not; but went and cast him into prison, till he paid the debt.—31. Now his fellow-servants seeing what was done, were very much grieved; and they came and told their lord all that was done.—32. Then his lord called him, and said to him: Thou wicked servant, I forgave thee all the debt, because thou besoughtest me;—33. Shouldst not thou then have had compassion also on thy fellow-servant, even as I had compassion on thee?—34. And his lord being angry, delivered him to the torturers, until he paid all the debt.—35. So also shall my heavenly Father do to you, if you forgive not everyone his brother from your hearts."

St. Peter now asks how often he is to forgive.

### I. ST. PETER'S QUESTION

St. Peter's question was doubtless occasioned by our Saviour's preceding instruction concerning fraternal correction (Matt. 18:15 seq.). The same lesson is here carried on, since our Lord now shows not only how we must seek to gain the offender by fraternal correction, but also how we must receive him when repentant.

The inquiry itself is addressed by St. Peter with the object of learning how often he should forgive personal offences and be reconciled. It is therefore not a question here of official remission of sins, but of the pardon of private injuries. Peter mentions for instance the number seven (Matt. 18:21). The scribes, in the spirit of their school, limited the number to three times, perhaps supporting this practice upon certain passages of Scripture (Amos

1:3; 2:1; Job 33:29). Peter wishes to know a definite limit (Matt. 18:21).

## 2. OUR DIVINE SAVIOUR'S ANSWER TO THE QUESTION

Our Saviour replies to St. Peter that he should forgive "not till seven times, but till seventy times seven times." The number is definite and yet indefinite. The meaning is that he should always forgive. The measure of forgiveness is inexhaustible and unbounded. It sounds almost as though our Saviour were alluding to the measure of vengeance for bloodshed (Gen. 4:24), and changing it into the measure of forgiveness.

## 3. ILLUSTRATION AND CONFIRMATION OF THE ANSWER BY THE PARABLE

Our Saviour adds to the answer already given the parable of the king and his two servants. The aim of the parable is indicated by the words: "So also shall my Heavenly Father do to you, if you forgive not every one his brother from your hearts" (Matt. 18:35). Our Divine Saviour wishes here to induce the Apostles and all of us to forgive offences against ourselves and others invariably and magnanimously, as our Heavenly Father also forgives us.

The parable contains two motives for this. The first is the example of God's magnanimity in forgiving us. This mercy of God is illustrated, first, by the immensity of the debt which the king forgives. The servant is a high official, a steward of the crown demesnes (I Par. 27:25), who has kept back from the king much money, indeed the income of a whole province, 10,000 talents, or about ten million dollars (Esth. 3:9). Thus the debt is enormous, beyond all repayment. Secondly, the mercy of God is shown by the manner in which the king remits this vast debt, viz. not merely in part, but wholly and entirely, upon a simple entreaty, without exacting any reimbursement or punishment, which latter was severe enough according to the laws and customs of the time, as is sufficiently evident from this very parable, where it relates the manner in which the unmerciful servant treats his debtor (Matt. 18:25, 28; IV Kings 4:1). As the king acted, so does God act towards man, when He forgives sin. Man, by virtue of his position towards God, is also an official of the Supreme King, and incurs an enormous debt by his misuse of creatures. He can do nothing but entreat pardon, and God forgives him the debt because of his entreaty.

The second motive is the unworthy behavior of the pardoned servant towards his debtor, and the punishment which he incurs thereby. The unworthiness consists, first, in his immediate forgetfulness of the favor just received (Matt. 18:27, 28); secondly, in his hard and cruel behavior in seizing and ill-treating his debtor in spite of his piteous entreaties (Matt. 18:28–30); lastly, in the insignificance of the debt, which amounted but to 100 denarii (about $20), and could in any case be paid. It is true that his conduct towards his fellow-servant was permitted by the law, but it was barbarous to exercise his rights under the circumstances. The unworthiness of his conduct is still further illustrated by the details given, in which we are told that his fellow-servants were grieved at this spectacle and reported the whole affair to the king, who was equally indignant and ordered the shameless servant to be called (Matt. 18:31–33). As a punishment the offender experiences the full severity of the king's wrath and of the penalty prescribed by the law. The remission of the debt is revoked and the hard-hearted servant delivered over to a dreadful prison, torturing fetters and hopeless captivity (Matt. 18:34). "So also," our Saviour significantly concludes the parable, "shall My Heavenly Father do to you, if you forgive not every one his brother from your hearts" (Matt. 18:35).

In this mystery the will of our Lord that we should forgive injuries generously is brought home to the Apostles as well as to all others, by clear and powerful motives. This forgiveness is required of us, first, by our Saviour's express statement to Peter; secondly, by the greatness of the mercy of God, Who so often forgives us many grievous offences, and always merely because we entreat pardon; further, by the unworthiness of implacability, and its punishment. The fifth petition of the Lord's Prayer is only a practical application of this teaching. Further, in addition to the mercy of God, His justice also is illustrated in this parable, as well as the nature of sin, which is rightly represented as an incalculable debt, impossible to discharge; the punishment of which is eternal, unending (Matt. 18:34).

## OUR SAVIOUR'S JOURNEY THROUGH SAMARIA TO JERUSALEM, TO THE FEAST OF TABERNACLES.

LUKE 9:51. And it came to pass when the days of his assumption were accomplishing, that he steadfastly set his face to go to Jerusalem.—52. And he sent messengers before his face; and going they entered into a city of the Samaritans, to prepare for him.—53. And they received him not, because his face was of one going to Jerusalem.—54. And when his disciples James and John had seen this, they said: "Lord, wilt thou that we command fire to come down from heaven and consume them?"—55. And turning, he rebuked them, saying; "You know not of what spirit you are.—56. The Son of Man came not to destroy souls, but to save." And they went into another town.

JOHN 7:1. After these things Jesus walked in Galilee; for he would not walk in Judaea, because the Jews sought to kill him.—2. Now the Jews' feast of Tabernacles was at hand.—3. And his brethren said to him: "Pass from hence, and go into Judaea; that thy disciples also may see thy works which thou dost.—4. For there is no man that doth anything in secret, and he himself seeketh to be known openly. If thou do these things, manifest thyself to the world."—5. For neither did his brethren believe in him.—6. Then Jesus said to them: "My time is not yet come; but your time is always ready.—7. The world cannot hate you, but me it hateth; because I give testimony of it, that the works thereof are evil.—8. Go you up to this festival day, but I go not up to this festival day; because my time is not accomplished."—9. When he had said these things, he himself stayed in Galilee.—10. But after his brethren were gone up, then he also went up to the feast, not openly, but as it were in secret.

## I. DEPARTURE FROM GALILEE.

The Feast of Tabernacles, which was celebrated towards the end of September, was drawing near (John 7:2), and our Saviour's kinfolk urged Him to go into Judaea, to Jerusalem, to the feast, in order that His adherents in Judaea might also see His wonderful works (John 7:3). No one, they said, who wishes to be known and celebrated, works miracles in such obscurity as is here in Galilee. If you will work miracles, show yourself to the world, i.e. the great Jewish world in Jerusalem, at the great national feast; that is the right time and the right place for the manifestation of the glory of the kingdom (John 7:3, 4). This, if it is not the utterance of worldly-mindedness, ambition and egotism, is at all events that of imperfect faith. St. John remarks, too, that our Lord's relatives did not believe in Him either (John 7:5), probably meaning that they had no correct idea who He really was and what He intended to do. They most likely expected, like the other Jews, a merely earthly kingdom, and it was therefore incomprehensible to them how He could remain in Galilee. They evidently wished to induce Him to make a sudden and forcible inauguration of His kingdom.

Our Saviour replied that they should go to Jerusalem, but that He would not go (John 7:8), i.e. either not with them, or not openly, or not with the intention they wished, viz. that of making a glorious revelation of Himself. The answer is equivocal. He also gives the reason of His answer. You can go, He says, "your time is always ready," because "the world cannot hate you," and you have nothing to fear from it, since you share its expectations and do not oppose it. "My time is not yet come," i.e. the time for My glorious entry into the city and subsequent death; for "Me it (the world) hateth, because I give testimony of it, that the works thereof are evil" (John 7:6, 7, 8). In this answer lay also the reason why He worked in Galilee particularly, why He would not go to Jerusalem openly, and why He had no intention of founding a kingdom at all in their sense of the word, least of all in Jerusalem, because He had nothing to expect there but hatred, persecution and death. In fact our Saviour actually did delay His departure for a time (John 7:9).

Our Lord did not start for Jerusalem until after His kinsfolk had departed, and then not openly, with an imposing following, teaching before crowds of people on the way, as was His usual custom; but accompanied only by a few, and by a circuitous route, first through Samaritan territory and then probably along the bank of the Jordan. And why did He do this? He Himself tells us the reason in His answer to His kinsfolk. He was, naturally speaking, not sure of His life if His departure for Jerusalem became known. For this reason He appeared there suddenly in the middle of the festival, when many people from Galilee who were devoted to Him had already assembled. And yet, in spite of this precaution, nothing but His divine power saved Him from death. Under these circumstances, then, our Saviour started on His journey to Jerusalem.

## 2. INHOSPITABLE RECEPTION IN SAMARIA AND INDIGNATION OF THE APOSTLES

The road to Jerusalem led for a time through Samaritan territory, and our Saviour sent messengers ahead to prepare for Him (Luke 9:52). This was a very wise precaution in the little towns through which He had to pass, and considering the somewhat numerous company of His Apostles (which included perhaps also some disciples); and He wished at the same time to practise His Apostles in the manifold duties of the Apostolate, in the exercise of prudence, intrepidity, and patient acceptation of humiliations. Perhaps He also intended to rid them by degrees of the prejudice which, like an impassable chasm, separated the Jews from the Samaritans.

At one place the Samaritan population would not receive Him, because, as the Gospel says, He was a pilgrim going to Jerusalem for the feast (Luke 9:53). Even out of the festival season, the tolerance of the Samaritans for the Jews probably did not extend to the exercise of hospitality.

James and John, who were perhaps themselves the messengers sent, were exasperated at this refusal, and asked if they should call down fire from heaven upon the despisers of their Master (Luke 9:54). In this question there certainly lay great esteem and love for our Saviour, and also zeal for His honor, together with childlike ingenuousness; but it nevertheless expressed also a zeal without discretion, a true Elias spirit (IV Kings 1:10), and a flagrant abuse of the miraculous gifts which had been bestowed on them for the purpose of edification, not of destruction. There may perhaps also have lain at the bottom of it a little irritated self-love and deep-rooted antipathy to the Samaritans. In short, the desire of the Apostles was not prompted by motives of the highest perfection. They signalize themselves here as very "sons of thunder" (Mark 3:17), although they are certainly entitled to some excuse, seeing that the refusal of hospitality was considered an odious fault by all Orientals, and by the Jews the refusal of hospitality to pilgrims on their way to Jerusalem was considered an atrocious crime which cried to heaven for vengeance.

### 3. OUR SAVIOUR'S BEHAVIOR TOWARDS THE APOSTLES AND TOWARDS THE SAMARITANS

Our Saviour had probably continued His journey immediately upon receiving the contemptuous repulse, without a word of reply, and was now addressed by the Apostles; for we are told that He turned round (Luke 9:55). He merely said to them: "You know not of what spirit you are. The Son of Man came not to destroy souls, but to save." "And they went into another town" (Luke 9:56). How beautiful and edifying is the calmness and humility of our Lord, as opposed to the inhospitable conduct of the Samaritans and the irritation of the Apostles! He does not retaliate, gives no rebuke, but goes quietly to another town, thus fulfilling His own precept (Matt. 10:14). We see another glorious example of our Divine Saviour's merciful love and zeal for souls, in His answer to the Apostles, in which He shows them how earnestly they should avoid such a misuse of their God-given powers as to turn them to selfish ends.

This departure from Galilee to Jerusalem is of great significance in the life of our Saviour. St. Luke's emphatic introduction to this narrative shows clearly that he is about to treat of an important turning-point in our Lord's life: "And it came to pass, when the days of His assumption were accomplishing, that He steadfastly set His face to go to Jerusalem" (Luke 9:51). This departure is the close of His ministry in Galilee. Henceforth He makes Judaea and Peraea the sphere of His activity, to accomplish there "the days of assumption," His Passion and glorification. His leaving Galilee is the signal for the real contest of the Jews against Him. About half a year later this combat ends with His Death, and in it Jerusalem has a special share, as He Himself impressively points out. The situation is already dangerous enough, as He plainly says in the above-mentioned answer to His kinsfolk; so dangerous that He does not think it advisable to go to Jerusalem openly or make known His arrival there. These circumstances, together with the feeling of being forsaken on all sides, and this to such an extent that even His own relatives did not believe in nor understand Him, must necessarily, humanly speaking, have saddened His Heart and caused Him anxiety, sorrow and fear.

All the more beautiful and touching, therefore, is the inexhaustible gentleness of His Heart, with which He subdues the outbursts of anger even of His disciples, and the decision, courage and undauntedness with which He sets His face towards Jerusalem in order to offer it salvation once more, and carries out His unalterable decree in spite of the foresight which He has of the events to come. It is this courage that our Saviour specially recommends to us here. Courage edifies, inspires with great thoughts and resolutions, accomplishes great things, and glorifies God by confidence in Him and in His protection. How many may already have been incited to vigorous action by these words of St. Luke (9:51) and the example of our Saviour!

## THREE CALLS TO THE APOSTOLIC LIFE

LUKE 9:57. And it came to pass as they walked in the way, that a certain man said to him: "I will follow thee whithersoever thou goest."—58. Jesus said to him: "The foxes have holes, and the birds of the air nests; but the Son of Man hath not where to lay his head."—59. But he said to another: "Follow me." And he said: "Lord, suffer me first to go, and to bury my father."—60. And Jesus said to him: "Let the dead bury their dead; but go thou, and preach the kingdom of God."—61. And another said: "I will follow thee, Lord, but let me first take my leave of them that are at my house."—62. Jesus said to him: "No man putting his hand to the plow, and looking back, is fit for the kingdom of God."

MATT. 8:19. And a certain scribe came and said to him: "Master, I will follow thee whithersoever thou shalt go."—20. And Jesus saith to him: "The foxes have holes, and the birds of the air nests; but the Son of Man hath not where to lay his head."—21. And another of his disciples said to him: "Lord, suffer me first to go and bury my father."—22. But Jesus said to him: "Follow me, and let the dead bury their dead."

We read of three vocations to the apostolic life on our Lord's way to Jerusalem.[1]

### 1. THE FIRST CALL

The first was that of a scribe, who offered himself to our Saviour that he might follow Him in the Apostolic life. He came to Jesus, saluted Him respectfully with the title of "Master," and declared himself ready to follow Him wherever He should go (Matt. 8:19; Luke 9:57). The words sound very respectful, determined and enthusiastic. But what his motives really were, whether he was actuated by merely temporal interests or higher ones, is uncertain. At all events our Saviour's answer shows that the scribe had not thought of the actual conditions of following Him.

Our Lord's answer was intended to test the candidate for apostolic life. He offers for his consideration the only condition upon which he can be accepted, viz. poverty, not merely inward and spiritual, but also outward, actual poverty, privation of external, material possessions; great poverty, such as our Saviour Himself practises. He explains this by the comparison of His own poverty with that of the animals. Generally speaking, the poverty of animals is greater than that of men; and amongst the former, again, the poverty of wild beasts is greater than that of domestic animals, which are provided for by their owners. But our Saviour's poverty is greater even than that of the poorest of the wild beasts. "The foxes have holes, and the birds of the air nests; but the Son of Man hath not where to lay His head" (Luke 9:58; Matt. 8:20). So it was in fact. He had no house of His own, no longer any fixed abode. The Samaritans have just turned Him away, and He must seek for shelter. Everything is uncertain, lodging and food. He receives whatever He uses as an alms from the charity of others. Such is indeed great poverty, and how touching it is, when we reflect Who He is, the "Son of Man," the God-Man, the Lord of heaven and earth, and what He might have possessed. But it is just this which makes His poverty also majestic and rich, that it is a voluntary poverty, chosen out of love for us and with the intention of enriching us. This, then, was the condition. If

[1] According to St. Matthew, the first appears to belong to another and earlier period.

the scribe sought only temporal advantages, his resolution of following our Saviour may well have been shaken, especially as our Lord made this condition on the way to Jerusalem. But if he sought to follow Him from supernatural motives, he would find the most powerful attraction in the very poverty which was so clearly and vividly laid before him.

## 2. THE SECOND CALL

The second call proceeded from our Saviour Himself, and the invitation was made in earnest and unmistakable form to a man whom He met on the way: "He said to another, Follow Me." (Luke 9:59).

The condition is made in this case by the one called. He asks to be allowed first to bury his father (Luke 9:59; Matt. 8:21). This may mean either: "Let me first tend my father until he dies," or, in the literal and immediate sense: "Let me go and bury my father today." In the East a dead person remains only one day unburied.

Our Saviour's answer, on the other hand, is most decided: "Let the dead bury their dead; but go thou and preach the kingdom of God" (Luke 9:60; Matt. 8:22). In the first sense of the request, the reason of this answer is clear. The condition was inadmissible, because unfitting and of fatal consequences for the man's vocation. Taken in the second sense, the answer seems hard. At all events we must not forget that our Saviour was acquainted with the Fourth Commandment, and knew how to show every delicate consideration for what was becoming. There must then have been important reasons for the refusal in this case, either that it was not at all necessary for the man whom He had called to be present at the burial in question, or that danger for his vocation awaited him there. As ever, our Saviour here lays very earnest stress upon the truth that God also has rights over us, more rights than anyone else, even than our parents; indeed all rights, so that before love of God all other duties of filial or fatherly love must stand aside (Deut. 6:5; Lev. 21:11; Num. 6:6). Even if our father would remain unburied, we must follow if God calls. If our country is in danger, we leave even a dying father in order to fight for it. The High Priest and the Nazarite were also dispensed by the law from burying their parents (Lev. 21:11; Num. 6:6). How much rather, therefore, is this lawful when the service of God's kingdom is in question!

God calls. That is the first motive, and it is contained in the first part of our Saviour's answer. The second part contains another beautiful motive, namely the great superiority of the apostolic vocation over a life in the world: "Follow Me" (Matt. 8:22), "Go thou and preach the kingdom of God" (Luke 9:60). The apostolic life consists in following Jesus, remaining, dwelling with Jesus; life in the world is intercourse with men and attachment to men. The apostolic life is yet further distinguished from life in the world in that it is concerned with the soul, is a service of life; whereas life in the world, especially family life, is concerned rather with the care of the body, and is therefore a service of death. It is probable that the man called by our Lord in this instance accepted His teaching and at once acted upon it.

### 3. THE THIRD CALL

It is not recorded whether the third man called presented himself of his own accord or was invited by our Saviour. He is willing to follow, only he wishes to go home first, either to put his affairs in order or to take leave of his relatives. In this case, then, the reason of the hesitation is probably solicitude for temporal affairs (Luke 9:61).

Our Saviour's answer requires complete detachment from all temporal interests, giving as a reason the peculiar character of the apostolic vocation. This vocation is such that it engrosses the entire man, his intellect, his will-power and his time. Our Saviour makes this clear by the simile of plowing and tillage (Luke 9:62). The plowman must look before him and exert his strength. If he looks back, he cannot hold the plow firmly, and makes crooked furrows. How much less, then, is looking back and the pursuit of earthly business compatible with the cultivation of the field of God's kingdom, the Church, which is to bear the fruit of God's glory and man's salvation, the fruit of eternal life! This vocation demands the entire man, all his strength and all his time. Whoever will not give this is unfitted for the service of God's kingdom.

These instructions of our Divine Saviour show us, before all, the virtues essential for the apostolic vocation, which every apostolic laborer must endeavor to acquire. He must have a perfect detachment from flesh and blood, home, possessions and temporal cares. The very manner in which our Saviour speaks of this necessity is a powerful motive. It is evident that He makes an important distinction between the different virtues which an Apostle must have. Whilst He is very moderate and indulgent, one might almost say reserved in the requirement of other virtues (Mark 2:19), He knows no reserve in this case, but is severe and inexorable. This shows us, as scarcely anything else does, the spirit of Jesus and the interior spirit of the apostolate. The apparent severity of our Saviour is not without its hidden reasons. This detachment is necessary first for God's sake, in order that we ourselves may fulfil the great commandment of the love of God, and that we may love Him with all our soul and with all our strength. Nothing can take the place of this. God will before all things have our heart; everything else is indifferent to Him. This detachment is necessary secondly for the sake of our neighbor, that we may be really useful to him. This will not be the case unless we have the strength which this detachment imparts, the edification which it gives, and the power of sacrifice by which it purchases souls. Without this virtue we are of no use to the souls of others; on the contrary, we only do them harm. Thirdly, it is necessary in order to ensure well-regulated love of ourselves. Only thus have we freedom or influence, and only thus do we obtain men's confidence. Otherwise we degrade ourselves and have not the compensating consciousness of disinterestedness, truth and fidelity towards God.

As regards the revelation of the character of Jesus, we have here an example of His frankness and rectitude. Openly and clearly He speaks out with regard to the conditions of following Him, conceals nothing, but yet requires no more than He does Himself. He too has left all, and now He is on His way to be received up into heaven through suffering and death. We have also a glimpse of the keenness of His intellect, in the play upon words: "Let the dead bury their dead," be it that He means by "the dead" worldly persons, or only wishes to signify that we must let the dead be buried by the dead, i.e. simply leave them unburied, rather than not follow the call of God.

### CHOICE AND SENDING OUT OF THE SEVENTY-TWO DISCIPLES

LUKE 10:1. And after these things the Lord appointed also other seventy-two; and he sent them two and two before his face into every city and place whither he himself was to come.—2. And he said to them: "The harvest indeed is great, but the laborers are few. Pray ye therefore the Lord of the harvest, that he send laborers into his harvest.—3. Go: Behold I send you as lambs among wolves.—4.

Carry neither purse, nor scrip, nor shoes, and salute no man by the way.—5. Into whatsoever house you enter, first say: Peace be to this house;—6. And if the son of peace be there, your peace shall rest upon him; but if not, it shall return to you. —7. And in the same house remain, eating and drinking such things as they have; for the laborer is worthy of his hire. Remove not from house to house.—8. And into what city soever you enter, and they receive you, eat such things as are set before you;—9. And heal the sick that are therein, and say to them: The kingdom of God is come nigh unto you.—10. But into whatsoever city you enter, and they receive you not, going forth into the streets thereof, say:—11. Even the very dust of your city that cleaveth to us we wipe off against you; yet know this, that the kingdom of God is at hand.—12. I say to you, it shall be more tolerable at that day for Sodom, than for that city.—13. Woe to thee, Corozain, woe to thee, Bethsaida; for if in Tyre and Sidon had been wrought the mighty works that have been wrought in you, they would have done penance long ago, sitting in sackcloth and ashes.—14. But it shall be more tolerable for Tyre and Sidon at the judgment than for you.—15. And thou, Capharnaum, which art exalted unto heaven; thou shalt be thrust down to hell.—16. He that heareth you, heareth me; and he that despiseth you, despiseth me. And he that despiseth me, despiseth him that sent me."

MATT. 10:23. "And when they shall persecute you in this city, flee into another. Amen I say to you, you shall not finish all the cities of Israel, till the Son of Man come.—. . . 40. He that receiveth you, receiveth me; and he that receiveth me, receiveth him that sent me.—41. He that receiveth a prophet in the name of a prophet, shall receive the reward of a prophet; and he that receiveth a just man in the name of a just man, shall receive the reward of a just man.—42. And whosoever shall give to drink to one of these little ones a cup of cold water only in the name of a disciple, amen I say to you, he shall not lose his reward."—11:20. Then began he to upbraid the cities, wherein were done the most of his miracles, for that they had not done penance.—21. "Woe to thee, Corozain; woe to thee, Bethsaida; for if in Tyre and Sidon had been wrought the miracles that have been wrought in you, they had long ago done penance in sack-cloth and ashes.—22. But I say unto you: it shall be more tolerable for Tyre and Sidon in the day of judgment, than for you.—23. And thou, Capharnaum, shalt thou be exalted up to heaven? Thou shalt go down even unto hell; for if in Sodom had been wrought the miracles that have been wrought in thee, perhaps it had remained unto this day.—24. But I say unto you, that it shall be more tolerable for the land of Sodom in the day of judgment, than for thee."

### 1. REASONS AND SIGNIFICANCE OF THE CHOICE OF THE SEVENTY-TWO DISCIPLES

On the way to Jerusalem our Saviour took a very important step. He chose from among the many followers who, besides the Apostles, usually accompanied Him, seventy-two (or seventy) for a special purpose, and sent them before Him into the towns to which He intended to go. The first reason for this is indicated by the words: "The harvest is great" (Luke 10:2), and there were few chosen laborers. Even now the harvest which He was about to reap in Judaea and Peraea was already great, and greater still was the harvest-field of the future Church, over which our Saviour glanced in spirit. The number "seventy" is rightly regarded as referring to the seventy nations (Gen. 10:1–32; 11:8) from which the whole human race sprang; the whole world, all ages and all nations are the great harvest of the Church. Our Saviour widens the view of His followers ever more and more, away beyond the little land of Judaea to a greater field of labor.

The second reason was the Apostles' need of assistance. The seventy-two disciples had the same vocation as they, and were to proclaim everywhere the coming of our Lord and prepare for Him in the places which He was to visit (Luke 10:1), by preaching and working miracles (Luke 10:9, 11). Our Lord sent them two and two (Luke 10:1), not merely as a symbol of charity and for mutual support (Prov. 18:19), but also to ensure the validity of their testimony (Matt. 18:16) as representatives of the Church (Matt. 18:20; Mark 6:7); and, as once the Apostles, so He now sends the disciples with the intention of letting them gain practical experience in the apostolic vocation, and inspiring them with courage and inclination for it (Luke 10:17). A type of this choice of the disciples may be seen in the seventy men whom God gave to Moses as his assistants (Num. 11:16).

The last and most profound reason was in this case also the goodness, wisdom and power of God, Who desired to receive not only the Apostles but also many others beside them and under them into the hierarchy, and to confer upon them the honor and happiness of sharing the dignity and work of the Apostles and acting as our Lord's representatives among men. This reason is indicated in the words: "Pray ye therefore the Lord of the harvest, that He send laborers into His harvest" (Luke 10:2). Vocation, therefore, proceeds from God as its deepest source, and is a mystery of His goodness and mercy.

The real signification of this mystery is, therefore, the extension of the hierarchy and the establishment of those hierarchical grades which are subordinate to the episcopate; and in the first place of the priesthood, i.e. the clergy both secular and regular. Even the ranks of the bishops were later on supplied from the number of these disciples (Acts 1:23). It is certainly worthy of note how greatly our Saviour extended the ecclesiastical hierarchy by this arrangement. All who have received a place in it must reflect upon this mystery with gratitude.

## 2. PREPARATION AND SENDING OF THE SEVENTY-TWO

Our Saviour equips the disciples in the same way as He had formerly done the Apostles, because the object of their mission is the same. Their preparation consisted of three parts. First, He gave them the apostolic authority to preach the kingdom of God (Luke 10:1, 9, 11). Secondly, He conferred upon them fitting miraculous gifts, viz. power to heal the sick and to cast out devils (Luke 10:9, 17). Thirdly, He gave them rules of conduct.

These rules of conduct specify the apostolic virtues which He recommends to the disciples. Before all things He requires apostolic zeal. They are to be laborers in the harvest (Luke 10:2), where there is hard work to be done. They are to reserve nothing, but to give all that they possess and have received for the welfare of souls; they are to show kindness and to give their blessing (Luke 10:5), to preach His doctrine (Luke 10:9), and to heal the sick (Luke 10:9). Further, as regards themselves, our Saviour bids them practise simplicity, modesty, poverty (Luke 10:4) and disinterestedness, so that they are to accept hospitality not according to private considerations, but only according to the necessity imposed by their office, and as long as this exacts it; they are to omit salutations by the way (which are very ceremonious in the East, and take up a great deal of time); not to go from house to house, lest they might wound the feelings of any or merely follow their own inclination, but to give edification (Luke 10:4, 7). On the other hand, they may take what is offered them, and are not bound by our Saviour to any special regulations with regard to food. Indeed, He lays special stress upon the right of the disciples to temporal sustenance (Luke 10:7, 8). Lastly, He bids them be prepared for opposition and an ill reception (Luke 10:3, 10, 11). He sends them as lambs among wolves. He requires of them therefore purity, gentleness, and the spirit of self-sacrifice without hope of recompense; and this as opposed to that wolfish craft, violence, covetousness and inordinate love of enjoyment which seemed incarnate in the Roman Empire. According to St. Matthew (10:16) our Saviour requires that they should be simple, peaceable as doves and wise as serpents; that is, wise in not exciting persecution unnecessarily, and in escaping from it, should it occur. We may here interpolate our Saviour's direction to flee persecutions (Matt. 10:23). This is also an exercise of apostolic prudence, and under certain circumstances even a duty. This implies that there will always be a place of refuge where the Church can exercise her apostolic office. Indeed, our Saviour here (Matt. 10:18–23) speaks of the entire period of the Church's life until the Last Judgment; He refers to the preaching of the Apostles and their successors amongst the Jews outside of Palestine, and hints at the mystery that Israel will not believe until after the Gentiles have entered the Church (Rom. 11:25). If people will not hear or receive the disciples, they are merely to shake off the dust from their shoes, publicly upon the spot, as a sign that they have no fellowship with those who contemn their mission, and to testify that the kingdom of God has come (Luke 10:11). It is evident that our Saviour now speaks much more plainly to His disciples of contradiction and persecution than He did to His Apostles at their first mission (Matt. 10:22). The situation has altered in the meantime. The great revelations of His Divinity have taken place, and on the other hand the enmity against Him has increased, the time of His Passion is approaching; He Himself has repeatedly revealed it, and now He is nearing a crisis.

### 3. DUTY OF THE WORLD TOWARDS THE MESSENGERS

Our Saviour foretells a severe chastisement of the world in case of its non-reception of His messengers. He says that the judgment upon those places which reject them will be severer than that upon Sodom, because the marks of grace shown to the latter were not so great (Luke 10:12; Matt. 11:20). He pronounces "woe" upon Corozain and Bethsaida, which had not been converted by miracles that would have brought even Tyre and Sidon to do penance (Luke 10:13; Matt. 11:21, 22). Capharnaum, which exalted itself in its pride up to heaven, will descend in darkness and silence to the depths of hell, where all greatness sinks into nothing (Luke 10:15; Matt. 11:23, 24).

Our Saviour justifies this judgment by their unbelief and stubbornness towards God, Whose representatives the messengers are by virtue of their mission. He says: "He that heareth you, heareth Me; and he that despiseth you, despiseth Me. And he that despiseth Me, despiseth Him that sent Me" (Luke 10:16). Unbelief and obduracy are worse and more deserving of punishment than sensual depravity; and for the same reason, friendly reception and every little mark of kindness which the world shows to God's messengers, from a good motive, will be rewarded. Everything depends upon the motive. Thus he who confers a benefit upon a prophet or other just man as such, i.e. as servants of God, will receive the reward of a prophet or just man; even a cup of water, given to the least disciple on account of his being a follower of our Lord, will not remain unrewarded (Matt. 10:40–42).

In this mystery another very important step has been taken in the erection of the ecclesiastical hierarchy, viz. the institution and authorization of the grades subordinate to the episcopate. In the pastoral instructions here given this grade also receives the necessary directions and regulations for exercising its functions with dignity and success. The appropriate virtues are all drawn from the model, our Saviour Himself: apostolic zeal, modesty in requirements, humility, poverty, disinterestedness and a noble liberty of spirit. The first duty which our Saviour imposes upon the world with regard to the disciples sent out is also a grave warning that the disciples themselves should undertake their office with all earnestness and fulfil it with all perfection. Taken in connection with the course of the whole life of Jesus, this mystery is as it were the solemn, and unhappily the painful, farewell of our Saviour to Galilee. His last words are a cry of pain, a sorrowful prophecy of the "woe" which shall come upon unbelief in this province; indeed the choice and sending out of the disciples, regarded in connection with the seventy nations and the great world-harvest, is like a taking away of salvation from Israel and an offering of it to the Gentile world. How our Saviour's curse has been fulfilled is shown by the present appearance of the lake, or rather of its surroundings. Of all the former splendor, nothing has remained but the lake itself, its rocky coasts, and the beautiful sky above. All else—shady trees, palaces and towns—have vanished. Thistles and ruins mark the former sites of Corozain, Bethsaida and Capharnaum. A veil of sadness and desolation lies over all. Gray walls of rock and blocks of basalt surround the clear, lonely surface of the lake, upon which scarcely a bark rocks. It is a gleaming emerald in a stained and broken setting (Schegg).

### RETURN OF THE SEVENTY-TWO

LUKE 10:17. And the seventy-two returned with joy, saying: "Lord, the devils also are subject to us in thy name."—18. And he said to them: "I saw Satan like lightning falling from heaven.—19. Behold, I have given you power to tread upon serpents, and scorpions, and upon all the power of the enemy; and nothing shall hurt you.—20. But yet rejoice not in this, that spirits are subject unto you; but rejoice in this, that your names are written in heaven."—21. In that same hour he rejoiced in the Holy Ghost and said: "I confess to thee, O Father, Lord of heaven and earth, because thou hast hidden these things from the wise and prudent, and hast revealed them to little ones. Yea, Father; for so it hath seemed good in thy sight.—22. All things are delivered to me by my Father. And no one knoweth who the Son is, but the Father; and who the Father is, but the Son, and to whom the Son will reveal him."—23. And turning to his disciples, he said: "Blessed are the eyes that see the things which you see.—24. For I say to you, that many prophets and kings have desired to see the things that you see, and have not seen them; and to hear the things that you hear, and have not heard them."

MATT. 11:25. At that time Jesus answered and said: "I confess to thee, O Father, Lord of heaven and earth, because thou hast hid these things from the wise and prudent, and hast revealed them to little ones.—26. Yea, Father; for so hath it seemed good in thy sight.—27. All things are delivered to me by my Father. And no one knoweth the Son, but the Father; neither doth any one know the Father, but the Son, and he to whom it shall please the Son to reveal him.— 28. Come to me, all you that labor and are burdened, and I will refresh you.— 29. Take up my yoke upon you, and learn of me, because I am meek and humble of heart; and you shall find rest to your souls.—30. For my yoke is sweet and my burden light."

## 1. RETURN AND JOY OF THE DISCIPLES

The mission of the disciples was limited to those places which our Saviour intended to visit (Luke 10:1); probably, that is to say, to the towns and villages along the banks of the Jordan, in the direction of Judaea and Peraea. This mission could be accomplished in a short time, on account of the close proximity of these places; and so it was probably after only a few days' absence that the disciples returned to our Saviour (most likely in Judaea), full of joy at their success.

They freely expressed this joy, saying: "The devils also are subject to us in Thy Name" (Luke 10:17). It need not necessarily be assumed that there was vanity in this. On the contrary, their pleasure seems to have been good and innocent. They say expressly that the evil spirits have been subject to them "in the Name of Jesus." They give our Lord the glory, therefore, and the object of their joy was the glorification of their Master, Who showed His power not only through the Apostles, but also through them (the disciples), and that in the most difficult of tasks, viz. the expulsion of devils. This joy after successful work is natural, sometimes even necessary, because it gives courage, zeal, and perseverance. In this the disciples show their open and childlike disposition.

## 2. OUR SAVIOUR'S RESPONSE TO THE DISCIPLES' DEMONSTRATION OF JOY

Our Saviour's answer contains three points.

First, He confirms the joy of the disciples, by giving them a still deeper insight into the cause of their power, which they have indicated by the expression "in Thy Name." This cause is the power of the God-Man over Satan, which originates in the first victory gained over him at the fall of the angels. "I saw Satan like lightning falling from heaven" (Luke 10:18). Even if we understand these words as referring to the present victory, gained by the disciples over Satan in the power of Christ, it is nevertheless connected with that first conquest and is a further triumph in the same warfare, which is continued in the defeat of heathenism in the world by the Apostles, and which will be finally completed on the Last Day at the universal Judgment. Our Saviour is probably alluding to all this, for He continues: Do not wonder at your success against Satan; I have conquered him, and "behold, I have given you power to tread upon serpents, and scorpions, and upon all the power of the enemy," i.e. against all that Satan employs as an instrument to injure you (Luke 10:19). It is obvious that our Saviour's words also contain an admonition to be humble.

Secondly, He elevates and perfects the joy of the disciples by pointing out to them a higher and truer reason for joy, viz. their predestination. "Rejoice in this, that your names are written in heaven" (Luke 10:20), in the Book of Life, which is often spoken of in the Scriptures (Ex. 32:32; Ps. 68:29; Dan. 12). All else is merely a gift of grace, imparted for the benefit of others, and does not of itself make the holder of it good or truly happy, but may even be found in one who is not pleasing in God's sight. As an example of this we need only recall Judas.

Thirdly, our Saviour points to Himself as the cause, author, center and aim of the glory of this election, and then casts a rapid glance over the wonderful plans and decrees of the Father with respect to predestination. He opens out to us a glorious revelation of the development of these divine plans. On the one hand He shows us the prudent and wise in worldly wisdom from Satan to the present time, and on to the end of the world's history; on the other hand the "little ones," the humble and the unlearned, from the good angels to all who recognize their own insufficiency, submit to God and adhere to Christ; while in their midst stands

Christ Himself, the Author and Intermediary of this gracious election by the Father, its guiding and determining principle. "All things are delivered to Me by My Father. And no one knoweth who the Son is, but the Father; and who the Father is, but the Son, and to whom the Son will reveal Him" (Luke 10:22). The God-Man, as the Word and only-begotten Wisdom of the Father, is the source of all knowledge of God and all salvation, and whoever would attain to these must come to Him, and through Him to the Father. He is thus truly the Book of Life. We have here a magnificent revelation of the greatness and Divinity of the God-Man. For this reason He "rejoices in the Holy Ghost," Who is the Author of all enlightenment and joy, praises the Father and thanks Him, the "Lord of heaven and earth," for His wonderful decrees in the communication as well as in the withholding of predestination, because the one as well as the other is a glorification of God and the God-Man; and He declares Himself at one with the Father in these plans (Luke 10:21). For this reason also He calls the Apostles "blessed" above all the prophets and kings, because no one stands nearer to the Saviour than they, and no one can see or hear the mysteries and counsels of God in the God-Man as they do (Luke 10:24), or share in them in the same measure.

### 3. CONCLUSIONS DRAWN BY OUR SAVIOUR FROM HIS ANSWER

Since our Saviour Himself is the Way to the Father and to the realization of the decrees of His election, He now invites all to come to Him by faith and love, to submit to Him, to take upon themselves the yoke of His doctrine, commandments and rule, and to become His scholars and learn of Him (Matt. 11:29, 30), especially the lessons of meekness and humility. We must belong to the "little ones"; we must lay aside all self-sufficiency, submit to Christ in humility and docility, and become His followers. Then and then only will He reveal to us the Father, and then only do we belong to the elect.

Our Saviour now gives us beautiful motives for complying with His invitation. The first motive is our exceeding need of knowledge, love, and happiness in the possession of God. We are full of trouble, sorrow, and labor of body and soul, from causes both natural and supernatural, and we sigh under the yoke of sin, the tyranny of the passions, and temporal evils. At that period there was in addition to all this the oppressive yoke of the ancient law

(Acts 15:10). Where is refreshment and deliverance from so many evils to be found, except with our Saviour (Matt. 11:29), with Christ?

The second motive is the Person of our Saviour, Who is so gentle, so kind and condescending a Master, in striking contrast to the haughtiness and selfishness of the world and the devil; for it is from Jesus that we are to learn humility and gentleness. Further, His yoke and His burden, His doctrine and commandments are sweet and light; because the doctrine is suited to our nature, consoling and elevating, and the commandments are few, but the graces and promises many and great (Matt. 11:30). Lastly, He will satisfy and "refresh" us in every respect: our intellect by His truth, our heart by His goodness, our senses by the beauty and sublimity of His Person and the glory of His heavenly, eternal kingdom. With Him alone shall we find perfect "rest to our souls" (Matt. 10:29).

What a precious revelation with regard to the Person of our Saviour this mystery affords us! If the words: "I saw Satan like lightning falling from heaven" refer to the fall of the angels, then we have here one of the few passages in which our Saviour speaks, always in a mysterious, awe-inspring manner, of His life before the Creation, in the bosom of the Godhead; and in this case a special connection of the angels' sin and fall with the mystery of the Incarnation seems implied. But if they refer to the victory of the disciples over the evil spirits, then we have here a majestic picture of our Saviour's might, since He can say, like a general who has vanquished the enemy by his army: I have seen the enemy fall at my feet. How kindly and sympathetically our Lord rejoices at the joy of His disciples, when they return, covered with glory! He does not take away nor lessen their pleasure at the success of their apostolic work. On the contrary, He confirms, raises and increases it by disclosures and glimpses of unthought-of degrees of glory and joy, which are the portion of the Apostolate. This Apostolate itself appears here in its full splendor, in the possession of marvelous gifts of grace, by means of which it rejoices men and makes hell tremble; in the immediate proximity of the God-Man; and in the most intimate connection with the great counsels of God, which underlie all His works. We have in this mystery, too, a surprisingly beautiful revelation of the life of prayer of the Sacred Heart: we see how constantly It is occupied with God, refers everything to the Father, lives in the closest union of will with Him; how the Holy Ghost dwells in this Heart, influences Its life and produces therein, by the gentle fluttering of Its joy and rapture, wonderful outpourings of adoration, love and praise of God on every occasion. And finally, what can link us more firmly or irrevocably to our Saviour than what has been said here? All motives for adhering to Him meet together as in a focus. He is our God from eternity; He is the keystone of all creation, the axis upon which all the destinies of angels and men revolve; He is the instrument of all election, the gracious and condescending Lord of us all, the God and Redeemer of the poor and oppressed, of the needy and of sinners; He is the full and satisfying answer and response to all our needs, the sweet love and rest of all created beings. Whither then shall we go, but to Him?

## THE PARABLE OF THE GOOD SAMARITAN

LUKE 10:25. And behold a certain lawyer stood up, tempting him and saying: "Master, what must I do to possess eternal life?"—26. But he said to him: "What is written in the law? How readest thou?"—27. He answering, said: "Thou shalt love the Lord thy God with thy whole heart, and with thy whole soul, and with all thy strength, and with all thy mind, and thy neighbor as thyself."—28. And he said to him: "Thou hast answered right; this do, and thou shalt live."—29. But he, willing to justify himself, said to Jesus: "And who is my neighbor?"—30. And Jesus answering, said: "A certain man went down from Jerusalem to Jericho, and fell among robbers, who also stripped him; and having wounded him, went away, leaving him half dead.—31. And it chanced that a certain priest went down the same way; and seeing him, passed by.—32. In like manner also a Levite, when he was near the place and saw him, passed by.—33. But a certain Samaritan being on his journey, came near him; and seeing him, was moved with compassion. —34. And going up to him, bound up his wounds, pouring in oil and wine; and setting him upon his own beast, brought him to an inn, and took care of him.— 35. And the next day he took out two pence, and gave to the host, and said: Take care of him; and whatsoever thou shalt spend over and above, I at my return will repay thee.—36. Which of these three in thy opinion was neighbor to him that fell among the robbers?"—37. But he said: "He that showed mercy to him." And Jesus said to him: "Go, and do thou in like manner."

### 1. OCCASION OF THE PARABLE

The parable was given in consequence of a lawyer's question concerning the greatest commandment. Probably our Saviour was still in Peraea or in the neighborhood of Jericho, and had just before called His disciples "blessed" because their names were written in heaven. He may have said this in presence of some of the people. The lawyer took occasion from this to ask a question concerning the way to heaven. These were probably the circumstances under which we are told: "And behold, a certain lawyer stood up" (Luke 10:25).

The actual question which gave rise to the parable was a double one. At first the lawyer simply asked how he might reach heaven. As our Saviour referred him to the great commandment of love of God and of our neighbor (Luke 10:26, 27, 28), he then inquired who the neighbor was, whom he must love as himself (Luke 10:29).

This double question was, in itself, good; but not so the intention of the questioner. He only wished to tempt our Lord (Luke 10:25). The first question, regarding the way to heaven, was much mooted at the time, and the Jewish schools were divided upon it. The "temptation" may therefore have consisted in the wish either to test our Lord's wisdom, or to make Him obnoxious to the one or the other school or party by His decision. In the second question also lay a certain insincerity. The lawyer merely wished to excuse himself (Luke 10:29) and to avoid the appearance of having asked what was so simple, or of having had the intention of tempting our Saviour. As a matter of fact the second question was of a much more seductive nature, because it was the subject of much dispute, and self-love had seized upon it in order to evade the duty of charity towards one's neighbor. It was a settled point that only the fellow-countryman, the Israelite, was to be understood by the terms "brother" and "friend" (Lev. 19:17, 18). On the other hand, the Pharisees disputed whether the Israelite owed love and mercy to the Gentiles and Samaritans, and even whether he might without sin exercise these virtues in their regard. At all events the degenerate Jews (and especially the Pharisees) wished to excuse themselves and evade the law by means of this dispute. The lawyer had therefore touched on one of the practical and burning questions of the day, and the answer was bound to be critical.

## 2. THE PARABLE

Our Saviour gave His answer in the parable of the Good Samaritan. In this parable He does three things.

First, He declares very plainly who is to be understood by the "neighbor" mentioned in the law, viz. everyone, even strangers, enemies, and those of other creeds. It is neither the circumstance of belonging to the same race or tribe, nor yet distress and need of help in itself which makes anyone our neighbor, but the mere fact of sharing the same human nature. This is the first thing taught by the parable in the example of the Samaritan, who manifests the greatest and most disinterested charity to a stranger, an unfortunate man and probably a Jew, that is to say, a hated adherent of another religion. No consideration, no prejudice, no example must prevent us from seeing in every fellow-man our neighbor, and treating him as such. Our Saviour emphasizes this point by putting an extraordinarily adroit question to the lawyer, and thus forcing him to give the decision himself. "Which of these three . . . was neighbor to him that fell among the robbers" (Luke 10:36), i.e. who showed himself to be the neighbor of the unfortunate man? Or in other words, since the word "neighbor" conveys the idea of a reciprocal relation, which of the three regarded the sufferer as his neighbor? The lawyer answers: "He that showed mercy to him." So the Samaritan regarded even a stranger, one of another creed and the enemy of his nation, as his neighbor, and treated him as such. "Go, and do thou in like manner," replies our Saviour, and with this the debated question was settled, and in reality by the lawyer himself.

Secondly, by this parable our Lord censures with severity, yet with consideration, the opposite teaching and practice of the Jewish schools. This He does by making one of the despised and proscribed Samaritans give the Jews this lesson; and moreover, in contrast to the Samaritan, He makes even officials of the Jewish Church play but a sorry part with regard to the unfortunate man. The motives of their selfish conduct were partly practical, such as fear of the trouble, cost and inconvenience of rendering aid, partly theoretical and moral, springing from scruples of their school and considerations of caste, for example fear of incurring contamination. Yet the priest and the Levite were probably just returning from the Temple service, where they ought above all things to have learned charity and the spirit of sacrifice. Lastly, our Lord censures the Jews by reproaching them with not showing proper charity even to their own fellow-countrymen, the Israelites, to whom the wounded man probably belonged; and by extending the reproach even to the priests themselves (Luke 10:31, 32). We can read this reproach also in the very wording of the question: "Which of these three . . . was neighbor to him that fell among the robbers?" Even according to the Pharisaic interpretation of the law, it should have been the priest or the Levite, because the unfortunate man was their brother and friend, one of their own race. But they forgot that, and did not help him. Thus did these faithless pastors usually treat the people.

Thirdly, our Saviour gives in this parable very beautiful motives for the exercise of charity towards one's neighbor. The first motive is the touchingly beautiful example of the Samaritan, who is so compassionate, energetic, self-sacrificing and heroic in his charity (Luke 10:33, 34, 35) towards one who is a perfect stranger to himself and an enemy of his nation. No scruples of school or caste have any weight with him; he sees in the unfortunate sufferer who so sorely needs succor only his fellow-man, and that is enough for his kind heart. Another motive is found in our Saviour Himself; viz. in the intention which prompted Him to give the parable, shown by His concluding words: "Go, and do thou in like manner" (Luke 10:37), and lastly in His example, which the holy Fathers regard as delineated trait for trait in the Good Samaritan. In truth, He went along the terrible, lonely, murderous path of this earth, and found the unfortunate human race robbed, bleeding from a thousand wounds, and half dead. Neither priest nor layman could or would help. He alone, the true Priest, has compassion and power, oil and wine; He binds up the wounds of the sufferer and brings him into the refuge which He has founded, the Church, where he is tended at the cost of the compassionate Saviour, until the latter returns to recompense the care bestowed upon him. Our Saviour is the true "Good Samaritan," who will reward us also for the pains we take for those whom He commends to our care. A third motive is the example of the saints, who have played this rôle of the Samaritan towards mankind, each according to his station in life, some by spiritual, others by corporal acts of mercy.

### 3. CONCLUSIONS TO BE DRAWN FROM THE PARABLE

The first conclusion is evident in our Saviour's words: "Go, and do thou in like manner"; we must exercise charity, then, after the example of the Good Samaritan, i.e. be Samaritans ourselves towards poor humanity, towards our brethren. We must therefore provide ourselves with the balsam of love, compassion and benevolence; with the wine of strengthening, cheering words and works; with plenty of the coin of prayer and of desire to do good; and with the patience, perseverance and contentment which are represented by the beast of burden. Such is the equipment of the Good Samaritan.

Another lesson we may draw from the parable is that of love and reverence for our Saviour, Whose character is so beautifully revealed in the meeting and colloquy with the lawyer. How instructive is the calmness and readiness with which He enters into all questions, even when they are not put with an honest intention; the modesty and prudence with which He answers, asking: "What is written in the law? How readest thou?" (Luke 10:26.) What wisdom is shown in the moderation and freedom with which He turns the question aside; in the fairness and sound judgment with which He acknowledges what is right even in His adversary (Luke 10:28); lastly, in the adroitness of mind with which He compels the lawyer to give such a crushing answer to his own question. The latter had asked who his neighbor was. Our Saviour in return inquires whose neighbor *he* is, by asking him at the conclusion of the parable who had been the neighbor of the wounded man. This turn of the question was perfectly justifiable, because the term "neighbor" has a reciprocal signification; and it also offered many advantages. In the first place, it facilitated the matter for the lawyer and almost compelled him to give the right answer. It was a much surer way of attaining this object, to ask him by whom he wished to be regarded and treated as a neighbor, than to ask whom he himself must treat thus. Our Saviour here appeals against the letter of the law to natural feeling. Secondly, He gives in this manner a very practical turn to the question, by intimating that only that man has charity who puts it into practice (Schanz). In this respect His conversation with the lawyer gives us a splendid model of a good discussion. —The parable altogether (if not a true narration) is a masterpiece of the inventive faculty of His wonderful intellect. Everything in it is so natural, adapted to the country and people: the road from Jerusalem to Jericho, a fearsome road through desolate valleys and ravines, notorious for robberies and murders, and actually often traversed by priests and Levites returning to Jericho after their service in the Temple; the inn, such as is still to be found on this road; the traveling-equipment of the Samaritan; in short, everything is so true to the life that the parable could not fail of its effect, especially if it was related by our Saviour in the vicinity of this district, as was very probably the case. In this grave reproach to the lawyers and leaders of Israel for their non-fulfilment of the law of charity, when He so markedly contrasts them with the Good Samaritan, we see our Lord severe indeed, even overpoweringly so, yet His words are not injurious. The teaching Church of Israel must pronounce its own sentence by the mouth of this lawyer.

## MARTHA AND MARY

LUKE 10:38. Now it came to pass as they went, that he entered into a certain town; and a certain woman named Martha received him into her house.—39. And she had a sister called Mary, who sitting also at the Lord's feet, heard his word.—40. But Martha was busy about much serving. Who stood and said: "Lord, hast thou no care that my sister hath left me alone to serve? speak to her, therefore, that she help me."—41. And the Lord answering, said to her: "Martha, Martha, thou art careful, and art troubled about many things.—42. But one thing is necessary. Mary hath chosen the best part, which shall not be taken away from her."

Proceeding on His journey to Jerusalem, our Saviour came to a town (probably Bethania), where He was hospitably received by a woman named Martha. Martha had a sister who was called Mary (Luke 10:38, 39). That our Saviour does not seek a lodging in Jerusalem, but in Bethania, still further proves how dangerous a stay of any length in the city was for Him. The two women were probably the sisters of Lazarus (John 11:1), and both hastened to do honor to our Lord, each in her own way. From the remotest times these two sisters have been regarded as types of the active and the contemplative life. Our Saviour stands between them as the type of the most perfect vocation, which combines both these kinds of life.

### 1. MARTHA, THE TYPE OF THE ACTIVE LIFE

Martha appears in a twofold manner as the type of the active life, since we find in her all its lofty and beautiful attributes, and also the imperfections which may be met with therein.

What is beautiful here (and indeed always in the active life, when this is exercised out of love for Christ) is the hospitality with which Martha so kindly received our Lord into her house and, as it seems, exerted herself to the utmost in order to entertain Him with the magnificence which became His rank; for we are told that she was "busy about much serving," "careful and troubled about many things" (Luke 10:40, 41). She seems to have been the elder of the two sisters, and also the housekeeper, and thus the entertainment chiefly devolved upon her. It is certainly very right to receive Christ and do Him all honor, when

He comes in the flesh, travels, works, hungers and thirsts. Further, it is very meritorious, for one must practise many virtues in the exercise of the active life, must overcome shyness and idleness, and exercise patience, zeal, and magnanimity; and therefore the reward also is great. What we do to the very least of our fellow-men, we do to Christ; and the kingdom of heaven is promised in recompense even for a glass of water. Lastly, this care, reverence and love for our Saviour is most touching and beautiful. We may be sure that, every time our Saviour stayed in Bethania, nothing was spared to show Him all the honor due to a guest. It is Martha's beautiful vocation to be the cordial, assiduous hostess of our Saviour.

But Martha also manifests a few imperfections which may occur in the active life. Our Saviour evidently gives her a reprimand, when she asks Him to bid Mary help her in serving. There must therefore have been something a bit faulty, not exactly about the action itself, but in the circumstances and the manner in which Martha wished to entertain our Lord. In the first place, her activity may have been prompted to a certain extent by an incorrect idea, namely the opinion that this outward service was the most important thing, before which all else must give way. For this reason she wishes Mary to help also. This is evidently not right, but yet it very often happens. Everyone is tempted to consider that for which he has talent and inclination to be the most important matter in life. Further, Martha's solicitude seems to have been exaggerated and unnecessary, as our Saviour says to her: "Thou art careful, and art troubled about many things" (Luke 10:41). She wishes to give not merely a worthy entertainment, but a splendid one; she wishes to do everything within her power; she thinks she cannot do enough. This is not necessary, and under certain circumstances not good even. Lastly, our Saviour reproves her especially for her uneasiness. "Thou art troubled about many things" (Luke 10:41). Uneasiness is never good, but often proceeds, when one is much occupied, from ill-humor or impatience, envy, and a little vanity. This caused her to come and stand before our Lord (perhaps after having repressed her impatience several times), and ask Him to bid Mary leave Him (Luke 10:40). She addresses herself to Him, because it would not have been polite to call her sister away from His side, and perhaps also because she thought that an admonition on His part would have more effect upon her. We see in all this the devotion and attachment of the disciple, but also the imperfection which lurked in her actions.

Our Lord's reproof is in accordance with this; it is familiar, impressive, and prudent. Familiarity is shown in His addressing her by her name, and repeating it. The reproof is impressive, because it exactly specifies the imperfection of her action, and takes Mary's part. It is prudent, because it does not condemn the thing itself, the exterior service, which is intrinsically good and justifiable and a way to God, and which also presupposes and produces good, practical common-sense. Perhaps it was just this practical turn which preserved Martha from the errors of Mary (assuming that this is Mary Magdalen); our Saviour only condemns the imperfections which cleaved to it—the self-exaltation, superficiality, uneasiness, impatience, bustle and officiousness. When we perceive anything like this in ourselves, let us think that our Saviour sees us, and calls to us: "Martha, thou art careful, and art troubled about many things."

### 2. MARY, THE TYPE OF THE CONTEMPLATIVE LIFE

It seems to have been Mary's natural disposition to think and ponder rather than to act. We see here how this natural disposition, which had perhaps been the occasion of her errors, now becomes an instrument of good and of her type of holiness. It makes her the pupil of Jesus *par excellence*. Whilst Martha attends to the outward service, to the material needs of the moment, Mary sits at His feet and listens to His words (Luke 10:39), and thus becomes the type of the interior, contemplative life. In this type there are two things to be noticed.

In the first place, there is a supposition or condition to make, under which alone Mary can be a type of the contemplative life worthy of imitation, and under which alone this contemplative life is of any value. This supposition is that Mary thought her help was not necessary for the entertainment of our Lord, that everything was sufficiently provided for by Martha, and that it was therefore not His wish that she should concern herself with it; that, on the contrary, she would honor Him more and be acting more in accordance with His wishes by sitting at His feet and listening to Him. If this were not so, Mary's conduct would not have been right. In like manner the service of contemplation is only then of value, when it is in accordance with our Lord's will, and when the other duties of our state are sufficiently attended to. Martha also is a disciple of our Lord, and He has need of her service too. As a matter of fact, Mary knew how to pass from the interior life to outward activity, when it was seemly and needful (John 12:3), and our Lord then acknowledges this also with complacency (John 12:7).

Secondly, our Saviour Himself reveals to us in Mary the value and excellence of the contemplative life, by the answer which He gives to Martha. He mentions three reasons for the superiority of the interior life over the exterior. First, its necessity: "One thing is necessary" (Luke 10:42). This "one thing" is God, the absolutely necessary Good of the soul; love of God, attachment to Him, intercourse with Him, by which we prepare ourselves to possess Him in heaven. All else, outward things, "many things," are necessary only under certain circumstances. Indeed, even for these other things, for the exterior service from which no one can be altogether exempt, the interior life is necessary to a certain degree. It is necessary, first, in order to make them meritorious for heaven, for merit can only come from interior motives; secondly, in order to ensure exterior success, whether as regards ourselves or others; lastly, for the proper performance of outward duties, and for perseverance under all circumstances, because this requires great self-sacrifice, which is only obtained as the fruit and effect of prayer and of the interior life. The second reason is the sublimity of the interior life. This is contained in the words: "Mary hath chosen the best (simply good) part" (Luke 10:42). What Mary has chosen is intercourse with God; that is, in reality, God Himself (Ps. 72:26; 141:6; Jer. 10:16; Lament. 3:24). But the supernatural value of this portion is intrinsic, whereas all else only acquires this value by being referred to God. Both Martha and Mary are friends of our Lord; but, whereas Martha expresses her devotion by active service, Mary is drawn to the service of contemplation. The third reason is the duration of the contemplative life. This portion "shall not be taken away from her" (Luke 10:42), not merely in the sense that the interior life and its practice are and will remain the permanent portion of Mary here below, from which no one is to dissuade her, whilst Martha has the gift of exterior service; but also in the higher signification that Mary's occupation does not end even with death, but is to be continued in eternity, because eternal life will be simply the vision, the joyful and loving embrace and possession of the Infinite Good, whilst outward service ends with death. Even upon earth the contemplative life has more stability, because it can be longer and more easily continued, and because it attracts, entices and satisfies the soul by its consolation and sweetness. This is our Saviour's answer to Martha's complaint. It ends with a solemn eulogy upon the contemplative life, which places upon it the seal of holiness.

### 3. OUR SAVIOUR, THE MODEL OF THE MIXED LIFE

The mixed life consists in the combination of the contemplative life with the active, so that outward activity arises and proceeds from the superabundance of contemplation and love. The contemplative life thus becomes the source and impulse of the active. Such outward activity is certainly better than contemplation alone, because it is more perfect to burn and at the same time to give light, than merely to burn; better to sanctify oneself and others, than oneself alone.

This, then, is the life which our Saviour leads, and teaches by His example to be the most perfect. Whilst Martha chose the active life as her portion, and Mary the contemplative, He combines both in Himself. He passes from the one to the other; without abandoning contemplation and communion with God, He performs active works, traveling, teaching, and healing, and draws from contemplation and love of God the impulse and strength to spend His energies upon the salvation of souls, as we see here. He does not lodge at Bethania merely for the sake of the visit, but because His way to Jerusalem led Him thither (Luke 10:38). While there He cannot remain inactive, but begins at once to teach. Whilst highly praising contemplation in Mary, He Himself exercises outward activity in an apostolic spirit. This apostolic spirit is also beautifully shown in the freedom with which He speaks to Martha. He blames His hostess, and does not fear to risk offending her. This presupposes a great detachment, liberty of spirit, and authority. Such, then, is the example which our Saviour gives us. It is difficult to combine the two lives, but their union is very sublime. It is the real evangelical perfection, the life of our holy Church and of all great apostolic men; it is the life of God Himself.

This mystery places vividly before us the truth that everything in the Gospel is life; all in it awakens and bestows life. The words, deeds and experiences of our Saviour, taking place in obscurity and as though incidentally, are in reality words of life; they conceal within themselves the germs of great things to come, and develop in the course of time into wonderful forms of activity. Thus the actors in this mystery and the words exchanged between them are true types and representatives of great vocations and states of life in the kingdom of Christ. The foundation is laid here for the active and the contemplative orders of the Church, and even for the more particular differences of these orders, according to their exterior, interior, and mixed activity; their life is characterized according to its nature, its laws, value, dangers, and good results. It seems as though St. Thomas must have had this scene before his mind, when he gave his judgment regarding the excellence of the various orders, and wrote that the contemplative life is better than the purely active (*Summa* 2, 2, q. 187, a. 1), but the mixed life still better than the purely contemplative (*Summa* 2, 2, q. 188, a. 6).

### E. The Public Life from the Feast of Tabernacles to the Feast of the Dedication of the Temple

With the Feast of Tabernacles begins the real life-and-death conflict of Judaism against our Saviour. In opposition to the great revelations of His Divinity made on this feast by miracles and teaching, the hatred of the Jews already goes so far as to make an actual attempt upon His life. From this date the work of Jesus continues until the Feast of the Dedication. On the one hand the animosity of the Pharisees increases more and more, and they give vent to it in the most disgraceful attacks and horrible blasphemies; and on the other hand our Saviour no longer spares them, but reveals their wickedness, regardless of all consideration, and speaks openly of the design of the Jews to murder Him and of His Death. But He strengthens His disciples by initiating them into the secret of prayer, and by recommending apostolic virtues to them, especially such as are calculated to strengthen and arm for battle, e.g. poverty, watchfulness, and courage in openly siding with the cause of His kingdom. The scene of the mysteries seems to have been Judaea throughout.

### The Feast of Tabernacles. First Part.
### Teaching of Our Lord

John 7:11. The Jews therefore sought him on the festival day, and said: "Where is he?"—12. And there was much murmuring among the multitude concerning him. For some said: "He is a good man." And others said: "No, but he seduceth the people."—13. Yet no man spoke openly of him for fear of the Jews.

—14. Now about the midst of the feast Jesus went up into the temple, and taught. —15. And the Jews wondered, saying: "How doth this man know letters, having never learned?"—16. Jesus answered them and said: "My doctrine is not mine, but his that sent me.—17. If any man will do the will of him, he shall know of the doctrine, whether it be of God, or whether I speak of myself.—18. He that speaketh of himself, seeketh his own glory; but he that seeketh the glory of him that sent him, he is true, and there is no injustice in him.—19. Did not Moses give you the law; and yet none of you keepeth the law.—20. Why seek you to kill me?" The multitude answered and said: "Thou hast a devil; who seeketh to kill thee?"—21. Jesus answered and said to them: "One work I have done, and you all wonder.—22. Therefore Moses gave you circumcision (not because it is of Moses, but of the fathers); and on the Sabbath-day you circumcise a man.—23. If a man receive circumcision on the Sabbath-day, that the law of Moses may not be broken; are you angry at me because I have healed the whole man on the Sabbath-day?—24. Judge not according to the appearance, but judge just judgment."—25. Some therefore of Jerusalem said: "Is not this he whom they seek to kill?—26. And behold he speaketh openly, and they say nothing to him. Have the rulers known for a truth that this is the Christ?—27. But we know this man whence he is: but when the Christ cometh, no man knoweth whence he is."—28. Jesus therefore cried out in the temple, teaching and saying: "You both know me, and you know whence I am; and I am not come of myself; but he that sent me is true, whom you know not.—29. I know him; because I am from him, and he hath sent me."—30. They sought therefore to apprehend him; and no man laid hands on him, because his hour was not yet come.—31. But of the people many believed in him, and said: "When the Christ cometh, shall he do more miracles than these which this man doth?"—32. The Pharisees heard the people murmuring these things concerning him; and the rulers and Pharisees sent ministers to apprehend him.—33. Jesus therefore said to them: "Yet a little while I am with you: and then I go to him that sent me.—34. You shall seek me, and shall not find me; and where I am, hither you cannot come."—35. The Jews therefore said among themselves: "Whither will he go, that we shall not find him? will he go unto the dispersed among the Gentiles, and teach the Gentiles?—36. What is this saying that he hath said: You shall seek me, and shall not find me; and where I am, you cannot come?"

## 1. POSITION OF AFFAIRS AT OUR SAVIOUR'S ARRIVAL IN JERUSALEM

The Feast of Tabernacles, one of the principal feasts in the Old Covenant, was just being held. It was celebrated shortly after the Day of Atonement, about the end of September or beginning of October, in thanksgiving for the harvest and in memory of the wonderful guidance of the people through the wilderness. The festivity lasted eight days, and was distinguished by great sacrifices, by the drawing and pouring out of water from the pool of Siloe, and by the erection of tabernacles, i.e. huts made with green boughs, under which the people dwelt during the feast. It was marked further by the carrying of branches of palm, myrtle and lemon, and by the illumination of the court of the Temple with torches, accompanied by dancing and music; in short, it was throughout a time of rejoicing and thanksgiving. This illumination and the drawing of water (in remembrance of the Messianic types, the pillar of cloud and the water from the rock in the wilderness) made the Feast of Tabernacles a true Messianic feast (Ex. 23:17; 34:23; Deut. 16:16; II Mach. 10:6, 7; II Esdr. 8:14–17).

Before our Saviour reached Jerusalem He had already become the subject of discussion there. The upper, leading classes of the Jews inquired for Him, in order to put Him out of the way. Among the lower classes too He was much spoken of. Some said that He was a good man; others called Him a seducer of the people (John 7:12). But all this was said secretly, because the fear of the watchful Jews predominated over all (John 7:13).

While public feeling was in this state, our Saviour appeared, not in the earlier part of the feast, but on the fourth day (John 7:14). His reason for this, as also for putting off His departure and then traveling so quietly, was probably the wish to avoid bringing on (or as it were challenging) the combat by appearing too conspicuously.

## 2. OUR LORD'S TEACHING

This instruction is not one long, connected sermon, but is probably composed of the most striking sayings of longer addresses which do not seem to have been preserved, or of answers to the remarks and objections of the hearers. Our Saviour speaks upon three points.

In the first place He defends Himself against two attacks on the part of the Jews. The first attack arose from their astonishment and vexation at the depth and beauty of our Lord's teaching of the Scriptures, since He had never gone through any course of instruction (John 7:14, 15). He answers that this doctrine is of divine origin; not His own, but that of the Father. He proves this divine origin of His doctrine first by appealing to the inward consciousness of anyone who sincerely seeks and does the Will of God; such a one will recognize from the accordance of the doctrine with his own disposition of soul that it comes from God (John 7:16, 17; cf. Matt. 6:23). A bad life hinders this perception, as was the case with the Jews. Secondly, our Lord proves the divine origin of His doctrine from the pure intention of the Teacher, saying that He sought therein not His own glory, but the glory of God; that whoever seeks his own honor speaks of himself, not from God (John 7:18). The human precepts or "commandments of men" (Matt. 15:9) of the Jews had this impure origin.

The second attack against which our Saviour defends Himself was based upon the violation of the law in healing the palsied man on the Sabbath (John 5:5–16), with which the Jews reproached Him in thought or word, and by which they justified their murderous designs against Him. He responded that they were not in a position to make such an accusation, since they themselves did not observe the law at all faithfully (John 7:19; Matt. 23:3 etc.); and as regarded the point in which they accused Him, they themselves were accustomed to circumcise children on the Sabbath, without considering this to be a violation of the law of Moses. On the contrary, they did it precisely in order to fulfil the law, because circumcision is of higher origin; not a part of the Mosaic law, but a tradition of the fathers or patriarchs (John 7:22; Gen. 17:10; 21:4; Lev. 12:3). Much less then ought they to be indignant at His having healed a man on the Sabbath, since He had thus given to this man health of the entire body and soul (John 7:20–23); they should not judge according to appearances, but they should base their judgment on truth and justice (John 7:24). Our Saviour had on this occasion spoken quite openly of the design of the Jews to murder Him, in order to deter those of them who stood amongst the people. The people in general knew nothing as yet of this murderous purpose, and insolently answered that He must be out of His senses to imagine such a thing (John 7:20). But our Saviour maintains His assertion, and also mentions the reason by which the Jews intend to justify the murder, viz. the healing of the paralytic on the Sabbath-day (John 7:21), in consequence of which they had formed the plan of killing Him.

In the second place our Saviour speaks of His origin and Divine Nature. He found an opportunity for this in the surprise of some Jews from Jerusalem at His being allowed to speak unpunished of His Messianic mission, thus openly and freely, in spite of the project against Him. They even wondered if the rulers themselves perhaps thought Him to be the Messias, although they reflected that this He could not possibly be, because His extraction was known, whereas no one would know that of the Messias. So the lawyers alleged (John 7:25–27), probably in false interpretation of many passages of the prophets (Mich. 5:2; Mal.

3:2). Our Saviour now officially testifies His divine origin with authoritative teaching (for we are told He "cried out in the Temple, teaching and saying"). He spoke in mysterious but yet plain terms both of His generation by the Father and of His mission from Him; and He rightly combined the two, for the divine missions are no other than the eternal procession of the Son from the Father and of the Holy Ghost from them both, revealed in a supernatural exterior effect. He says: "You both know Me" (i.e. with regard to My natural extraction), nevertheless "I am not come of Myself, but He that sent (and generated) Me is true, whom you know not (as My Author). I know Him, because I am from Him, and He hath sent Me" (John 7:28, 29). Thus our Saviour confirmed at once His divine mission and divine origin, and proved Himself to be the Messias, because the prophetic passages concerning this mysterious origin exactly applied to Him. This testimony was understood by the Pharisees well enough, for they now wished to use violence and arrest Him on the authority of a warrant from the Sanhedrim.

In the third place our Saviour predicts to the Pharisees and chief priests that He would "go to Him that sent Him," i.e. He foretells in obscure terms His own Death and subsequent Ascension. This prediction of our Lord's was occasioned by the fact that armed men were sent out to apprehend Him, because the Pharisees heard that many of the people believed in Him on account of His teaching and miracles. "When the Christ cometh," they said, "shall He do more miracles than these which this man doth?" Upon these words the Pharisees obtained an order from the Sanhedrim for the despatch of some Temple soldiers (John 7:31, 32). With regard to His Death our Lord makes two statements. First, that it will be free and voluntary. Although armed men already stand there to apprehend Him, He nevertheless declares that He will still remain with the Jews for some time, that they had therefore no power over Him. Secondly, He foretells that this departure (or "going to Him who sent Him") will be of the most fatal consequences for themselves. They will seek Him, His Person and His help, in their distress at the destruction of the city and at their own death, and they will not find Him; they will perish in time and in eternity, if they do not believe in Him (John 7:33, 34). Our Saviour's statement concerning His Death was received by the Jews with mockery and unbelieving scorn. "Whither will He go, that we shall not find Him? Will He go unto the dispersed (Jews) among the Gentiles, and teach the Gentiles?" (John 7:35, 36.) This is the very climax of unbelief, and without knowing it, they uttered in their own mocking words the prophecy of their judgment and punishment. Faith and the Church pass over to the Gentiles (Isa. 49:6), and they themselves go also, but as slaves, blind and infatuated; they are henceforth "the dispersed," without pastors or altar. And in fact no one dared to lay hands upon our Lord, because the hour of His Passion, in which He voluntarily yielded Himself up to His enemies, had not yet come (John 7:30).

### 3. SIGNIFICANCE AND EFFECT OF THESE WORDS

These, then, were some of the occurrences which took place during the Feast of Tabernacles, either on one day of it or on several. How many glorious revelations are contained in these discourses regarding our Lord's authorization for His teaching office, regarding His Divine Nature and origin and the voluntariness of His Death for our redemption! How magnificently the acuteness, depth and versatility of His intellect are here again displayed! He refutes with irresistible force the reproach of violating the Sabbath. How mysteriously and profoundly He speaks of His Divine Nature, on the one hand veiling from this unholy and contentious people the complete revelation of His Divinity, and on the other hand plumbing the very depths of the mystery by the justness and precision of His words! With open hands He offers to the Jews salvation and the revelation of divine truths, and at what a cost! How trying must these scenes have been for Him, how fraught with menace! We see with what reason our Saviour had removed His ministry from Judaea to Galilee, and why He, naturally speaking, required all His courage to turn His face towards Jerusalem and make another attempt there. Every revelation is met only by unbelief, irritation, mockery and hatred, and leads to a further step in their plot to put Him to death. Only a few of the people believe. Our Saviour is already beset by the myrmidons of the law, and the prophecy of His Death and the coming judgment upon the unhappy nation breaks in with startling effect upon the rejoicings of the feast.

## SECOND PART OF THE FEAST OF TABERNACLES.
## OUR SAVIOUR THE LIVING SPRING

JOHN 7:37. And on the last and great day of the festivity Jesus stood and cried, saying: "If any man thirst, let him come to me and drink.—38. He that believeth in me, as the Scripture saith, Out of his belly shall flow rivers of living water."—39. Now this he said of the Spirit which they should receive who believed in him; for as yet the Spirit was not given, because Jesus was not yet glorified.—40. Of that multitude therefore, when they had heard these words of his, some said: "This is the prophet indeed."—41. Others said: "This is the Christ." But some said: "Doth the Christ come out of Galilee?—42. Doth not the Scriptures say: That Christ cometh of the seed of David, and from Bethlehem the town where David was?"—43. So there arose a dissension among the people because of him.—44. And some of them would have apprehended him; but no man laid hands upon him.—45. The ministers therefore came to the chief priests and the Pharisees. And they said to them: "Why have you not brought him?"—46. The ministers answered: "Never did man speak like this man."—47. The Pharisees therefore answered them: "Are you also seduced?—48. Hath any one of the rulers believed in him, or of the Pharisees?—49. But this multitude, that knoweth not the law, are accursed."—50. Nicodemus said to them, he that came to him by night, who was one of them:—51. "Doth our law judge any man, unless it first hear him, and know what he doth?"—52. They answered and said to him: "Art thou also a Galilean? Search the Scriptures, and see that out of Galilee a prophet riseth not."—53. And every man returned to his own house.

### 1. OUR SAVIOUR TESTIFIES THAT HE IS THE MESSIAS

The circumstances of this testimony which Jesus bore of Himself were as follows.

It was the last, that is the eighth and most solemn day of the feast (John 7:37), marked like all the other days by the solemn drawing of water from the pool of Siloe and the festive procession in which the water was carried in a golden urn into the Temple, and there mixed with wine and poured out upon the altar. During this ceremony the Great Hallel (Psalms 112–136) was sung, first in thanksgiving for the harvest, secondly in remembrance of the miraculous water in the desert, and thirdly as both an expression and also a renewal of the faith in the Messias, Who was to be the true renewal and refreshment of the world. For this reason also the words: "You shall draw waters with joy out of the Saviour's fountains" (Isa. 12:3) were sung in the procession.

Our Saviour, it would seem, took occasion from this ceremony; as He stood there teaching and the procession passed by, He cried out loud enough to be heard above all the rejoicing: "If any man thirst, let him come to Me, and drink. He that believeth in Me, as the Scripture saith, Out of his belly shall flow rivers of living water" (John 7:37, 38). With these words our Saviour revealed Himself as the One with Whom all the abundant grace of the Messianic period was to be found, the object of the Messianic expectation, the very Messias Himself. He explains the words "come . . . and drink" by the word "believeth." The whole ceremony reminded the people of the exodus from Egypt, which was a type of Christ's kingdom and of Christ Himself. He is the true Manna, and also the Rock from which the water of life flows (I Cor. 10:4; Ex. 17:6; cf. John 4:10); indeed He is the Fountain itself (Isa. 12:3; 49:10; 65:13). The spring of Siloe, which rises in the Temple hill, also signified the Messias (John 9:7; Isa. 8:6). Lastly, our Saviour indicates as an effect of faith in Him the reception and communication of living water. According to many passages of Holy Scripture (Isa. 44:3; 55:1; Ez. 47:1–11; 36:25; 39:29; Joel 2:28; Zach. 14:8) which our Saviour does not quote but only gives the sense of, this water signifies the pouring out of the Holy Spirit, His graces and miraculous gifts; and again, this communication of the Holy Ghost and the manner in which it was made is an effect of our Saviour's Life, Death, and glorification (John 7:39; 16:7). He already sees in spirit this glorification and the stream of grace of the holy Feast of Pentecost breaking forth from it, as a torrent from a mountain, overpowering all hindrances and reviving the whole world. The Holy Spirit, it is true, was in the world and in souls, even before the Death and glorification of our Saviour, but less abundantly and according to less definite laws; now He is present constantly, in a new manner and in all the faithful. Therefore our Saviour invites all to come to Him and drink. Hitherto they drew the water from the pool of Siloe only to pour it out again, and did not drink of it, because all this was only a type, but now they are confronted with the reality and fulfilment.

#### 2. EFFECT OF THIS TESTIMONY OF HIMSELF

The effects produced upon the people and upon the Great Council were very various.

Some among the people believed in our Saviour through these words (John 7:40). Some of them considered Him to be a prophet and forerunner of the Messias, like Elias or Jeremias (John 7:40); others even held Him for the Messias Himself (John 7:41). Others again doubted, thinking that the Messias could not come from Galilee, since the Scripture said that He would belong to the family of David and come from "the town of Bethlehem, where David was" (John 7:41, 42; Isa. 11:1; II Kings 7:12; Mich 5:2; I Kings 16:4; 17:12). Both these prophecies were fulfilled in our Saviour. But they did not inquire, or would not acknowledge the truth, and so our Lord remained silent and gave them no further information with regard to this. Others, probably of this faction or partisans of the Pharisees, wished to apprehend Him (John 7:44). In short, opinions varied greatly with regard to our Saviour; but no one actually laid hands upon Him (John 7:43, 44).

The Great Council was meanwhile awaiting in intense expectation the result of the warrant for His arrest. On account of the general excitement and the crowd of pilgrims assembled for the feast, the moment was most critical and might even become dangerous. When the soldiers returned without our Lord and were asked why they had not arrested Him, they answered that the majesty, power, and force of His words had cast a spell upon them, never had any man spoken thus (John 7:45, 46). Possibly they were converted. The Pharisees, furious at their reply, asked if they too were seduced, and employed two very popular arguments against them: first, that none of the rulers or Pharisees believed in Him (John 7:47, 48); secondly, that only the common people adhered to Him, and they understood nothing of the law, and were therefore accursed (John 7:49). Thus speaks pride of intellect.

Nevertheless they were not unanimous amongst themselves. Nicodemus, the Pharisee and member of the Great Council, with whom we are already acquainted through his conversation with our Saviour (John 3:1, 2), took up the defence of our Lord, though not openly and directly, probably because he feared to do this, and because it would not have been of any use. He confutes his colleagues by calling their attention to the fact that they too were ignorant of the law, or else most guiltily violated it, when they neglected to observe the fundamental principle of jurisprudence, that no one should be condemned unheard (Deut. 17:6; 19:15; Num. 35:30). If he did not openly declare himself to be an adherent of Jesus, still he showed courage. And under these circumstances his method of procedure was a prudent one and the best that could be adopted. His representation was answered only by the evasive, insulting question if he too was a

Galilean; let him search the Scriptures, and see if a prophet ever came from Galilee (John 7:52). In this reply lay three falsities: Jesus was not from Galilee, but in reality from Judaea; further, the Scriptures nowhere say that Galilee would produce no prophet; and Jonas at least was a Galilean (IV Kings 14:25). Moreover the answer reveals the unbounded presumption of the Jewish synagogue and also its contempt of the populace and of Galilee, where our Saviour had the most adherents. They tried by the name of "Galilean" to make Him contemptible to the Jews and destroy His influence. This much at least seems to have been attained by Nicodemus, that for the present no further proceedings were taken against Jesus by the Great Council, and that all dispersed in dissension and indecision (John 7:53).

### 3. POSITION OF AFFAIRS

Thus passed the Feast of Tabernacles. It was a Messianic feast, a feast of faith and longing for the Redeemer, and now it has become the commencement of mortal hatred and cruel persecution of Him. The stirring events during these festive days at Jerusalem make the whole position clear. The Pharisees and Sadducees, the scribes and priests, all the authoritative circles have formed a conspiracy against our Saviour; they are obdurate in unbelief and full of implacable hatred against Him, especially now that He dares to make Jerusalem the scene of His activity. The threads of their policy are laid bare. These are: false insinuations, injuries, abuse, spying, intimidation, and violence. Beside and around these leaders move the throngs of people, at one time believing, at another malicious; now doing homage to our Lord, now bowing down before those in power; altogether powerless, irresolute, inactive, and carried away by the ruling party. How brightly the figure of our Saviour stands out against these shadows, in all its purity, majesty, undauntedness, and wonderful divine power! Not without reason does St. John so often remark that "no man laid hands on Him, because His hour was not yet come" (John 7:44; 8:20; 10:39; 18:4). The soldiers stand round Him, spellbound and overawed, like craven hounds before a mighty lion, and become His panegyrists before the Great Council. His own persecutors are witnesses of His glory. How magnificent and how glorious is His testimony and revelation of Himself as the Messias, in the Temple itself, in the midst of the surging, rejoicing throng of people and chanting priests, at the beautiful ceremony of the libation of water! This revelation opens out boundless views in two directions: backwards into the age of types, and forwards into the time of their fulfilment. Our Saviour is the Living Rock and Fountain from which the miraculous water flowed for the Fathers; from Him the stream of grace and of the Holy Ghost will flow for the future ages of the Church. Thus He is the center, the source of faith and salvation for all ages. For the first time, though obscurely, our Saviour speaks publicly of the Holy Ghost.

### THE WOMAN TAKEN IN ADULTERY

JOHN 8:1. And Jesus went unto Mount Olivet.—2. And early in the morning he came again into the temple, and all the people came to him, and sitting down he taught them.—3. And the scribes and Pharisees bring unto him a woman taken in adultery; and they set her in the midst,—4. And said to him: "Master, this woman was even now taken in adultery.—5. Now Moses in the law commanded us to stone such a one. But what sayest thou?"—6. And this they said tempting him, that they might accuse him. But Jesus, bowing himself down, wrote with his finger on the ground.—7. When therefore they continued asking him, he lifted up himself and said to them: "He that is without sin among you, let him first cast a stone at her."—8. And again stooping down, he wrote on the ground.—9. But they hearing this went out one by one, beginning at the eldest; and Jesus alone remained, and the woman standing in the midst.—10. Then Jesus lifting up himself, said to her: "Woman, where are they that accused thee? Hath no man condemned thee?"—11. Who said: "No man, Lord." And Jesus said: "Neither will I condemn thee. Go, and now sin no more."

Our Saviour passed the night after the close of the Feast of Tabernacles upon the Mount of Olives (John 8:1), probably in the country-house of Gethsemani, which had most likely been placed at His disposal by some friend, and whither He often retired for prayer and repose (Luke 21:37). Early on the following morning He was again in the Temple, teaching before a large assembly (John 8:2), probably consisting of pilgrims who had come for the feast and were now preparing to start on their homeward journey. He was interrupted in His address by the scene with the adulteress.

#### 1. THE ACCUSATION

The accused was a poor woman, probably betrothed or just married, who had been taken in the act of breaking conjugal fidelity (John 8:3) and was now to be brought before the ecclesiastical court. The accusers were scribes and Pharisees (John 8:3), probably members of this court of justice, partly accusers and partly judges, otherwise they could scarcely have left the woman in the hands of Jesus (John 8:9).

This method of procedure is evidently calculated to attract attention and make a sensation. They bring the poor creature there publicly, into the Temple, to the very place where Jesus was teaching before a crowd of people, and set her before Him in the midst of them all. The people are to witness the decision.

The conduct of the accusers was certainly not prompted by zeal for the law and for morality, however great a show they might make of this; but by insincerity and hostility to our Saviour, "that they might accuse Him" (John 8:6). Before judging this disagreeable case, or in order to avoid having to pronounce upon it, they brought the sinner before our Lord, that He might decide whether she should be stoned or not (John 8:4, 5). The plan was so maliciously designed that He could not, naturally speaking, avoid a decision which would in any case be of fatal consequences for Himself. The accusation was publicly brought against the criminal in her own presence and in that of the people; the crime was certain, more witnesses could not be required; if our Lord decided in favor of her pardon, they would accuse Him of despising the law of Moses, contrary to His assertion that He was not against the law (John 7:19, 23). This appears to have been what they most desired; for this reason they laid stress upon the Mosaic law (Lev. 20:10; Deut. 22:22), reckoning, however, upon His well-known clemency towards sinners. But if He decided that she should be stoned, they could at any rate get Him into trouble with the executive power, for the Romans would scarcely pass sentence of death for adultery, and did not readily meddle in religious affairs at all. At least, no matter what His verdict, they could agitate and intrigue on the strength of it, and lead Him into a contradiction of Himself in one way or another. Their proceeding, therefore, was prompted by insincerity and hypocrisy. Though displaying indignation against the adulterous act, yet they themselves were destroyers of the marriage-bond (Matt. 19:3), and caused Israel to fall away from God (which is often described in the Scriptures as adultery), by drawing away the people from the Messias and trying to work His destruction. This and nothing else was their intention in bringing forward this accusation against the woman.

## 2. HOW THE PHARISEES WERE PUT TO CONFUSION

The attitude of our Saviour was at first simply repellent; He maintained silence, stooped down (probably sitting) and wrote upon the ground with His finger (John 8:6). He does not expressly repulse them, nor does He take the part of the sinner, out of respect for the law and in order to bring the guilty woman to a consciousness of her wrong-doing. But neither does He enter upon the accusation brought against her; first because it was a most painful case, for which a competent court of justice already existed, and which did not really concern Him, at least not outwardly; and secondly because He knew what the intention of the accusers was, and wished to let them feel this. Paying no heed to the matter, therefore, He wrote on the ground with His finger, which was with the Greeks and the Jews a sign that a person did not wish to discuss a topic proposed, and that it was distasteful (in this case because of His purity, kindness of heart and justice). Some say that He wrote upon the ground merely unmeaning signs and characters; others, that it was the answer which He was about to give the Pharisees, or the text from Jeremias: "They that depart from thee shall be written in the earth" (Jer. 17:13), which was certainly very applicable to the behavior of the accusers and to our Saviour's own thoughts. At all events it might have sufficed to show that He did not wish to meddle in the matter.

But the Jews pressed for an answer, and so our Lord raised Himself from His stooping posture and said: "He that is without sin among you, let him first cast a stone at her." Then He bent down again and continued writing (John 8:7, 8). This was a prudent answer. He does not say that the woman should not be stoned, and does not therefore decide against the law; but in the case in question He deprives the accusers of all right to stone her, since it is unseemly to accuse another when one is guilty of worse crimes oneself. To this end He cites the passage of the law according to which the witness must cast the first stone (Deut. 17:7). As the lawyers resigned the right to judge the criminal and left the decision to our Lord, the whole affair devolved upon His view of the law and the sentence He chose to give. He therefore transferred the matter from the jurisdiction of human laws to that of the divine justice, and judged according to this higher law (Rom. 2:1). The answer was thus not only wise, but also just, lofty, and at the same time forbearing towards the accusers, since He did not name their sins, but stooped down again and left them time to retire one after another, without increasing their confusion by His glance. And they actually did retire; not all together, in order not to appear defeated as a body, but one after another, the eldest first, because they, as the wiser of the party, saw very well that there was nothing else to be done, or because they felt themselves more guilty and had more to fear from our Lord (John 8:9). The woman alone remained, standing before our Lord; or, as St. Augustine says, only two remained behind, misery and mercy. By not leading the guilty woman away from our Saviour to the appointed court, they proved clearly enough that it was not their object to punish the crime, but to bring our Lord into a dilemma.

### 3. JUSTIFICATION OF THE WOMAN

The poor woman who had stood there so abashed had also good reason for flight. She does not attempt it, however, but remains, penitent, contrite, and trustful. It may be that she had cast herself down at the feet of Jesus. When He speaks to her, she addresses Him respectfully as "Lord" (John 8:11). Surely grace has been doing its work in her heart all this while that she has been standing so close to Jesus.

Our Saviour, Who had not yet looked up, now raises Himself and encourages her, asking who has condemned her and where her accusers are (John 8:10). He thus rouses her to a consciousness of the benefit of deliverance from her judges. But one Judge still remains, He Himself, and from Him she has the most to fear. But neither does He condemn her (John 8:11). There are no accusers, and He will not be a Judge, but a Redeemer. He dismisses her in peace (John 8:11). "Sin no more": that is the only thing He says and the only condition He imposes. He does not speak a single harsh word. He thus condemns the sin but not the sinner, and grants her the life of the soul as well as that of the body.

This mystery opens out to us yet further the wondrous beauty of our Saviour's character. It shows Him triumphing over all the devices of craft by His superiority in intellect and in the gift of counsel. It is a fresh revelation of His goodness and mercy, which is so great that it becomes the occasion of a temptation, and which is able to defend, correct and convert sinners, without infringing upon the rights of justice. Lastly, it is a further manifestation of His Divinity, by right of which He here makes use of that most beautiful privilege of forgiving sins by His own power (Luke 5:24). Thus the mystery is a true proof of the Divinity of Christ, and perhaps it may have been on this account especially that St.

John included the incident in his Gospel. On the other hand, the characters and dispositions of the enemies of Jesus appear black enough; we see the cunning, insincerity and hypocrisy which caused them to make a show of zeal for the law, whilst they were in reality occupied with murderous plans against the Messias. This very event was to give rise to a new attempt at murder, and is only the introduction to the following scenes, which are described in the eighth chapter of St. John.

### Our Saviour the Light of the World

JOHN 8:12. Again therefore Jesus spoke to them, saying: "I am the light of the world; he that followeth me walketh not in darkness, but shall have the light of life."—13. The Pharisees therefore said to him: "Thou givest testimony of thyself; thy testimony is not true."—14. Jesus answered and said to them: "Although I give testimony of myself, my testimony is true; for I know whence I came, and whither I go; but you know not whence I come, or whither I go.—15. You judge according to the flesh, I judge not any man.—16. And if I do judge, my judgment is true; because I am not alone, but I and the Father that sent me.—17. And in your law it is written, that the testimony of two men is true.—18. I am one that give testimony of myself; and the Father that sent me, giveth testimony of me."—19. They said therefore to him: "Where is thy Father?" Jesus answered: "Neither me do you know, nor my Father; if you did know me, perhaps you would know my Father also."—20. These words Jesus spoke in the treasury, teaching in the temple; and no man laid hands on him, because his hour was not yet come.—21. Again therefore Jesus said to them: "I go, and you shall seek me, and you shall die in your sin. Whither I go, you cannot come."—22. The Jews therefore said: "Will he kill himself, because he said: Whither I go, you cannot come?"—23. And he said to them: "You are from beneath, I am from above. You are of this world, I am not of this world.—24. Therefore I said to you, that you shall die in your sins. For if you believe not that I am he, you shall die in your sin."—25. They said therefore to him: "Who art thou?" Jesus said to them: "The beginning, who also speak unto you.—26. Many things I have to speak and to judge of you; but he that sent me is true, and the things I have heard of him, these same I speak in the world."—27. And they understood not that he called God his father.—28. Jesus therefore said to them: "When you shall have lifted up the Son of Man, then shall you know that I am he, and that I do nothing of myself, but as the Father hath taught me, these things I speak;—29. And he that hath sent me is with me, and he hath not left me alone; for I do always the things that please him."—30. When he spoke these things, many believed in him.—31. Then Jesus said to those Jews who believed him: "If you continue in my word, you shall be my disciples indeed.—32. And you shall know the truth, and the truth shall make you free."—33. They answered him: "We are the seed of Abraham, and we have never been slaves to any man; how sayest thou: You shall be free?"—34. Jesus answered them: "Amen, amen I say unto you: that whosoever committeth sin, is the servant of sin.—35. Now the servant abideth not in the house for ever; but the son abideth for ever.—36. If therefore the son shall make you free, you shall be free indeed.—37. I know that you are the children of Abraham; but you seek to kill me, because my word hath no place in you.—38. I speak that which I have seen with my Father; and you do the things that you have seen with your father."—39. They answered and said to him: "Abraham is our father." Jesus saith to them:

"If you be the children of Abraham, do the works of Abraham.—40. But now you seek to kill me, a man who have spoken the truth to you, which I have heard of God; this Abraham did not.—41. You do the works of your father." They said therefore to him: "We are not born of fornication; we have one Father, even God." —42. Jesus therefore said to them: "If God were your Father, you would indeed love me; for from God I proceeded, and came; for I came not of myself, but he sent me.—43. Why do you not know my speech? Because you cannot hear my word.—44. You are of your father, the devil, and the desires of your father you will do; he was a murderer from the beginning, and he stood not in the truth, because truth is not in him; when he speaketh a lie, he speaketh of his own, for he is a liar, and the father thereof.—45. But if I say the truth, you believe me not. —46. Which of you shall convince me of sin? If I say the truth to you, why do you not believe me?—47. He that is of God heareth the words of God. Therefore you hear them not, because you are not of God."—48. The Jews therefore answered and said to him: "Do not we say well that thou art a Samaritan, and hast a devil?"—49. Jesus answered: "I have not a devil; but I honor my Father, and you have dishonored me.—50. But I seek not my own glory; there is one that seeketh and judgeth.—51. Amen, amen I say to you: if any man keep my word, he shall not see death for ever."—52. The Jews therefore said: "Now we know that thou hast a devil. Abraham is dead, and the prophets; and thou sayest: If any man keep my word, he shall not taste death for ever.—53. Art thou greater than our father Abraham, who is dead? And the prophets are dead. Whom dost thou make thyself?"—54. Jesus answered: "If I glorify myself, my glory is nothing; it is my Father that glorifieth me, of whom you say that he is your God.—55. And you have not known him, but I know him; and if I shall say that I know him not, I shall be like to you, a liar. But I do know him, and do keep his word.—56. Abraham your father rejoiced that he might see my day; he saw it, and was glad." —57. The Jews therefore said to him: "Thou art not yet fifty years old, and hast thou seen Abraham?"—58. Jesus said to them: "Amen, amen I say to you, before Abraham was made, I am."—59. They took up stones therefore to cast at him; but Jesus hid himself, and went out of the temple.

Our Saviour appears to have resumed His address after the interruption caused by the scene with the adulteress, but at another place; namely in the court where the treasury stood.

### 1. GENERAL CHARACTER OF THE DISCOURSE

The whole of this address is in reality a dispute with the Jews. Our Saviour propounds some truth, the hostile Jews reply by raising some objection, and He immediately gives an answer to their retort and follows it up by continuing the revelation of Himself, until at last it is broken off by an attempt upon His life. The whole discourse was probably held after the close of the Feast of Tabernacles. Whether it was delivered continuously, on the same day and at the same time, is uncertain.

### 2. THE DISCOURSE IN DETAIL

The discourse may be divided into two parts, according to the train of thought contained in it. The first part (John 8:12–

30) is directly occupied with the unbelieving Jews; the second part is devoted in the first instance to those of the Jews who believed in Jesus upon these words of His, and only incidentally to the unbelieving and refractory hearers (John 8:30–59).

The first part gives us at once the truth which our Saviour here reveals of Himself; secondly, we have the objection made by the unbelieving Jews; thirdly, our Saviour's answer to their resistance and unbelief.

The truth which our Saviour propounds as the subject of His address is contained in the words: "I am the Light of the world; he that followeth Me walketh not in darkness, but shall have the light of life" (John 8:12). The figure of light was probably suggested by the illumination of the Temple during the Feast of Tabernacles, which was at once the emblem of the pillar of fire in the wilderness and of the Messias. Like the spring of water, light and flame were also symbols of the Messias, and the prophets often employ this figure when speaking of Him (Num. 24:17; Hab. 3:4; Isa. 9:2; 42:6; 49:6). These words, therefore, simply contain a testimony and revelation of Himself as the Messias. He says that the light of the feast is extinguished, but that the true Light of the Temple is now shining, in Himself, over the whole world. The Jews understood this very well (Luke 2:32). It was equivalent to an assertion of His Divinity, for God alone is the "light of life"; here below by faith, and in the world to come by sight. Only God can speak of Himself thus (John 1:4). This is the witness borne by our Lord of Himself. Upon this the Pharisees base their opposition. They first deny the validity of His witness, because He had borne it of Himself (John 8:13); then, as He gives them plain intimations with regard to His origin from the Father and to His own Person, they ask Him where His Father is (John 8:19) and who He is Himself (John 8:25); finally, they persist in their design of murdering Him (John 8:20, 21), and mock at the prediction of His departure from this world with the insulting remark that perhaps He intended to commit suicide and go to hell (John 8:22). To this our Saviour replies, first, that the testimony which He bore of Himself was nevertheless true, and proves this by two reasons. The first consisted in His clear consciousness of His absolute holiness, His Divinity, His origin (eternal generation), and His goal, the Ascension (John 8:14); they pronounced Him to be an ordinary man, judging from appearances and from His insignificant extraction, and they

may therefore be mistaken, whilst if He judges, He does not err (John 8:15). The second reason consisted in the fact that the Father also bore this witness together with Him, the Second Person of the Godhead, and therefore this evidence was legal (John 8:16, 17, 18). Secondly, our Lord replies evasively to the question as to the abode and identity of His Father: if they knew Him, they would also know the Father (John 8:19); and with regard to Himself He answers: (I am) "the beginning, who also speak unto you" (John 8:25), or according to others: "I am what I have told you from the beginning," or: "I am what I have just told you, neither more nor less." He could judge them with regard to many things, and that not by Himself, but according to the judgment of Him Who had sent Him, and Who was true (John 8:26). Lastly, our Saviour attests the unbelief of the Jews, which arises from their worldly character and manner of thought (John 8:23) and from their blind infatuation (John 8:27), and which will even go the length of murdering Him by crucifixion (John 8:28). He announces to them the most terrible punishments, viz. not being able to find in Him a helper in their distress (at the destruction of the city), impenitence in death, and exclusion from eternal bliss (John 8:21, 24). Only His Death and the subsequent Descent of the Holy Ghost will open their eyes to His Nature, His rank as the Messias, and His Divinity, which He shares with the Father in community of nature and operation (John 8:28; cf. John 5:19, 20; 30:36); and by this revelation salvation will be brought to many. In all that He says and does, the Father is with Him by His cooperation, authority and guidance; the token and the meritorious cause of this is His unerring fulfilment of the Father's good pleasure (John 8:29). As a matter of fact many Jews were converted after the Death of Jesus.

The second part of the discourse is occupied in the first instance with the faithful; for many of the people believed in Jesus on seeing His miracles and hearing these doctrines (John 8:30). In order to fortify and at the same time test these new converts, our Saviour adduces four motives for faith. First, the happiness and honor of being His true disciples; secondly, the knowledge of the truth, which He preaches; thirdly, freedom through this knowledge (John 8:31, 32). This third motive gave rise to vehement contradiction on the part of the neophytes, in whom the "Jew" was not yet extinct, and who felt themselves wounded in their national pride by the idea of being first made free by our Saviour.

Indeed, this was a remarkable feature of Jewish nationalism. In spite of the numberless times they had fallen into slavery, they regarded themselves alone as free-born people, simply because they were descended from Abraham and belonged to the Covenant (John 8:33). The highest benefit which they expected from the Messias and from their religion was national, political freedom. Our Saviour gives a twofold answer to this. First, He tells them in what true freedom consists, namely in freedom from sin (John 8:34) and in being His followers. Without freedom from sin one is only a slave in God's house, and may at any time be driven out; the son alone has the right to inherit and dispose of the property. But God has only one natural Son, and only by being followers of this Son can we obtain the remission of our sins and the divine adoption (John 8:35, 36). He is the Truth, and thus in Him the truth really makes us free (John 8:32). This is the true deliverance through the Messias. If they lack this, our Saviour seems to hold out to them only the prospect of sharing the fate of Ismael (Gal. 4:22, 30, 31). Secondly, He refutes the grounds upon which the Jews supported their supposed freedom, namely their descent from Abraham (John 8:33, 39) and outward alliance with God by the Government; by reason of which they held that they were not heathens (John 8:41). Our Saviour shows, on the contrary, that they are descended from Abraham only according to the flesh (John 8:37), but not according to the spirit, for His words have no effect upon them (John 8:37) and they follow the promptings of another father (John 8:39), not of Abraham, for he would not have sought to kill the Messias (John 8:40); neither have they God as their Father, as they pride themselves in contrast to the Gentiles, for in that case they would love our Saviour as the Son and Messenger of God, and would hear His word (John 8:47). He tells them that on the contrary they are the children of the devil, and proves this from the fact of their doing the works of the devil (John 8:38, 41), viz. murder and lying (John 8:44), which he has practised from the days of Paradise until now. He Himself speaks the truth (John 8:45), because He cannot be convicted of sin, and yet they do not believe Him; therefore they are not of God (John 8:46, 47). The Jews reply to this grave reproach by words of reviling, urging His very zeal as a proof that He was a Samaritan and possessed by an evil spirit, meaning that He was as foolish as He was wicked (John 8:48); whereupon our Saviour answers that His emulation is zeal for the glory of God, and that their words are an insult to Him (John 8:49), for which they will be judged by Another (John 8:50).

After this digression our Saviour brings forward a fourth motive to incite the newly converted to hold fast to their faith, viz. the promise that whoever will keep His words shall escape everlasting death (John 8:51). By steadfast faith in Jesus we avoid condemnation at the Judgment, and this promised immortality is the glorious contrast to the punishment inflicted by this Judgment, which is no other than everlasting death. The Jews see in this a new proof that He is possessed and does not rightly know what He is saying, since He promises to His disciples exemption from bodily death, greater things than fell to the lot of Abraham and the prophets, and ask angrily whom He makes Himself (John 8:52, 53). Our Divine Saviour answers this both directly and indirectly. He first says that His glorification would certainly be void if He exalted Himself, but that it is the Father, not He, Who has glorified Him, given Him the glory, by begetting Him from all eternity and making Him that which He now declares Himself to be, and to which the Father in turn bears witness,—"the Father . . . of whom you say that He is your God. And you have not known Him (as My Father, nor honored Him in practice by accepting His testimony); but I know Him (as My Father) and keep His word . . . (by declaring Myself to be His Son, otherwise I should) be like to you, a liar" (John 8:55). Our Lord then passes on to a direct answer, and explains His relations to Abraham, upon whom the Jews take their stand. In the first place, He says, Abraham honored Him and hailed His coming with joy, whether upon receiving the revelation and promise vouchsafed to him here in his temporal life (Gen. 18:18; 22:18), or in Limbo. Abraham, therefore, is less than our Saviour (John 8:56). And as the Jews now malevolently misinterpret this mental vision as an actual one, and ask how Abraham can have seen Him, since He has not yet attained the full maturity of man (John 8:57), Jesus declares quite openly not only that He is a contemporary of Abraham's, but that He even existed before him as an Uncreated and Divine Being from all eternity: "Before Abraham was made, I am," as Jehovah, He who is (John 8:58). So also the Jews understood it, and would have stoned our Lord as a blasphemer (John 8:59; Lev. 24:16). For this purpose they may have taken up the stones which were lying there for the building of the Temple, or our Saviour may then have been in the fore-court of the Gentiles, where there was no stone pavement, but loose stones enough lay about within reach. But He "hid Himself," i.e. disappeared amongst the people or made Himself invisible, as at Nazareth, and went out of the Temple (John 8:59).

### 3. RESULT AND EFFECT

Side by side appear two very different results, viz. the progress of our Lord's testimony and revelation of Himself, and on the other hand the increase of opposition on the part of the Jews.

Our Lord terms Himself very fittingly the Light of the world. The light of His Divinity is being more and more fully disclosed. We have here three kinds of utterances with regard to it. First, those in which He refuses a plain statement, because the Jews would only have made a bad use of it (John 8:19, 25). Secondly, utterances in which He declares plainly enough, although in a mysterious manner, His Godhead, His generation by the Father (John 8:14, 18, 25, 42), the unity of Their nature, the attributes of His knowledge and operation (John 8:18, 19, 26, 28, 38, 40) and of the communication of light and blessedness (John 8:12, 51). Thirdly, we have utterances in which He openly declares His Divinity, so that the Jews accuse Him of blasphemy.

In proportion as He reveals Himself more fully, the Jews grow more bitter in their rage and hatred. We see their increasing irritation in their more and more frequent and excited contradiction; in the scorn and derision which now mark their retorts and with which they respond to our Lord's prediction with regard to His decease (John 8:22), here with far more malevolence than on the Feast of Tabernacles (John 7:35); lastly, in the open affront and curse which they hurl in His face before all the people, calling Him a Samaritan and a demoniac (John 8:48, 52; 7:20). Our Lord also becomes more severe in His language, and upbraids them with very bitter truths, predicting their impenitent death and temporal and eternal ruin (John 7:34; 8:21, 24), and calling them plainly children of the devil (John 8:44). The severe and humiliating defeat in connection with the adulteress must already have excited and exasperated these perverse hearts to the very utmost, and now that our Lord so unsparingly castigates their national and personal pride, their hatred and fury break out into a wild act of violence, and they wish to stone Him in the Temple.

Our Saviour's divine power alone frustrates their attempt. It is as though we see the combat between light and darkness actually before our eyes, and as if the words of St. John: "The light shineth in darkness, and the darkness did not comprehend it" (1:5) were here enacted in a living scene (Keppler). The Jews are not only the real adulterers, by their violation of the Covenant with their God, but also His persecutors and murderers; they wish to stone their Messias in the midst of His Temple, and thus to extinguish the Light of the World with their own hands. How marvelously beautiful and majestic the figure of our Saviour appears against this dark background, in His calmness and self-possession, His childlike fidelity and love for His Father; in His pure zeal for the honor and the mandate of His Heavenly Father; and lastly, in the courage He displays in the midst of the infuriated people, and in His divine power, since He does not flee or bend down to avoid the stones cast at Him, but simply withdraws from them like the light, which cannot be seized and stoned! The Godhead was His shield and refuge. But the situation had become so strained by the preceding events that a crisis was unavoidable.

## THE MAN BORN BLIND

JOHN 9:1. And Jesus passing by saw a man who was blind from his birth;—2. And his disciples asked him: "Rabbi, who hath sinned, this man or his parents, that he should be born blind?"—3. Jesus answered: "Neither hath this man sinned, nor his parents; but that the works of God should be made manifest in him.— 4. I must work the works of him that sent me, whilst it is day; the night cometh when no man can work.—5. As long as I am in the world, I am the light of the world."—6. When he had said these things, he spat on the ground, and made clay of the spittle, and spread the clay upon his eyes,—7. And said to him: "Go, wash in the pool of Siloe" (which is interpreted, Sent). He went, therefore, and washed, and he came seeing.—8. The neighbors therefore, and they who had seen him before that he was a beggar, said: "Is not this he that sat and begged?" Some said: "This is he."—9. But others said: "No, but he is like him." But he said: "I am he."—10. They said therefore to him: "How were thy eyes opened?"—11. He answered: "That man that is called Jesus made clay, and anointed my eyes, and said to me: Go to the pool of Siloe, and wash. And I went, I washed, and I see."—12. And they said to him: "Where is he?" He saith: "I know not."—13. They bring him that had been blind to the Pharisees.—14. Now it was the Sabbath when Jesus made the clay and opened his eyes.—15. Again therefore the Pharisees asked him, how he had received his sight. But he said to them: "He put clay upon my eyes, and I washed, and I see."—16. Some therefore of the Pharisees said: "This man is not of God, who keepeth not the Sabbath." But others said: "How can a man that is a sinner do such miracles?" And there was a division among them.—17. They say therefore to the blind man again: "What sayest thou of him that hath opened thy eyes?" And he said: "He is a prophet."— 18. The Jews then did not believe concerning him, that he had been blind and had received his sight, until they called the parents of him that had received his sight.—19. And asked them, saying: "Is this your son, who you say was born blind? How then doth he now see?"—20. His parents answered them and said: "We know that this is our son, and that he was born blind;—21. But how he now seeth, we know not; or who hath opened his eyes, we know not; ask himself; he is of age, let him speak for himself."—22. These things his parents said, because they feared the Jews; for the Jews had already agreed among themselves, that if any man should confess him to be Christ, he should be put out of the synagogue. —23. Therefore did his parents say: "He is of age, ask him."—24. They therefore called the man again that had been blind, and said to him: "Give glory to God; we know that this man is a sinner."—25. He said therefore to them: "If he be a sinner, I know not; one thing I know, that, whereas I was blind, now I see."—26. They said then to him: "What did he to thee? How did he open thy eyes?"—27. He answered them: "I have told you already, and you have heard; why would you hear it again? Will you also become his disciples?"—28. They reviled him therefore, and said: "Be thou his disciple; but we are the disciples of Moses.—29. We know that God spoke to Moses; but as to this man, we know not from whence he is."—30. The man answered, and said to them: "Why, herein is a wonderful thing that you know not from whence he is, and he hath opened my eyes.—31. Now we know that God doth not hear sinners; but if a man be a server of God, and doth his will, him he heareth.—32. From the beginning of the world it hath not been heard that any man hath opened the eyes of one born blind.—33. Unless this man were of God, he could not do anything."—34. They answered and said to him: "Thou wast wholly born in sins, and dost thou teach us?" And they cast him out.—35. Jesus heard that they had cast him out; and when he had found him, he said to him: "Dost thou believe in the Son of God?"—36. He answered and said: "Who is he, Lord, that I may believe in him?"—37. And Jesus said to him: "Thou hast both seen him, and it is he that talketh with thee."—38. And he said: "I believe, Lord." And falling down he adored him.—39. And Jesus said: "For judgment I am come into this world; that they who see not, may see, and they who see, may become blind."—40. And some of the Pharisees, who were with him, heard; and they said unto him: "Are we also blind?"—41. Jesus said to them: "If you were blind, you should not have sin; but now you say: We see. Your sin remaineth."

Our Lord's meeting with the blind man probably took place immediately upon His leaving the Temple.

### 1. OCCASION AND REASON OF THE MIRACLE

It may have been in passing through one of the gates of the Temple, where poor and infirm persons were wont to gather in order to solicit alms (Act 3:2), that our Saviour saw a man who had been blind from his birth. This glance was the first occasion of the miracle. It was a glance of heartfelt sympathy and compassion for his blindness and poverty (John 9:8). Possibly our Saviour stood still before the poor man, and looked at him significantly (John 9:1).

The disciples gave occasion for the disclosure of the second motive. The special attention paid by our Lord to this poor blind man probably aroused their sympathy also, and they asked to whose fault this misfortune was due, to his parents' or his own (John 9:2). Generally speaking the question is correct, and proceeds from the religious view that temporal evils are very often punishments for sin, which view finds its confirmation in the whole history of the nation (Ex. 20:5; Deut. 5:9; Jer. 32:18; John 5:14). Our Saviour answered that neither the man nor his parents were in fault, but that his blindness was permitted by God in order that His works might be manifested (John 9:3). These "works of God" signify here not only His omnipotence and goodness as seen in the working of miracles, but also many other works of His love and power for the welfare of souls, which are typified in this miracle. The circumstances of the miracle are arranged with this end in view; our Saviour's chief object in working it is to reveal all this. The second motive, therefore, is the glory of God and the salvation of souls.

Our Lord explains and confirms this motive by a third, which shows at the same time the connection of this miracle with the previous mystery. He says: "I must work the works of Him that sent Me, whilst it is day; the night cometh when no man can work. As long as I am in the world, I am the Light of the world" (John 9:4, 5). In other words: I am the Light of the world, and as light by virtue of its nature cannot help shining, so it is My vocation, as long as I live here below, to glorify God by revealing and performing His works. But this life is nearly over, since the Jews have resolved to kill Me; therefore I feel Myself urged to let My light shine now by this miracle, which is emblematic of Me as Light and as the Giver of light, even as I have let it shine in the Temple by My teaching. This miracle therefore is only a fresh token that our Saviour is the Light of the world, and a further effort to manifest Himself as this Light, i.e. as Messias and God. This shows us the connection of this mystery with the preceding one. What a beautiful example our Lord here gives us, and what an earnest exhortation to make a good use of life as long as we have it at our command! Here, too, we see again exemplified His custom of explaining and confirming an important statement concerning Himself by an appropriate miracle.

## 2. THE MIRACLE

There are two things to be considered in this mystery: first the miracle itself, and secondly how it became known and substantiated.

The miracle itself is, as regards its nature, extraordinary, indeed absolute, if the visual faculty did not exist, and in this respect the healed man is right in saying that it had never yet been heard that one born blind had received sight (John 9:32); but if the visual faculty was present, then the means employed by our Saviour are still by no means proportionate to the effect. In any case, therefore, it was an extraordinary miracle. As regards the manner in which it was worked, our Saviour requires from the blind man no other cooperation than that he should go in faith and confidence to the pool of Siloe, and wash. The following are the ceremonies He employs: He prepares clay from dust and His own saliva, spreads it upon the eyes of the blind man, and bids him wash himself with water from the pool of Siloe (John 9:6, 7). The ceremonies which our Saviour often performs in working miracles either have the object of preparing the person in question for the benefit he is about to receive, or they correspond to the nature of the sickness, or else symbolize spiritual truths and things to come. There is in this case no natural relation between the means and the effect; on the contrary, such a remedy might prevent even the best eye from seeing. It is therefore the symbolic signification which predominates here. Perhaps our Saviour intended, by employing dust, to indicate that the visual faculty did not exist at all, and must therefore be created, as Adam had once been formed out of the dust of the earth. But it seems more probable that it is Holy Baptism which is here signified. Baptism is not merely a cleansing, but also a new creation. The spreading of clay upon the eyes denotes the stain of sin and the complete deficiency of supernatural life. The impurity of sin and natural blindness to supernatural truth are removed by the water of baptism, which flows from the Temple mountain (the Church) and in the first instance from the side of the Redeemer, and which is typified by the water of Siloe.

Lastly we see that our Saviour doubtless wished to indicate Himself as the Author of the miracle, by sending the blind man to the pool of Siloe, i.e. (as St. John remarks, certainly not without reason) to the pool of the "Sent" from God, and only healing him upon his washing with this water. Our Saviour is the One "Sent" from God, and the still waters of Siloe were always regarded as a symbol of the Messias and a pledge of His graces and blessings (cf. Introd., p. 5). Since the miracle was now worked by Him, and of its very nature bestowed light and the faculty of sight, and was performed by means of water; and since the Feast of Tabernacles was especially distinguished by the libation of water and the illumination of the Temple, this miracle is united to the feast as an epilogue and after-type, and proves our Saviour to be the real "pool of Siloe" and "Light of the world." Thus regarded, the miracle really typifies all the divine mysteries of the Redemption and of the Church, and truly reveals the works of God; without these mysteries humanity would lie, like this poor man, blind, wretched and mendicant before the doors of the Church and of heaven.

Another attendant circumstance of this outstanding miracle is that our Saviour performed it on a Sabbath-day (John 9:14). He does not choose the Sabbath in order to irritate and annoy His enemies, but because it was His special day of grace for the performance of God's works; and also because the Jews needed instruction and explanation with regard to this point, and it was upon this that they were to declare themselves and take their stand. As a matter of fact they founded their opposition on this very circumstance, and made use of it to support their unbelief (John 9:16, 24). Thus we have in the cure of the man born blind one of our Saviour's most wonderful miracles. He now withdrew from the Temple and from the hands of the enraged people, having cast by this miracle a fiery brand in their midst. They weary themselves in the wild endeavor to extinguish it, but only fan the flame and burn themselves.

A miracle only does its work and, so to speak, really becomes a miracle when it is known and substantiated. So also in this case. Our Saviour disposed the circumstances excellently for this end, and the Pharisees helped towards it. They themselves were to substantiate the miracle brilliantly, and this by the very pains they took to deny and nullify it. In order to make the fact of the miracle known and to establish it, it was necessary, first, that the event should come to the ears of our Lord's enemies and become generally known; further, the fact of the blindness and of its cure, and also the identity of the healed man with the one who had been born blind, must be established. All this took place in four successive scenes.

In the first, that is, the one between the people and the man born blind, the identity of the latter, which was doubted by the people on account of the altered expression of his face, is established by himself (John 9:8, 9), as also the manner of the cure, and the fact that Jesus is its Author (John 9:10, 11, 12). The people take care that the miracle becomes known in the right quarter; they bring the healed man before a small assembly of Pharisees, prompted either by a rightful zeal for the reporting of the event to the proper authorities, or by fear of the Pharisees, or by antipathy to our Saviour (John 9:13).

In the second, the man's examination by the Pharisees, the former confirms the facts of the cure and the manner in which it had taken place (John 9:15). This now gives rise to dissension amongst the Pharisees. The evil-disposed among them fix upon the circumstance that our Lord has healed the blind man on the Sabbath by the application of a remedy, and this is in their eyes a violation of the Sabbath. They reason thus: God gives to no sinner the power to work miracles; but this man (i.e. our Saviour) is a sinner and a despiser of the Sabbath, therefore he cannot have worked the miracle. Others, on the contrary, hold fast to the fact of this and other miracles, and maintain that a sinner could not work such (John 9:16). However, the miracle might be attacked from other sides. It was important for the antagonists to know what the healed man himself thought of our Saviour. If he agreed with them that Jesus was a sinner, it would already be something gained. But he answered that he considered Him to be a prophet (John 9:17).

Thereupon they now tried to call in question the fact of the miracle, through the parents of the healed man. This forms the third scene. They questioned the parents in precise and definite terms as to whether the man was their son or not, and how he had received his sight. The first question was boldly answered in the affirmative by the parents, but they feared to reply to the second, lest they should incur the excommunication with which the chief priests had threatened the adherents of Jesus (John 9:18–23).

Thus we are led to the fourth scene, the scene in which the Pharisees urged the healed man with all the authority of their office, by their unerring theological knowledge ("We know") and by means of a kind of adjuration (Jos. 7:19; I Kings 6:5), to declare with them, as a matter of conscience and to the glory of God, that Jesus was a sinner (John 9:24). The man will not pronounce himself upon this point; but he maintains in the most decided manner the fact of the cure (John 9:25). After they had once more asked information as to how the miracle had been performed, and again expressed themselves in terms condemnatory of our Saviour (John 9:26–29), the healed man opposed to their verdict the following proposition: If he were a sinner, he could not have worked the miracle, because God does not work miracles to confirm imposture; but he has worked it; therefore he is no sinner, but of God (John 9:30–33). There cannot then be much in this charge of Sabbath profanation. The Pharisees could give no reply to this but the insulting question how he, who had been born blind, evidently in consequence of sin, dared to try to teach them; then they forcibly ejected him from the court (John 9:34), and probably also excommunicated him from the synagogue.

In this way, then, the miracle is made known and triumphantly established by the statements of the parents of the healed man, by his own frankness, integrity and intrepidity, and by the perplexity, rage and violence of the Pharisees. Our Saviour could stand quietly in the background and watch the pains they took to make the miracle known and established. By their excommunication of the recalcitrant they did but increase the number of our Lord's adherents.

### 3. RESULTS AND EFFECTS OF THE MIRACLE

Our Saviour now came forward in order to complete and confirm the effects of the miracle in two directions.

First, with regard to the healed man. Our Lord probably went to seek him, in order to reward him for his fidelity and courage and to comfort him in his desolation, since He heard that the Pharisees had cast him out of the synagogue. So He approached him and revealed Himself to him, tentatively at first, asking him if he believed in the Son of God (John 9:35). The poor man responded readily to His advances, inquiring who this Son of God was, that he might believe in Him. Our Saviour replied with simple candor that He Whom he saw (in consequence of the miracle) and with Whom he was speaking was the Son of God (John 9:37). How kind and touching are these advances made by our Lord! He made such to very few persons, and the man to whom He now addressed them was poor and unfortunate, yet precious in His eyes for his sincerity of soul. On hearing the words of Jesus he fell at once upon his knees, made his confession of faith, and adored Him as the Son of God (John 9:38).

Turning to the bystanders (or rather to those of them who

were Pharisees), our Saviour declared that He had come into the world for judgment, that those who did not see, i.e. the "little ones," the humble and simple-minded, who were not hindered by fancied knowledge from opening their eyes to the truth (Matt. 11:25; Luke 10:21; John 7:49), might receive sight; and that those who saw, i.e. the wise and enlightened, who considered their imperfect knowledge as the highest and most perfect wisdom, might become blind (John 9:39). Upon their inquiring whether He reckoned them amongst the blind (John 9:40), there follows the weighty answer: "If you were blind, you should not have sin; but now you say: We see. Your sin remaineth" (John 9:41). Their sin is that of hardened impenitence (Matt. 12:32; Rom. 10:3).

We have now reached the full significance of the mystery. Our Saviour gives in it a true revelation of Himself and a new proof that He is the Light of the world. He opens the natural eyes of the poor blind man, in order to prove that He is come to free mankind from its spiritual darkness. His saying that He thereby becomes the cause of judgment is also confirmed here. The man born blind, who kneels at the feet of Jesus and makes his confession of faith with such grateful and childlike dispositions, and the Pharisee who stands by proud and scornful and thinks himself, in his belief, the very opposite of blind, are a proof of both statements; the blind receive their sight, and those who see become blind. The light enlightens the willing, but blinds the proud and deprives them of their reason. They wish to prove that something cannot have happened, which nevertheless has happened, and which they themselves cannot deny. But unhappily their blindness is their own fault, and an unpardonable one, because it is sin against the Holy Ghost. This mystery contains also a lesson for all those who approach Christ by baptism, which is typified by this cure of the man born blind, and teaches them that they must be prepared to suffer persecution, and be ready also to make a firm confession of their faith in Christ. If their constancy can stand this test, comfort and reward will surely follow.

## THE GOOD SHEPHERD

JOHN 10:1. "Amen, amen I say to you: he that entereth not by the door into the sheepfold, but climbeth up another way, the same is a thief and a robber.— 2. But he that entereth in by the door is the shepherd of the sheep.—3. To him the porter openeth, and the sheep hear his voice; and he calleth his own sheep by name, and leadeth them out.—4. And when he hath let out his own sheep, he goeth before them; and the sheep follow him, because they know his voice.—5. But a stranger they follow not, but fly from him; because they know not the voice of strangers."—6. This proverb Jesus spoke to them. But they understood not what he spoke to them.—7. Jesus therefore said to them again: "Amen, amen I say to you, I am the door of the sheep.—8. All others, as many as have come, are thieves and robbers; and the sheep heard them not.—9. I am the door. By me if any man enter in, he shall be saved; and he shall go in and go out, and shall find pastures.—10. The thief cometh not, but for to steal and to kill and to destroy. I am come that they may have life, and that they may have it more abundantly. —11. I am the good shepherd. The good shepherd giveth his life for his sheep.— 12. But the hireling, and he that is not the shepherd, whose own the sheep are not, seeth the wolf coming, and leaveth the sheep, and flieth; and the wolf catcheth and scattereth the sheep.—13. And the hireling flieth, because he is a hireling; and he hath no care for the sheep.—14. I am the good shepherd; and I know mine, and mine know me.—15. As the Father knoweth me, and I know the Father; and I lay down my life for my sheep.—16. And other sheep I have, that are not of this fold; them also I must bring, and they shall hear my voice; and there shall be one fold and one shepherd.—17. Therefore doth the Father love me; because I lay down my life, that I may take it again.—18. No man taketh it away from me; but I lay it down of myself, and I have power to lay it down; and I have power to take it up again. This commandment have I received of my Father."—19. A dissension rose again among the Jews for these words.—20. And many of them said: "He hath a devil, and is mad; why hear you him?"—21. Others said: "These are not the words of one that hath a devil. Can a devil open the eyes of the blind?"

The parable of the Good Shepherd probably followed immediately upon the preceding event, in which the hostile ruling parties had shown themselves to be such unworthy pastors of the ancient Church of the Covenant, whilst the rightful Shepherd met with such a ready response from His sheep. The preceding event is here resumed in the form of a parable.

### 1. THE PICTURE OF THE GOOD SHEPHERD AND THE BAD ONE

The reason why our Saviour speaks of the heads and teachers of Israel as "shepherds" is probably that Scripture very often represents the guidance of the nation by God and His representatives under the figure of a shepherd leading his sheep (Gen. 48:15; Ps. 22; Isa. 40:11; Jer. 23:1; Ez. 34:1–23; 37:24; Zach. 11:17; 13:7; Matt. 9:36). And this was quite in keeping with the character of peace and benevolence which this guidance bore. The simile was equally well-founded as regards the economical conditions of the country, since the wealth of Palestine, especially in the highlands, consisted chiefly in pasture-land, meadows and flocks. These flocks fed in the meadows from spring until winter. In the evening the sheep, which were separated into different flocks by day, were brought into a common fold surrounded by a wall, which was provided with a gate or door and a little lodge. The door was given into the charge of a door-keeper or porter. In the morning he opened the door to admit the shepherds; each of these called the flock belonging to him, and the sheep obeyed the call of their shepherd and followed him to their own place of pasture. Our Saviour now takes the chief features of His parable from this picture of Oriental rural life. But the immediate occasion of the parable was given by the Pharisees, through their unjust and unauthorized measures against the adherents of Jesus. Not content with not believing in Him themselves, they wished forcibly to draw away from Him those who did believe, and therefore expelled them from the synagogue. They hereby arrogated to themselves the supreme pastoral office, and guarded violently and arbitrarily the entrance to the kingdom of God.

Our Saviour now draws for us in the parable the picture of the true shepherd and the false one. He mentions as the characteristics of the true shepherd: first, legitimate authority or valid appointment to the exercise of the pastoral office. The legitimacy of this authority is expressed in his admittance by the door-keeper, and in his going in to the sheep through the door (John 10:2, 3). The second characteristic, which corresponds to the first (but on the side of the sheep), is the attachment of the flock to their rightful shepherd; they know his voice and follow him when he calls them and walks on before them (John 10:3, 4). But the characteristics of the false shepherd are the very opposite of these. In the first place, his illegitimate method of procedure, going in without being admitted by the door-keeper, not openly and honestly throught the door, but climbing over the wall (John 10:1); and in the second place the intractability and dislike of him on the part of the sheep. They do not know nor follow him, but on the contrary instinctively flee from him (John 10:5). This marks the thief and robber; he arrogates to himself the right to the sheep and robs them of well-being and life.

In this parable our Saviour indicates by the fold the means of salvation in the Old Covenant; by the sheep, God's people; by the door, Himself; by the door-keeper, the Heavenly Father; by the thieves and robbers, unlawful pastors; and by the rightful shepherd, those lawfully appointed. The parable was only propounded in general, without any particular application or specification; and therefore the Pharisees either could not or would not understand it (John 10:6).

## 2. APPLICATION OF THE FIGURE TO OUR SAVIOUR AND TO THE PHARISEES

Our Saviour now applies the parable in detail, first to Himself and then to the Pharisees.

He shows how all the traits which mark the good shepherd are found in Himself, in contrast with the Pharisees. There are two chief characteristics. First, lawful authority. He is not only a legitimately appointed Shepherd, but the source and necessary condition of all real authority. Therefore He does not say merely that He has been admitted through the door by the door-keeper, but that He Himself is the door; and He repeats this statement again (John 10:7, 9). The God-Man is the holder of all power and pastoral authority. Whoever does not enter the sheepfold through Christ and His appointed representatives cannot be a shepherd or teacher, and is not even a member of the flock. Our Saviour is the source of all authority and of salvation. Whoever enters through Him will find, as a shepherd of God's flock, pasturage (i.e. God's help and care) for himself and the sheep (John 10:9). Christ is the door for the shepherds. No one admits at this door but the door-keeper, who is no other than the Heavenly Father; without Him no one can come to our Saviour (John 6:44), or arrive either at faith in Him or at participation in His pastoral authority. Whoever therefore enters by this door is the shepherd of the sheep; whoever breaks in elsewhere is a thief and a robber. The sheep do not belong to him; he himself does not belong to the fold (John 10:1, 2). Our Saviour now applies this part of the parable to the pastors, teachers and leaders of the people of His own time. Since they do not believe in Christ, but wish to murder Him, they are no rightful shepherds, because they do not enter by the door of divine appointment; they are simply robbers, if they arrogate to themselves any right over the sheep (John 10:8). By the word "all" our Saviour means all the then ruling parties—Pharisees, Sadducees and Herodians, who sought under the cloak of religion to gain adherents among the people, and persecuted one another for purely worldly ends, in order to attain to power and honor. The misfortune was not that single individuals were opposed to the true Messias, but that closely united parties were against Him. They were, every one of them, destroyers, not shepherds of souls. In their inordinate desire of money and honor they oppressed the people (Matt. 9:36) and hid from them the key to wisdom and salvation (Luke 11:52); they laid down the law with regard to faith and eternal bliss, disposed of the kingdom of heaven (Matt. 23:13), and hunted the people to temporal and eternal ruin (John 10:1, 10). They were no better than wolves (Zach. 11:16), and therefore God's true sheep did not know them, but fled from them (John 10:5), as the man born blind had done, together with all who already believed in our Saviour.

The second characteristic of the true shepherd which our Saviour applies to Himself is that He exercises his pastoral power aright, with disinterested labor, tender charity and a real shepherd's care, such as He had already described in the first part of the parable. He knows and calls His sheep, choosing them out, exhorting and urging them to good, and warning them against evil; He goes before them by His example (John 14:6) and protection; He feeds them by doctrine, grace and guidance; and all this from the loving desire that the sheep may have life, and may have it abundantly, i.e. by justification, resurrection and glory (John 10:3, 4, 10).

Yes, in this pastoral care and love our Saviour goes so far as to deliver Himself up to death for His sheep, to protect and defend them against the wild beasts and wolves: the world and the Evil One (John 10:11, 15). Our Lord does not here contrast Himself with unlawful pastors, but with those who, though rightfully appointed, are unfaithful, rather "hirelings" than shepherds; who flee at the approach of danger and forsake the flock, leaving them to disperse and perish (John 10:12). He also gives the reason of this different behavior. The hireling is not the owner of the flock, it does not concern him; only self-interest and his own profit have led him thither and keep him there; if he finds no advantage for himself, but on the contrary danger, he leaves them to their fate and makes his own escape (John 10:13). Not so our Saviour. He is the Only-begotten Son of the Heavenly Father. Sharing the same nature, He recognizes and loves His Father in all His paternal relations, in His whole Fatherhood, natural and adoptive; since He is not only His Father, but also the Father of all men, especially by sanctifying grace, which is an imitation of the Divine Sonship. He sees that the Father regards and loves all men as His children, and wills that the Son should regard and love them as His brethren.

Thus our Saviour sees in us His Father's property and His own and cherishes us as His sheep with the love with which He loves the Father and Himself (John 10:15); not only Israelites, but Gentiles also. For this reason He adds that He has other sheep outside of the sheepfold of Israel; that He will bring them too, and there will be one fold and one shepherd, namely in the Church (John 10:16). In order to accomplish this great union of all men under the Chief Shepherd and thus to honor the Father, He delivers Himself up to death of His own free will; no power can otherwise deprive Him of life. "I lay down My life of Myself" (John 10:18), "that I may take it again" (John 10:17). "This commandment have I received of My Father" (John 10:18), and "therefore doth the Father love Me" (John 10:17), because I glorify Him by My Death (by this union of the whole human race which will result from it, and by My glory). What a shameful picture of the hireling was presented by the Pharisees, to whom the greater part of the priesthood and of the leading circles of Israel belonged, as opposed to this sublime and touching love of the Good Shepherd, our Saviour! They did not exactly deliver the people into the hands of the Romans, but they incited them to fight against them, and when ruin came, many of them tried to make their escape (Schanz).

The whole parable and teaching of our Saviour here is a magnificent and glorious revelation of Himself as the Messias, the supreme Shepherd of all nations, a priestly King who asserts His rights over all shepherds and peoples, and who will unite them all under His peaceful and beneficent pastoral staff in one great kingdom of happiness and glory, which will arise from His voluntary Death for all. How many glorious prophecies are here blended together in one grand fulfilment! The prophecies of the Messias, who is to be also the Shepherd of Israel (Ez. 34:23; Isa. 40:11); of the king of the nations (Ps. 2:8); of the redeeming Death of the Messias (Isa. 53:7); of the great kingdom that will spring from this Death (21:28). All is of tremendous import, yet full of charm; all is perfectly in keeping with the character of our Saviour.

These words of His, spoken with majestic calmness and judicial severity, did not fail of their effect. The enemies of Jesus sought to weaken this effect by calling His sayings senseless and attributing them to possession by a devil (John 10:19, 20). Others, again, replied that no demoniac would speak like this; no evil spirit could make the blind to see (John 10:21). And so there was dissension among them.

### 3. APPLICATION OF THE FIGURE TO OURSELVES

The application to ourselves consists in this, that we give ourselves unreservedly to this Shepherd of our souls. The motives are as follows. First, He is our rightful Shepherd, because He is our God and Lord. The pastoral office is only one title and one manifestation of his royal sovereignty, which is His peculiar birthright as Man-God. Secondly, He is really and in all the mysteries of His life a Shepherd, and the *Good* Shepherd. In His Incarnation He forsakes high heaven and the bright choirs of angels for our little earth, that He may seek after us poor strayed sheep, and He assumes our nature in order to win us. In His public life He is again the Good Shepherd. He hastens after poor sinners over mountain and vale, through thorns and thickets; He carries them gently back, heals them by His grace, leads them to the good pastures of His teaching and example, and nourishes them with His own Flesh and Blood. In His Passion He dies in our stead, that we may live. In His Resurrection He gathers His sheep together again, comforts them, gives them the Holy Ghost and eternal life. He is everywhere the Good Shepherd. Oh, let us never forget His tender, all-embracing, all-sacrificing, faithful love, and all that we owe to it! Our Saviour is everything to us: fold, door, way, pasture and shepherd. Thirdly, let us reflect that we must have a shepherd. We must belong to some flock and some shepherd. We have only the choice between Christ and the world or the Evil One. Is there a more selfish and cruel tyrant than the world and its prince? In what powerful and terrifying characters our Saviour depicts its sway! And what a terrible fate it prepares for us, whilst our Saviour promises us life, abundant, beatific, eternal life!

Let us therefore be good sheep of the Good Shepherd. Let us learn to know Him by His word, His example, His footprints. This is a mark by which the true sheep of Jesus may be known, this pleasure, this joy in everything that concerns Him. Let us follow Him, let us permit ourselves to be guided aright, when He wishes to hold us back from the poisonous pastures of worldly joys and from lurking wolves. Let us offer Him the poor gift of our life, our body, our sufferings and labors. Who deserves it more than He?

Let us follow Him everywhere, to Bethlehem, to Thabor, or to Mount Quarantine, Gethsemani and Calvary. If the Good Shepherd is with us, we shall want for nothing. "Dominus regit me, et nihil mihi deerit" (Ps. 22:1).

## INSTRUCTION UPON PRAYER

LUKE 11:1. And it came to pass that as he was in a certain place praying, when he ceased, one of his disciples said to him: "Lord, teach us to pray, as John also taught his disciples."—2. And he said to them: "When you pray, say: Father, hallowed be thy name. Thy kingdom come.—3. Give us this day our daily bread.—4. And forgive us our sins, for we also forgive every one that is indebted to us. And lead us not into temptation."—5. And he said to them: "Which of you shall have a friend, and shall go to him at midnight, and shall say to him: Friend, lend me three loaves,—6. Because a friend of mine is come off his journey to me, and I have not what to set before him.—7. And he from within should answer and say: Trouble me not, the door is now shut, and my children are with me in bed; I cannot rise and give thee.—8. Yet if he shall continue knocking, I say to you, although he will not rise and give him because he is his friend, yet because of his importunity he will rise, and give him as many as he needeth.—9. And I say to you, Ask, and it shall be given you; seek, and you shall find; knock, and it shall be opened to you.—10. For every one that asketh, receiveth; and he that seeketh, findeth; and to him that knocketh, it shall be opened.—11. And which of you if he ask his father bread, will he give him a stone? Or a fish, will he for a fish give him a serpent?—12. Or if he shall ask an egg, will he reach him a scorpion?—13. If you then being evil, know how to give good gifts to your children; how much more will your Father from heaven give the good Spirit to them that ask him?"

MATT. 6:7. "And when you are praying, speak not much, as the heathens. For they think that in their much speaking they may be heard.—8. Be not you therefore like to them; for your Father knoweth what is needful for you, before you ask him.—9. Thus therefore shall you pray: Our Father who art in heaven, hallowed be thy name.—10. Thy kingdom come. Thy will be done on earth as it is in heaven.—11. Give us this day our supersubstantial bread.—12. And forgive us our debts, as we also forgive our debtors.—13. And lead us not into temptation. But deliver us from evil. Amen."

MATT. 7:7. "Ask, and it shall be given you; seek, and you shall find; knock, and it shall be opened to you.—8. For every one that asketh, receiveth; and he that seeketh, findeth; and to him that knocketh, it shall be opened.—9. Or what man is there among you, of whom if his son shall ask bread, will he reach him a stone?—10. Or if he shall ask him a fish, will he reach him a serpent?—11. If you then being evil, know how to give good gifts to your children; how much more will your Father who is in heaven give good things to them that ask him?"

It was probably a few days after the Feast of Tabernacles, whilst our Saviour was still in the neighborhood of Jerusalem, that He gave the instruction upon prayer. Tradition points out as the site of its delivery the Mount of Olives, whither He often resorted for prayer (John 8:1), and that spot upon the mountain where the "Paternoster" Church stands at present.

## 1. THE OCCASION OF THE INSTRUCTION

Our Saviour Himself furnished the occasion which led to this instruction by applying Himself to prayer in the presence of the disciples, probably at the above-mentioned spot upon the beautiful, quiet Mount of Olives (Luke 10:1). His prayer may have lasted very long, and the disciples, who were not as yet blessed with such a copious gift of prayer, perhaps regarded Him with astonishment and reverence, and probably also with the secret desire of being taught how they too could pass the time in prayer. A second occasion was afforded by the request of one of the disciples, which seems to have been prompted by this very wish: "Lord, teach us to pray" (Luke 11:1). He bases his request upon the example of John the Baptist, who had also taught his disciples a method of prayer (Luke 11:1; cf. Luke 5:33).

This motive also indicates the inner reason of the instruction, and shows why it was desirable that our Saviour should give His disciples and the Church definite directions and precepts with regard to prayer. Prayer is of too great importance for the spiritual life and for religion altogether, external as well as internal, for our Saviour to allow this point to remain in obscurity. It is one of the chief practices of the worship of God, the soul of public religious service, and the chief means of grace for the interior life. No religious or monastic founder has omitted to give the most minute regulations with regard to prayer. To organize prayer is to organize religion and life. Our Saviour must provide for unity, conformity and uniformity in prayer, as in all else. This was certainly one of St. John the Baptist's reasons for thus acting, and it also lies in the request of the disciple in this case, whilst it was this which induced our Saviour to comply with the request.

## 2. THE INSTRUCTION ITSELF

The instruction upon prayer includes three points.

Our Saviour first teaches us for what we are to pray, what the subject of our prayer is to be. And He gives us in the "Our Father" a complete and all-embracing formula of prayer (Luke 9:2–4; Matt. 6:9–13).

Secondly, He also teaches us the spirit in which we are to pray and the qualities which our prayer must have. These qualities are contained in the two little parables which our Saviour subjoins to the "Our Father" (Luke 11:5–8, 11–13; Matt. 7:9–11), and in a passage from the Sermon on the Mount (Matt. 6:7, 8). They are three in number. The first is the spirit of faith. We must not, as the Gentiles and (as it appears) the Jews also sometimes did (Eccli. 7:15; III Kings 18:26), estimate the value of prayer by its length or by the number of prayers we utter, or indeed pray at all with the idea that we must represent our wants to God because He does not know them, or that we must or can so influence Him by our prayers as men are influenced by reasoning (Matt. 6:7, 8). All this is erroneous. God knows much better than we what we need, and He will give it to us if it is good for us. We do not dispose God in any way by our prayer, but we must dispose ourselves, by removing the obstacles which might prevent Him from granting it; and this is exactly what we do by prayer, which is such a beautiful confession of our poverty, insufficiency, and unworthiness, and on the other hand a glorious acknowledgment of the power, goodness, and fidelity of God. The second quality is confidence. God is represented in the two parables as our Friend (Luke 11:5), our Father even (Luke 11:2, 11). We can therefore pray to Him with full confidence and childlike trust, especially when we ask for what is necessary and absolutely good. We are kind to our children and friends, and certainly mean them well from our hearts. Surely God is better than we (Luke 11:11–13). Confidence, then! The third quality is importunate perseverance. We must, like the man at his friend's door, call, entreat, knock, and leave our Lord, as it were, no peace until He grants our prayer. A special promise is given to this perseverance (Luke 11:7, 8). These are the qualities which our prayer must have.

Thirdly, our Saviour also mentions motives which encourage us to prayer. Besides His own example (since He not only teaches us to pray, but also prays Himself), there are two principal motives, which are contained in this very instruction. The first is the necessity of prayer. If we consider the formula given and examine into the words of the parables, we find included in it everything that we need, even to our daily bodily wants. From this we may conclude that we must pray for everything, and that God wishes to be asked by us for everything, from the highest to the lowest, from heaven and the Holy Ghost (Luke 11:2, 13) to an egg, a piece of bread, or a fish (Luke 11:3, 11, 12). God is not bound to give us anything, except as a consequence of prayer. Prayer, then, is a necessary means of life for body and soul. Yes, as theologians say, prayer is as necessary as grace, without which there is no salvation and no beatitude; simply because, in the ordinary course of things, no grace is obtained without prayer. God has placed everything under the necessity of prayer, and all confidence which does not rest upon prayer is vain and worthless, and only leads to destruction. The second motive given by our Saviour for prayer is its power and efficacy. As it is a necessary means for everything, so it is also sufficient for everything. This power and efficacy of prayer are due above all things, as our Saviour here so beautifully shows, to the promise that He makes to prayer (Luke 11:9, 10; Matt. 7:7, 8). His promise is a solemn one by which He pledges His Divine Word (Luke 11:9); it is a comprehensive and unconditional promise, limited only by our welfare and the glory of God. Miracles are not excluded. Prayer has worked plenty of them. Even heaven is included; indeed heaven especially, and before all else. The power and efficacy of prayer are due, further, to the infinite goodness and mercy of God. We cannot emphasize this too much. The reason why our petitions are granted is not our worthiness and merit, but the infinite mercy of God. If our merit were the reason, we should not petition, but demand; but as it is, we petition, and so we rest upon the basis of God's goodness and mercy. Just as far as this extends, so far also reaches the power of prayer. What can encourage us to pray, more than this?

### 3. CONCLUSIONS

The first conclusion must certainly be to thank our Saviour for this important instruction. How to pray, and how to pray well, is a question of vital importance for us, and we could not have solved it of ourselves. For "we know not what we should pray for as we ought" (Rom. 8:26). Now our Saviour comes, and tells us quite clearly and plainly what we are to pray for, and how we are to pray. This surely deserves our gratitude.

The second conclusion is that we must follow out this instruction. Our Saviour teaches us here how we are to pray, and also that we must pray; for He does not merely teach us a method of prayer, but also gives us motives which encourage us to pray much and often. We must observe both these precepts. The model of prayer which our Saviour has set up for us must always be before our eyes, as the compass within which our wishes and petitions move, in order that they may be conformable to God's Will and tend to our salvation. And we must also take to heart the motives by which He urges us to pray. He enjoins upon us the practice of prayer by word and example. We must pray, because our Lord recommends and commands us to do so; we must pray because He also prays, and His example is equivalent to a command; and we must pray, because prayer is for us the means of salvation. Prayer is necessary for all, and suffices for all. These are the ties which bind us to prayer.

### THE "OUR FATHER." INTRODUCTION

MATT. 6:9. "Thus therefore shall you pray: Our Father who art in heaven, hallowed be thy name.—10. Thy kingdom come. Thy will be done on earth as it is in heaven.—11. Give us this day our supersubstantial bread.—12. And forgive us our debts, as we also forgive our debtors.—13. And lead us not into temptation. But deliver us from evil. Amen."

LUKE 11:2. And he said to them: "When you pray, say: Father, hallowed be thy name. Thy kingdom come.—3. Give us this day our daily bread.—4. And forgive us our sins, for we also forgive every one that is indebted to us. And lead us not into temptation."

There are two points upon which we may meditate, as an introduction to the explanation of the "Our Father."

#### 1. EXCELLENCE OF THE "OUR FATHER"

The excellence of the Our Father arises from extrinsic and intrinsic causes.

The first extrinsic cause is the origin, or rather the Author of the prayer. The sublimity and holiness of the Author make the prayer which He originates more holy, more powerful and worthy of reverence. The Author of the Our Father is no other than our Saviour, our God, the Eternal Word, the Founder of our religion, our Lord. For this reason it is also called the Lord's Prayer. We pray through Him, through Whom we also live. It is an example of extraordinary graciousness and condescension on the part of the Lord to Whom we pray, that He Himself vouchsafes to compose the petition which we are to present to Him. In repeating the Our Father we rely not only upon the merits but also upon the very words of Christ, upon the words of eternal life. The second extrinsic cause for our esteem and love of the Our Father is the thought of the multitudes by whom it has been uttered. All ages and all Christian races from the time of Christ until the present day have said this prayer, have praised and honored God by it, and thereby gained heaven. It has become a prayer still more universal than the Psalms, an instrument of great honor and glory to God, a means of great graces and consolations, a very ladder to heaven for the human race. The third reason is the frequency with which we repeat it. It is the usual form of prayer, whether in private or at public worship. There is no prayer which we use so often to praise God and obtain graces for ourselves. It is therefore of great importance to know it and recite it well. For the same reason, too, more grace is derived from this prayer than from any others.

The internal reasons consist in the intrinsic worth, construction, and qualities of the prayer itself. The qualities of a good prayer are brevity, clearness and completeness. The Our Father possesses all these. As regards completeness, a good prayer embraces, first, a suitable form of address; and secondly, the presentation of the petitions. All this is found in the Our Father. With respect to the petitions, it contains all that we can reasonably wish for, and in the manner and order which are most fitting. Thus the Our Father not only instructs our intellect, but also gives the right direction to our will. All our wishes and prayers should be directed only to the end which we have to attain and the means which may assist us towards it. Such is also the arrangement of the seven petitions of the Our Father. After the invocation, our first request concerns the end for which we have been created, and since this end has a double relation, inasmuch as it includes the honor and glory of God and our own beatitude, the attainment of it forms the subject of the first two petitions. The subject of the other five is the means by which this end is attained. We may also distinguuish two kinds of means: those which are absolute and necessary for all, or in other words *positive* means, the subject of which is some necessary good; and *conditional* means, which are necessary under certain circumstances, and which may also be called *negative* means, because their object is to avert some evil. These five petitions are so arranged that the first two contain positive means, the other three negative; and our need of means to our end is thereby sufficiently provided for. Thus the Our Father is a truly model prayer, the perfect pattern of all prayers indeed an abstract of our whole religion, an abridgment of all the commandments and the whole Gospel, as the holy Fathers say. These surely are reasons enough to love and highly esteem the Our Father.

## 2. THE WAY TO SAY THE "OUR FATHER"

We must therefore recite the Our Father with devotion. This devotion includes several things.

First, we must say it with right comprehension. The Our Father must be understood in its depth, sublimity and compass, if we are to value it as we ought. And therefore we must now study it and meditate upon it.

Secondly, we must say the Our Father with great reverence. The Church introduces the repetition of the Our Father at Holy Mass with these beautiful words: "Admonished by salutary precepts, and taught by divine instruction" (or institution), "we venture to say: Our Father. . . ." The reason is that the words we use are revealed, holy and divine, the words of our Divine Saviour Himself.

Thirdly, we must be animated by great confidence when we say the Our Father, and for the very same reason, viz. that the words we use in our address to God are the words of our Saviour. Without doubt the Father will recognize the words of His Son and grant our petitions for His sake. Our Saviour then prays with us in a special sense, and we with Him and through Him.

Lastly, we must unite ourselves in spirit to our Saviour, and recite the beautiful prayer with His thoughts, intentions and dispositions, in union with the love and reverence for His Heavenly Father with which He uttered it, and with the ardent desire by which He was animated, to promote the glory of God and our salvation by the institution of this prayer. The Our Father is a beautiful and eloquent expression of the all-embracing love of our Saviour for God, the Church and the human race. He has comprehended in it not merely the wishes and needs of individuals, but those of all nations and of the whole Church, even the interests of God and of heaven. The Our Father is the prayer of Jesus Christ and the Church for the use of the family and nation. In these dispositions, then, we must recite the Our Father; it will thus certainly tend to the honor of God, the joy of our Saviour, and the advantage of the Church.

## THE FORM OF ADDRESS USED IN THE "OUR FATHER"

MATT. 6:9. "Thus therefore shall you pray: Our Father, who art in heaven!" LUKE 11:2. And he said to them: "When you pray, say: Father!"

### 1. HOW WE MUST ADDRESS OURSELVES TO GOD

Every perfect prayer, like every address and every presentation of petitions to those of high position among men, must be properly introduced by a name or title. This title must be before all things true, and also honorable to the person addressed and useful to the speaker. Its aim should be to obtain the favor of the person addressed, and at the same time to put the petitioner in the proper dispositions. The former is to be favorably disposed and won by recognition of his position, rank, and qualities. The speaker is to be reminded of his relation to the person whom he addresses, and admonished to acquit himself of his task in a becoming manner. The first point is not necessary in the case of an address to God, inasmuch as He does not need to be made favorable to us. But *we* must be in good dispositions; we must remove the hindrances to the granting of our prayer, and this takes place by the humble and joyful acknowledgment of God's supreme dominion. The recollection of the greatness and majesty of God and of His gracious relation to ourselves aids us to acquire reverence, confidence and all other suitable dispositions.

### 2. HOW THE INVOCATION OF THE "OUR FATHER" ANSWERS TO THESE REQUIREMENTS

The invocation of the Our Father has three parts.

The first is the little word "our." Our Saviour intended by this prayer to unite us men not only to God as our Father, but also to one another as children of God and brethren. He could call the Heavenly Father in a special sense "His" Father, because He alone is the natural Son of God; but we could not do this. This word therefore reminds us of our equality before God; subdues pride, presumption, envy and indifference, and awakens the spirit of fellowship, love and care for one another. Christ wished by this word to remind and encourage us to pray for all and in the name of all, because we all, angels and men, just and sinners, are children of God. In the name of all these we praise God, acknowledge Him as our Father, return thanks and intercede for all. Thus the effect of prayer is increased, God is more glorified, and we ourselves pray with more fervor, because we pray with many and for many. Our Divine Saviour wished to draw us completely out of a certain narrowness of heart and exclusiveness; we are always to feel ourselves members of one great body, and to think, act and pray accordingly. So He Himself thought, acted and prayed, and wished hereby to imprint this character of common fellowship upon our life and prayer. With this little word He strikes the keynote of the entire Our Father.

The second point is the title of "Father." It is addressed not only to the First Person of the Holy Trinity, but also to the other Persons, inasmuch as they all possess one and the same Divinity and creative power. This title of "Father" is, first, true. Even in the Old Covenant God was so called (Deut. 32:6, 18; Isa. 1:2; 63:16); indeed, it was His Will to be so called (Jer. 3:4). He is in very deed our Father, because He is all to us and does all that is incumbent upon fatherhood. He gives us existence by creation, and we enter thereby not merely into relations of complete dependence, but also into the most intimate connection with Him; further, He maintains us continually and finally provides for us in heaven. Thus He is even in a natural manner our Father, precisely because He is our Creator. Much more and in a far higher sense is He our Father by adoption through our Saviour. We are really children of God, and bear in us the communication of the supernatural adoption of God with all its titles and rights, in sanctifying grace. This adoption is the characteristic mark of the New Covenant (John 1:12; 15:15; Rom. 8:15; Gal. 4:6; Hebr. 2:17). Our Saviour reveals the Father to us here also (Luke 10:22). We are therefore really God's "children," and call Him with full right "Our Father." This title is secondly very honorable and glorious for God. It reveals His most beautiful attributes, His majesty, wisdom and goodness, fidelity and mercy; and not less His divine operation in creating, preserving, governing and beatifying. The name of "father" is a name of power and love. Lastly, this mode of address is also useful to us. It brings us at once into the right position to God as our Father, and awakens in our hearts sentiments of reverence, submission, love and confidence. We must above all things approach God as children. Christ teaches us to do this, and God wills it. By how many other titles He might have caused Himself to be addressed! He chooses this one. It is the most glorious for Him and the most advan-

THE "OUR FATHER" 531

tageous for us. It unites by the closest tie our intellect and our heart to God, our last end, in faith and in love.

The third part of the address contains the words: "Who art in heaven." By these words our Saviour directs not only our intellect, but also our imaginative faculty and our will to the place where God dwells. God indeed dwells everywhere and is present everywhere, by virtue of His nature. But heaven is especially mentioned as His abode, because God nowhere so reveals His majesty, power and goodness, and nowhere so visibly communicates Himself to His creatures as in heaven, by the beatitude which He there bestows upon them; and which essentially consists in the direct contemplation and possession of God (that is, in the knowledge and love of Him), and also in the secondary joys which the glorified bodies of the blessed experience. Heaven is a kingdom of quite inconceivable joys and honors and exceeding power, where God, like a ruler in his own city, displays all the treasures of His goodness and communicates them to His Saints. We are therefore to think of this glorious heavenly kingdom, first in order to recollect our thoughts and direct our imagination; secondly, to fill our hearts with reverence for God, for He is not only our Father, but also our Lord and King; thirdly, to awaken in our hearts, by the representation of this beautiful heaven, love and desire for our end and object, the heavenly home. The petitions for this glorious end and for the means to attain it will then be all the more fervent.

## THE FIRST PETITION

MATT. 6:9; LUKE 11:2. "Hallowed be thy name!"

### 1. SUBJECT OF THE PETITION

The subject of the first petition is our last end; and this with relation to God Himself, inasmuch as it includes the honor and glory (or in other words the service) rendered to Him by men. The "Name" of God signifies here the Nature, Attributes and Person of God, God Himself, as far as He is revealed, and therefore also the invocation, the honor and glory, worship and service of God on the part of men (Deut. 28:58; 32:3; Ps. 19:2; 75:2; Isa. 30:27). To "hallow" the Name of God means to keep it holy, to regard it and treat it as sacred, not to dishonor it, but to glorify it by acknowledgment, reverence, veneration, love and service (Ex. 20:7, 8). We do not, therefore, ask that God's Name may be hallowed in itself, for that it is already; but that men may honor it by the observance of the first three commandments, and especially by interior and exterior worship.

## 2. MOTIVES

This is only right; because, in the first place, no one is so worthy of acknowledgment, honor and glory as God. His Name is great (Ps. 75:2), His Name is admirable (Ps. 8:2), His Name is holy and terrible (Ps. 110:9), worthy of praise (Ps. 112:3), high (Isa. 12:4), and sweet (Ps. 134:3). He is our God and our Father, and no created good is greater than the honor of God, for this is a divine good. How just it is, therefore, that we should pray for the glorification of God!

Further, it is a matter of justice and a simple duty to acknowledge God; indeed it is our first duty and the foundation of all other duties, the duty of all men without exception. And yet, in reality, how far the greater part of the world is from acknowledging God! We can therefore procure for Him by our service a good which He does not as yet possess, and which He expects to obtain from us.

Then, also, we can do nothing better and more salutary for our fellow-men than to pray for the realization of this petition. How much peace and joy there would then be in the world! And how much more greatness of soul would be produced by glorifying God than by glorifying oneself and other men, which is so often the result of not giving glory to God!

Lastly, let us thus turn our thoughts and endeavors to the great aim of God, and labor at the work of His glorification, which He has begun and continues from all eternity, and towards which all His outward creation is directed. There is nothing greater. It is the highest intention that we can have; it is God's own intention, and that of our Saviour.

## 3. MEANS

The first means to this end is prayer, as it is here practised. In all our prayers this should be the first petition; even when we pray for ourselves or for others, the intention should be that God may be glorified by the favorable hearing of our petition. Our prayer may be powerfully supported by the hearing of Holy Mass, where Christ Himself prays with and for us.

The second means of attaining the object of this petition is the example which we give to others of glorifying God's Name. Other active efforts form the third means; such as the exercise of the priestly functions in the pulpit, good conversations, and the support of the missions to heretics and heathens, by which the honor of God's Name is promoted.

## THE SECOND PETITION

MATT. 6:10; LUKE 11:2. "Thy kingdom come!"

### 1. WHAT WE REQUEST IN THE SECOND PETITION

By this kingdom of God, the advent of which we pray for in the second petition, is not to be understood the absolute sway which God exercises over His creatures by His absolute power and permission. He has this already. On the contrary, what is here meant is that sway, the realization of which depends not only upon the grace of God but also upon the free will of man; that is, the kingdom of God among men, or in other words the attainment of our last end, inasmuch as it is our welfare, our happiness and our blessedness. Only in this sense can the kingdom of God be the subject of a petition.

Thus understood the kingdom of God comprises three things, of which the one depends upon the other. Before all things and in the highest sense of the word, we pray for heaven and our eternal bliss under the conception of a "kingdom"; assuredly the most glorious and magnificent idea by which heaven can be imagined, and the utmost that anyone can wish for in the shape of power, honors and joys. But we arrive at this kingdom only by means of the kingdom of God's grace within us. Heaven is the kingdom of holiness and of the children of God; but we have holiness and are God's children solely through grace. God must therefore first reign in our hearts by sanctifying grace, by faith, hope, and charity. The kingdom of God in heaven must begin in this world, in our hearts; for "the kingdom of God is not meat and drink, but justice, and peace, and joy in the Holy Ghost; for he that in this serveth Christ, pleaseth God, and is approved of men" (Rom. 14:17, 18). It is therefore secondly this kingdom of grace that we ask for by this petition. This grace and the right divine service are to be found only in the Catholic Church, because she alone possesses the true faith and the true means of grace. Whoever therefore wishes to arrive at the kingdom of faith and of heaven, must be a citizen of the Church. Heaven is nothing but the development and glorious completion of the Church, which is the kingdom of God upon earth. It is a kingdom here and in the world beyond; the one is the step to the other. One Lord and Christ reigns here and there; there in glory, here through faith, the commandments, and the Sacraments. For this reason Christ sometimes designates the Church and sometimes heaven itself, in Scripture, by the expression "kingdom of heaven." We ask then in this petition that the kingdom of the Church may spread over the whole human race, receive all men into her bosom and guide them to heaven; in other words, that all that God has appointed for the realization and development of the economy of salvation, here below and in the world beyond, may be accomplished in the heart of each one individually and in the social life of the nations.

### 2. FOR WHOM WE MAKE THIS PETITION

We pray for the advent of the kingdom of God in the abovementioned sense for all men: in the first instance for those who are not yet in the bosom of the Church, the heretics and infidels; and secondly for all members of the Church, that they may arrive at an interior state of grace, persevere therein and become possessors of heaven. No one is excluded from the petition, except the souls of the lost in hell.

### 3. WHAT THE MOTIVES OF THIS PETITION ARE

In the first place, there is nothing more glorious for God than the realization of this petition. God is nowhere glorified so much as in the Church, in souls in the state of grace, and in heaven. There He really rules, there he is served as He desires, there He is loved as He deserves, and reveals Himself in the most glorious manner. In this threefold kingdom He attains the great end of Creation.

Secondly, there is also for us men nothing more salutary and necessary than the advent of this kingdom. What are we then and what have we, without the Church, without grace and heaven? We can therefore wish and ask for nothing more beneficial for ourselves and for all men. Dominion, a crown, a kingdom, is the highest thing that human ambition can aim at, the summit of temporal felicity. But what is all earthly power in comparison with the kingdom of eternal beatitude?

By this fervent prayer for the advent of God's kingdom in the hearts of all men, we pave for ourselves the road to this glory, and secure for ourselves an exceptional position in the heavenly kingdom. This praying for God's kingdom makes us think of, desire and strive after heaven at any cost; it reanimates our love for our Holy Church and our zeal to work for her. Whoever has received the grace and happiness of the priestly vocation should support this prayer by his apostolic zeal. We thus become really claimants and conquerors of heaven and promoters of Christ's kingdom upon earth; and no one has a richer share in heaven than he who seeks to defend, exalt and extend this kingdom here below.

## The Third Petition

MATT. 6:10. "Thy will be done on earth as it is in heaven!"

Here we begin the petitions for the means of attaining our end, and first we are to ask for positive means, i.e. for the granting of blessings. Among these positive blessings we must reckon before all, and in all circumstances, the fulfilment of God's Will, a spiritual blessing.

### 1. WHAT IS TO BE UNDERSTOOD BY THE WILL OF GOD

By the Will of God, the fulfilment of which we pray for in this petition, is to be understood not only the absolute but also the conditional Will of God, inasmuch as it is revealed to us in commandments and inspirations, or in dispensations and permissions of God. In the first case we ask for the grace to accomplish this Will of God by our cooperation; in the second, to submit with all readiness to what He permits to take place. We ask, then, that the Will and good pleasure of God, however it may be manifested, whether in commandments, inspirations or permissions, may be fulfilled by us, upon us, and in us, in all cases.

### 2. WHAT MUST BE THE MANNER OF THIS FULFILMENT OF GOD'S WILL

The manner in which God's Will must be fulfilled is specified in the words "as it is in heaven." The angels and Saints enjoy the direct contemplation of God, and in this contemplation they also see the plans of Divine Providence in their wisdom, holiness, and bounty. They therefore admire and adore these plans, submit to them completely in love and reverence, accomplish them zealously, and have but one desire, viz. to see them fulfilled in the most perfect manner.

We conform ourselves to this disposition of heart by taking the angels and Saints and our Saviour Himself as our models. We ask for the grace to resign ourselves to God's Will with perfect conformity of our intellect and will, and to accomplish it in all reverence and submission, love and joy, like the angels (Ps. 102:20) and the God-Man Himself (Matt. 11:26; John 8:29).

### 3. WHY WE ASK FOR THIS GRACE

The accomplishment of God's Will is a very important grace, not only for our perfection but also for our salvation. Our free will is a great blessing and the source of all merit and holiness; but it is also a great danger and the source of all sins. "Get rid of self-will, and hell will no longer exist," says a Doctor of the Church. But by the accomplishment of God's Will, which we here ask for, we unite our frail and faulty will with this Will of God, which is the guide to all holiness and perfection. We become one with God, and God rules in us. Of sin there is no question. In order to lead us to perfection quickly and easily, no other means is needed than to resign ourselves readily and in a childlike manner to everything we know to be God's Will, and to lose ourselves therein.

Nothing unites us so closely to God as this conformity to His Divine Will. We thus participate in His infallibility, power and wisdom. God grants our wishes in return (Ps. 144:19); and "to them that love God, all things work together unto good" (Rom. 8:28). This childlike, unconditional resignation to God's Will and dispensations is such a glorious act that it at once merits heaven for us.

This submission is also quite in accordance with the nature of God's Will, which is wisdom, justice, omnipotence, and goodness. There is nothing better or more worthy of love on earth or in heaven than the Will of God. And it would be vain for us to oppose it. What God has decreed takes place, even against our will. His plans and dispensations are often incomprehensible, inexplicable, and painful to us, and look like the wrong side of a woven picture. Their lovable and beautiful side is turned towards heaven. Looked at from that side, all is not only holiness, justice and wisdom, but also goodness and divine benevolence towards us. We must therefore always raise our thoughts to God and heaven, and regard and consider everything from this point of view. In all things and in all occurrences, let us say with our whole heart: "May the holy, just, wise, and all-gracious Will of God be fulfilled in my regard and in me, at all times and in all things!"

### THE FOURTH PETITION

MATT. 6:11. "Give us this day our supersubstantial bread!"
LUKE 11:3. "Give us this day our daily bread!"

This petition also has for its subject a positive means or benefit, though a temporal one.

#### 1. WHAT THE SUBJECT OF THIS PETITION IS

The preceding petition had for its subject a spiritual good, a blessing of the soul; this one is directed towards the preservation of the life of the body. By the bread for which we ask is to be understood everything that is necessary and useful for the preservation of the body and of life, such as food, clothing, and shelter (Luke 14:1). Our Saviour Himself in another place mentions as "daily bread" eggs and fish, the usual provisions taken on a journey in the East (Luke 11:11, 12).

#### 2. HOW WE ARE TO ASK FOR THE FOOD OF THE BODY

Our Saviour Himself gives us a few rules as to the manner in which we should ask for bodily food; and there are others which we ourselves can easily think of.

In the first place our Saviour hints that we should not only ask for food for ourselves, but for all men; for this reason He says: "Give us." In this respect also the spirit of fellowship is to reign. And we have all the more reason to do this when we think how many needy poor there are in the world. We then assist them at least by our prayer.

Secondly, our Saviour indicates that we should ask for our bread with modesty and moderation, not with excessive eagerness, anxiety and uneasiness. For this reason we are to say: "Give us *this day* our *daily* bread," or our necessary, sufficient bread (Matt. 11:34; Luke 12:15).

Thirdly, we should ask for our bodily sustenance in reasonable conformity with the dispensations of Divine Providence. We must cooperate with the Divine Providence of God not only by prayer but also by work, and by proper care and management of what God bestows upon us, especially by liberality in almsgiving (Prov. 19:17). In any case we must ask for our bodily nourishment and endeavor to procure it, inasmuch as it does not injure the welfare of our souls, but is even conducive to it.

Lastly, we should ask for our bread trustfully, as a child asks his father. The child needs bread, and the father knows this very well (Matt. 6:32; Luke 12:30).

### 3. WHY GOD WISHES US TO ASK FOR OUR BREAD

In the first place, God is the Author and Giver of all blessings, temporal as well as spiritual. It is therefore fitting that we should recognize Him as such, and acknowledge that we cannot and will not do without Him, even in this respect.

Secondly, it is very good for us to be reminded that all temporal things also come from God; otherwise we misuse His benefits, regard them as our deserts, and do not use them as God wishes. Thus we alienate God's blessing from us and fall into temporal want and distress. God often inflicts such punishments because we do not give Him glory by returning thanks to Him and recommending ourselves to Him (Luke 12:18, 19).

Thirdly, such temporal want and distress is dangerous and a source of sin and crime, just as much as are superfluous riches (Eccli. 27:1). For this reason the wise man prays to be preserved from poverty as well as from riches (Prov. 30:8). In the right comprehension of this petition and in adhering to its truths there lies moreover a very important solution of the social question. We see too how good our Saviour is, how truly a Father to us, by His putting this petition also in the "Our Father."

## THE FIFTH PETITION

MATT. 6:12. "And forgive us our debts, as we also forgive our debtors."
LUKE 11:4. "And forgive us our sins, for we also forgive every one that is indebted to us."

Now follow the petitions whose object is to avert the evils that hinder us from attaining our end. Of these evils there are two kinds, present and future; or the evil of the guilt of sin, and the evil of its punishment.

## 1. SUBJECT OF THIS PETITION

The subject of the fifth petition is the removal of the present evil of the guilt of sin, and of the punishment which we deserve for it. In this petition then we ask for remission of sins, whether mortal or venial, and for remission of the punishment due to them. Both sin and its punishment are debts which we owe to the divine justice (Luke 11:4).

As regards the guilt of sin, venial sin is actually remitted by contrite prayer for pardon, if there is no opposing evil disposition in the will; the guilt of mortal sin, however (setting aside actual, perfect contrition) is only indirectly remitted through the Our Father, inasmuch as in it we ask only for the grace of conversion.

We also obtain by this prayer the remission (or at all events the partial remission) of the temporal punishment due to sin, because all prayer is a work of satisfaction, and in the Our Father especially we make the express petition for remission of punishment, and this in our Saviour's own words.

## 2. MANNER IN WHICH THE PETITION MUST BE MADE

We must present this petition, first, in all sincerity and earnestness, with sentiments of penitence and contrition, and with a firm purpose of amendment. Everyone, even the just, can in all truth implore forgiveness of sins, whether for himself or for others. Everyone can acknowledge himself to be a sinner, and fear with reason that all has not yet been forgiven him (Eccli. 5:5).

Secondly, our Saviour Himself adds a motive, or rather a condition of the forgiveness of our sins, by saying: "As we also forgive our debtors." We must therefore present this petition with a disposition of readiness to be reconciled to those who have offended us. This spirit of forgiveness is not only a condition, but also the measure of pardon which we ask of God for our own sins. If we have not this disposition, we condemn ourselves by these words. We must and can pray in this spirit, whether we pray thus in the name of the Church and all the faithful, or whether we ask for the grace of this disposition for ourselves (Eccli. 28:1–4; Matt. 6:14, 15; Mark 11:25, 26).

## 3. MOTIVES

The first motive that we have for actually presenting this petition is the consideration that sin is the greatest, indeed the only, hindrance to the attainment of our end. Only through sin can anything else become a real hindrance, which excludes us from our end or retards us in the attainment of it. Sin is therefore our great and only evil, the source of all other evils. How much reason we have, then, to pray right heartily and earnestly for forgiveness of our sins and their punishment, especially since we commit so many sins! And what an easy means to free ourselves from them we have here at our command!

Secondly, sin is also the source of all social evils. Sin disturbs the order of justice, and calls down upon men the chastisement of God. When we reflect on the many and shocking crimes committed every day, must we not be anxious to destroy the source of these manifold evils, at least as far as we can, by prayer and penance?

Thirdly, the glory of God is especially connected with this petition. As sin is our own evil, so also is it the evil and the enemy of God. It diminishes His honor and service upon earth; it is an injury, an act of disobedience, of contempt of the divine majesty, and destroys all His works and institutions for the salvation of men. It is therefore a beautiful act of love to God and zeal for His honor, to work at the extirpation of sin.


## The Sixth Petition

MATT. 6:13; LUKE 11:4. "Lead us not into temptation!"

### 1. WHAT WE PRAY FOR IN THIS PETITION

This petition has for its object to avert a future evil, namely temptation to sin. Everything within and without, which tends to lead us into sin, is a temptation.

What do we really ask for with regard to temptation? We do not pray that we may have no temptations; that would be asking for a miracle, in this world, where everything may (and does, more or less) become a temptation to us. The wicked world, the wicked Enemy, and the wicked nature within us are a continual source of temptation. It would not be at all a good thing to be free from temptations. That would only nourish our pride and self-confidence, make us narrow and slothful in striving after perfection, and deprive us of much merit. On this account the Holy Ghost calls that man blessed who stands the test of temptation and receives the crown of life (James 1:12). "What doth he know, that hath not been tried?" (Eccli. 34:9.) What we ask, then, is that God may not expose us to dangerous temptations in which we shall fall. We pray that He may either avert such temptations from us or give us the grace to resist them victoriously.

### 2. WHY WE SHOULD MAKE THIS PETITION WITH FERVOR

The first inducement is the fact that we cannot live long without being exposed to temptations. The occasions of temptation are too frequent, whether from ourselves, our surroundings, or the Evil One, whose business it is to tempt and try men.

Secondly, not only is it impossible for us to live long without being tempted, but we cannot overcome all great temptations without grace. This, in our fallen state, is a moral impossibility. And therefore we must pray, in accordance with our Saviour's exhortation: "Pray that ye enter not into temptation" (Matt. 26:41).

Thirdly, the consequences of temptation are of such importance for the welfare of souls, that we should make them the subject of prayer. Temptations are in the spiritual life what battles are in a campaign. The destinies of Christ's kingdom depend upon the result of temptations. For this reason Christ also willed to be tempted, to encourage us and to teach us by His example and His prayer how we are to resist temptation. Prayer is all the more necessary here, since the Evil One besets everyone with his temptations; men themselves allow him to use them as his tools, and poor tempted souls even seek his snares and perish miserably in them. By our prayer we share and support the endeavors of the holy angels to check the inroads and ravages of the evil spirits in Christ's kingdom.

### 3. WITH WHAT DISPOSITIONS MUST WE MAKE THIS PETITION?

We must make this petition, first, with heartfelt humility, in the full consciousness of our frailty and weakness. It was in order to remind us daily of this weakness that our Saviour placed this petition in the Our Father.

Further, we must pray with confidence in the power of these words of our Saviour, Who uttered them Himself and taught them to us. By doing this He prayed for us all and prepared graces for us for the time of temptation.

Lastly, we must not overlook our Lord's precept to unite vigilance with our prayer. "Watch ye, and pray, that ye enter not into temptation," He said to the Apostles (Matt. 26:41; Mark 14:38). To watch is to flee dangerous occasions, and not to give oneself up to self-confidence and carelessness. The petition also reminds us of this.

## THE SEVENTH PETITION

MATT. 6:13. "But deliver us from evil. Amen."

This petition also aims at averting an evil.

### 1. WHAT EVIL IS TO BE AVERTED BY THIS PETITION

There remains no other evil for the prevention of which we can pray but temporal evils, such as war, famine, pestilence etc., in fact every kind of misfortune (unless we assume that this is a repetition of a former petition, which is scarcely admissible). On account of the little word "but," some interpret the petition to mean "Protect us from the Evil One," who is certainly the originator of all evil, and therefore of temporal evils also. However, the word "but" may also have the same meaning as "further" or "moreover."

### 2. WHY WE PRAY THAT THESE EVILS MAY BE AVERTED

In the first place, because they *are* "evils," and if not always effects and punishments of sins, yet consequences of the first sin.

Secondly, these evils may often be the occasion of sin.

Thirdly, they often hinder great blessings and disturb peace and general good order.

Lastly, God wishes to be acknowledged as our Helper in such needs and distresses. It is to lead us to put our trust in God in such matters that our Saviour has placed this petition in the Our Father.

### 3. HOW WE SHOULD ASK FOR THE PREVENTION OF THESE EVILS

We must ask for this, first, with childlike confidence; secondly, with perfect conformity and resignation to the Will of God; and lastly, for all men. How much misfortune men meet with every day! We have therefore sufficient reason to make this petition most fervently for all who are in trial and affliction.

The Our Father concludes with the word "Amen," which is a confirmation, ratification, and short recapitulation, the seal, as it were, of all the petititons.

# JOURNEYS OF JESUS
## during His public Life.

I. *Nazareth, Bethania across the Jordan, desert near Jericho, Galilee (Cana, Capharnaum). (Dec. 29 till Spring 30. — John 1. 2; Luke 3. 4; Mark 1; Matt. 3. 4.)*

II. *Capharnaum, Jerusalem, Judaea, Sichem, Galilee (Cana, Nazareth, Capharnaum), Galilee, Capharnaum. (Passover 30 till about Pentecost 31. — John 2—5; Luke 4—7; Mark 1—3; Matt. 4—9.)*

III. *Capharnaum, Naim, Judaea, Jerusalem, Galilee, Chapharnaum. (From about Pentecost till autumn 31. — John 5; Luke 7. 8; Mark 3. 4; Matt. 11—13.)*

IV. *Capharnaum, Gadara (or Gerasa), Capharnaum, Galilee, Capharnaum. (Autumn 31 till about Passover 32. — Luke 8. 9; Mark 4—6; Matt. 8—14.)*

V. *Capharnaum, desert near Bethsaida Julias, Genesar, Capharnaum. (About Passover 32. — John 6; Luke 9; Mark 6; Matt. 14.)*

VI. *Capharnaum, Tyre and Sidon, Decapolis, Magedan and Dalmanutha; desert near Bethsaida Julias, Caesarea Philippi, Galilee (Thabor), Capharnaum. (May till Sept. 32. — Luke 9; Mark 7—9; Matt. 14—18.)*

VII. *Capharnaum, Galilee, Peraea, Jericho, Bethania, Jerusalem, Judaea. (Sept. till Dec. 32. — John 7—10; Luke 9—13; Mark 10; Matt. 19. 8. 11. 12. 23. 24.)*

VIII. *Judaea, Jerusalem, Bethania across the Jordan, Bethania near Mount Olivet, Ephrem. (Dec. 32 till Feb. 33. — John 10. 11; Luke 13—17.)*

IX. *Ephrem, Samaria, Galilee, Peraea, Jericho, Bethania on Mount Olivet, Bethphage, Jerusalem. (Feb. till Passover 33. — John 11. 12; Luke 17—19; Mark 10. 11; Matt. 19—26.)*

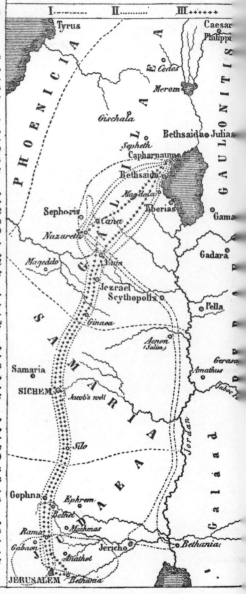

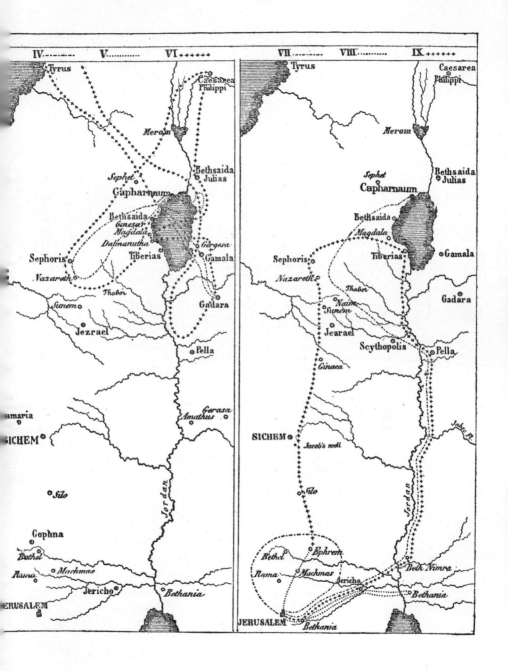